The
Employee Assistance
Handbook

S0-BJK-268

The Employee Assistance Handbook

Edited by

James M. Oher

JOHN WILEY & SONS, INC.

New York • Chichester • Weinheim • Brisbane • Singapore • Toronto

This book is printed on acid-free paper. ∞

Copyright © 1999 by John Wiley & Sons, Inc. All rights reserved.

Published simultaneously in Canada.

No part of this publication may be reproduced, stored in a retrieval system or transmitted in any form or by any means, electronic, mechanical, photocopying, recording, scanning or otherwise, except as permitted under Section 107 or 108 of the 1976 United States Copyright Act, without either the prior written permission of the Publisher, or authorization through payment of the appropriate per-copy fee to the Copyright Clearance Center, 222 Rosewood Drive, Danvers, MA 01923, (978) 750-8400, fax (978) 750-4744. Requests to the Publisher for permission should be addressed to the Permissions Department, John Wiley & Sons, Inc., 605 Third Avenue, New York, NY 10158-0012, (212) 850-6011, fax (212) 850-6008, E-Mail: PERMREQ@WILEY.COM.

This publication is designed to provide accurate and authoritative information in regard to the subject matter covered. It is sold with the understanding that the publisher is not engaged in rendering professional services. If legal, accounting, medical, psychological or any other expert assistance is required, the services of a competent professional person should be sought.

Designations used by companies to distinguish their products are often claimed as trademarks. In all instances where John Wiley & Sons, Inc. is aware of a claim, the product names appear in initial capital or all capital letters. Readers, however, should contact the appropriate companies for more complete information regarding trademarks and registration.

Library of Congress Cataloging-in-Publication Data:

The employee assistance handbook / edited by James M. Oher.
    p.   cm.
    Includes bibliographical references and index.
    ISBN 0-471-24252-7 (alk. paper)
    1. Employee assistance programs—United States—Handbooks,
manuals, etc.   I. Oher, James M.
    HF5549.5.E42E468   1999
    658.3′82—dc21   98-31699

10 9 8 7 6 5 4 3 2

To my wife Susan and my sons Sam and Jake
who fill my life with joy and purpose.

Editor

James M. Oher
President
Oher & Associates, Inc.
Chappaqua, New York

Contributors

Thomas M. Amaral, PhD
President
EAP Technology Systems, Inc.
Yreka, California

Bernard E. Beidel, MEd, CEAP
Director
Office of Employee Assistance
U.S. House of Representatives
Centreville, Virginia

Keith D. Bruhnsen, MSW
The University of Michigan
Human Resource & Affirmative
   Action
Ann Arbor, Michigan

Wayne N. Burton, MD
FVP and Corporate Medical Director
First Chicago NBD Corporation
Chicago, Illinois

Tamara Cagney
CEO
TC Consulting
Pleasanton, California

David Cambronne, MA
Employee Assistance Consultant
Wells Fargo Bank/Norwest
Minneapolis, Minnesota

Kenneth R. Collins, LCSW, CEAP
Executive Vice President
EAP Technology Systems, Inc.
Orienda, California

Daniel J. Conti, PhD
Vice President and EAP Director
First Chicago NBD Corporation
Chicago, Illinois

Arlene A. Darick, LCSW, CEAP
Executive Director, EAPs
Magellan Health Services
Maryland Heights, Missouri

Bruce N. Davidson, CSW, CEAP
formerly, Manager EAP and Work/Life
   Services
Digital Equipment Corporation
Maynard, Massachusetts

W. Dennis Derr, CSW, CEAP
Mobil Oil Corporation
Fairfax, Virginia

Regina Dickens, EdD
formerly, Manager Employee and Family
    Assistance Services
Champion International, Inc.
Area Director
Riverston Counseling & Personal
    Development
Littleton, North Carolina

J. Chip Drotos
Associate Publisher
*Behavioral Healthcare Management
    Magazine*
Bloomfield Hills, Michigan

T.J. Elliott
Director, Consulting Design
Cavanaugh Leahy & Company
White Plains, New York

Barbara Feuer, PhD
Managing Director
The Catalyst Group
Bethesda, Maryland

Mark R. Ginsberg
Chair, Department of Counseling
    and Human Services, Graduate
    Division of Education
The Johns Hopkins University
Baltimore, Maryland

Paula G. Gomes
President
Gomes & Associates
Washington, D.C.

Robert Grossmark, PhD
First Chicago NBD Corporation
New York, New York

Kate Harri, MA, LP
Private Consultant
Minneapolis, Minnesota

Paul W. Heck
Senior Consultant–Global Employee
    Assistance Services
Integrated Health Services
E.I. DuPont de Nemours Co., Inc.
Wilmington, Delaware

Patricia A. Herlihy, PhD
Research Analyst
Boston College
Center for Work and Family
Boston, Massachusetts

Jeffry P. Kahn, MD
President
WorkPsych Associates, Inc.
New York, New York

Richard R. Kilburg
Senior Director of Human Services
The Johns Hopkins University
Baltimore, Maryland

Garry M. Lindsay
Mobil Oil Corporation
Fairfax, Virginia

Donald L. Oberg, PhD, CEAP
President
The Oberg Group
Greenbelt, Maryland

Ted Rooney, MPH
Manager, Employee Health Management
L.L. Bean, Inc.
Freeport, Maine

Donald A. Rothschild
President
Peak Paths, a division of Rothschild's
    Files, Inc.
Littleton, Colorado

Jerry Shih, MA, LP
Clinical Supervisor
Neighborhood Involvement Program
    Counseling Center
Minneapolis, Minnesota

Geoffry B. Smith, LCSW, BCD
EAP Consultant
L.L. Bean, Inc.
Freeport, Maine

Linda Stoer-Scaggs, PhD, LPPC
Director University Faculty/Staff
    Assistance Programs
Ohio State University
Columbus, Ohio

Rudy M. Yandrick
Behavioral Risk Institute
Mechanicsburg, Pennsylvania

James K. Zimmerman, PhD
Oher & Associates, Inc.
Chappaqua, New York

Preface

When I was an adolescent, I saw a play that profoundly affected the course of my professional life. It was *The Kitchen* by Arnold Wesker. Although I later learned that Wesker was often criticized for his overtly socialist political point of view, what struck this young impressionable theatergoer as overwhelmingly powerful was the impact of a group of workers and their personal problems on the functioning of the workplace. Up until that point, the world of daily work had seemed a somewhat remote and faraway place. In the play, an interpersonal work conflict mobilizes the rebellion and fear of the other kitchen employees as an act of violence erupts. When the restaurant owner demands that the employees focus on the tasks at hand—preparing and serving food—the workers, now exhausted and weary, are unable to. Wesker's view of the workforce only reinforced certain fears about its coldness and lack of compassion. Although it was a few years before I found the right venue and outlet for my interests, the field of employee assistance programs (EAPs) provided the perfect format where I could help people with psychosocial problems as well as influence the organizations where these people worked.

Many things have changed since I entered the EAP field more than 25 years ago. Over the past 10 years, the healthcare and human resource fields have been in a state of progressive change that is profoundly affecting the structure and delivery of their services. These changes are impacting allied services such as EAPs, whose evolution and development are firmly grounded in both these areas. As worksite-based resources that prevent, identify, and resolve personal problems affecting productivity and health, EAPs are intricately connected to other central workplace functions. But to what degree have they established, maintained, and strengthened these linkages? In part, this book addresses this question. Many of the EAPs discussed in this book have survived and prospered because they have coordinated their activities and services with other workplace operations such as human resources, health and safety, healthcare, and benefits.

This book shows how several EAPs are playing that role. Many of the professionals who have contributed to this book are stepping forward to take a leadership role in addressing these workplace issues with their management colleagues in the workplace. As a result, they are creating viable, innovative services that are particularly suited to their unique workplace settings. It is fair to speculate that those EAP professionals who are not meeting the challenge to articulate their value and collaborate with colleagues in strategic thinking, planning, and programming may continue to lose their position and voice within the workforce.

As the workplace becomes even more aware of the costs of a wide range of personal problems affecting workers and the workplace, EAPs will play an increasingly pivotal role in creating and providing services.

There is a strong historical connection between substance abuse problems and EAP programming. Following the lead of and with the assistance of both federal and state legislative mandates, EAPs have become the legitimate promulgator of many initiatives to combat, identify, and refer for treatment of substance abuse in the workplace. Many EAPs are actively involved in drug testing and drug-free workplace activities. EAPs are also involved in encouraging and stimulating new treatments, interventions, and educational approaches for people with alcohol problems. The Institute of Medicine has reported that innovative approaches to helping people with alcohol problems pose one of the great challenges to medicine throughout the next century. This book provides information on these relevant and timely issues.

It has been said that the only common element of various EAP programs is their differences. In truth, there are differences and similarities to EAP services. The programs described in this book show that the workplace has provided enormous opportunity for unique growth and adaptability in diverse workplace settings with many kinds of issues and needs.

This book provides mental health clinicians with an array of state-of-the-art EAP programming and emphasizes the unique contributions EAPs make in addressing health and productivity issues. The contributors conceptualize the ever-changing skills clinicians may need to make the transition into EAP practice. We hope it becomes essential reading for any behavioral healthcare providers who want to expand their services to include aspects of EAP services. This will be particularly important as direct contracting by providers—bypassing the administrative intermediary—gains in popularity. The book also is of value to people who are interested in aspects of EAP service development and administration, and those seeking insights into new strategies that promote EAP effectiveness in the changed workplace landscape.

Based on their technology-based tasks and responsibilities, EAPs are naturally called on to serve workplace productivity and health. This book tells you how, where, and to what effect. Let the authors speak for themselves!

JAMES M. OHER

Acknowledgments

I would like to thank Kelly Franklin and Alexandra Mummery of John Wiley & Sons for their encouragement and technical competence. They demonstrated an effective combination of patience and persistence. Tracey Thornblade was invaluable in keeping this product focused and clear. Vicki Strebel helped enormously with tireless organization and word-processing skills, as she has for over 10 years. Harvey and Marcia Levine provided masterful assistance with the use of the English language as well as loving unconditional support. I also want to thank the Employee Assistance Professional Association (EAPA) and the Employee Assistance Society of North America (EASNA), its members, and all employee assistance practitioners throughout the world, who—sometimes despite great odds—work diligently to improve the well-being of individuals and the organizations they serve. Our talks and discussions over the past 25 years have moved and inspired me. Because of your efforts and accomplishments—often unappreciated and unrecognized—this book was developed.

Contents

PART ONE

Developing and Managing Employee Assistance Services

CHAPTER 1

Clinical Practices and Procedures

ARLENE A. DARICK

The clinical practice and procedures an EAP clinician follows can help determine the type of intervention necessary for successful resolution of workplace or personal problems for both the individual client being treated and the employer. Both customers make up the dual-client relationships inherent in the EAP practice. In this chapter, clinical practice guidelines that incorporate procedures to ensure dual client satisfaction are discussed. The issues reflect EAP practice guidelines as developed by Magellan Behavioral Health Services. Magellan has a large EAP service center based in St. Louis, Missouri, as well as service centers in other areas of the USA and Canada, and a continuum of staff offices located throughout the United States. The St. Louis Service Center holds contracts with approximately 600 organizations to provide employee assistance services to over 3½ million people.

The factors that make EAP services an integral part of any workplace setting are important to examine. Most companies are very interested in providing easy access to their EAP program both for employees wanting clinical services and for supervisors wanting to consult about the problems inherent in managing a workforce. Good EAP practice ensures easy access for both of these service requests. An internal EAP program is often located on company premises or at an off-site location nearby. An external vendor is usually off-site. Location of the program is important as easy access is necessary; however, clients must feel that the setting maintains their confidentiality. An internal program or external EAP company can operate a 24-hour-a-day toll-free service line staffed by service representatives or clinicians to meet the needs of customer requests. Most internal EAP programs have contracted the 24-hours-a-day service delivery through answering services or larger external vendors. This allows clients calling to investigate EAP services or supervisors calling to request services for an employee with work-related problems flexibility in seeking assistance at any hour of the day or evening. Magellan has implemented a 24-hour call center to ensure this flexibility and access to the customers served. EAP internal program staff and external program consultants work closely with human resources personnel to ensure that information about access and flexibility is communicated to the employee and dependent population. In an external EAP model, which is the type of programming contracted for by the client companies of Magellan, customers who contact the company's EAP toll-free line are connected directly to an intake service representative, an administrative support assistant, or an intake clinician. Magellan's EAP product line allows a client company flexibility to choose a mode of access to the program that the client company desires to purchase for the employee population and dependents. Access to an external or internal program, however, must be simple, direct, and confidential, or EAP services will not be used.

At the St. Louis Service Center, Magellan uses highly trained intake representatives and clinicians who function as the initial contact for EAP services. Intake service representatives who are not clinicians receive initial and ongoing training in listening and empathy skills, call management, and client risk assessment. Intake service representatives also receive ongoing training in identifying and managing callers in crisis, as they may encounter callers who are potentially homicidal or suicidal. A set of questions designed to screen for risk is standard procedure for every call. After the intake representative has gathered the initial demographic information, explored the presenting problem, and completed a risk assessment, the clinical process begins.

Clinical EAP services can be provided to clients by utilizing resources through a comprehensive system. An EAP clinical delivery system might include a company's onsite counselors strategically located to serve a large population. Many EAP companies also have staff offices; employees can leave the work site and travel to an off-site location to see a counselor. Counselors are available to provide clinical diagnostic assessment, short-term counseling, and comprehensive follow-up services to clients. Many EAP companies have chosen to provide services over the phone without direct face-to-face client consultation. These programs have limitations in that a clinical assessment includes a client's appearance and body language, as well as eye contact, affect, and mood. These are hard to determine over the phone. Most EAP practitioners would agree that a comprehensive diagnostic assessment is always best performed in person. Magellan's large external EAP staff office and affiliate network continuum of care system allow clients throughout the country to be referred to EAP offices within a designated radius of their homes or offices. Where staff offices are not convenient, for the client customer calling in, the network of EAP affiliates is used to provide face-to-face service delivery for clients with in-person service.

THE DIAGNOSTIC ASSESSMENT PROCESS

When a client steps into a counselor's office for the first appointment, a series of events occurs that is the basis for developing an action plan designed to assist the client resolve the issue or concern that brought him or her into the EAP program. A first step in initial interviews is to assist clients to thoroughly understand their rights and responsibilities as EAP clients. This process is essential for both internally and externally based EAPs and should be standard practice to ensure that all clients using the program understand its capabilities. This process incorporates a Statement of Understanding form to educate clients of the terms under which EAP services are provided. Terms in the Statement of Understanding can include quantity of sessions, designated follow-up procedures, and confidentiality limitations. Counselors provide each client with a written and oral description of the terms under which services are provided, consistent with the particular client organization's policies and procedures. The Statement of Understanding, signed by the client, is filed in each client's case record. EAP firms adopt different versions of the Statement of Understanding for different client organizations and their employees because of the variances in corporate expectations. For example, one client company designates that if a client exhibits at-risk behavior for potential violence, the client company will be notified. This notification may be made to the referring supervisor or to the Human Resources department and may result in a fitness-for-duty examination for the employee who is a potential risk. Many companies have now established risk or threat assessment teams, and EAP clinicians are often a part of that team. Another client company may designate that a substance abuse situation be reported if an employee is in a safety-sensitive position. A report of this nature might be made to a medical review officer or a supervisor in charge of performance at the work site. When participation in the EAP is made a condition of keeping the employee's job, usually following a positive drug test, a mandatory Statement of Understanding allowing communication with the work site is used.

An EAP counselor or an affiliate acting on a company's behalf reviews the Statement of Understanding form orally at the beginning of the client's first session, giving examples of situations such as child abuse and threats to harm others that might require disclosing confidential information. The counselor also explores whether the client is involved in a lawsuit and, if so, advises the client that the case file could be subpoenaed. Although it is unlikely that these events will happen, it is important that the EAP counselor cover all aspects involving legal interaction. The EAP counselor also orally informs the client about service payment, including that the client is responsible for the fees of third-party providers that may be incurred following a referral. The counselor ensures that the Statement of Understanding and the EAP process is understood by the client and both then sign the form.

If a client refuses to sign the initial Statement of Understanding, the counselor documents that the client reviewed the form with the counselor but refused to sign it. The counselor will then terminate the session. It is important for the client to understand the terms under which EAP services are provided and to agree to them at the onset of the process. The refusal to sign a Statement of Understanding is an indicator of the client's refusal to abide by the EAP procedures a company has arranged. This situation may occur when an employee is formally referred to an EAP program and does not believe it will provide real assistance for problems or the employee is experiencing anger and mistrust over the formal referral. This situation is particular to the EAP field and the dual-client relationship and is always present as a dynamic in EAP work. A clear understanding of program parameters sets the stage for the diagnostic assessment:

> Assessment is an ongoing activity that dominates the treatment process. Each interaction with a client requires assimilating information, weighing it, responding to the meaning, and again assimilating information about the client's response. It is one of the most important clinical functions. Although data collection is a significant part of the assessment process, it is not synonymous with it. Data collection serves as the foundation, but the evaluation of the data is the linchpin. Reporting data without evaluating represents only partial completion of the assessment process. (Joint Commission on Accreditation of Healthcare Organizations, 1997, p. 23)

Assessment is one of the EAP's most important clinical functions. The assessment process can last up to several hours over the course of several sessions. The goal of this initial assessment is to identify the problem areas that the client and clinician believe are the cause of the client's emotional discomfort.

It is the experience of most clinicians, and informed practice demonstrates, that a client's presenting issue is typically only part of the underlying problem. The assessment stage is viewed as an opportunity to:

- Unmask the potential constellation of contributing problems.
- Organize the problems in priority and probability of resolution.
- Develop an initial treatment or action plan.

During the assessment process, the following areas are discussed:

- Work-related issues and the impact the problem is having at the work site.
- Work history.
- Family history.
- Alcohol and drug history.
- Mental status.
- Legal history and military history.
- Dependent care issues including child care or elder care concerns.
- Medical history and past hospitalizations.
- Career concerns.
- A thorough risk assessment, including suicidal/homicidal ideation and evidence of domestic violence or child/elder abuse.

In addition, as noted in the *Practical Guide to Clinical Documentation* of the Joint Commission on Accreditation of Healthcare Organizations (JCAHO; 1997), completing a cultural and spiritual assessment with the client is useful as well. If the employee is formally referred, the goal is to gather key psychological information and, together with the client, develop a treatment plan tailored to the client's needs that will assist the employee to resolve personal and work-related issues. It is an additional goal in clinical assessment to screen for any underlying problems and not focus only on the client's presenting problem.

To assist in screening, standardized assessment tools may be used including:

- Beck Depression Scale or Zung Depression Scale. These tools are helpful in making a preliminary diagnosis of depression in clients who utilize EAP Services.
- The CAGE. This simple four-question test is used widely in assessing alcoholism. It can be nonthreatening to the client and help create awareness of a possible drinking problem.
- The Michigan Alcohol Screening Test (MAST). This 25-question self-report tool is used to assess for alcoholism. The MAST scoring system puts the test subject in one of four categories: probable social drinker, borderline, possible alcoholism, probable alcoholism. This test is longer and a more comprehensive screen for alcohol problems than the CAGE.
- The Hazelden Questionnaire for Women. This clinician-administered test identifies chemical dependency in women. Questions focus on issues such as preoccupation with alcohol or other chemical substances, increased tolerance, rapid intake, premeditated use, blackouts, and other potential indicators of abuse.
- The Lowell Institute's Cocaine Involvement Test. This 75-question self-report tool addresses the client's frequency and extent of cocaine use, the drug's effects on feelings, and physical and psychological reactions to cocaine use. Although

the Lowell Institute no longer exists, this tool can be helpful in diagnosing co-caine use.

- The Global Assessment of Functioning or GAF Scale-M, a part of the *Diagnostic and Statistical Manual of Mental Disorders, Fourth Edition* (*DSM-IV*; American Psychiatric Association, 1994). This tool gives a numeric indicator, from 0 to 100, of overall psychological, social, and occupational functioning as a means of determining the degree of overall mental health or illness. An assessment tool like the GAF can provide benchmarks against which progress made during and following treatment can be measured. There are many and varied assessment tools that can assist clinicians in the diagnosis of other problem areas like gambling, money concerns, and eating disorders. An EAP clinician should become familiar with the vast array of questionnaires and tools available for assessing the myriad problems employees may be facing that affect their performance on the job.

An aspect of the diagnostic assessment process including the questions developed at the former Merit Behavioral Care Corporation, now Magellan, and used in the initial assessment phase is the WHY NOW? The WHY NOW? is a critical, clinically sophisticated process essential to determining the most effective way to deliver care to the client. The WHY NOW? was developed for use to assist clinicians to understand the cause of a client's request for assistance. By asking this question, the counselor is trying to determine why the client is seeking services. The WHY NOW? process consists of delineating the precipitating event, the proximal event, and the internal failure or inability to adapt to the proximal event. Each aspect of the process will be discussed. The precipitating events include birthdays, marriage, interpersonal conflict, death or significant loss, job change, change in health status, and so on. It is from this first event that a series of worsening events or stresses may follow. The proximal event is the event that prompts the client to access treatment. Like the proverbial "last straw," this event triggers an inability to otherwise cope or adapt to the increasing stresses. For example, a client who has recently experienced the loss of a loved one may be expected to experience some level of abandonment. As additional stresses are experienced in this time of loss, the last straw may be the one that sends the client into a state of being overwhelmed with a fear of losing everything. Other examples of precipitating and proximal events follow:

- A married couple has had an increasing number of arguments over the past 3 months about the husband's inattentiveness to their relationship (precipitating event). While the wife (client who calls in) has been increasingly distressed by these arguments, she has also been able to effect some reasonable coping mechanisms for herself. The night before she calls in, she overhears her husband on the phone with his mistress and discovers the affair she has suspected he's been having and denying over the past several weeks. This discovery surpasses her internal coping mechanisms, and she is thus prompted to seek out professional counseling resources to further cope. The overheard phone call is the proximal event.
- A parent has suspected her child of using drugs due to behavioral changes she's observed over the past month (precipitating event). Upon delivering clean laundry to the child's room she discovers a bag of dried leafy substance and cigarette

papers (proximal event). Not knowing how to confront her child (the inability to cope), she calls in to ask advice.

- A woman has become increasingly anxious over the past six months; her husband started a new job as a firefighter approximately six months ago as well (precipitating event). Last night on the news she saw a report about a firefighter in another community who was severely injured while on the job and may be permanently disabled as a result of his injuries (proximal event). She calls in to the EAP unable to calm her nerves the next morning (inability to cope).

The WHY NOW? process is essential to determine the most effective way to deliver care to the client because it analyzes specific strengths and weaknesses of the client at the moment the client decides to enter care. Questions clinicians can use in the WHY NOW? process include:

- What was it about today that made you want to pick up the phone and call?
- What was the cause of distress that made you ask for help today?
- What prompted you to call at this precise time?
- What brings you into treatment now, rather than one week ago or one month ago?

The clinical assessment should reflect the clinical case formulation, including the WHY NOW? Good care formulation creates treatment plans that are individualized and that optimize clinical outcomes.

The WHY NOW? process can give an EAP clinician insight into the client's problem area and the client's current ability to cope with the identified problem. Merit Behavioral Care's Utilization Management Guidelines for 1997–1998 state:

Not only does the "WHY NOW?" contain the patient's unique distress and motive for seeking help, it also contains the patient's expectations and attitudes toward changing. For these reasons, attempts to probe and understand the precise timing of the patient's decision to seek help have important implications for structuring treatment fostering alliance, developing a focus, and using time and resources efficiently. In constructing the road-map of treatment (the treatment plan) the WHY NOW? is the point of departure for the therapeutic journey to be taken.

Using WHY NOW? for Supervisory Consultations

The WHY NOW? process is also effective to use with supervisors calling in to EAP service for a management consultation on a specific employee who may or may not be in treatment. The WHY NOW? questions that a clinician poses to a supervisor can help the clinician and supervisor further clarify the job performance issues or conduct-related issues that are the basis of the supervisory concern. A counselor can utilize the same questions with a supervisor to determine the precipitating event regarding job performance. Some questions that can be used with supervisors include:

- How long has this been going on or how long have you been feeling this way about the job performance or conduct-related problem with this employee?
- What was it about today that made you pick up the phone and call us about this employee?

- Did something happen today that gave you the idea that you needed to call and ask for assistance with this employee?
- What is the difference between yesterday and today with this employee?

Utilizing the entire WHY NOW? process with supervisors, managers, and union officials can enhance the understanding of the nature of the referral and assist the clinician to better determine appropriate steps for providing service to the referring party.

Release of Information

Another very important step in the process of the initial assessment is the explanation of the necessity for the release of information to be signed when a referral is made by a manager, supervisor, or union official. There is an implied warranty of confidentiality in every case that is opened by an EAP counselor. If the policies of the EAP require or permit disclosures other than by the consent of the client, except as the law requires, it becomes mandatory that the conditions of disclosure be made known to the client. Written confidentiality terms are highly recommended and consent is always required for disclosure of client information except as provided by law. A written consent form should include the following five items:

1. The person or agency to which the information will be disclosed.
2. The address of the person or agency.
3. The purpose for the disclosure of the information.
4. The date signed.
5. The length of time the consent to disclose is valid and a secondary disclosure clause that is a prohibition against redisclosure without client consent.

It is highly recommended that an EAP counselor take time during the initial assessment phase to thoroughly explain this process of confidentiality and to also explain the benefits of signing a release of information to the referring party to allow certain types of information to be shared. The type of information generally shared with a referring entity is attendance and compliance with the EAP process. Under some conditions, it is also recommended that the nature of the treatment and compliance with the treatment plan be made accessible to the referring entity. An EAP client should also be aware that a consent is revocable anytime at the client's will.

A client should also be made aware of the conditions under which confidentiality can be broken. As noted, EAP counselors may be required to disclose information without consent in the following two circumstances:

1. If a client poses a threat of harm to others or to him- or herself, an EAP counselor may need to breach confidentiality to get the client to a safe place or to keep others from harm.
2. Instances of child abuse require mandatory reporting in all states, as does abuse of elderly or handicapped individuals in many states.

At times, exceptions to confidentiality are presented to the client as part of the Statement of Understanding or as the basis on which the EAP and client will work together. An example of this exception is the disclosure often mandated under the United States Department of Transportation (DOT) regulations where various persons, including the supervisor and medical review officer can be informed of a client's test results. A thorough understanding of the confidentiality process is essential to the initial assessment phase of treatment. There is often a great deal of confusion in the EAP world regarding what information can be shared between an EAP professional and the employer. As previously stated, the dual-client relationship exists whether the program is externally or internally based. Generally, the supervisor making the referral or the employer can disclose any information about a referred employee to the EAP; however, the EAP can only provide information about a referred employer or supervisor in accordance with the policies and procedures of the program, the conditions of the Statement of Understanding, and the client's signed consent form. As a guide for good EAP practice, an EAP clinician can allow a supervisor to discuss concerns about or complaints against an employee; however, an EAP clinician should not confirm knowledge of an employee's attendance in EAP without the signed release of information or as a result of the aforementioned mandatory disclosure exceptions mentioned. At all times, the EAP should work in a consulting capacity with a referring supervisor or union official to assist with concerns regarding employees.

Treatment Planning

Following completion of a thorough diagnostic assessment is the formation of an action plan or plan of treatment to best address the client's needs. A treatment plan is a blueprint, a design, a projected strategy. It is not an edict, an order, or a mandate. A treatment plan in EAP practice can take several forms, however, the two most common ways to address the need identified in the diagnostic assessment process are (a) to continue to see the client for short-term problem resolution or (b) to refer the client for long-term assistance. This is a critical point in any EAP case because a clinician must gauge the severity of the presenting problem and decide where the client can get the best care for problem resolution. An EAP clinician must decide whether the client can be treated successfully using short-term problem-solving methodology, often within the EAP, or would be better served through a referral to a longer-term level of care covered by the client's insurance program or paid for by the client out of pocket. This decision point is often a difficult one for the EAP clinician and several questions must be asked. First, an EAP clinician must assess his or her ability to assist the client with short-term counseling care. A clinician who is unable to assist the client using short-term techniques must refer the client to the most appropriate resource. When a referral is made, a standard follow-up program must be instituted. In cases where short-term counseling is the agreed-on treatment, both the client and the therapist will decide on the desired outcome. Short-term counseling can be effective in many situations where employees have chosen to contact their EAP. At Magellan, St. Louis Service Center, approximately 70% of EAP client concerns can be resolved in a short-term counseling mode that includes up to eight sessions.

To be effective in an EAP setting, short-term counseling must be focused and must contain direct objectives for the EAP sessions. Problem areas must be identified and prioritized and objectives must be established for resolution of the concern. This is often accomplished by giving employees reading assignments or other "homework" to complete between sessions and by identifying the expectations and outcomes of every session. Short-term counseling can be effective in areas of job stress and job-related issues as well as myriad personal problems about which employees contact their EAP. When appropriate for problem resolution, short-term counseling can also result in cost savings both for the client company and the employee who may be involved in an insurance copay plan.

When short-term counseling is not sufficient to resolve the issues identified in the assessment, it becomes necessary to refer an employee to long-term care. Generally, these are cases where substance abuse or a more serious emotional concern or illness is present. It then becomes essential that the EAP clinician evaluate the employee's situation and refer the employee to the appropriate level of care. This referral process also includes a thorough discussion of the employee's benefit plans and an exploration of coverage that is available to the employee. Often it becomes necessary for an EAP clinician to become an advocate to appropriate levels of care (a process that often includes communication with a primary care physician).

FOLLOW-UP

An important aspect of EAP care is follow-up services to the employee who is referred for longer term treatment. Follow-up is also necessary for employees who remain in short-term counseling within the EAP. Follow-up takes many forms depending on the type of initial referral; however, at a minimum, an employee utilizing EAP services should receive follow-up by phone or in person at least monthly during the course of treatment to ensure that the program is effective and the employee is improving. Monthly follow-up with an employee is necessary if an employee is self-referred; however, for mandatory referrals, a more comprehensive follow-up becomes necessary. Supervisors who have referred an employee to an EAP have a need to know whether the employee has followed the supervisor's recommendation, as the supervisor must make decisions based on the work performance and conduct of the employee. In mandatory referrals where an employee's job may be in jeopardy, a supervisor should receive follow-up on a weekly basis for a specified time period, often a month, to ensure the supervisor that the employee is complying or to inform the supervisor the employee is not complying with the referral to the EAP program. This compliance follow-up can only be completed with a signed release of information from the employee allowing the EAP counselor to continue contact with the supervisor. Many employees will sign such a release to involve their supervisor and to show good faith that they are trying to rectify the work-related problem for which they were referred. A release to allow supervisory follow-up is usually limited to compliance with treatment recommendations and will generally not have information about the nature of the problem area. Supervisory follow-up with an appropriate release usually continues until the case is closed and the job-related issue is resolved. A specific and mandatory follow-up procedure is required for employees in organizations that are regulated by the Department of Transportation (DOT). It is essential for an EAP clinician to provide close monitoring and follow-up services to the employer and the employee in these cases.

Follow-up is an integral part of the therapy process and supports the gains made during therapy. Follow-up can be used to maintain a therapeutic relationship until the client feels strong enough to take the next treatment step. Follow-up can also ensure that the client does not need further treatment. Follow-up is done for the following four reasons:

1. It is the clinically appropriate procedure to follow to ensure that gains made during short-term counseling are sustained.
2. It is a core technology to EAP service and is an integral part of ensuring job performance gains at the work site.
3. It is a method of communication from the EAP to the work site allowing the work site to make decisions about the employee's status at work.
4. It is clinically appropriate to ascertain whether an employee who has received a referral to longer-term care has been able to access that treatment resource.

Standards for follow-up include prearranging contact in the last in-person session including selecting convenient times for contacting the client. The EAP clinician should confirm whether or not it is acceptable to contact the client at home or at work and whether or not the client can be contacted by mail.

An EAP clinician should make three attempts at follow-up. If the client does not return those calls, the clinician should send a brief letter (if the client has given permission to contact by mail) wishing the client well and offering the services of the EAP if the need should arise again for services. The case can then be closed.

In cases of chemical dependency, follow-up is important to the recovery of the individual. There also needs to be close contact with referring supervisors and treatment facilities. Most cases are open a year for follow-up before being closed.

Case closure is an important juncture in EAP because after a case is closed, no further contact can be made with the client. It is very important from the standpoint of legal liability to close a case because an EAP clinician can remain liable for a client's well-being as long as the case remains active and open. At the point of case closure, these areas should be evaluated:

- An EAP clinician should evaluate whether the clinical intervention provided to the client resulted in improvement of the client's assessed problem.
- Evaluation should also include the degree of improvement or nonimprovement in job performance or conduct at the work site.
- The EAP clinician should evaluate whether the client will access treatment or if the EAP will be utilized again.
- A concise summary of services provided to the client is helpful along with the compliance or noncompliance report. This will assist if the case should reopen at a later point in time.

If the client decides to use EAP services again for a similar problem or if the same problem recurs, the information in the case closing can be very helpful to the clinician handling the reopened case. Case closure can be a time for evaluation and for measuring outcomes. EAP companies purchasing services expect a positive outcome at the work site for the money they spend to fund these services. The EAP must strive to show the positive impact at the work site and demonstrate a positive impact on absenteeism, safety, and productivity.

THE FUTURE OF EAP CLINICAL PRACTICE

In future years EAP will probably expand into areas that were more traditionally human-resource based. EAPs will need to show a positive impact with regard to disability, work-life concerns, threat management, and the issues facing productivity at the work site. The EAP field seems to be in a position to grow and expand as companies downsize and continue to emphasize increased productivity for the remaining workforce. Companies are also interested in additional services that will assist their employees to be more productive, such as benefits addressing dependent care issues and the provision of emotional support throughout the disability process. An EAP program, whether internal or external, will need to continue to be flexible to meet the needs of companies as an increase in employee productivity continues to be at the core of business today. According to the January 1998, issue of *Open Minds,* an expanded human resource consultation model is emerging in the EAP field with more services to managers. Some of these services include stress management related to organizational change, disability management, drug-free workplace compliance, critical incident debriefing, crisis management services, and dependent care. Workplace consultation for managers and full spectrum support services for employees will be the product of the next decade. An EAP program that continues to be flexible and to meet the needs of the dual customer base will grow and expand in importance in the organization it serves.

REFERENCES

American Psychiatric Association. (1994). *Diagnostic and statistical manual of mental disorders* (4th ed.). Washington, DC: Author.

Joint Commission on Accreditation of Healthcare Organizations. (1997). *A practical guide to clinical documentation in behavioral health care* (pp. 23–30). Oakbrook Terrace, IL.

J. Clary, & Oss, M.E. (1998, January). EAPS are evolving to meet changing employer needs. *Open Minds.*

Utilization Management Task Force, Merit Behavioral Care. (1997). *1997–1998 utilization management guidelines* (pp. 13–14). St. Louis, MO.

CHAPTER 2

EAP Accreditation and Credentialing

J. CHIP DROTOS

Program accreditation and individual credentialing organizations have been around as long as people have been successfully completing courses of study. Program or organizational accreditation has also been a major topic of discussion among employee assistance program (EAP) and behavioral health providers in the behavioral healthcare field as well. The question for many EAPs is: "Which type—accreditation or certification—will best fit my needs?" Should professionals seek out individual EAP credentialing or EAP program accreditation? In doing some investigating, here is what I found. The Employee Assistance Professional Association (EAPA) serves as one of two member organizations for employee assistance (EA) professionals and has developed a certification procedure that includes years of experience, continuing education (called PDHs—professional development hours), and a written exam. The other EAP member organization is called the Employee Assistance Society of North America (EASNA). EASNA accredits entire Employee Assistance programs.

So, which to choose?

Well, wait, there's more. The Council on Accreditation (COA) and the Committee on Accreditation for Rehabilitative Facilities (CARF) accredits EA programs, too. So does the Joint Commission on Accreditation of Healthcare Organizations (JCAHO). To add to all these accreditation and credentialing choices, the behavioral health field itself is rapidly evolving. Mergers and acquisitions have made some small to midsize mental health/substance abuse/ EA providers into large conglomerates. Because purchasers of EAP/Behavioral Health programs are concerned about the quality of care, many are demanding accreditation as a condition of doing work for them. Since accrediting entities are there to ensure that EAPs have met standards of quality services, they have become very important when considering growth.

Add this to the mix as well: the federal government is under pressure from Congress to turn more control of the mental health dollars over to the states. There is some fear, though; that the states may not have as much experience as does the federal government in these matters. Once again, enter accrediting entities because that is their job—to ensure quality.

Back to the question: "Which accrediting entity do I choose?" If I am accredited or credentialed by one and the purchaser demands I belong to another, will I be excluded from doing the work altogether? What are the costs of either (or even both)? Do we need more than one credential for the EA field? What if the purchaser demands a different accrediting body, say the National Committee for Quality Assurance (NCQA)? Do I then commission more than one? Does the initiation of another credential duplicate services already out there?

Few contend that some form of accreditation or credentialing isn't becoming more necessary. EAPs face many difficult decisions confronting the rise of managed care. (Reprinted by permission from *Behavior Health Management Magazine.*)

This column entitled, "The Accreditation Dilemma" appeared in an edition of *Behavioral Health Management* magazine (Drotos, 1996). It points out the myriad choices and decisions EAPs must make regarding accreditation and credentialing. Since that column appeared, 2 of the approximately 25 Employee Assistance/Behavioral Health companies have requested reapplication as a provider in their networks. Both organizations cited an accreditation process as the reason for reapplication. When asked about the specific accrediting bodies chosen, both companies said that it was the federal government who made the choice for them. Companies offering EA services to CHAMPUS and MEDICAID clients would be required to become accredited or lose their provider status. Although 2 companies out of 25 may not seem significant, both requests came from large provider organizations regarded as trendsetters in the field.

Accreditation is a timely concern. The medical field has embraced it. Several behavioral health organizations have, too. Internal and external EAPs have wavered, some adopting it and others opting for certification or adopting a "wait and see" attitude. The EAPA has opted for an individual credentialing process. The trend, however, is becoming clear: if the EA profession does not take the lead in both accreditation and certification procedures, someone else from the outside will. As accreditation takes on a more and more important role, each EAP should become more familiar with the options. This chapter will help an EAP make those choices and answer some questions about the accreditation and certification process. This chapter explores accreditation, what it is, and how it differs from credentialing and licensure. It examines five organizations that do accrediting and one organization that does credentialing.

TERMINOLOGY

The terminology used to discuss accreditation and credentialing can be confusing. EA professionals have used terms like accreditation, credentialing, and licensure. They are not the same. Adding to the confusion is the changing landscape of the behavioral healthcare market. Yesterday's credentialing process may not be enough today for some behavioral healthcare/EAP services purchasers. We will examine that changing marketplace and discuss how accreditation can be useful, even vital, to the EA provider.

Harms and Miller (1994) in their book *Family Child Care Quality Recognition: A Comparative Study of Credentialing and Accreditation Systems,* give perhaps the best definition of the terms accreditation, credentialing, and licensure.

Accreditation

Accreditation "is the process whereby an agency or association grants public recognition to an organization that meets certain predetermined qualifications or standards" (Harms & Miller, 1994, p. 7). It "is a voluntary, peer review process that evaluates the quality of a program or an institution. The profession establishes an accrediting institution (or institutions) for the purpose of self-regulation and self-improvement through the use of pre-established standards. The purpose of the accreditation organization is to verify that an institution has well-defined, appropriate objectives and that it meets set standards" (p. 5). Medicom International, a managed care company, defines accreditation programs as "giving an official authorization or approval to an organization against a set of industry-derived standards."

Accreditation is given to networks, programs, groups, facilities, or organizations—not to individuals.

Accreditation refers both to networks of behavioral health organizations, and to stand-alone EA programs, rehabilitation facilities, and family service agencies.

Credentialing and Certification

According to Harms and Miller (1994), certification "is the process by which a professional organization or external agency recognizes the competence of individual practitioners." (p. 7) "Professional associations develop certification programs to meet several goals including increased visibility of the field, increased recognition of qualified workers in the field, improved performance and qualifications of the membership, and enhanced prestige of the association and its members" (p. 8). Harms and Miller identify seven purposes for credentialing:

1. "To protect the client and the employer.
2. To avoid external regulations.
3. To improve . . . programs.
4. To enhance the prestige of the field.
5. To increase the influence of the society/association.
6. To assure professional competence.
7. To stabilize individual job security." (p. 8)

Medicom defines credentialing as "an examination of a physician or healthcare provider's credentials to determine whether he or she should be entitled to clinical privileges at hospitals or to contract with a managed care organization" (Medicom International, 1997, p. 19).

Licensure

Harms and Miller (1994) describe licensure as a mandatory legal requirement for certain professions established to protect the public from incompetant practitioners. Licensing procedures are generally established or implemented by a political governing body that proscribes practice without a license (p. 7). The Greater Detroit EAPA Chapter newsletter (Nov/Dec 1996) defined licensure as "the process by which licenses—permits to conduct a certain activity—are issued by state governments and cover individuals. Set criteria must be met and can be mandatory or voluntary. Licensure is thought by some to offer protection to the user of EAP services because the state would be the issuer of the license and would ensure the EA practitioner had the training and experience necessary. Licensure laws also provide confidentiality and legal protection of records and communications" (p. 3). The newsletter further stated: "During the 1996 EAPA National Conference it was noted that it (licensure) . . . offers consumer protection of the profession and consistent standards, ethics, accountability and quality to the EAP field" (p. 3). Dan Feerst pointed out in his Washington, DC, EAPA/Metro/EAP newsletter (March 1997), "Licensure is the only way to accomplish the identity of a discipline while protecting the consumer against the purveyors of 'less than services' who masquerade as experts of that trade."

OVERVIEW

There are two tiers of accrediting bodies; however, some accrediting bodies belong to both groups. The first tier accredits the large behavioral health networks that provide the behavioral health carve-out to large corporations in the private sector and, more recently, governmental entities in the public sector. Organizations in the first tier include the NCQA and JCAHO and, to some extent, COA. The second tier includes organizations that accredit programs, facilities, and providers who make up those networks. JCAHO, COA, CARF and EASNA make up this group. EAPA credentials individuals rather than programs.

Two of these organizations are directly related to the EA field:

1. The Employee Assistance Professionals Association (EAPA) is the largest membership organization for EA professionals. EAPA credentials members and nonmembers and awards professional development hours (PDHs) for the Certified Employee Assistance Professional (CEAP) credential. Applicants for the CEAP must sit for an exam.

2. The Employee Assistance Society of North America (EASNA) is a smaller organization with chapters in Canada and the United States. EASNA accredits EAPs, sending surveyors to review the EAP for EASNA established standards. To date, it has accredited 35 EAPs with more than 65 awaiting accreditation.

Four other accrediting bodies are independent of the EA field:

1. The National Committee for Quality Assurance (NCQA). NCQA accredits independent managed behavioral health organizations (MBHOs) as well as those connected with managed care organizations (MCOs). NCQA accredits networks and organizations, rather than individual providers, and has accredited over half the HMOs in the United States.

2. The Joint Commission on Accreditation of Healthcare Organizations (JCAHO) has offered accreditation for inpatient and outpatient providers for more than 20 years. Their standards are applicable to both structurally integrated networks of care and functionally linked delivery systems. The survey procedure includes site visits and examines not only an organization's central managed care operations, but also its provision of care at the provider level. JCAHO traditionally has focused on the medical setting but has developed behavioral standards including EA providers.

3. The Council on Accreditation (COA) has accredited more than 700 agencies providing more than 4,000 behavioral health care and social service programs. Sites are accredited based on standards that apply to generic as well as

57 service-specific standards. They offer a set of standards for freestanding EAPs. COA has traditionally focused in the family and children services area, but it, too, has broadened its focus to include behavioral and EA providers.

4. The Rehabilitation Accreditation Commission (CARF) has accredited 2,000 mental health and alcohol-based programs and includes EAP-specific standards. The survey focus is on processes of care and outcomes. CARF has had extensive experience with community-based rehabilitation facilities.

Each accrediting or credentialing body has different standards and procedures for attaining accreditation or credentialing. This can be confusing for EAPs or individual providers seeking approval. To untangle this web, this chapter will focus on the accreditation or credentialing practice of each of the aforementioned organizations.

RATIONALE FOR ACCREDITATION

Accreditation within the healthcare industry is not a new phenomenon. It is, however, relatively new to the EA field. EA accrediting standards have been available since 1987 and updated as recently as 1996. It is important to examine why accreditation, credentialing, or licensure became a requirement in the first place. Primarily, these requirements are being driven by accountability demands throughout the entire healthcare industry. As managed care continues to increase its grasp on the American workforce, employers are demanding more and more accountability from behavioral health providers for their services.

Second, as behavioral healthcare companies continue to merge and expand from numerous small entities to fewer and larger providers, employers have less choice. Therefore, quality and assurance of quality providers moves to the foreground. Employer liability also becomes an issue. Increasing numbers of for-profit EA vendors have pressured EAPs to become more accountable and connected to company benefits plans. Accrediting bodies were only too eager to join with employers to develop standards for measuring provider qualifications, values, and operations.

During the past 15 years, behavioral healthcare service purchasers, employers, unions, and consumer groups have become increasingly aware of the costs of their services, which have skyrocketed along with healthcare costs in general. Historically, EAPs contributed to skyrocketing costs by referring troubled employees to substance abuse and mental health facilities regardless of length of stay or cost. The emergence of managed behavioral health organizations signaled a gatekeeping function to reel in high costs and introduce a structured continuum of care. The growth of the behavioral health industry and its close relation with EAPs has become the rule rather than the exception. Two-thirds of Americans with health insurance—140 million lives—are now covered by managed mental health care plans, according to a May 6, 1997 *Washington Post* story (Boodman, 1997). Of those, an estimated 125 million are enrolled in specialized behavioral health plans that function like health maintenance organizations (HMOs). That's twice the number who were enrolled in 1993, the story later reported. According to the NCQA Public Comment Form, behavioral healthcare now provides service to over 100 million covered lives in more than 300 managed behavioral health organizations.

This rapid growth of managed care and subsequently managed behavioral healthcare organizations spurred demand for objective criteria by which these organizations could be measured. These standards may also encourage improvement in the overall quality of the managed behavioral healthcare industry. By encouraging the adoption of a "best practices" approach to continuous improvement, the standards may strengthen clinical decision-making and foster the development of more effective quality improvement systems. Finally, widespread implementation of these standards may offer an opportunity for strengthening the partnership between behavioral health delivery and medical care delivery to achieve a higher quality of care for the consumer. (NCQA handout, 1997)

Joan Betzold, a consultant for programs seeking accreditation wrote: "Accreditation and licensure came into being because of the lack of accountability and history of abuses in healthcare" (1996, p. 22). As lower costs became important to purchasers of EAP/behavioral health products and services, quality also became a paramount issue.

Thus, quality assurance, outcomes management, client satisfaction, risk management, information systems, and operational and procedural standards entered the picture, as well as added emphasis on the credentials of the EA professional. Today, many major employers and insurers expect EAP provider organizations to verify their professional credentials through a process called "primary source verification." The process includes verification of education, residencies (or in some cases training in a certain area), board certification, hospital privileges, insurance coverage, Drug Enforcement Agency and state licenses, and work history. Malpractice claims are reviewed against standard criteria. As well, some credentialing bodies require the applicant to attest to statements regarding health status and absence of impairment caused by a history of substance abuse, mental illness, physical fitness, or a combination thereof. These requirements have helped some purchasers of EAP services ensure they are contracting for quality services. Prior to this verification process, although the EAP had many organizations' employee benefits and negotiated union contract, little was known about the EAP's precise services, who performed them, or, more importantly, how much these services cost.

With the proliferation of behavioral health managed care plans came competition. EA services that cost x dollars per employee per month now cost x minus y dollars in a competitor's bid. This was another reason that standards helped to level the playing field for what was being purchased.

Another contributing factor to the rise in accreditation requirements came as the federal government began to get out of the business of healthcare and asked the states to take over the care of the chronically mentally ill and/or substance-abusing populations. Shortly thereafter, the federal government required some form of standards before turning the work over to a provider. For example, Medicaid funds became contingent on some form of standards to be met by companies that were willing to care for these disturbed populations. As this trend continues, it is more likely legislation will follow encouraging Medicare beneficiaries to enroll in managed care organizations.

There may even be some case to be made legally for accreditation. The *Hospital Law Manual* (Kucera & Ator, 1996) states that historically hospitals were rarely held liable for damages arising from negligent treatment rendered by physicians using its facilities. However:

Recent case law indicates a change which broadens considerably the scope of a hospital's liability. Under this rationale the courts have recognized a public expectancy that the hospital owes a duty to its patients that transcends the rigid line previously drawn between the hospital administration and the medical staff and that increasingly involves the hospital in the adequacy and quality of care provided to its patients. (p. 3)

[In addition], . . . the Pennsylvania Supreme Court broadly defined a hospital's independent duty as a responsibility to ensure its patients' safety and well-being during hospitalization. To satisfy this duty, the court explained a hospital must not only select and retain competent physicians, but must also use reasonable care in maintaining safe and adequate facilities and equipment, oversee all persons who practice medicine within its walls, and formulate, adopt, and enforce adequate policies to ensure quality care for its patients. Specifically, a hospital is obligated to exercise reasonable care in the selection of staff members. To this end, the hospital is responsible for obtaining reasonably available information on prospective staff members regarding their credentials, licensing, and any prior negligent conduct. (pp. 4–5)

Despite the increased accountability for EAPs and EA providers, as the behavioral health care field grows, there are increasing opportunities for EA professionals and EAPs to provide services. For example, the Department of Transportation (DOT) mentions the EAP as an integral part of the Department of Transportation regulations, as does the Occupational Safety and Health Administration (OSHA). The Drug Free Workplace (DFWP) Acts also mention EA professionals: "Licensure of EA professionals and eventually EAPs will provide continued focus on workplace-oriented core technologies and not just assessment, problem resolution, or referral. A proactive protection of the concept of EAP and its success in benefiting the bottom line is vital" (Legislative & Public Policy Committee, 1996, p. 1). Similarly, *Principles for Behavioral Healthcare* (National Council for Community Behavioral Healthcare, 1997) states:

Organizations should establish internal credentialing programs to assure that their treatment staff are well-qualified for their positions and will be able to provide quality care. Further, the organizations should take all necessary steps to assure that they will meet the credentialing requirements of any payors or partners with whom they may contract and that they conform to the standards of external credentialing organizations. Organizations should measure themselves by appropriate national standards for the delivery of behavioral healthcare. (p. 3)

ACCREDITATION PROCESS

Although each accrediting organization is somewhat different, there are many common elements. Generally, each program completes an accreditation application, followed by a self-study. Next, a surveyor or a group of surveyors from the accrediting entity performs an on-site evaluation. The survey generally offers program personnel an opportunity to consult with surveyors to enhance the delivery of quality services. Some accrediting entities solicit input from consumers during the on-site survey. An accreditation report is then generated regarding the program's compliance with the standards and the program is given time to review and comment on the surveyor's report. Next, the accrediting body provides an objective evaluation of the report. Accreditation can be unconditionally granted for 3 years, provisionally granted for 1 year, or denied. An appeals process for programs denied accreditation also exists. Those programs granted accreditation are publicly identified and acknowledged.

Recognition generally means the program has demonstrated that it meets nationally recognized standards. The accrediting body then monitors compliance during the accreditation period.

BENEFITS OF ACCREDITATION

Accreditation reinforces a commitment to enhance and monitor the quality of EA services to the consumer. An EASNA brochure (1995) adds that accreditation ". . . shows your program possesses a body of useful knowledge values and skills; has completed a specified period of successful performance; showed your program has reached an approved level of competence; has been accepted as a member of a community of professionals recognized by experts from similar fields with similar purposes; created a vehicle for continuous quality improvement; attracts business from companies looking for accredited programs" (p. 6).

A CARF handout (1996) also adds that accreditation shows that the accredited organization ". . . has provided experts and consumers an active involvement in developing standards for your program; established a level of program expectation; removed any inappropriate influence from political pressure; offered evidence of the effective use of budgeted dollars to run the program; subscribed to a set of standards used to evaluate and improve other like programs on an ongoing basis" (p. 5).

COA's handout (1996) states that accreditation ". . . identifies organizations worthy of public and private funding support; protects programs against pressure to lower standards; provides a solid risk-management strategy; enables organizations to meet measurement and reporting requirements of payors and regulators; demonstrates accountability in management resources; builds staff morale and increases program effectiveness" (p. 1).

SURVEY SUMMARY

The six accrediting or credentialing bodies listed earlier were surveyed because they have or shortly will have measures for surveying and accrediting the Employee Assistance field. Each organization responded to a 12-item questionnaire that outlined their respective organizations' histories, procedures, and costs. Table 2.1 shows the questions each organization was asked. The responses serve as a guide to EAPs choosing an accrediting body. Each credentialing or accrediting body's answers are compared and contrasted to show the different audiences and approaches of each organization. Although the purpose of the accreditation is the same, the process may be different, and different service purchasers may prefer a different accreditor.

HISTORY OF EACH ACCREDITING OR CREDENTIALING ORGANIZATION

Each organization surveyed was founded with a different audience and purpose. Knowing this background and history makes it easier for a prospective EAP to choose an accreditor.

Table 2.1   Questionnaire Sent to Each Accrediting Body

1. Please enclose a short history of the organization including its founding date, and reason for beginning in the behavioral health area. Specifically, list the number of facilities and types accredited to date.
2. Are your professional standards published? If so, please enclose a copy under separate cover.
3. Does the organization accredit individual providers? Programs? Networks? Each of the above? Other aspects of the organization? Please include a sample client list.
4. What does it cost to become accredited? Please be specific on how costs are determined—by size of company? Type of company? Other means?
5. How long does the process usually take from application until some decision is made?
6. Does the organization furnish consultants to help with the process?
7. Does your organization make site visits?
8. How long does the accreditation period last?
9. What percentage of sites starting the process are ultimately accredited?
10. What are some reasons sites fail to become accredited?
11. Advice for potential candidates?
12. In addition to the Joint Commission on Accreditation of Healthcare Organizations (JCAHO), the National Committee for Quality Assurance (NCQA), the Council on Accreditation (COA), the Committee on Accreditation for Rehabilitative Facilities (CARF), the Employee Assistance Society of North America (EASNA), and the Employee Assistance Professionals Association (EAPA), are there any other accrediting organizations that need to be included?

National Committee for Quality Assurance

The NCQA is an independent, not-for-profit organization that assesses and reports on the quality of managed health plans, including HMOs and behavioral health plans. It became independent in 1990 and began accrediting managed care organization (MCOs) in 1991 in response to the need for standardized, objective information about quality. In 1997, the NCQA expanded to include managed behavioral care organizations. Currently, the NCQA accredits 335 managed care organizations, which includes just about one-half of all health maintenance organizations (HMOs). Since the fall of 1996, NCQA has offered an educational program for organizations seeking accreditation under its newly published Behavioral Health Standards. The standards are organized into seven categories:

1. Quality management and improvement.
2. Accessibility, availability, referral, and triage.
3. Utilization management.
4. Credentialing and recredentialing.
5. Members' rights and responsibilities.
6. Preventive behavioral healthcare services.
7. Clinical evaluation and treatment records.

Generally, NCQA accredits HMOs and PPOs. Its 50 standards fall into one of six categories: quality improvement; physician credentials; members' rights and responsibilities;

preventive health services; utilization management; medical records. The board that guides NCQA consists of two purchasers; two consultants; six representatives of healthcare systems and one consumer; one attorney; one former member of Congress; and one member each from NCQA, the American Medical Association, and a labor association. The board's mission is to provide information that will enable purchasers and consumers of managed health care to distinguish among plans based on quality.

Joint Commission on Accreditation of Healthcare Organizations

Founded in 1951, JCAHO is an independent not-for-profit organization that has accredited 16,000 healthcare organizations; it is the oldest and largest accreditor of such organizations. JCAHO accredits healthcare networks, HMOs, and mental health and chemical dependency centers ranging from nursing homes to outpatient treatment centers. JCAHO began accrediting behavioral health organizations in 1972. Currently, JCAHO accredits 1,200 behavioral/managed behavioral health accreditation services, including chemical dependency treatment centers, inpatient, residential, outpatient, and partial hospitalization settings. JCAHO has established an advisory panel of BH leaders and consumer representatives and works in consultation with healthcare experts, providers, researchers, purchasers, and consumers. Accredited organizations use JCAHO accreditation to improve quality and health care outcomes, demonstrate accountability, and increase participation in managed care and other contracted arrangements. The *Comprehensive Accreditation Manual for Managed Behavioral Health Care* includes management of the delivery system and benefits and an evaluation of the clinical care provided. The standards include the following sections:

- Rights, responsibilities, and ethics.
- Continuum.
- Assessment.
- Care.
- Education improving organizational performance.
- Leadership.
- Management of the environment of care.
- Management of human resources.
- Management of information.
- Surveillance, prevention, and control of infection.
- Behavioral health promotion, and illness prevention.

Council on Accreditation

Founded in 1977, COA was established by the Child Welfare League of America and the Family Service Association of America (now Family Service America). The nonprofit organization grew out of the anticipation of national health insurance. COA's intent was to have a system of accreditation for social services to improve the quality of public and private services and, at the time, to offer an alternative to JCAHO's medical model. The early sponsors did not want to distort their practice to fit the expectations then present in the JCAHO. COA accredits 700 organizations that oversee 4,000 programs. Over 1,000 of these are behavioral health care services. In 1997, COA published the *Integrated Service Provider Network Standards* and the Canadian Edition of the *Behavioral Healthcare Services.* The new standards are found in a freestanding section on EAPs distinct from family counseling and emphasize traditional EAP features, especially the EAP as a work-site-based program. In addition, COA standardized more recent EAP functions such as managed care interface, work/life services, and outcomes management. The general provider standards include the following sections:

- Organizational purpose and relationship to the community.
- Continuous quality improvement process.
- Organizational stability.
- Management of human resources.
- Quality of the service environment.
- Financial and risk management.
- Professional practices.
- Person and family-centered assessment planning.
- Person and family-centered delivery processes.

The EAP section includes:

- Definition.
- Access to service.
- Service elements.
- Educational and consultation services.
- Human resources.
- Design and implementation.
- Benefits information.
- Record keeping.
- Complaint resolution.
- Outcomes.

An additional section includes 57 behavioral healthcare service standards including EAPs, mental health and family and individual counseling services, substance abuse services, crisis services, day programs, and residential programs. COA features a balance between generic and service specific standards as well as outcome standards for each service accredited.

Committee on Accreditation for Rehabilitative Facilities

CARF is a nonprofit organization founded in 1966 and accredits programs including detoxification, outpatient, residential, case management, inpatient, and community housing. They also accredit child and adolescent programs, corrections, and methadone programs. Currently, there are over 12,500 facilities of which 2,100 are behavioral healthcare organizations. CARF accreditation provides consumer-focused organizational and practice standards to ensure quality care and continuous outcome evaluation for mental health, alcohol, and other drug and community rehabilitation programs.

CARF standards are developed with input from consumers, rehabilitation professionals, state and national organizations, and third-party purchasers. CARF's *1998 Standards Manual* and *Interpretive Guidelines for Behavioral Health* include:

- Organizational quality.
- Quality improvement systems.
- Accessibility, health and safety, and transportation.
- Program quality.
- Specific program standards.
- Specific EAP standards such as employment services, employment case management/service coordination, employment planning services, comprehensive vocational evaluation services, employee development services, employment skills training services, organizational employment services, and community employment services.

Behavioral health standards also include alcohol and other drugs, mental health programs, psychosocial rehabilitation programs, and employment services credentials.

Employee Assistance Society of North America

Founded in 1984, EASNA is an international group of professional leaders with competencies in workplace wellness, employee benefits, and EAPs. The overwhelming majority of members are EA professionals, meaning they have advanced study and degrees in some aspect of counseling. EASNA provides staff development, peer review, training, and accreditation services. EASNA's first standards were approved in 1980 and have been updated every 3 years. To date, 35 programs have been accredited, and 65 programs are waiting to be accredited.

EASNA accreditation requires documentation and implementation in the following 11 areas:

1. Administration.
2. Design and implementation.
3. Program operations.
4. Record keeping.
5. Confidentiality.
6. Staffing.
7. Staff supervision.
8. Staff development.
9. Managed alcohol, drug abuse, and mental health care in an EAP setting.
10. Evaluation.
11. Research.

Employee Assistance Professionals Association

EAPA was founded in 1971 and was originally called the Association of Labor-Management Administrators and Consultants on Alcoholism. The group began as workplace occupational alcoholism programs. In 1985, the board of directors established a credentialing program for EA professionals called the Employee Assistance Certification Commission. It requires potential applicants to have worked within an EAP for 3 years or 3,000 hours. Once the fieldwork is completed, individuals can sit for an examination. The examination is valid for 5 years. On successful completion of the application and examination, the applicant is awarded the Certified Employee Assistance Professional (CEAP) distinction. Currently, there are 5,000 CEAPS. Professional development hours (PDHs) are hour-long units of EACC-approved training required to maintain certification and are in the following six areas:

1. Work organizations.
2. Human resource management.
3. EAP policy and administration.
4. EAP direct services.
5. Chemical dependency.
6. Personal and psychological problems.

Workers can obtain PDHs at their local EAPA chapter meetings or at national conferences. In 1995, representatives from CARF and the Employee Assistance Professionals Association (EAPA) met to discuss EAP standards for the EAPA membership. Those discussions ceased and no further talks are scheduled with CARF or any other accrediting body. At this time the EAPA endorses the Certified Employee Assistance Professional (CEAP) individual.

Other Survey Responses

Following are the specific questionnaire results. The tables (see Tables 2.2–2.5) are a comparison of the services offered by each surveyed accrediting/credentialing organization.

Table 2.2 Founding Date, Behavioral Health Accreditation Founding Date, and Number of Behavioral Health Facilities Accredited

Name	Founding Date	Behavioral Founding Date	Accredation Type and Number Accredited		
			Network	Organizations	Programs
NCQA	1990	1997	305		
JCAHO	1951	1971		1,800	16,000
COA	1977	1980		700	4,000
CARF	1966	1985		2,100	5,513
EASNA	1984	1990			20

Table 2.3 Professional Standards Published

NCQA	JCAHO	COA	CARF	EASNA	EAPA
Yes	Yes	Yes	Yes	Yes	NA

Table 2.4   Organization Accreditation or Credentialing of Networks, Programs, and Individual Providers

Name	Networks?	Programs?	Individuals?
NCQA	Yes	No	No
JCAHO	Yes	Yes*	No
COA	Yes	Yes	No
CARF	No	Yes	No
EASNA	No	Yes	No
EAPA	No	No	Yes

*JCAHO calls programs organizations.

Table 2.5   Accreditation Costs

Each surveyed organization based charges on the size of the entity to be accredited. Some gave ranges of costs included here. Others listed the application fee charge and amount charged per surveyor per day.

NCQA	JCAHO	COA	CARF	EASNA**
$40,000–$100,000	$5,655-up d.o.s.*	$2,900 d.o.s.*	$550 application/ $950 surveyor/day	$750–$5,000 d.o.s.*

*d.o.s. Dependent on size of entity accredited.
** All but EASNA offer a series of training programs given at different times through the year and at different locations. They don't offer consultants.

EAPA credentials and does not accredit. EAPA charges $250.00 to take the CEAP exam for members of EAPA and $395.00 for nonmembers. The exam includes 250 multiple choice questions that change over time and is offered twice yearly. Certification lasts 3 years (see Table 2.6).

Most accrediting bodies offer a series of regional training programs where individuals or organizations can send representatives to learn more specifically about the accrediting process (see Tables 2.7–2.10).

Most sites that begin the accreditation process eventually become accredited. For example, COA states that nearly all who start the process eventually attain accreditation if they give enough time to coming into compliance through self-study and to remediation during referral. Nevertheless, EASNA notes that although many EAPs have plenty of desire and start the process, they drop out due to lack of time to prepare the materials. Time seems to be much more of an issue than commitment or accreditation fees. COA has this advice for those who are planning to start the accreditation process:

> See this as an unparalleled opportunity for the pursuit of excellence, for a participatory change process, and for employee morale building through affirmation of the valuable and sound work many are doing. Make it part of your teamwork as an organization. Engage the board as well as the staff, wherever possible and appropriate. Use the self-study process to bring the organization into compliance. (Council on Accreditation Handout, 1996, *The CARF Story*)

Table 2.6   Length of the Accreditation Process from Application to Approval

NCQA	JCAHO	COA	CARF	EASNA
3–5 months	3–6 months	Approximately 1 year	Approximately 6 months	9–18 months

Table 2.7   Availability of Consultants to Help with Accreditation Process

NCQA	JCAHO	COA	CARF	EASNA*
No, trainings	No, trainings	No, trainings	No, trainings	Yes, mentors

*All but EASNA offer a series of training programs given at different times through the year and at different locations. They don't offer consultants.

Table 2.8   Availability of Site Visits

NCQA	JCAHO	COA	CARF	EASNA
Yes	Yes	Yes	Yes	Yes

Table 2.9   Length of Accreditation Period

NCQA	JCAHO	COA	CARF	EASNA
3 years	3 years	4 years	3 years	3 years

Each organization also awards a 1-year provisional accreditation if survey results are less than merit the full 3-year accreditation. EAPA certifies for 3 years.

Table 2.10   Percentage of Sites Starting the Process That Are Ultimately Accredited

NCQA	JCAHO	COA	CARF	EASNA
Approximately 90%	98%	Most	75%	All

Likewise, EASNA advises:

Be sure the administration of your facility is as committed to accreditation as you are. You'll need their support to get: funds for the accreditation fee; time to work on the study guide; the entire administration must be up to speed on the EAP's operations because site reviewers will interview all executives of the program and need to get the right answers before accreditation is awarded. (EASNA Handout, 1995, *Accreditation: A Step-by-Step Guide*)

Once an EA program decides to proceed with the accreditation process, certain steps can speed successful completion. Janet Williams and Jo Anderson, copartners of Alternatives, an accreditation firm, urge:

Set aside the time. It may take from one to three years from start to finish. Once you have decided to proceed, collect everything available from the prospective accrediting body—guidelines, standards, manuals, fee schedules, goals and philosophy of the prospective accrediting body. Then get your information together—your organization's goals, standards, procedures, focus, mission and service philosophy.

Next, select a member from the staff or an outside consultant to coordinate the project. JCAHO literature suggests one to two full time equivalent (FTEs) staff. Selection should be based on overall knowledge and understanding of the organization, organization and time management skills, ability to motivate people and facilitate change, attentiveness to detail, and previous experience with the accreditation process. Perform a self-assessment to see how well the organization is currently measuring up to the selected standards. Take advantage of the pre-survey process some accrediting bodies provide, although there is a cost for this service.

Once these steps are completed, an organization should have a clear picture of their deficiencies and needed improvements. Formulate an action plan and set priorities to accomplish the improvements with dates of completion. Once completed, put the plan into operation and monitor progress. Then complete a mock survey within the organization to gauge self-readiness. Now it is time to apply for the formal survey by the accrediting body. While waiting, continue to drill the staff and prepare for the survey. Once the surveyor(s) is (are) known, request a resume of the surveyor(s). This will help prepare for the orientation of the person(s) conducting the site visits. The day before the surveyor(s) arrive, collect all the documents the surveyor will want to read and put it in one location. Pass out the surveyor's schedule to staff and offer encouragement to the staff. When the day of the survey arrives, do a last minute check of the grounds and relax. The preparation has been done. Now it is up to the accrediting body. Plan a celebration.

THE FUTURE OF ACCREDITATION

Future speculation about behavioral health accreditation is tied to the overall future of managed care. According to E. Clarke Ross (1997), Executive Director of the American Managed Behavioral Healthcare Association (AMBHA), ". . . three tenets underpin managed care: (a) documented performance by managed care companies and providers as a basis of continued business; (b) positive clinical outcomes and consumer satisfaction as a basis for such documented performance; and (c) the management of innovative and comprehensive service delivery networks in order to deliver individualized, appropriate and flexible service arrangements." If these tenets are valid, then more and evolving forms of behavioral healthcare will dominate the market. Accreditation fits snugly into a philosophy where quality service and accountability are key. What better way to document practice than to comply with accepted and tested standards? Accreditation also fits the EAP adage: "Document. Document. Document." It simply adds a twist: Document according to an accepted body of knowledge. As consumers of mental health care become more vocal about the quality and choice of care, managed care will continue to be forced to be more responsive. Federal parity legislation within overall healthcare has moved the behavioral healthcare providers closer to using standardized healthcare guidelines.

Capitation and risk management programs have entered the marketplace as rapidly as managed care plans did 10 years ago. As EA providers become more at risk for the services delivered, it makes financial and practice sense to have the most qualified individuals and organizations providing the service. As the entire field moves more toward measurement and more purchasers of behavioral care demand it, accreditation of programs becomes more necessary.

As the field burgeons, consolidates, and shifts, someone is going to have to monitor best and consistent practice. Accreditation organizations will continue to develop tools to refine the process. NCQA has adopted a "Behavioral Report Card" called Health Plan Employer Data and Information Set (HEDIS) that Medicaid and Medicare requires as an assessment document. NCQA's first "Report Card" developed in 1989 was an effort by employers and health plans to collaborate on an integrated set of uniform standards to gauge quality and the value of the health plan's performance. The HEDIS gauges effectiveness of care, access/availability of care, satisfaction with the experience of care, health plan stability, use of services, cost of care, informed health choices, and health plan descriptive information. AMBHA has developed a tool called Performance Measures for Managed Behavioral Healthcare Programs (PERMS) that assesses care, consumer satisfaction, and quality of care. JCAHO has developed ORYX, a set of initiatives requiring their accredited organizations to choose performance and outcomes standards slated to go into effect in late 1998.

The Center for Mental Health Services published "MHSIP: Consumer-Oriented Mental Health Report Card" for assessing access to care, appropriateness of care, and outcomes. Charles Jacobs, in "Credentialing for Practice Privileges" (1996) noted:

> As medicine becomes more technologically advanced and more dangerous, society is insisting that hospitals take reasonable steps through credentialing to protect patients from preventable harm. . . . In the future, health plans will be more at risk financially for adverse patient outcomes because of their failure to exercise due diligence by extending the provider credential to practice privileges. . . . Practice privilege credentials will provide some of the back up managed care plans need to support assertions of attention to the quality of care. (p. 52)

This has become the era of purchaser-driven and user-driven accountability. With the emphasis on measures and standards, the EA field is likely to draw more closely together. Future EA firms will utilize the same measurements and standards, rather than developing individual standards.

Barbara Marsden is the current Chairperson of the EASNA Accreditation Committee. She pointed out in a recent phone interview (January 25, 1997): "There will always be a core of Employee Assistance Professionals who will be involved in accreditation."

Tamara Cagney (1996), formerly of EAPA's Standards Committee remarked in her article "The Future Holds Great Promise:"

> How EAP services are delivered will continue to change. More and more services are being delivered by affiliates in the field. Standards for affiliate management will be a challenge as will program accreditation. The question: Who can deliver Employee Assistance services? will not be answered until our standards clearly address the differences between employee assistance and clinical services. (p. 44)

CONCLUSION

The trends toward accreditation have been in place in the overall healthcare industry for some time. The behavioral health field is now encompassed. Whether the federal government continues to dictate which standards EA providers use or whether EA professionals, associations, or others step in, the issues are clear. It is not whether accreditation will be part of the EA field, but when and who will take the lead for its direction. Will the focus be on the cost of care or the care itself that is furnished to the troubled employee? The EA field has the responsibility and ability to make the decision.

CONTACT INFORMATION FOR SURVEYED ACCREDITING (AND CREDENTIALING) ORGANIZATIONS

National Committee on Quality Assurance (NCQA)
    2000 L Street, NW Suite 500
Washington, DC 20036
(202) 955-3500 Main (202) 955-3599 Fax
Website: http://www.ncqa.org
Contact person: Brian Schilling

The Joint Commission on Accreditation of Healthcare Organizations
One Renaissance Boulevard
Oakbrook Terrace, IL 60181
(630) 792-5000 Main (630) 792-792-5005 Fax
Website: http://www.jcaho.org
Contact Person: Mary Cesare-Murphy

Council on Accreditation of Services for Families and Children (COA)
120 Wall Street
11th Floor
New York, NY 10005
(212) 797-3000 Main (212) 797-1428 Fax
Website: http://www.coa.org
Contact Person: Jean Elder

CARF. The Rehabilitation Accreditation Commission (CARF)
4891 East Grant Road
Tucson, AZ 85712
(520) 325-1044 Main (520) 318-1129 Fax
Website: http://www.carf.org
Contact Person: Timothy Slaven

Employee Assistance Society of North America (EASNA)
435 North Michigan Avenue Suite 1717
Chicago, Illinois 60611-4067
(312) 644-0828 Main (312) 644-8557 Fax
Contact Person: Barbara Marsden

Employee Assistance Professionals Association (EAPA)
2101 Wilson Boulevard, Suite 500
Arlington, VA 22201
(703) 522-6272 Main (703) 522-4585 Fax
Contact Person: Kimberly Willis

REFERENCES

Accreditation: A step-by-step guide. (1995). Handout. EASNA.

Benefits of accreditation. (1996). Handout, p. 1. Council on Accreditation.

Betzold, J. (1996). Accreditation—A growing phenomenon. *Paradigm, 1*(4), 22.

Boodman, S. G. (1997, May 6). Managed care comes to mental health. *Washington Post.*

Cagney, T. (1996). The future holds great promise. In *Many Parts One Purpose* (25th Anniversary Commemorative Journal).

The CARF story. (1996). Handout. The Rehabilitation Commission.

Drotos, J.R. (1996). The accreditation dilemma. *Behavioral Health Management, 16*(32), 32.

Feerst. (1997, March). EAPA/METRO/EAP *Newsletter* (p. 7). Greater Detroit Chapter Newsnotes. (1996). vol. XVIII, no. 10, p. 6.

Harms, T., & Miller, K. (1994). *Family child care quality recognition: A comparative study of credentialing and accreditation systems.* Frank Porter Graham Child Development Center. University of North Carolina at Chapel Hill.

Hines, J., & Lewis, D. (1996). Alternatives to EAP Accreditation. *Employee Assistance, 8*(7), 32.

Jacobs, C.M. (1996, May/June). Credentialing for practice privileges. *Infocare, 52.*

Kucera, W.R., & Ator, N.E. (1996). The hospital's duty to warn with respect to medical treatment. In *Principles of hospital liability hospital law manual* (pp. 3–4, 5). Gaithersburg, MD: Aspen.

Legislative & Public Policy Committee. (1996). *Why do members need to work toward licensure?* (Handout). EAPA 25th Conference, Chicago.

Medicom International. (Ed.). (1997). *A thru Z managed care terms* (pp. 1, 19). Bronxville, NY: Medicom International.

National Council for Community Behavioral Healthcare. (1997). *Principles for behavioral healthcare* (p. 3). Author.

NCQA. (1997). Handout (pp. 2, 6). Public Comment Form, Washington, DC: National Committee for Quality Assurance.

Ross, E.C. (1997, June). Managed behavioral health care premises, accountable systems of care and AMBHA's PERMS. *Evaluation Review, 21*(3), pp. 318–321.

CHAPTER 3

Employee Assistance Programs in Higher Education

The Ohio State University Faculty and Staff Assistance Program

LINDA STOER-SCAGGS

Employee assistance programs (EAPs) within higher education have assisted in meeting the needs of faculty and staff for more than 20 years. The intent of these programs has been to provide appropriate intervention, assessment, counseling, referral, follow-up, and case management for employees with personal or workplace problems that may affect job performance. Other names, including Faculty and Staff Assistance Programs, Personnel Counseling Services, Personnel Assistance Programs, Occupational Chemical Dependency Programs, and Employee Counseling Services have been used to designate such workplace services, and denote the vested interest of an organization in helping its employees overcome problems that impact their jobs (Campbell & Langford, 1995; Masi, 1992; Scanlon, 1991). However titled or described, EAPs are basically job-based strategies for helping employees solve problems that affect workplace performance (Sonnenstuhl & Trice, 1990).

EAPs have become widely accepted by private industry and large government organizations; however, institutions of higher education have been slow to embrace the idea, presumably because these organizations have a greater tolerance for varying attitudes and behaviors (Baxter, 1979; Dugan, 1989; Thoreson & Hosokawa, 1984). One of the great strengths of higher education, especially within the faculty, is having the flexibility of time and schedule to explore, conduct research, create innovative programs, investigate new ideas, and develop new protocols. The freedom to be creative that is essential to these activities can also provide protection for those who need assistance and are nonproductive members. EAPs in higher education may be viewed as invading the hallowed sanctions of the faculty as well as the directorate of the staff, which may choose to manage their own troubled employees even if that may include enabling problem behavior. Roman (1980) noted that EAPs in higher education began to develop in the mid-1970s through federal funding from the National Institute on Alcohol Abuse and Alcoholism (NIAAA). Since that time, implementation of EAPs in higher education has grown rapidly as a result of the value they offer individual and systems problems as well as conflict resolution and a focus on the health and wellness of the employees. Mermis (1990) estimates that approximately 5% (or 200) of the colleges and universities in the United States have some type of EAP in place.

The world of academe constitutes a special culture with norms for conduct of its members, specification of valued behaviors, and a mythology surrounding its form and functions (Thoreson & Hosokawa, 1984). Mintzberg (1979) describes colleges and universities as representing a type of "professional bureaucracy," in which employees are given considerable autonomy and control over their work. However, higher education is evolving through a change process that is driven by elements not unlike corporate America. "Higher education . . . enters an era of scarcity of resources where an important segment of its mythology, for example, academe as a protected and revered community of scholars unfettered by outside pressures who can, in leisurely fashion, pursue and advance the frontiers of knowledge, seems no longer applicable" states Thoreson and Hosokawa (p. 47, 1984). Despite the image of the university as an institution insulated from the marketplace, higher education faces many of the same market risks as business and industry. Shrinking revenues, rising costs, and an increased emphasis on financial and academic accountability are all reflections of societal pressures on higher education (Austin & Gamson, 1983; Shuster & Bowen, 1986).

An examination of the workforce in higher education indicates that significant differences exist between the work environments of staff and faculty (Thoreson & Hosokawa, 1984). Staff are described as working in a businesslike environment, depending on their status and role, which includes a more precise schedule and measurable productivity that embraces attributes of the corporate climate including performance reviews and a greater scrutiny of the work area. Faculty, who function in a so-called professional environment, have greater freedom through tenure, which provides opportunities for research, creative endeavors, and a less defined approach within the workplace. The challenges include being published (and the greater number of articles the better), as well as completing research that has value to the world, the organization, and the academic department. Roman (1980) and Thoreson and Hosokawa (1984) suggest that in relationship to EAPs, the work environment found in colleges and universities poses some interesting problems. Because deteriorating job performance is more difficult to monitor and detect in terms of faculty performance especially at the level of a tenured professor or dean, it becomes less useful as a criterion on which to base a referral to an EAP (Grosch, Duffy, & Hessink, 1996). Also, because supervisors have less direct contact with employees, strategies such as constructive confrontation (Trice & Roman, 1972) become less applicable. Experts in the field have argued that EAPs in higher education should place greater emphasis on self- and peer-referrals, as opposed to the more traditional supervisory referral (Gottlieb, 1984; Roman, 1984).

Hampton (1997) states that as many as 20% of employees in any workplace including institutions of higher learning are likely to be affected by personal problems severe enough to impact performance of work duties. Problems an employee is experiencing can result in increased costs to the employer due to adverse effects on health, productivity, safety, security, public confidence, and trust (Masi, 1992).

Sullivan and Poverny (1992) suggest that EAPs may assist with problems ranging from alcohol and drug abuse to family discord, along with adaptation to physical illness, child rearing, and career mobility; sexual harassment; occupational stress; and financial worries. EAP programs are designed to cover a broad spectrum of personal problems employees encounter including stress, financial difficulties, marital problems, and the use of drugs or alcohol by employees and family members. Brunson (1988) identified a profile of services used through the EAP: 23% of the problems clients reported were related to alcohol and drugs, 19% were related to marriage and family, 16% were job related, and 7% reflected legal and financial concerns. Mermis (1989) profiled presenting problems of clients as follows: 29% indicated marriage and family concerns, 23% mental health concerns, and 18% were career- and job-related problems. Baxter's research (1979) indicated that 22% of the services used were related to alcohol and drugs, 19% were job related, 19% marital problems, 18% personal adjustments, and 17% family problems. Financial, legal, health, and housing problems constituted the remaining 3%. Although the proportional magnitude of the problems differ in Baxter's and Mermis's studies, the profile of identified client problems is similar.

Developing an EAP reflects institutional commitment to the human and economic concerns of both individuals and organizations, because it represents intent to improve quality of life for the entire workforce (Hampton, 1997). This improvement includes enhancing the work performance of individuals and profitability of the sponsoring organization (Gerstein & Sturner, 1993). Masi (1992) suggests that with the help of an EAP work can be a means for people to get assistance with personal problems if (a) supervisors and workplace peers are educated to appropriately confront troubled employees, (b) job performance is used to measure treatment success, (c) job leverage is used to encourage workers to seek help, (d) EAPs focus on personnel issues and job performance, (e) cost-effectiveness is addressed, and (f) the EAP is staffed by clinically licensed mental health professionals familiar with addictions.

The pros and cons of internal versus external EAPs have been discussed in the literature (e.g., Roman, 1990), and research indicates that these two approaches produce different referral patterns. Blum and Roman (1989) reported in a study of more than 400 private firms that external EAPs led to a higher percentage of self-referrals for alcohol-related problems than internal programs; however, internal programs had a higher percentage of supervisory referrals. Internal programs also reported a slightly higher percentage of employees with alcohol-related problems who returned to adequate job performance within a 12-month period.

An internal EAP is frequently a product of human resources, operating either as a separate department or attached to health, wellness, or benefits services. This type of EAP is most common in settings with large, geographically centralized employee populations making it more economically feasible to operate an internal program than to contract for these services (Cunningham, 1994). Within institutions of higher education, internal EAPs can offer a greater distinction for the unique issues within this system—problems related to status and hierarchy versus lack of productivity, the isolation and flexibility of faculty and administrative staff who need assistance, and the political climate and "ivory tower" protection can make intervention very challenging. In a positive way, internal EAPs give the sponsoring organization an opportunity to control the quality of the program, and to ensure that company goals and objectives are well understood by the employee (Hampton, 1997).

In-house EAP staff are more likely to understand a company's inner workings than an outside provider would, and are also more likely to be empathetic to worker concerns than someone without an understanding of the company (Campbell & Langford, 1995). Moreover, contracts for EAP services with outside mental health providers may be less costly but can be far less effective in preventing chronic or severe problems, largely because off-site locations are intimidating to persons with sensitive issues that need professional attention (Masi, 1992).

Although higher education has been slow to embrace EAPs, the integration of these programs within academic institutions is a strong indicator of the value they offer to faculty and staff members in addressing problems experienced within the workplace. The past decade has been a time of significant change, as evidenced by corporate and institutional downsizing, outsourcing, and reengineering; and higher education has not been immune to these changes. Colleges and universities have experienced major cost-cutting efforts to provide more services with fewer resources. The change masters of academe may appropriately look to employee assistance programs for support and a sustained vision of health and well-being in preparation for the year 2000.

Internal EAPs are frequently found in U.S. institutions of higher education. Internal programs exist at the University of Michigan, West Virginia State University, University of Missouri, University of Maine, Arizona State University, University of Southern California at San Diego, Harvard University, Rutgers University, University of Minnesota, University of North Carolina, and The Ohio State University, to name a few.

The Ohio State University is one of the largest universities in the world. As of autumn quarter 1998, faculty and staff numbered 18,009 and the student population numbered 55,233. The development of the EAP program began in 1985 and has been expanded and modified during that time. The following discussion is presented as an example of an internal EAP and the components that are important in the program's composition.

A UNIVERSITY FACULTY AND STAFF ASSISTANCE PROGRAM— THE OHIO STATE UNIVERSITY

The Office of Personnel Services (presently the Office of Human Resources) at The Ohio State University initiated the Faculty and Staff Assistance Program (UFSAP) in September 1985 to provide professional consultation, counseling, and referral services to university faculty and staff members (including families) seeking assistance for problems that could interrupt or cause deterioration in work performance. The University recognized that colleges and universities, like other institutions, are affected by many macroscopic changes in the organization of work. This included the recognition that faculty and staff members throughout the University may, from time to time, experience behavioral and medical problems, such as substance abuse and emotional difficulties. The University continues to seek ways to assist faculty and staff members whose personal or professional lives have become adversely affected by personal predicaments and health problems, which in time affect job performance.

Since the University's goals include supporting the physical and emotional well-being of staff, as well as increasing morale and productivity, considerable effort is expended to develop programs that will assist faculty and staff in resolving problems that affect job performance. In addition to being responsive to individual needs, cost considerations cannot be overlooked. Higher education, not unlike corporate America, has come to realize that addressing work productivity problems is a good business practice that improves the bottom line. As indicated by Roman (1982) and Trice and Beyer (1984), there are a number of reasons for the corporate trend toward adopting emotional health programs, but primarily, managers believe that helping employees solve their personal problems is good business.

The UFSAP emphasizes confidentiality and addresses a comprehensive range of personal and professional issues including substance abuse; emotional stress; relationship problems relative to marriage, family, or significant others; psychological problems;

financial, legal, career, and medical issues; or problems that are specifically job related. Several factors have influenced management's belief in compassion and emotional health programs: government support, escalating healthcare costs, corporate liability for work stress, and society's tendency to make troublesome behavior a medical problem (Sonnenstuhl & Trice, 1986).

Policy Statement

The UFSAP policy statement informs the campus community that The Ohio State University has long recognized that members of the University community may occasionally encounter personal problems that affect the person's ability to meet performance expectations. To address this concern, the UFSAP offers professional consultation and referral services for University faculty and staff members (and their families) seeking assistance for personal or workplace problems as part of its overall benefits program. A main objective of UFSAP is to provide personal, confidential information and referral services for a broad range of issues and problems. Whenever possible, expenses incurred for recovery services are provided through the University insurance plan, subject to appropriate benefit guidelines (Reis, 1985). Depending on the choice of insurance plan from the menu of offerings, employees' behavioral health services are covered after a deductible cost and/or a copay charge. Beginning in 1994, a new insurance plan was initiated called PRIME Care which has lower monthly premiums and a more restricted network of providers; it allows members to access mental health counseling with a $10 copay. All services provided by the UFSAP are free.

Eligibility

UFSAP services are available to all currently employed Ohio State University faculty and staff members and their families. For the most part, participation is voluntary although department heads, supervisors, and coworkers are encouraged to recommend the program's services to individuals whose problems have led to less than satisfactory job performance. The first consultation with UFSAP may be during work hours in conformance with area work rules; however, follow-up contacts are arranged so that they do not interfere with job duties.

Program Description

The UFSAP is a confidential resource developed to address disruptive issues and help employees return to the work setting and lead productive lives. UFSAP services include comprehensive consultation and assessment, appropriate and equitable referral services, short-term counseling when appropriate, case monitoring of client progress, and posttreatment review and recommendations for faculty and staff within the main campus area. In cases involving persons outside this designated area (i.e., Cooperative Extension Services and Regional Campuses), assessment, referral, and case monitoring will be provided between UFSAP and appropriate local resources. Providing services to our five regional campuses has been a challenging venture as three of these sites are two hours' driving time from main campus. As well as working with resources in that area, two staff members of UFSAP have made monthly trips to provide services to employees at regional campuses.

Confidentiality

UFSAP records are retained for continuity of care and are subject to the same rules of confidentiality as all medical records. Individuals seeking assistance will not have their condition of employment jeopardized by their involvement with the program. All information is confidential and will not become part of the individual's employment record. Moreover, neither job security nor promotional opportunities will be jeopardized solely because of diagnosis, counseling, or treatment in the UFSAP. Information will be released only by the written request and consent of the employee or in response to a subpoena issued pursuant to legal proceedings.

Responsibilities

The UFSAP is designed to enhance the existing benefits programs administered by the Office of Human Resources. The program director assigned to UFSAP is responsible for the overall administration of the program and acts as a liaison to any department seeking services from the program, such as consultation regarding problems in a department, strategies to assist a troubled employee, mediation, debriefing employees in crisis, and problem-solving. The UFSAP assists in the early identification of problems and provides proper linkage between the individual and appropriate resources. The University, however, believes that the decision to address personal problems is the sole responsibility of the individual. The University will not force treatment; nevertheless, if an employee's job is on the line versus going to treatment, a powerful lever exists to encourage treatment.

UFSAP Development and Implementation

The decision for the development of a Faculty and Staff Assistance Program was made by the Office of Personnel Services in January 1985. The Assistant Vice President began researching the major universities of the nation to investigate other programs that existed at that time. Information was obtained from the University of Missouri, University of Southern California, Michigan State University, and the University of Maine. Memorandums were sent within the University to inform the faculty and staff of the forthcoming UFSAP Program. A search committee was formed to interview applications for a director of the program. This committee was representative of the University's population including student health, psychology, social work, preventive medicine, nursing, the research center, labor unions, maintenance, senior management, and art. That search committee was later to become the UFSAP advisory committee. A director was chosen and came on board in September 1985. The director of UFSAP would be responsible for developing and implementing the components of the program including training, consultation, assessment, referral, follow-up, and short-term counseling. The director would later add two additional counselors and one secretary. By December of that year, extensive training to make the University aware of the program and ways to utilize its services had taken place. Faculty and staff had started utilizing the program.

In 1985, the UFSAP was quickly initiated and implemented into the University system. Many of the essential ingredients of an EAP were established early on, including policy statements, eligibility requirements, responsibilities, confidentiality concerns, staffing patterns, location considerations, and program services. In addition, physical evidence of the program's presence was realized at a rapid rate. Before implementing the UFSAP, effective efforts were made to market the program and encourage the campus community to participate in the groundwork and definition of this forthcoming service. As a result of the efforts of program staff and members of Personnel Services, the UFSAP office provided services to several clients the first week of its existence. The office is located at the University Hospitals Clinic, which provides a comprehensive range of medical and clinical services. This location was chosen because it offers clients privacy and confidentiality.

UFSAP Advisory Board

The Advisory Board, composed of a diverse composite of faculty and staff members, is a great strength as well as an astute guiding strategy for UFSAP. The Board consists of members of the search committee for the Director of the UFSAP which included campus leadership (a vice president, an associate vice president, two deans, and department chairs) as well as appropriate additions to ensure that a representative cross-slice of faculty and staff were included. Campus leadership claimed some ownership of UFSAP and opened doors for employees to use the program. They also helped to market the program through affirmation and support. Having diverse representation on the Advisory Board assisted in making UFSAP acceptable for any employee to use.

The Advisory Board membership comprises not less than 6 and no more than 11 members, drawn from regular faculty and staff. Upon consultation with the committee, among others, the chairperson will be appointed by the Vice President of Human Resources.

Each Advisory Board appointment shall be for two years and appointments will be structured in such a manner that not more than one-half of the board members' terms shall expire in any one year. Board member appointments may be renewed once; however, after board members have served two consecutive terms they will be ineligible to serve on the Advisory Board for one year. UFSAP professional staff members are ineligible for membership; however, they are required to attend all board meetings.

The purpose and responsibility of the UFSAP Advisory Board is to make program recommendations to UFSAP and professional staff. The board does not have direct financial or management responsibility for the UFSAP operation.

The Advisory Board has been actively involved in the development process of UFSAP. Through regular quarterly meetings, board members have had an opportunity to offer critical feedback regarding new program initiatives that have opened doors to assist the campus in program utilization; when the National Research Center at the University lost a multimillion dollar grant, the UFSAP was asked to provide crisis intervention, stress workshops, and individual counseling to assist employees. Recently, a campus policeman was shot and killed on campus. The UFSAP was called in to provide critical incident stress debriefing and individual counseling to employees and family members.

The Advisory Board assists UFSAP in developing future goals and objectives of the program including marketing the program to University faculty and staff, creating an optimum atmosphere for training, orientation, and consultation, and facilitating an awareness of the needs and interests of University faculty and staff; perhaps most important, the board offers visionary support for present program delivery and future expansion of the UFSAP within the University community.

A harmonious and collegial relationship is nurtured between the vice president who serves as chair of the Advisory Board and the director of UFSAP which provides a positive check and balance regarding the interaction of the board. Networks to EAPs have been established at the international, national, state, and local levels as the program continues to posture itself for leadership roles. UFSAP staff members are continually challenged in their professional role of being responsive, professional, and caring.

Training and Education

Supervisors play a key role by encouraging employees to seek assistance through the employee assistance program. Training and education have proven to be key marketing tools of the UFSAP to make faculty and staff more aware of the program's services. Clients have traditionally sought EAP services either through self-referral or on a supervisor's recommendation. To successfully refer an employee to the EAP, however, a supervisor must possess the necessary skills to assess a troublesome situation and intervene in the most supportive, constructive manner possible. (Donohoe, Johnson, & Stevens, 1997). Thus, the overall goal of EAP Supervisory Training Programs has been to enhance supervisory skills to identify employees experiencing personal difficulties through declining job performance, and to facilitate intervention and referral through the supportive confrontation strategy (Heyman, 1976). As a result, nearly all EAP programs have implemented some form of supervisory training program (Trice & Roman, 1972).

The UFSAP provided an intensive training and education program for management, staff supervisors, and each University college shortly after beginning the program. A stand-up presentation was used to present the guidelines and tenets of the program with a time for questions and answers following each training session. A video presentation that incorporated the key issues of the UFSAP through creative photography was presented with the University fight song playing in the background (Nicholson, 1987). Members of UFSAP staff, who served as models, role-played problem situations to demonstrate how to access UFSAP services. Following the video presentation, an overhead presentation detailed key issues for supervisors in making an EAP referral. When the training group was small (up to 15 members) a roundtable discussion encouraged questions and dialogue that facilitated understanding of the process of assisting troubled employees and referring them to UFSAP. The overarching message was that the UFSAP is a broad-brush EAP offering professional assistance to employees and their families for problems including, but not limited to, the following areas:

- Financial concerns.
- Alcohol and drug abuse and dependency.
- Marital and family issues.
- Stress and emotional disturbances.
- Job-related problems.
- Legal concerns.
- Health and medical concerns.
- Conflict in the workplace.
- Any other problems that cannot be handled alone.

Training supervisors for their role in implementing University policies (including those related to drugs and alcohol and Americans with Disabilities Act guidelines) comprises four stages: (a) definition of program policy; (b) emphasis of University support of such policies; (c) explanation of the supervisor's role in implementing the policy (including confrontation and documentation); and (d) clarification about how the supervisory role should be integrated into existing responsibilities in regard to employee job performance (Johnson, 1995).

Supervisors are encouraged to use the following guidelines for making referrals to the UFSAP:

- Monitor job performance and attendance.
- Document issues related to work performance.
- Informally discuss with the employee a need for improvement.
- Provide a time frame in which improvements must be demonstrated.
- Refer employee to UFSAP.
- Discuss the case with department manager.

The UFSAP is currently utilizing a faculty model that was developed by UFSAP and is proving to be a successful tool in effecting a level of sensitivity and change among the most challenging population within institutions of higher education, the faculty (Stoer-Scaggs, 1990). This model includes seven objectives that were followed in a long-term strategy to facilitate awareness of the UFSAP and develop a responsive faculty network to assist in the utilization of employee assistance services by faculty members:

- Develop a planning committee network within each department and office to function as a liaison between the UFSAP and the department or office represented. This committee is tasked with creating options and opportunities for the department or office to utilize the UFSAP in ways that could include team building, problem solving, clinical services, in-service educational presentations and consultation services concerning issues or personality interaction.
- Create an opportunity for informal dialogue through sharing program ideas related to departmental needs. The intent is to deepen the faculty's understanding and interaction between the UFSAP and the academic department or office thus amplifying ways that needs and services can be appropriately matched to enhance the mission and the wellness of the UFSAP system.
- Provide appropriate training and orientation for both staff and faculty including competent and therapeutic approaches for dealing with troubled employees or employees who have become a serious problem for the University. This step involves professional coaching in many cases. Additional training would include topical presentations on issues of interest and importance to the department or the University at large including stress management, substance abuse, mental health issues, health, and wellness.
- Develop an appropriate bridge between the faculty and the UFSAP for continued and ongoing dialogue focusing on open and supportive communication between the academic faculty and the UFSAP.
- Establish a high level of professional integrity that encourages and supports program utilization. The primary emphasis for this tenet comes from the UFSAP,

which identifies the three major cornerstones of EAP development as professionalism, confidentiality, and caring. The integration of these cornerstones inspires trust in the staff and academic community thus keeping the doors of the UFSAP open for faculty and staff utilization.

• Provide a secure information and support base. The mandate and vision of the program is twofold: the integrity, sensitivity, and clinical expertise of UFSAP staff members focusing on the needs of the client as well as expanding outside parameters, gleaning new information, and offering support to the discipline of employee assistance locally, nationally, and internationally.

• Develop an ongoing needs assessment and evaluation process that includes linking individual colleges and departments with the University and UFSAP goals. This is the most challenging objective of the long-term strategy and involves being sensitive and responsive to faculty members through the UFSAP and its interdisciplinary network allowing accurate communication between the UFSAP and faculty. Stoer-Scaggs (1990) discussed the importance of the UFSAP's keen awareness to messages communicated directly and indirectly regarding UFSAP involvement. A key component of this objective is to establish communication links outside the program that can provide a quick and accurate response to faculty who need a referral to UFSAP. This provides a check-and-balance procedure between the colleges and the UFSAP through frequent contacts and evaluation of help being given to the colleges by the UFSAP.

Stoer-Scaggs (1990) stated that since the integration of the faculty model in 1987, the UFSAP has experienced a threefold increase in the number of faculty members who have utilized the program. Previous to the use of this model, faculty members using UFSAP represented 6% of the total number of employees using the program. The UFSAP has offered services such as prevention strategies for substance abuse problems, conflict mediation, stress workshops, interventions on chemical use or mental health problems, and other types of difficulties where an objective clinical professional may be helpful.

The evaluation of the UFSAP faculty training module and regular campus presentations has been informal and based on the following indicators:

• Increased EAP referrals including self-referrals and supervisor referrals.
• Increased requests for information from units that have received training.
• Increased requests for training as word spread of the program's ability to work with problems.
• Informal verbal feedback across the campus about the value of or improvement needed in the provision of training.

Young, Reichman, and Levy (1987) cited that supervisory perception of EAP effectiveness was the best predictor of referrals regardless of the sex of the employee being referred. Nord and Littrell (1989) suggest that their study indicates familiarity with the EAP and the level of support the EAP receives from upper-level management, employee's immediate supervisor, the union, and whether the referring supervisor was in middle or upper-level management were factors associated with referrals and the support given employees who sought assistance.

In summing up this discussion of training and education in higher education, Maiden (1993) discusses W. Edwards Deming's concept of "Institute Leadership," (1986) in which he views leadership as helping people do a better job and learning by objective methods who needs individual help. This approach moves away from "victim blaming" whereby the fault is placed on the individual, to looking at organizational deficiencies that may have contributed to a worker's poor performance. Another way of expressing this philosophy is to look beyond the manifestation of the problem and examine the factors that contribute to the problem. Examples include poor or inconsistent supervision that leaves employees unclear about their job objectives; inadequate support services for employees that make completing work projects difficult and time consuming; or lack of human resource support services, which would contribute to an employee's inability to maintain a constant focus on the job and possibly produce a less than satisfactory work product.

Training focuses on the big picture as well as all the facets that comprise this picture. An example might be a training that focuses on substance abuse in the workplace and all the signs and symptoms that are evident in revealing this problem as well as strategies that can be used to assist the troubled employee and other employees affected by this problem. Employees are encouraged to be active participants in solutions to "workplace problems," thus facilitating a cooperative spirit of collegiality and support instead of polarization and blaming, which results in a much more satisfying workplace.

Evaluation

Evaluating services is essential to justify the existence and to demonstrate the effectiveness of EAPs, thus allowing the sponsoring organization an opportunity to assess the extent to which objectives are reached: (a) training for the employee population; (b) assessment, referral, and follow-up services for employees who are in need of mental health and substance abuse services; (c) conflict resolution and organizational development strategies for the population; and (d) development of strategies to improve performance. A variety of evaluation methods can be used, but they should include a process evaluation as well as an outcome evaluation (Loo, 1994; Masi, 1992).

Csiernik (1995) discusses a process evaluation that includes a review and analysis of monthly statistics to determine whether the EAP is reaching the appropriate number of employees, as well as ascertaining types of problems being dealt with and components of the population being served. Masi (1992) discusses outcome evaluations in quantitative as well as qualitative terms. Quantitative analyses determine the cost-effectiveness of the EAP based on factors such as absenteeism, disability claims, health claims, sick leave accidents, and leaves without pay. Yamatani's (1993) belief is that an EAP could become outdated and stagnant without continual review to strengthen EAP programs. Yamatani discussed evaluation in terms of service needs, compliance and legality, program adequacy, external resources, program effort, program effectiveness, program benefit equity, client satisfaction, cost benefit, and program analysis.

The UFSAP developed three forms, as shown in Forms 3.1–3.3, for a three-part evaluation procedure that examines all aspects of the services provided including client satisfaction with UFSAP services and the referral to a clinician or treatment center; clinician or treatment center satisfaction with the UFSAP's handling of the referral and

Form 3.1 Follow-Up Assessment
(3 Weeks after Client Visit)

Name: _____   Problem: _____

Case number: _____   Phone: _____

Date of service: _____   Follow-up date (attempts): _____

A. Phone Call (showing personal concern and support for the client).

1. How are you doing (emotional state, status of presenting problem):

   Same ___   Better ___   Worse ___   Comments: _____

2. Did connection with referral work out successfully? Yes ___   No ___   N/A ___

   If not, why? _____

   Who were you referred to? _____

   Do you want another referral? Y ___   N ___   Referral: _____

   After you called the counselor, how long was it until your first appt.? _____

   Do you feel the counselor you were referred to was an appropriate match? Y ___   N ___

   Would you recommend that counselor to someone else? Yes ___   No ___

   If no, why? _____

3. May we send you a questionnaire? (encourage client to return it)

   Yes ___   No ___   What address would you prefer?

   Address: _____

4. We would like to call you in six months. Do you anticipate any change in your phone number?

   Yes ___   No ___   Change: _____

   Comments: _____

Form 3.2 Client Satisfaction Questionnaire

1. How did you become aware of UFSAP?

   Friend ___   Brochure ___   Supervisor ___   Training ___

   Campus newspapers ___   ___ Other: _____

2. Did you find UFSAP services easy to contact and use? Yes ___   No ___

3. Was your initial contact with UFSAP efficient and courteous? Yes ___   No ___

4. Was appointment scheduled promptly? Yes ___   No ___

5. Was UFSAP counselor helpful? Yes ___   No ___

   If not, why? _____

6. Was service that you were referred to (if any) appropriate and helpful? Yes ___   No ___

   If not, why? _____

7. Would you recommend UFSAP to someone else? Yes ___   No ___

8. Would you utilize UFSAP services again if there was a need in your life?

   Yes ___   No ___

9. How would you rate your experiences with UFSAP?

   Very Helpful ___   Moderately helpful ___   Not helpful ___

10. We would appreciate any comments, compliments, criticism or suggestions relative to our service.

    _____

    _____

11. Do you have any questions you would like to ask?

    _____

    _____

Name (optional): _____   Case #: _____

Follow-up Assessment: Form 2   Reviewed: _____

Form 3.3 Follow-Up Assessment
(6 Months after Client Visit)

Name: _____   Problem: _____

Case number: _____   Phone: _____

Date of service: _____   Follow-up date (attempts): _____

1. Referred to (counselor, treatment center, etc.): _____

2. Did you follow our referral/recommendation? Yes ___ No ___ N/A ___
    Why? _____

3. How long did you participate in counseling or other services?
    Number of sessions/months: _____

4. Are you participating in follow-up or aftercare treatment? Yes ___ No ___ N/A ___
    Day care ___   O/P counseling ___   AA type meetings ___   Other support group ___

5. Was the counseling service or treatment program helpful?
    Very much ___   Moderately ___   Not helpful ___   Other: _____

6. Were your expectations met?
    Very much ___   Moderately ___   Not met ___   Other: _____

7. Would you recommend this counselor or treatment service to someone else?
    Yes ___ No ___ N/A ___

8. In relationship to the problem you were dealing with, how would you define your present situation?
    A. Problem resolved ___
    B. Problem being resolved ___
    C. Problem in active state of being resolved ___
    D. Problem in initial stages of being resolved ___
    E. No progress ___
    F. Other: _____

9. Are you feeling more able to use your resources to deal with the situation you face?
    Yes ___ No ___

10. Do you feel your work performance has improved? Yes ___ No ___

11. Are your significant relationships more satisfactory? Yes ___ No ___
    Describe: Very much ___   Moderate ___   Not satisfactory ___

12. Do you wish to make any recommendations for improvement or change?
    Yes ___ No ___

whether the referral was appropriate; and most important, whether the client is improving and moving toward a more positive level of health. The three components are:

1. *Form 1.* The clinician conducts a 3-week follow-up after the first client visit: during this phone call, the clinician asks how the client is feeling and finds out whether the connection to a referral resource was made (see Form 3.1; Stoer-Scaggs, Marlor, & Nicholson, 1988). The clinician also inquires whether a questionnaire may be sent to the client concerning the client's satisfaction with UFSAP and the referral to clinical services.

2. *Form 2.* A questionnaire is sent 1 week after the follow-up telephone assessment. The questionnaire assesses program effectiveness and client satisfaction (see Form 3.2; Stoer-Scaggs et al., 1988) and addresses such issues as the convenience and ease of using the EAP and the efficiency and effectiveness of the program for the client. It also requests comments and suggestions relative to the EAP.

    Oher (this volume) states that the EAP research literature offers few references regarding the use of survey questionnaires as a vehicle to provide feedback about EAP functioning or effectiveness. This is not surprising considering that the employee assistance field is still in the early evolutionary phase of professional development.

3. *Form 3.* Six months later, an additional telephone assessment is administered (see Form 3.3; Stoer-Scaggs et al., 1988). This assessment of the client addresses the value of counseling or other types of treatment that the client experienced from the client's perspective as well as the EAP expectations. The assessment considers the client's present status and acknowledges changes that may or may not have occurred as a result of the EAP visit (e.g., assistance with mental health or substance abuse problems; workplace problems; support provided through difficult situations involving self, family, or workplace; financial or legal issues). The EAP will be appropriately responsive to the inside-outside assessment and evaluation of the faculty and staff of the University.

Park (1992) discusses a client satisfaction survey used at the California State University, Chico, which was part of a study "to investigate the level of integration of the Faculty Staff Assistance Program into the university work environment as perceived by employees and client satisfaction with the services provided by the FSAP" (p. 15). The objectives of the Client Satisfaction Survey include the following:

- Determine the extent of faculty and staff awareness regarding availability of EAP services and define a profile of individuals who were aware of the services versus those who were not.
- Examine employee's perceptions of whether or not the EAP is a viable resource for themselves and their coworkers.
- Assess effectiveness of the EAP by identifying whether clients received the services they needed, as well as level of client satisfaction with quality of services and appropriateness of referrals.
- Identify possible areas of improvement in services.
- Indicate whether respondents perceive the EAP as successful and able to handle confidential issues such as racial or sexual harassment.

Park (1992) found that a Client Satisfaction Survey provided a wealth of information in support of the efficiency and need for expansion of services of any EAP under investigation. The survey can be designed by the EAP director focusing on objectives of the program, a review of the literature, and the guidance of a researcher. Park suggests that these survey instruments would serve not only as an excellent evaluation instrument but also as a public relations tool.

The UFSAP follows clients through the previously described steps of evaluation including an evaluative survey. After the mailing of the UFSAP brochure in 1987 and use of our Faculty Model, approximately 7% of University faculty and staff utilized the UFSAP; on average, 87% of the clients were willing to participate in the evaluation procedure. UFSAP clients responding by phone and written survey indicated that 97% were satisfied with the program. Client feedback has continued to reflect that faculty and staff value the employee assistance program through the past decade and this information has been invaluable in helping UFSAP staff better serve clients and be responsive to their needs. Since 1988, UFSAP utilization has remained consistently between 5% and 7%. The follow-up telephone survey assures that a referral was a positive connection for the client or provides an opportunity to select another referral provider. It also allows the client to inform the UFSAP of any dissatisfaction with services. The UFSAP has made a concentrated effort to encourage clients to offer constructive criticism.

CHANGE AGENTS IN INTERNAL EAPS

Cunningham (1994) reminds us that EAPs were originally designed to help clients with chronic or late-stage drinking problems, who were in denial and experiencing declining work performance. EAP clients today are likely to receive services for more universal problems in social, emotional, and relational areas, such as use of other addictive substances along with or instead of alcohol, resulting in the development of new EAP paradigms. Other addictive substances or behaviors would include shopping, gambling, prescription drugs, street drugs, sex, and food. Hampton (1997) states that in the past EAP sponsors were large organizations, typically with a full-time employee assistance staff. As an awareness of the need for and advantage of EAP functions increased, these services began to be marketed by a range of outside organizations. Thus, even large companies began to use a combination of in-house and contracted EAP services to address different client needs or provide services to varied locations. Types of EAP service contractors, originally small groups of mental health practitioners, now range from individual contractors to large, for-profit, multinational firms. Changes in the field of employee assistance have resulted in blurred definitions of loyalties and ethics in response to the socioeconomic realities of the business world (Cunningham, 1994; Heaney & Van Ryn, 1990). The implications of this statement within academic institutions make it essential to know who the client is (the organization, the employee, or both); define boundaries regarding confidentiality and providing services to the employee and the organization; and offer strategies for therapeutic assistance to employees that encourage healing and accountability in the workplace.

Escalating medical care costs during the 1990s, with the resulting uncertainty about availability and quality of medical and behavioral health services, motivated the introduction and use of managed care procedures. The controversy surrounding managed care, often referred to as "managed cost," has polarized employee assistance professional opinion: many EAP professionals have joined managed care organizations, whereas others express concern about trends toward reduced range and quality of treatment, and free choice by employees in selection of healthcare providers (Cunningham, 1994).

Hampton (1997) summarizes that privatization of social welfare services, including management by private industry of state, university, and corporate-initiated EAPs, is a relatively recent development. Ten years of federal deregulation and free market spending produced chronic inflation of employer medical costs, fiscal crises at the state, university, and corporate levels, and the emergence of medical entrepreneurs selling cost containment systems, including for-profit psychiatry. Attempts to save money resulted in states, universities, and large medical insurers contracting with private, entrepreneurial, medical corporations to manage their EAPs on a per client fee basis (Denzin, 1995).

Private industry-managed EAPs appear to be the wave of the future (Finkle, 1993). More than 2,000 companies now compete in the arena of managed healthcare and employee assistance. Money is saved through cost containment practices that include restricting reimbursements; increasing subscriber out-of-pocket payments; limiting number and length of treatment plans; using limited networks of preferred providers who provide services at cut rates to the managed care company; hiring utilization reviewers who often overrule providers; promoting least costly forms of treatment; implementing a philosophy of short-term treatment that often counters more efficacious models; and using primary care networks, point-of-service plans, and third-party administrators (Denzin, 1995). It will take some time before the effects of these changes will be reflected on EAPs and the populations they serve. Careful data collection regarding effectiveness and reactions by workers and families will assist in future development.

SUMMARY

Employee Assistance Programs can be an extremely good investment. On average, every dollar invested through organizational contributions for EAP services saves from $5 to $16 for the organization. The excellent return on employer investments reflects improved worker well-being resulting in improved job performance. In general, EAPs are supported by the concept that improving a worker's quality of life results in increased employee productivity and increased profitability for the employer, and that EAPs can help troubled employees attain improved quality of life by helping them solve their problems (Every & Leong, 1994).

The formal process of addressing deteriorating workplace behavior includes training supervisors and peers to recognize symptoms of troubled behavior, confronting these behaviors in constructive ways within the policies and procedures of the company, and encouraging troubled employees to seek the help available through EAP services (Hampton, 1997). The major tenet of EAP is confidentiality, which ensures that the use of EAP services will not have a negative impact on the employee's employment record. In addition, the services are free to employees and their families.

Internal EAPs were initially the industry standard, but in the emerging managed care climate of the 1990s, contracting with managed care organizations of all types and sizes for EAP services appears to be the trend (Hampton, 1997). Outsourcing the EAP may appear at first glance to be more cost-effective than hiring professional on-site staff to serve employee needs; however, research has yet to show that the criteria of productivity and profit will be supported in the long term.

EMPLOYEE ASSISTANCE PROFESSIONAL TRAINING COURSES

Numerous institutions of higher education are now offering academic courses on employee assistance or courses that address related topics. In the January/February EAPA Exchange, 1996, Paula Harney, LPC, and Susan Frissell, PhD, provided information on current EAP curriculum in higher education within the United States. Highlighting a few of these courses, the University of Maryland at Baltimore offers an EAP Specialization; Occupational EAP within the School of Social Work that includes all six content areas (Work Organizations, Human Resource Management, EAP Policy and Administration, EAP Direct Services, Chemical Dependency/Other Addictions, Personal and Psychological Problems), plus emphasis on research, social policy, and brief therapy. Dr. Dale Masi, Professor of Social Work, describes the curriculum as a "living laboratory" of EAPs. Arizona State University at Tempe offers a Certificate in EAP, Program Development and Administration, or Certificate in EAP, Direct. Dr. William Mermis, professor, includes all six content areas, plus independent study/professional issues. Franklin University in Columbus, Ohio offers an undergrade specialization in EAP that includes all six content areas, plus marriage and family counseling, human growth and development, cross-cultural awareness, and workplace diversity. Dr. Brian Maze is the program director. California University of Pennsylvania, California, Pennsylvania, offers an EAP specialization within the Industrial Counseling Department of Counselor Education, which includes 46 credits on EAPs or EAP-related subjects, with all six content areas represented. Dr. William Parnell is Chairperson, Department of Counselor Education and Services. The George Washington University, Washington, DC, offers a Master in Counseling degree with an EAP specialization that includes four EAP courses that focus on EAP specialization. Dr. Janet Heddesheimer is Chair, Department of Human and Organizational Studies. Rutgers, The State University, New Brunswick, New Jersey, offers three EAP specific courses within the Summer School of Alcohol Studies. This listing of EAP courses in higher education names but a few of the excellent programs offered to students at this time.

EMPLOYEE ASSISTANCE PROGRAM—DEVELOPMENT, IMPLEMENTATION, EVALUATION, AND GRADUATE CERTIFICATE COURSE SEMINARS

In 1990, the UFSAP expanded its traditional EAP services and forged a series of graduate level seminar courses on EAP to be taught as a certificate group (three courses) within the College of Education as a part of Educational Services and Research. The three courses would be taught over the period of a year and cover the following areas:

- EAP I. Development, implementation, evaluation.
- EAP II. Substance abuse and addiction.
- EAP III. Health and wellness within organizations.

Students from various disciplines were invited to enroll.

Rationale

The concept of employee assistance through systems' program development is an important approach to be explored and developed in the counseling profession to ensure that the comprehensive needs of people in the workplace are identified and addressed. The seminars prepare students to understand the concept of EAP in the corporate world as well as higher education and the way that it can be integrated into the workplace to concretely enhance the employee and the organization. Of considerable importance is the ability to assist employees in general to understand the organization or system in which they work and to become aware of the skills and expertise they can offer to enhance the mission of the workplace. This knowledge and the definition of EAP skills provides the foundation for exploring counseling experiences in which students may participate during the masters program and, in some cases, toward a doctoral program.

Description

The purpose of these seminars is to provide graduate level students with the knowledge and defined skills required to develop, implement, and manage an EAP. The seminars address knowledge and skills defined by the credentialing board as necessary for the Certified Employee Assistance Professional Certification. The seminars focus on the major factors involved in developing and implementing an EAP within a system and the counselor's primary role not only with regard to comprehensive training and approach to problem-solving and process issues but also the professional and ethical concerns involved with the employees serviced. The seminars are appropriate for masters or doctoral level counselor education students as well as interdisciplinary students who desire to participate in the courses as electives. Courses were originally designed to be taken respectively as I, II, and III; however, students had such difficulty taking them in order along with the required curriculum that taking classes in order was waived.

Seminar classes are structured to enhance dialogue and participation regarding the topic under discussion. Guest speakers offer their expertise on topics that follow the syllabus for a particular quarter. Various formats are adopted, including panel discussions, student presentations from EAP manager interviews, treatment center visits or projects that focus particularly on students' own wellness, and regular sessions taught by the professor of record.

Course Objectives—EAP I

- Increase knowledge and understanding concerning the concept of EAP.
- Outline policies and procedures of EAP relative to the organization and the population to be served.
- Prepare basic models for EAP I, II, and III.
- Introduce client assessment and referral procedures.
- Discuss systems' implementation: parameters and responsibilities.
- Explain modes of service delivery for the client (internal and external service providers).
- Cover ethical responsibilities of EAPs to the populations they serve.
- Highlight marketing strategies for raising awareness and utilization of the program.

- Discuss training issues within an EAP.
- Cover evaluation methods and issues within an EAP.
- Outline prevention approaches within an EAP.
- Discuss critical issues relevant to an EAP including social policy issues and ethical questions concerning employees.
- Outline organizational development in the workplace.

Employee Assistance II and III are seminars with presentations, dialogue, and "being in community" as the primary modes of behavioral interaction. These courses focus on EAP in relationship to addressing addictions and ensuring individual and organizational health and wellness in the workplace. The value of these classes to each student and to the group is directly related to the contribution and energy investment of each student.

Course Objectives—EAP II

- Introduce a systems approach to EAP addressing the critical issue of addictions in the workplace.
- Present strategies for assessment, diagnosis, referral, and treatment of addictions for the employee and the organization.
- Explain the concept of "community building" (Peck, 1993) in relationship to the class and the organization and the implications for the future of the world.
- Present materials and guidelines for drug testing in the workplace and discuss the role that unions play in assisting employees into treatment.
- Outline prevention strategies in an EAP and the integration of health and wellness. Discuss coordinating health promotion by educating employees in the areas of chemical dependency and stress management.
- Provide requirements for state-certified Chemical Dependency Counselor credential.
- Discuss critical issues relevant to the EAP including ethical questions concerning employee assistance, alcoholism as a major focus, opportunities for improving mental health and quality of worklife programs (the reorganization of the workplace).
- Introduce *Merry-Go-Round Named Denial* developed by Reverend Joseph Kellerman (1970) which is a psychodrama depicting how alcoholism affects the impaired individual, the family, and the larger community. This drama unfolds the effects of the disease of alcoholism/other drug addiction and demonstrates the mental, emotional, physical, and spiritual deterioration that occurs. Intervention strategies are demonstrated that can help each member of the family make best decisions for recovery.
- Explore intervention as a bridge to opportunities for health and recovery through discussion, education, and experiential strategies.
- Outline treatment program and discuss the opportunities offered for wellness and recovery.
- Examine the role that each individual plays in the scheme of life regarding health and wellness and the power of the individual in the organization regarding the role employee assistance plays in utilizing this concept.

Course Objectives—EAP III

- Illustrate the interrelationship of wellness and employee assistance programming.
- Explore a wellness program at a university setting and the components involved in development and implementation.
- Understand a health risk appraisal and its importance to a wellness program.
- Understand the role of managed care in relationship to health and wellness within a systems orientation.
- Provide a greater understanding of the role each individual plays in the wellness of the world.
- Experience an extended workshop entitled "Journey in the Spirit" and focus on the way strategies including the use of art in mandalas, music, relaxation, meditation, and games used to teach wellness to an organization.
- Introduce the "New Paradigm of Wellness."
- Develop a vision for a personal and systems wellness that can carry the message of health and well-being to the world.

Class Process

At the beginning of each quarter, students are asked four questions that set the stage for the 10-week curriculum:

1. Why did you choose to attend this class?
2. What do you hope to learn from this class?
3. What are you willing to give to the class and its members?
4. What is your commitment to the class?

These questions open the dialogue among the class members and lay the foundation for an exchange of ideas as new material is presented within the class. Students are urged to lead balanced and healthy lives because it is recognized that human service professionals can only give the level of health they possess to clients, students or the employees that they serve. The class becomes an EAP laboratory through this type of interaction. Principles and concepts of employee assistance are applied as lectures are given. Guest speakers are invited to share specific topical expertise.

Each week, the class decides what assignments will be given regarding student health. Class members often suggest things that would be helpful to them and frequently commit to the class beginning steps toward positive movement in this area. For example, John (not his real name) was a doctoral student preparing for general exams and experiencing high stress levels. During the class community time, he would discuss his past week and the class would listen and offer suggestions. John and others have mentioned the value of applying the principles discussed in class to improve the quality of their own lives. Thus, these activities showed them the value of sharing these principles with future clients.

As these principles are discussed and applied, class members challenge each other regarding policies and practices. Because most students are in professional positions, already working as counselors and so on, they can offer valuable information and insight within the class discussions. Some students are already working informally within the employee assistance profession and the class can assist in framing and amplifying their work as well as offering a perspective that the student may not have previously understood. As the tenets of EAP are presented to the class, each member brings the unique experience of his or her individual workplace to the class discussion making for varied and rich dialogue.

Class assignments take the students to chemical dependency treatment centers and EAP programs for interviews and discussions with directors of these services. Assignments are made individually or in dyads or triads with the information later compiled and presented to the class. As a result of these assignments, all class members share in the comprehensive information gleaned by each member. The class informally evaluates the quality of the presented programs and services in relationship to their understanding of EAP.

Class members are also expected to attend an Employee Assistance Professionals' Association (EAPA) meeting. This allows students to immerse themselves among other EAP professionals and begin to have a distinction for the true purpose and activity of EAP. They can begin building a network within the state and an understanding of the vast connection that EAP has nationally and internationally. EAPA and EASNA (Employee Assistance Society of North America) are discussed and membership encouraged. Articles from the various EAP journals are given to class members weekly.

The final project for the Employee Assistance I course is to design and implement a comprehensive EAP complete with personnel requirements, budget, and operating policy statements suitable for the population being served. The designs are presented to the class and critiqued by class members. The students' creativity, skillfulness, and knowledge are a testimony to the strength and value of the discipline of employee assistance.

The EAP I, II, and III classes are taught in support of the Certified Employee Assistance Professionals' examination to provide comprehensive and foundational information to assist students if they choose to take the exam. But these courses are not designed specifically to help students pass the exam. It is gratifying to note that many past students who participated in the EAP certificate courses are working in the field of employee assistance programming today and enjoy coming back to the class as guest speakers. This maintains a positive cycle of information and learning to help the discipline of EAP move forward.

REFERENCES

Austin, A.E., & Gamson, Z.F. (1983). Academic workplace: New demands heightened tensions (Research Report 10). Washington, DC: Clearinghouse on Higher Education, George Washington University.

Baxter, A.K. (1979). University employees as people: A counseling service for faculty and staff. *CUPA Journal, 30,* 44–49.

Blum, T.T., & Roman, P.M. (1989). Employee assistance programs and human resources management. In K. Rowland & G. Ferris (Eds.), *Research in personnel and human resources management* (Vol. 7, pp. 259–312). Greenwich, CT: JA Press.

Brunson, K. (1988). A cost benefit analysis of the medical center: The University of Michigan. *The Almacan, 18,* 23–30.

Campbell, R.L., & Langford, R.E. (1995). *Substance abuse in the workplace.* New York: CRC Press.

Csiernik, R. (1995). A review of research methods used to examine employee assistance program delivery options. *Evaluation and Program Planning, 18*(1), 25–36.

Cunningham, G. (1994). *Effective employee assistance programs: A guide for EAP counselors and managers.* London: Sage.

Deming, W.E. (1986). *Out of crisis.* Cambridge, MA: MIT Center for Advanced Engineering Study.

Denzin, N.K. (1995). Living and dying in an employee assistance program. *Journal of Drug Issues, 25*(2), 363–378.

Donohoe, T.L., Johnson, J.T., & Stevens, J. (1997), An analysis of an employee assistance supervisory training program. *Employee Assistance Quarterly, 12*(3), 25–34.

Dugan, P. (1989, July/August). Peer intervention in higher education. *EAP Digest,* 47–53.

Every, D.K., & Leong, D.M. (1994). Exploring EAP. *Employee Assistance Quarterly, 10*(1), 1–12.

Finkle, M.L. (1993). Managed care is not the answer. *Journal of Health Politics, Policy and Law, 18,* 105–112.

Gerstein, L.H., & Sturner, P. (1993). A Taoist paradigm of EAM consultation. *Journal of Counseling and Development, 72*(2), 178–184.

Gottlieb, B.H. (1984). The informal system of employee assistance on campus. In R. W. Thoreson & E.P. Hosokawa (Eds.), *Employee assistance programs in higher education.* Springfield, IL: Thomas.

Grosch, J.W., Duffy, K.G., & Hessink, T.K. (1996). Employee assistance programs in higher education: Factors associated with program usage and effectiveness. *Employee Assistance Quarterly, 11*(1), 43–57.

Hampton, E.M., (1997). *Discussion of the development and implementation of an internal EAM program in a corporate setting (30,000 employees) or an institution of higher education (serving 43,000 persons).* General Examination, Doctor of Philosophy.

Harney, P., & Frissell, S. (1996, January/February). EAP curricula in higher education. *EAPA Exchange,* 10–14, 33.

Heaney, C.A., & Van Ryn, M. (1990). Broadening the scope of worksite stress programs: A guiding framework. *American Journal of Health Promotion, 4*(6), 413–421.

Heyman, M. (1976). Referral to alcoholism programs in industry: Coercion, confrontation, choice. *Journal of Studies on Alcohol, 37*(7), 900–907.

Johnson, A.T. (1995). Employee assistance programs and employer downsizing. *Employee Assistance Quarterly, 10*(4), 13–27.

Kellerman, J.L. (1970). *Alcoholism: A merry-go-round named denial* (Pamphlet). Center City, MN: Hazelden.

Loo, R. (1994). The evaluation of stress management services by a Canadian organization. *Journal of Business and Psychology, 9*(2), 129–136.

Masi, D.A. (1992). Employee assistance programs. In D.A. Masi (Ed.), *The AMA handbook for developing employee assistance and counseling programs.* New York: American Management Association.

Maiden, R.P. (1993). Principles of total quality management and their application to employee assistance programs: A critical analysis. *Employee Assistance Program Quarterly, 8*(4), 11–39.

Marlor, F.N. (1996) *University faculty and staff assistance program assessment forms: Participant's information form, medical history, employee information record.* The Ohio State University, Columbus.

Mermis, W.L. (1989). *Employee assistance programs in colleges and universities* (Unpublished report).

Mermis, W.L. (1990, February). The college and university EAP network. *EAPA Exchange,* 34–35.

Mintzberg, H. (1979). *The structuring of organizations.* Englewood Cliffs, NJ: Prentice Hall.

Nicholson, P.E. (1987) *University faculty and staff assistance program training video.* The Ohio State University, Columbus.

Nord, J., & Littrell, J. (1989) Predictors of supervisors' referrals of employees to an employee assistance program. *Employee Assistance Quarterly, 5*(2), 21–40.

Park, D. (1992). Client satisfaction evaluation: University employee assistance program. *Employee Assistance Quarterly, 8*(4), 77–100.

Peck, M.S. (1993). *A world waiting to be born: Rediscovering civility.* New York: Bantam Books.

Reis, F.W. (1985) *University faculty and staff assistance program policy statement.* The Ohio State University, Columbus.

Roman, P.M. (1980). Employee alcoholism and assistance programs: Adapting an innovation for college and university faculty. *Journal of Higher Education, 51,* 135–149.

Roman, P.M. (1982, Fall). Barriers to the use of constructive confrontation with employed alcoholics. *Journal of Drug Issues,* 369–382.

Roman, P.M. (1984). Barriers to the initiation of employee alcoholism programs. In *Occupational alcoholism: A review of research issues* (pp. 139–168). Rockville, MD: National Institute on Alcohol Abuse and Alcoholism.

Roman, P.M. (1990). *Alcohol problem intervention in the workplace: Employee assistance programs and strategic alternatives.* New York: Quorum Books.

Scanlon, W.F. (1991). *Alcoholism and drug abuse in the workplace: Managing care and costs through employee assistance programs* (2nd ed.). New York: Praeger.

Shuster, R. & Bowen, T. (1986). *American professors: A national resource imperiled.* New York: Oxford University Press.

Sonnenstuhl, W.J., & Trice, H.M. (1986). *Strategies for employee assistance program: The crucial balance.* Ithaca, NY: ILR Press.

Sonnenstuhl, W.J., & Trice, H.M. (1990). *Strategies for employee assistance programs: The crucial balance* (2nd Rev. ed.). Ithaca, NY: ILR Press.

Stoer-Scaggs, L. (1990). Faculty model and evaluation strategies in higher education: The Ohio State University EAP. *Employee Assistance Quarterly, 6,* 67–73.

Stoer-Scaggs, L., Marlor, F.N., & Nicholson, P.E. (1988). *University faculty and staff assistance assessment forms #1, #2, & #3.* The Ohio State University, Columbus.

Sullivan, R., & Poverny, L. (1992). Differential patterns of EAP service utilization among university faculty and staff. *Employee Assistance Quarterly, 8*(1), 1–11.

Thoreson, R.W., & Hosokawa, E.P. (Eds.). (1984). *Employee assistance programs in higher education.* Springfield, IL: Thomas.

Trice, H.M., & Beyer, J.M. (1984). Employee assistance programs: Emotionally disturbed employees. *Research in Community and Mental Health, 4,* 245–253.

Trice, H.M., & Roman, P.M. (1972). *Spirits and demons at work: Alcohol and other drugs on the job.* Ithaca, NY: New York State School of Industrial and Labor Relations, Cornell University.

Trice, H.M., & Roman, P.M. (1978). *Spirits and demons at work* (2nd ed.). Ithaca, NY: New York State School of Industrial Labor Relations, Cornell University.

Yamatani, H. (1993). Suggested top ten evaluations for employee assistance programs: An overview. *Employee Assistance Quarterly, 9*(2), 65–82.

Young, D., Reichman, W., & Levy M. (1987). Differential referral of women and men to employee assistance programs: The role of supervisory attitudes. *Journal of Studies on Alcohol, 48*(1), 22–28.

CHAPTER 4

Models of Service Delivery

TAMARA CAGNEY

Employee assistance programs (EAPs), like other human resource services and health care entities, have experienced much change in the past 10 years. All service delivery systems are being modified, merged and integrated and EAPs are no exception. Traditionally, EAPs were internal programs based inside the host organization and staffed by employees of the organization. The EAP field has experienced outsourcing as have many industries. Today, the majority of EAPs are external programs provided to the employer organization through outside contracting EAP vendors. These EAP firms have, in many cases, also been integrated into other behavioral health delivery systems such as behavioral health managed care organizations (MCOs).

The challenge for EAPs is to maintain their clarity of vision and purpose, as the models of EAP respond to the market place. Recent human resources issues—such as the Drug-Free Workplace Act, new interpretations of the Americans with Disabilities Act, recent Economic Employment Opportunity Committee (EEOC) rulings, child and elder care concerns and workplace violence—are triggering a closer look at employee assistance programs.

Historically, EAPs dealt with alcohol and drug issues in the workplace. They expanded their focus in the 1970s to include other personal and mental health problems. Over the intervening two decades, EAPs have evolved further to incorporate a broad spectrum of clinical tools and organizational services geared for promoting productivity.

With the advent of prepaid behavioral health managed care organizations (MCOs), there were some who felt that EAPs were merely mental health HMOs and that no distinction in services could be made. MCOs saw EAPs as duplicative services to the mental health access numbers and provider panels that they were offering. Some MCOs designed EAPs that were merely a loss leader to be offered to employers to channel employees into the managed health care benefits. In the early 1980s, there were many predictions by managed care organizations (MCOs) of the demise of EAPs. But MCOs have learned over the intervening years that the contracting employer, the one paying for the services, values highly the work-site-focused services offered by EAPs and, in fact, EAP enrollment has increased 45% since 1994.

EAP SERVICE COMPONENTS

It is important to delineate what services and components combine to create the unique EAP approach to productivity problems. The pressure from MCO has helped develop more clarity about EAP services and the development of EAP standards of practice. Employee assistance programs have several core components that are not present in other delivery systems. EAPs are defined by the Employee Assistance Professional Association (EAPA) as work-site-based programs designed to assist (a) work organizations in addressing productivity issues and (b) "employee clients" in identifying and resolving personal concerns (including but not limited to health, marital, family, alcohol, drug, legal, emotional, stress, or other personal issues) that may affect performance. Although traditional behavioral health clinical skills are employed to this end, the key focus is on work-site problems as the trigger for case finding. The focus on performance problems, combined with self identification, positions the EAP to intervene early on in the development of many problems. The EAP deals with *DSM-IV* clinical diagnosis, such as depression, but the EAP is also in a unique position to intervene in non-*DSM-IV* Axis I classified issues such as parenting issues, marital stress, and financial and legal concerns that may be distracting the employee and could be the precursor to more serious psychological problems.

PROGRAM DESIGN

Program design depends a great deal on the goals of the EAP. Some EAPs deliver assessment and referral services only, others add clinical services in the form of short-term problem resolution. Still others are fully integrated with behavioral health benefits and take on a more clinical appearance. Whatever the collateral services offered, and no matter how they are packaged, the core EAP functions must be present. These seven core components combine to create a unique approach to addressing work productivity issues and client concerns that affect job performance. EAP core technology is:

1. Consultation with, training of, and assistance to work organization leaders (managers, supervisors, and union stewards) seeking to manage the troubled employee, enhance the work environment, and improve employee job performance; and outreach to and education of employees and their family members about EAP services.
2. Confidential and timely problem identification/assessment services for employee clients with personal concerns that may affect job performance.
3. Use of constructive confrontation, motivation, and short-term intervention with employee clients to address problems that affect job performance.
4. Referral of employee clients for diagnosis, treatment, and assistance, plus case monitoring and follow-up services.
5. Consultation with work organizations in establishing and maintaining effective relations with treatment and other service providers, and in managing provider contracts.
6. Consultation with work organizations to encourage availability of and employee access to health benefits covering medical and behavioral problems, including, but not limited to, alcoholism, drug abuse, and mental and emotional disorders.
7. Identification of the effects of EAP services on the work organization and individual job performance.

ACCESS TO SERVICES

EAPs target both:

1. Employees whose performance shows a pattern of decline which is not readily explained by supervisory observation of their job circumstances.
2. Employees who are aware of personal difficulties that may be affecting or may start to affect their work lives.

The majority (up to 90%) of EAP clients are from this second group and access the EAP through self-referral (see Figure 4.1). These are employees who have some insight into their problems and avail themselves of the easy access offered by the employers' EAP. Employees who self-refer are given assurances that their personal issues will be kept confidential and that the employer's interest is in maintaining a safe and productive workforce. These employees contact the EAP to receive assessment services and referral to qualified local providers or to receive short-term solution focused counseling provided within the EAP system.

Of the employees who access EAP services, up to 80% receive the guidance that they need to clarify their issues, contact appropriate resources, and effect change if necessary. Therefore, these employees do not access their mental health benefit. Early intervention when symptoms are milder results in a considerable savings to the employer and benefits cost containment.

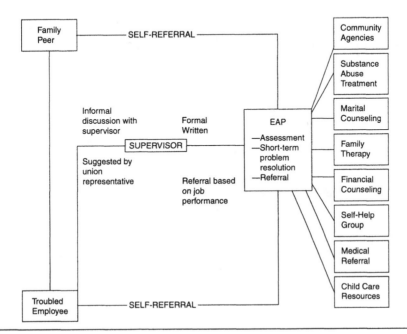

Figure 4.1   General EAP structure.

SUPERVISORY REFERRALS

As valuable as self-referral services are, it is the EAP services delivered to the remaining 10%, the employees referred on the basis of job performance problems, that make EAPs unique and have made EAPs valuable to employers. When an employer has a functional EAP, they do not have to wait for the employee to contact one of their panel providers, or wait for the problem to escalate to a point where fitness for duty or workers' compensation systems are called into play. Effective management always involves understanding and responding to people as individuals. In the case of behavioral health problems, some of these individual characteristics can become a management issue. Emotional problems at work cause a dilemma for most managers. There is a tendency to want to leave charged emotional issues alone, but there is also a natural desire to help. Employee problems do need to be recognized before they can be addressed and recognition can be difficult. Less enmeshed in the personal emotional turmoil of the employee, often workplace colleagues and management recognize problems before the family or the employee has to confront them. Problems at work show up in subtle ways such as decreased productivity, ambition, quality, or interpersonal effectiveness.

EAP offers a tool that allows supervisors to combine their concern with an offer of assistance and progressive disciplinary action. The employee does not have to possess insight into the problem, admit to a problem, or have motivation to seek help. The supervisor is provided with a means to intervene at an early stage of dysfunction and to refer the employee to a professional for assessment and assistance (see Figure 4.2).

As part of their specialized services, EAPs provide supervisors with training and consultation to determine the appropriateness of an EAP referral and to guide the

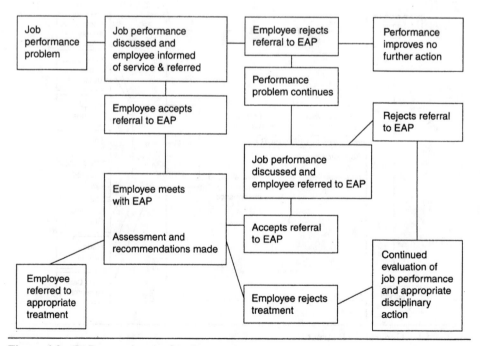

Figure 4.2   EAP supervisory referral.

manager through the intervention and referral. This intervention process was historically referred to as "constructive confrontation." The EAP intervention consists of documenting examples of performance problems to overcome denial, precipitate concern or a crisis, and offer assistance. The next steps involve following progressive discipline procedures but also assuring the employee that assistance is available.

The EAP intervention has evolved to encompass normal supervisory intervention and to combine it with professional assistance through six steps:

1. Supervisory observation of a performance problem.
2. Documentation of observed performance deficit.
3. Review of the performance with the employee.
4. Identification of specific problem areas and delineation of improvements sought.
5. Referring to the EAP for assistance in resolving personal problems that may be contributing to poor performance.
6. Establishing follow-up steps and the consequences if performance does not improve.

The availability of the EAP relieves supervisors and, for that matter, union representatives, of the need to counsel employees and to provide assistance that is most often outside their areas of expertise. Supervisors are encouraged to stress that the referral to the EAP helps the employee get assistance to improve performance. Supervisors are coached to state the facts of the performance problems and to have the EAP focus on the causes with the employee.

In this highly litigious age, supervisory EAP intervention also provides the employer a way to fulfill their social role and helps to assure due process for the employee. The use of the EAP provides an alternative to discharging valuable trained employees and encourages the return to an effective performance level of employees in whom the employer has invested time and training.

ORGANIZATIONAL SERVICES

EAP programs deliver services to both the individual employees and the work organization. Larger scale problems of the organization itself can creep up gradually, invisible to management until the organizational effects are pressing or severe. EAPs can be designed to deliver services with an aim toward productivity restoration as well as productivity enhancement. The expertise of EAP professionals and their unique view of the organization can be valuable during periods of organizational change, such as layoffs and restructuring.

EAPs have expanded the human resource consultation model to offer more services to employers (see Figure 4.3). They have evolved to offer education and prevention services including health promotion, stress claim prevention and supervisory coaching programs. Coordination with other departments and organizational services that lend themselves to productivity enhancement, such as supervisory training, violence teams and work group team building make optimal use of the EA professional's training. EAPs also help employers comply with legislative and regulatory mandates such a Drug-Free Workplace Act and Department of Transportation Drug Testing.

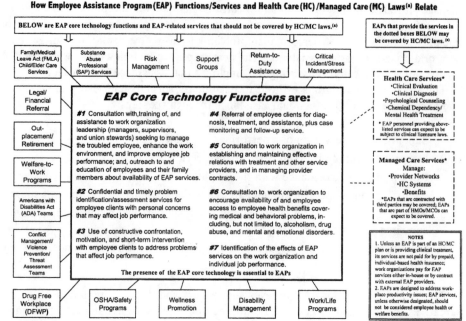

How employee assistance program (EAP) functions/services and health care (HC)/managed care (MC) laws[a] relate.

© Reprinted with permission from the EAP Association, 2101 Wilson Blvd, Suite 500, Arlington, VA 22201.

Figure 4.3   How employee assistance program (EAP) functions/services and health care (HC)/managed care (MC) laws[a] relate.

The challenge, however, is to build all these collateral services around the core EAP activities and to not lose sight of the EAPs' primary purpose.

PROGRAM MODELS—INTERNAL EAP

EAP services are delivered through a variety of program models. The earliest EAPs and many in large corporations today are structured as an internal department of the employer. Internal EAPs, like all the EAP models, have their strengths and their drawbacks. The major concern about internal EA programs is that they may be perceived as being too closely identified with any particular department, group, or person in the organization and that the confidentiality of employee problems may be difficult to protect. These concerns result in some structured isolation within the organization. This necessary separation and neutrality is balanced by developing links to the other parts of the organization. These internal linkages build one of the internal EAP's most unique strengths. The internal EAP knows the work organization in a way that few external vendors ever will. Internal EAPs are positioned to deliver high-quality organizational services designed for that specific organization (see Figure 4.4).

Internal EAPs can be more integrated with the employer organization than an external vendor. The EAP logically fits into the constellation of human resources. The

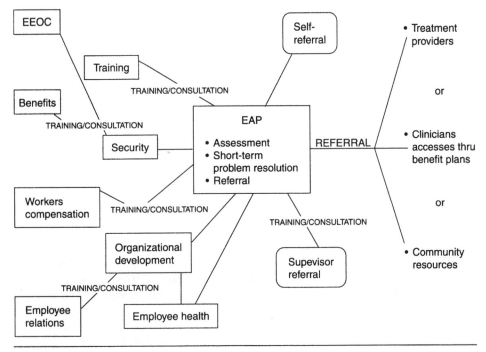

Figure 4.4   Internal EAP model.

internal EAP, while focusing on its core components, is also in a unique position to contribute to other areas in the organization and to identify collaborative tasks between the various human resource areas. The developing areas of HR consultation fit well with this model.

The internal EAP model also allows for closer management of EAP professionals. Clinical supervision and quality assurance functions are routinely performed. The EAP is not relying on a far-flung panel of independent affiliates to deliver services.

MEMBER ASSISTANCE PROGRAMS

The labor organization corollary of an internal corporate EAP is a member assistance program (MAP). Many labor organizations, including the AFL-CIO, are strong supporters of EAP systems. The unions have in some cases established member assistance programs that are totally union run such as the Teamsters and the Longshoreman. These programs deliver EAP services to union members and their families. MAPs are an efficient arrangement for employees who work out of a hiring hall or by the job. These workers often are not on one job with consistent supervision for any extended period. Patterns of poor performance can go undetected by short-term supervisors but are more visible to the union. MAPs also offer a consistent source of assistance for mobile employees' groups (see Figure 4.5).

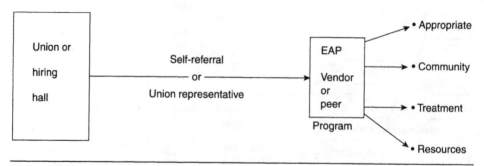

Figure 4.5 Member assistance program.

EXTERNAL EAPS

Many small employers began contracting with external vendors to have ready access to behavioral health services that were not covered in their benefit plans. This model also gave small employers access to human resource consultation services that they were lacking. But the external vendor model has expanded far beyond just meeting the needs of small employers. As corporations sought to outsource any services not related to their primary product and needed to provide access to EAPs in multiple sites, external vendors became the norm rather than the exception. The external vendor model is now the most prevalent regardless of type of industry or work-site size. The external model allows vendors to take advantage of economies of scale and centralized administrative services that lower the contract cost for the employer. The advantages of using EAPs outside the employer organization lie largely in the availability of a greater breadth of expertise and in diminished concern about confidentiality and potential conflicts of interest.

The models of delivering external EAP services are as varied as the organizations that contract for the services:

- A traditional external model has a centrally located employer contracting with a local external vendor. The external EAP has offices near the employer and operates on a staff model or may form alliances with other EAP firms and individual clinicians who deliver care in outlying areas.

- Another example of an external EAP model is one in which the employer contracts with an outside vendor who has a management system in place that verifies eligibility and screens the employee to determine the major complaint. The employee is then channeled to the appropriate affiliate clinician for assessment, short-term problem resolution, or referral for more intensive treatment. Any ongoing treatment is accessed through the employee benefit plan or community resources.

- In another variation, the employer contracts with one external vendor that offers both EAP and managed care services. The employee can access the EAP or can directly access treatment providers who are part of the network. Some MCOs separate these two functions. The EAP affiliates refer those employees needing a higher level of care to the MCO. It is generally recommended that EAP affiliate clinicians not be the clinicians who would take over ongoing care. This blurring of roles is confusing to the employer and the employee. Separating

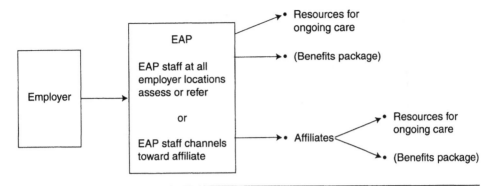

Figure 4.6   External EAP staff model with affiliates.

these functions allows the EAP affiliate to deal with supervisory referrals through case management and to have the clinical care delivered by a therapist (see Figures 4.6–4.8).

USE OF EAP AFFILIATES

If affiliates are used, specialized training in EAP is a must. A routine psychological assessment performed by clinicians without an EAP focus may not address the workplace issues. Although the clinical skills processed by EAP professionals mirror those of MCO clinical providers, an EA professional must also be well versed in the structural

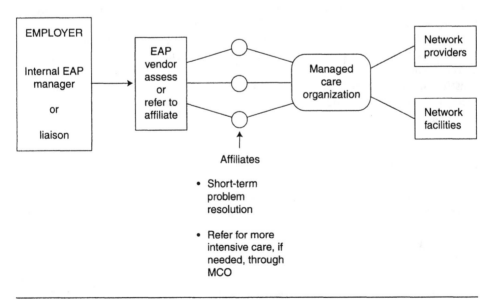

Figure 4.7   External EAP with affiliates and managed care organization.

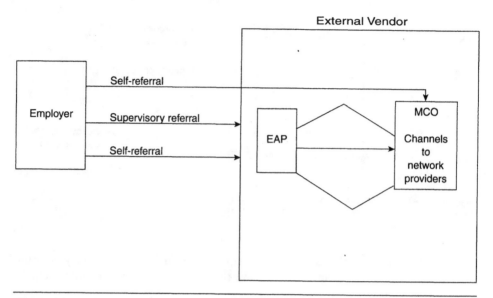

Figure 4.8   Integrated EAP.

functions of work organizations, human resource management issues, labor law, and legislative and regulatory mandates that impact the workplace. It is also essential that affiliates know the difference between an EAP service that includes the interests of the company and a private treatment relationship.

An EAP professional's role varies from a clinical provider in shortened terms of engagement, the limits of confidentiality, the need to respond to various constituencies, and the focus on job performance. Clinicians are traditionally trained to regard the relationship of the therapist and the client as sacrosanct. As an EAP affiliate, they are working with an "employee client." The focus of their work together is to identify problem areas, explore possible solutions and engage in short-term problem resolution.

The EAP professional has multiple constituencies including the supervisor, the employer organization, the EAP vendor, and at times, even public safety. All the EAP constituencies have legitimate interests in the outcome of the case. This complex relationship has to be understood by both the affiliate and the client and managed by the EAP vendor.

INCREASINGLY COMPLEX PROGRAM DESIGNS

The advent of managed care has brought changes in program design. Many employers who contract for EAP services also contract for managed care services. These services can be delivered by two different entities but the preferred model for large self-insured employers and union groups is an integrated model. A single vendor reduces the possibility of the programs working at cross-purposes and increases administrative efficiencies. Because the managed care firms focus on channeling clients to the most appropriate level of care and functioning as an access barrier, the MCO may at times appear to work at cross-purposes with the EAP. The EAP focuses on early intervention and increased case finding and utilization. Well-designed integrated systems have proven to work well. By integrating both EAP and managed behavioral health care, the focus is on behavioral health benefit management, with an integrated gatekeeping function for access to both employee assistance and behavioral health benefits. The MCO benefits from the early intervention activities of the EAP.

An increasing number of employees are enrolled in EAPs. This has created renewed interest among managed care organizations and hospital systems in acquiring EAPs. As a result, EAP market share is experiencing rapid consolidation. The 20 largest EAP vendors now service 34,500,000 employees. According to a recent Open Minds industry survey, EAP enrollment has increased 45% since 1994. The largest percentage increase in enrollment has occurred in the integrated EAP/MCO model. It is estimated that the total national EAP enrollment of 49 million represents 42% of the potential market of employees in businesses with 50 or more employees. It is reasonable to assume that by the year 2000, penetration could rise to 65%, with a potential for 20 million new EAP enrollees.

A dozen national players each have enrollment of over 800,00 lives. But these large vendor organizations are having difficulties managing their far-flung acquisitions and assuring consistency of services. These drawbacks are opening the market to small local and regional EAPs. Smaller vendors have the flexibility to customize services and can establish direct relationships with the purchasers.

These are just a few of the designs in use to deliver EAP services. EAP design is tailored to suit the workforce and the variations are infinite. What is definite is the increasing pressure on employers to respond to employees' personal problems and to minimize the impact that these personal problems have on the workplace. The concerns of organized labor, public opinion, employee morale, federal regulations, and cost/benefit considerations are making it increasingly difficult for employers to simply deal with these issues by terminating the employee. Additional pressure is being added by drug and alcohol testing in the workplace and the desire to provide employees with an opportunity for rehabilitation while safeguarding the public. Employee assistance programs can be designed and implemented in such a way that they strike a balance and satisfy both individual employee and organizational needs.

REFERENCES

American Psychiatric Association. (1994). *Diagnostic and statistical manual of mental disorders* (4th ed.). Washington, DC: Author.

Employee Assistance Professional Association. (1997). *Standards of practice* (3rd ed.). Arlington, VA: Author.

Employee Assistance Professional Association. (1990). *EAP solutions to the employer health crisis.* Arlington, VA: Author.

Mayberry, A. (Ed.). (1993). *Benefits communications, 4th quarter.* Washington, DC: Retirement, Safety and Insurance Department, National Rural Electric Cooperative.

Phillips, D., & Older, H. (1981, May/June). Models of service delivery. In *EAP digest* (pp. 12–15). Troy, MI: Performance Resource Press.

Sonnenstuhl, W.J. (1986). *Inside an emotional health program.* Ithaca, NY: ILR Press.

Spicer, J. (1987). *The EAP solution: Current trends and future issues.* Center City, MN: Hazelden Foundation.

CHAPTER 5

Cultural Diversity and Employee Assistance Programs

ROBERT GROSSMARK

CULTURAL DIVERSITY IN THE U.S. WORKFORCE AND IN EAPS

The past decade has witnessed a growth in awareness and attention to the challenges and rewards of the culturally diverse U.S. population. Articles, academic and otherwise, have proliferated about cultural diversity in the workforce (Dreyfuss, 1990; Geber, 1990), in the mental health field (McGoldrick, Pearce, & Giordano, 1982; Perez-Foster, Moskowitz, & Javier, 1996; Rogler, Malgady, Constantino, & Blumenthal, 1987; Sue, 1988), and of course in the field of EAP, where, for example, special issues of *EAP Exchange* (1997) and *Employee Assistance Quarterly* (Hooks & Weinstein, 1991) have been devoted to diversity in the workplace and the role of EAPs.

The changes in the U.S. population and workforce that have prompted the interest in cultural diversity are by now familiar to most readers. A 1990 report by the U.S. Department of Labor (National Alliance of Business, 1990) included projections that by the year 2000, 80% of the U.S. workforce will be non-Whites, females, and immigrants (Foxworth-Kern, 1989). We all live in a culturally diverse society, and all EAP professionals function within this diversity. Whether it is the consideration of the appropriate referral for psychotherapy for a person of color, the structuring of a management training workshop, critical incident debriefing, or assisting in a return-to-work plan, the issue of diversity is a constant presence for the EAP professional.

DIVERSITY, CULTURE, AND INTERGROUP RELATIONS

The word "culture" is often applied solely to minorities, people of color, or simply to those who are different. I have often been struck, while conducting "cultural sensitivity" and "diversity training" workshops that White men and women often express the view that they are not the ones with diversity or culture; it is the minorities or people of color who are diverse or have culture. Their perspective is often that the workshops are not about them but about the "others." Similarly, writings about cultural diversity that admonish therapists or managers to be sensitive to the cultures of specific patient or employee groups and that outline the particular features of different ethnic groups, can inadvertently compound and reinforce the view that culture and diversity reside solely in minority groups. This chapter argues that cultural diversity is not a thing that exists in isolation or is about a "them," or even an "us" (as opposed to a them); rather, we all live and work in a multicultural society. Our histories and cultures are present, in conscious and unconscious ways, in every aspect of our work in this multicultural matrix.

Group and organizational researchers have long alerted us to the ubiquity of intergroup relations (Alderfer, 1986; Rice, 1969). Whether it is in one-to-one interaction with clients and their families, consultation to managers, or other EAP interventions (internal or external), we are always consciously and unconsciously experiencing and being experienced according to membership in any number of groups. It is common—perhaps always the case—that EAP professionals are experienced at least in part, as representing the organization of the employer, and most often are seen as representing the leadership and therefore power center of that organization, whether the EAP is internal or external. Variations in the position of the employee and the nature of the organization can create a host of assumptions about and experiences of the EAP. Moreover, the EAP professional will experience him- or herself differently depending on the intergroup features of the situation. Certainly we can also state that all other intergroup aspects of the situation, including race, gender, age, and social class, among others, are facts of the situation. Every interaction between the EAP professional and the organization or employee contains some version of an interaction between these variables. Awareness of the nature of these variables, how they interact and how they affect the EAP professional's thinking, emotional response, and action (e.g., while conducting an assessment interview, consultation with a manager, considering a referral) can only illuminate the role and enhance the effectiveness of EAP professionals.

This chapter describes the functions of the EAP at First Chicago Trust Company and will discuss the many ways in which cultural diversity impacts on and is integrated into EAP practice at the company.

THE EAP AT FIRST CHICAGO TRUST COMPANY OF NEW YORK

First Chicago Trust Company of New York is the stock transfer agent for First Chicago NBD. Approximately 1,250 employees are involved in the transfer of stocks and shares when they are traded, reimbursed, or otherwise assigned. The business relies on a large management information systems operation, a large number of telephone customer service operators, a large mailing and printing operation, a marketing division and a senior management level. Due to the overall relatively small size of the organization, the EAP has been able to establish a presence and involvement at all levels of the organization and become part of the community.

The racial mix of the employee population is fairly typical of a current corporate environment in the eastern United States and roughly matches that predicted by the Workforce 2000 Report with White men accounting for 23% of employees. Although overall White employees make up 42% of the workers, the largest single group is that of Black women (27.4%); there are more women (57.3%) than men at First Chicago Trust Company, with a substantial number of Hispanics and Asians in the workplace.

The EAP

The EAP at the Trust Company is a satellite of the First Chicago NBD EAP, which serves the parent organization and is described by Conti in this volume. The approach is that of a "broad brush" internal EAP that is a part of the company's community, and services all levels of employees. The EAP offers services that are typical of this type of EAP: bio-psychosocial assessment, short-term counseling and referral, the management of short-term disability, wellness and prevention interventions, management training and consultation and critical incident intervention. In all these areas, there is a commitment to proactive and preventive interventions. Many opportunities are taken to present the EAP to the employees, and hence there are many different opportunities to consider the role of cultural diversity in the EAP and to integrate issues of diversity into the EAP function.

SHORT-TERM COUNSELING

Credibility and Giving

Like most EAPs, short-term counseling together with referral is the basic core technology of the program. The chief question here is how to establish a culturally competent EAP. Historically, minorities have been underserved by mental health services and there has been considerable controversy about the effectiveness of psychotherapy with minority clients. Since the late 1970s when the President's Commission on Mental Health (1978) concluded that minorities "are clearly underserved or inappropriately served by the mental health system" much attention has been paid to how to remedy the situation. Consideration has been given to external factors such as the location and availability of mental health services, and internal factors, such as the substance and appropriateness of the services themselves (Sue, 1988). The general finding has been that whatever the utilization rates, there tends to be a significantly higher dropout rate for minorities from mental health services, and the unavoidable conclusion has been that minorities have been underserved by the mental health system in general and by the therapy community in particular (Gorkin, 1996; Ponterroto, Casas, Suzuki, & Alexander, 1995; Sue & Zane, 1987).

In considering the reasons for this, we can point to factors such as the lack of bilingual therapists and therapists' discrimination toward and stereotypes of ethnic clients. Beyond these, the most salient reason is the inability of therapists to provide "culturally responsive forms of treatment" (Bazron, Dennis, & Isaacs, 1989; Sue & Zane, 1987). Many therapists are not familiar with the different cultures and lifestyles of their clients and therefore minority clients frequently find mental health services strange, foreign, or unhelpful. For example, a therapy with a Hispanic client might be impeded if the therapist is unaware that as a group Hispanics may tend to value linearity, that is, role-structured rather than egalitarian relationships (Szapocznik, Santisteban, Kurtines, Hervis, & Spencer, 1982), or that with an African American, therapy may be less effective because of an underestimation or underappreciation of traditional Black values such as group identification and collectivity, spirituality, and the role of the history of oppression of African Americans in this country (Jones, 1985). White and Parham (1990) pointed out that development of pro-Black attitudes may indicate healthy psychological adjustment for African Americans whereas striving to be White may be a symptom of maladaptive adjustment. This is a complicated issue within corporate or other environments where the power centers tend to be predominantly White and many African Americans and other minorities are upwardly mobile within these organizational systems. Issues of identity, loyalty, betrayal, and self-abnegation are often present in these situations.

Although *no* knowledge of the client's culture is most likely to be detrimental to the therapeutic process, a clumsy application of "cultural knowledge and techniques" in psychotherapy can also be detrimental to a successful intervention. These techniques can be applied in inappropriate ways. Insufficient cultural knowledge can be naively applied and can be characterized by overgeneralizations and the neglect of within-group heterogeneity (Sue & Zane, 1987). Furthermore, I do not support the idea that minorities require different types of therapy altogether. To simply steer clear of traditional insight-oriented therapies and appropriate assessment with minorities is itself a form of bias (Evans, 1985).

Rather than proposing that minorities be treated in one particular way or another, I suggest that two concepts, *credibility* and *giving* are especially relevant to working with culturally diverse groups. These are not the only factors that are important with culturally diverse groups, nor are they relevant only for diverse groups, but these features are *particularly* relevant for culturally diverse groups. These concepts seem to have real usefulness when applied to the EAP situation.

Therapist or EAP "credibility" refers to the employee or client's perception that the EAP professional or program is offering effective and trustworthy help. "Giving" refers to the employee or client's experience of bringing something away from the encounter with the EAP (Sue & Zane, 1987).

Credibility would seem particularly relevant in the EAP situation where perceived utility and credibility are always issues. Credibility is enhanced by two factors: *ascribed status* and *achieved status.* Ascribed status is that which is or is not ascribed to the clinician or the program according to intrinsic factors. These factors can be obvious or subtle; large or small. For example, many may ascribe status to a clinician on the basis of his or her age. In some cultures, authority and status are intrinsic to the role of professional or doctor. Ascribed status may be enhanced or diminished according to many factors such as gender or sexual orientation, skin color, or even hairstyle or texture (Baker, 1988; Williams, 1996).

An EAP program may have ascribed status due to many factors such as location, personnel, perceived closeness to the employer, rank of EAP staff (in a corporate setting) and involvement with wellness initiatives, to name a few. However, status and credibility can also be *achieved.* Achieved credibility comes from the actual effectiveness and experience of the therapist's skills and how he or she works. EAP professionals and EAP programs can achieve status by their own actions. The degree to which their behavior engenders faith, trust, confidence, and hope is the degree to which they will have achieved status, along with, or despite a lack of, ascribed status. For example, an EAP may have a low ascribed status within an organization where ideas of mental health and counseling are devalued. However, a strong and useful presentation about stress can accomplish a gain in achieved status among employees and thus help the EAP immeasurably. Similarly, minority clients might be skeptical about mental health services due to the historical lack of provision of culturally responsive services, and assign the EAP little ascribed credibility. But attending a wellness seminar where they felt understood, included, and joined with might redress their skepticism and the EAP will accrue achieved status. Likewise a meaningful experience with an EAP counselor where a minority client feels understood, valued, and helped will increase achieved credibility for the EAP. A culturally responsive EAP will achieve credibility and thereafter gain in ascribed credibility.

The idea of *giving* stresses the value that is accrued when clients feel that they have taken something away from their encounter with the EAP, which, in corporate parlance is called the "take-away" or the "value added" of the encounter with the EAP. With all employees, and in particular with culturally diverse clients, there is much to be gained from a sense that the employee has received something from their encounter with the EAP. This is by no means unique to minority clients, nor does it mean that the "gift" that is given is a concrete thing (The concept of the "gift" in psychotherapy is grounded in Asian culture where the idea of gift-giving is central to interpersonal relations; Sue & Zane, 1987.). Rather, there are numerous possible forms of "gifts" to be given to the clients. These might include a soothing of the most present and pressing symptoms, however slight; a small sense of some cognitive clarity and the idea that feelings and symptoms can be understood and controlled; the normalization of symptoms, the idea that the reactions make some coherent sense or a sense of hope, or that a useful process has begun.

It is important to stress that this is not a recommendation for short-term treatment nor for quick-fix problem solving. Rather, the sense of a meaningful experience that engenders some hope is important and can make or break the usefulness of the contact with the EAP. In the absence of such an experience, employees may fail to follow EAP recommendations, avoid the EAP altogether and fail to utilize EAP services. EAP professionals therefore must attend to the cultural variables that will determine meaningful credibility and giving for each employee.

The ideas of credibility and giving are construed within the theoretical approach of the British psychoanalyst D. W. Winnicott. His ideas of the transitional object (Winnicott, 1953) are well-known. The child will carry around a "security blanket," which is experienced as containing elements of what is safe and known (the mother) and what is unsafe and unknown—it allows the child to be away from the mother and explore his or her own space. In this way, the child can separate and negotiate the transition from dependence to some new autonomy. I have proposed (Grossmark, 1996b) that the EAP functions in this manner, helping employees transition into a new kind of space: that of the EAP, therapy, and personal change. Credibility and giving are important factors in establishing a successful therapeutic encounter particularly where there is cultural diversity and can help shepherd the employee into this transitional space (Grossmark, 1996b).

Credibility and giving are necessary but not sufficient features of a useful therapy experience, and a host of other client and therapist features are active in the therapy matrix. However, it does seem that the ideas of credibility and giving are especially relevant to EAP practice with cultural diverse clients (whether the contact with the EAP will involve short-term counseling or a referral) because the EAP task is to guide the employee into the new space of therapeutic endeavor.

The Dynamics of Race and Symptomatology: Credibility and Giving

Awareness and consideration of the experience of diversity in the work environment can also widen the scope of mental health diagnosis and problem conceptualization. The dynamics of race, discrimination, and the experience of one's identity are always present and can play a major role in symptom formation.

Consider the following fairly typical hypothetical situation based on discussions with other EAP professionals. An African-American man in his late 40s comes to the EAP complaining of feelings of anxiety, depressed affect, and sleeplessness. The employee's family situation is stable, notwithstanding the expectable life transitions for him and his wife of approaching middle-age and of their children growing into adolescents. On inquiry, he reports that both his parents and his parents in-law have passed away during recent years, but he is most interested to talk about his current situation at work. He reports to a White woman some years his junior who generally conducts herself in a friendly manner and has seemed more than satisfied with his performance. Typically, he has received good reviews and he has felt generally well established and situated. On examining the onset of his symptoms, he notes that some days prior, he had not been invited to attend a meeting that was pertinent and central to his role. On further exploration, he notes that there have been a number of times when he has anticipated inclusion in these meetings, has actually prepared much material for them, but has been excluded, on occasion only learning of the meeting after it has taken place. Of particular poignancy is the realization that these are all meetings that involved an interface with representatives of another organization. As he discusses the situation in the EAP, the employee begins to evidence and describe increasing rage.

In this situation, the EAP professional can ask whether race is a factor. Other EAP professionals report that in this kind of situation, the addressing of race can be a major relief and help for the employee. This hypothetical employee then may have an opportunity to work through the complex mix of rage, shame, impotence, and sadness at being treated in a perceived oppressive manner and the fear that many minorities can experience when feeling rageful, that to their detriment, they will become another angry minority in the eyes of their employers. In such situations, the EAP professional can work with the employee on strategies for addressing the situation at work and for finding support that is trusted from other sources, such as friends, colleagues, and family. I have collected many informal examples, where symptoms are then alleviated.

Multiple themes are evident in the previous situation. In terms of conceptualization of the clinical problem, the dynamics of race are always present and can often be the source of symptom formation. In this hypothetical situation, the presence of family transitions and the death of parents could certainly have been taken as the precipitants for a depression. However, by following the employee's lead and listening to the race dynamics that may be at work in his department, the EAP is able to help the employee on his terms and in a way that is meaningful to him. This is the kind of problem formulation and intervention that is suggested by the ideas of credibility and giving.

The EAP professional's credibility was enhanced by following the employee's lead; he was most interested to talk about his work situation, rather than other aspects of his life. His assessment of the situation was never interpreted as a paranoid orientation and most importantly, he was asked about the issue of race. This enhanced the EAP professional's credibility and also permitted the employee to explore the source of his depressed and anxious reaction. The inquiry into whether race may be a factor can be couched as a simple open-ended inquiry. The employee can therefore be said to have received some viable gifts from his encounter, in particular, cognitive clarity, recognition of his feelings, a means for understanding his depression, and a plan of action that was comfortable and reasonable for him.

This hypothetical situation is not offered as a guideline for practice, but as an example of how credibility and giving can be particularly useful in the sphere of culturally diverse EAP situations when tied to an appreciation of how race and diversity dynamics can play a role in symptom formation. However, such conclusions can only be reached with confidence when all other possible psychological and work-related variables that may account for the poor relationship between the employee and his superior have been considered and examined, so that race is not erroneously made an issue. There are situations where it would be incorrect to ignore the possibility of a paranoid reaction, where work issues are a screen for deeper and more troubled character pathology, family dysfunction, and so on. However, when the assessment of psychological structure suggests a lack of deeper pathology, a path that brings the EAP credibility and the patient a sense of having been given something useful via affirming his or her reality and allowing the issue of race to be discussed, can help achieve a successful and meaningful outcome.

Countertransference

It is always important to consider countertransference when discussing any interaction between a mental health professional and a client or employee. It is even more pertinent when thinking about the culturally diverse situation. This chapter regards the idea of countertransference not simply as a feature of the therapist's mental life that is affected by a particular client or situation and that might impede the therapeutic process, but rather as a ubiquitous phenomenon that, when understood and clarified, can shed much light on the unconscious and conscious elements of the therapeutic interaction (Slakter, 1987) and therefore can inform the therapist or EAP professional about the employee's internal life and his or her effect on others and can certainly add more depth to decisions about further treatment or referral.

When divergent cultures are present in the EAP situation, the EAP professional must be aware of any biases he or she may hold based on race, class, gender, or sexual orientation. The mental health field has historically not been free of bias, manifesting biased attitudes in areas of assessment, diagnosis, and treatment (Clark, 1972). Needless to say, such negative biases will interfere with successful contact with the EAP, probably harming the employee in the process. When people hold negative biases about others, anxieties are raised within the relationship. In the therapy and counseling situation, this can lead not only to minority clients leaving therapy, but to therapists unconsciously pushing them away to alleviate the anxiety (Grace, 1997). In the EAP situation, this pushing away can take subtle and unsubtle forms, including inappropriate interventions, premature or inappropriate referral, lack of therapist interest, or hesitation to offer the gifts of therapy described previously. Any situation where negative biases are present can certainly be said to diminish the ascribed and achieved credibility of the EAP.

It must also be recognized that everyone carries many subliminal assumptions and expectations that may operate in a barely acknowledged manner where there is diversity. Many therapists will freely admit that they experience different dynamics when working with a person of the opposite gender or when working with older clients, or with children, and so on. Arguably the same holds for work with clients of different races, skin color, social class, and sexual orientation. The task of the EAP professional is not to eliminate these dynamics (they are in the very fabric of human interaction) but to attend to them and be aware of what is evoked in any given situation.

There is a growing literature on countertransference in the culturally diverse therapy situation (Abel & Metraux, 1974; Basch-Kahre, 1984; Gorkin, 1996). Among the typical forms of countertransference in the culturally diverse clinical situation is an excessive and ambivalent curiosity about the client's culture. EAP professionals may become curious about meeting someone from a different culture and may let their curiosity or stimulation interfere with their task of helping the client. The clinician might find the client exotic or fascinating, or alternatively may have some contempt or irritation with the client's culture or the distance between the two cultures. A client who has a different sexual orientation to the EAP professional can evoke issues of curiosity, arousal, fear, and discomfort. This need not only apply to situations where there is a *difference* in culture, class, or orientation. Therapists with unresolved issues relating to their own identity may similarly idealize or denigrate or imagine a natural familiarity with a client of similar race or culture, all of which might interfere with the EAP task.

There can also be a countertransference reaction that seeks to eliminate cultural difference from the therapy situation. Certainly we might all agree with Harry Stack Sullivan's dictum (1953) that "everyone is much more simply human than otherwise" (p. 22), but many can use this as a way of not dealing with cultural difference in the therapy encounter. Gorkin (1996) cited a compelling example of an Israeli therapist working with Arab clients who insisted that cultural differences never emerged in his work with these clients. To the reader, it would seem hard to believe. Any time there is an attempt to ignore cultural realities and create "an island of the treatment situation" (Gorkin, 1996, p. 163), countertransferences are at work. This can be an attempt to avoid discomfort and abrasion in the interaction. EAP professionals may slip into functioning in a way that will avoid consideration of racial, class, and gender dynamics and history; they then disavow bias of any sort and maintain the island of the EAP interaction. Such island making may often point to a need to not consider these issues.

There can also be manifestations of guilt in the countertransference. The idea of racial guilt has been suggested as a feature of race relations in this country (Greene, 1985; Williams, 1996). Guilt might manifest itself in the EAP encounter as overconcern to be useful to the client, to "make up" for perceived abuses or discrimination; as an over-eagerness to identify and understand the culturally different patient; or an attempt to minimize one's own cultural identification. The issue of guilt is particularly pertinent when the client is from a lower socioeconomic class. Therapists may dilute aspects of their own social status to unconsciously be more like the client. An informal observation of mine comes from my experience working in a public health clinic in an impoverished inner-city neighborhood. I often observed male clinicians removing their neckties on entering, and replacing them later before leaving to work in their private practice offices. Although this "dressing down" could be construed as helpful in establishing a better rapport between therapist and client, by creating the impression that the client is on a more equal footing with the therapist, it can also illustrate an acting-out of a guilt countertransference; the therapists did not want to remind themselves or their clients of the socioeconomic reality and the vast gulf on that dimension that lay between them. Such attempts run the risk of being perceived as false and ingratiating by the clients.

In terms of class, the EAP professional can also consider the countertransference that is stimulated when working with clients who are of greater affluence and societal position. Reactions to this situation can include feelings of envy, threat, excess scrutiny, self-devaluation, or the need to prove one's usefulness. In the internal EAP, such situations are pregnant with meaning. It may be the case that the client is senior to the EAP professional in the organization and may even have some involvement with the EAP's tenure.

As in all these situations, the goal is not to act as if there is no assumption, or re-action; countertransference is ubiquitous. Much is to be gained from studying and understanding one's countertransference. Much light can be shed on the cross-cultural situation from appreciating and being informed by the countertransference that is stimulated. Needless to say, errors and poor interventions can result from a blindness to the issue of countertransference in all situations, and especially in the culturally diverse interaction.

Future Directions: Short-Term Counseling and Cultural Diversity in EAPs

When engaged in short-term counseling, a culturally competent EAP professional will value and enhance credibility and giving; will strive to attend to what will be mean-ingful for each client given his or her culture and ethnicity, will consider the dynamics of race in the formation of mental health symptomatology, and will appreciate the role of the culturally diverse aspects of the encounter. The EAP can consider what level of ascribed credibility exists with a particular client and what might enhance the EAP's ascribed and achieved credibility. The EAP can focus on what kind of a gift will be meaningful for a particular employee to take away from an encounter. The EAP will not preclude or preemptively prescribe the type of therapy according to ethnicity or as-pects of diversity. Alternative therapies and interventions indigenous to the client's culture can always be considered as possibilities but, like other treatment, need not be introduced simply by virtue of the client's culture. Furthermore, the EAP professional should always ask and inquire about cultural information where it is needed to attain clarity. It is a simple suggestion but often clinicians do not feel authorized to ask for cultural information, sometimes assuming that they are expected to have all this infor-mation as part of their professional status. A loss of ascribed status is feared by asking questions that seem naive or uncomfortable. The more of a feeling the clients have that all aspects of their life can be spoken about and are not off limits, the greater chance of success. Race and ethnicity are sometimes felt to be the deepest taboo and are avoided by therapist and client alike.

Countertransference should always be considered, especially in situations of cul-tural diversity. Just as a common and accepted recommendation for therapists of all types is to undergo a therapy experience themselves to clarify their personal issues and blind spots, a cultural identity self-examination is also recommended, so that all EAP professionals can have some clarity about their own psychological and cultural iden-tity, and about their issues and blind spots in this dimension. Just as important as be-coming knowledgeable about the client's culture, perhaps even more so, is knowing one's own cultural identity and clarifying what may be the psychological issues associ-ated with it.

Regarding program evaluation in terms of short-term counseling and cultural di-versity, EAPs can follow two simple recommendations. First, they can measure whether the demographics of the employees utilizing the EAP approximates what would be expected given the demographics of the employee population (i.e., are mi-norities underrepresented in the population that utilizes the EAP?). If so, the reasons must be explored. Second, given the history of minorities and dropout rates in therapy, appropriate follow-up data can be collected to measure whether minority employees are dropping out faster or more often than others. Again, if so, the EAP can consider itself to be lacking in cultural competence and can search for causes.

REFERRALS AND CULTURAL DIVERSITY

The Psychodynamics of Referral and the Question of Matching

The field of referrals is an underexamined area of EAP practice. Grossmark (1996a) pointed out some of the many different possibilities for complex psychological dynamics in the "referral moment," (i.e., the process of deciding which clinician is appropriate for a particular patient). Among these is the perennial question of whether it is beneficial to match the employee with a therapist along ethnic, cultural, gender, or sexual-orientation criteria. There are studies whose data can support all of the four possible answers to the question; "yes" (Sattler, 1977), "no" (Griffith & Jones, 1978), "it depends" (Parloff, Waskow, & Wolf, 1978), and "can't tell" (Abramowitz & Murray, 1983). There is also an interesting discussion by Sue (1988) of the role of the ethnicity of the researcher in these outcomes. This chapter posits that the ethnic or cultural match is one of many variables that are present in the therapy encounter that can affect a client's ability to enter the therapy experience in a useful manner.

There can be cultural and linguistic mismatches that can have clear and detrimental effects on therapy outcome. Referrals of employees for treatment with a therapist who is not able to communicate in the preferred language of the employee are already at a disadvantage. There are numerous situations where referring to a therapist of a different ethnicity or sexual orientation would be an error, and there are situations where a simple cultural match would be deleterious. The factors relevant here can only be determined by a thorough evaluation of the employee, a joint discussion of the kind of therapist the employee would feel comfortable working with, and a thorough knowledge of the clinician who is being considered for referral. In the days of assessments conducted anonymously over the telephone and referrals made according to zip codes, such a prereferral evaluation can seem something of a luxury but, nevertheless, essential.

This points to the idea that the key issue in the area of referral is the issue of choice. It is incumbent on every EAP to be in a position to offer an appropriate choice of therapists of diverse ethnicity, age, gender, sexual orientation, and language for referral to employees. Moreover, it is important to consider that while seeking to avoid mismatches based on culture, ethnicity, and language, a simple one-to-one matching need not be successful. More important than therapists' demographics is the degree to which they have examined their own cultural and ethnic identity issues, whatever their ethnicity and culture. Among the host of psychological features, we might include any feelings about their own social status, their own ethnicity in relation to the larger society, their own biases and fears, their feelings of shame or superiority, guilt, denial of these issues, or overzealous application of these issues. For example, a gay therapist who is openly gay may have a complicated reaction to a gay employee who is unwilling to disclose his or her homosexuality to family or the employer. Conversely, a referral of an African-American employee to a White therapist who would seek to make an island of the therapy situation and avoid consideration of race in the therapy situation, would seem to be a poor match.

Once again the issue is one of self-knowledge and countertransference. The crucial variable is not simply a demographic characteristic of the therapist (gay or straight, Black or White, etc.), but the degree to which the therapist brings self-knowledge, clarity, and an appreciation of the dynamics of race, gender, and sex to the dimension of diversity. This, needless to say, may not be evident from a curriculum vita, or even a simple interview or list of qualifications. There are countless informal examples of clinicians who are held in the highest esteem by their colleagues, who are often reported by minorities or particular minority groups to be unhelpful.

The EAP must strive to know the providers to whom they refer in a much more personal and intimate manner than is often the case. Simple ethnic matching can be detrimental for therapy, if the therapist has little awareness of his or her own identity issues. In fact, we can surmise that the deleterious effects of a negative therapy experience with someone who is of the same background, let's say a Latino therapist, could raise a further layer of psychological complications for a Latino employee. Deeper issues of loneliness, fear, and confusion could be evoked, as well as problems with loyalty and betrayal, if the patient must return to the EAP and ask for a new referral. Worse would be a feeling of needing to stick with or drop out of the therapy because of a mix of disappointment and loyalty to the therapist of the client's own culture.

The meaning of an ethnically matched referral can contain vastly different meanings for the employee depending on his or her own identity issues. An employee who has positive self-image and positive associations to his or her own identity may feel grateful, well-understood, valued, and cared for by such a referral. Employees who have unresolved feelings, perhaps of shame, fear, or guilt in relation to their own identity (dynamics that are not uncommon across all diagnostic categories, and certainly a feature in the personality disorders according to the *DSM-IV*) may feel slighted, fearful, or even aggressed upon by an ethnically matched referral.

Relationship of the EAP to Minority Providers

Frequently, minority therapists express the desire to not simply serve clients from the same demographic group. Other minority therapists are willing, eager, and proud to provide services perhaps exclusively for other minority clients. It is incumbent on the EAP to know its providers well and to treat them in a way that acknowledges their multiple and particular abilities. It may be a form of racism to only refer African Americans to an African-American therapist, or a form of homophobia to only refer gay patients to a gay therapist.

Here, once again, we can consider countertransference. In a presentation on the psychodynamics of referrals, Grossmark (1996a) suggested that the referring EAP professional may have psychological responses to the receiving provider as well as the employee being referred. These might include feelings of having given a gift to the provider, feelings of envy when referring a "good" patient, feelings of fear or hostility when assigning a particularly difficult patient, and feelings of exposure or incompetence when referring a patient to an admired senior provider. In the realm of cultural diversity, other layers are added to this matrix of psychodynamics. Just as the chapter outlined forms of countertransference with minority employees, much can be gained from a consideration of similar possibilities with minority providers.

Simply matching, let's say Latino employees with a Latino therapist could be a way to avoid dealing with the complexity not only of the EAP's relation to the Latino employees but also of avoiding the EAP's relation to the Latino therapist. Simple ethnic matching may be an attempt by the EAP to find a shortcut to feeling culturally competent and good. It may also disguise feelings of discomfort or distrust with the minority providers. Conversely, there may be envy and idealization of minority providers, or an attempt to repair hurt based on feelings of guilt. Once again, these possibilities are outlined to alert the EAP professionals to possible dynamics that may interfere with clear and effective work. Each referral situation is different and contains a matrix of numerous and possibly complicated dynamics. Informed and considered action is recommended rather than the simple rote application of matching or other automatic mechanisms.

Future Directions: Referrals and Cultural Diversity

The EAP must be able to offer a relevant variety of providers, to meet the multicultural needs of the employees. Each referral situation must be considered individually. The EAP can involve the employee in considering the features that would be desired in a therapist. The rote application of ethnic or cultural matching is not recommended. Rather the EAP is urged to know its providers well along the dimension of identity and cultural awareness and to base referrals on as thorough a consideration of all the many variables involved as possible.

Likewise the EAP needs to consider its relationship to the multicultural providers that will constitute the provider network. A referral is a communication to the employee and to the provider. It can contain information that can enhance the therapy process as well as information that can be deleterious. The EAP is urged to put effort into knowing the providers and to considering the possible dynamics of every referral situation as it arises.

THE CULTURE OF THE EAP

Each EAP can be said to have its own culture. When an employee contacts and meets with an EAP professional, there can be said to be a meeting of these two cultures. And when members of two cultures meet, information about the two cultures is communicated, perceived and reacted to in numerous conscious and unconscious ways. The degree to which the employee can feel that the EAP culture is going to offer understanding and help is a crucial variable in the outcome of the interaction. Similarly, in the many events and opportunities where the EAP can present itself in wellness programs, management training, or consultation, the EAP can be said to be presenting its culture to the culture of the organization.

The elements that make up the culture of each EAP include such features as the cultural and socioeconomic mix of the EAP staff, psychological orientation of the staff, authority structure within the EAP, relation to the clients (if external) and to the employer (if internal), conception of the task of the EAP, and its stated mission. Some EAP cultures will value and give attention to issues of diversity. Each EAP should examine how and whether the issue of diversity is attended to in its operations. Is the attention to cultural diversity a stated part of the EAP's task; is there a commitment to attend to the diverse employee population that is being served; and is there an attempt to create a culturally diverse staff within the EAP? Just as in the case of therapist-client matching, demographics of the staff are by no means the only variable that will affect the cultural competence of the EAP; nevertheless, employees will comprehend and respond consciously or unconsciously to the demographic makeup of the EAP, affecting the ascribed credibility of the EAP in the process.

In addition to the EAP staff, there are often opportunities for the EAP to represent its commitment to cultural diversity. Guest speakers on wellness issues can be drawn from a diverse population, and the EAP can integrate and bring the issue of diversity to the table when presenting the EAP to the employees. In the following section, the manner in which themes of cultural diversity can be integrated into wellness and management training are explored. In all these situations, the EAP can be said to be presenting its own culture to the culture of the organization.

WELLNESS AND PREVENTIVE INTERVENTIONS AND CULTURAL DIVERSITY

Wellness, Credibility, and Diversity

Wellness initiatives, typically involving presentations or workshops about mental health issues or involving screenings for vulnerabilities to mental health problems are central to an EAP's proactive approach to the issue of cultural diversity. These offer numerous opportunities for employees to encounter the EAP and its culture, to learn whether the EAP has anything to offer, to ascertain whether its services will relate to them in particular and to dispel any concerns they may have about the EAP. These are opportunities to enhance the ascribed and achieved credibility of the EAP.

At the First Chicago NBD, the EAP takes as many opportunities as possible to present information about and therefore advertise its services. In addition to the content of these presentations, employees gain a sense of the attitudes the EAP holds (i.e., whether it is an open-minded and attuned EAP or didactic and closed-minded). In particular, these presentations allow culturally diverse employees to experience the EAP culture and to ascertain whether it will be a comfortable, responsive, and culturally competent service.

Stress and Diversity

One of the most common forms of wellness intervention is the stress management workshop or presentation, and the EAP at the First Chicago Trust Company is not unique in regularly offering these. These may be lunchtime presentations open to all, half-day workshops for managers in training, or presentations to the employees of a particular department or group. The stress management workshop is a particular opportunity to address the diversity of the employee population. The workshops are always highly interactive with the participants invited to share their experiences of stress and to work collaboratively with the help of the presenter to reach strategies for coping with stress. Although the EAP has abundant information and guidelines for teaching about stress and stressors, the greatest utility can be gained by collecting the employees' own experiences. Consequently, presentations are oriented to the particular stressors of this population. The cultural mix of employees attending an EAP presentation can vary greatly from one presentation to the next. It is essential to recognize who the employees are culturally. Just as the stressors addressed with a group of managers would be different from the stressors addressed with a group of telephone-response customer-service representatives, the stressors of a White, single mother, customer-service-representative are distinct from those of a married Latina mother who is a department supervisor. As well as considering participants' actual life situations, the presentation can also include cultural differences.

As part of the discussion of stressful situations, participants always raise questions about whether these situations are the same for men and women, White or other races, and so forth. It is rare that these questions do not open up further discussion and material that in turn deepens and makes more real the whole experience for all participants. The questions are raised in a spirit of investigation and interest that invites candor, rather than in a polemical or intrusive manner. The closer to employees' actual experience the presentation or workshop is, the greater will be the utility. Moreover, they will experience an EAP that addresses the real issues of the employees and is prepared to ask about and discuss cultural aspects of their experiences. This in turn can only increase the achieved and therefore ascribed credibility of the EAP for all employees and in particular those from minority groups. It is not only minorities who benefit from an open and frank inclusion of issues of cultural diversity in stress and other wellness presentations. Typically race, class, and cultural difference are taboo and anxiety-arousing topics in the work environment; they must be addressed with sensitivity and thoughtfulness so that employees who are not open-minded do not have a negative experience. An EAP that conveys to all employees that these can be addressed in an open, intelligent, and helpful manner is helpful to the whole employee community.

Similarly, presentations on stress can address the issue of discrimination. The *DSM-IV* cites discrimination as one of the problems related to the social environment included in Axis IV diagnostic classification. In conditions where the psychosocial and environmental problem is severe and the primary focus of clinical attention, the *DSM-IV* recommends including it in Axis I. Discrimination is given as much prominence as other psychosocial stressors. Many of the other stressors outlined by the *DSM-IV* are commonly the theme of EAP wellness presentations, such as family health problems, disruption of family life through divorce or other separations, and threat of loss of job, to mention a few. It is therefore incumbent on the EAP to address discrimination and racism as issues of preventive mental health. To talk about stress in a multicultural environment and *not* raise cultural mix as a potential source of stressors arguably would be unrealistic and may implicitly undermine the credibility of the presenter and the EAP. This highlights a recurrent theme when discussing cultural diversity; that messages and words are often given great value and meaning and that what is *not* said is often as significant as what is said. By not bringing up the issue of cultural diversity in an open manner, a piece of the participants' reality is left unrecognized and unspoken. Like a therapist who does not mention a crucial and perhaps anxiety-arousing piece of reality, one's credibility is ultimately undermined and effectiveness depleted.

The same rules of thumb, to always address discrimination and the cultural differences present in the room, can be applied to every type of preventive, wellness endeavor. When presenting on anxiety, depression, and alcohol and drug use, it is useful to address cultural differences in incidence and utilization of services, and to solicit discussion of this data. Once again, to *not* mention cultural differences, as a matter of course, itself will convey a message.

In some cases, specific cultural issues can be the topic of wellness interventions and initiatives. For example, such topics as "Depression in the African-American Community" and "Mental Health and the Latino Community" can be considered. However, these should not supplant the inclusion of cultural diversity themes in all wellness and preventive activities.

Future Directions: Wellness and Cultural Diversity

Wellness and preventive mental health initiatives are opportunities to expose employees to the EAP and therefore are opportunities to enhance the EAP's ascribed and achieved credibility, especially for minorities. The rule of thumb is to address diversity in a proactive manner wherever possible and therefore to integrate themes of cultural diversity into all areas of mental health prevention. To reiterate, when presenting the EAP, what is *not* addressed can be as important as what is addressed.

MANAGEMENT TRAINING, CONSULTATION, AND CULTURAL DIVERSITY

Management Training

The EAP at First Chicago Trust Company is involved with various management training initiatives. Classes entitled "Managing the Troubled Employee" are regularly taught to managers attending the company's training college, and a "Forum for Managers" is offered in which the psychological aspects of management are discussed and management cases are examined. In many ways, these are opportunities for preventive interventions by the EAP. The same rule of thumb can be followed. Cultural diversity can be addressed as part of these training experiences. Just as with the approach to wellness initiatives, these are opportunities for the EAP to impact in a proactive manner on the community of the organization and to enhance the ascribed and achieved credibility of the EAP.

Diversity Training

Many organizations in the United States have initiated diversity training workshops and interventions for employees. There is a growing literature that addresses the content and structure of such training (Geber, 1990). A couple of observations are relevant here. Overall, there is a great variation in the design and content of such training sessions. Those with the most utility seek to engage the participants in as much realistic experiential dialogue as possible. Those that seek to impart principles alone, without allowing for the experience, and examination of a here-and-now process are less likely to be experienced as real and successful by employees. To facilitate such processes, trainers are best equipped if they have experience and training in group process and have themselves been a part of a process-oriented diversity training. The reliance on the didactic imparting of principles or the rote application of prepared structured exercises alone can lead to sterile, "as-if" training experiences. When used in a process-oriented experiential format, however, such exercises can have much power and lasting impact.

Nevertheless, reliance on diversity training has a pitfall. It can convey that cultural diversity is a reified and isolated feature of organizational life that can be addressed in an unintegrated manner. The approach expressed here in relation to wellness, management training, and all other opportunities for the EAP to impact on the organization, is one of integrating themes of cultural diversity into all aspects of organizational life, and all aspects of EAP functioning, where relevant.

Diversity training along with other EEO initiatives, obviously has tremendous usefulness, but when the benefits are not integrated into the daily life of the organization, they can function as a "social defense" (Menzies, 1988). This is a concept that points to the tendency of organizations to create procedures and policies around aspects of organizational life that are most anxiety producing, in a manner that prevents the organization and employees from actually experiencing the anxiety in a more psychologically real and therefore lasting manner. Subsequent to the classic example of a hospital where staff policies and procedures contain anxieties and complicated psychological processes that might otherwise be aroused by considering the impact of such close contact with sickness and death (Menzies, 1959), many organizational theorists and practitioners have demonstrated much evidence to support the idea that unconscious anxieties are often reflected in organizational structures that then function as a system of social defense (Diamond, 1993; Hirschorn, 1990). Similarly, procedures, mission statements, and didactic diversity training can sterilize the issue rather than actually create a space to work it through and create lasting personal and organizational change. Such training can function as an avoidance of the issue and consequent anxiety, and can convey a false message of having dealt with diversity, rather than creating a truly culturally diverse environment.

SHORT-TERM DISABILITY MANAGEMENT AND CULTURAL DIVERSITY

The short-term disability (STD) management strategy of First Chicago NBD's EAP is outlined in detail in Chapter 17 in this book. Proactive involvement by the EAP staff in short-term disability cases has proven to be effective, not only in reducing the length of the STD event but also reducing the likelihood of future events. One of the primary reasons for these compelling findings is that the proactive interventions by the EAP staff can ensure a higher quality of mental health care for the employee on short-term disability and a smoother return to work transition.

The interventions that characterize short-term disability management are manifold and depend greatly on the needs of the particular employee. A few features seem to be common to these situations. They tend to be situations where there are deeper and more prolonged episodes of psychopathology. They also can involve greater involvement of the EAP in liaison with management, family, and outside providers and agencies. They are also situations where there is more likelihood of suspiciousness of the EAP's motives, by clients, families, and providers. It has sometimes been the case, that the family, the client or the treating agency will assume that the EAP is an arm of the employer and is approaching the client in an aggressive manner solely with the intention of bringing the employee back to work, regardless of clinical need or reason. Generally these fears and concerns are quickly allayed once communication has begun, and it becomes clear that the EAP places the clinical agenda as paramount. However, the STD situation is one where fears of the EAP, and trust issues in general are often in the forefront. Trust issues are also always present in the cross-cultural matrix. This being so, the EAP must pay careful attention to any cross-cultural features of the clinical situation and how they may impact on the successful management of a short-term disability episode.

Particular attention needs to be paid to establishing the EAP's credibility not only with the employee, but also with the other players involved in the STD situation such as family members, treating agencies, and individuals. Any suspiciousness of the EAP as representative of the employer may be compounded when there are cultural differences between the employer, EAP personnel, employee, family, and treating clinician. Achieving credibility in these situations can take many forms, including conveying to a treating clinician or agency that the EAP can coordinate a smooth return to work, or conveying to family members that the employee's well-being is paramount. Credibility and giving are always important aspects of the EAP's role in STD events, but they are particularly useful when there are cultural differences.

Countertransferences can also play an important role in the STD situation. Because these situations often involve more severe psychopathology, and more involvement with family and other systems, it follows that the countertransferences will also be more primitive and can evoke more pronounced acting-out on the part of the clinician when unacknowledged. Similarly, countertransferences relating to culture, class, gender identity, and other differences outlined earlier are magnified in the STD situation. There may be an overinvolvement with family or treating systems (perhaps out of racial guilt), an aggressive urgency to bring about a return to work (perhaps as a result of diminishing the gravity of the employee's symptoms, as a result of bias toward the employee with regard to race or other such issues), an identification with the "policing" function of the employee (as a defense against anxiety caused by the greater complexity and involvement required by an STD event), an identification with the employee together with a need to fight the employer on behalf of the employee (out of racial guilt and anxiety), and so forth.

Future Directions: Short-Term Disability Management and Diversity

The EAP can pay special attention to the concepts of credibility and giving in the culturally diverse STD situation, and must pay particular attention to possible countertransference acting out.

Regarding program evaluation, a measurement of whether short-term disability is being managed in a culturally competent manner is the comparison of the length and frequency of STD events for different groups. Any significant differences will point to areas that need to be examined.

CONCLUSION

No EAP can afford not to examine the cultural competence of its services. Each section of this chapter has included specific recommendations for the future delivery of culturally competent services. The overriding principle is that diversity is not a separate issue or topic, but a feature of every EAP activity and treatment, and indeed of modern-day life. The greatest barriers to effectively integrating an awareness of diversity issues into EAP practice have been bias and countertransferences that have prevented EAP professionals from addressing diversity organizationally and in personal, clinical terms. The future offers an opportunity not only to evaluate the cultural competence of

EAP interventions, but also for EAP professionals to consider their own cultural identity themes and how they "wear" them and bring them to the task of employee assistance.

REFERENCES

Abel, T., & Metraux, R. (1974). *Transference and countertransference in culture and psychotherapy.* Connecticut College and University Press.

Abramowitz, S.I., & Murray, J. (1983). Race effects in psychotherapy. In J. Murray & P. Abramson (Eds.), *Bias in psychotherapy* (pp. 215–255). New York: Praeger.

Alderfer, C.P. (1986). An intergroup perspective on group dynamics. In J. Lorsch (Ed.), *Handbook of organizational behavior* (pp. 190–222). Englewood Cliffs, NJ: Prentice Hall.

Baker, F.M. (1988). Afro-Americans. Comas-Diaz & E. Griffith (Eds.), *Clinical guidelines in cross cultural mental health* (pp. 151–181). New York: Wiley.

Basche-Kahre, E. (1984). On difficulties arising in transference and countertransference when analyst and analysand have different sociocultural backgrounds. *International Review of Psycho-Analysis, 11,* 61–67.

Bazron, B., Dennis, K., & Isaacs, M. (1989). *Towards a culturally competent system of care.* Washington, DC: Georgetown University Child Development Center.

Clark, K.B. (1972). Foreword. In A. Thomas & S. Sillen (Eds.), *Racism and psychiatry* (pp. 11–13). New York: Brunner/Mazel.

Diamond, M. (1993). Bureaucracy as externalized self-system: A view from the psychological interior. In L. Hirschorn & C.K. Bennet (Eds.), *The psychodynamics of organizations.* Philadelphia: Temple University Press.

Dreyfuss, J. (1990, April). Get ready for the new workforce. *Fortune.*

EAP Association Exchange. (1997, March–April). Vol. 27, 2.

Evans, D.A. (1985). Psychotherapy and black patients: Problems of training, trainees and trainers. *Psychotherapy, 22,* 457–460.

Foxworth-Kern, M. (1989, August). Minorities 2000: The shape of things to come. *Public Relations Journal,* 14–22.

Geber, B. (1990, July). Managing diversity. *Training.*

Gorkin, M. (1996). Countertransference in cross-cultural psychotherapy. In R.M. Perez-Foster, M. Moskowitz, & R.A. Javier (Eds.), *Reaching across boundaries of culture and class.* Northvale, NJ: Aronson.

Grace, C.A. (1997). Clinical applications of racial identity theory. In C.E. Thompson & R.T. Carter (Eds.), *Racial identity theory: Applications to individual, group and organizational interventions.* Erlbaum.

Greene, B. (1985). Considerations in the treatment of black patients by white therapists. *Psychotherapy, 22,* 389–393.

Griffith, M.S., & Jones, E.E. (1978). Race and psychotherapy: Changing perspectives. In J.H. Masserman (Ed.), *Current psychiatric therapies* (Vol. 18, pp. 225–233). New York: Grune and Stratton.

Grossmark, R. (1996a). *The psychodynamics of referral.* Paper presented at meeting of Occupational Clinical Professionals Group, New York.

Grossmark, R. (1996b, April). *Winnicott goes to work: An integrated psychotherapy and consultation approach.* Presented at Society for Psychotherapy Integration conference. Berkeley, CA.

Hirschorn, L. (1990). *The workplace within—The psychodynamics of organizational life.* Cambridge, MA: MIT Press.

Hooks, J.M., & Weinstein, S. (1991). *An emerging paradigm. Diversity in the workplace: EAP strategies.* Employee Assistance Professional Association.

Jones, A. (1985). Psychotherapy and counseling with black clients. In P. Pedersen (Ed.), *Handbook of cross cultural counseling and therapy* (pp. 173–179). CT: Greenwood Press.

McGoldrick, M., Pearce, J.K., & Giordane. J. (Eds.). (1982). *Ethnicity and family therapy.* New York: Guilford Press.

Menzies, I.E.P. (1959). The functioning of social systems as a defence against anxiety: A report on a study of the nursing service of a general hospital. *Human Relations, 13,* 95–121.

Menzies, I.E.P. (1988). A psychoanalytic perspective on social institutions. In E. Bott-Spillius (Ed.), *Melanie Klein today: Developments in theory and practice: Mainly practice* (Vol. 2). London: Routledge.

Parloff, M.B., Waskow, I.E., & Wolfe, B.E. (1978). Research on therapist variables in relation to process and outcome. In S. L. Garfield & A. E. Bergin (Eds.), *Handbook of psychotherapy and behavior change: An empirical analysis* (2nd ed., pp. 233–282). New York: Wiley.

Perez-Foster, R.M., Moskowitz, M., & Javier, R.A. (Eds.). (1996). *Reaching across boundaries of culture and class.* Northvale, NJ: Aronson.

President's Commission on Mental Health. (1978). *Report to the President.* Washington, DC: U.S. Government Printing Office.

Ponterroto, J.G., Casas, J.M., Suzuki, L.A., & Alexander, C.M. (1995). *Handbook of multicultural counseling.* Thousand Oaks, CA: Sage.

Rice, A.K. (1969). Individual, group and intergroup process. *Human Relations, 22,* 565–584.

Rogler, L.H., Malgady, R.G., Constantino, G., & Blumenthal, R. (1987). What do culturally sensitive mental health services mean? *American Psychologist, 42*(6), 565–570.

Sattler, J.M. (1977). The effects of therapist-client racial similarity. In A.S. Gurman & A.M. Razin (Eds.), *Effective psychotherapy: A handbook of research* (pp. 252–290). Elmsford, NY: Pergamon Press.

Slakter, E. (1987). *Countertransference.* Northvale, NJ: Aronson.

Sue, S. (1988, April). Psychotherapeutic services for ethnic minorities: Two decades of research findings. *American Psychologist,* 301–308.

Sue, S., & Zane, N. (1987, January). The role of culture and cultural techniques in psychotherapy: A critique and reformulation. *American Psychologist,* 37–45.

Sullivan, H. S. (1953). *The interpersonal theory of psychiatry.* New York: Norton.

Szapocznik, J., Santisteban, D., Kurtines, W.M., Hervis, O.E., & Spencer, F. (1982). Life enhancement counseling: A psychosocial model of services for Cuban elders. In E.E. Jones & S.J. Korchin (Eds.), *Minority mental health* (pp. 296–330). New York: Praeger.

U.S. Department of Labor. (1990). National Alliance of Business, *Partners shaping our American workforce,* 7.

White, J.L., & Parham, T.A. (1990). *The psychology of Blacks: An African American perspective* (2nd ed.). Englewood Cliffs, NJ: Prentice Hall.

Williams, A. L. (1996). Skin color in psychotherapy. In R.M. Perez-Foster, M. Moskowitz, & R.A. Javier (Eds.), *Reaching across boundaries of culture and class.* Northvale, NJ: Aronson.

Winnicott, D.W. (1953). Transitional objects and transitional phenomena. *International Journal of Psycho-Analysis, 34,* 2.

CHAPTER 6

Internal Marketing Strategies to Maximize EAP Visibility and Effectiveness

BERNARD E. BEIDEL

For most employee assistance programs, the marketing of the program and its services is its bread and butter—not only in promoting the services to the workforce, but often in forming the foundation of expectations on which the program's effectiveness will be measured. Whether promoting the assessment and referral services of the program, announcing a training activity, or advancing a new service component, the marketing of those efforts is as important as the activity or service being promoted.

Although the perspective taken in this chapter is that of an internal EAP administrator, many of the ideas and comments for marketing an internal EAP apply equally well to externally or contractually-provided employee assistance programs. In exploring the traditional techniques and activities that most programs employ in marketing their services, we also examine the challenges of marketing those services within sensitive work organizations or to sensitive employee populations. In addition, we review nontraditional and newer marketing strategies that have emerged with the advancement of technology and electronic media in the workplace. Like most such advances, they present difficulties as well as opportunities, and administrators must make certain that the marketing of the program does not compromise its integrity or neutrality and objectivity within the organization.

Finally, we review the common and universal concerns in developing a marketing campaign for one's program and in promoting the employee assistance services on an ongoing basis. Whereas the techniques and activities are important in and of themselves, much of the commentary focuses on the marketing process and the importance of integrating it into the ongoing activities and services of the EAP. The unique role of the employee assistance professional in the program's marketing campaign is also explored. The discussion concludes with a summation of critical issues and concerns that must be considered in developing an internal marketing effort.

MARKETING GOALS AND OBJECTIVES

As with any marketing campaign, an EAP promotional effort must have clear and distinct goals and objectives. Generally, those objectives can be summarized in five primary areas:

1. To increase employees' knowledge of the EAP and its services, activities, and key components (e.g., confidentiality policy, referral procedures).
2. To increase familiarity and comfort with the EAP's operations and to enhance the acceptance and use of the service by employees, managers, labor representatives, and the organization's leadership.
3. To increase utilization of the program at all levels throughout the organization.
4. To enhance the integration of the EAP within the host or contract organization and to promote a feeling of ownership for the program on the part of the organization and its managers and employees.
5. To maintain the visibility of the EAP and its presence as a vital contributor to the organization's productivity and efficiency and to the well-being and general work life of the employees and managers.

It is imperative that an EAP identify its goals for the overall marketing campaign and its objectives for any specific marketing or promotional activity. A general informational brochure on the program might be the strategy of choice to introduce the EAP to the workforce or to announce a new provider of the EAP contract. On the other hand, the program may consider a different activity and employ other materials if it is targeting managers and labor representatives to increase the rate of job performance-based referrals to the EAP. Whether initiating an EAP and formulating the program's initial marketing effort within the organization or building on or modifying the ongoing promotional efforts of an established program, the organization and the EAP are best served when the marketing strategies and activities are carefully planned and coordinated with other information dissemination efforts within the organization. These coordination activities themselves play an informal part in the program's marketing campaign—exposing other operations within the organization to the services of the EAP and increasing the knowledge of and familiarity with the program among other key personnel who, by virtue of this liaison role, become an extension of the EAP's promotional efforts.

The key to an employee assistance program's successful internal marketing plan is rooted not only in the knowledge of where the program currently is and where the organization wants it to go or ultimately be, but also in the carefully identified strategies and activities that will get it there. The goals of the plan must be specific, whether it be expanding services (e.g., child and other dependent care service; preretirement or other transition services), increasing client utilization, meeting specific service delivery goals (e.g., frequency of follow-up contacts), or improving the image of the EAP within the workplace or within specific targeted underserved populations. But the strategies to reach those goals must be as carefully defined and as targeted. Very often, the applicable strategy is determined by the stage of the life cycle of development of the EAP. In general, the program moves through three distinct stages of development: (a) the missionary stage when the principal objective is to sell the program to the organization and its employees and managers; (b) the modification stage when the program adapts to changes within the organization and trends among the organization's populations; and (c) the maturity stage when the EAP has realized and begins maximizing its influence as a significant change agent within the organization.

Beyer and Trice (1978) described similar stages of program integration in terms of (a) the diffusion phase, when the program becomes known within the organization;

(b) the receptivity phase, when the members of the organization learn about and accept the principles and procedures of the program; and (c) the utilization phase, when individuals are willing to use the program, actually use it, and are satisfied with the program's services. These developmental phases reflect the EAP's progression and evolution as it becomes more entrenched and influential in the organization. In two separate accounts, Reichman and Beidel (1989, 1994) provide a thorough discussion of a 10-year study of an internal EAP as it moved through these phases of integration within a law enforcement agency—ultimately positioning itself as an agent of organizational change.

An EAP that recognizes these stages of development and their respective influence on its ongoing promotional efforts will be careful to adapt its overall marketing plan and its individual promotional activities to meet these unique needs in the service delivery continuum and the program life cycle. What worked early in the program's history may fall far short of meeting the needs of a more sophisticated employee population and an organization with enhanced expectations for the program and for the level of information concerning the program's services and activities in response to the organization's changing and evolving needs.

UNIQUE WORKPLACES AND WORKFORCES AND THEIR IMPACT ON PROMOTIONAL EFFORTS

Whereas clarifying the objectives of the marketing campaign is a critical task, tailoring the marketing strategies and promotional activities to the unique dynamics of the organization and its workforce is as important as the message itself. The EAP must weigh many issues and factors as it develops a marketing plan. An organization that is constantly in the public eye may be particularly concerned about promotional materials emphasizing a service available to employees to assist with personal difficulties or performance problems. Although EAP acceptance has increased greatly over the years, there are still many misconceptions and misrepresentations about organizations that aggressively promote their employee assistance services. Employee assistance professionals need to be cognizant of and alert to an organization's possible underlying ambivalence about how the public, or even its stockholders, might view its promotion of the EAP.

Similarly, many organizations employ individuals who identify with specific professional or occupational groups. Often these associations and affiliations bring forth their own issues, which need to be considered in the planning stages of the marketing campaign. Law enforcement personnel often perceive themselves as part of a separate and distinct occupational group with unique needs that set it apart from those outside the profession. These distinctions and perceptions can have tremendous implications for an EAP that is attempting to service the law enforcement agency. Imagine the perception of a police officer who initially sees the EAP as an affront to the self-sufficiency of his occupation and/or the demanding performance requirements of her organization. Reichman and Beidel (1994) provide an excellent overview and additional discussion of the unique influences of a sensitive law enforcement workforce on the organization in general and more specifically on the EAP itself.

Similarly, other occupational groups—physicians, nurses, politicians, lawyers, firefighters—and a host of crafts and trades workers bring myriad perceptions and preconceived notions that may have an initially negative impact on their view of the EAP. An EAP does itself and the employees it is charged with serving and that it intends to reach a tremendous service when it spends the time up-front meeting with those very employees in the workplace, getting to know the particular dynamics and perceptions of the relevant occupational groups, and formulating a marketing plan and relevant promotional materials that incorporate this knowledge and address these perceptions.

In addition to the unique dynamics of a particular workforce or occupational group, other considerations also come into play as the EAP carries out its marketing campaign. One organization with which the author is familiar has a high annual employee turnover rate and routinely experiences significant organizational transitions that result in the regular and systematic departure and influx of employees. The implications for an ongoing marketing campaign are straightforward; at a minimum, the program needs to avail itself of strategies to keep the EAP services visible to the ever-changing workforce. Such a workplace demands a more frequent information distribution schedule and specifically targeted promotional activities for the new hires.

A third element affects the marketing strategies employed by an EAP. Beyond frequent turnover or the initial skepticism of an occupational group, a workforce that is constantly in the public eye or under the continuous scrutiny of the press will bring another set of concerns that the EAP must address in its marketing or promotional efforts. An EAP that looks to promote its services in a very public way may be tagged with a perception that the employee population using these services will be subject to similar public view. One need only think about several political campaigns over the past 20 years that have been impacted by the revelation or exposure of a candidate who sought counseling or treatment for a particular mental health, family, substance abuse, or other personal problem. Similarly, the succession planning of some corporations has been influenced by the behavior and resultant treatment sought by a corporate executive under previous consideration for promotion. The test of the success of a particular marketing strategy by the EAP—and the success of the EAP itself in reaching its targeted populations—will depend on its sensitivity to these perceptions and concerns and its ability to respond to these issues and to reassure the employees and managers that the use of the EAP is indeed in their best interest and of minimal risk in both an immediate and long-term sense.

An Organization's Culture

Possibly the most important consideration for the EAP marketing plan, however, is the culture of the organization itself—the unique and particular way that the organization functions and gets things done, on both a formal and informal level. Although this culture is difficult to assess, particularly for the staff of a newly implemented EAP, it is nevertheless the most critical aspect of the EAP's ability to formulate its marketing strategies into the "language of the organization"—a task that is vital to the integration and utilization of the program within the organization. Morrison and Beidel (1984) and Reichman and Beidel (1994) talk specifically about these influences within a large law enforcement agency.

As both discussions reflect, the difficulty often is identifying and understanding the components of the organization's culture. It is critical to look at the primary influences in the organization, not the individuals or the operational components of the organization, but the processes that are followed to get things done. Myriad processes no doubt exist in any organization, but experience indicates they generally can be reduced to five key ones:

1. The way the organization is *led*. The degree of delegation and participation in the organization, which is often at the root of the trust, initiative, and risk-taking found within the workforce.

2. How the organization *motivates* its workforce. The degree to which managers take risks and the effectiveness of their supervision as well as their ability to carry out the business, administrative, and operational decisions of the organization.

3. How the workforce *communicates*. The degree to which and the effectiveness of the information that flows not only down the organization, but up and across the organization as well. The ability of the organization to maximize both the informal and formal channels for the exchange of information in the workplace and the solicitation of feedback from the workforce.

4. The level of *interaction* within the organization. The degree of cooperation and teamwork among individuals, work groups, departments, or organizational functions. The amount of interaction that is promoted among these groups and the amount of information that flows within and between them.

5. The *decision-making* process within the organization. The degree to which decisions are made as part of an individual or group process, ultimately influencing the quality of those decisions.

These are the elements that become the benchmark against which the success of the organization's communications activities, and hence the EAP's marketing plan and promotional efforts, can be measured. An EAP that understands these organizational determinants and taps into these cultural influences will have a better grasp of the strategies that are most likely to meet the EAP's overall marketing goals and objectives.

Although these influences may be as simple as understanding whether the organization employs written (e.g., executive memorandums or directives) or oral (e.g., announcements by the CEO) avenues to promote a new initiative or service for the employees, they can also be as complex as knowing whether the organization is inclined to deal with organizational problems or crises through its defined functional areas or by an ad hoc task force organized around the crisis at hand. In any event, the organization is spelling out its preferences in its day-to-day operations and functions, and the EAP that is sensitive to those elements is in the best position to maximize its marketing approach within the organization. As indicated in another publication (Morrison & Beidel, 1984), "when in Rome do as the Romans do"; tailor marketing strategies to the organization and utilize strategies that the organization's leadership, and its managers and employees, recognize as acceptable activities and promotional avenues within that specific organization. The first step for the EAP can be as simple as the name of the program. For example, in one particular organization, "programs" are strictly transient activities and often are viewed in time limited or operationally restrictive terms. Thus, the employee assistance service bears the title "Office of Employee Assistance," as opposed to Employee Assistance Program, to reflect an operation that is consistent with the other routine and permanent functions, departments, or operating units of the organization. The chosen title represents a service striving to become or already better integrated into the organization's culture and positional on the established table of organization.

Timing, Timing, Timing

Although it is critical to understand and align employee assistance promotional efforts with the organization's preferred style of doing things, it is equally important to time promotional efforts so that they do not conflict with other organizational events or efforts. An initial effort to promote the EAP in the midst of significant labor-management difficulties or during very difficult labor-management contract negotiations may cause labor to view the employee assistance program with skepticism or to question the motives of management. Even though a joint labor-management agreement concerning the operations of the EAP would probably alleviate any potential misunderstandings concerning the employee assistance service's role in the organization and in relation to the bargaining agreement, an EAP would nevertheless be wise to scrutinize the goals of its promotional activity and carefully plan any significant promotional effort. This is particularly important if it is to be undertaken in the midst of such tumultuous labor-management relations. Additional thoughts on the timing of a marketing effort and the corresponding promotional activities are provided at the conclusion of this discussion.

The Changing Customer Base and Their Values

As indicated earlier, occupational groups represented in the organization may directly influence the goals of an EAP's internal marketing effort and the strategies used to meet those goals. Similarly, the changing dynamics of the customer base in the organization impacts the marketing plan. Whereas many EAPs undertake a single promotional activity to reach the entire organization, the workforce is made up of a variety of "customers"—employees, referring managers, upper management, line supervisors, union representatives and shop stewards, family members, specific work groups, and other diverse or special interest groups (e.g., single parents, employees with specific disabilities).

Each of these customer bases challenges the EAP to address or respond to a complex array of special concerns and specific values that are particularly important to that group. While one group may be focused on the perception of the quality of the employee assistance service, another is more interested in the convenience, availability, and the accessibility of the services. The business manager for the union may be most interested in the confidentiality of the EAP when used by one of its members, but a line supervisor may want the assurance that the EAP staff will remain objective in its assessment process and view the performance problem from both the employee's and the supervisor's perspective. Meanwhile, upper management may be most interested in the overall reputation of the EAP and its services as it continues to integrate itself into the organization and evolves through its own developmental and implementation stages. The list in Table 6.1 illustrates a few of these varied and frequently changing customers and the types of questions that reflect their potential interests and areas of concern .

The significance of these customers and their interests cannot be overstated. Most students of organizational development understand that every organization that succeeds

Table 6.1   Concerns of an EAP's Varied Customers

Upper Management	Line Supervisors	Union Personnel	Employees/Families
How does the EAP interface with our health insurance carrier?	How does the EAP referral process interact with our disciplinary process?	Will the EAP referral process conflict with the arbitration process specified in our contract?	Will the EAP be confidential?
What is the EAP's impact on health care costs, absenteeism levels, and productivity in the organization?	Will it be easy to refer employees to the EAP?	How will management deal with our members who voluntarily use the EAP?	What will it cost me?
How well is the EAP integrated into the organization's day-to-day operations?	How realistic is it to expect improvement in employee performance as a result of a referral to the EAP?	How will the EAP's confidentiality be handled should a member file a grievance with the organization?	How will the EAP work with my health care provider and the organization's managed care program?

does so largely because of the efforts of both its formal and informal change agents. So too does the success of the EAP depend on its ability to equally identify the customers unique to its organization and their particular interests and concerns. But most important will be the EAP's ability to devise a plan and formulate the corresponding strategies that meet those identified needs and its success in engaging those customers through its ongoing promotional activities. Indeed, meeting the customers' information needs becomes part of the expansion of the EAP marketing force beyond the EAP staff and beyond the EAP promotional materials. The achievement of these tasks allows the EAP to benefit from the influence of the organization's formally designated and informally operating change agents. In essence, the EAP promotional efforts move from a program of written and electronic materials and dedicated educational and training programs to a combination of these EAP-generated efforts and the informal discussions that occur in every organization on a day-to-day basis. The EAP that meets the information needs of its customers in a timely manner and with direct and targeted responses to their specific interests will expand its marketing force beyond the employee assistance staff and well into the operational and functional heart of the organization.

TRADITIONAL PROMOTIONAL EFFORTS

Most employee assistance services have employed traditional promotional materials to meet many of the marketing goals detailed earlier. In his discussion of leadership, Hitt (1988) offers a paradigm of leadership that includes communication as an essential component. He goes on further to enumerate four essential components of organizational communication: (a) written communication, (b) oral presentations, (c) meetings, and (d) interpersonal communication (p. 130). These four elements provide a convenient framework from which to explore the promotional and marketing efforts of an EAP.

Written Materials

Table 6.2 provides a list of written materials and strategies that have been effective in several distinctive organizations and settings.

Although such a list of promotional materials can serve as a menu of options for the novice as well as the seasoned employee assistance professional, there are some basic rules or guiding principles to the development and delivery of these written materials. Any marketing or advertising text may offer suggestions and recommendations to drive the preparation and distribution of these materials, but the efforts should be rooted in sound communication practices. In that context, the work of Olson and Olson (1993) has been particularly helpful in its comprehensive examination of the communication process at all levels in an organization. They specifically detail the following effects of communications:

> When you communicate: You teach others how to treat you. You influence others whether you intend to or not. Your communication is persuasive. You usually operate on the basis of perceptions and feelings more than facts. You reveal and exchange values. You are responsible for your expectations. You do more than communicate information; you also comment on your relationship. (Olson & Olson, 1993, p. 6)

As their list illustrates, the role of communications in an organization is to teach, persuade, influence, set expectations, exchange values, and establish or enhance relationships—a definitive set of communications principles and objectives from which to guide any employee assistance promotional material or marketing strategy.

How the EAP achieves these objectives, however, is a critical part of the marketing effort. Whether distributing an initial brochure on the program or publishing an article in the corporate or departmental newsletter, the EAP needs to follow some basic guidelines for its written material. As discussed earlier, it may be necessary to target a specific audience in response to a situation being faced or a need that must be met. For example, the EAP may develop a brochure for the managers and line supervisors in the

Table 6.2   Traditional EAP Written Promotional Materials

- Brochures
- Flyers
- Newsletters
- Paycheck inserts
- Posters
- Informational memos
- Stress cards
- Rolodex cards
- Tabletop information tent cards
- Fact sheets
- Fax informational announcements
- Training calendars
- Seminar announcements

organization to provide them with information on dealing with employees who will be facing a significant reorganization or other corporate transition. The brochure may look at the role of the manager in keeping employees informed throughout the reorganization process and the supportive services available through the EAP to assist the employees and the manager alike in managing their stress throughout the transition.

In addition, some basic rules for any printed promotional materials apply. Keep the copy brief and have the intended audience in mind when laying out the format, content, and design of the informational piece. Likewise, the intent and goal of the material should be specific, targeted, and simple. Do not attempt to accomplish too much within a single brochure. An announcement to introduce the EAP may cover the rationale for the program, the types of services provided and problems covered, the confidentiality of the operation, the process for contacting the services, and may define those who are eligible for the service. Information beyond that may be more appropriately handled in a subsequent, more targeted discussion piece. For example, the interface between the EAP and the organization's health insurance carriers and their managed behavioral health programs may warrant a separate discussion either during the organization's health insurance open enrollment season or as part of the new employee orientation when employees are more focused on the selection of their insurance coverage.

As indicated, any written material should also be clear in its call to action or its expectations of the reader. A newsletter article describing the EAP's new service component for child, elder, and other dependent care should specifically state the EAP's expectations that employees in need of such services will make the EAP their first point of contact for additional information and/or referral to appropriate resources.

In the end, the written materials should reflect a consistent service image of the EAP, and newly developed materials should build on previously generated promotional pieces. These materials are most effective when they employ simple language and use simple persuasive techniques to reach simple objectives for the EAP.

In addition to brochures, newsletter and corporate magazine articles, periodic flyers, posters, paycheck inserts, and other standard written promotional materials, several more targeted and often indirect promotional devices are also of value, particularly when looking for diverse approaches to communicate the EAP's message. Informational transmittal memos to executive level personnel within the organization are often excellent devices for summarizing particularly relevant business, human resource, health care, mental health, or other developments with implications for the EAP's service delivery. This technique can be useful in calling attention to recent regulatory or legislative developments and their impact on the EAP's operations and the recommended response from the organization and/or the EAP.

Many employee assistance services have also used promotional materials such as stress cards, Rolodex cards, and referral handbooks to promote the EAP service or to provide specific guidance for managers, supervisors, and shop stewards in making referrals to the program, and employee assistance professionals should never overlook the benefit of the often forgotten thank-you note. Whether acknowledging a referral from a supervisor or a supportive gesture from either labor or management, a thank-you note often goes a long way to instill an appreciation for the EAP and to encourage and foster an expectation that the referring manager will call on the employee assistance professional again in the future. In building upon these varied suggestions, the employee assistance professional should never be lacking for appropriate employee assistance, business, human resource, or related material to keep the

EAP in the forefront of the awareness of the organization's leadership, managers, labor representatives, and employees.

Orally Transmitted Information

Very often, the employee assistance professional's most effective strategies for promoting the EAP and the acceptance and use of its services involve some form of oral presentation. These efforts offer several advantages because the professional can use his or her persuasive skills and interact with the targeted population, thus fulfilling one of the intents of communications as Olson and Olson (1993) described—to establish or enhance a relationship. Table 6.3. offers a list of traditional forms of oral communications available to the EAP and examples of programs and strategies that have been effective in a variety of labor and management settings. Most of the oral promotional efforts employed by EAPs occur as part of a formal training or educational program or within the context of a structured or informal briefing to a targeted population in the organization.

Although EAP training programs are frequently intended to provide specific information about the current operations of the EAP and the process for making referrals or accessing the services, these programs are also a means to raise organizational awareness of needs that may be met through the addition of a future service component or the planned development of another activity within the EAP. For example, while employed by a law enforcement agency experiencing an increase in traumatic incidents, several of which resulted in line-of-duty deaths or injuries, the author became keenly aware of the organization's lack of a formalized critical incident stress debriefing (CISD) process for the officers, families, and coworkers impacted by such situations. As a result, the idea for such a response was incorporated into the EAP's standard stress management training program. In addition, a discussion of the benefits of a CISD stress management response policy and the related operating procedures was included in the EAP's supervisory and mid-level management training programs as well as being added to the Stress Management and Employee Assistance Development seminar provided to senior police executives. The training program became a vehicle for "planting the seed" or "raising the consciousness" of a need within the employee population. These training programs served as a catalyst to promote grassroots support for the concept and the development of a specific critical incident stress management service component. The promotional effort of a routine training program became the primary activity for marketing a new service component before it was actually established. When the CISD

Table 6.3   EAP Orally Communicated Promotion Activities

- New employee orientation sessions.
- Supervisory and management training sessions.
- Shop steward training.
- Brown bag luncheon seminars.
- Health fair or wellness program information booths or tables.
- Presentations to specific work groups, (e.g., senior management, union officials, organization task forces).
- Ongoing educational programs dealing with work and family issues; alcohol and drug awareness; smoking cessation; conflict resolution; transition and change management.

stress management response procedure was finally introduced to the organization three years after the initiation of the concept in the training programs, it was brought into an organization that had been primed for its development and was receptive to its implementation. The EAP found that the initial oral presentation of a concept was an effective tool for advancing the recognition, acceptance, and ultimate utilization of the needed service component.

Meetings and Partnerships with Other Organizational Operations

Most employee assistance professionals recognize that their training and educational activities are an essential and vital part of the program's overall marketing efforts. They provide opportunities to dialogue with other key personnel and, through the process of persuasion, offer a chance to enlist other personnel in marketing and promoting the employee assistance service throughout the organization.

Most organizations, however, offer other forums for an EAP to market its services and to promote its image to the workforce. Many EAPs in their early development often make use of advisory committees to provide liaison between the EAP and other functions and operations in the organization. These advisory committees still play an important role in the marketing of the program because they promote, establish, and enhance the relationship between the EAP and other parties within the organization. Reichman and Beidel (1994) offer a specific discussion of the role that an advisory committee and other key organizational personnel played in promoting a newly established EAP within a large law enforcement organization, as well as their collective role in advancing an EAP evaluation effort within the organization's unionized workforce and encouraging participation in and support of the evaluation effort by both labor and management.

Most EAPs also participate in other events in the workplace such as health fairs and other wellness efforts. The EAP may participate in the annual health insurance open enrollment fair and provide information to employees regarding the EAP's services as well as its interface with the health insurance carriers and the managed care organizations that oversee mental health, substance abuse and other behavioral healthcare benefits.

Interpersonal Communication

As the employee assistance professional becomes more engaged with the organization by attending the myriad of meetings that arise, the opportunity for establishing these strategic partnerships proportionately increases. These expanding partnerships in return provide a variety of avenues for the professional to more fully develop an interpersonal communication style that demonstrates the commitment of the EAP to serve the workforce and support the business interests of the organization. Through these interpersonal communication opportunities the EAP professional can model an appreciation for balancing the demands of the business with the interests and well-being of the workforce. It is often easier to communicate this important EAP marketing message through these dynamic interpersonal communication exchanges than through the traditional written materials and formal presentations. As is evident in the training experience, real learning often results from the more dynamic and interactive training opportunities where the participants have the opportunity to engage each other as well as the training facilitator. This issue will be more fully explored in a later discussion of the EAP professional as a marketing agent for the program.

Promotion of New Service Activities and Components

As EAPs have evolved over the years, their services have as well. Employee assistance efforts trace their roots to the occupational alcoholism movement and the related, but limited, assessment and referral services provided for alcoholic employees; but today's EAP offers expanded services that have emerged in response to the general changes in most work environments and to the specific needs of individual work organizations. Although these services sometimes are as varied as the programs providing them and the organizations they serve, they can be characterized in several general categories, a few of which are provided as examples.

Many EAPs are providing conflict resolution and negotiation services as an expansion of their core short-term problem resolution services. As discussed, many EAPs have also developed critical incident stress management processes as part of their standard service delivery continuum. For many organizations, this stress management response includes individual grief or bereavement services for employees and specific work groups impacted by the death or terminal illness of a coworker, or trauma response services for larger work groups impacted by a natural disaster or other tragedy in the workplace. With the emergence of workplace violence and enhanced awareness of domestic violence as issues facing many organizations, the EAP is frequently at the head of the organization's collective response. Such issues have generated fitness-to-perform policies, return-to-duty procedures, and other preventive and protective services, many of which involve an interface between the EAP and other operational entities within the organization, thus providing another opportunity for the EAP to promote other aspects of its service delivery continuum within the organization.

With the developments over the past 15 years of drug testing and the related regulatory guidelines that primarily impact the testing activities in the transportation industry, many employee assistance efforts have also incorporated an interface with the drug-testing operation within the organization. In fact, some EAPs also oversee the substance abuse professional (SAP) activities in their organization or incorporate the SAP services as a separate and distinct component of the EAP's overall service delivery system. While these services are discussed elsewhere in this book, the EAP and SAP interface provides another avenue for the EAP to market its principal services often with an emphasis on its role as an organizational consultant.

As indicated, many EAPs have found that the numerous changes and reengineering efforts within organizations have given rise to specific transition services to assist affected employees and managers. In addition, EAPs have responded to issues such as work-life balance, career management, retirement planning, and disability and behavioral risk management (Yandrick, 1996), that have provided excellent opportunities to promote services throughout the organization in areas beyond the traditional EAP role. These efforts reflect the changing demands of today's workplaces and the corresponding needs of the organization and its managers and employees.

NONTRADITIONAL AND EMERGING PROMOTIONAL STRATEGIES

The emergence of electronic media in the workplace has given rise to alternative strategies to support an organization's and EAP's internal marketing efforts. Alongside the opportunities presented by these technologies, however, new issues, concerns, and challenges have emerged. An EAP must be prepared to address them to be certain that the strategies and activities used by the program are consistent with its image and role within the organization and that they take into consideration the perceptions held by the employees in the workplace.

Electronic Media

Over the past few years, e-mail has become an increasingly popular system of communications in the workplace, often replacing memos and other forms of written correspondence or oral communications. Although many welcome the ability to leave messages for colleagues via e-mail, particularly when coworkers are unavailable or away from their desks, EAP professionals must use e-mail in a guarded fashion. Using e-mail to broadcast or widely announce an EAP training session might be the most expedient way of getting the announcement to the targeted audience. On the other hand, use of e-mail to communicate with a manager following a referral to the program raises serious considerations about the security of the e-mail system, especially for managers who have other personnel screening e-mail in their absence. An EAP considering e-mail as a resource should probably limit its use to the marketing of the services and activities of the program. In general, e-mail is not an appropriate system for providing feedback or follow-up information to referring managers, supervisors, or labor representatives.

Other electronic media have also emerged over the years and have brought EAPs considerable options for marketing their efforts within the organization. Facsimile transmissions can be an effective and quick promotional method. In many cases, the fax is the quickest means of responding to specific inquiries about the program's operations. In fact, the author has used an "employee assistance fact sheet," which provides answers to basic questions about the EAP, as a standard part of all his informational responses transmitted by fax. Like any other electronic transmission, the fax necessitates extreme care by the sender to be certain that the fax transmission arrives at the intended destination and that the content of the transmission itself does not compromise the privacy of the office or the individual to whom the fax is being sent. Before sending a fax in response to an inquiry by an individual in a specific work setting the EAP should first determine from the individual whether a fax is an acceptable form of relaying the information and whether the individual will be available to receive the fax directly. To use this method of transmission, both conditions must exist.

The final three electronic methods for marketing one's program raise fewer security issues and are probably more in line with the marketing goals or objectives outlined at the beginning of this chapter. Intranet or internal Web sites, internal television broadcasting systems, and video teleconferencing have become viable methods for providing the most current information on an EAP's services, operations, and activities, for announcing new training programs, and for the delivery of in-house developed and produced videos to support those promotional, training, and educational activities. Each of these systems brings the EAP a capability of providing the most up-to-date information to the entire workforce or to specifically targeted segments of the employee population in an expedient and efficient fashion. An internal, organizationwide Web site is a most effective method for providing not only standard information on the EAP, but also for day-to-day updates on any time-limited services being offered or training programs being provided. In particular, a Web site provides a great avenue for an EAP to highlight the services it may be providing in response to a traumatic event or critical incident that has occurred in the workplace, such as a planned plant closing, a natural disaster, or a reorganization of a major operational unit that has affected a significant segment of the organization. The emergence of these and other electronic media has greatly enhanced an EAP's ability to promote its services in a proactive and timely manner. They offer the additional advantage of reaching even the smallest number of employees dispersed in remote locations or in multiple operational units around the world.

Information Transmissions to Key Personnel

Although EAP-developed written promotional materials and these newer electronic methods have become standard practice, an age-old method of marketing is often underused in the workplace—the transmission of journal articles and other news pieces to key personnel. All too often, EAP professionals miss the opportunity to promote their efforts to the organization's leadership when they do not forward articles of interest or of related subject matter to the organization's key personnel or decision makers. An EAP making an effort to position itself as a critical player within the organization's managed care review and decision-making process should consider the benefits of being seen by the organization as a source of information on the managed care issue in general and the experiences of other comparable organizations in particular. This can be readily achieved through the transmission of related articles and other materials on the issue.

In a similar way, it is extremely valuable for the EAP to become viewed as an information resource within the organization. With that objective in mind, this author has guided several EAPs in gathering and providing an array of materials on ongoing and emerging issues in the organization—from the management of people with disabilities to the risk management associated with workers' compensation cases, from the supervisory implications of family and medical leave to the interface between the EAP and the organization's human resource function. Although many of these issues go beyond the EAP's traditional concern for the employee's personal problems and their ultimate impact on job performance and productivity, professionals can promote EAP services by simply using these informational materials as a periodic reminder to the organization's decision makers that the EAP is a vital resource, even when it is not providing specific services for an employee experiencing performance difficulties or struggling with a personal problem.

Surveys

Surveys provide another indirect, and often subtle, method to effectively promote the EAP within the organization. In particular, needs assessment and satisfaction surveys have been exceptionally beneficial. Some EAPs have also employed focus groups to assess the needs of the entire organization or of particular populations within the workplace. Needs assessments have traditionally looked at identifying new or emerging trends within the organization that may require the development of specific service components or training and educational programs to meet those needs. The mere fact that an EAP is using a survey to gather information for further service development reflects its attentiveness and responsiveness to the changing needs of the organization—a critical promotional goal for any EAP.

On another level, satisfaction surveys can serve a similar promotional function. Whether telephone, mail, or face-to-face processes are utilized for the survey, employee assistance professionals who take the time to solicit information from their customers actively promote the EAP as an operation focused on the needs, satisfaction, and feedback of its clients. The EAP can use a random process to select those clients who will receive a satisfaction survey or can distribute a survey to every EAP client. Whatever process is followed, however, the end result is the same; the employees, managers, union personnel, and other clients will see the EAP as an operation that is interested in improving its services and enhancing its responsiveness to its customers—the employees, managers, and family members who actually use its services or will consider using them in the future.

Evaluation Efforts

Another indirect method to promote an EAP within an organization is through the evaluation of the program. The author was involved in a 10-year project that utilized an evaluation model developed by Beyer and Trice (1978) to measure the integration of an EAP within an organization. Over the life of the evaluation project, written surveys were periodically mailed to a random sample of the entire employee population soliciting information on the following:

- The employees' knowledge of the EAP and its operational procedures (e.g., referral processes, confidentiality).
- Their attitude about the EAP and its use.
- Their perception of the EAP and its key operational provisions.
- Their actual use of the EAP.
- Their willingness to promote the EAP's use to their coworkers.
- Their willingness to refer a subordinate or peer to the EAP.

Although the surveys were designed as part of an overall evaluation to measure the integration process and determine the stage that the EAP had achieved at any particular time, the survey questions themselves became a means of providing information throughout the organization. The surveys became promotional devices because they were mailed to employees who in most cases had not used the EAP services themselves. On another level, many of the survey responders became more knowledgeable of the EAP by simply answering the questions on the survey instrument. After the first survey was distributed at the initiation of the evaluation project and shortly after the introduction of the EAP, the subsequent surveys included additional questions and information pieces regarding future service activities and programmatic developments. So each survey built on the expanding knowledge and receptive attitudes within the organization. In reality, the survey instrument acted as an informational handout on the EAP's policies, operational procedures, and services.

The ultimate promotion, however, occurred when the EAP and the researcher prepared their collective presentation of the survey results for the organization's leadership, its managers and employees, and representatives of the various bargaining units. The EAP and the evaluation research consultant seized the opportunity to portray the

EAP in a positive light as a service that responded to the needs of the organization and that was prepared to modify its service delivery systems if necessary, and adjust its operations in response to the feedback provided or the shortcomings identified through the survey. Reichman and Beidel (1989, 1994) also illustrate how the EAP evaluation was able to incorporate a series of key questions for the organization's leadership about organizational issues and developments that went well beyond the focus of the EAP. The incorporation of these issues into the evaluation played a major role in promoting the EAP as an integral component of the organization's operations, a significant contributor to the well-being, health, and performance of the workforce, and a service delivery system responsive to the interests of both labor and management.

An evaluation offers an EAP a unique opportunity. While not a traditional promotional activity, the evaluation becomes an indirect means to communicate with the organization, with the union, and with the employees and managers in the workforce. Through a series of surveys and other measurement tools, the EAP maintains visibility and advances itself as an operation that is sensitive to the employees' needs and one which recognizes its collective role in partnering with others in the workplace to successfully integrate the EAP into the organization. The evaluation becomes another means of marketing the EAP's services, programs, and ongoing activities throughout the organization.

In several other discussions, the author has examined the initiation of this evaluation effort and the EAP's promotion of the evaluation to a sensitive employee population and an initially skeptical work organization (Morrison & Beidel, 1984), the actual steps undertaken and the processes followed to carry out the evaluation over its 10 years of operation (Reichman & Beidel, 1989), and the role that the evaluation played both to enhance the EAP as a change agent and to act as a significant EAP promotional activity through its interface with the organization's and the union's decision makers and their respective formal and informal leaders (Reichman & Beidel, 1994).

The Individual EAP Professional as a Marketing Agent

Although traditional and nontraditional marketing strategies are valuable and essential for any successful EAP, the EAP professional is often the most critical marketing device within the organization. No matter how effective the written materials or electronic media are in promoting the program, the professional may be the consummate marketing tool having the opportunity to reach customers and influence their perceptions each and every day he or she operates within the organization or interacts with any employee, manager, or family member. This discussion offers some guidelines for maximizing one's individual influence in the organization and capitalizing on the EAP professional's role in marketing the EAP through personal behavior and actions.

The EAP professional is held to a high standard in most organizations. And with that standard is the responsibility to carry oneself in the most positive light and to live by the principles, policies, and procedures advocated by the EAP. EAP professionals represent their programs in all their interactions in the workplace. The reality for the workplace is still, "First impressions are indeed the lasting ones." As a result, a number of expectations and principles provide the basis for an EAP professional's effective marketing of a program. The following are proposed for consideration.

Perception Is Reality

EAP professionals must demonstrate the ability to handle their own workload and balance their work and family demands in a healthy and positive way. Imagine the perception of the EAP if it is viewed as a service staffed by professionals who do not seem able to strike a balance in their own professional lives. On another level, the EAP professional's preparedness in meeting the demands of the workplace may be perceived as reflecting the EAP's ability to meet the needs of the employees seeking its services. If the EAP professional is unaware of the organization's business plan, will managers feel confident about referring employees to the EAP when the performance issues in question are related to the financial goals and business objectives of the organization? No manager or employee will be confident in working with an EAP that it perceives as operating in a vacuum void of any true partnership with the organization as a whole or out of touch with its strategic direction.

In addition, as an EAP professional interacts with coworkers and colleagues throughout the organization, his or her attitude will be assessed on an ongoing basis. Does he have a "can do" spirit and look for the opportunity to be found in any dilemma or problem that arises? Does she tend to criticize others in the organization or question the motives of management or labor to the point that her objectivity is suspect? And on still another level, the individual's ethics as a professional and business partner are observed on a daily basis. Coworkers will view the way that EAP professionals handle confidential business or organizational information as a reflection of their ability to maintain the confidentiality of the information gathered through the EAP itself.

The challenge for EAP professionals is to establish themselves as service and information experts who can be highly visible promoters of the EAP service while also being effective internal consultants who respect the business plan of the organization and demonstrate and espouse the principles at the core of the EAP's strategy to restore and maintain the performance of employees in the workplace.

EAP Professionals as Internal Consultants

The EAP professional also plays a vital role in the organization as an internal consultant. Very often, the professional's availability and ability to consult with the organization's leadership, its managers, and employees about issues beyond the EAP's traditional areas of focus promotes the EAP's value in a broader sense within the organization. The EAP that emphasizes and carries out this consultation function creates a series of ongoing promotional and marketing opportunities throughout the life of the program. In general, these consultative functions arise through two or three primary methods: (a) responding to specific inquiries from managers or employees, (b) serving on task forces or ad hoc working groups, and (c) speaking with or making presentations to groups within the organization.

Every inquiry that comes into the EAP is an opportunity to market the program in a broader sense and often to a wider audience. Although the initial request may be to meet with an employee who is experiencing an attendance problem, the EAP professional might have the additional opportunity to provide the referring manager with information on a service component that will be of particular value as the manager interacts with the work group in carrying out a planned reorganization. The EAP's primary responsibility is to meet the immediate needs of the manager or employee making an initial inquiry or requesting specific information, but the EAP should never overlook that a client who turns to the EAP for a specific issue the first time may come back at a later date for an entirely different one. That possibility is greatly increased when the EAP aggressively promotes its services and educates its potential return customers to the variety and diversity of its services and programmatic components. All too frequently, EAPs are still viewed primarily as programs that react to problems that arise in the workplace. This consultative role offers an EAP the opportunity to market the preventive and proactive nature of its broader range of services.

Serving on task forces and ad hoc working groups is particularly effective for marketing the EAP within the organization. In one organization in which the author has managed an EAP, he has served on the following task forces: personnel policy development, violence in the workplace, performance management system development, corporate communications, and organizational strategic planning. Each of these groups provided the EAP with the chance to interact with other managers and employees at all levels and from a variety of operations throughout the organization. Through the interactions with these working groups and the diversity of employees represented, the EAP integrated itself more fully within the organization, particularly within the Human Resources function, and interfaced with other functional and operational entities in the organization. With the diverse issues facing today's workers and the complex situations that arise in today's workplaces, an EAP can no longer afford to operate in isolation if it expects to have an impact on the work life of employees. In fact, an EAP that does not connect with other operations in the workplace misses the opportunity to promote the value of the EAP partnership across operational and functional lines in the organization. Over years of EAP experience, the author has worked closely with many organizational entities in addressing workplace issues. Table 6.4 details some of those operations as well as others that are worth any EAP's consideration.

No matter what the relationship, the ultimate end is an opportunity for the EAP to promote its services, develop and enhance its partnership with other operations, and demonstrate its value to the organization and its work teams—a definitive sign of the EAP's integration within the organization, its ability to weave its services into the very fabric of the organization, and its role in supporting the heart of any organization—its people.

But with this integration comes a caution. As an EAP serves in these advisory and working group functions or establishes linkages and working partnerships with other organizational functions, it must be careful to not become so aligned with these operations that it loses its independence and objectivity. The EAP may become part of a functional group but not to the point that it loses its identity within the context of that group.

The final consultative function comes from the speaking opportunities that present themselves from time to time. Although an EAP professional should seize any opportunity to speak about or on behalf of the program, caution needs to be exercised in terms of understanding the context in which the EAP will be speaking. Appearances at certain organizational functions, particularly those with strong internal or external political overtones, may warrant extreme scrutiny before the EAP commits to the presentation. The author was once invited to speak at a union meeting in the midst of bitter contract negotiations. The intent of the discussion and the information to be presented required significant clarification to maintain the EAP's neutrality and

Table 6.4   Organizational Entities or Functions for Partnership Consideration

Benefits	Marketing
Compensation/Payroll administration	Medical/Occupational health
Conflict resolution/Mediation/ Alternative dispute resolution	Operations
Corporate ethics office	Organizational/Workplace diversity
Corporate ombuds office	Professional/Career development
Corporate planning	Public relations
Crisis/Emergency management	Quality control/Process improvement
Drug-free workplace/Drug testing	Recruiting/Hiring
EEO/Affirmative action/Compliance	Relocation/Expatriate services
Employee relations	Research and development
Environmental health/Safety	Retirement planning
Family/Work-life programs	Risk management
Finance	Security
Fitness for duty	Training/Development
Human resources	Wellness
Labor relations	Worker's compensation/Disability management
Legal	

prevent the program from being caught in the middle of a long-standing dispute between labor and management.

Similarly, when the EAP commits to appearances at any organization function, whether a retirement gathering or an organization health fair, the EAP professional needs to be vigilant of the EAP's primary role in the organization and to approach the appearance cognizant of the context of the gathering and the professional's ever-present responsibility to promote the EAP and market its services in the most positive light. Professionals who are able to see their roles as a representative of the EAP and as a workplace colleague with clear delineation must realize that such distinctions are not as readily apparent or even evident to other personnel in the organization. The best practice is to expect that the employee assistance professional is always viewed in the context of the EAP in every interaction in the workplace.

Common Courtesies

Before moving on to some final considerations and concerns about the EAP marketing process, a few comments about the role of some common courtesies in the EAP professional's role as the marketer of the program are in order. All too often, these "tried and true" practical courtesies have become lost in the workplace. When they are present, however, they go a long way to promote the EAP professional and ultimately the program.

Making it a practice to send thank-you and condolence notes brings a distinctive personal touch to the program reflecting the concern and compassion of the professionals affiliated with it. Returning calls promptly and following through with commitments should result in many employees perceiving the EAP with a high degree of integrity. Offering to go the extra mile, beyond one's normal areas of responsibility, also enhances the normal promotional and marketing activities of the program. And finally, responding to requests in person as frequently as possible will provide the added opportunity to meet directly with your customers—a basic strategy of any marketing campaign, whether being driven by the organization as a whole or by the EAP itself.

CONSIDERATIONS AND CONCERNS; CHALLENGES AND OPPORTUNITIES

Throughout this discussion, we have examined the principles behind and the fundamental goals of a successful marketing campaign, the traditional and nontraditional or emerging EAP marketing strategies and activities, and the role of the EAP professional as an effective marketing agent. Individually and collectively, however, these marketing strategies raise issues and concerns for further consideration. This discussion concludes with an examination of a few of these issues and the challenges they present and the opportunities they provide.

Targeted Marketing Strategies

As with any promotional efforts or overall marketing plan, the EAP professional must first recognize that the message to be communicated, the information to be exchanged, and the marketing activity employed may vary drastically depending upon the intended audience. As discussed elsewhere, the concerns and interests of managers may vary greatly from those of the shop stewards. Similarly, upper management's interests in the EAP during an economic downturn are going to be very different than those of the employees and their family members at the same time. The EAP must address these audience variations in its marketing plan and develop and utilize varied promotional strategies and tools to reach the intended audience and to meet their informational needs, at all times recognizing the need to be flexible and responsive to the changing circumstances and situations that can occur on a moment's notice impacting the organization and its workforce.

Meeting the Future

As discussed in our examination of the non-traditional and emerging marketing and promotional tools, the challenges that lay ahead and the related opportunities they present may be limitless. The implications for the EAP professional, however, are clear. One of the most important partnerships that the professional can cultivate within the organization or through a network of professional colleagues is with the marketing department or comparable association. EAPs must be on the cutting edge of packaging their message in the formats that their employees and organizations are accustomed to seeing. Clearly, the knowledge of the emerging trends and resulting successful strategies employed by an organization's marketing department can be of great benefit to the EAP as it plans and develops its own strategies. The EAP needs to move beyond its reliance on traditional methods when the future is demanding creative and bold techniques to meet a more demanding and enlightened customer, whether an individual employee or the broader organization.

Striking a Balance

In promoting the EAP throughout the organization, an EAP must be vigilant that its promotional efforts be viewed as an effort to market the program and not the professionals affiliated with it. There is often a fine line between what the employees may perceive as promotion of the EAP and self-promotion of the EAP professional. The risk of the latter is generally greater when the popular press or public media is used in the promotional effort. When an EAP professional seems to welcome the opportunity to talk with the press, even if about very general programmatic or related issues, employees may question why the EAP professional is so public in these comments and whether the professional will exercise due discretion in discussions concerning confidential matters that the press may inquire about on another occasion. Every EAP must evaluate the pros and cons and ultimately the utility of the popular press in its marketing campaign. An EAP is wise to formulate in advance clearly defined policies and procedures that are strictly followed and adhered to in dealing with the press, press inquiries of any nature. An EAP always needs to consider the precedent that is set and the expectations established through its initial contacts with the media. The immediate benefits of press coverage for an EAP initiative may be greatly diminished by the long-range consequences of an EAP that becomes perceived as having a "too cozy" relationship with the press.

Technology and Confidentiality

As discussed, the emergence of technology in the workplace in and of itself raises many considerations, particularly around confidentiality and privacy issues. On one level, the EAP's use of that technology in its promotional efforts may raise questions among the workforce about the EAP's process for handling confidential information in the information technology age. The EAP's ready use of an intranet or internal Web site may prompt employees to question the program's procedures for assuring that the confidential information maintained as part of the EAP's management information system (MIS) has no chance of being compromised by other organizationwide and generally easily accessible technologies. Specific procedures for dealing with this problem and security precautions must be developed in advance and periodically updated. The best practice may be to maintain the EAP's MIS on an independent network that is self-contained and not linked with any other computer system within the organization.

The use of surveys in the organization can prompt employees to question why they have received a survey. The author encountered this problem in his work with a law enforcement agency. When employees received surveys as part of the evaluation effort, some questioned why they specifically had received the survey. Although the survey sample was randomly selected by a computer, some recipients who had been clients of the EAP were concerned that they might have been selected because of their involvement with the EAP or because their participation had been revealed, even if only to the researcher conducting the evaluation. Others asked whether they had received the survey because someone within the organization or within the EAP itself had perceived them as having a problem. Although none of these scenarios were reality, such erroneous perceptions within the workplace can derail the best program promotional efforts or marketing activities. This experience suggests the need to spell out the survey sample selection and data collection process at the time any survey is undertaken. Although the preceding scenario occurred with the "confidentiality sensitive" and image-conscious employee population of a law enforcement agency, the cautions implied and the recommended remedies are appropriate for any organization; employees in most organizations still rank confidentiality as their issue of primary concern when they seek the services of their EAP.

Building Flexibility into the Marketing Plan and Process

While the emergence of electronic communication formats in the workplace presents a number of challenges for the EAP, the flexibility they provide offers the EAP a number of opportunities as well, particularly in terms of flexibility. As discussed, today's workplaces are subject to a variety of changes and external influences that impact employees, managers, and the organization as a whole. Whether the emergence of a drug testing requirement imposed on the organization through regulation, or the introduction of a new wellness program as a result of a recently negotiated bargaining agreement, the EAP may be initiating new services or adjusting existing procedures as a result of an expanded or altered role in the organization. The marketing plan should be fluid enough to meet these changing information demands. Electronic formats offer the EAP the capability of making these immediate and timely adjustments in each marketing plan in anticipation of these changing informational needs.

Seizing Special Opportunities

This need for immediacy is particularly evident when the workforce or the organization is thrust into a crisis, whether internally or externally driven. An incident of workplace violence, an industrial accident, or a natural disaster that affects the community where the organization is located or in which may of the employees live—each is a situation that demands immediate information from the EAP in terms of the services it provides, the availability of its staff, and the immediate steps it is taking to assist employees and the organization through the crisis.

While traditional EAP promotional materials may address some of the generic EAP services provided at such a time, electronic formats and other emerging marketing tools offer the EAP the chance to address the unique circumstances of the particular situation in its informational dissemination efforts. This enables a more direct connection with employees as they look for resources to help them manage the situation. Many EAPs are finding that a Web page offers an easy vehicle for transmitting information necessitated by an immediate event impacting the organization. Similarly, voice mail messages can be directed to the homes of employees when they are unable to get to the office or plant. In order to reach the organization's employees impacted by large scale natural disasters, some EAPs have relied on press releases to engage the local media in the dissemination of appropriate information concerning the trauma response services being provided by the EAP. The EAP that plans for these types of situations, adjusts and alters its promotional activities and tools, and employs the latest technology in its marketing is in the best position to portray its image as a partner with the employees and the organization—a partner capable of meeting both in the moment of the situation.

Timing of Promotional Activities

As indicated earlier, the timing of a promotional effort can be as critical as its content. The example of promoting the EAP in the midst of an extensive and bitter labor dispute exemplifies the importance of being sensitive to other developments and events in the organization. In addition, the EAP must always recognize that it is one of many organizational operations, departments, or events competing for the employees' attention. Thus it is imperative to develop the EAP marketing campaign in conjunction with the organization's overall marketing and promotion of other activities, programs, and services to the employees. The EAP should be aware at all times of the organization's other promotional campaigns and informational efforts and schedule its promotional activities in relation to those efforts—recognizing that at times some EAP efforts go hand-in-hand with other organizational activities, while at other times they need to stand alone.

Another experience of the author provides a good example of this issue. When sending out the EAP's initial promotional brochure within a law enforcement agency, the EAP decided to mail the brochure to the homes of all employees to be certain that family members would see it as well. Considering that this was a novel undertaking within the law enforcement community and that many of the police officers initially questioned the intent and goals of the organization's EAP initiative, the officers were similarly skeptical of the EAP's intent to get information to their families. Thus, when the brochures were mailed, many of them were delivered on a Saturday, which afforded some officers an opportunity to intercept the brochure before their families saw it. This promotional activity served as a tremendous learning experience for the EAP and assured that all future mailings were scheduled in such a fashion that they did not arrive at the employees' homes on a weekend. It also demonstrated the ever present need to discuss the marketing plan and the specific promotional activity in advance with the decision makers and formal and informal change agents at all levels in the organization.

Other Concerns

Several other concerns must be considered when generating a marketing campaign within the organization. Some of them do not matter whether the EAP is internally managed or provided by an external contractor or provider. Others differ depending on whether the EAP is an internal or external one.

The rate of turnover of the organization's workforce will necessitate promotional activities that are sensitive to the movement of personnel in and out of the organization as well as within it. The author has managed an EAP in a very stable law enforcement environment and another EAP in an organization that experienced a considerably greater turnover rate in any given year. To say the least, the overall goal of the EAP marketing campaign and the schedule of related promotional activities varied drastically between these two organizations. Promotional efforts undertaken within the law enforcement agency built on each other over the years and were based on a finding in the evaluation that knowledge of, attitudes toward, receptivity of, and comfort in using the EAP were steadily increasing in the employee population over time. Thus, promotional efforts could move beyond the basic and fundamental EAP operational and service delivery information. On the other hand, the promotional efforts within the other organization more routinely revisit these basic informational needs because the EAP cannot be assured that the information disseminated six months or a year ago is still prevalent: the workforce has probably undergone significant transition within that time frame. Thus, informational efforts are kept basic and are regularly scheduled around the operational schedule of the institution.

Another consideration is the dispersion of the employee population. Marketing the EAP to a localized employee population requires completely different strategies and activities from those used in an organization that is dispersed throughout the country, around the world, or in remote geographic areas. The marketing campaign becomes even more complex and challenging when promoting the EAP to a worldwide employee population with its multiple cultural influences and considerations. Although the impact of these cultural and international influences in the workplace probably warrants a separate and dedicated discussion, an EAP must consider these issues in every promotional effort, whether it serves an international, multiple location corporation or the auto repair shop down the road.

As with any marketing strategy, the EAP must always be evaluating the reliability of the internal promotional strategies and activities within the organization. What may have been a reliable vehicle for promoting the service in the past, may not be today. What may have worked with the union membership in the organization may not work with upper or mid-level management. In addition, a well-integrated EAP must always be looking at marketing strategies with the potential to reach all facets of the organization. That includes the use of alternative format materials (e.g., Braille, large-print format, audiotapes) for people with disabilities and appropriate alternative language translations for employees who require information in their primary language. As indicated, the EAP that recognizes the influence of cultural differences in the workplace, the importance of valuing those differences, and the role and impact of other diversity issues will be more successful in reaching a diverse employee population with an appropriately developed and comparably tailored array of promotional materials and marketing strategies.

Many of these issues are common whether the EAP is an internal or external effort, but undoubtedly, a central issue in any marketing campaign is an honest self-assessment of the advantages and disadvantages that the particular EAP may have because of its position as an internal or external provider of the EAP service. Although debating the merits of either approach is beyond the scope of this discussion, each program must weigh its position with the parent or host company, or contracting organization to maximize those respective advantages and minimize the disadvantages that come with its position within or in relation to the organization. Many EAP professionals may argue that few externally provided EAPs can match the accessibility and organizational sensitivity of the internal EAP; however, there is no guarantee that an internally provided program has an upper hand in marketing the program within the organization. Likewise, an externally contracted EAP that is marketing its services to an extremely sensitive population of employees has no assurance that those employees will perceive the EAP as a service that is detached and far enough removed from the organization simply because it is provided by an outside organization. Neither an internal nor external provision of employee assistance services is any guarantee of confidentiality—which is generally a major focus of the EAP's initial marketing or promotional effort.

In the end, the critical formula for effectively addressing these concerns and considerations is the EAP's ability to develop creative and divergent strategies for marketing the program, recognizing that a diverse organization and a diverse employee population require similarly diverse promotional materials and strategies—all the while maintaining a commitment to the EAP's ultimate mission, its operating values, its policies and procedures, and to its fundamental marketing goals and promotional efforts.

CONCLUSION

This chapter has provided an examination of the traditional and nontraditional avenues for marketing an EAP within an organization. Although most of the discussion is based on the experiences of an internal EAP, the general marketing guidelines, specific strategies, tools, and activities, and the considerations discussed apply whether the EAP is an internally or externally provided service. In particular, the discussion about the role of the EAP professional as a marketing agent has applications across the EAP service delivery spectrum. The EAP that sees the marketing of its services and programs as a day-to-day operational activity of the highest priority positions itself to receive the maximum return on the investment of time, resources, and personnel. It continually strives to keep the EAP visible, its services accessible and effective, and its staff approachable while the program evolves and moves toward realizing the dynamic partnership that is possible when an EAP becomes fully integrated within the organization and accepted by the worforce—the measure of its true effectiveness. Such an integration always begins with a well-planned marketing campaign and continually relies on a series of diverse, creative, targeted, innovative, and at times flexible promotional activities.

REFERENCES

Beyer, J., & Trice, H. (1978). *Implementing change: Alcoholism policies in work organizations.* New York: Free Press.

Hitt, W.D. (1988). *The leader-manager: Guidelines for action.* Columbus, OH: Battelle Press.

Morrison, H.D., & Beidel, B.E. (1984, September 20–21). *Data collection and research maintenance within the organization.* Paper presented at the National Occupational Research Conference on Alcohol, Drug Abuse and Mental Disorders at the Worksite, Washington, DC.

Olson, S.K., & Olson, P.M. (1993). *Communicating in the workplace.* Aloray, Inc.

Reichman, W., & Beidel, B.E. (1989). Implementation of a State Police EAP. *Journal of Drug Issues, 19,* 369–383.

Reichman, W., & Beidel, B.E. (1994). The evaluation of an employee assistance program as an agent for organizational change. In A.K. Korman & Associates (Eds.), *Human dilemmas in work organizations: Strategies for resolution.* New York: Guilford Press.

Yandrick, R.M. (1996). *Behavioral risk management: How to avoid preventable losses from mental health problems in the workplace.* San Francisco: Jossey-Bass.

CHAPTER 7

Survey Research to Measure EAP Customer Satisfaction: A Quality Improvement Tool

JAMES M. OHER

The use of a survey questionnaire to gather information is a widely accepted technique in the organizational development field. Traditionally, the survey instrument gathers quantitative and qualitative data and the summarized survey results provide specific feedback. The goal is to improve overall functioning by viewing the whole organization as client (French, Wendall, & Bell, 1978). This process can be modified to evaluate and incrementally improve EAP services, no matter whether services are provided internally, by an external vendor, or by a combination thereof.

The EAP research literature offers few references about the use of such survey questionnaires to provide feedback about EAP functioning or effectiveness. Only recently have two studies been published (Harlow, 1997; Harris, 1997) This fact is not surprising because the employee assistance field is still in the early evolutionary phase of professional development. Several EAP managers have noted that client satisfaction surveys are one vehicle for measuring program activity toward the goal of continuous advancement. Based on this author's experience as a purchaser of EAP services as well as a consultant, few EAP vendor firms appear to do this. Some request service users to complete a brief evaluation of the assessment process. There are only a few questions and the instrument is often a postcard. Results are occasionally incorporated into a client company report.

However, this mechanism is primarily a broad quality assurance check to detect aberrant counselors and untimely processes. Rarely are suggestions solicited, analyzed, or incorporated in the EAP product or service delivery system. This lack of solicitation and feedback is a major programmatic deficiency, particularly for services that need to be customer sensitive yet are easily exposed to legal liabilities and employee relations problems if perceived as inappropriate.

HISTORY OF THE PROJECT

The author was requested by a benefits manager at a Northeast corporation to evaluate its corporate EAP. Sixteen months previously, the company had implemented a program administered and operated off-site by an external EAP firm. Due to increasing corporate pressures to reduce expenses, the client feared EAP service curtailment or even elimination. Equally important and a compounding concern, the benefits manager had no mechanism to determine these aspects of the firm's performance: (a) the clinical and informational services for directing clients (employees and dependents) in need of clinical intervention, assessment, problem resolution, or referral and follow-up; and (b) procedures, processes, and content for management consultation regarding information and guidance about specific job performance issues. The benefits manager anticipated many questions from senior management:

- Do the employees like the service?
- Do they perceive the service as a reliable dependable resource?
- Does lack of any direct complaints guarantee quality service?

Anecdotal reports indicated the affirmative to only the first two questions, leaving the company with no hard data regarding customer satisfaction. In addition, the utilization reports received from the EAP firm were of little value providing only basic demographic information and indicating approximately 4% utilization by the workforce. This figure is slightly less than a suggested benchmark of 5% to 10% annual utilization after a program's first year of operation (Jones, 1983). Others have noted a range of 4% to 8%.

SURVEY GOALS

After reviewing several evaluation vehicles, the author and client decided to develop and set in motion customer satisfaction surveys. Since management had not articulated EAP service standards or expectations prior, during, or after service implementation, positive program feedback was anticipated. This is usually the case with newly implemented EAPs because service users are by and large appreciative of all aspects of service, most particularly of the no-cost assessment/counseling, guidance, and support. However, the survey process was designed to accomplish more than the task at hand of program justification. The survey process itself could educate and make company employees more aware of the array of services that the EAP firm could provide. This education would, in turn, shape expectations and indirectly introduce the concept of performance standards and periodic review toward the goal of continuous improvement. In addition, the feedback information would identify areas that could be targeted for refinement and serve as a baseline for future evaluations. Last, but not least, the survey feedback could identify current operational or clinical service problems that the organization needed to address.

An identification of specific customers is an essential prerequisite for any focused improvement initiative. This is particularly true for EAP services because of the large customer base. In their book, *Curing Health Care*, Berwick, Godfrey, and Roessner (1990) note that sound customer-supplier relationships are essential for modern quality management and that customers are defined as anyone who depends on the vendor/supplier. They define external customer-supplier relationships as those between a company and its customers and internal customer-supplier relationships as those that lie within the organization and work process. One could apply their customer definitions to the EAP constituency without compromising the integrity of their conceptual framework. Separating that base into internal and external customer groups, the external customers are the employee, and dependent; the internal customer the companies' medical, benefits, human resources staff, and referral community practitioners and treatment programs.

To simplify the evaluation process, the author and client singled out human resources managers as the internal customer, and employees as the external client. Initially, two surveys were developed—one tailored to each group. However, because employees receiving EAP service had not given their permission to participate in such an evaluation prospectively, the survey for this group was abandoned, putting to rest any potential employee relations liabilities regarding alleged breach of confidentiality. The EAP satisfaction survey is presented as Figure 7.1. The reader should recognize that this instrument is not statistically standardized.

The surveys were designed primarily to obtain data regarding:

- Service satisfaction.
- Factors in one's decision to use/not use services.
- Recommended service changes.
- Types of problems for which employees and management utilized the program.
- Effectiveness of services relative to its key components.

To obtain this information, questions were developed that focused on the user's perception of service availability, accessibility, clinical capability and perceived expertise, and acceptability. The survey also requested information in these areas:

- Program confidentiality.
- User demographics.
- Correlation between program use and changes in employee behavior.

The survey instrument administered to human resources staff is displayed as Figure 7.2.

The Human Resources Manager as EAP Client

The client and author targeted the human resources manager as a primary EAP customer for several reasons. First, human resources managers have a direct, ongoing relationship with benefits personnel. On a regular and frequent basis, human resources managers transmit salient benefits information to their divisional unit employees. This practice is fairly common at a majority of large, geographically diverse companies throughout the country. Second, human resources managers have on-the-line accountability to resolve work site problems that compromise productivity, albeit at times in consultation with others. In this role, they are responsible for retaining valued employees and, if necessary, are expected to enlist EAP services to accomplish this task. An ancillary role is to ensure that due process takes place before an employee is disciplined, and that the process is fair. Many of these specific job functions relate to EAP central goals as articulated by Blum and Bennett (1990):

- To help retain services of valued employees.
- To aid in managing troubled employees.
- To provide for due process for those employees whose personal problems may be affecting the job.

1. How many times have you used the Employee Assistance Program (EAP) Program? (please check one)

___ (1) One

___ (2) Two

___ (3) Three

___ (4) Four

___ (5) More than four

2. For how many situations have you used the EAP Program? (please check one)

___ (1) One

___ (2) Two

___ (3) Three

___ (4) Four

___ (5) More than four

3. Thinking about your most recent experience, who referred you to the EAP Program? (please check all that apply)

___ (1) Myself

___ (2) Supervisor suggested

___ (3) Supervisor directed/insisted I go

___ (4) Co-worker

___ (5) Spouse

___ (6) Parent

___ (7) Other (Please describe)

4. Think about your initial call to the EAP Program. How satisfied were you with each of the following? (Please circle appropriate response for each one)

	Very Satisfied	Satisfied	Neither Satisfied nor Dissatisfied	Dissatisfied	Very Dissatisfied
a. The hours during which you were able to call.	1	2	3	4	5
b. The ease with which you could get through by telephone.	1	2	3	4	5
c. The responsiveness of the person answering the call.	1	2	3	4	5
d. The number of different office locations available to you.	1	2	3	4	5
e. The amount of time between calling and seeing a counselor.	1	2	3	4	5
f. The availability of counselors and other services.	1	2	3	4	5

Figure 7.1   Employee assistance program satisfaction survey.

5. Is your not being able to leave during the business day a major problem, a minor problem, or not a problem at all for you when using the EAP Program? (please check one)

___ (1) A major problem

___ (2) A minor problem

___ (3) Not a problem at all

6. And, how would you rate your counselor on each of the following factors? (please circle appropriate response for each one)

	Excellent	Good	Fair	Poor
a. Being able to understand your situation.	1	2	3	4
b. Helping to clarify your problem(s).	1	2	3	4
c. Helping to resolve your problem(s).	1	2	3	4
d. Being competent.	1	2	3	4
e. Being well-organized.	1	2	3	4
f. Being responsive to your needs.	1	2	3	4
g. Being attentive.	1	2	3	4
h. Being thoughtful.	1	2	3	4
i. Being trustworthy.	1	2	3	4

7. Do you agree with the counselor's assessment of your problem/situation? (please check one)

___ (1) Yes

___ (2) No

___ (3) Uncertain

8. Do you agree with your counselor's suggested plan of action? (please check one)

___ (1) Yes

___ (2) No

___ (3) Uncertain

9. Which of the following did the counselor recommend? (please check *all* that apply)

___ (1) Continue in counseling with him/her for a *fixed* amount of time (for example, 3 months).

___ (2) Continue in counseling with him/her for an *undetermined* amount of time.

___ (3) Go to a different counselor/mental health professional for counseling.

___ (4) Rely on community resources (for example, a local clinic with a sliding payment scale) for counseling.

___ (5) Go to a local support group (such as AA/NA, etc.) for on-going assistance.

___ (6) Hospitalization.

___ (7) Referred back to your HMO for services.

___ (8) Call/return as needed.

___ (9) No additional referral—problem resolved (skip to Question 12).

___ (10) Other (specify).

Figure 7.1   *(Continued)*

10. Which option did/will you choose to do? (please check one)

    ___ (1) Continue with counselor (fixed time).

    ___ (2) Continue with counselor (undetermined time).

    ___ (3) Go to different counselor/mental health professional.

    ___ (4) Rely on community resources.

    ___ (5) Go to a local support group.

    ___ (6) Hospitalization.

    ___ (7) Go back to HMO.

    ___ (8) Call/return as needed.

    ___ (9) Other.

11. How much assistance has your counselor offered in getting this additional help? (please check one)

    ___ (1) A great deal

    ___ (2) Some

    ___ (3) Not too much

    ___ (4) None at all

12. In your opinion, do you feel the EAP Program is confidential? (please check one)

    ___ (1) Yes

    ___ (2) No

    ___ (3) Uncertain

13. How likely are you to recommend the program to another employee or family member? (please check one)

    ___ (1) Very likely

    ___ (2) Somewhat likely

    ___ (3) Somewhat unlikely

    ___ (4) Very unlikely

    ___ (5) Uncertain

14. All in all, how satisfied are you with the EAP Program? (please check one)

    ___ (1) Very satisfied

    ___ (2) Somewhat satisfied

    ___ (3) Somewhat unlikely

    ___ (4) Very unlikely

    ___ (5) Uncertain

15. In your opinion, should the EAP Program be continued? (please check one)

    ___ (1) Yes

    ___ (2) No

16. Why/Why not?

Figure 7.1   *(Continued)*

17. If you could make one improvement to the EAP Program, what would it be?

18. My sex is: (please check one)
    ___ (1) Male
    ___ (2) Female

19. My age is: (please check one)
    ___ (1) Under 21   ___ (4) 31–35   ___ (7) 46–55
    ___ (2) 21–25   ___ (5) 36–40   ___ (8) Over 55
    ___ (3) 26–30   ___ (6) 41–45

20. My family status is: (please check one)
    ___ (1) Single/divorced/widowed without dependents
    ___ (2) Single/divorced/widowed with dependents
    ___ (3) Married without dependents
    ___ (4) Married with dependents

21. Relation of person using EAP Program to employee/retiree: (please check one)
    ___ Employee/retiree
    ___ Spouse
    ___ Child
    ___ Parent

22. Other Comments:

---

*This instrument may not be reproduce or used without prior consent by the author.

Figure 7.1   *(Continued)*

1. Approximately how many times have you contacted or used the Employee Assistance Program (EAP) for employees? (Record below)

   Number of times:

IF NEVER USED, SKIP TO QUESTION 8

2. For which of the following problems have you contacted/used the EAP Program? (please check all that apply)

   ___ (1) Employee absenteeism

   ___ (2) Employee tardiness

   ___ (3) Employee attitude problem

   ___ (4) Aggressive behavior displayed by employee

   ___ (5) Productivity/performance problem with employee

   ___ (6) Possible alcohol/drug use by employee

   ___ (7) An employee emergency

   ___ (8) Unusual behavior displayed by employee—please describe:

   ___ (9) Other—please describe:

3. How important were each of the following factors in your decision to use the EAP program? (Please circle appropriate response for each one)

	Very Important	Somewhat Important	Neither Important nor Unimportant	Somewhat Unimportant	Very Unimportant
a. Prior experience you've had with this EAP Program.	1	2	3	4	5
b. Prior experience you've had with another EAP.	1	2	3	4	5
c. The ease of access.	1	2	3	4	5
d. Wanting to have an active involvement in employee problems.	1	2	3	4	5
e. Confidentiality concerns.	1	2	3	4	5
f. Encouragement by management.	1	2	3	4	5
g. Other (please describe):	1	2	3	4	5

Figure 7.2   EAP Evaluation Human Resources Staff.

4. And, in your opinion, how effective is the EAP Program for each of the following? (Please circle appropriate response for each one)

	Very Effective	Somewhat Effective	Neither Effective nor Ineffective	Somewhat Ineffective	Very Ineffective
a. Crisis intervention.	1	2	3	4	5
b. Offering specific guidance on how to address the problem employee.	1	2	3	4	5
c. Offering consultation on whether you have a problem employee.	1	2	3	4	5
d. Ease with which the program operates/functions.	1	2	3	4	5
e. Assistance with documenting employee performance concerns or problems.	1	2	3	4	5

5. How satisfied are you with the EAP Program for the following attributes? (Please circle appropriate response for each one)

	Very Satisfied	Satisfied	Neither Satisfied nor Dissatisfied	Dissatisfied	Very Dissatisfied
a. The timeliness of responses.	1	2	3	4	5
b. The thoroughness of responses.	1	2	3	4	5
c. The level of understanding of the presenting problem/ situation.	1	2	3	4	5
d. Wanting to have an active involvement in employee problems.	1	2	3	4	5
e. The level of "team play" demonstrated by the EAP counselor.	1	2	3	4	5
f. The level of understanding of business realities.	1	2	3	4	5

Figure 7.2 *(Continued)*

6. What changes, if any, have you observed in employee patterns with respect to the following for anyone you have referred to the EAP? (Please circle appropriate response for each employee referred)

	Change for the Better	No Change	Change for the Worse
a. Attitude	1	2	3
b. Absenteeism	1	2	3
c. Tardiness	1	2	3
d. Performance/productivity	1	2	3
e. Sickness	1	2	3
f. Error rate	1	2	3
g. Cooperation	1	2	3

7. Have you observed changes in department/unit where an employee was referred to the EAP with respect to the following? (please circle one)

	Yes	No
a. Morale	1	2
b. Attitude	1	2
c. Performance/productivity	1	2
d. Absenteeism	1	2

8. Did you ever decide to use the EAP Program for specific situations? (please check one)

____ (1) Yes

____ (2) No (Skip to Question 10)

9. How important was each of the following factors in deciding *not* to use the EAP Program? (Please circle response for each one)

	Very Important	Somewhat Important	Neither Important nor Unimportant	Somewhat Unimportant	Very Unimportant
a. Prior experience you had with the program.	1	2	3	4	5
b. Prior experience you had with another EAP program.	1	2	3	4	5
c. Pressure to resolve the problem on your own.	1	2	3	4	5
d. Employee resolving the problem him/herself.	1	2	3	4	5
e. Problem disappeared.	1	2	3	4	5
f. Employee quit or was fired.	1	2	3	4	5
g. Confidentiality concern.	1	2	3	4	5
h. Other (please describe):	1	2	3	4	5

Figure 7.2   *(Continued)*

10. All in all, how effective is the EAP Program? (please check all that apply)

    ___ (1) Very effective

    ___ (2) Somewhat effective

    ___ (3) Neither effective nor ineffective

    ___ (4) Somewhat ineffective

    ___ (5) Very ineffective

    ___ (6) Have not used it yet

11. In your opinion, is the EAP Program truly confidential? (please check response)

    ___ (1) Yes

    ___ (2) No

    ___ (3) Uncertain

12. Should the EAP Program be continued? (please check one)

    ___ (1) Yes

    ___ (2) No

13. Why?/Why not?

14. If you could make one change in the EAP Program, what would it be?

15. Your sex is: (please check one)

    ___   (1) Male

    ___   (2) Female

16. For how many total years have you been with your company?

    ___ (1) Less than one year

    ___ (2) One year to less than three

    ___ (3) Three years to less than five

    ___ (4) Five years to less than ten

    ___ (5) Ten years to less than twenty

    ___ (6) Twenty or more

Figure 7.2 *(Continued)*

17. And, for how many years have you been in your current position?
    ___ (1) Less than one year
    ___ (2) One year to less than three
    ___ (3) Three years to less than five
    ___ (4) Five years to less than ten
    ___ (5) Ten years to less than twenty
    ___ (6) Twenty or more

18. In what city is your current position?

19. Other comments:

* This instrument may not be reproduce or used without prior consent by the author.

Figure 7.2 *(Continued)*

The human resources function is also often accountable for a key component of the EAP core technology as described by Blum and Roman (1989), "to evaluate employee outcomes (in utilization) on the basis of job performance." Human resources managers are involved in the review and analysis of workforce productivity and the trends and factors that affect this central issue.

In addition, on a more pragmatic level, for the purposes of this project and because of the employee relations' aspects of their position, it was assumed that HR managers would generate a fairly high survey response rate. They are responsible for promulgating company programs and policies—much more so those direct supervisors who have other divergent responsibilities. In fact, many supervisors do not know what EAP services are nor how to access them (Vaccaro, 1991). Human resources managers are often responsible for the distribution of the EAP communication materials as well as interpretation of the service policies. Interestingly, the survey response rate was less than anticipated.

CUSTOMER SATISFACTION SURVEY FINDINGS

Respondents' Profile

Only 55 respondents out of 205 Human Resources managers returned a completed survey. Due to the small sample size, the findings are more qualitatively as opposed to statistically significant. They are not scientifically valid nor a definitive assessment of services provided. Only the most significant data is noted here. Please refer to the tables for more complete response information.

Respondents tended to be female and located in Washington DC. Just over half (55%) were employed by the corporation for less than 5 years, and an even greater percentage (85% of all respondents) had been in their current position for less than 5 years (Table 7.1).

Use of the Services

Over half (55%) of the respondents never contacted or used the EAP. These respondents report significantly shorter tenures with the corporation—48% of those never using the program have been with the company less than three years. In contrast only 8% who have used the program have been with the company for such a short time.

Among the respondents who used the service, over half (57%) contacted or used the program four or more times, as opposed to 25% who used it only once.

Most frequently mentioned problems that led respondents to contact or use the service include productivity/performance problem with an employee (46%) and an employee emergency (46%) (Table 7.2).

Importance of Various Factors in One's Decision to Use Services

Users of the service were presented with six factors and were asked to rate how important each was in their decision to use the EAP (Table 7.3). Of the factors presented to respondents, confidentiality concerns were most important to their decision—63% rated this as being "very important" and 17% as "somewhat important."

Table 7.1   Demographics of EAP Respondents

Demographics	# of Times Contacted EAP		
	Total (N − 55)	None (N = 31)	1 + (N = 24)
1. Gender			
−Male	20%	20%	21%
−Female	80	80	79
2. Number of years with . . .			
−Less than 1 year	8%	7%	8%
−1 year but less than 3 years	17	31	0
−3 years but less than 5 years	30	24	38
−5 years but less than 10 years	24	21	29
−10 years but less than 20 years	15	14	17
−20 years or more	6	3	8
3. Number of years in current position			
−Less than 1 year	15%	17%	13%
−1 year but less than 3 years	37	60	8
−3 years but less than 5 years	33	17	54
−5 years but less than 10 years	13	6	21
−20 years or more	2	0	4
4. In what city is your current position			
−Princeton, New Jersey	2%	0%	4%
−Chicago, Illinois	4	0	0
−Washington, DC	94	100	88

Table 7.2   Use of Employee Assistance Program for Employees

	Total (N − 55)
1. Approximately how many times have you contacted or used the EAP for employees?	
−none	56%
−one	11
−two	4
−three	4
−four	11
−five or more	14
2. (IF "CONTACTED") For which of the following problems have you contacted/used the EAP Program?	
−Productivity/performance problem with employee	46%
−An employee emergency	46
−Aggressive behavior displayed by employee	29
−Employee attitude problem	25
−Possible alcohol/drug use by employee	25
−Employee absenteeism	17
−Employee tardiness	13
−Unusual behavior displayed by employee	13
−Other behaviors	25

Table 7.3   Importance of Various Factors in One's Decision to Use the EAP Program (among "users")

	Total (N = 24)
1. Prior experience you've had with this EAP Program:	
–very important	35%
–somewhat important	35
–average importance rating*	2.22
2. Prior experience you've had with another EAP:	
–very important	5%
–somewhat important	58
–average importance rating*	3.63
3. The case of access:	
–very important	48%
–somewhat important	35
–average importance rating*	1.74
4. Wanting to have an active involvement in employee problems	
–very important	48%
–somewhat important	17
–average importance rating*	2.00
5. Confidentiality concerns	
–very important	63%
–somewhat important	17
–average importance rating*	1.58
6. Encouragement by management:	
–very important	9%
–somewhat important	41
–average importance rating*	2.64

* Using a 1–5 rating scale. The lower the average rating, the more important the factor in one's decision to use the EAP Program.

Service Effectiveness

Respondents were presented with five factors and were asked to rate the effectiveness of the service with respect to each (Table 7.4). Respondents gave the highest effectiveness ratings relative to the ease with which the program operates—61% of the users rated the services as being "very effective" with respect to this factor.

Areas in which respondents perceive the program as being less effective include offering consultation on whether they have a problem (30% rated it "very effective") and offering assistance with documenting employee performance concerns or problems (only 10% rated the program as being "very effective").

Service Satisfaction

EAP service users from the HR department were presented with six attributes and asked how satisfied they were with the service relative to each attribute (Table 7.5). Users are most satisfied with the timeliness of responses (67% "very satisfied") and least satisfied with the level of understanding of business realities (25% "very satisfied"). Approximately half of the users reported being "very satisfied" with the program relative to the other attributes: level of understanding of the present problem/situation (50%); thoroughness of responses (46%); level of "team play" demonstrated by the EAP counselor (46%); and the degree of expert consultation (44%).

Table 7.4   Effectiveness of the EAP Program Relative to Certain Factors (among "users")

	Total (N = 24)
1. Crisis Intervention:	
−very important	50%
−somewhat important	46
−average importance rating*	1.55
2. Offering specific guidance on how to address the problem employee:	
−very important	48%
−somewhat important	48
−average importance rating*	1.57
3. Offering consultation on whether you have a problem employee:	
−very important	30%
−somewhat important	35
−average importance rating*	2.13
4. Ease with which the program operates/functions	
−very important	61%
−somewhat important	35
−average importance rating*	1.43
5. Assistance with documenting employee performance concerns or problems:	
−very important	10%
−somewhat important	24
−average importance rating*	2.62

* Using a 1–5 rating scale. The lower the average rating, the more effective the Program.

Table 7.5   Satisfaction with the EAP Program with Respect to Certain Attributes (among "users")

	Total (N = 24)
1. Timeliness of response	
−very important	67%
−somewhat important	33
−average importance rating*	1.33
2. Thoroughness of responses	
−very important	46%
−somewhat important	54
−average importance rating*	1.54
3. Level of understanding of the present problem/situation:	
−very important	50%
−somewhat important	50
−average importance rating*	1.50
4. Degree of expert consultation:	
−very important	44%
−somewhat important	48
−average importance rating*	1.65
5. Level of "team play," demonstrated by the EAP counselor:	
−very important	46%
−somewhat important	41
−average importance rating*	1.68
6. The level of understanding of business realities:	
−very important	25%
−somewhat important	50
−average importance rating*	2.04

* Using a 1–5 rating scale. The lower the average rating, the more satisfied the respondent.

Changes in Employee Patterns

Respondents who used the service were asked what changes, if any, they have observed in employee patterns for anyone they have referred to the EAP (Table 7.6). Areas where the greatest change has been seen include employee attitude (50% report change for the better) and employee performance/productivity (46% report change for the better).

Factors in Decisions to Not Use Services

One in five (21%) respondents decided not to use the EAP for specific situations—33% of the users and 10% of the respondents have not used the EAP (Table 7.7). Factors most important to these individuals in their decision include confidentiality concerns (56% rated "very important"); self-resolution of the problem by the employee (43% "very important"); and departure of the employee—quit or was fired (38% "very important").

Table 7.6 Changes in Employee Patterns Among those Referred to the EAP (among "users")

	Total (N − 24)
1. Attitude:	
–change for the better	50%
–no change	8
–uncertain	42
2. Absenteeism:	
–change for the better	21%
–no change	25
–uncertain	54
3. Tardiness:	
–change for the better	8%
–no change	25
–uncertain	67
4. Performance/Productivity:	
–change for the better	46%
–no change	25
–uncertain	29
5. Sickness:	
–change for the better	13%
–no change	29
–uncertain	58
6. Error Rate:	
–change for the better	13%
–no change	25
–uncertain	6
7. Cooperation:	
–change for the better	29%
–no change	21
–uncertain	50
8. Percentage observing changes in department/unit where an employee was referred to the EAP with respect to the following:	
–morale	25%
–attitude	21
–performance	13
–absenteeism	4

Table 7.7   Factors Important in One's Decision to Not Use the EAP Program

	Total (N = 55)
1. Did you ever decide to *not* use the EAP Program for specific situations?	
−yes	21%
−no	79
2. (IF "YES") How important were each of the following in deciding *not* to use the EAP Program?	
a. prior experience with the program:	
−very important	11%
−somewhat important	22
−average importance rating*	3.00
b. prior experience with another EAP Program:	
−very important	11%
−somewhat important	11
−average importance rating*	3.33
c. Pressure to resolve the problem on your own:	
−very important	22%
−somewhat important	0
−average importance rating*	2.78
d. Employee resolving the problem him/herself:	
−very important	43%
−somewhat important	14
−average importance rating*	2.00
e. Problem disappeared:	
−very important	25%
−somewhat important	25
−average importance rating*	2.50
f. Employee quit or was fired:	
−very important	38%
−somewhat important	0
−average importance rating*	2.50
g. Confidentiality concern:	
−very important	56%
−somewhat important	0
−average importance rating*	1.89

Perceived Effectiveness of Services

Over half (52%) of the respondents perceive the services as being effective. Not surprisingly, users are more likely than nonusers to rate the program as being "very effective" (Table 7.8). Respondents are split as to whether the EAP is truly confidential: 42% believe it is; whereas 51% are uncertain. Fewer than one in ten (7%) feel the program is not confidential. Again, data reveal that the users are more likely to feel the program is truly confidential (75%) and nonusers are more likely to be uncertain (74%).

Whether or not respondents have used the services, the majority (89%) believe the program should be continued. One could argue that this large percentage indicates a response bias. Not surprisingly, all the users feel the company should continue the program, and among the nonusers, 81% answered in the affirmative. In fact, no one felt the program should be discontinued—the remaining nonusers were uncertain because

Table 7.8   Perceived Effectiveness of the EAP Program

	# of Times Contacted EAP		
	Total (N – 55)	None (N = 31)	1 + (N = 24)
1. How effective is the EAP Program			
–very effective	26%	3%	54%
–somewhat effective	26	14	42
–neither effective nor ineffective	2	0	4
–haven't used yet	46	83	0
2. In your opinion, is the EAP Program confidential?			
–yes	42%	16%	75%
–no	7	10	4
–uncertain	51	74	21
3. Should the EAP Program be continued?			
–yes	89%	81%	100%
–no	0	0	0
–don't know	11	19	0

they have not used it. This response is expected because employees typically support EAPs as a valuable employee relations and human resources service with the potential to resolve workplace and personal problems.

DATA CLARIFICATION AND VERIFICATION

The survey results offer extensive information and serve as the springboard for further exploration and clarification. The results also stimulate research questions relating to the role of the human resources managers in relation to EAP service activation. The data also challenge some firmly held assumptions regarding the value of EAPs as effective workplace resources that resolve problems. For example, traditionally EAPs have viewed manager/supervisor referrals as a mainstay activity. In terms of a benchmark, it has been suggested that a minimum of 10% of all EAP clients be referred from this source (Jones, 1983). However, the present survey results suggest that this approach to manager referral benchmarking is inadequate. Only half of the managers who completed the survey ever used the EAP. And those who used it, did so often. Therefore, when establishing benchmarks, one should first determine how many and what kind of managers are in a position to refer employees for EAP service, and what the referral expectation might be, based on prevalence of employee problems that can affect workplace performance. Only after doing this planning and analysis can one determine what the target range might be for each manager within company divisions. After this process is complete, one can then determine whether it has been reached. This methodological procedure is a more realistic and comprehensive strategy to determine an appropriate number of manager referrals.

Another noteworthy finding is that managers who did not use the EAP had far less corporate service than HR managers who used the service frequently. The professional literature does not address the issue of varying EAP referral pattern by managers based on years of service, yet this seems to be influencing program utilization. It would be useful to find out whether this experience is the case in other work settings and to discover the underlying cause as well.

Survey results also indicated that although managers noted a change for the better in the productivity of EAP users, many fewer human resources managers noted an improvement in error rate, sicknesses, absences, and tardiness. The possible discrepancies in these answers also deserve further exploration.

That EAP service users were least satisfied with the EAP's level of understanding of the business realities of the company was another finding worthy of reflection and further examination. One of the unique features of EAPs is the ability to simultaneously advocate for the individual while representing the overall interests of the sponsor (company or union), thus balancing the needs of both parties while focusing on the primary goal of resolving workplace problems (Oher, 1987). One wonders whether the EAP examined was at times functioning more like a social service or mental health agency and not reflecting, supporting, or acknowledging the company's distinct values or workplace priorities. Further clarification and verification could determine if this was the case.

Survey response findings in the areas of service effectiveness and, in particular, aspects of service where respondents found the program less than effective also support further inquiry. Two prominent areas noted were offering consultation on whether the managers had a problem and offering assistance in documenting employee performance concerns or problems. Only 10% of the managers thought the EAP was effective with this last task. Whether this EAP vendor incorporates these services into its manager referral protocols and procedures, or conversely, fails to carry them out effectively, is open to question. Regardless of the answer, the company should strive for greater customer satisfaction from the vendor in this identified area. Further exploration could provide answers to the low rating and guidance on how to improve this service.

Other findings in need of further clarification indicated that the HR customers were not sure that the program was confidential. This information is intriguing, particularly since confidentiality concerns were the most important factor in one's decision to use the services. Questions that might lead to answers to clarify this data include: What constitutes confidentiality? Is the definition clear? Are there differentiations of meaning and its application at the workplace? What would constitute a breach of confidentiality? Is this concern inhibiting program outreach, usage, and effectiveness? Answers to these questions might provide organizational information that sheds new light on the company's modus operandi and values. What the EAP does with this information focuses on the inherent contradiction embodied within EAP philosophy: Are EAPs mechanisms of social control or potential agents for social change?

The next scheduled step in the improvement process was to clarify and verify the survey results. Due to the low survey response rate, this process was essential. The author planned to conduct a telephone format focus group with a statistically significant number of HR managers because this method usually commands a higher response rate, and ensures more control over the process. It also offers less probability of data contamination.

An equally important goal of the focus groups was to gain a better understanding of the HR managers' specific concerns. Regrettably, as indicated, only after reviewing the survey responses did it become clear that some of the questions could have been more detailed and precise. Ambiguous answers might have been minimized. However, one could speculate that had the survey been more lengthy or less "user friendly," the response rate might have even been lower. The focus groups would also offer the clients an opportunity to provide additional information about aspects of service not sufficiently covered in the survey, as well as solicit suggestions about how to improve the survey itself. Budgetary constraints, however, forced the abandonment of the data clarification/verification process, as well as the development of an action plan to ensure continuous EAP service improvement.

IMPLICATIONS FOR EAPS

As the results from this corporate survey indicate, many aspects of EAP service that reflect firmly held beliefs may not be present in programs that are, nonetheless, perceived as worthwhile. Because of this fact, consensus concerning what is effective EAP service will be very difficult, if not impossible, to achieve. This is a significant concern facing the EAP profession as it attempts to solidify its distinct identity. The external threats to identity consolidation, both from the managed mental health industry as well as from the allied health care professional groups (clinical psychology and social work) are as prevalent as ever. The dominance of these forces in the shaping of EAP products could lead to dilution of a strong independent professional identify that is related to, but distinct from, other human resources and health care disciplines. This dilution could result in an insufficient emphasis on EAP human resources related aspects of service. The survey responses reviewed and discussed in this chapter justify this concern.

Although less critical (and as already indicated), survey projects can yield more useful information if specific program and performance standards and measurement/monitoring techniques are mutually determined by the EAP firm and the client corporation prior to program implementation. Customer feedback can then be compared with predetermined standards, thereby paving another road toward evaluation and continuous quality improvement. In fact, although this project was driven by realistic concerns about program survival, the program might have been less vulnerable to cost-cutting pressures if clear goals and expectations, as well as an evaluation methodology, had been articulated prior to implementation and, equally important, sanctioned by senior management. In addition, the planning and strategic thinking should go into setting specific program clinical and operational standards and utilization targets, such as percentage (of entire population) of referrals; type of manager referrals; and even expected types of problems based on specific workplace demographics, health care benefit utilization, and EAP referral/caseload patterns. Knowledge of prevailing psychosocial stresses in the community environments should also be factored in when developing these targets. The greater the information one can request and receive, the more meaning the data will have.

As EAPs embrace the quality process, identify customers, and help articulate and satisfy their needs, more EAP sponsors will use increasingly sophisticated survey questionnaires to evaluate and continually improve their products and services. Progressive EAPs rely on finely tuned, exacting technologies that have taken several decades to develop. However, more scientific investigation and research will separate actual EAP service content and effectiveness from myth and marketing. This activity will help EAPs gain needed credibility as a unique human resource function within work settings.

REFERENCES

Berwick, D.M., Godfrey, A.B., Roessner, J. (1990). *Curing health care: New strategies for quality improvement* (p. 37). San Francisco: Jossey-Bass.

Blum, T., & Bennett, N. (1990). Employee assistance programs: Utilization and referral data, performance management, and prevention concepts. In P.M. Roman (Ed.), *Alcohol problem intervention in the workplace* (p. 144). Quorum Books.

Blum, T., & Roman, P. (1989). Employee assistance programs and human resource management. In K.M. Rowland & G.R. Ferris (Eds.), *Research in personnel and human resource management* (pp. 251–312). Greenwich, CT: JAI Press.

French, W.L., & Bell, Jr., C. (1978). *Organization development: Behavioral science interventions for organization improvement* (p. 149). Englewood Cliffs, NJ: Prentice Hall.

Harlow, K.C. (1997, November/December). Perceptions of supervisors and managers of an internal employee assistance program. *Employee Assistance Research Supplement of the EAPA Exchange, 1*(2), 5–8.

Harris, S.M. (1997, November/December). Validating the EAP philosophy: Listening to satisfaction survey. *Employee Assistance Research Supplement of the EAPA Exchange, 1*(2), 2–4.

Jones, D. (1983) *Performance benchmarks* (pp. 20, 28). Minneapolis, MN: Hazelden.

Oher, J.M. (1987). EAPS: Key elements of an in-house program. *Occupational Health and Safety, 56*(13), 23.

Vaccaro, V.A. (1991). *Depression: Corporate experiences and innovations* (p. 23). Washington Business Group on Health, Prevention Leadership Forum.

CHAPTER 8

Occupational Psychiatry and the Employee Assistance Program

JEFFREY KAHN

Organizational and occupational psychiatry dates back at least to the 1920s. Over the years, many psychiatrists have studied workers, leaders, and work organizations. In recent decades, though, psychiatric attention to the workplace has been only a minor part of the field. During the same period, employee assistance programs (EAPs) emerged as an essential way to provide workplace mental health services. Most recently, there has been a resurgence of psychiatric interest in the workplace. This change has occurred as organizational and occupational psychiatrists renewed a focus on workplace issues important for patients and for companies. In addition, many EAPs have sought out a psychiatric perspective to enhance their own work.

PSYCHIATRIC PERSPECTIVE AND THE PSYCHIATRIST'S ROLE

The psychiatrist's value to the EAP lies primarily in the benefit of a psychiatric perspective. Psychiatrists have broad training in psychiatric evaluation and diagnosis, psychotherapy, psychopharmacology, and medical illness. Organizational and occupational psychiatrists have further expertise in work and workplace concerns and with how those concerns interact with organizational, career, family, and psychiatric issues.

Workplace mental health symptoms and dysfunction result from a complex interaction of these individual and workplace factors. The psychiatric perspective can be essential to understanding and simplifying this complexity. As in any medical model, accurate evaluation is the result of comprehensive assessment and understanding of the issues. Accurate diagnosis leads to more specific and effective treatment.

Psychiatric knowledge and perspective enhance the work of all clinicians in an EAP setting. Psychiatrists can offer this perspective in a wide variety of ways (see Table 8.1). For example, psychiatrists can educate (through seminars, supervision, case review) EAP clinicians and business managers, in addition to evaluating and treating particular cases. The psychiatric perspective is valuable in all areas of EAP functioning, including initial assessment, diagnosis, and treatment.

Table 8.1 Psychiatric Roles

- Broad clinical viewpoint.
- Clinical training and supervision.
- Outside perspective, consultation, and treatment.
- Independent medical examination and legal needs.
- Case management and managed care issues.

INITIAL ASSESSMENT

Good mental health care requires careful attention to issues of confidentiality, empathic understanding, and alertness to historical detail. Mental health care in the EAP setting requires particular caution about confidentiality and perceived conflicts of interest.

Presenting symptoms are usually the best place to start, and attentive listening allows employees to open up about their important and personal concerns. Additional history about other emotional or behavioral symptoms will later help to formulate diagnoses. For example, emotional disorders typically involve multiple stressors, symptoms, and dysfunctions. It is important to understand early on those stressors and impairments that the employee already recognizes. Employees will rarely describe irrelevant events or factors. Frequently, though, the most disturbing stressors and symptoms are not described unless specific history is obtained. For this reason, EAP assessment of emotional problems should include a standardized psychiatric history, even if time constraints preclude a fully detailed evaluation. Only by attempting to identify all principal areas of stress and dysfunction can clinicians make specific diagnoses and effective treatment recommendations.

Psychiatric History

Each area of the employee's history is explored in order to obtain a general overview and to pinpoint areas of particular stress, symptoms, and dysfunction. It is also useful to recognize areas of strength and support, which may be helpful in formulating diagnosis, planning treatment, and encouraging compliance (see Table 8.2).

Personal History

General History

The nature of the presenting complaint must be examined. Have there been similar episodes in the past? What does the employee think is going on? Is there past or

Table 8.2 Evaluation Overview

- Offer supportive, understanding, confidential evaluation.
- Identify perceived cause of stress.
- Identify stressors and general history.*
- Identify symptoms and dysfunction.*
- Identify common syndromes (e.g., anxiety, depression, substance abuse).
- Identify urgent referral need (see "Indications for Immediate Referral").
- Review and facilitate evaluation, treatment, and referral options.

*Personal, work, family, social, medical, psychiatric.

current treatment? What kind of treatment is the employee looking for or expecting? Why did the employee decide to come for help now? Is substance abuse a problem for the employee?

Stressors

The nature of the physical and psychological stressors at the individual level should be cataloged and explored. Potential stressors are many, and a full listing is beyond the scope of this chapter. Examples of individual level stressors might include diagnosis of physical disease, change in residence, job promotion, or a car accident. Because the employee often does not identify the most significant stressors, stressor history typically relies on a "parallel history." In other words, symptomatic history is obtained separately from a careful review of significant life events, looking for chronologically associated events and symptoms.

Symptoms/Dysfunction

Exploration of individual symptoms is the most essential component of the diagnostic evaluation. In cataloging symptoms, the clinician must be most attuned to those symptoms most frequently found in emotional disorders (see differential diagnosis below). These include mood disturbance (such as depression, hopelessness, elevated mood), anxiety symptoms (anxiety, panic attacks), cognitive disturbance (memory, concentration), and psychotic symptoms (paranoia, hallucinations), as well as the common physical manifestations of psychiatric disorders (changes in energy, sleep, appetite). Care should be taken to consider all of the symptoms relevant to common or otherwise important disorders. For each symptom and dysfunction, the clinician can explore severity, past history, timing of current episode, exacerbating and mitigating factors, and coping strategies.

Work History

The history of the employee in the workplace is an essential element for the diagnosis of emotional and behavioral disorders. Work is a central function for most people. The workplace is a frequent source of physical and psychological stressors that trigger emotional disorders. And the workplace is frequently where emotional disorders produce symptoms and reduced function. Thus, an adept workplace history is essential in the evaluation of an individual presenting with emotional complaints, even when no work-related context is initially presented.

General History

Any workplace phenomena must be viewed in the context of individual work history and the general history of the specific workplace. Key elements of the individual's history include length of employment, reasons for past job or function changes, level of job satisfaction, and the nature of past and present relationships with managers, colleagues, and subordinates. It is important to explore where the employee sees himself or herself in terms of the life cycle of the job and to gain some understanding of the meaning of the job and job function to the employee. It is only within this job context that the clinician can begin to understand the specific workplace stressors and symptoms that the employee may be describing.

Workplace Stressors

The workplace is a complex environment with a wide variety of psychosocial stressors. Workplace stressors may be physical or psychological, acute or chronic. One kind of stress comes from traumatic workplace events. For example, employees may witness or participate in violent events or accidents, death or injury of a coworker, harassment, or a rescue or a rescue attempt. Other stressors include the following types of change:

Organizational.   Change is a normal part of all successful organizations, and a degree of stress is a normal part of the individual's adaptation to change. However, any change in organizational structure, function, goals, leadership, ownership, stability, profitability, union activity, or location has the potential to serve as a significant stressor to individual employees.

Interpersonal.   Personnel changes, such as changes in manager, employees, customers, or suppliers, affect the complex network of interpersonal relationships and supports of an individual in the workplace. As in any social setting, interpersonal conflict is commonplace, varied, and always important.

Job Function.   Jobs are more changeable these days than ever, and any job change can be stressful. The long list of possibilities includes changes in job function, salary, or title; actual or pending demotion, sanction, pay cut, job loss, job insecurity, promotion, or raise.

Poor Work Role or Organizational Fit.   Some employees might be troubled by assignments exceeding or incompatible with skills, by excessive or insufficient work quantity, by work inconsistent with personal beliefs, by irregular or changing work assignments, or by harassment. Excessive job demands might include decreased sleep, excess travel, or even poor nutrition.

Workplace Symptoms/Areas of Dysfunction

For any employee presenting with emotional complaints, it is essential to explore the full extent of workplace symptoms and dysfunction. Depending on circumstances and confidentiality, this information may come not only from the individual employee, but also from workplace colleagues, managers, and human resource staff. Typical examples of workplace dysfunction include decreased productivity, increased interpersonal conflict, bizarre behavior, increased tardiness or absenteeism, increased work accidents, and on-site substance abuse.

Family and Social History

General Family/Social History

Employees spend most of their lives outside of work. Exploring the general family and social context is essential to understanding problematic stressors, symptoms, and areas of dysfunction. Who are the members of the family? What are the living arrangements? Who are the past and present sources of emotional and financial support? How have family and friends dealt with serious problems in the past? Who would the employee like to involve in the evaluation and treatment?

Family/Social Stressors

The employee's family and social situation may be the most significant source of stressors. A careful evaluation of all acute and chronic family and social stressors is a necessary part of the history. Acute family stressors include any recent change in family circumstances, such as household membership, financial status, a spouse's career, or the health of a relative. Chronic family stressors can include marital difficulties, chronic illness, elder care, parent/child conflict, and substance abuse. Stressors also may be found in the entire range of any individual's social context. Examples of social stressors are illness or relocation of a friend, termination of a supportive group experience, or social change within the community. It is important to note that family and social stressors may be quite subtle, yet unwittingly significant to the employee. In addition, some of the most stressful events are changes for the better.

Family/Social Symptoms and Dysfunction

Emotional disorders may manifest themselves as family or social difficulties. Thus, any change in the individual's family or social functioning should be considered a possible symptom of an underlying emotional disorder. Typical family and social manifestations of emotional disorders include marital difficulties, parent/child conflict, social withdrawal, and abrupt termination of long-term relationship(s).

It is important to note that with all family/social stressors and symptoms, causality is often ambiguous. The same family phenomenon (e.g., marital difficulties) may be either a stressor helping to trigger an emotional disorder or a symptom resulting from an emotional disorder. Untangling these complicated situations may be difficult but can promote accurate diagnosis and effective intervention.

Medical History and Evaluation

It is important to remember that physical illness can be a hidden physical cause of anxiety, depression, or other emotional distress. A few examples might include thyroid disease, anemia, vitamin B_{12} deficiency, unrecognized cancer, and medication side effects. HIV/AIDS can also first present as cognitive or emotional symptoms. In addition, there are many physical complaints. Some examples would include—chest pain, nausea, dizziness, loss of appetite, trouble sleeping—that may reflect either an emotional disorder or a physical illness. Although these are important issues to be aware of, fully ruling out contributing medical disorders is beyond the scope of a routine EAP evaluation.

An evaluating psychiatrist (or other physician) might consider whether thorough examination by an internist is needed. Commonly, an evaluation might include a medical history, physical examination, and such standard blood tests as a blood count, a chemistry panel, and a thyroid panel. Many other tests and procedures might be appropriate for some employees.

Psychiatric History

Current problems are often related to past problems. It is helpful to know if the employee has ever had counseling, psychiatric consultation, or psychiatric hospitalization in the past, and if so, for what reasons. In particular, it is important to know about past and present mental health diagnoses.

Although the list of possible psychiatric disorders is long, there are only a few common psychiatric diagnoses. A presenting complaint of stress or depression is common to most of these diagnoses, and an acute stressor may exacerbate almost any psychiatric disorder. It is worth remembering that anxiety disorders, mood disorders, and substance abuse are the most prevalent of the disorders described. Thus, recognition and treatment of these disorders should be given the highest priority. Some other diagnoses, although less common, are also especially important to recognize (see Table 8.3).

Anxiety Disorders

Anxiety disorders include the group of disorders whose primary symptom complex includes prominent anxiety. These disorders appear commonly in the workplace and are often exacerbated by workplace stressors. On outward appearance, many employees with anxiety disorders will appear merely tense or sad or will show little clear evidence of anxiety at all. Others may exhibit concrete symptoms such as phobias (panic disorder), stage fright (social phobia), or hoarding (obsessive-compulsive disorder). Whenever anyone has significant anxiety for more than a short period of time, there is usually an underlying anxiety disorder. Although benzodiazepines (like diazepam) and buspirone (a nonbenzodiazepine, nonaddicting antianxiety medication) can seem useful for symptomatic anxiety, they will have little effect on the underlying anxiety disorder. Identification of anxiety disorders, and other diagnoses, allows prompt consideration of appropriate medication strategies to combine with psychotherapy. There are several common anxiety disorders.

Panic Disorder. *Panic disorder* is characterized by recurrent and unexpected panic attacks. *Panic attacks* are defined by the *Diagnostic and Statistical Manual of Mental Disorders, Fourth Edition (DSM-IV)*, (American Psychiatric Association [APA], 1994) as "a discrete period of intense fear or discomfort" during which at least four of the specified physical or emotional symptoms are present. Symptoms include palpitations, sweating, trembling, shortness of breath, a choking feeling, chest pain, nausea, abdominal pain, lightheadedness, derealization, fear of going crazy, fear of dying, numbness,

Table 8.3 Common or Important Psychiatric Disorders

Common Disorders
- Panic disorder.
- Social phobia.
- Major depression.
- Dysthymia and atypical depression.
- Adjustment disorders.
- Substance abuse.

Other Important Disorders
- Obsessive compulsive disorder.
- Traumatic stress disorders.
- Bipolar disorder.
- Personality disorders.
- Primary psychotic disorders.
- Malingering/Factitious disorders.

and chills or hot flashes. Panic disorder is often associated with fears or phobias of driving, flying, enclosed spaces, or even of leaving the house (agoraphobia).

Panic disorder responds well to treatment with tricyclic antidepressants. The selective serotonin reuptake inhibitor (SSRI) antidepressants are less reliably effective for panic disorder, and some other antidepressants have little direct antipanic effect. Choice of antipanic medication is often determined by side-effect profile, as described below. Most importantly, antidepressants can cause an initial increase in anxiety, with relief of symptoms only coming after 3 or 4 weeks. This can sometimes be appropriately dealt with by concurrent short-term dosing with clonazepam.

Clonazepam and alprazolam are considered effective antipanic agents. Because clonazepam has a longer half-life, it has a much lower abuse and withdrawal potential than alprazolam. It is not clear whether any other benzodiazepines have specific antipanic properties. Because of its ease of use, rapid onset, and low side-effect profile, many clinicians advocate the use of clonazepam for long-term treatment of many panic disorder patients. However, in view of the potential for addiction, noncompliance, and abuse, caution is advised. Special care should be taken in patients who have a history of substance abuse. Abrupt discontinuation of any benzodiazepine can produce dangerous withdrawal syndromes, as well as exacerbation of the treated symptoms. Psychotherapeutic issues in panic disorder may include overcoming phobias, dealing with separation or loss, medication compliance, and relationship problems. With appropriate treatment, panic attacks will usually go into full remission in a month or less. At that point, there will be gradual improvement in phobias, anxiety, and other symptoms.

Social Phobia. *Social phobia* is persistent anxiety about situations where there is a fear of social scrutiny. Common social phobic situations include meeting new people (shyness) and public speaking (stage fright). Fear of embarrassing oneself is a central symptom, commonly accompanied by racing heart and sweating. Unlike abrupt-onset panic attacks, social anxiety has a more gradual onset. Symptoms can be severe enough to cause significant social and occupational limitations. Some employees have learned how to endure social anxiety without avoiding the feared situation. Although the anxiety remains distressing, it can also help to hone some speaking and social skills.

Social phobia is generally responsive to SSRI antidepressants, with therapeutic benefits starting to appear after some 3 to 6 weeks at an effective dose. Beta-blockers (such as propranolol or atenolol) can be used to relieve physical symptoms just before a speech or a presentation. Psychotherapeutic issues commonly include public-speaking fears, shyness, and feelings of social isolation. Cognitive-behavioral approaches use systematic desensitization and other approaches to reduce avoidant behavior. Psychotherapy works best in combination with medication.

Obsessive-Compulsive Disorder.   Obsessive-compulsive disorder (OCD) is a syndrome of obsessions and compulsions (or both) that cause significant distress or that interfere with social or occupational functioning. *Obsessions* are persistent and unwanted thoughts that can be about orderliness, religion, anger, nonsensical, and other thought. *Compulsions* are repetitive behaviors in response to an obsession or to a set of stereotyped rules. Examples include counting, cleaning (handwashing), checking (stove, lights, locks), and hoarding. Compulsions are often intended to neutralize obsessive thoughts and can consume vast amounts of time. Overly perfectionistic, slow, or rigid job performance can suggest OCD.

Effective OCD treatment includes medication and psychotherapy. Medications that can be effective include the SSRI antidepressants and clomipramine. Doses are typically much higher than for depression, and the full medication benefit may not occur for several months. Medication effect can be further improved with the addition of a second medication to enhance the effect of the first. Optimal treatment includes cognitive-behavioral approaches to address obsessions and compulsions, and interpersonal approaches to understand issues of anger and control, ingrained behaviors, and family dynamics.

Traumatic Stress Disorders.   These disorders are included among the anxiety disorders in *DSM-IV.* They occur in response to the observation or experience of an emotionally traumatic event outside the range of ordinary experience. *Posttraumatic stress disorder* (PTSD) is characterized by persistent reexperiencing of the traumatic event through memories, dreams, flashbacks, or hallucinations, with consequent distress and decreased functioning. Apparent PTSD may often reflect exacerbation of longer term anxiety or mood disorders. *Acute stress disorder* refers to short-term dysfunction (less than 4 weeks) marked by derealization and other symptoms similar to those experienced with PTSD. Some clinicians have suggested that these stress disorders typically occur in people with preexisting anxiety or depressive disorders and that they are often associated with legal or entitlement claims.

Treatment of traumatic stress disorders typically involves diagnosis and medication management of component anxiety and depressive disorders (i.e., panic disorder or major depression). Concurrent psychotherapy focuses on the details and the effects of the stressful event, other family and work issues, and returning to normal functioning. Group psychotherapy may focus on issues of understanding and overcoming the traumatic event. Prognosis is variable, with many employees having a full recovery. Others may have ongoing symptomatic or entitlement issues.

Mood Disorders

Mood disorders refer to the group of syndromes in which dysregulation of mood is the most prominent symptom. Mood disorders are common and generally responsive to treatment. There are several common mood disorders that present in the workplace.

Major Depression.   *Major depression* is marked by the presence of severely depressed mood, often accompanied by diminished pleasure, sleep changes, appetite changes, psychomotor changes, fatigue, memory or concentration difficulties, suicidal thoughts, feelings of hopelessness, and feelings of worthlessness or guilt. It is important to remember that most cases of depression do not include *all* of these symptoms. However, the presence of any of these symptoms is an indication for a full evaluation for depressive symptoms. It is also useful to remember that major depression may first present without a complaint of mood disturbance. However, the presence of other depressive symptoms should trigger a closer evaluation for depression. Major depression is often comorbid with panic disorder.

Mood disorders are responsive to specific treatment. Antidepressant treatment and appropriate psychotherapy are the cornerstones of most treatment of depressive disorders. Antidepressants must be prescribed in an effective dose and continued for at least 3 to 6 weeks before a response can be expected. The choice of antidepressant should largely be determined by the side-effect profile, the medication cost, and concurrent medical considerations. Tricyclic antidepressants (desipramine, imipramine, nortrypti-lene, and others) are generally lowest in cost and are unsurpassed in efficacy for major depression. Tricyclics do have a side-effect profile that includes anticholinergic effects, such as dry mouth, constipation, and orthostasis. In addition, the cardiac arrythmogenic effects of the tricyclics make them contraindicated in most cases of heart block.

The newer SSRIs, such as fluoxetine, paroxetine, sertraline, and fluvoxamine, are just about as effective and have a more limited side-effect profile that makes them the most common choice. Even so, SSRIs have been noted to cause uncomfortable agita-tion, nausea, and appetite or energy changes that may be unacceptable to the patient. In addition, sexual side effects of the SSRIs (decreased libido, delayed or retrograde ejac-ulation) can be problematic. Other useful antidepressants include buproprion and tra-zodone. Benzodiazepines or other sleep medications may help with insomnia until an antidepressant can begin working.

Dysthymic Disorder and Atypical Depression.   *Dysthymic disorder* refers to a long-term (at least 2 years) presence of consistently depressed mood with neurovegeta-tive signs that does not meet the full criteria for major depression. Many employees with dysthymic disorder may actually suffer from the long-term *atypical depression* subtype. This common diagnosis reflects depressed but reactive mood, increased desire for sleep, increased appetite, decreased energy (sometimes feeling physically heavy in arms or legs), and a chronic pattern of heightened sensitivity to interpersonal rejection. Chronic atypical depression is often comorbid with panic disorder or acute major de-pression. The SSRIs are the preferred treatment for treating atypical depression. They have the advantage of treating major depression as well, although they offer unreliable relief of panic disorder.

Psychotherapeutic issues in depression may include grief, loss, hopelessness, and frustration. Careful attention should be paid to suicide risk, especially around the time of medication response. Hospitalization may be indicated for major depression when there are questions of poor self-care, treatment noncompliance, or suicidal risk.

Bipolar Disorders.   *Bipolar disorders* (e.g., manic depression) refer to a group of mood disorders characterized by marked fluctuations in mood, including the presence of periods of mania or significantly elevated mood. All employees evaluated for de-pression should be questioned about a history of manic or hypomanic episodes. Manic symptoms may include persistent elevated, expansive, or irritable mood, grandiosity, decreased sleep, fast speech, psychomotor agitation, or abnormally increased activity (spending, sexual, or other). Manic episodes are also often accompanied by psychotic symptoms. Primary medications for bipolar disorder include lithium, carbamazepine, and valproic acid. Medication compliance is often a major focus of psychotherapy. Al-though the prognosis for control of manic and depressive episodes is excellent, there can still be infrequent manic breakthroughs.

Adjustment Disorders

Adjustment Disorder with Anxiety.   Adjustment disorder with anxiety (not a for-mal anxiety disorder in *DSM-IV*) requires the presence of an identifiable major stressor in the 3 months preceding onset of marked distress or diminished functioning. A diag-nosis of *adjustment disorder with anxiety* should be made only after specifically estab-lishing the absence of all other anxiety disorders.

Adjustment Disorder with Depressed Mood.   Adjustment disorder with depression (not a formal mood disorder in *DSM-IV*) reflects the presence of a recent specific major life stressor and consequent depressed mood. A diagnosis of *adjustment disorder with depressed mood* should be made only after specifically establishing the absence of all other mood disorders.

Substance Abuse/Dependence

Substance abuse and dependence are common disorders that present frequently in the workplace. The clinician must be aware of signs and symptoms of common drugs of abuse and should be aware of the drugs of choice in the local geographic or socioeconomic environment. Every employee presenting with an emotional complaint should be asked about alcohol abuse/dependence.

Substance Abuse.   The cardinal feature of *substance abuse* is maladaptive behavior (continued use despite adverse consequences). Adverse consequences may include failure to fulfill role obligations, legal problems, exposure to hazardous situations, or recurrent social or interpersonal problems.

Substance Dependence.   *Substance dependence* indicates substance abuse with the additional presence of the following phenomena (three of the following phenomena are required by *DSM-IV* to make a diagnosis of dependence): tolerance, withdrawal phenomena, greater than intended use, persistent efforts to cut down, a great deal of time spent in substance-abuse-related activities, and neglect of other activities.

Substance Withdrawal.   Withdrawal phenomena with marked physical or psychological phenomena are common with all major drugs of abuse. Evidence of physical withdrawal indicates a need for immediate medical attention.

Substance Abuse/Dependence.   All clinicians should have some familiarity with the basics of the diagnosis and treatment of substance abuse even if they do not treat substance abusers themselves. Treatment of the substance abuser requires identification of the problem, decision of the employee to receive treatment, detoxification, rehabilitation, and relapse prevention. The successful treatment of substance abuse requires choosing appropriately among a wide variety of treatment modalities. Inpatient or structured outpatient treatment may be indicated. Medication (naltrexone, sleep medication, antidepressant medication, antianxiety medication) may be helpful for relapse prevention and treatment of comorbid symptoms. Psychotherapy (individual, group, family) may be indicated. Involvement in an AA-model self-help group is almost always appropriate.

Psychotic Disorders

Psychotic disorders are characterized by prominent and generally persistent psychotic symptoms including delusions, hallucinations, or paranoia. When these symptoms appear in the workplace setting, they are often secondary to major depression, bipolar, or substance abuse disorders. Employees may appear eccentric, preoccupied, withdrawn, or out of control. Primary psychotic disorders such as schizophrenia are less likely to have their first presentation in the workplace setting. As previously noted, the presence of any psychotic symptoms is an indication for immediate evaluation by a clinician skilled and comfortable in evaluating psychotic symptoms.

Treatment of schizophrenia usually starts with an antipsychotic medication. Such older medications as chlorpromazine and haloperidol are being replaced by newer antipsychotics such as risperidone and olanzepine. These newer "atypical" antipsychotics offer improved benefit with significantly fewer side effects. Treatment often includes antidepressant or antipanic medication as well. Psychotherapy is largely supportive at first, though many patients benefit from group psychotherapy and more involved individual therapy. It is important to remember that psychotic symptoms are generally responsive to antipsychotic medication these days.

Personality Disorders

Every individual has recognizable personality traits and styles. Those personal styles generally have both advantages and disadvantages. Personality disorders, though, are rigid and exaggerated personality styles that generally interfere with relationships and functioning. A poor fit between personality and job function or organizational structure can be a major source of stress in the workplace. This poor fit may be detrimental to the individual or to the organization. Although a full discussion of personality disorders is beyond the scope of this chapter, some attention to personality issues is always warranted in the evaluation of an emotional complaint. Personality disorders are often associated with diagnosable anxiety and mood disorders. The categories of personality disorders recognized by *DSM-IV* include paranoid, schizoid, schizotypal, antisocial, borderline, histrionic, narcissistic, avoidant, dependent, and obsessive-compulsive.

In general, personality disorders are most responsive to psychotherapy. However, medication can be used to promptly treat comorbid syndromes while psychotherapy is initiated. Medication treatment of concurrent anxiety and mood disorders will typically reduce personality rigidity and will allow psychotherapy to work faster and more easily.

Malingering/Factitious Disorder

No discussion of workplace mental health complaints is complete without some attention to fabricated symptoms. Feigned symptoms may be deliberate or unwitting. Symptoms may be intentionally produced in the presence of external incentives (malingering) or without any external incentives (factitious disorder, where the goal is a sick role). Symptoms may be physical or psychological.

Careful evaluation for malingering or factitious disorder is indicated when symptoms are inconsistent with likely diagnostic categories, where legal and entitlement issues are involved, and where there appears to be noncompliance with full evaluation. Importantly, fabricated symptoms can coexist with genuine psychiatric disorders.

Malingering (feigning symptoms for external benefit) is not an emotional disorder and does not generally respond to psychotherapy or medication. Factitious disorder (feigning symptoms without external benefit in order to be considered ill) is an emotional disorder that may be treatable with appropriate psychotherapy.

Stress Complaints without Underlying Physical or Psychiatric Disease

Emotional complaints (either physical or psychological) may also be present without apparent underlying physical or psychiatric illness. This should prompt another review of the history and differential diagnosis. The presence of limited or inconsistent symptoms that still do not meet criteria for any of the previously mentioned disorders may nonetheless require symptomatic treatment.

When psychological symptoms of stress are present without a diagnosable psychiatric disorder, symptomatic treatment is indicated. Antianxiety medications are often useful for brief or intermittent treatment of anxiety. Antidepressant medications are not indicated for the treatment of depressed mood in the absence of any of the cited psychiatric diagnoses. Brief supportive psychotherapy is also frequently useful in the treatment of anxiety or depressed mood in the absence of the diagnosis of a psychiatric disorder.

Mental Status Examination

The Mental Status Examination (MSE) supplements the employee's psychiatric history in the same way that a physical examination complements an employee's medical history. A detailed MSE might include specific questions about or tests of memory, abstraction, concentration, orientation, knowledge, suicidal and violent thoughts, and self-reported mood. Perhaps most importantly, though, the MSE includes careful observation about affect (observed emotion), anxiety, judgment, self-awareness, behavior, personal interaction, thought process, and speech content.

Differential Diagnosis

Having identified the principal stressors, symptoms, and areas of dysfunction, the next step is to systematically consider the differential diagnosis. *DSM-IV* (or the primary care version, *DSM-IV-PC*) of the American Psychiatric Association offers standard psychiatric diagnoses for EAP clinicians. *DSM-IV-PC* also offers a straightforward diagnostic algorithm for the evaluation of common emotional symptoms. It is important to note that emotional disorders have a high level of comorbidity; for example, an employee who has been demoted may present with a major depression, as well as a long-term history of panic disorder. Most importantly, an exaggerated stress reaction indicates the likelihood of a diagnosable disorder, even when there is a clearly identifiable workplace stressor.

INDICATIONS FOR IMMEDIATE REFERRAL

It is important for all clinicians to recognize conditions that urgently require specialized expertise (see Table 8.4). The following is a noncomprehensive list of indications for immediate referral to a psychiatrist or other mental health professional. Many of these indications reflect risk of harm to self or others.

Table 8.4   Indications for Prompt Psychiatric Referral*

- Risk of suicide or self-harm.
- Risk of violence to others.
- Significant anxiety, depressive, psychotic symptoms.
- Cognitive disorganization or acute cognitive changes.
- Substance abuse.
- Child abuse.
- Urgent life issues or overwhelming emotional state.

*Referral to a specialized evaluator is indicated whenever these phenomena are present and are beyond the expertise of the initial evaluator. Always consider possible need for urgent referral.

Risk of Suicide or Self-Harm. Current or recent thoughts of suicide are indicative of significant psychopathology and require evaluation by a psychiatrist or a therapist experienced and comfortable with the assessment of suicidal risk.

Risk of Violence to Others. Violent behavior and threats of violence require immediate and appropriate evaluation.

Significant Anxiety, Depressive, or Psychotic Symptoms. These symptoms typically require psychiatric evaluation for diagnosis and possible medication. Anxiety and depression can be overwhelming for an employee, even when the initial complaint is about a more practical concern. Concern should be further heightened when there are suggestions of hopelessness or when there is an inability to function at work, at home, or during the interview. Psychotic symptoms (including paranoia, auditory or visual hallucinations, delusions, bizarre beliefs) are also usually indicative of severe pathology and require immediate appropriate evaluation.

Cognitive Disorganization or Acute Cognitive Changes. Before completing an initial evaluation, the clinician must be comfortable that the employee is organized and functional enough to follow through with basic treatment recommendations. Disorganization or cognitive dysfunction interfering with self-care or with the ability to follow basic treatment recommendations are indications for referral. In particular, any signs of acute cognitive change that suggest delirium or of significant neurologic or psychiatric pathology should indicate immediate evaluation by a neurologist or a psychiatrist.

Substance Abuse. Medical and mental health clinicians (EAP clinicians, psychiatrists, psychologists, primary care physicians, social workers) vary widely in their experience and expertise with substance abuse. General guidelines for indications for immediate referral for acute treatment by a substance abuse clinician include either the presence of active symptoms of withdrawal, past history of serious withdrawal phenomena, the desire or indication for structured inpatient or outpatient detoxification or rehabilitation, or the presence of any of the previously described symptoms (suicidal ideation, psychotic symptoms, threats of violence, disorganization, or acute cognitive changes).

Child Abuse. Many states have mandated reporting standards for evidence of child abuse. Notify appropriate authority where required.

Urgent Life Issues or Overwhelming Emotional State. Any situation of immediate or overwhelming crisis requires immediate attention and may require immediate referral for rapid and integrated treatment. Any situation requiring an employee to make prompt or immediate significant life decisions may also require referral.

Case A: Urgent Referral

Ernest Lee is a 50-year-old married man, a line manager in a large manufacturing company. He first went to his company's medical department complaining of dental pain. The evaluating nurse noticed that Ernest asked for an urgent appointment that morning, even though the pain had been going on for many weeks. On interview Ernest talked more about his boss than about his teeth. He looked angry, spoke rapidly, and was barely able to sit still in his chair. "I don't know what is wrong with this company—they are letting that SOB ruin my life. I'm sick to my stomach . . . now my teeth . . . I just don't know how long I can take this." The evaluating nurse realized that the primary problem was emotional rather than medical. She was concerned that Ernest could be in a dramatic emotional crisis. She made an immediate referral to the in-house EAP.

On interview with the EAP counselor, Ernest talked about his job situation. The counselor knew that rumors of impending downsizing had raised the levels of stress throughout the corporation, and she was experienced with stress management issues. Ernest seemed like a typical client, a middle-aged man temporarily overwhelmed by work stress. But as she took the history, she was struck by the bizarre nature of some of his complaints: "My boss is ruining my whole life. He is friends with everyone my wife and I used to be friends with. . . . He has told everyone to stay away from us. I don't know what he is after. Last night, we were at a party, and he had a whole group of people laughing at me and telling jokes about me." The counselor was concerned that these unusual complaints may be paranoid psychotic symptoms. Evaluation and treatment of these urgent symptoms were beyond her expertise. She called the EAP's consulting psychiatrist, who offered to see the patient immediately.

The psychiatrist performed a complete psychiatric evaluation. He learned that Ernest has a past history of "a breakdown in college. . . . I had to take a couple of months off. . . . It's the only time I've seen a psychiatrist in my life . . . and all he wanted to do was give me medications that made me feel sleepy." The psychiatrist confirmed that Ernest was psychotic, with paranoid delusions about his boss. He immediately started treatment with olanzapine (an antipsychotic medication) and recommended medical leave of absence. After three weeks of medication and therapy, Ernest was nonpsychotic and ready to work again. Further psychotherapy and medication adjustments helped him figure out what happened and how to be sure it won't happen again. Because the evaluation and referral process was so effective, a valued employee kept his job, and a more acute crisis was averted.

TREATMENT

As outlined previously, stressors and symptoms may appear in the employee as an individual, in the workplace, or in the family and social context. Similarly, treatment may be directed at the individual (for example, medication or psychotherapy), the workplace (modified job requirements or modified workplace), or at the family/social context (family or marital treatment, legal or financial assistance). In most cases, a specifically selected combined therapeutic approach will be most effective. Accurate diagnosis leads to appropriate and effective treatment.

For most of the common psychiatric diagnoses, a combination of psychotherapy and medication is the most effective treatment. The following general discussion outlines some of the general psychotherapeutic issues in the treatment of mental health problems.

Psychotherapeutic Approaches

Whether counseling an employee about performance improvement, the effects of a downsizing, family crises, or treatment of a depression, psychotherapy is an important part of all EAP care. Even in taking an initial history, the clinician's effectiveness is improved by sensitivity to an employee's expressed and unexpressed concerns. In all of these cases, counseling requires attention to some of the same basic principles (see Table 8.5).

Table 8.5   Some Basic Concerns in Psychotherapy

- Treatment alliance and compliance.
- Education about the problem, treatment, prognosis, and time frame.
- Practical issues posed by the current problem.
- Empathic understanding of expressed and unexpressed emotions.
- Real and perceived conflicts of interest.
- Real and perceived progress in treatment.

Emotional disorders require particular attention to the emotional distress itself. There are a number of ways to do this. For many employees, an appropriate treatment plan would include review of practical coping strategies for the disorder. Depending on the stressors and the syndromes involved, those skills might include breathing or relaxation techniques, exercise, self-care, and changing goals or expectations. EAP treatment of these disorders might also include brief, focused psychotherapy to address stressors, syndromes, work, family, and recovery issues. Much of the time, employees will respond well and return to their usual lives. Care must be taken not to assume poor prognosis and overlook treatment options and not to underestimate risk of suicide or violence. In addition, the employee and clinician emotions that can arise in any treatment can be particularly intense and problematic with some employees.

Optimal treatment is sometimes beyond the time constraints of EAP care or may require additional expertise. In addition to the indications for *immediate* referral, nonurgent referrals for treatment or consultation should also be considered at times (see Table 8.6).

Formal psychotherapy training is a detailed and lengthy process. It generally involves didactic training in theory and technique, supervised treatment experience, and often personal psychotherapy. In different ways, most of the appropriate psychotherapies offer a better understanding of self and others, as well as education about the mental health problem and its treatment. When referral is indicated, employees will do best with a broadly trained clinician. The various psychotherapy practitioners differ in the range and depth of their training. The most common practitioners are psychiatrists, psychologists, and social workers.

Table 8.6   Nonurgent Psychiatric Referral

- Support during an emotional crisis.
- Long-term life issues.
- Interpersonal or personality issues.
- Concerns about suicide or violence.
- Inadequate response to treatment.
- Reconsidered or more definitive diagnosis or treatment planning.
- Troublesome employee or clinician emotions (interfering with treatment).
- Significant concurrent medical illness.
- Distressed executives (heightened confidentiality concerns).
- Management consultation issues.

Case B: Nonurgent Referral

Hope Fernandez is a married 36-year-old woman in a financial services firm. A graduate of a prestigious college and business school, she was recognized right away as a rising star employee and held a series of increasingly important jobs within the firm. The mother of a 2-year-old, she recently was made partner in the firm. Soon after, she went to the EAP with complaints of stress and work-life-balance issues. The evaluating social worker suggested brief treatment at the EAP, with a focus on stress management. The social worker was a superb therapist and had treated several other women struggling with work/family issues in this demanding firm. Hope appeared to be an excellent patient. She arrived promptly for each session, seemed insightful about her situation, and followed every suggestion made by the social worker. After four sessions, she was exercising regularly, meditating daily, drinking less wine, and eating lunch with old friends twice each week. Nonetheless, she wasn't feeling a whole lot better. The social worker suggested an evaluation with a psychiatrist.

The psychiatrist performed a full evaluation. He learned that Hope had not felt like herself since the birth of her child 2 years before. She has had poor sleep, decreased concentration, brief periods of tearfulness, and feelings of hopelessness. Although she wasn't on a diet, she had steadily lost weight, until she was 15 pounds lighter than before pregnancy. The tearful episodes increased after her promotion, which was particularly confusing to her ("I thought that I would feel much better once they made me a partner").

The psychiatrist and the social worker agreed that Hope was experiencing a complex set of biological and psychological stressors. The subtle depressive symptoms that began after childbirth were consistent with a major depression. The increase in symptoms after making partner suggested powerful underlying psychological factors. The psychiatrist and the social worker agreed that antidepressant treatment and long-term psychotherapy were needed. This more comprehensive and longer treatment was beyond the usual scope of the EAP program. Hope was referred for treatment to a psychiatrist. After one month, her depressive symptoms were much improved. After three months, she understood some of her reaction to making partner.

Workplace Interventions

Job Modification (Short- or Long-Term)

Untreated stress disorders may raise questions about interim deficits in interpersonal skills, attentiveness, energy, judgment, memory, and concentration. The EAP clinician should understand the essential functions of the job to assess the need for job restrictions or modified duty. The clinician can then match impairments with essential job functions. Considerations include the nature and the time course of the impairment and issues of special provisions for work or treatment. As in all treatment, care must be taken to avoid real or perceived conflict of interest. In particular, treatment of emotional symptoms can be impeded when a treating clinician is also responsible for determining impairments or entitlements.

Workplace Modification

Presentation of a mental health complaint may indicate the need for workplace modification. In the simplest case, modification of a physical stressor may be useful. However, the mental health complaint may also indicate the need for organizational restructuring. Examples of restructuring include placement and transfer, changing systems of information exchange or reward determination, and changing chains of command. Evaluation by an organizational psychiatrist, psychologist, or other organizational professional may be indicated.

Workplace Interventions (Group)

Organizational interventions are appropriate in several situations. Group interventions by a qualified professional are almost always appropriate in situations of significant workplace trauma (accident, violence, sudden death). In addition, group interventions may be appropriate if a cluster of stress reactions is seen, if major organizational change has occurred, or if there is a particular need to prevent problems in a given employee segment.

Family and Social Interventions

There are a wide variety of family or social interventions that may be appropriate in the treatment of emotional disorders.

Marital/Family Treatment

The presence of significant marital or family dysfunction should prompt consideration of marital or family therapy, regardless of any diagnosis. Similarly, marital treatment may be indicated even when the marital problem is caused by other stressors.

Treatment of Other Family Member

It is not unusual for the evaluation of an employee complaining of an emotional problem to reveal significant emotional difficulties in another family member. In these cases, evaluation and treatment of the other family member may be indicated.

Other

A wide variety of life difficulties may cause stress to an individual. Support in dealing with these difficulties may allow an employee to resume his or her potential level of functioning. Examples of such support might include referral to appropriate legal or financial help or help in making child care or elder care arrangements.

WORKPLACE PREVENTION

The prevention of emotional disorders in the workplace involves several key elements (see Table 8.7). Achieving the goal of prevention requires sophisticated coordination between the corporate operating management structure, human resources, and the medical department. Appropriate flow of information, with due attention to legal and confidentiality issues, is the key to early identification of problems, diagnosis, treatment, and relapse prevention.

Table 8.7   Workplace Prevention

- Identification of potential workplace stressors.
- Workplace education.
- Early identification of distressed workers.
- Available and appropriate treatment.

Prevention requires an educated workforce, with employees, supervisors, and managers who are aware of typical workplace stressors, symptoms, and avenues for evaluation and treatment. Treatment must be available in a convenient, confidential, supportive environment. Prevention is the key to any effective workplace strategy for dealing with emotional symptoms and disorders in the workplace.

Early recognition of emotional distress can be enhanced with programs for both employees and supervisors. For example, there are now programs that allow employees to complete a brief self-assessment or telephone screening to see if they are depressed. Although the most depressed employees are less likely to participate, the programs do encourage a treatment-friendly atmosphere. Similarly, other programs train managers to recognize the signs of emotional distress in the workplace and to know how to point employees toward help.

Other programs focus on issues of organizational change. Change is stressful for people who lose, change, or keep their jobs. Often, employees who do well while others suffer career or financial hardship are the most stressed. Properly designed programs can reduce distress while improving morale and performance.

Finally, mental health benefits are in a constant state of flux these days. Benefits packages that do allow access to optimal treatment are not common. Instead, managed mental health care typically addresses immediate problems at best, without sufficient attention to diagnostic, social, career, and long-term issues. Concerns about confidentiality can further erode quality of care. Current legislative and judicial activities may help to improve this situation soon. In the meanwhile, clinicians and employers need to evaluate mental health programs with a keen eye toward these quality-of-care issues.

INDEPENDENT MEDICAL EVALUATION

Beyond treatment itself, there are a number of circumstances in which it is important to obtain a formal psychiatric evaluation for an employee. Where these examinations are conducted at the company's request, they are called *independent medical examinations* (IMEs). IMEs are paid for by the employer and typically involve a written or oral report back to the EAP, medical department, or human resources. Commonly, IMEs are used to evaluate employees who file claims for psychiatric disability. An IME is useful to the company in assessing diagnostic accuracy, treatment effectiveness, and degree of disability. When employees return to work from an episode of psychiatric illness, they are sometimes asked to have a return-to-work evaluation. This is especially important for jobs that would have a higher level of concern about residual psychiatric symptoms, such as drivers, pilots, and police. Violence assessments are often requested after an employee has spoken or acted in a way that appears threatening or violent. Finally, companies will often suggest or offer confidential psychiatric second opinions to employees, either working or on leave, who have illness or distress that does not appear to be improving.

The 1997 Equal Employment Opportunity Commission (EEOC) psychiatric guidelines for the 1990 Americans with Disabilities Act (ADA) address issues of reasonable accommodation for psychiatric disability in the workplace. As the guidelines are written, they appear to limit the scope of an IME conducted to determine reasonable accommodation for an established employee. For example, the guidelines discourage questions about psychiatric history and treatment. Whether these guidelines will be applied by the courts remains to be seen at this time.

Because IMEs are usually conducted for the company, it is very important to clarify confidentiality issues with the employee in advance. Employees should be told both by the company's representative and by the evaluating psychiatrist that the IME is not confidential and that information will be reported back to the company. The employee should sign a written release of information that indicates who will have access to the report. Although IMEs are not conducted for clinical purposes, they can often help the employee to obtain improved diagnosis and treatment.

An optimal IME is conducted in much the same way as a clinical psychiatric evaluation. Information is typically obtained from the employee and from medical and employment records supplied by the employer. Treating clinicians can also be a source of important information. A formal IME report includes a summary of relevant clinical information, diagnostic impression, disability (or violence) assessment, prognosis, and treatment recommendations. In some cases, a briefer and less specific report is preferred.

EAPs are often asked to assist with psychiatric IMEs. Common questions include whether an employee is able to continue at work, is receiving adequate treatment, is well enough to return to work after leave, or has a risk of violence. Perhaps most commonly, employees on disability are referred for evaluation of their ability to work, for treatment, and for prognosis. This case report summarzies the evaluation of an employee on long-term disability leave.

Case C: Independent Medical Examination

Faith Stevens is a divorced 37-year-old Acme Software employee who was seen in a two-session IME after signing a release of information form. History is obtained from the employee and from written records provided by the Acme EAP.

Faith has been on disability since leaving work 15 months ago because of "a nervous condition." She noted that her supervisor was writing her up on "crazy stuff." As a result, she "got a note that I couldn't work for him anymore."

Faith has episodes of abrupt anxiety, tachycardia, palpitations, shortness of breath, chest pain, fear of loss of control, dizziness, lightheadedness, depersonalization, and derealization. Some of these panic attacks occurred out of the blue. Although less frequent than when she was working, they still happen about once a day. The attacks started about 7 years before. She is afraid to return to work but otherwise has no phobias. She currently takes lorazepam, 0.5 milligrams twice a day, with limited benefit.

Faith has also had a mild chronic/intermittent depression for about 20 years. The depressive episodes included hypersomnia, loss of energy, lethargy, increased appetite, sweet cravings, and mood reactivity. She has always had increased emotional sensitivity to social rejection. Her symptoms of atypical depression seem to get worse during the winter.

She reports social alcohol use and denies drug use. There is no evidence for current major depression, social phobia, psychosis, bipolar disorder, or other common syndromes

Faith's psychiatric history is notable for hospitalization 7 years earlier, after her divorce. Symtoms then included anorexia, depressed and unreactive affect, severe anxiety, and reverse diurnal mood variation. She was treated with imipramine, lorazepam, and psychotherapy, with full resolution. Since then, she was followed by her internist on lorazepam only. His current diagnoses are depressive disorder (not otherwise specified), and personality disorder (not otherwise specified). She has had infrequent supportive psychotherapy sessions with him, but few or none in the past 3 months.

Medical review of systems is noncontributory, though her last complete physical exam and blood work were 18 months ago.

Some parts of her personal, career, and family histories are relevant. Faith worked for Acme Software for 12 years. Three years ago, she was moved into a new department. The new supervisor was "weird . . . treated me as if I were a student intern." She says she does not know if she wants to return to work, even if her symptoms resolved. Her major concerns are about stress and whether she is qualified to do her work. She maintains a very limited social life. Her mother and one of three siblings have a nervous condition. Although two siblings live locally, she sees them rarely. Faith last visited her retired parents in Miami about 5 years ago.

On mental status examination, she is cooperative, talkative, and pleasant. She seems very anxious. She is cooperative with the interview and appears to answer questions openly and honestly. Her affect is reactive and appropriate to content. There is no evidence of psychosis, mania, disorientation, or suicidal ideation.

Diagnostic Impression

1. Panic disorder.
2. Probable chronic atypical depression.
3. Probable major depression 7 years ago.
4. Denial current drug or alcohol abuse.
5. Life stresses including significantly restricted social and family life.

Functional Impression

Panic disorder is the primary psychiatric cause of distress. Panic attacks can cause significant anxiety and can impair concentration; they can also contribute to phobic avoidance of work.

Prognostic Impression

Currently documented diagnosis and treatment has not been adequate. Referral to a psychiatrist for appropriate treatment for panic disorder should be considered. For example, an initial dose of clonazepam (0.5 milligrams every 12 hours) could be raised steadily to the point where all panic attacks cease. An SSRI antidepressant could also be considered for atypical depression and should offer some benefit after 4 weeks. Reduction in rejection sensitivity would possibly take longer. SSRIs are sometimes insufficient for panic disorder, and further medication adjustment or augmentation may need to be considered over time. Routine medical evaluation and blood tests (especially thyroid) should be reviewed.

Weekly psychotherapy is indicated to discuss issues of family relationships, social relationships, successes, losses, and separations, as well as work concerns. Psychotherapy might also explore the commonplace possibility of emotions from personal-life changes displaced to the workplace. Especially once panic and depressive symptoms are controlled, therapy should also be able to usefully address underlying dynamic issues.

With appropriate medication and psychotherapy, Faith could be able to return to work within 1 month. Initial apprehensiveness should then diminish with time and psychotherapeutic work. She should then be able to return to her previous level of work functioning, if not higher. Should problems persist after implementation of these suggestions or should there be problems in adopting them, then reevaluation may be of some benefit.

Conclusion

As the preceding discussion suggests, the diagnosis and treatment of workplace mental-health-related disorders can seem complex. The complexity springs both from the diverse nature of life stressors and the diverse symptoms that may result from these stressors.

However, two key principles apply in trying to make sense of the complexity. First, a clear diagnostic framework is the key to understanding diffuse symptoms in a rational way. Diverse and diffuse symptoms can be organized into symptom complexes that are likely to suggest specific diagnostic categories. Specific diagnosis leads to specific and appropriate treatment. Second, it is important for all clinicians evaluating emotional complaints to recognize the limits of their expertise. Emotional complaints can indicate a wide variety of minor to severe psychological, physical, neurologic, or psychiatric disease. It is essential that each clinician recognize the signals that indicate the need for specialized evaluation.

The psychiatric perspective can be helpful, though finding the right psychiatric consultant is not always easy. Names can be obtained from medical schools, hospitals, the local medical community, other EAPs, or the local branch of the American Psychiatric Association. The Academy of Organizational and Occupational Psychiatry (aoop@degnon.org; 703–556–9222) is a good source for organizational and occupational psychiatrists. Credentials, recommendations, and a personal interview are good places to start evaluating a consultant, but clinical outcomes are most important in the long run.

References

American Psychiatric Association. (1994). *Diagnostic and statistical manual of mental disorders* (4th ed.). Washington, DC: Author.

Kahn, J.P. (Ed.). (1993). *Mental health in the workplace: A practical psychiatric guide.* New York: Van Nostrand Reinhold.

CHAPTER 9

Benchmarks and Performance Measures for Employee Assistance Programs

THOMAS M. AMARAL

Total quality management, continuous quality improvement, and other quality initiatives have become a visual part of the American business and industry landscape. From manufacturing concerns to service industries, from big companies to small ones, organizations now realize that their competitive position and survival may well depend on the effectiveness of their quality control programs.

Benchmarking has emerged as an essential component of these quality initiatives (Camp, 1989). It involves isolating key metrics in specific functions (e.g., production, distribution, billing, marketing) and comparing one's own practices with those of organizations that have established themselves as leaders or innovators in that specific business function. In benchmarking, the focus extends beyond measuring outcomes to understanding the processes of how products or services are developed and delivered.

While some quality initiatives have occurred in the employee assistance program (EAP) field (see Foster, 1994; Maiden, 1993), very little on benchmarking has been included in this work. In a critical appraisal of the status of benchmarking within employee assistance (EA), Googins (1994) stated that "the absence of benchmarking principles and techniques puts EA programs outside of the core business and brings into question their perceived linkage with the business goals of the organization" (p. 13).

Today, when organizations are questioning more than ever the value of their EAPs, these programs need to demonstrate their worth and to align themselves with their organizations' missions. Benchmarking offers a potent strategy for accomplishing this while also providing data that a program can utilize for continuous quality improvement.

This chapter will describe specific performance measures for benchmarking EAPs. These measures were selected based on the following criteria:

- They track core activities of employee assistance work.
- They can be easily calculated.
- They are derived from process data that are readily available to most EAPs.
- They are easy to standardize.
- They are applicable to a wide variety of organizations and programs.

UTILIZATION RATE

Utilization rate is the most commonly calculated performance measure in the EAP field and by far generates the most controversy. EA professionals have used many different formulas to derive utilization rates (see Korr & Ruez, 1986), and calculations are more often driven by program managers' marketing needs than by any industry standard. Up to this point, lack of a consistent definition has rendered this performance measure meaningless and has led to confusion over its interpretation.

Benchmarking Value

When compared to benchmarking data from comparable programs or similar industries, an accurate utilization rate can provide a general understanding of how well an EAP is engaging the organization's employees in its services. Although utilization rate does provide a good starting point for understanding an EAP's outreach efforts and casefinding strategies, when viewed in isolation, a utilization rate's value is limited because it can only yield an overall indication of the extent to which employees are participating in the program. For instance, a low utilization rate might suggest that an EAP needs to increase its promotional activities, but it does not provide specific direction on what the program should do differently.

Improvements in EAP processes and practices can come about by examining utilization rate in combination with other performance indicators that provide specific information about who participated in the EAP and how each participant reached the program. For example, a utilization rate of 3%—which most would agree is relatively low—and the additional knowledge that few supervisors have referred employees to the program suggest that the EAP could increase its overall utilization rate by engaging in outreach efforts that target supervisors, such as EA orientation sessions or substance abuse awareness training.

The push for high utilization rates reflects a commonly held misconception that the more cases an EAP opens, the more successful it is. Although this may be true for those rare programs with low employee-to-staff ratios, the reality in most EAPs is that this "head counting" comes at the expense of other services that go into making the program successful, such as consistent follow-up. Unfortunately, the head-counting approach reduces the program's success for those individuals who receive limited services and, consequently, diminishes the EAP's value to the organization.

Benchmarking can be defined as a systematic process for understanding the services that are recognized as representing best practices for the purpose of continuous quality improvement (Spendolini, 1992). Benchmarks are set based not on the highest achievable levels for a service, but on what one considers best practices. For this reason, a particular EAP's utilization rate should be set at an optimal level of performance that will yield the greatest possible success for that program.

One can determine an appropriate rate by taking into consideration a program's available human resources as well as the extent to which it provides services in areas other than traditional assessment and referral. For instance, individual EA counselors often develop signs of burnout when they open more than 200 new cases per year. With similar knowledge about the capacities of their own professional staff members, EA managers can set a utilization rate based on what can reasonably be expected of their staff rather than on an arbitrary level derived from the size of the organization's workforce.

Caveat Emptor

Utilization rates have been important both in contract proposals submitted by external EA vendors and in accountability reports submitted by in-house programs to their organizations' upper-management team. Rates have often been submitted, however, without any indication of how they were derived. As a consequence, the recipients of this information may have made decisions regarding a program's merits based on unwarranted assumptions.

To enable management to make well-informed program decisions, EA professionals should provide the exact formula, and its underlying assumptions, used to calculate utilization rates. Furthermore, programs should provide decision makers with other key indicators that capture the broad spectrum of EAP services, including measures of at least the following areas:

- Employee and dependent cases opened.
- Follow-up services provided to clients and supervisors.
- Supervisory case consultations.
- Employee education programs.
- Management training activities.
- Organizational and noncase services (e.g., critical-incident stress debriefings, work group consultations).

Unfortunately, a long history of reporting inflated utilization rates has created its own pressure to continue the practice. How, for instance, can a program report a 5% utilization rate this year when last year it presented one that was 12%? EA professionals should resist this momentum to manipulate the rate's formula to make their EAPs look good and, instead, should give an honest and comprehensive accounting of the program's services. In the long run, this approach will yield a better understanding of the EAP's true worth to the organization.

Creative Number Crunching

Utilization rates can range from lower than 2% to higher than 30%. Why do rates vary so greatly? Some variation is due to differences in program success: Some EAPs are better than others at engaging employees in their services. Most of the variation in reported rates, however, is an illusion created by differences in calculation methods rather than by true differences in program practices. Because rates have been largely determined by their underlying formulas, their value as benchmarks has been significantly reduced.

The most common rate-calculation methods that create inflated utilization figures are:

- Combining dependents and employees.
- Including supervisory case consultations.
- Adding employees who have participated in EAP-sponsored support groups or workshops.
- Including brief, information-only telephone calls.
- Counting all active cases.

Combining Dependents and Employees

The common practice of combining dependent cases with employee cases to derive the utilization rate mixes apples and oranges. Dependents arrive at the EAP through different referral routes than employees, they are different demographically, and they have different problems. Because of these significant differences, including dependents in the utilization-rate formula obscures the rate's primary purpose of benchmarking the program's employee-outreach efforts.

Because dependents comprise an important client group of an effective EAP, reporting the number who participate in the program is important. This reporting should be done, however, through a separate statistic.

Including Supervisory Case Consultations

Supervisory case consultations are important EAP services, and they, too, should be counted, but not in the utilization rate. Because the recipient of consultation services is not the employee with a potential need for EAP services, including consultations in the utilization rate once again interferes with the rate's capacity to provide information on employee casefinding processes. Including supervisory case consultations in the rate calculation also double-counts those particular employees who are the focus of the consultation and later become EAP clients.

Adding Support-Group Participants

Employees who participate in EAP-sponsored support groups, workshops, and educational programs are frequently already EAP clients who have been referred to these groups or who are exploring the possible need for individual EAP services. Including these participants in the utilization rate potentially double-counts many of them. In addition, because these activities (e.g., parenting groups, stress management classes) often serve as casefinding vehicles for the EAP, including their participants in the rate calculation once again confuses these activities with the benchmark that is attempting to measure their impact.

Including Information-Only Telephone Calls

In traditional EAPs, information-only telephone calls are relatively rare because EA professionals try hard to engage all employees who call in a thorough assessment-and-referral process. Information-only referrals, without an assessment, are typically given only as a last resort when an employee declines any other offer of help. In some "1-800 programs," however, which provide assistance only by telephone, these brief calls can comprise a large percentage of the services provided. These programs, if they call themselves EAPs, generate the highest apparent utilization rates of all.

Brief information-only services should not be included in the utilization rate because they do not reflect core EAP work. Also, they do not require an EA professional to deliver the service. If anything, they should be monitored so that their number does not become too large.

Counting All Active Cases

Many utilization-rate formulas count all employee cases that were opened during the reporting year plus all active clients from previous years who had contact with the program at some time during the reporting year. Mixing previously opened cases with current ones again decreases the utilization rate's value because it contains many cases that are not a consequence of the program's recent outreach efforts.

Even without including active cases, a program's policy on when to inactivate and close cases can still have a significant impact on the overall utilization rate. If cases are routinely closed quickly after the initial assessment date (e.g., less than 6 months), they have a greater likelihood of being reopened—and counted again—within the reporting year.

One way to mitigate this potential problem is to adopt a guideline like the "6-month/12-month rule." Under this rule, (1) no case is closed before 6 months after the client's initial assessment date; and (2) all cases are closed at 12 months after the initial assessment unless still active in treatment or follow-up, with *active* defined as ongoing quarterly or more frequent contact. This policy yields an accurate utilization rate and reduces the administrative burden associated with needlessly reopening case files.

Standard Definition

A standard operational definition for *Overall Employee Utilization Rate* (UR) is:

$$UR = \frac{\text{Employee cases}}{\text{Eligible employees}} \times 100\%$$

where "Employee cases" = Number of employee cases that the EAP opened
during the reporting year

"Eligible employees" = Number of employees who were eligible to
participate in the EAP during the reporting year

This definition is restricted to *employee cases* in order to exclude dependents, as well as supervisors who sought assistance with managing an employee. However, supervisors who seek help for their own personal problems would be included. Also included would be reopened employee cases—those employees who sought help in previous years and whose previous case file has been closed and who sought help again during the reporting year. Previous-year employee cases that are still active (i.e., those with case files that have not yet been closed) would not be included.

For purposes of the definition, a case is considered *opened* whenever an EA professional performs a clinical assessment and reviews the case for possible referral for additional services. Because of the requirement for an assessment, this definition excludes information-only telephone calls and employees who only participated in training or education programs. The definition does include, however, telephone calls during which an assessment was conducted by an EA specialist. Because not all employees who seek help through an EAP require additional assistance beyond that which they receive from the program itself, this definition does not require a referral to outside services.

Eligible employees are defined by each organization's EAP policy, which typically specifies all full- and part-time employees who work for the organization. Technically, to calculate the utilization rate, this number should include all employees who were working for the organization on the first day of the reporting year plus any employees who were hired during the year. An easier-to-obtain alternative—and close approximation to this figure—is the average number of employees in the workforce during the year.

An annual rate is recommended to standardize the reporting period and to ensure that adequate data are available for benchmarking. For programs with large caseloads (i.e., greater than 1,000 cases opened per year), annualized rates can also be calculated at midyear or at each quarter to engage in more frequent quality-improvement efforts.

Sample Utilization Rates

Using the standard definition presented here, Table 9.1 shows utilization rates calculated for five internal EAPs. The sample programs presented in this chapter include:

- Program A: A mostly centralized EAP in a widely dispersed utility company with approximately 20,300 employees; during the time period of these analyses, the program was 15 years old with four full-time equivalent (FTE) professional staff members.

- Program B: A regionalized EAP in an international petroleum company with approximately 35,000 employees; a long-standing program with 14 FTEs.

- Program C: A centralized EAP in an aerospace company with 17,250 employees; two full-time professionals; data for these analyses were gathered from the time period just prior to the EAP's conversion from an alcohol program to a broad-brush one.

- Program D: A mostly centralized EAP in a municipality with 11,600 employees; very broad-brush program offering a wide diversity of services; 10 years old with seven FTEs.

- Program E: A new EAP in a federal agency with 8,500 employees; three full-time professionals; all calculations derived from data gathered during the program's first year of operation.

As shown in Table 9.1, utilization rates vary across the sample programs from a low of 1.6% to a high of 7.0%. Two factors that significantly impact rates are an EAP's age and the number of FTE staff professionals who work in the program. The effect of age can be seen in Figure 9.1, which charts utilization rates for Program D during its first 10 years of operation. As shown, this program experienced rapid growth in its utilization rates during the first few years, followed by a slowing down in rates until it has

Table 9.1   Overall Employee Utilization Rate (UR) for Five Sample Programs

Sample Program	EAP Cases	Eligible Employees	Utilization Rate
Program A	695	20,300	3.4%
Program B	2,451	35,000	7.0
Program C	276	17,250	1.6
Program D	510	11,600	4.4
Program E	132	8,500	1.6

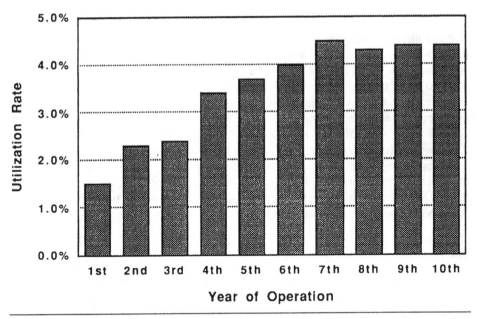

Figure 9.1   Utilization rates for sample program D during the first ten years of operation.

now reached a relatively stable rate of approximately 4.4%. This growth pattern is typical for most EAPs.

One factor that limits a program's utilization rate is the number of EA professionals providing services. Dividing the number of each sample program's cases opened during the year by the number of its FTE staff members yields the "Cases per Staff Professional" ratios presented in Table 9.2. As can be seen, ratios for Programs A and B are nearly identical and are similar to Program C's ratio, even though their utilization rates differ greatly. The EAP specialists in Program D, which is very broad-brush in its services, spend only half of their time providing direct client services, and, as a consequence, their yearly caseload sizes are only about half of those found for Programs A, B, and C. Program E's relatively low ratio reflects that this program is in the growth phase of its evolution.

Table 9.2   Average Caseload Size per Full-Time Equivalent Staff Professional

Sample Program	EAP Cases	Full-Time Equivalent Professionals	Cases per Staff Professional
Program A	695	4	174
Program B	2,451	14	175
Program C	276	2	138
Program D	510	7	73
Program E	132	3	44

Setting a Benchmark

One can use projected average-caseload sizes per staff professional to derive a rough range of utilization rates for any particular program: Multiply the number of FTE professionals working in the EAP by 175 and then again separately by 200 (which appears to be an optimal range of cases opened by each professional per year), and divide the two results by the number of eligible employees. Substituting Program C's numbers into these equations, for example, yields a lower benchmark figure of 2.0% ($2 \times 175 \div 17,250$) and an upper benchmark figure of 2.3% ($2 \times 200 \div 17,250$). Knowing that its utilization rate of 1.6% is below this range, Program C should consider developing an action plan to increase its casefinding activities. (Program C did in fact change its operations significantly during the year after these data were collected. At that time, it converted from an alcohol program to a broad-brush one and added additional staff professionals.)

The Effect of Formulas on Rates

To illustrate the degree to which the calculation method can influence the final rate, consider the utilization figures derived for Program D. Using the standard definition offered earlier yields a utilization rate of 4.4%, illustrated previously in Table 9.1. Calculating the rate by counting everything—dependents, supervisory case consultations, workshop participants, and all active cases—yields a rate of 23.6% ($2,734 \div 11,600$).

Utilization Rate versus Penetration Rate

Utilization rate as defined here is not the same as *penetration rate,* which measures the proportion of troubled employees who received EAP services. To calculate a penetration rate, a program must have available an estimate of the number of troubled employees in the organization. Because of the difficulties associated with accurately estimating problem prevalence rates, this performance indicator is impractical for benchmarking purposes. Other, more easily determined measures, such as the Alcohol Cases Participation Rate that will be presented next, can serve the purpose of understanding how well the program is reaching the organization's specific troubled employee groups.

PARTICIPATION BY TROUBLED EMPLOYEE GROUPS

In their field-defining papers on the core technology of employee assistance, Roman and Blum (1985, 1988) recognized the unique role of EAPs in successfully dealing with workplace alcohol and drug problems: "The EAP focus on employees' alcohol and other substance abuse problems offers the most significant promise of producing recovery and genuine cost savings for the organization in terms of future performance and reduced benefit usage" (p. 21).

Even though today's EAPs evolved from yesterday's occupational alcohol programs, the historically important focus on alcohol has diminished in recent years. This marks an unfortunate trend because employees who have alcohol problems continue to present significant risks for organizations, themselves, and other employees. Studies have shown that alcohol use by employees is associated with workplace accidents, excessive absenteeism, turnover, high medical-benefits utilization, and other work-place performance problems (see Normand, Lempert, & O'Brien, 1994). Further, the Exxon *Valdez* incident demonstrates vividly the potential liability associated with an unsuccessfully treated alcoholic employee who remains in the workplace.

EAPs have shown good success intervening in the workplace with alcohol and other drug problems (see Blum & Roman, 1995). One recent investigation conducted by the author and several associates (Conlin, Amaral, & Harlow, 1996) looked at the unique role of EAP case management in reducing healthcare claims filed by employees with substance abuse problems. The study compared total medical claims filed by employees with substance abuse problems and managed by the EAP with total medical claims filed by employees with substance abuse problems and managed solely by the organization's preferred provider organization (PPO) medical benefits plan. During a 30-month period following initiation of substance abuse treatment, the average healthcare claims for employees who first sought help through the organization's EAP were approximately $6,900 less than the average claims for those employees managed by the PPO.

Alcohol Cases Participation Rate

The continued importance of these cases to the successful functioning of an EAP can be tracked by an *Alcohol Cases Participation Rate* (APR) performance measure. APR is defined as:

$$APR = \frac{\text{Alcohol cases}}{\text{Eligible employees}} \times 1,000$$

where "Alcohol cases" = Number of employee alcohol cases that the EAP
opened during the reporting year

"Eligible employees" = Number of employees who were eligible to participate in the
EAP during the reporting year

As with utilization rate, this performance measure is restricted to employee cases only. What constitutes an alcohol case often varies with the professional degree and background of the EA specialist who performs the assessment. To facilitate benchmark-ing across programs, organizations should use an all-inclusive definition that counts employees who have any level of assessed alcohol abuse, dependence, or problem, regardless of whether alcohol has been identified as primary, secondary, or tertiary.

The denominator for this performance measure is identical to the one used for uti-lization rate. This reflects the indicator's primary function of measuring the pro-gram's penetration into the alcoholic segment of the organization's entire employee workforce. Multiplying the ratio by 1,000 to yield a number that is greater than 1 makes the resulting figures easier to deal with than small decimal numbers. The APR is expressed as a number per 1,000 employees, as shown in Table 9.3, for the five sam-ple programs.

As Table 9.3 shows, Program B has the highest participation rate among the sample EAPs. This reflects, no doubt, the petroleum industry's understandable concern re-garding alcohol in the workplace and the fact that this program has an arrangement under which it has primary responsibility for managing the organization's substance

Table 9.3   Alcohol Cases Participation Rate (APR) for Five Sample Programs

Sample Program	Alcohol Cases	Eligible Employees	Participation Rate
Program A	34	20,300	1.7/1,000
Program B	173	35,000	4.9/1,000
Program C	57	17,250	3.3/1,000
Program D	40	11,600	3.4/1,000
Program E	26	8,500	3.1/1,000

abuse cases. Ironically, Program A, which today has the lowest APR of the five sample programs, began as an occupational alcohol program with early APRs in excess of 7/1,000. Unfortunately, when the recovering alcoholic who started the program retired, the EAP lost its alcohol focus.

Establishing an APR Benchmark

How best to establish an ideal APR benchmark is not clear. As mentioned previously in the discussion on penetration rate, alcohol-problem prevalence rates are difficult to determine for specific organizations. It is safe to assume, however, that the stresses associated with today's society in general and with the workplace specifically will continue to supply EAPs with a steady stream of alcoholic clients. Given the likely number of current and future employees in need of alcohol-related services, a participation rate of 5/1,000 would seem to be a reasonable and desirable minimum threshold for most programs. This benchmark can be achieved through rigorous alcohol casefinding and outreach methods, such as supervisory training and alcohol education programs.

A Family of Benchmarks

APR is one member of a potential family of performance measures that can be used to track an EAP's ability to engage in its services those employees who have specific kinds of problems. One companion metric is the *Drug Cases Participation Rate* (DPR), defined as:

$$DPR = \frac{Drug\ cases}{Eligible\ employees} \times 1,000$$

where "Drug cases" = Number of employee drug cases that the EAP opened
during the reporting year

"Eligible employees" = Number of employees who were eligible to participate
in the EAP during the reporting year

As with APR, the challenge with this performance measure is defining what constitutes a drug case. Again, to facilitate benchmarking across EAPs, a definition that counts all drug-related cases without regard to their level of severity or particular type of drug used is recommended.

One can similarly define performance measures for other types of employee problems, such as psychological/emotional disturbances, family/marital problems, work-related issues, and financial problems. The recent workplace interest in depression suggests that this employee problem area might warrant specific tracking as well. Use of these additional measures is best driven by each particular EAP's interest in them and by the availability of benchmarking partners who are willing to share definitions and data.

REFERRAL INTO THE EAP BY GATEKEEPERS

Roman and Blum (1985, 1988) articulated three separate core technologies to describe the crucial role of supervisors in the operation of EAPs:

1. Use by supervisors of job performance issues as the criteria for identifying troubled employees.
2. Provision by EAP specialists of expert consultation to supervisors on how to take appropriate steps in utilizing the program's services.
3. Supervisors' use of constructive confrontation to motivate troubled employees to contact the EAP.

In everyday use, these three technologies combine, through job-performance monitoring and job leverage, to create a powerful circumstance that strongly encourages employees whose behavioral problems are rooted in denial, such as substance abuse, to seek appropriate help.

The value of supervisors to the success of an EAP was shown in a study conducted by the author and a colleague (Amaral & Cross, 1988). This study compared sickness absenteeism taken 1 year before and 1 year after participation in an EAP by two groups of clients with alcohol problems. One group consisted of formal supervisory referrals and were compared with a second group made up of voluntary referrals. During the year after EAP referral, sickness absenteeism for voluntary referrals increased by 49%, whereas for formally referred alcohol-abusing employees, sick leave showed a decrease of 33%. Savings in reduced sickness absenteeism for the supervisory-referred clients were estimated at approximately $350,000 over a 4-year period.

Supervisory Referral Ratio

The role of supervisors can be tracked by a *Supervisory Referral Ratio* (SRR) performance measure defined as:

$$SRR = \frac{\text{Supervisory-referred cases}}{\text{Employees cases}} \times 100\%$$

where "Supervisory-referred cases" = Number of employee EAP cases that were referred by supervisors during the reporting year

"Employee cases" = Number of employee cases that the EAP opened during the reporting year

This performance measure is expressed as a percentage of the program's employee cases opened during the reporting year. Because percentages of all types of referrals must necessarily add up to 100%, this definition places the percentage of supervisory referrals and the percentage of self-referrals in opposition to one another. In other words, when one of these two values goes up, the other must go down (unless a third type of referral source also changes significantly during the year, which is uncommon in most programs).

SRR is defined in this way to emphasize the importance of striking a balance between self- and supervisory referrals. With little effort beyond routine program promotion and a history of providing effective services, EAPs typically have no difficulty obtaining large numbers of self-referrals. In contrast, programs must continuously expend energy through outreach activities and training to maintain high levels of supervisory referrals. Involving supervisors in the program is well worth the effort, however, because these individuals provide the EAP with those employees whose personal problems are having the most deleterious impact on work performance and attendance and, therefore, those cases with the greatest potential return on investment for the program's services (see Amaral, 1986).

In the numerator of the definition, *supervisory-referred cases* include all those in which the supervisor is the primary referral source. For those programs that distinguish between informal/voluntary/suggested and formal/involuntary/recommended supervisory referrals, further differentiation of performance submeasures for these two referral types can also be of value (see Amaral & Cross, 1988). They might be described as *Informal Supervisory Referral Ratio* and *Formal Supervisory Referral Ratio,* respectively.

Sample Referral Ratios

Supervisory Referral Ratios (SRRs) for the five sample programs are shown in Table 9.4. Table 9.4 shows that SRRs vary widely across the sample programs. Programs C, D, and E, for instance, all have ratios of approximately 30%. Program C, which at the time of these data analyses had a strong alcohol orientation, likely achieved its high ratio by conducting frequent, ongoing supervisory training. Similarly, Program E, although new, reached its relatively high SRR by promoting itself almost exclusively to supervisors during its first year, rather than following the typical approach of launching itself through a promotional campaign to the general employee population. Program D is somewhat unique in that it maintains its very high visibility,

Table 9.4 Supervisory Referral Ratio (SRR) for Five Sample Programs

Sample Program	Supervisory Referrals	EAP Cases	Referral Ratio
Program A	113	695	16.3%
Program B	190	2,451	7.8
Program C	95	276	34.4
Program D	154	510	30.2
Program E	39	132	29.5

credibility, and utilization among supervisors through its comprehensive trauma-response services.

Ironically, older programs with well-established track records among employees, like Programs A and B, must work doubly hard to achieve high SRRs. Because of their long-standing positive reputations, they receive large numbers of self-referrals, especially among employees who sought help in the past and who return for additional assistance when new problems arise. These kinds of program differences highlight the importance of selecting SRR benchmarking partners that are comparable.

Other Gatekeeper Benchmarks

Supervisors have historically been the primary referring agents for EAPs from within organizations. Human resources (HR)/personnel representatives, medical department professionals, and union stewards have also traditionally referred many employees to programs. An extended family of gatekeeper benchmarks can track participation by these additional referring parties and could include *HR/Personnel Referral Ratio, Medical Referral Ratio,* and *Union Referral Ratio,* respectively. Definitions for these metrics would be analogous to the one previously presented here for supervisory referrals.

In recent years, as EA professionals have partnered with other workplace players who have an interest in behavioral issues, referrals have been increasing from sources such as security officers, workers' compensation case managers, and disability case workers. Someday, when the absolute numbers of these types of referrals have increased, they, too, may warrant consideration as formally defined performance measures.

REFERRAL OUTSIDE OF THE EAP FOR ADDITIONAL SERVICES

In their presentation of the core technologies, Roman and Blum (1985, 1988) emphasized the vital importance of micro- and macrolinkages between EAPs and outside counseling, treatment, and other resources. In microlinkages, "the individual case is the focal point of this technique, which calls upon the EAP specialist's skills in creating efficient and effective linkages between each troubled employee and treatment/counseling services in the community" (1988, p. 20). Macrolinkages are "the result of a continued pattern of community-resource usage. It calls upon the skills of an EAP coordinator to create and utilize a management information system based on employee use of different services relative to their clinical conditions and job circumstances" (p. 21).

Embodied within these two core technologies is an important truth about EAP work that is easy to overlook: An EAP's effectiveness is directly linked to the effectiveness of the service providers in its resources network. Because EAPs are primarily a case management function, they must rely heavily on external resources to provide the therapeutic interventions that lead to behavioral changes in troubled employees. Consequently, an EAP's ability to select resource providers appropriate to the organization's employees and their problems and to engage employees in these services is crucial to the program's ultimate success.

A common frustration among EA professionals has been the perceived erosion of their own effectiveness because of managed care, which often limits an EAP's ability to screen and to select resource providers. Fortunately, new cooperative relationships between EAPs and managed care organizations have mitigated many of these concerns.

Furthermore, market pressures during the past several years have prompted managed care organizations to focus attention on the quality of their providers' services. This focus is evident today by the development of clinical-outcomes measurement systems that managed care organizations hope will show their effectiveness in reducing costs without sacrificing quality (see Donchez, 1997).

Four separate performance measures can be used to track EAP processes associated with referral of employees for additional services:

1. Overall Referral Rate.
2. Referral Acceptance Rate.
3. Referral Follow-through Rate.
4. Services Completion Rate.

These four measures mark steps in an employee's participation in the additional services that the EAP recommends. The sequence begins with the EA professional's determination of whether the employee needs assistance beyond that which was provided during the initial assessment, and, if successful, the sequence ends when the employee completes the EAP-recommended services.

Overall Referral Rate

Overall Referral Rate (ORR) provides a starting point for understanding EAP referral processes and is defined as:

$$ORR = \frac{\text{Cases that were given recommendations}}{\text{Employee cases}} \times 100\%$$

where "Cases that were given recommendations" = Number of employee cases to which the EAP gave at least one outside referral recommendation

"Employee cases" = Number of employee cases that the EAP opened during the reporting year

This performance measure tracks the percentage of cases that are given referral recommendations for additional assistance outside the EAP. These outside recommendations might include self-help groups and community-based service agencies and practitioners, as well as departments or services external to the EAP but still within the employee's organization.

In programs adhering to a strict assessment-and-referral model, ORRs often exceed 90% because the only employees not referred are those who decline all assistance or whose problems are resolved during the assessment process itself. For many internal programs, however, referral rates are frequently much lower than 90% (often between 50% and 75%) because they opt for providing in-house short-term counseling as an alternative to referral or because they have in place models that allow for three, five, or eight sessions, which is often sufficient time to resolve many employees' problems.

The question of whether it is to an EAP's advantage to provide in-house counseling has not yet been answered by research or by sound economic analysis of its potential cost-saving value. Roman (1992a, 1992b) argued that provision of short-term counseling presents grave risks to EAPs because of an intrinsic conflict of interest, increased vulnerability to litigation, licensing concerns, and diversion of staff away from providing core EAP services. Until this issue is resolved, appropriate benchmarks for ORR must be established on an individual program basis, taking into consideration its implicit- or explicit-services delivery model.

Referral Acceptance Rate

Once the EA professional has determined that additional assistance is appropriate, he or she must then motivate the client to accept the services that have been recommended. This step can be tracked with a *Referral Acceptance Rate* (RAR) performance measure defined as:

$$RAR = \frac{\text{Cases that accepted recommendations}}{\text{Cases that were given recommendations}} \times 100\%$$

where "Cases that accepted recommendations" = Number of employee cases that accepted at least one of the EAP's outside referral recommendations

"Cases that were given recommendation" = Number of employee cases to which the EAP gave at least one outside referral recommendation

RAR is expressed as a percentage of those referred cases (as specified previously in the ORR) that accept at least one of the EAP's referrals. *Acceptance* is defined as the client's expressed willingness, during the assessment interview or interviews, to seek assistance at the agency, the practitioner, or the service recommended. At this step in the sequence of participation, whether the employee will actually follow through with the recommendation is unknown.

In recent years, managed care and health maintenance organizations have complicated the referral process because these organizations often must grant approval for the EAP-recommended services. This makes the EA professional's job more difficult now than in the past because he or she must convince both clients and approving organizations of the appropriateness of the recommendations. To establish benchmark figures for RAR, therefore, EAPs must consider their unique relationships with partner managed care and health maintenance organizations.

Referral Follow-through Rate

As EA professionals know all too well, some employees express a willingness to seek additional help but never actually engage in the services that have been recommended. This prompts definition of a third performance measure in the participation sequence, *Referral Follow-through Rate* (RFR):

$$RFR = \frac{\text{Cases that contacted recommendations}}{\text{Cases that accepted recommendations}} \times 100\%$$

where "Cases that contacted recommendations" = Number of employee cases
       that followed through with
       and initiated contact at the
       accepted outside EAP
       referral recommendations

"Cases that accepted recommendations" Number of employee cases
       that accepted at least one of
       the EAP's outside referral
       recommendations

The phrase "followed through with and initiated contact at" in the definition of RFR means that the employee attended at least the first session or appointment at the EAP-recommended service. Because this performance measure tracks the next step in the employee's participation in services, its denominator is identical to the numerator for the previous RAR measure.

The RFR performance measure emphasizes that employees can drop out at many points along the continuum of help seeking and that EA professionals have primary responsibility for ensuring that they do not. In an ideal world, all clients would follow through with their service plans; hence, the ideal benchmark for RFR would be 100%. Unfortunately, EAPs are prevented from achieving this level of performance by such real-world constraints as benefits coverage limits and outside influences that change an employee's motivation to seek help. RFR allows EA professionals to track the impact of these constraints and then to take corrective actions to remove them whenever possible.

Services Completion Rate

Many employees who begin treatment or services do not finish them. This suggests the fourth and final performance measure for tracking an employee's participation in services, the *Services Completion Rate* (SCR) defined as:

$$SCR = \frac{\text{Cases that completed services}}{\text{Cases that contacted recommendations}} \times 100\%$$

where "Cases that completed services" = Number of employee cases that
       completed the accepted outside
       services recommended by the EAP

"Cases that contacted recommendations" = Number of employee cases that
       followed through with and initiated
       contact at the accepted outside
       EAP referral recommendations

This performance measure tracks the percentage of cases that completed all of the EAP-recommended services that were accepted by the client. For benchmarking purposes, one should calculate SCR at a standard follow-up period of 1 year after each employee's EAP initial-assessment date. For treatment plans with long-term follow-up or continuing-care components, SCR can be calculated using the employee's level of participation in treatment on the 1-year, follow-up date.

SCR and the three preceding performance measures do not themselves measure the effects of the EAP-recommended services: They merely track the program's ability to keep employees engaged in services. Standard workplace outcome measures are required to determine the impact of EAPs on the actual behavior of troubled employees (Roman, 1990). The EA field must wait for the development of these standard outcome performance measures before advancing to the next level of benchmarking.

CONCLUSION

Benchmarking is a valuable methodology that belongs in every EAP's quality-improvement tool chest. The benchmarking performance measures presented in this chapter are formulated based on the EAP core technologies as presented by Roman and Blum (1985, 1988). Consequently, they track crucial EAP policies and procedures associated with problem-employee casefinding, participation by supervisors and other gatekeepers, and referral for additional services.

The metrics defined here are offered not as an all-inclusive list, but as a starting point to stimulate the development of a core set of benchmarking indicators that will stand the test of time. By establishing a common set of indicators, it is hoped that the EAP field will focus attention on identifying which policies and procedures are most effective and that, in time, a comprehensive set of employee assistance best practices will emerge based on solid benchmarking data.

REFERENCES

Amaral, T.M. (1986, October). *How important are supervisory referrals to the cost-effectiveness of an employee assistance program?* Paper presented at the Los Angeles chapter meeting of ALMACA.

Amaral, T.M., & Cross, S.H. (1988, November). *Cost-benefits of supervisory referrals.* Paper presented at the National Conference of ALMACA, Los Angeles.

Blum, T.C., & Roman, P.M. (1995). *Cost effectiveness and preventive implications of employee assistance programs* (DHHS Publication No. SMA 95-3053). Washington, DC: U.S. Government Printing Office.

Camp, R. (1989). *Benchmarking: The search for industry best practices that lead to superior performance.* Milwaukee, WI: American Society for Quality Control.

Conlin, P., Amaral, T.M., & Harlow, K. (1996). The value of EAP case management. *EAPA Exchange, 26*(3), 12–15.

Donchez, P.F. (1997, November). *Innovative method for improving outcome effectiveness of chemical dependency treatment.* Paper presented at the National Conference of EAPA, Baltimore.

Foster, B.J. (Ed.). (1994). TQM: What is your EAP bringing to the table? [Special issue]. *EAPA Exchange, 24*(3).

Googins, B.K. (1994). Missing the benchmark. *Employee Assistance, 7*(3), 13–14.

Korr, W.S., & Ruez, J.F. (1986). How employee assistance programs determine service utilization: A survey and recommendations. *Evaluation and Program Planning, 9,* 367–371.

Maiden, R.P. (Ed.). (1993). Total quality management in employee assistance programs [Special issue]. *Employee Assistance Quarterly, 8*(4).

Normand, J., Lempert, R.O., & O'Brien, C.P. (Eds.). (1994). *Under the influence? Drugs and the American work force.* Washington, DC: National Academy Press.

Roman, P.M. (1990). Seventh dimension: A new component is added to the EAP "core technology." *Employee Assistance, 2*(7), 8–9.

Roman, P.M. (1992a). Short-term counseling risks. *Employee Assistance, 4*(12), 10–12.

Roman, P.M. (1992b). The case against short-term treatment. *Employee Assistance, 5*(1), 10–11.

Roman, P.M., & Blum, T.C. (1985). The core technology of employee assistance programs. *ALMACAN, 15*(3), 8–9, 16, 18–19.

Roman, P.M., & Blum, T.C. (1988). The core technology of employee assistance programs: A reaffirmation. *ALMACAN, 18*(8), 17–22.

Spendolini, M.J. (1992). *The benchmarking book.* New York: American Management Association.

CHAPTER 10

Behavioral Risk Management: The Pathway to a New Generation of Workplace Services

RUDY M. YANDRICK

Employee assistance programs (EAPs) have a long and well-documented history of helping to restore productivity to substance abusers and to other employees with serious personal problems. In fact, some EAPs have been able to show that their clients have become *model* employees by experiencing less absenteeism and incurring lower healthcare costs after rehabilitation than nonclient employees.

Such findings are commendable, and they speak to the value that an EAP brings to its organization. However, the findings are limited in that the EAP's impact is felt almost exclusively among a company's highest-risk, "Pareto group" employees. Perhaps this is why, despite the apparent fact that EAPs have increased their presence over the past several decades among North American employers, other evidence suggests the field is not fully appreciated by employers for its importance as a productivity-enhancement tool. Specifically, many longtime observers of the field report that today's programs:

- Are poorly positioned in the structures of their host or client organizations, limiting their influence in department-wide or organization-wide problems.
- Are increasingly external models with little if any work-site presence.
- Have fewer and fewer work deficiency-based management referrals.
- Are often viewed by management more as a clinical practice or substance abuse program than a workplace service that optimizes organizational performance.
- Are increasingly reliant on public policy initiatives such as the Drug-Free Workplace Act and Department of Transportation testing regulations for sustenance.
- Are, as a result of these factors, financially undervalued.

Some business decision makers actually view EAPs as a function that increases healthcare costs! Clearly, there is a disconnect between what EAPs are or are intended to be and what many business decision makers perceive them to be. As the EAP field moves forward, it needs to have its value affirmed in the eyes of decision makers and, with a continuing trend toward employer demand for increasing services, to do so as part of a more comprehensive service-delivery mechanism. Behavioral risk management, which is a new operating paradigm for delivering workplace services that embodies a set of core workplace practices, does both.

This new paradigm accommodates the expansion of services delivered by EAPs and service providers that has occurred since the field originated in 1971. However, the services have been stacking on top of one another, often without benefit of a strategy for galvanizing them or for critically assessing which new services should be added and which should not. For example, many EAPs today offer managed behavioral healthcare services, long-term counseling, drug-free workplace activities, drug testing, work/family services, organizational development, or conflict management, or some combination of these. By contrast, there are few, if any, substance abuse–only programs left, and not many rely entirely upon assessment and referral as their only bread-and-butter service.

Instead of replying "yes, we can do that" to employer requests for new services, which often arise out of crisis situations, behavioral risk management provides a master plan that enables programs and service providers to assert, "There is a better way." By definition, *behavioral risk management* is the holistic management of behavioral issues that adversely impact work organizations. Behavioral risk management can be applied by EAPs as a next-generation set of workplace services that:

- Refocuses on workplace problems and deemphasizes clinical services.
- Addresses the broader range of behavior-related problems with which many workplace-focused programs—typically those that are either internal or external ones with local or regional service areas—deal.
- Builds on established practices that are codified in the Employee Assistance Certification Commission's Scope of Practice.

Behavioral risk management, then, neither replaces nor cannibalizes employee assistance; it facilitates the addition of workplace activities that continue the field's evolution. At the same time, it meets employer needs by:

- Positioning EAPs and other non-revenue-producing workplace services as loss-prevention specialists rather than experts in improving productivity. This distinction is critical because there are already many initiatives in the workplace to improve productivity, including geometric tolerancing, process mapping, 360° feedback technology, and many others. There are far fewer loss-control specialists, however. EAPs should help companies to understand that as they aim high for productivity and profit gains, they simultaneously need resources to prevent the organization from being eroded by behavioral losses from the bottom up.
- Offering solutions to the problems of a larger proportion of the worker population.
- Calling for a strong organizational focus and visible work-site presence.
- Continuing to move service delivery forward from early intervention toward prevention.
- Placing priority on those services that have visibility in the organization and whose results are experienced on the ground floor of the organization.

As a preview of discussions later in the chapter, among the solutions that will control behavioral risks (which are listed in Table 10.1) are a specialized audit of the organization, adoption of conduct criteria for earlier identification of high-risk employees in addition to those identified by work-performance deficiencies, use of conflict management services, training on behavioral change and related workplace issues, and introduction of a broadly applied critical-incident policy.

First, however, a brief primer will specify the workplace problems that are germane to behavioral risk management, will explain the five areas of intervention, and will describe how a new job classification now in its formative stage—the behavioral risk manager (BR Manager)—builds on existing EAP knowledges and skills.

A Brief Primer on Behavioral Risk Management

Several features make this workplace problem-prevention and problem-solving concept different from others. To parse the term *behavioral risk management,* behavior is the criterion for defining the work-related problems, and it takes three forms: (1) individual, (2) interpersonal/group, and (3) organizational. The three behaviors can be thought of as existing on a continuum. This understanding is essential because if behaviors are viewed as occurring only on the individual end of the continuum—where the behaviors are most visible, the losses are most easily quantified, and EAPs have traditionally intervened—the problems will often recycle themselves because the underlying interpersonal/group and organizational factors that induce the negative behaviors remain intact. This is often the case even after the individual problem is thought to be resolved by a change of personnel!

Interpersonal and group behaviors at work are increasingly a threat to organizational performance. This is evidenced by the continuing trend by companies of replacing vertically integrated management structures with horizontally integrated, team-oriented ones. This horizontal revolution elevates in importance the ability of groups of two or more workers to be able to communicate and to interact effectively, as well as to resolve problems that surface.

Although workplace interpersonal/group behavioral problems have always existed, in traditional environments the problems are often covert because of the unilateral decision-making authority of managers and supervisors. If the problem is not resolved to the satisfaction of the disputants, the problem becomes suppressed and can resurface as redirected communication, backbiting, favoritism and clique formation, an us-versus-them mentality between management and employees, and other residual forms of conflict that are usually nonconfrontational but equally divisive. This is most likely to be the case when the manager is one of the disputants, is a causative factor of the conflict, or is perceived to be biased in his or her decision making. In such a situation, the conflict and its resolution is shaped by the fact that at least one party in the dispute has power while another one does not.

In a work environment where there is not unilateral decision making, negotiation, or brokering of solutions by a manager, the interpersonal and group problems are more likely to be expressed overtly, meaning that the problem is more visible, is less likely to resurface in another form, and can be addressed more openly. In this situation, the locus of control in resolving interpersonal and group conflict also shifts, from the manager to the disputants themselves, who are called upon to put their problems on the table and to arrive at a mutually acceptable decision. The egalitarian relationship of the disputants gives rise to a need for an impartial, third-party intervenor.

Employers EAPs are increasingly asking to be that intervenor, both in horizontally integrated environments and, as is often the case today, in settings where management is striving to be less heavy-handed, more impartial, or more accommodating to employees. This intervention is made at the second point of the behavioral continuum—interpersonal and group behavioral problems. Compared with the role of assessor, the conflict intervenor must get a broader, multiple-perspective view of the problem, must remain neutral, and must safeguard against bias that can arise from empathizing with one of the parties at the expense of another.

Organizational behavior occupies the third, and final, point on the behavioral continuum. Organizational behaviors exist as inanimate policies and procedures that run an organization, as cultural phenomena that determine what it feels like for an employee to work in the organization, and as management policy-making practices.

How does an organization develop its behaviors? Consider the experiences of one company over several decades of sustained growth. It developed from a mom-and-pop operation into a company of over 1,000 people through a succession of business developments and execution of strategic plans. These developments included the owner's relinquishment of daily management and supervision in order to concentrate on marketing and sales, addition of new managers and employees when the company won its first major contract, departmentalization when the size of the organization reached about 40 employees, introduction of formalized personnel policies and procedures, changes in communication channels (such as increasing use of memos), introduction of a formalized human resources (HR) department, relocation to a larger facility, changeover to computerized equipment and Internet e-mail communication, development of short- and long-range plans, implementation of total quality management and reengineering initiatives, merger with another organization, establishment of a board of directors, opening of other facilities outside of the immediate locality with subsequent relocation of employees, offering of private stock, establishment of franchises, offering of public stock, sale of a division, and change of senior executive leadership.

Each change allowed the organization to grow, but it also allowed for the possibility of company-wide problems that could lead to increased behavioral risks and subsequent loss. Examples of systemic dysfunction that can arise from organizational change are the so-called *law of diminishing competence*—a pattern in which managers promote subordinates who are less competent than themselves in order to prop themselves up; a family-like codependent system in which coping mechanisms from elevated stress result in behavioral alterations; severed communication and feedback loops; emergence of enforcers who intimidate people in order to force compliance with a new culture and values; chronic turnover from people bailing out of a company that they consider to be a sinking ship; and a rash of accidents arising from employee preoccupation as a result of the stressful environment coupled with the presence of safety hazards. Under these circumstances, an organization that would otherwise continue to grow steadily and reliably will typically start performing at a suboptimal level.

Another distinguishing feature of behavioral risk (BR) management is the process by which problems are identified and resolved (see Figure 10.1), which is an adaptation of a generic risk management process. The five steps of the process are:

1. Identify the organization's behavior-related risks and determine what its risk exposures have been.
2. Take stock of current activities that affect risks and risk exposures.
3. Gather two sets of data that indicate or suggests (a) the individual, interpersonal and organizational risks and risk exposures, and (b) the effectiveness of behavioral risk management activities.

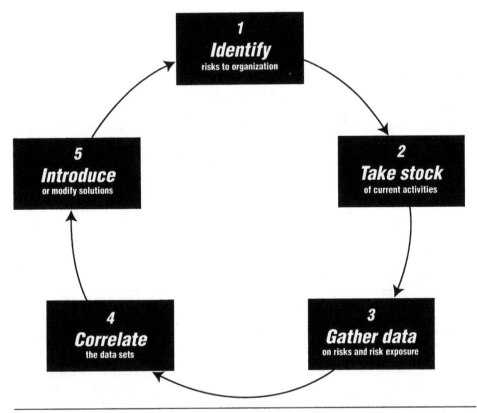

Figure 10.1   Yandrick's behavioral risk management process. (© 1999 by Rudy M. Yandrick.)

4. Correlate and analyze the data, looking for relationships between the two sets of measures.
5. Introduce (or modify existing) interventions.

Based on the five-step behavioral risk management process in *Behavioral Risk Management: How to Avoid Preventable Losses from Mental Health Problems in the Workplace,* Rudy M. Yandrick, San Francisco: Jossey-Bass Publishers, 1996, p. 18.

A third distinguishing feature of a BR management strategy is that it seeks to systematically progress from costly, late-stage intervention with behavioral problems to early intervention and finally to prevention. Characteristics of late-stage intervention include employee lawsuits, frequent and expensive treatment episodes for behavioral health problems, and a work culture that harbors inappropriate or destructive behaviors. Early interventions typically include some integration of programs and services, uneven management approaches to dealing with employee problems, and earlier identification of people with behavioral health problems. Preventive approaches include an integrated BR management strategy, a work culture that conscientiously looks after employee needs, and effective early interventions to behavioral problems. (*Secondary prevention* interventions, which are made after a behavioral problem sets in and seek to prevent further losses, such as those due to a problem recycling itself, are considered to be early interventions.)

THE BEHAVIORAL RISK AUDIT

The first step in the BR management process is to identify the risks to the organization and determine what its risk exposures have been, which is accomplished by a behavioral risk audit. Those that cut across nearly all organizations are listed in Table 10.1. Others may be added that are endemic to a particular industry or organization.

Some measuring instruments now in use by workers' compensation insurers, management consultants, and others measure only actual losses, such as work days lost due to absenteeism. These instruments help employers to quantify the amount of productivity and of financial loss. That information is then used to recommend to employers interventions that can be used to resolve the problem. Such an instrument is deficient in that it doesn't provide information about the root causes. How effective can the interventions be when there is not a clearcut understanding about the causes of the problems?

Other instruments available to employers, such as manager and employee surveys, yield qualitative results. Such perspective-based findings show underlying attitudes

Table 10.1 Behavioral Problems in the Workplace

Behavioral Risks	Business Losses	Risk Factors
Excessive turnover	Recruitment and replacement costs for turnover	*Personal Factors*
Preventable accidents	Excessive lost-work-time costs	Lack of lifestyle and health management
Theft, sabotage, and blackmail	Excessive benefit costs for behavioral healthcare and medical healthcare due to lifestyle factors	Social and family problems
Self-medication with food, alcohol, and other substances		Poor attitudes toward employer, work, or supervisor
Emotional and psychological problems, including workaholism and other compulsive behaviors	Cost of supervisor time spent handling employee behavioral problems	Poor communications and other interpersonal skills
Malingering and procrastination while on disability	Poor productivity and other inefficiencies	Exhaustion and lack of concentration
Excessive or pattern absenteeism	Equipment or property damage costs	Racial or gender bias
Interpersonal and group conflict	Lost business	*Organizational Factors*
Violence	Regulatory compliance costs	High-demand, low-control jobs
Employee lawsuits	Legal costs	Poor internal communications
Disruptive behavior		Lack of management-employee trust
Racial and gender bias		Lack of a supportive organizational culture
		Lack of supportive programs, services, and benefits
		Sustained high level of organizational stress
		Lack of controls in hiring and promotion
		Tolerance of confrontational or avoidance work behaviors
		Dysfunctional and untrusting relationships among managers and employees
		Dysfunctional work teams
		Unsafe or overly stressful working conditions
		Continuous crisis management

and other factors that precede behavioral problems, and the findings reveal areas where managers and employees have strongly differing views. For example, those views might pertain to beliefs about whether management hears and is responsive to the concerns of rank-and-file employees.

A well-designed BR audit instrument should include both quantitative and qualitative indicators so that the data can be juxtaposed to establish relationships. To illustrate, indicators of workplace violence that assess both actual losses and the risk factors include:

- The number and severity of violent acts of the company, the work site, or the work unit (quantitative).
- The number of reported threats (quantitative).
- The beliefs among managers and employees about whether the threat of violence is imminent, moderate but increasing, moderate but decreasing, or remote. If a great disparity exists between manager and employee feedback, there may be additional risks in the area of employee-management relations (qualitative).
- The incidence of supervisor-supervisor, supervisor-employee, and employee-employee conflicts (qualitative), which is a major cause of workplace violence.

According to the Society of Human Resource Management, 62% of violent incidents have a personality conflict as a causative factor ("Workplace Violence," a survey report, Alexandria, Va., 1996).

The BR audit should also accommodate indicators of business performance, such as output per employee, missed deadlines, work defects, and revenues. There may be other behavioral risk exposures to the organization, but they should always be considered vis-a-vis structural and operational problems, where other factors—or in research parlance, confounding variables—come into play. Although there are likely to be multiple variables involved in business performance, repeated audits—performed across an organization or operating unit perhaps twice a year—may reveal patterns suggesting losses due to behavioral risk exposure.

Once the data are gathered, they should be correlated and analyzed to find relationships among the risk exposure, risk factor, and business-performance data. Employers can turn to implementing solutions. Just as the problems are holistic in their manifestation, the solutions need to be systemic. In such a system, the solutions fall into five general categories:

1. *Programs and services,* which are intervention tools for problems at the interpersonal and group level.
2. *Organizational culture development,* which involves adjusting various workplace "levers" to influence how employees perceive their relationship to the work organization. Organizational culture is the composite response to the question, "What does it feel like to work here?"
3. *Policies and procedures,* which support the culture through management and organizational directives.
4. *Training,* which educates managers and employees about how behavioral risks manifest in the context of both the work environment and their personal lives.
5. *Benefits,* which provide pathways to help outside of the organization for people with behavioral health problems.

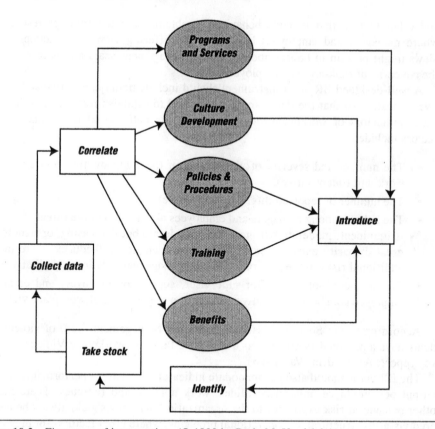

Figure 10.2   Five areas of intervention. (© 1999 by Rudy M. Yandrick.)

Figure 10.2 relates the solutions to the five steps of the behavioral risk management process.

BUILDING A BEHAVIORAL RISK PROGRAM

The use of BR management as an operating paradigm gives rise to many questions: Who is the *process owner?* To whom does that person report? Does the program have a central administrative function, or is it, in effect, a confederacy of services? Does it have a core set of practices that constitute the heart of a discipline? Does it have a centralized data management system? How is it integrated with the organization?

In order to achieve its full potential, the application of BR management needs to have an identifiable leader and a discrete, programmatic entity—the individual and office to whom behavioral risk problems can be taken—regardless of whether the delivery of services is performed by individuals and groups who are internal or external to the organization. A behavioral risk program (herein called "BR Program") should be positioned in the organization as independently as possible. It should have a process owner, the BR Manager, who at a minimum is the central point of contact for management, coordinates the deployment of services in the organization, manages information, and protects confidential information.

The BR Manager is a natural outgrowth of the position of EAP manager, just as a BR Program is a logical next step for an EAP. The BR Manager will function best not as a part of the formal management chain of command, because the individual is privy to confidential and other sensitive information that can be pursued by other managers (some of them with higher rank and able to exert influence), but as an independently positioned function. The person ideally reports to a senior-level manager in the company, who is likely to have less interest in the behavioral problems of individual employees than a manager who is situated closer to line operations. Consistent with the five steps of the BR management process, the BR Manager should have the ability to perform a BR audit or to direct the activities of an independent consultant who can, in addition to correlating the audit's datasets, introduce or modify solutions to the organization, and assess progress by performing a follow-up audit. Whereas a company might expect to have an internal EAP manager if it has 3,000 to 4,000 full-time employee equivalents (FTEs), a company with even 1,500 to 2,000 FTEs should consider an internal BR Manager.

A BR Program should be designed to attack problems at all three points on the behavioral risk continuum. Fortunately, this can be done by expanding on the activities of an existing EAP. In this respect, of the five areas of intervention cited in the previous section, the BR management process will be driven by the programs-and-services area of intervention, from which the other four areas of intervention will be impacted. Under this scenario, training is recommended as an activity for BR Program staff, and the BR Manager can provide coaching support to managers and teams in the area of management processes. Further, the BR Manager can provide organizational consultation in the areas of culture development, benefits, and noncoaching aspects of management processes, such as policy development.

As an EAP expands its services to become a full-fledged BR Program, it needs to focus on (1) expanding services to intervene at the interpersonal/group and organizational points of the behavioral continuum and (2) developing expertise in the delivery of new programs and services and in the other four areas of intervention.

For reasons cited earlier, the most powerful way of intervening with interpersonal and group problems is by adding conflict management services. Examples of conflict areas are employee-on-employee, employee-on-supervisor, supervisor-on-supervisor, team-on-team, department-on-department, and professional staff versus rank-and-file.

Some EAPs have already integrated problem assessment and conflict management, doing so because companies increasingly are recognizing that conflict is a destructive, insidious problem that, if ignored, can lead to significant loss for the organization and can leave a residual aftertaste with employees for years. It also, by necessity, involves the program staff in the everyday affairs of the organization. (This is contrasted with activities such as behavioral health case management, which can be provided with little or no workplace presence or interaction.) With their assessment skills, EAP professionals often find that one or more disputants in a conflict is experiencing elevated personal and emotional problems, which may be related to home or work life or both. In a personality conflict, for instance, problems at home may be taken out on a coworkers. (The reverse is also true.) Periodic stressors such as this can give rise to conflicts that recycle themselves if no intervention is made.

Exacerbating interpersonal conflict is the fact that most co-worker relationships are arranged marriages, of sorts—management directs who will work with whom and sets the ground rules for how the work will be accomplished. These two or more coworkers, then, will spend more time together during the work week than with their spouses—

even though they might not otherwise consider socializing with that person or people. It is little wonder, then, that conflicts arise, even if the work environment is stable and doesn't instigate conflict, such as through continuous crisis management!

With information that a BR Manager receives through problem assessments and conflict interventions, as well as the rich data derived from periodic BR audits, he or she is positioned to be an internal consultant with unique insights to the organization. If an organization is thought of as a garden, the BR Manager not only views the flora above ground, but also knows the root system below ground. In the work organization, then, the BR Manager may be knowledgeable about problems before they become visible to others! With this depth of understanding about the organization, over time the BR Manager can become an increasingly relied upon player on an organizational transition team.

With what types of organizational problems can a BR Manager expect to have useful information and be able to play a constructive role? Start with those problems that come to the EAP's attention. In 1998, 25 experienced EAP managers were surveyed about the organizational problems they saw as a result of confidential employee assessments. Their top 10 responses were:

1. Chaos and stress arising from organizational change and downsizing.
2. Poor communication vertically and laterally in the organization.
3. Lack of effective leadership or managerial skills.
4. Poor line manager and employee relations.
5. Short-term business solutions at the expense of a long-term company vision.
6. Lack of work performance and conduct accountability.
7. Lack of supervisor and employee training and development.
8. Lack of human resource expertise and support programs.
9. Excessive work demands.
10. Favoritism by management and unevenly applied policies.

The data would undoubtedly be enriched by additional information produced by a BR audit and as a result of conflict interventions, which provide new vantage points.

Another core BR service is the ombuds, or ombudsman. The ombuds intercedes with conflicts that exist between a worker or a group of workers and the organization itself. The ombuds seeks to clarify issues and offer possible solutions. The final core service, executive intervention, is fundamentally the same as problem assessment, except for the fact that executives are in highly sensitive and political positions in their organizations, and their decisions usually have organization-wide implications and are not localized in impact to a particular department, work group, or project. Furthermore, executives reach their positions of influence as a result of an organization's business priorities and its hiring and promotion practices. Therefore, executive interventions are more appropriately situated on the organizational end of the behavioral risk continuum than on the individual end.

Examples of other BR management interventions are found in Table 10.2. These activities can be provided in addition to the aforementioned core services, depending on the interests of organizational decision makers and on findings from the behavioral risk audit.

Table 10.2   Recommended Behavioral Risk Program Activities

- Behavioral risk audit
- Case identification activities
  — Consultation with and coaching for line managers on how to approach problem employees.
  — Consultation/coaching managers and work teams on using the conflict resolution resource.
  — Constructive confrontation.
  — Peer or team-member confrontation.
- Interventions to individual behaviors
  — Problem assessment (core activity).
  — Consultation on work/family conflict issues.
  — Problem solving or referral.
  — Reintegration of worker following behavioral health counseling or treatment.
- Interventions to interpersonal and group behaviors
  — Assessment of behavioral problems on work teams and in work units.
  — Conflict intervention (core activity).
  — Diversity-based mediation.
  — Mentoring (in participatory work environments).
  — Critical incident debriefing.
- Interventions to organizational behavioral problems
  — Ombuds (core activity).
  — Executive interventions (core activity).
  — Humor programming and other creative stress-reduction activities.
  — Consultation on organizational development issues (core activity).
- Specialized interventions
  — Workers' compensation case management.
    - Periodic offers of support to injured worker.
    - Reintegration of employee into workplace.
- Training
  — Understanding organizational behavioral change (for board members and senior management).
  — Constructive confrontation of employees with problems (for line managers).
  — Effective communication and interaction (for line managers and workers).
  — Stages of permanent behavioral change (for line managers and workers).
  — The relapsing nature of behavioral change (for line managers and workers).
  — Resiliency during continuous organizational change (for line managers and workers).
  — Ways to access helping resources (for workers).

Other interventions
These activities can potentially position the BR program in an adversarial role to the employee and therefore may best be conducted by an individual not affiliated with the program.

- Preemployment testing, such as personality or integrity tests.
- Substance abuse testing.
- Preauthorization and utilization review of behavioral health treatment cases.
- Fitness-for-duty testing.

STRUCTURING THE BR PROGRAM

An employee assistance program or service provider may ask, how can a BR Program build onto an existing EAP? Although much depends on program size and staff composition, a BR Program may wish to be structurally segmented into three divisions: Employee Behavioral Risk Services, Organizational Behavioral Risk Services, and Management Consultative Services. Each of the divisions may have its own dedicated staff and information management system that is integrated only at the level of senior program management, particularly the BR Manager.

Employee Behavioral Risk Services would include confidential employee assessment and referral, conflict interventions, work/family consultation, and specialized services provided at the employee level, including support services for workers out on disability.

Organizational Behavioral Risk Services can include consultation on organizational culture development and management processes, executive intervention, work-team development, and other areas that impact behavioral risks departmentally, across a worksite, divisionally, or organization-wide.

Management Consultative Services can include all BR training and coaching activities; consultation on behavioral health, benefit-plan development; data generation such as from BR audits and program evaluation; account management; and internal administrative and operational activities.

One procedural issue that a BR Program will need to resolve with the employer and the employer's managed behavioral health care (MBHC) provider is that of preauthorization, continuing care, and discharge planning of clients with behavioral health problems for which the employer's health plan needs to be accessed. In such cases, the BR Program may wish to seek a "bypass agreement" that will allow access to the benefit plan without preauthorization from the MBHC provider. The BR Program may need to have a well-placed senior manager in the organization intercede in this matter because it may involve negotiation with the employer's benefits department.

Because the BR Program focuses on the workplace, it may wish to transfer responsibility for problem assessment of family members to the MBHC provider, with the possible exception of situations where a family member's problems have a direct linkage to the employee's performance problems. In such a case, collaboration between the BR Program and MBHC provider may be to the advantage of both the employee and the family.

Protecting Client Confidentiality

Issues of confidentiality are more critical in a BR Program than in an EAP setting. Problem assessment services are confidential. Conflict interventions are usually quasi-confidential in that the problems are generally visible to other people in the organization, although the private discussions with the intervenor (and EAP, if there is a subsequent cross-referral of one or more of the disputants) usually are not. Executive interventions are confidential, as well.

EAP professionals will no doubt ask, "With the behavioral risk management model and its multiple levels of confidential services, how can client confidentiality be protected?" This question is critical because the same client may be seeing the EAP and may be involved in a conflict intervention. One solution is to assign a different staff person for each service and to maintain separate files for problem assessment and conflict interventions (which are in the same division of the aforementioned BR Program structure) and another file for executive interventions (which is in a separate division). In some cases, it may be desirable for BR Program staff to recuse themselves from executive intervention, for example, when there is a linkage between the BR Program and the reporting structure, when the technique and objective of the intervention is contrary to corporate philosophy, or when the politics of the organization pose a conflict of interest.

As a further precaution to prevent accidental leakage of confidential information, the BR Manager can incorporate into the Program's management information system walls through which only she or he has authorization to pass. As BR management continues to grow as a mainstream workplace practice, more detailed confidentiality standards that cover a range of situations will be needed.

Integration of the Behavioral Risk Service with Other Workplace Functions

A BR Program needs to be well integrated with other workplace delivery systems for optimal positioning, benefit, and visibility in the organization, regardless of whether the program is managed internally or externally or the services are delivered internally or externally. Among the other delivery systems with which a BR Program can integrate are:

- *Performance management,* involving the HR department and line management.
- *Disability management,* involving Medical, HR, Vocational Rehabilitation, occupational nurses, managed care, and providers of rehabilitation services.
- *Theft deterrence,* involving Security, Risk Management, and Legal.
- *Litigation prevention,* involving Legal and Risk Management.
- *Labor relations,* involving HR and union representatives.

The BR Program can become involved in each of these other service-delivery systems either as a consultant or as a person who provides specialized, behavior-related interventions, or as both. In the area of disability management, for example, the BR Program can serve as a voice to management advocating better integration of disability services; it can be a resource both to prevent malaise from setting in with the injured worker (which is a deterrent to the behavioral risks of malingering and procrastination in the return to work) and to serve as a return-to-work facilitator who does periodic follow-ups (which is a deterrent to the risk of disability syndrome).

Three Case Studies

To illustrate BR management in action, here are case studies of three behavioral problems: one each of individual, interpersonal/group, and organizational problems. The case studies will bring to light how BR interventions can offer a more balanced, multidimensional view of the problems.

Case 1: Individual Behavioral Problem

Susan was an eighth-year employee who was a steady performer for the organization. Her attendance and performance records were consistently high. During the fourth year, she was promoted to a low-level management position, one without the authority to discipline, promote, hire, or terminate workers. In this position, she began to have panic attacks due to the daily pressure of production deadlines and to her frustration in dealing with other employees' problems. Her condition was compounded by the fact that, as a single mother, her teenage son recently had become part of an unruly crowd and was being rebellious. She also fluctuated between self-medicating with food and dieting while visiting a health spa. Over time, though, her weight increased.

Concerned about her panic attacks, Susan visited the EAP, which referred her to a psychiatrist, who prescribed medication for her. Susan was demoted after 6 months—a mutual decision between her and her supervisor—and eventually moved to a different department. But her behavioral health condition only intensified instead of diminishing following the demotion and transfer. She complained to the psychiatrist that she felt like she was on an accelerating merry-go-round and unable to jump off.

Case 2: Interpersonal/Group Behavioral Problem

An attractive but physically imposing woman had a verbal disagreement with a male coworker over the use of a microwave oven during lunch. She verbally attacked and repeatedly slapped the coworker, who was known to irritate his coworkers because of his idiosyncratic behavior and effeminate voice and mannerisms. The woman also had a reputation as being exploitive, aggressive, and glib. Further, she admittedly used sex in prior employment situations to obtain favors and advancements from male managers.

Several people were witness to the slapping incident, including a contract employee who provided technical support to the organization. The shift supervisor, who on prior occasions had shielded the imposing woman from others whom she had offended, seemed determined to protect her from the consequences of her actions. In fact, he advised two of his subordinates to not report the incident to corporate human resources, and he blackmailed the technical support person with threat of loss of contract.

Other employees did not see the incident but heard about it from the two coworkers. One employee discussed the incident with the site manager but was advised, "What happened is none of your business." Eventually the employees found out that two layers of sexual blackmail existed: (1) the female employee had information on her supervisor that prevented him from disciplinary action against her; and (2) the supervisor had information on the site manager that prevented him from taking action against the supervisor.

Case 3: Organizational Behavior Problem

A company had numerous internal issues that contributed to people problems throughout the organization. It had poor hiring practices, using a temporary agency with minimal screening standards to meet its personnel needs; problems between its three shifts; high turnover, especially among highly educated, and professional and technical staff; persistent employee threats of litigation; a prior contract devaluation with the company's primary customer because of quality defects; interpersonal clashes and production problems resulting from information management specialists who did not communicate computer system changes with the operators who used the software; and many boring jobs that failed to keep people's minds occupied and that contributed to various forms of self-medication, such as food and alcohol. During spurts of heavy workload and deadline pressure, mild conflict between workers intensified.

These three actual behavioral risk situations did not occur in separate organizations; they were a part of the same 250-person production site that was part of a major corporation. These examples illustrate how different the behavioral problems of a company can look from various perspectives—yet the problems are all related.

Solutions to the Three Sets of Problems

With a behavioral risk strategy, all three sets of problems can be addressed comprehensively instead of each in isolation. In Susan's case, a structured behavioral risk solution could include education on human resilience, behavioral change, and time management (such as through behavioral risk training for all employees or through referral of Susan to a community resource); and one-on-one problem solving with the EAP for both work and personal problems. Supervisor training and coaching, along with a periodic, visible work-site presence (perhaps with two office hours, three times a week), might have augmented a self-referral by Susan before her anxiety reached a state wherein psychoactive medication was necessary. Additionally, her son could have been referred to a group teen-counseling program. Finally, a more supportive work culture that addresses the organizational behavior problems in the third case study and that reduces workplace stress could have helped control her anxiety problem.

In Case 2, the company took no remedial steps to rectify the injustices caused by the female employee, her supervisor, and the site manager. Had conflict management services been available—services that included individual problem assessments as part of the intervention—the injustices that prevailed could have been proactively addressed. Furthermore, they might have been avoided because the persons involved would know that the company was vigilant against aggression and sexual perpetration.

The perpetrating employee might also have been identified for intervention if the company had a broadly applied critical incident policy that was promoted throughout the organization. Such a policy, whose purpose is to minimize the damage caused by potentially trauma-producing events, should be broad enough to flag situations in which a potentially serious workplace problem could lead to a critical incident and to flag actual incidents whose aftermath could include emotional and psychological trauma. In this case, *other* nonmanagement employees could have sought to invoke the policy. These indicators and events include:

- Physical violence or threat of physical violence.
- Injury or accident while on duty.
- Physical or mental impairment, from mild to gross.
- Bizarre conversation or behavior.
- Threats of suicide.
- Sudden death of a coworker.
- Intimidating, threatening, or abusive language or behavior.

In Case 3, had the BR Manager been part of an organizational development team that makes constructive change, the myriad problems in the work setting could have been reduced. For example, a BR audit would have produced data that quantify the losses, identify underlying risk factors not necessary visible on the surface of the organization, and foretell the likelihood of future behavioral problems.

From a business standpoint, this company did not face imminent threat of extinction from these problems. It was, in fact, a company that had a track record of mediocre performance and whose risk exposures were typical of those of other employers. Nevertheless, it could have significantly improved its loss control with a BR Program. Furthermore, if the industry experienced a new influx of competition or required rapid change with the advent of new technology, it would have had difficulty motivating a demoralized workforce to quickly respond to change. In order for this company to become a world-class organization—as senior management said was its want—it would have to be more proactive in controlling its behavioral risks.

How ready is an EAP to become a BR Program? Some questions that should be asked are:

- Does the EAP have a consistent work-site presence?

- Do EAP staff know and are they known by the production managers or work teams?

- Are the new services that the EAP provides ones that impact daily productivity and the overall performance of the organization?

- When a departmental or interdepartmental problem of a behavioral nature occurs, is the EAP called in?

- Does the EAP definition of *success* include nontraditional performance criteria such as reductions in injured-worker time on disability, in number of employee lawsuits, in absenteeism and turnover rates, and in excessive healthcare claims for employee lifestyle-related diagnoses, and qualitative measures such as the belief that management does not intervene effectively in disputes between employees and that the organization faces a high risk of violence?

- Does the EAP regularly have formal and ad hoc meetings with representatives of other workplace delivery systems such as performance management, disability management, and safety management? Is the EAP involved in their strategic planning initiatives?

- Is the EAP one of the first or one of the last programs to fall victim to budget cuts?

BEHAVIORAL RISK MANAGERS NEED KNOWLEDGE-AND-SKILL SETS

In order to transition from an EAP to a BR management operating paradigm, EAP managers will need new knowledge-and-skill sets. BR management addresses a wider spectrum of workplace issues than does traditional employee assistance. This has two implications for EAP professionals. First, BR management provides greater career development without having to move into another workplace discipline, such as HR management. Second, related to the acquisition of new knowledge and skills, BR management will also lead to greater curricula development in higher education.

There has been a conspicuous lack of EA degree programs in higher education. By and large, the pinnacle of EAP educational achievement is either a continuing education certificate program or an EAP specialization as part of another graduate curriculum, such as human services. As a rapidly evolving, highly specialized field requiring a broader knowledge and skill base than that of employee assistance, BR management will increasingly interest colleges and universities as a discipline worthy of its own graduate-level degree program.

There are at least 11 recommended knowledge-and-skill sets for employee assistance professionals interested in becoming full-fledged BR Managers. They include Problem Solving and Intervention Skills, Workplace Knowledge, Risk Management, Organizational Development, Training and Consultation, Business and Professional Ethics, Information Management, Program Administration, Community Resource Development, Public Policy, and Other Specialized Knowledges. These sets include all of those encompassing traditional EAP practice and others required for delivery of BR services.

The following overview was prepared in collaboration with Elizabeth Miceli, MS, LSW, a corporate human resource director, behavioral management and program development consultant, and mental health clinician in New Cumberland, Pennsylvania.

Intervention and Problem-Solving Skills

This skill set involves the use of techniques to address personal and interpersonal/group behavioral problems, as well as methods for coaching supervisors and team leaders who must deal with subordinates or coworkers about the problems. These techniques include such traditional EAP practices as constructive confrontation, supervisor referrals, and peer interventions, as well as new ones that are necessary for the delivery of BR services.

Personal Behavioral Problems

Counseling and clinical skills can be helpful with the problem-assessment and referral processes and in any case-management activities following referral to the treatment community. Additionally, a degree, certification, or licensure in a mental health discipline can provide a measure of protection against malpractice claims, given the litigiousness of U.S. society today, as well as safeguard confidentiality obligations that are espoused in codes of ethics or of professional conduct in the mental health disciplines.

However, mental health diagnosis, treatment, and use of pharmaceuticals is often overemphasized in EAP practice today at the expense of focusing on behavioral change. Because the assessment process limits the identification of the problem behavior and the motivation of the person to change it, the client does not stigmatize herself or himself as having an illness, or a disorder, or a disability, that might be used to excuse his or her own behavior; nor is the client stigmatized by others as being mental, unbalanced, or damaged goods. Thus, behavioral change should be the primary goal of the intervention, and referral to the treatment community should focus on detoxification, stabilization, and education about obsessive, compulsive, and addictive behaviors. One eating disorders clinic used the slogan, "You're not alone, it's not your fault." Rather than a slogan that addressed the issue of who's to blame, a better one would be, "Others have successfully recovered, so can you."

To illustrate the distinction between a mental health orientation and a behavioral orientation to workplace problems, the *Wall Street Journal* broke a story in 1996 about an airline pilot who was known to "fly off the handle." According to the article, over the course of several years, this former Marine Corps drill instructor threatened to kill both himself and his wife, was ordered committed to a locked psychiatric ward for evaluation, had a screaming cockpit argument with his flight engineer, and had a profane argument with a copilot over a dinner bill, which was heard over the intercom by passengers including a Federal Aviation Administration (FAA) inspector. The pilot was a self-avowed alcoholic and was variously diagnosed by psychiatrists as having dysthymic disorder involving bouts of depression, "narcissistic personality disorder with compulsive traits," and "intermittent explosive disorder." He was grounded on several occasions, but neither the FAA nor the airline could keep him grounded, in part because in other evaluations he was found fit to fly. It appeared to the reader of the article that the pilot was adept at changing his behavior and at manipulating the diagnostic evaluations in order to retain his pilot's license and continue flying.

Perhaps the best diagnosis by one of the psychiatrists quoted in the article was that the pilot was "stubborn, pompous, self-centered, domineering, belligerent, and aggressively intimidating." These were not psychiatric diagnoses, but behavioral descriptions! Further, his behavior, which was not in dispute, might have kept him grounded had the FAA and the airline based its decisions on conduct criteria instead of evaluations that led psychiatrists to recommend differing courses of action. To make a further point favoring the use of conduct criteria, as many EAP professionals have long known, threat of job loss is often the most effective motivation for reforming counterproductive pattern behavior. Particularly for male employees, the common EAP wisdom is that threat of loss of job is a more motivating factor for behavioral change than is loss of family. (For women, loss of relationships is the greater motivating factor for accepting help, according to conventional wisdom. However, this may be changing as more women strongly identify with their jobs and careers.)

One can conjecture from the article that the pilot may have rationalized that any threat of job loss using conduct criteria could be circumvented by manipulating the outcome of psychiatric evaluations on which the company and the FAA ultimately relied. This is not to suggest that that pilot did not have a psychiatric disorder or that he should not have been treated for the conditions. Consideration as to whether he should fly or be grounded, however, should have been based first and foremost on conduct and work performance criteria.

For a BR Manager, knowledge from the pages of behavioral science will be at least as useful as psychological or psychiatric know-how. The following is an overview of clinical and behavioral knowledge, presented in the form of descriptions of three suggested graduate-level, three-credit courses. The descriptions assume that a BR staff member will not be assigning diagnoses to clients, performing intensive clinical case management, or doing psychological evaluations as part of fitness-for-duty examinations.

Biopsychosocial Foundations of Assessment (in two parts)

This course will strengthen skills necessary for early intervention. Course content will explore general systems theory as a foundation for effective interviewing during the intake process. The intake process is very important in comprehensively assessing the presenting and underlying problems, as well as the particular personal-life circumstances of the individual seeking help. Knowledge sets include the signs and symptoms of addictive and compulsive behaviors, including alcohol and drug abuse; the stages leading to behavioral change, including the occurrence of relapse; the grieving process, essential to helping employees understand how they cope with permanent change; human resiliency, which is a coping mechanism to help people deal with environmental change beyond their control; the ways that change occurs on an organizational level; and other manifestations of behavior in the workplace.

The second Biopsychosocial Foundations course will bring a general understanding of the various modalities of behavioral health treatment, recognizing that the employee may have had previous treatment episodes and/or preconceived issues regarding the need for treatment, the type of treatment, or follow-up recovery concerns. The other aspect of training that will be valuable during early intervention is a basic understanding of psychopharmacology. With first-time clients, psychopharmacological issues usually surface in one of two forms:

1. Fears that medication is the only form of treatment, as well as media-related fears such as those surrounding Prozac.
2. Questions regarding the use/effects of their current prescription of psychotropic or other medication.

Finally, education on the manner and the depth of information that should be divulged to the client will be useful, as well as education on the process of coordinating medical expertise.

Psychological Modalities and Ethics

This course will provide in-depth knowledge of clinical methods and an overview of ethical practice. The student will receive exposure to several of the more common modalities relating to cognition, behavioral modification, addictions, and crisis intervention. Focusing on symptoms to stabilize the individual and on problem identification is essential to early intervention and subsequent referral. BR Managers will need a strong understanding of and practical experience with coping skills and grief management. This course will establish practical guidelines for monitoring progress and safeguarding confidentiality.

Interpersonal and Group Behavioral Problems

One useful frame of reference to understanding interpersonal and group behavioral problems at work is that of family systems. Experts in marital relations and family systems understand the mechanics of how people clash and, in order to cope with their situations, assume roles that create and perpetuate a dysfunctional system. This, in effect, produces a situation where one dysfunctional, codependent behavior counterbalances another. For example, the personalities of a codependent family may include, among the authority figures, one abusive parent and one apologetic parent and, among the dependents, a troublemaker, a rescuer, a beauty queen, a person of relaxed virtue, a perfectionist, a withdrawn loner, a person who is calm under extreme pressure but has difficulty handling daily life with equanimity, and other personality manifestations. This type of social splitting can occur in the workplace, too, and its effects can result in behavioral risk exposures.

Whereas in a family the members are ensnared in the dysfunctional situation by economic factors and by the use of love to perpetuate family bonds by inducing guilt, in the workplace people are bonded by economic factors, by productivity pressure, and by an inability to leave the organization because a person lacks the confidence to obtain employment elsewhere or has a "black mark" on his or her employment record.

There is much useful literature on dysfunctional relationships in both families and the workplace, as well as the use of conflict (or dispute) interventions at work for the purpose of dealing with the conduct and the work-performance problems caused by the relationships. One research paper references five "dimensions," or turning points, of managerial third-party dispute resolution, which are also the same dimensions that apply to a BR intervention. Interestingly, the same dimensions can be overlaid on EAP problem assessment and resolution. The dimensions are:

1. *Attention is given to the stated problem versus underlying problem.* An EAP seeks to resolve the underlying or primary problem to prevent recurring symptoms or treatment episodes. As with personal problems, unresolved interpersonal conflicts tend to recur.

2. *Commitment is forced versus encouraged.*

3. *Decision control lies with the manager (intervenor) or with participants (EAP client).*

Dimensions 2 and 3 are related. Supervisory and fitness-for-duty referrals to an EAP often require the client to comply with a treatment plan. By contrast, conflict interventions initiated by a manager may force participants, as a condition of continued employment, to accept an intervenor's solution, whereas voluntary conflict interventions may be mediational in that control rests with the participants.

4. *Manager approaches conflict versus manager avoids conflict.* As with EAPs, supervisory involvement is important in identifying and resolving the most difficult workplace problems, especially in traditional, command-and-control work environments. A manager who is proactive, who welcomes conflict, and who seeks to resolve it is likely to be more effective than one who avoids conflict. By contrast, when conflicts fester, the result may be enabling, formation of an oppressive "bully" environment, and behavioral risk exposures ranging from absenteeism to emotional problems to workplace violence.

5. *Dispute is handled publicly versus privately.* Except in certain fitness-for-duty situations, problem assessment and referral is a confidentiality-based process. Ideally, conflict interventions are, too. However, coworkers are more likely to be aware of a conflict due to its interpersonal nature, making it semipublic by definition. Nevertheless, the conflict intervention, as with problem assessment, is best handled in private.

EAP managers who seek to become BR Managers will want to familiarize themselves with the types, causes, and consequences of interpersonal and group conflict at work, along with various intervention modalities. Armed with these skills, a BR Program can help to resolve a host of people problems that beset organizations, such as those related to age, gender, and race and to different classifications of work (i.e., professional, technical, managerial, rank-and-file). Furthermore, a BR intervention can help to prevent these problems from later becoming legal issues for the organization.

Societal and Personal-Life Issues

Some workplace problems have their roots in society and personal-life problems, which have prompted some employers to undertake such activities as work/family consultation and policy development. A BR Manager will want to become familiar with the nature of work/family conflicts, techniques for structuring solutions, roles the workplace can play in reducing conflicts (such as a flextime policy), community resources that are available for services such as dependent care, and benefits (such as flexible benefit spending accounts) that augment the solutions. The ability to identify and to help structure solutions for work/family conflicts is within the purview of the BR Program's problem assessment activity.

Therefore, a work/family initiative could be part of a BR Program, or if such an initiative is already established as a distinct program, it could be another delivery system with which the BR Program can integrate. An inherent advantage of work/family activities is that, according to William L. Mermis, PhD, they are conducive to partnering with other functions, including human resources, benefits, affirmative action, and occupational health and wellness. The potential for cross-pollination of ideas, goals, and activities almost speaks for itself.

Work-Site Wellness Issues

A secondary focus of a BR Program can be physical health and wellness because employers are the primary payers of the private healthcare system and because health-related behaviors can impact productivity and lost work time. For example, education about behavioral aspects of diet and nutrition, prenatal care, fitness, smoking, and lifestyle management can augment the behavioral expertise of a BR Manager. This expertise, in turn, can be used in client problem solving and in managerial and employee training and, in organizations with separate wellness programs, for better integration of services and cross-referral of clients. It is not recommended, however, that health and wellness become the primary focus of a BR Program.

Workplace Knowledge

At least five sets of workplace knowledge will be useful to the BR Manager: management theory, history of labor and industrial relations, personnel management, discipline procedures related to employee-problem resolution, and issues related to responding to specific organizational factors that elevate behavioral risks.

Relevant management theory includes the one that espouses traditional, vertically integrated work structures, reflected by "Theory X," whose assumption about human nature at work is that people are best motivated by being told what to do and that sanctions in the form of punishment should be used to control behavior. Newer, participatory work structures, reflected by "Theory Y," hold that people are best motivated by participating in decision-making processes and that rewards for positive behavior should take precedence over sanctions for negative ones. "Theory Z," invented as a midrange solution that reflects mainstream employment practices today, has elements of both. It will be useful to the BR Manager to be grounded in management practices that reflect all three theoretical foundations.

Labor and industrial relations provide useful information about navigating and delivering services in a unionized work environment. Personnel management provides additional knowledge about how a HR management department functions and acts as the main interface between the organization and its employees.

Knowledge of the disciplinary process encompasses three subprocesses: (1) continuous performance appraisal, (2) progressive discipline, and (3) a four-step problem-resolution technique. These processes allow for shared responsibility with the HR department, which controls the appraisal and the discipline processes. The problem-resolution technique, in particular, helps the supervisor to deal with the counterproductive behavior and to keep the intervention from having the appearance of a personal attack on the employee. The technique's steps include corrective feedback, problem solving, consultation, and corrective interviews, the last two of which can be addressed with the employee as part of the formal progressive-discipline steps.

The final area of workplace knowledge pertains to specific organizational risks, including those listed in Table 10.1. To illustrate, one such risk is poor work design. Research has shown that high-demand, low-control jobs pose long-term health risks, including cardiovascular disease, because of long-term buildup of residual strain. As millions of workers already know, boring and repetitive jobs that do not provide meaningful work and keep employees' minds occupied can lead to other problems such as inattentiveness, lack of production, internecine conflict and backbiting, turnover, and self-medication with food. Work design is an area in which most employers have not adequately done any formal risk analysis, and it is where the BR Manager, with adequate training on the subject, can make an impact.

To make a further point, many work cultures support professional, managerial, and technical people whose impact on work design can actually lead to elevated behavioral risk. In one highly automated manufacturing unit, a multimillion dollar computer system was designed to run an entire production floor, with workers needing only to perform mundane tasks. The head software engineer offhandedly told one of the production managers, "We made a system so advanced that it only takes one employee and a monkey to run the entire floor, and the only reason the employee is there is to feed the monkey!" At this company, many of the employees were heavy utilizers of health benefits, which constitute the bulging part of the balloon that represents behavioral risk exposures to the company. Yet senior management failed to recognize the relationship between health problems and the meaningless work it provided to its employees.

Other work-related problems include poor ergonomic design of equipment, mismatches between skills and jobs, lack of step-up to more sophisticated jobs, shift work that leaves employees in a continuous state of torpor, and so forth. It will be helpful for the BR Manager to be familiar with the "hierarchical approach to the evaluation of human work." Two of the levels of evaluation are practicability and endurability, which are evaluated using ergonomic criteria. Two other levels occupying the lower end of the hierarchical scale are acceptability and satisfaction, which are evaluated using economic and sociopolitical criteria. Similarly, criteria that define *humane* work are associated with the structural and the process levels. These criteria, in turn, are useful in understanding whether and to what degree the work is meaningful to the individual.

A BR Manager is not likely to play a lead role in developing solutions to organizational problems such as poor work design, but he or she can make a contribution to this area by using information from the BR audit and as a result of individual problem assessments.

Risk Management

The thought of linking EAP practices with risk management gives rise to anxiety for some employee assistance professionals, whose *modus operandi* has traditionally been, "By doing all I can to help the individual, I am helping the organization." The plain fact is, though, that EAPs have always had a hand in managing workplace risk. Being versed in risk management principles is fundamental to becoming a BR Manager.

There are four ways to deal with risk: (1) Accept risk. (2) Eliminate risk where possible. (3) Transfer risk where possible. (4) Manage the remaining risk. BR management is different from some other forms of risk management, however, because one of its premises is that an organization cannot transfer its risks. Because of the multidimensional nature of behavior, without reducing the environmental factors that foster risk exposure, an attempt to squelch one type of behavioral risk will result in the behavioral problem resurfacing in another form. Once the environment has been changed, then, managing the remaining risk involves providing resources such as EAPs and conflict management.

As employers seek to address problems earlier on the behavioral continuum, the pinnacle of success is preventing the problems from occurring in the first place. Because employees bring their own risks with them to the workplace, there may be a need for measures that actually *reduce* the risks imposed by outside society. This can be done, for example, by screening employees more carefully, such as through the use of psychometric tests, and by creating a work environment that positively motivates employees.

To formulate a risk management strategy, one common practice among risk managers is risk mapping, which provides a visual frame of reference of the relative impacts of various risks and their attendant solutions. As shown in Figure 10.3, X and Y axes can be used to show the objectives of behavioral risk management, to plot the impact of problems and solutions, and to implement solutions. These maps follow a sequence that corresponds with the steps of the BR management process, from measuring the risk to developing solutions. They are adaptations of generic business risk management maps.

The behavioral risks listed in Table 10.1, along with others specific to the organization, can be plotted along the X and Y axes as shown in the risk map after completing a BR audit. Note that some risks are low in terms of frequency of occurrence, which is plotted on the X axis, but high in terms of organizational impact, which is plotted on the Y axis. Such a risk might be workplace violence or employee litigation. Other risks, such as excessive employee healthcare utilization, occur frequently, and their organizational impacts are cumulative.

The objectives map can be used to identify preferred strategies for attacking behavioral problems, with organizational impact plotted on the Y axis and difficulty of achieving the objective plotted on the X axis. Information used to determine the difficulty of achieving the objective can be derived from qualitative information from the BR audit, as well as from the experiential input of an organizational development team working in collaboration with the BR Manager.

Because BR management invokes solutions both after behavioral problems manifest and in the prevention of problems from occurring in the first place, control map–early intervention and control map–prevention address those two objectives separately. The early intervention map is provided first because employers need to ensure that their behavioral risk exposures are under control before focusing on preventive activities. Early-intervention strategies also include so-called "secondary prevention" interventions, which prevent behavioral exposures from becoming worse or from recycling themselves.

Examples of early-intervention strategies are the core BR services, work-site wellness, work/family services and benefits, management of the behavioral aspects of disability, managed behavioral healthcare activities that promote cost-effective care, and fitness-for-duty evaluations of drug-abusing and other employees prior to their return to work.

Control map–early intervention should include activities that reflect time and expenses associated with integrating BR services.

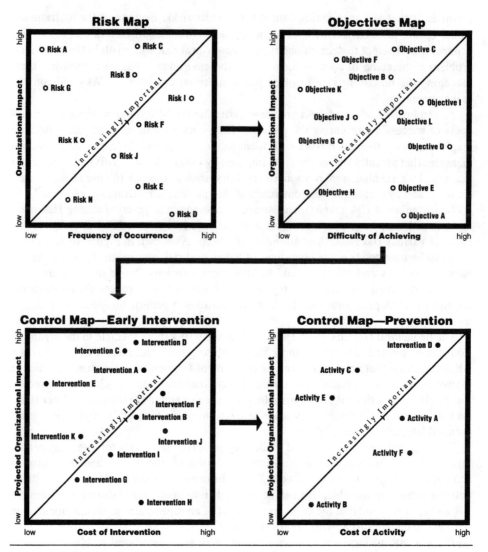

Figure 10.3   Risk map.

Examples of preventive strategies are preemployment testing and hiring practices that identify hidden behavioral risks; management training on effective communication, problem solving, and conflict resolution; and organizational culture developments that are preventative.

Preventive activities are likely to involve other workplace resources that are only partially concerned with behavioral risks. Therefore, control map–prevention should reflect time and expenses associated with coordinating or integrating a company's BR Program with other workplace departments and other functions.

Community Resource Development

This is an EAP core technology embodied in the term *macrolinkages*. It requires competence in locating, interviewing, selecting, interacting with, and evaluating vendors for all types of referral outside of the program. Further, it requires knowledge of the organization's benefit plan coverage and alternatives for funding.

This activity has changed significantly in the past 10 years due to the influence of managed behavioral healthcare firms. In most cases, this is no longer informal network building between EAPs and addictions treatment centers. It often involves contract writing, negotiation, and volume purchasing instead of ad hoc, case-by-case referral.

The *microlinkages* of the core technology pertain to the referral to treatment, case management, and successful return of the individual to work. The BR Manager should be thoroughly familiar with this knowledge subset, also.

Organizational Development

With the information that a BR Manager has about an organization, produced by a BR audit and by interventions with individual and interpersonal/group behavioral problems, he or she is ideally situated to be part of an organizational development (OD) team. Culture development is the aspect of OD work in which a BR Manager is likely to have the greatest influence because it directly impacts the environment in which employees work.

Organizational development, is a specialized area of workplace consultation, and there are many activities and models available. Some of the activities include participating on a transition management team, developing strategic plans, being a team leader in one aspect of the OD process and a participant in others, providing training for managers and employees in groups and individually, measuring outcomes, and providing reports and recommendations to senior management. One model of OD intervention is the "organizational counseling" model presented by Ginsberg, Kilburg, and Gomes in this book.

Cultures need to be understood as organic and subject to continual change because of such external business factors as business growth, acquisitions and mergers, and changing divisional structures and such internal factors as work design, communication patterns, management processes, and management and nonmanagement personnel changes. A BR Manager's role, then, should normally be one of regulating the internal factors while seeking some stability and predictability of external factors. BR audit data will be particularly valuable, showing, for example, that certain elevated risk factors make external change to be inadvisable at a particular time or that certain internal changes are working or not working.

Training and Consultation Techniques

Effective training is a critical element in the successful implementation of any occupational program. Marketing a concept to key organizational executives also requires the expertise of someone apt in basic training skills, many of which are interpersonal and communicative in nature. In addition, training incorporates the ability to read an audience in order to effectively communicate key points of concepts. Training skills, such as those espoused in train-the-trainer seminars, will also be beneficial in the consultative process and in other parts of program development.

Professional and Business Ethics

Ethics are morals applied to the business and work setting. Both business and professional ethics apply to BR management. Professional ethics apply to such operational issues as the handling of confidential client data; the divulgence of information under subpoena; involvement in behavioral risk interventions when a conflict intervention and problem assessment, as separate cases, involve the same individual; and other situations that could compromise the integrity of the BR Program. Professional ethics are increasingly important because, whereas in an EAP the manager handles only one set of confidential information (problem assessment), in a BR Program there are three sets (with the addition of conflict management and the BR audit).

Business ethics are vital for anyone in a workplace decision-making role. A working knowledge of business ethics will be important in order for BR Managers to intervene with higher-level workplace personnel, whose business ethics frequently underlie their management and executive behavior. For example, ethical behavior is an important part of how managers communicate with rank-and-file employees. Can a manager withhold information from employees or make exaggerated claims? Is it ever excusable to outright lie?

One ethics standard is a six-part litmus test for business actions:

1. Is the potential action/decision legal?
2. What happens when you apply the benefit cost costs, in other words, the utilitarian perspective of greatest good for greatest number?
3. Do you want the action in which you are about to engage to become a universal standard (i.e., if it's good for the goose, it's good for the gander)?
4. Will your actions pass the light-of-day test (i.e., if your actions were made public, would you be proud)?
5. Would the Golden Rule ("Do unto others . . . ") apply to your decision? Would you be happy if the same thing were to happen to you?
6. On further reflection, does your course of action still remain ethical? Obtain a second opinion from a friend with no investment in the outcome of your actions.

The ethical boundary is crossed when an individual or a corporate entity fails one or all of the tests but continues to proceed with the intended plan of action.

Information Management

A BR Manager needs competence in computerized information management to aggregate and correlate the large amount of information derived from a BR audit. Information management (IM) will also be useful for program evaluation and for daily administration and operations. Having the capability to use computer equipment and programs may not be enough because it may be necessary to design, shop for, and perform basic maintenance. An ancillary ability to train staff may also be necessary.

Therefore, suggested working knowledges for a BR Manager include IM terminology (in order to communicate with a management information systems [MIS] programmer), analyzing hardware and software need, computer languages, types of MIS (e.g., peer-to-peer network, server, mainframe), system design, file management, records confidentiality, protecting systems, and other areas.

Program Administration

The BR Manager must be viewed as a highly specialized, researched, and accredited part of the corporate structure. In order to do this, BR Managers need to earn respect, support and authority from executive management and boards of directors. BR management has to overcome the obstacle of being viewed as a department that provides "soft" services as opposed to revenue-enhancing operational units. The BR Manager's career path will require both skills of traditional management, which includes a general understanding of core business practices, and an understanding of basic human behavior/psychology.

In order to maintain ethical standards essential for a BR Manager, it is important for this career path to be reserved for professionals in employee assistance or for those in mental health with workplace expertise. It would be naïve to assume that current HR professionals, in particular, will not also view the BR field as an opportunity to advance their careers. HR managers will tout their management experience as the ingredient to build resilience and stability for their own survival in the corporate arena. BR management could become a competitive field where HR managers are able to exploit home-court advantage by being familiar with their organizations and by exercising marketing skills that they have fine-tuned during the last decade.

Additionally, corporate BR Managers need to be strategic thinkers who can not only deliver a service, but can also drive change in terms of organizational policy while contributing to the bottom line. Therefore, EA professionals, who have traditionally had little training/experience in core competencies, will have to include a basic understanding of budgets and financial management, results orientation, marketing, strategic planning, and change management, which can be incorporated into or added to the aforementioned skill sets. In addition, motivational theory and emotional intelligence are also becoming competency areas that BR Managers will need to leverage in order to link the vision, mission, and strategy or BR management to corporate performance. The BR Manager needs to align behavioral technology with business strategy in order to transform the workplace to achieve cross-functional success.

Public Policy

Employers must be increasingly aware of the impact of employment law in the workplace. Whereas labor union formation was once the prevalent solution to unfair work practices and policies as perceived by employees, employment law has been the prevalent solution since the 1980s. A sampling of public policy today includes Title VII of the Civil Rights Act, which prohibits discrimination in hiring and employment; the employment provisions of the Americans with Disabilities Act, which extends protections to individuals with a disability; the Family and Medical Leave Act, which provides up to 12 weeks of unpaid, job-protected leave; Employee Retirement Income and

Security Act, which, among other things, ensures that employee benefits are provided on a nondiscriminatory basis; Occupational Health and Safety Act, which requires employers to provide a safe workplace, including preventing workplace violence; Health Insurance Portability and Accountability Act, which allows employee to ratain their health care benefits as they move from one job to the next; state whistle-blower laws, which protect employees from retaliation or discrimination as a result of good-faith reporting of wrongdoing or waste.

BR Managers will need to have a general working knowledge of the laws and will need to understand their ramifications for work organizations and their employees because (1) employment laws are organizational-risk exposures to employers because, in each case, significant body of disgruntled individuals organized and successfully lobbied for the laws' passage; and (2) senior management will expect a BR Manager to understand how the laws impact the organization and the nature of an intervention.

Other Specialized Knowledges

There are some ancillary specialized knowledges that are useful in delivering BR services. They address aspects of behavioral problems and solutions that are not likely to be core issues and that, in fact, may be handled by other practitioners in the workplace. For example, in work-team environments, the BR Manager may be called on to manage the behavioral aspects of team performance.

This could involve the BR Manager in building work teams from scratch or in intervening with conflicted teams. If the BR Manager has the luxury of helping to build a team from scratch, he or she may wish to become familiar with the work of Isabel Briggs Myers, who researched the ability of different types of people in team activity. The types include extroverts, introverts, sensing types, intuitive types, thinking types, feeling types, judging types, and perceptive types.

However, it is more likely that skills, experience, and competence will be the overriding concern in the formation of a work team, not people types. Therefore, a BR Manager may also wish to become knowledgeable about educational and evaluation tools such as the DiSC, which is published by the Carlson Learning Company and helps people to understand why they have problems communicating and interacting. DiSC assumes that a person is one or more of four types: Domineering, Intuitive, Steadiness, and Conscientious. In team environments, DiSC can be an effective intervention tool for addressing interpersonal conflict. Similarly, in team environments, mentoring is an important tool to help people understand the behavioral expectations, both written and unwritten, of the organization.

BR Service Delivery Means Doing the Dirty Work in Organizations

Will the EAP field ultimately evolve into a BR service? Much depends on the field's desire to return to a stronger workplace role at the expense of the more healthcare-oriented role of managed behavioral health care and on a desire to acquire more workplace knowledges. Typically, an EAP counselor who sits on one end of an 800 line wearing a telephone headset is neither knowledgeable about nor has any genuine interest in the work environment that is so often a part of client problems. Longtime EAP professionals often talk about the dirty work associated with dealing with the organizational politics, complex interpersonal relationships, skeletons in the company closet, extenuating circumstances, and other hurdles that go along with resolving genuine workplace problems. The ability to find solutions to the personal and interpersonal issues of employees while taking these problems head-on will be the most difficult and the most rewarding work for the BR Manager.

Returning to the bulleted set of indicators cited at the beginning of this chapter, BR management can help EAPs by strengthening their position and clout in work organizations, by increasing their work-site presence, by involving them more with the bread-and-butter work of the organization, and by aligning their value and performance with the performance of the organization.

REFERENCES

At Orange County (Florida) Public Schools, a Success Formula: EAP Services + MIS Capability = Program Accountability. (1992, July). *EAPA Exchange, 22*(7), 24–25.

Brannigan, M. (1996, March 7). When is mental state of a pilot grounds for grounding him? *Wall Street Journal*, p. 1.

Briggs Myers, I. (1974). *Type and teamwork* (p. 8). Gainesville, FL: Center for Applications of Psychological Type.

Employee Relations Bulletin. (1997, October 21). Waterford, CT: Bureau of Business Practice.

Karasek, R., et al. (1981). Job decision latitude, job demands, and cardiovascular disease: A prospective study of Swedish men. *American Journal of Public Health, 71,* 694–705.

Kwasha Lipton Group of Coopers & Lybrand. (1997, November/December). Based on the format of risk control maps accompanying the article, business risk and control at work. *Kaleidoscope, 6*(3), 4–6.

Luczak, H. (1992). 'Good work' design: An ergonomic, industrial engineering perspective. In *Stress and well-being at work: Assessments and interventions for occupational mental health* (pp. 96–112). Washington, DC: American Psychological Association.

Mermis, W.L. (1996, November 7–9). *The changing face of higher education: The need to integrate work/family life.* Paper presented at the second annual Conference of the College and University Work/Family Association, Stanford University, Stanford, CA.

Phillips, D.A. (1994). *Management training: When problems persist* (training program). Washington, DC: COPE.

Pinkley, R., et al. (1995). Managerial third-party dispute intervention: An inductive analysis of intervenor strategy selection. *Journal of Applied Psychology, 80*(3), 386–402.

Workplace Violence. (1996). A survey report. Alexandria, VA: Society for Human Resource Management.

Yandrick, R. (1995). How external service providers can structure services to help employers control their behavioral risks. *Behavioral Healthcare Tomorrow, 4*(5), 34.

Yandrick, R. (1998, June 14). A survey performed for the Annual Retreat of the Keystone Chapter of Employee Assistance Professionals Association, keynote presentation, Hershey, PA.

Yandrick, R.M. (1996). Making the case for conflict management, II. *EAP Digest, 16*(6), 27.

CHAPTER 11

EAP and SAP Interface Issues in Small Businesses

DONALD I. ROTHSCHILD

More than 90% of all businesses in the United States are small businesses that employ less than 50 people and that are probably the most underserved by the employee assistance profession. These businesses, sometimes mom-and-pop organizations, often have minimal employee benefits and little knowledge or patience with poorly performing employees. Rarely are these businesses interested in appropriately referring troubled employees to agencies capable of restoring them to fit condition that would allow them to effectively perform their work. The solution of many small business owners is to replace the individual because they do not fully understand how cost-effective it is to rehabilitate and support experienced employees.

Yet when the federal Omnibus Transportation Employee Testing Act (OTETA) of 1991 was passed, an increased burden was placed on these small businesses. The resulting federal testing regulations are spelled out in 49 CFP Part 40 and are directed to employers of individuals in safety-sensitive positions that are involved in interstate commerce and regulated by the Department of Transportation (DOT). The regulations state that employers are responsible to maintain a drug-free workplace by implementing drug testing programs. Covered employees are tested under the following instances: preemployment, random, reasonable suspicion, postaccident, return-to-duty (following a positive test), and follow-up (following treatment/education for misuse of drugs or alcohol). The implementation of these regulations affected about 8 million workers holding commercial drivers licenses (CDLs) or involved in other safety-sensitive jobs related to airlines, railroads, pipelines, or commercial marine traffic.

In 1994, the DOT added alcohol to the list of prohibited drugs as a safety move following a study of serious accidents involving alcohol, notably one in Chevy Chase, Maryland, in 1992 that took 16 lives. Employees and union officials opposed the addition because alcohol is a socially acceptable legal substance, as opposed to the legally controlled substances (marijuana, cocaine, amphetamines, opiates, and phencyclidine [PCP]) that were prohibited by law and by the preexisting DOT rules.

If generally accepted figures are valid, the numbers of positive drug and alcohol tests may be in the order of hundreds of thousands. According to SmithKline Beecham Clinical Laboratories, the positive rate in 1997 in the general population for the five drugs prohibited by the DOT is in the order of 5%. Although The Compliance Alliance does only about 5,000 tests per year, its positive rate was more in the order of 1% in 1997.

Each of the six DOT administrations—Federal Aviation Administration (FAA), Federal Highway Administration (FHWA), Federal Railway Administration (FRA), Federal Transit Administration (FTA), Research and Special Programs Administration (RSPA), and U.S. Coast Guard (USCG)—set the rates at which the covered workers are randomly selected for testing; and although all agreed that a 50% figure should be affective for drugs, each may change the rate if and when the rates of positive tests became significantly lowered.

The testing rate for alcohol, which began at 25% in 1994, was lowered by all administrations except FRA in February 1997 to a rate of 10%.

The original Part 40 required employers to refer an employee testing positive for a prohibited drug to be referred to an employee assistance program (EAP); but when alcohol was added to the testing regimen, the Department went a step further: Should an employee test positive for one of the five prohibited drugs (marijuana, cocaine, amphetamines, opiates, or PCP) or alcohol in excess of 0.04% blood alcohol content (BAC), the employer must refer the employee to a *substance abuse professional* for an assessment and referral to a specific venue of education or treatment. Thus, by federal mandate, the substance abuse profession (SAP) was born!

Regulations specifically covering the six DOT administrations (FAA, FHWA, FRA, FTA, RSPA, and USCG) each specifically state that the covered employee testing positive for prohibited drugs or greater than 0.04% BAC shall be evaluated by an SAP.

It is the duty of the SAP to provide a comprehensive, face-to-face assessment and clinical evaluation of those individuals testing a BAC at or above 0.04% or a positive urine test result for any of the five prohibited drugs. The evaluation should determine the employee's needs for assistance in resolving problems associated with the use of alcohol or other drugs. Referrals may be made, allowing the employee to seek a venue of education or therapy as recommended by the SAP.

Most large businesses (those with greater than 50 employees) have a formal human resource department that would handle the testing program internally, but few small businesses have a specific resources department to handle the job of setting up a drug/alcohol testing program in compliance with the complex regulations. This responsibility in the small company may either be farmed out to a third-party administration or ignored with the hope that they will not be found to be noncompliant.

Nevertheless, passage of the OTETA may refocus small businesses not only on the problems concerning safety in the workplace, but also on the value of working with troubled employees to improve their performance and to increase profit for the employer. It also spotlights the liability issues related to safety and drug-related behavior along with rights to privacy and confidentiality.

Some small business owners believe that using the mandated SAP services would eliminate the need of any EAP services. This is a simplistic response to a complex problem. The fact is that with an EAP, employee performance—the critical factor in business profit and the focus of the EAP—is the driving force. But the SAP is used only in the case of a positive drug or alcohol test.

There is a distinctive difference in both the responsibility and the focus of the EAP and the SAP: Whereas the EAP has always had primary responsibility to the employee with the focus on solution of life problems (an employee benefit) in order to help improve job performance (an employer benefit), the SAP's primary responsibility may either be to the employer with the focus on compliance with DOT regulations on the behalf of public safety or to the employee who may be left to pay for the services and is seeking reinstatement into his or her safety-sensitive job.

This chapter spells out the scope of a drug/alcohol testing program with emphasis on the responsibility of the SAP and the relationship of the SAP to the EAP. Working with small businesses will be stressed, giving examples of the third-party administrator (TPA) concept and the formation of small business consortia.

THE PROBLEM

A quandary of small business is how to keep employee performance at an optimum level. The federal government's intrusion to enforce safety rules has helped to focus on the problem. Furthermore, ever-increasing liability issues are present, such as those relating to damages directly or indirectly related to irresponsible behavior caused by illegal drug use or alcohol misuse.

The small business whose employees are the object of the testing mandates must create a company policy implementing a drug/alcohol testing program. And, should an employee test positive for drugs or alcohol, the small business owner is compelled by Part 40 to seek the services of an SAP. For those already having an EAP, the solution is simple: A certified employee assistance professional (CEAP) qualifies as an SAP.

If an EAP is not in place, many of these businesses may seek the name of an SAP from the medical review officer (MRO) who reports the drug positive. Although regulations state that the MRO may be a source for SAP referrals, it does not ensure a quality assessment regarding the extent of the employee's dependency.

Today, many therapists present themselves as SAPs. Although the regulation is clear on the professional accreditation required to serve as an SAP, there is no guideline on measuring the experience or the ability required to make accurate assessments or viable referrals. For example, a licensed clinical social worker (LCSW) with appropriate licensure applied for SAP status in the Colorado SAP Network; however, the candidate's addiction experience was in eating disorders. An assessment referral from this individual would be of questionable quality, thus doing an injustice to the employee, the employer, and the general public for whose protection the OTETA was created.

In order for the federally mandated drug testing program to work effectively in the public interest, there must be some self-regulation and some standards set by the SAP for the benefit of the public, in general, and the employee and the employer, in particular. The federal guidelines for SAP qualification have no measure of the experience and the scope of knowledge of diagnosis and treatment of substance abuse disorders. Inadequate knowledge and experience may result in an inappropriate venue of treatment or therapy, which may, in turn, present the employer with the problem of repeat offenders and the resulting inability to remain in compliance with federal regulations.

THE SOLUTION

To the employee assistance professional, the answer is simple: Get an EAP! However, economics are the most important factor in any small business. Each and every business owner asks, "How do I comply with the law?" which is immediately followed by

"How do I avoid costly litigation in this litigious age, continue to offer valuable goods and services to my customer at a fair price, and still make a recover my investment at a fair profit?"

Three possible effective methods of addressing the situation and creating solutions for small businesses are: (1) to contract with an external EAP, (2) to join a consortium or to work with a third-party administrator, or (3) to contract with an SAP who will act as a third-party administration (TPA). Each method will be addressed in the pages ahead.

In order to make the appropriate selection of the method of compliance, the problem must be further defined.

SUBSTANCE ABUSE PROFESSIONAL DEFINED

The DOT defined the *substance abuse professional* in '40.3, 49 CFR Part 40, as follows:

> A licensed physician (Medical Doctor or Doctor of Osteopathy); or a licensed or certified psychologist, social worker, or employee assistance professional; or an addiction counselor (certified by the National Association of Alcoholism and Drug Abuse Counselors Certification Commission [NAADAC] or by the International Certification Reciprocity Consortium/Alcohol & Other Drug Abuse). All must have knowledge of and clinical experience in the diagnosis and treatment of alcohol and controlled substances-related disorders.

The DOT did not include state-certified alcohol and drug counselors in the definition because education and experience qualifications varied greatly from state to state.

The most important part of the definition of an SAP is its last sentence that addresses the knowledge and the experience in both diagnosis and treatment of the presenting problem. It is unfortunate that the DOT definition does not state the amount of expertise in the field or knowledge of appropriate referral sources that may be required. Yet, for this type of program to be effective, it is of utmost importance to the business owner that the troubled employee be referred to an appropriate facility for the appropriate venue of education or therapy. Imagine the complexity of potential legal issues when an employee, after completing SAP-recommended treatment, is involved in a serious drug/alcohol-related accident.

Furthermore, because this requirement for knowledge and experience is so vague, it opens the doors for charlatans wishing to exploit the system. Early in the period following the SAP definition, some organizations offered SAP services via telephone, but DOT soon updated the regulation to mandate only face-to-face assessments. There has been movement to certify SAPs, and some states now license EAPs. But until there is more supervision of the SAP qualification process, it is a buyer-beware process, and small businesses should be cautioned to investigate the credentials if their SAP.

The SAP should have a knowledge of the rules specific to each DOT Operating Administration: FAA, FHWA, FRA, FTA regulating public transportation safety, RSPA regulating pipeline safety, and USCG regulating marine safety. Rules pertaining to testing and assessment vary with each administration.

In order to make an appropriate referral, each SAP must have a working knowledge of quality programs and qualified counselors as well as of insurance, benefit plans, and payment requirements of the client company. To best serve the employer, the SAP must be able to present an assessment and referral of value to both employer and employee.

Standard assessment tools, such as MAST, ORBIT, or SASSI, should be used in order to get uniform and repeatable results. For a comprehensive list and description of assessment tools, please refer to Cagney and Springer (1995).

Referrals should likewise be made using standard placement criteria, such as that prescribed by the American Society of Addictive Medicine (ASAM). Use of a standard assessment tool assures fairness and consistency of assessments, increasing reliability, and decreasing liability.

DOT rules state that SAPs may not refer to themselves, except in specific managed care settings. This would occur when the health organization responsible for the company medical benefits provides SAP services.

Referrals are made allowing the employee to seek a venue of education or therapy as recommended by the SAP. It is important the SAP not imply that the treatment venue is a form of punishment. If the evaluation results in referral to an intensive or a residential program, the employee must complete the initial phase of treatment before being reassessed for return to a safety-sensitive position. However, if a less restrictive educational program or treatment modality is prescribed, the SAP determines the time frame of involvement and compliance that the employee must complete before a return-to-duty evaluation is conducted. Therefore, the SAP may conduct ongoing case management services in order to monitor employee compliance with the recommended level of care until the employee is scheduled to return to the SAP for a return-to-duty evaluation.

The SAP should learn company policy relating to sick leave and conditions for returning the employee to duty. The SAP must do the best job possible in creating a simple answer within the limits of company sick leave and good reason so the employee will be allowed to return to work with the company where he or she is employed or will be qualified to find other suitable work, if terminated.

The return-to-duty evaluation is a process to determine the employee's compliance with the SAP's initial recommendations and to assess risk factors associated with the employee's return to safety-sensitive job duties. Conditions of returning to work include, but are not limited to, a clean drug/alcohol screen followed by at least six random tests during the subsequent year. The period for random follow-up tests may extend up to 5 years. These random tests are over and above the company's standard random-testing pool.

A typical return-to-duty (RTD) evaluation would be on the SAP's letterhead and would contain the following:

- Employee's name and social security or company ID number.
- Employer's name and address.
- Reason for evaluation, including date and rule violations.
- Summary of initial evaluation and treatment plan, including date.
- Name and address of treatment provider.
- Inclusive dates of treatment.
- Summary of clinical evaluation by provider.
- SAP clinical evaluation of employee's compliance with treatment plan.
- Recommendation for support system, if any.
- Follow-up testing plan.

THE SCOPE AND VISION OF A DRUG/ALCOHOL TESTING POLICY

A legally flawless drug/alcohol testing policy statement is critical in creating a testing program in any small (or large) business. Although the purpose and validity of the federal testing mandates have been tested in the courts, it is in the employer's best interest from a liability standpoint to have such a flawless policy in place before beginning any testing program.

Unfortunately, the DOT is silent on policy statements, and each company reaches out to whatever source is available for its drug-free workplace policy. Often such policies are written by the company's legal counsel. But equally often, they are plagiarized from another company policy. The Compliance Alliance offers several boilerplate policies from which our clients can choose.

Testing of bodily fluids (urine and breath) has been determined in court to not be in violation of Fourth Amendment privacy rights, provided that it is done properly in the name of public safety.

Although federal regulations state rules regarding testing procedure and whether a covered employee may or may not operate within their assigned position, it is the company policy that controls employee wages, benefits, and discipline.

Who Pays What?

Inasmuch as there are various appurtenant costs involved in facilitating a drug/alcohol testing program, company policy should state whether the employer or the employee pays for each of the charges involved. DOT regulations are silent on this subject. The company usually pays for the random, reasonable-suspicion, and for-cause tests because it is in the best interest of the company. However, some company policies state that a prospective employee must pay for any preemployment test that shows a positive test for a prohibited drug. In addition, some companies require an employee to pay for reasonable-suspicion testing, but the employee is reimbursed if the test is negative.

The federal mandates are silent on who pays for the SAP services. Some medical benefits may cover some of this charge. Some companies will pay for the SAP assessment, and some companies will have the employee pay up front and will then reimburse the fees to the employee upon the employee's completion of the venue of education or therapy and signing of a return-to-duty agreement.

Inasmuch as SAP services are a rare occurrence, it would be most cost-effective for small businesses to contract out for them on an as-needed basis. They may be made available via their EAP, their drug-testing consortium, or in some instances their MRO.

Lost Time

The federal mandate is clear on the fact that an employee testing positive for any of the five prohibited drugs or alcohol greater than 0.04% BAC may not return to duty until the employee has been assessed by the SAP and has completed at least a minimal required education or treatment and has had a negative return-to-duty drug/alcohol test. Company policy will dictate if this enforced leave is with or without pay.

Federal regulations do not state that the employer must return this specific employee to his or her job. Indeed, company policy may state that an employee may be terminated if found positive for drugs or alcohol in any instance. Some companies may allow a second-chance policy. In this case, the policy must be clear on the conditions of reinstatement, and it is normal to have a formal written agreement upon return to duty. Regardless of the employment status, an individual having a positive drug/alcohol test must be referred to an SAP.

A well-written company policy will address ways that costs of drug/alcohol treatment and education, if needed, will be met. The policy may go on to state specific treatment facilities or medical coverage to be utilized.

Small businesses may seek direction and help in drawing up a drug/alcohol policy from their lawyer, their EAP, their insurance provider, or a TPA. A consortium, such as The Compliance Alliance, provides consultation service as a part of the consortium fee to advise on company policy, but TPAs seldom provide this service. In all instances, the organization's legal counsel should give final approval.

THE ROLE OF THE SAP

The role of the SAP is narrowly focused upon evaluation of affected employees for the sake of public safety. It is the SAP who decides if and when an employee testing positive for drugs or alcohol greater than 0.04% BAC shall return to a safety-sensitive position with the employer or shall be fit to apply for work with another employer.

And because of the invasive appearance of drug/alcohol testing, there is always the possibility of legal action, especially by those wishing to evade detection of irresponsible use of drugs or alcohol. The SAP must take due diligence in record keeping, in preparation of appropriate releases, and in protecting confidentiality on behalf of the employee being assessed. The SAP must have a thorough knowledge of every aspect of the laws and regulations pertaining to confidentiality.

Confidentiality

Employee records relating to DOT-mandated drug/alcohol testing are generally confidential. However, under certain circumstances, this information must be released to others. For example, information pertaining to positive drug/alcohol tests must be disclosed to persons within the employee's organization responsible for carrying out the drug-free workplace program.

The drug/alcohol test information may be released, upon request, to the Secretary of Transportation, to any DOT agency with regulatory authority over the employer, or to a state agency with regulatory authority over the employer (as authorized by DOT agency regulations).

The mandates require that upon a subsequent employer's request and with written consent of the employee, all previous records pertaining to the employee's use of drugs or alcohol be furnished to the subsequent employer in order to comply with regulations. Furthermore, at the request of the National Transportation Safety Board, as part of an accident investigation, the employer must disclose information related to postaccident drug/alcohol test performed following the accident.

ADDRESSING THE ISSUES FOR SMALL BUSINESS

For a small business to handle the responsibilities thrust upon them by federal regulation, they must first make a policy decision on the type of contractor they will use to administer the drug/alcohol testing program and on how to involve an SAP should an employee have a resulting positive drug test. The three possible solutions mentioned earlier must now be considered.

External EAP

The external EAP is a contractor serving the employer and the employee to help resolve problems in employee performance by assessing the problems and by either offering solutions or referring to a therapist, agency, or facility offering solutions within the scope of company benefits or the ability of the employee to handle either financially or emotionally.

Problems may range from mental health to addiction to financial to legal to social, and solutions may be provided by therapists within the company benefit package, by support groups, or by nonprofit assistance organizations.

The external EAP may well serve the small business as adviser on drug-free workplace policy, provide required supervisor training, employee education and function as the SAP. This choice can be very cost-effective in solving more than just the federal drug and alcohol testing problems because it addresses any problems related to job performance.

Certified EAPs (CEAPs) qualify by definition as SAPs, and because it is their primary function to perform an assessment-referral process, they are probably an excellent choice for this assignment, should an employee test positive for drugs or alcohol. However, as previously mentioned, the client-clinician relationship with an SAP is entirely different than the relationship with an EAP.

The use of an external EAP is an ideal solution for a small company interested in optimizing work performance because a CEAP can act as an SAP when required, and can work with management and labor in solving other problems that may inhibit work performance. The only distinction in this case would be the focus of responsibility, as mentioned in the introduction.

Drug/Alcohol Testing Consortium

The drug/alcohol testing consortium is a new concept, but it is similar to the EAP small business consortium* in which members share EAP services with the other consortium members, thus saving expenses. These consortia offer a full array of services required for the operation of the drug/alcohol testing program and are very cost-effective because they have the ability to consolidate and pool such services as training and record keeping. Furthermore, by pooling the total consortium employee population for random testing, a more mathematically effective selection system is made available to the client company.

If the small business has no contracted EAP, the drug/alcohol testing consortium offers a simple solution. Not only would this employer be assured of reliable SAP services, but it would also be able to contract out the distasteful obligation of testing employees for drugs and alcohol.

---

* The structure and operation of our company, The Compliance Alliance (formerly UA Express) documented in *Alcohol and Drug Testing for Small Businesses: The Consortium Concept*, by Don Rothschild, EAPA Exchange, Sept./Oct. 1995.

When the mandates were put into place in the early 1990s, employers were not prepared to initiate a drug test program to strictly comply with the federal regulations. This required contracting with federally approved laboratories for the lab work, acquiring drug test supplies, modifying and securing an isolated collection site (toilet), and having collectors trained in protocol for chain of custody procedures. To the small independent trucker, for example, this was a foreign operation having nothing to do with his business operation!

In those early days, companies providing services in compliance with hazardous materials transport and services related to commercial driver's physicals jumped into the business, providing consortium services. One of the earliest was STA-United of Omaha, Nebraska, which provided random selection of employees and collection kits for their member companies.

Clinics serving workers' compensation needs also began drug testing for their customers. It seemed like a logical move, inasmuch as these organizations already were capable of urine screens and had registered nurses and physicians on hand.

Today, specialty companies, such as The Compliance Alliance, Transportation & Small Business Consortium, and others, offer an array of services that help the employer to comply with the regulations and see that the legal requirements are met in both collection and record keeping.

Services provided by such a consortium may include:

- Drug/alcohol testing program design, to meet specific governmental mandates and to correspond with the corporate culture of the organization.
- Assistance in developing a drug/alcohol company policy statement and an implementation plan designed to fit each specific consortium member.
- A random testing pool, including employees from the entire consortium, for selection by a computer-generated randomizer.
- Urine, breath, and saliva collection and testing in strict compliance with DOT regulations by trained and certified collection technicians.
- Educational materials for employees, including handouts and breakroom posters for employee education.
- Supervisor training for recognition and documentation of drug/alcohol affected behavior and procedures to affect reasonable suspicion and postaccident testing.
- Record maintenance and annual reports.
- SAP services as required.
- Various options for on-site testing devices and general consultation.

A good deal of time is spent around developing a good company policy that will protect both the employer and the employee from any errors, false accusations, and DOT audit proceedings. It is this personal service that helps the relationship between the employer and the consortium.

Should an employee test positive, the consortium should be able to provide a qualified SAP for assessment. The Compliance Alliance, for example, has created the Colorado SAP network, an alliance of qualified SAPs who have met federal standards and who have been trained in uniform standards of assessment and referral.

Colorado SAP Network is composed of about 20 clinicians who qualify as National Association of Alcoholism and Drug Abuse Counselors (NAADAC)-certified counselors or Employee Assistance Certification Commission (EACC)-certified EAPs. Inasmuch as the federal drug/alcohol program is safety oriented, and failure to remove from duty and appropriately refer individuals with drug/alcohol use or abuse problems may result in litigious situations, it is critical to the employer that the SAP be well-grounded in assessment and referral. The candidates for the Network are carefully screened for credentials, experience in substance abuse assessment and referral, appropriate clinical supervision, and sufficient liability insurance coverage. They are provided standard forms and trained to follow set procedures. The objective is to achieve uniformity to such an extent that the assessment could be repeated on the same person by different SAPs with the same results.

Because of the close alliance of these clinicians, there is a free exchange of information regarding court cases relating to drug testing and updates of the various regulations pertaining to the procedure. Furthermore, these Network members may refer to each other, as long as the referral is within the organization of their primary employer.

Third-Party Administrator (TPA)

A third-party administrator is a party that may offer singular services such as drug/alcohol collection and testing services, and that is often associated with the workers compensation provider serving the company. The services offered would be limited by the function of the provider.

The employer either administering its own drug/alcohol testing program or contracting the testing program through a third party, such as their occupational health or workers' compensation clinic, may seek another third-party administrator to provide SAP services. There are numerous SAP providers available, both on national and local levels.

These SAP providers are structured in the same way as the Colorado SAP Network, however, it is usually the only service provided addressing the federal drug/alcohol testing programs.

In addition, there are associations of SAPs who set their own qualifications and standards, contracting their services on an as-needed basis. Several of these exist nationwide, such as STA United and Totally Positive, and in specific geographic areas, and may be found in local yellow pages or on the Internet.

FUTURE IMPLICATIONS

As government becomes more safety conscious, being aware that the highways are paths of missiles weighing tens of tons moving at speeds of over a mile a minute, increasing burdens are placed on companies that employ drivers guiding these vehicles. The safety rules apply to public transportation and to movement of material on road, rail, sea, and pipeline. Over time, governmental regulation can be expected to increase rather than lessen.

Small businesses must be made aware of their obligations and must be able to make wise choices in meeting the obligations of these mandates. Some five states (e.g., Florida) have assisted in lowering the financial burdens to employers by giving discounts in worker's comp rates. Similar bills are in the process of legislation in nine more states. Some insurers may give discounts to businesses with drug-free workplace policies.

A useful function of an SAP should be to inform and consult with the local small businesses on their obligations to maintain a drug-free workplace and on the up-to-date status of federal and state mandates and to assist them in designing a company policy to work within. The SAP should work with them to overcome barriers to implementation as follows:

- Within the context of public safety through maintaining a drug-free workplace lie opportunities for positioning an EAP where none previously existed.
- Benefit coverage should be reviewed keeping in mind the employee presenting a positive drug/alcohol test.
- Company resources should be allocated to maintain a drug-free workplace program.

Opportunities lie ahead for the employee assistance professional providing SAP services to work with both the small business employer and employee within EAP core technology in helping them overcome the burdens imposed on them by ever-invasive government mandates.

REFERENCES

Cagney, T., & Springer, K. (1995, September/October). EAP assessments: Tools of the trade. *EAPA Exchange,* p. 8 ff.

Drug Detection Report. (1998. April 9). Vol 8, No. 8, p. 59. Silver Spring, MD: Business.

NACS. (1998). *The red book: Federal drug and alcohol testing rules.* Arlington, VA: Author.

Parker, C. (1996). *Where the DOT guidelines leave off . . . your decision making begins: A comprehensive guide to designing and setting up substance abuse programs.* Mill Valley, CA: Buckley.

Rothschild, D. (1995). *Alcohol and drug testing compliance for small business: The consortium concept* (Vol. 25, No. 8, p. 18 ff). Arlington, VA: EAPA Association Exchange.

Rothschild, D., & Hermanson, M.K. (1996). *The SAP network: Colorado alliance acts as clearinghouse, referral source for state's substance abuse professionals* (Employee Assistance, Vol. 8, No. 4, p. 32 ff). Waco, TX: Stevens.

Substance Abuse Professional Procedures Guidelines for Transportation Workplace Drug and Alcohol Testing Programs. (1995, June). Washington, DC: U.S. Department of Transportation, Office of the Secretary, Drug Enforcement Program Compliance.

CHAPTER 12

Brief Interventions and Moderation Approaches for Preventing Alcohol Problems

KEITH D. BRUHNSEN

Nothing in excess.
—Solon (7th–6th c.b.c.)

This chapter will describe my experience developing a brief intervention approach for problem drinkers at the University of Michigan. In addition I will present the addiction field's current understanding of the use of brief intervention approaches for problem drinking and make a case for its application to employee assistance programs (EAPs) as a method for prevention and wellness services targeting problem drinkers. I have found that providing a brief intervention program to our faculty, staff, and students is an effective and efficient means of reaching a previously ignored population of problem drinkers. Clients who participated in our brief intervention program significantly reduced their individual levels of alcohol use and related consequences from this use and, as a result of these reductions, our campus has expanded its efforts to identify and to prevent alcohol problems early on.

ALCOHOL USE AND EPIDEMIOLOGY OF U.S. DRINKERS

Alcohol Use, Problems, and Definitions

Alcohol is the most widely used and abused drug in the world and has become a permanent part of the American social fabric. Only a few cultures forbid the social and sensible use of alcohol for pleasure, recreation, or religious ceremony. Most adult Americans use alcohol recreationally without any problems but not without inherent risk. It is a widely documented fact that alcohol use in the United States poses a major public health problem because of alcohol's links to diseases and death. Misusing or abusing alcohol has enormous negative impact on healthcare cost, legal systems, occupational safety and productivity, and family relationships.

There is no consensus on general terminology in the alcohol field, and there is considerable disagreement about what constitutes alcohol problems and who has them. This is a major obstacle in establishing a common language within the health professions and in considering any new or alternative options for treating those with alcohol problems. It appears the general public is even more confused than the professional community on the difference between social drinking, alcohol abuse, alcohol dependency, addiction, alcoholism, and problem drinking. Any discussion of alcohol use needs to begin with a clear understanding of who the problem drinkers are and how serious their problems are; otherwise, miscommunication and frustration dominate the debate.

Epidemiology of U.S. Drinkers

The American public and many health professionals have often mistakenly divided drinkers into two groups: those who are social drinkers and those who are alcoholics. Over the past several decades, substantial epidemiological data from national surveys show we are actually addressing a wide spectrum of alcohol use and levels of severity. The Institute of Medicine (IOM) review developed a Terminology Map found in Figure 12.1 that dramatically illustrates this point.

Hence, we can identify four major groups among the adult population based on consumption levels and related problems: (1) abstainers (or nondrinkers), (2) social drinkers who are problem free, (3) problem drinkers with mild- to moderate-level problems, and (4) a population that drinks heavily. The last group is the one most likely diagnosed as alcohol dependent or as alcoholics.

One-third of the adult population never drinks for health, religious, or personal reasons. Within this group are those who should be advised not to drink alcohol—pregnant women, those operating machines, those with health conditions or required medications

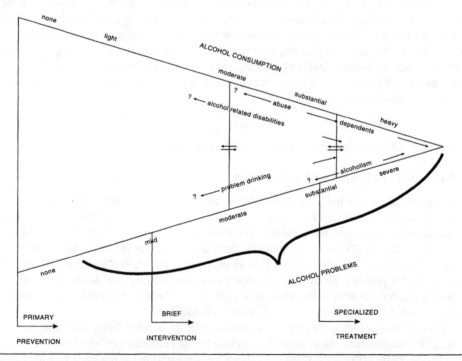

Figure 12.1 Terminology map. (Reprinted with permission from *Broadening the Base of Treatment for Alcohol Problems.* Copyright 1990 by the National Academy of Sciences. Courtesy of the National Academy Press, Washington, DC.)

that prohibit it, those underage, and those in alcohol or drug recovery. The remaining two-thirds are drinkers with light or mild, moderate, or heavy consumption patterns. Despite the depth of available research, there is still variation in the data on what percentage of drinkers fall within the three drinking groups. This variation may depend on various survey techniques and on the criteria and time periods used in measuring consumption, symptoms, or consequences.

If we apply one commonly used criteria system for measuring the severity of symptoms (that of the *Diagnostic and Statistical Manual, Third, Edition,* or *DSM-III*) for any individual with a diagnosable condition (abuse or dependence), then several major U.S. epidemiological population studies, using this criteria, show that about 13 to 14% of adults over their lifetime will have an alcohol dependence problem and that more than 7% will be dependent in the past 12 months (Kessler, McGonagle, & Zhao, 1994; Reiger et al., 1990). Michigan's Department of Public Health (MDPH, 1995), in conjunction with the Center for Disease Management, conducts annual random surveys (as do most state governments) of various risk behaviors, including alcohol use. In Michigan we have consistently shown that about one-third of adults are abstainers and two-thirds of adults are drinkers. Among drinkers, 4% have severe dependency, about 20 to 25% are at-risk or problem drinkers, and about 60 to 70% are sensible drinkers.

The recent IOM report (1990) of the U.S. National Academy of Sciences (USNAS) stated, "Approximately one-fifth [of the population of the United States] consumes substantial amounts of alcohol, and approximately 5 per cent drink heavily" (pp. 30–31). The IOM classified the former group as "problem drinkers" and the latter group as "alcohol dependent or alcoholics."

Using the IOM data, we can estimate that the group of problem drinkers is four to five times larger in size than the group of alcohol dependents. This substantial population of problem drinkers include both those with mild-to-moderate consumption patterns who experience mild-to-moderate consequences and those with drinking patterns that place them "at risk" for developing problems. It is this population that often goes unaddressed and for whom brief interventions are appropriate. This group is most responsible for burdening all levels of American society—the family, the healthcare and legal systems, and the workplace. Compared to the size of the severely alcohol dependent population, the size of this group is disproportionate and demands attention.

After analyzing problem drinkers and the available methods for treating them, the IOM report called for the development and use of primary prevention for those at risk for serious problems and the use of brief intervention for those with mild-to-moderate-level problems. These interventions, the report suggested, should not occur in specialized treatment sectors but in a variety of community agencies, including EAPs. If we are ever to have a substantial impact on alcohol use and abuse in this country, we must try new approaches aimed at this larger population of problem drinkers.

PREVENTION MODELS

The bulk of our primary prevention efforts in the United States have been aimed at educating the American populace and limiting access to alcohol. Our tertiary efforts have been aimed at helping those with severe alcohol problems. But we need new program efforts for secondary prevention. Secondary prevention should try to reduce or eliminate alcohol problems early on for current users.

   In beginning this discussion, it is important to have a comprehensive framework that demonstrates a continuum of prevention strategies, which can be found in Figure 12.2, issued by the Ontario Ministry of Health (OMH, 1993). I have added to the bottom of the continuum the range in which brief interventions and moderation approaches are viable for clients who drink at risk or who have mild- to moderate-level alcohol problems. Lastly, it is critical to emphasize that brief interventions and various moderation approaches are not intended for clients whose drinking has produced permanent damage or for those with alcohol problems so serious that they deserve to be diagnosed as "alcoholic." I equate the layterm *alcoholic* to those diagnosed with severe alcohol dependence.

   Central to understanding or applying any secondary prevention approach are two key public health concepts: risk and severity. When individuals engage in certain drinking practices (e.g., binge drinking, daily drinking) or exceed guidelines for moderate drinking (e.g., more than two drinks per day for men, one per day for women), there is a direct increase in the risk of developing drinking problems. Therefore, any intervention aimed at reducing alcohol consumption will have a preventative impact, reducing the risk and decreasing problems. Alcohol problems don't develop overnight. They often take many years and build from mild to moderate in intensity. Thus, early identification of the severity of the drinking problem is fundamental and requires prompt attention before the condition worsens. In contrast, those with chronic alcoholism often experience the end stage consequences from long-term, heavy, chronic use of alcohol. Often we find that alcoholics avoid help, believing their drinking will correct itself.

   We know that any use of alcohol entails some level of risk (P. Anderson, Cremona, Paton, Turner, & Wallace, 1993). Some adult drinkers make informed personal choices about alcohol use and what risks they are willing to accept by making those choices. This is similar to other behavioral risks and personal choices that individuals make in their lives: how much to smoke, how fast to drive, whether to snow-ski, or whether to

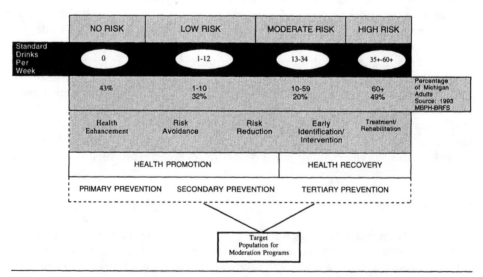

Figure 12.2 Continuum of prevention strategies. (Reprinted with permission of the Ontario Ministry of Health, Partners in Action-Ontario Substance Abuse Strategy, "1993.")

have unprotected sex. So, to reduce the risk level, it is critical for drinkers in a brief intervention or prevention activity to receive basic education on alcohol, its properties, and its impact on the risk level.

On the other hand, confusion mounts for clients making personal choices about drinking as new evidence continues to be reported in the media and as research fields show the potential physical benefits of moderate alcohol consumption (Camargo et al., 1997; Chou, Grant, & Dawson, 1996; Figueredo, 1997; Hanna, Chou, & Grant, 1997; NIAAA Alcohol Alert—Moderate Drinking, 1995; Yuan et al., 1977). As a result the attention on the subject both informs drinkers on the complexity of their personal choices and risk factors and, at the same time, reduces some of the negative stigma that surrounds social use of alcohol. Between the new evidence on positive health benefits and the introduction of moderation programs, the debate has intensified over the need to try to reduce the harm from drinking instead of trying to make clients give up alcohol entirely (Bradley, Donovan, & Larson, 1993; Turke, 1995). Advocates for harm-reduction programs argue that these programs may be a more efficient approach to drinking problems because they often focus on minimizing occasions for heavy use of alcohol, which the heavy use of alcohol predicts the development of later problems while still allowing people to enjoy the possible health benefits from moderate use (Single, 1996).

The New Option

Initially, I was very skeptical, as I expect readers of this chapter will be, about shifting away from the traditional *disease concept* of alcoholism to a brief intervention model for less severe cases of problem drinking. The program we adopted was intended to teach individuals how to control their drinking or to moderate their use of alcohol. Moderation training is technically called *behavioral self-control training,* and is aimed at teaching techniques or strategies that modify how often and how much a person drinks, why and in what context. Behavioral self-control training is one of several cognitive-behavioral approaches that addresses alcohol dependence as a learned behavior by using behavior modification interventions to teach clients the skills needed to confront or to avoid everyday situations that lead to drinking (Kadden, 1994). Heather (see Hester & Miller, 1995, p. 107) suggested that it is best to describe brief interventions as educational, in order to avoid the negative labeling of clients and the stigma-associated diagnosis of an alcohol problem.

The brief intervention approach teaches individuals strategies for dealing with high-risk situations most often associated with their overuse of alcohol. The moderation approach we adopted is an educational prevention program based on cognitive-behavioral principles, delivered in a fixed-format curriculum, and intended to lower consumption levels to within specific suggested guidelines. We have found that individuals who have experienced elevated alcohol use and mild- to moderate-level problems for 4 to 5 years commonly seek a program that will help them reduce their drinking to a more healthful, lower, and safer level without requiring abstinence.

Client choice in treatment goals has been found to be a critical factor in the success of brief intervention approaches. Sanchez-Craig and Wilkinson (1993) stated: "Allowing clients to choose between abstinence and moderation is still anathema to many in the field of treatment. Others, with equal passion, see the denial of choice as a denial of the dignity and respect that they are ethically bound to accord their clients.

This furious controversy has been portrayed as a clash of ideologies, or as a straightforward disagreement about the interpretation of scientific facts" (p. 127). One consistently reported concern that inhibits people from changing their behavior is finding a treatment approach that is acceptable. Offering clients a menu of treatment options increases the chances that they will find an acceptable one.

For the client, a brief intervention experience often involves a combination of education on alcohol and its effects and behavior modification, such as standardizing drinks, conducting a functional analysis of drinking patterns, goal setting and rewarding attainment, self-monitoring progress, management consumption techniques, and learning constructive alternatives. Usually individual instruction is supplemented with self-help manuals that provide a structured format for learning. In using a harm-reduction approach, if the individual still chooses to drink, lowering consumption and remaining problem-free may be both a short- and a long-term goal. Although I have found that many clients undertake a moderation approach to see if they can modify their drinking, in the end they decide to abstain because it is easier and more desirable. Either way, the final choice is left to the client. This learning process occurs for several reasons. First, clients' threshold for initial commitment is lower so they can attempt to moderate their drinking. Second, clients can explore different goals and strategies in a supportive, respectful environment. Third, clients can modify their drinking patterns without being judged and without having to follow a counselor's prescriptive solution. With this new level of awareness, clients can reevaluate for themselves such future goals as continued moderation or abstinence because many of the strategies they learn to moderate drinking can be adapted if they want to abstain.

This approach is only one form of brief intervention available today, but we found that, given our target population and culture, it was a program supported by the greatest amount of empirical evidence for its effectiveness. Admittedly, using any type of alcohol-management program ran contrary to all of my previous knowledge and instruction and required a fundamental shift in my beliefs and attitudes. It was not until I learned the facts about brief intervention approaches and considered how they applied to the population of problem drinkers at my organization that I came to support this change in my approach to alcohol-problem prevention. Substantial empirical data support the brief intervention approach, which enjoys specific advantages that EAPs should consider in the prevention services they provide at their work sites. One major emphasis EAPs need to consider in planning their prevention services is the healthcare services' shift from managing the supply of services at reasonable costs to managing the demands for such services. Drinkers increase the demand for health services, and innovative prevention programs can impact these demands. This impact is demonstrated in Figure 12.3 by the University of Michigan's Fitness Research Center work with Steelcase Corporation.

This research quantifies the rates at which high- and low-risk groups affect annual healthcare cost in relation to seven modifiable risk factors. The study shows that risk status alone can predict whether a heavy or a moderate drinker uses healthcare. Previously, it was believed that current risk status was simply a predictor of future illness and disability and that it had no direct bearing on the present. In addition, changes in risk status from heavy to light drinker or vise versa results in a corresponding change in how often a drinker uses healthcare services and the cost of this use. This means that helping clients lower their risk status reduces the demand for health services by the amount of the differential. According to L.T. Yen, D.W. Edington, and P. Witting (1991), the potential yearly savings in their study for heavy

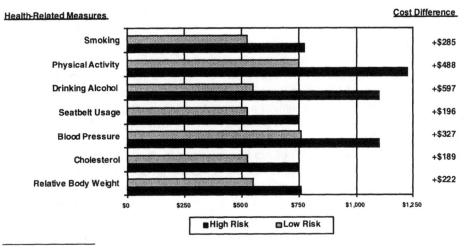

Health-Related Measures   Cost Difference

Smoking	+$285
Physical Activity	+$488
Drinking Alcohol	+$597
Seatbelt Usage	+$196
Blood Pressure	+$327
Cholesterol	+$189
Relative Body Weight	+$222

■ High Risk   ▦ Low Risk

For smoking, low risk = non-smoking, high risk = any smoking
For drinking, low risk = less than 14 drinks/week on average
          high risk = 15 or more drinks/week on average

Figure 12.3 Medical claims costs by health risk levels average cost/employee/year. (Reprinted with the permission of the University of Michigan Health Management Research Center, (1994).)

drinkers is $597 and exceeds the potential savings for other risk factors measured. Hence, preventative programming aimed at heavy drinkers as a risk practice is amenable to change through cost-effective interventions.

The University of Michigan Experience

The University of Michigan is a large, public, research institution, located in the Midwest, with approximately 30,000 faculty and staff and 35,000 students. As the prior Manager of our Faculty and Staff Assistance Program, EAP, I was asked to play a leading role in the University's Task Force on Alcohol and Other Drugs (1991). This was a unique opportunity to gain both applied and scientific knowledge on a broad array of substance abuse issues on our campus that I could incorporate into our EAP prevention programming.

I was one of a 70-member task force made up of many senior researchers in substance abuse, administrators, students, community professionals, and other faculty. Together, we drew upon available research, demonstration projects, and information about programs besides our own so we could evaluate our existing program's efforts and recommend changes in order to develop a different plan to address the alcohol-and-drug problem among our students, faculty, and staff. One of our goals was to create and sustain an environment that would support responsible use of alcohol and prescription drugs, that promoted health, that assisted individuals to make informed personal decisions, and that reduced the likelihood of excessive consumption and other destructive behaviors associated with alcohol and other drugs (U-M Task Force, 1991, pp. 7–8). Our task force worked for 3 years and involved a thorough review of policies, prevention, and intervention efforts on our and other peer campuses. We made major recommendations for change, made numerous suggestions based on creating a community approach to our problems, and developed guidelines for adopting new policies, prevention activities, and intervention efforts across our campus units. The final product may be one of the most comprehensive reports on campus substance abuse to date.

After disbanding the task force, we established a formal office responsible for implementing the recommendations. This office conducted a random survey on campus, funded by the State of Michigan Department of Public Health, to guide us in planning and developing programs. We mailed a survey to a representative sample of faculty, staff, and students that asked about their perceptions, attitudes, and behaviors related to alcohol and other drugs. Over 4,400 surveys were sent, with return rates representing 63% of undergraduates, 69% of graduate students, 67% of faculty, and 57% of the staff selected for our sample population. We found the predominate drug of choice on our campus, by all groups, was alcohol. Our survey found 6.5% of our faculty and staff, 9% of our graduate students, and 18% of our undergraduates had a serious alcohol problem. Despite the wide range of behavioral problems that our respondents reported in our survey about alcohol consumption, our standardized alcohol screening instrument (CAGE) indicated that most faculty and staff members had only mild to moderately serious problems with alcohol (UM Initiative, 1993). We faced the dilemma of finding new, alternative strategies for addressing our current and future problems with alcohol on campus, but our task force did not recommend prohibiting the legal use of alcohol on campus at that time, even though we also did not want to condone or promote alcohol use by individuals under the age of 21.

During the work of our task force, one nationally recognized EAP researcher, Andrea Foote, Ph.D., reviewed and classified the current prevention models in substance abuse (see Table 12.1) which identified the causes of inappropriate alcohol or drug use, as well as the range of suggested intervention strategies and programs organizations could consider adopting (UM Task Force, 1991, p. 25).

Our campus survey data on patterns of alcohol use, which was consistent with the epidemiological and empirical prevention literature we reviewed, led us to conclude that, from a public health perspective, we needed to identify and to adopt some form of a secondary alcohol-prevention program (defined as preventing the regular practice of harmful behavior) for our campus. Such a program would, at best, be a brief, educational intervention for those with mild- to moderate-level problems with drinking. Underlying our decision to adopt a brief intervention approach was the knowledge that we were at the time limited to one conventional approach to alcohol treatment for quite different groups within our university population, and this single approach was not meeting our needs. In addition, when we turned to the empirical literature and research on alcohol problems, we found the most recent, and valid, way to classify alcohol use and its related problems is to understand that:

- "Alcohol problems are not heterogeneous" (there is not one problem but rather many problems).
- "Most people have no alcohol problems, many people have a few alcohol problems, and some people have many alcohol problems."
- "There is no single treatment approach that is effective for all persons with alcohol problems."
- "Brief interventions can be quite effective compared with no treatment, and they can be quite cost-effective compared with more intensive treatment" (IOM, 1990, pp. 147–148, 214).

Table 12.1   Prevention Models Identified in the Literature

Causes of Inappropriate Use of Alcohol and Other Drugs	Suggested Intervention Strategy
(1) Normative behavior within larger context	(1) Change norms: • Adopt formal rules/regulations on availability (sellers/servers) • Change societal/institutional cues about use (e.g., advertisements)
(2) Normative behavior within peer group	(2) Change norms: • Adopt formal rules/regulations re when/where use is appropriate • Institute procedure for examining norms and comparing across groups
(3) High availability	(3) Reduce availability through changes in pricing, sales outlets, or qualifications necessary to purchase.
(4) Lack of desirable alternative activities	(4) Develop alternatives: • Social events not centered on alcohol • Wellness interventions to help individuals develop healthy lifestyles
(5) High stress	(5) Develop alternative stress-management methods: • Stress management training • Develop healthier alternatives for managing stress • Reduce the causes of stress (esp. stressful work environment)
(6) Low self-esteem; isolation from others	(6) Personal counseling; organizational strategies to integrate isolated individuals or subgroups.
(7) Inadequate skills in decision-making or action-taking, resulting in high vulnerability to peer pressure	(7) Skills training (e.g., training in lower-risk behaviors; resistance training). Values clarification is also used in these programs.
(8) Inadequate knowledge or understanding of the dangers of use	(8) Education interventions: • Medial publicity • Classes/seminars • Health promotion/wellness interventions

Several other facts converged to influence my perspective. These included my EAP experiences, which demonstrated a consistent gap in being able to offer appropriately matched services to the array of problem drinkers who would use our campus EAP, and more than 20 years of credible, scientific research that has established the effectiveness of brief intervention approaches. These approaches had success rates far greater than efforts with more severely alcohol-dependent persons. Finally, my interaction with several prominent scholars and scientific researchers in the addiction field, as well as health professionals at the University of Michigan, encouraged me to launch our new prevention program because it was well researched and long overdue, and it could be applied both on our campus and in our local community.

We researched the available programs and selected *DrinkWise,* developed in Canada, because it was well researched and extensively tested. I also made contact with other EAPs and local addiction centers, but I could not identify any EAPs or local professionals that would publicly admit that they were currently helping problem drinkers to moderate, rather than instructing them to give up their alcohol consumption completely. This reticence to admit to helping clients achieve moderate drinking goals meant we would be the first major educational or health institution to publicize offering a professionally led, brief alcohol-moderation approach in the country. As a result, the media overwhelmed us with attention when we opened the program. The exposure provided a good source of referrals both on campus and within our state region. It supported the legitimized model for a "responsible use" approach for many health professionals in our community as a valid means to help certain drinkers because they felt this type of program was long overdue. We ran our program out of the health promotion office on our medical campus and extensively trained social workers, nurses, and health educators in our program's philosophy, in the research supporting it, and in ways to deliver our program to clients. If it was that easy for me and other health professionals in our moderation program to make the shift, why, I asked, weren't more EAPs and health-promotion professionals using this type of model, which had the ability to help so many more problem drinkers?

Historical Background for Alcohol Services in EAPs

Employee assistance programs (EAPs) have been recognized since the 1970s by the health and business communities as leaders in establishing alcohol intervention in the workplace (i.e., identifying and assisting those with symptoms of chronic alcoholism) even though the roots of EAPs in job-based alcoholism programs can be traced back earlier, to around the 1930s, when the influence of Alcoholics Anonymous and recovering alcoholic employees reached out to other workers with known problems. EAP professionals have long been dedicated to the idea of making such work-site interventions both a central and a primary priority because they comprise a large percentage of the typical EAP caseload. EAPs try to identify cases of alcoholism based on problems in job performance. If the threat of losing one's job is the "stick" that motivates the employees to alter their drinking patterns, EAPs are the "carrot" offering help to them. EAPs have strived and succeeded in making a fundamental shift in the human resource field's practice and management of substance abuse problems. As a result of EAP efforts, most work sites today have a more progressive and enlightened view of addressing substance abuse. And countless numbers of employees with alcohol and drug problems have been successfully identified, motivated, and helped, without losing their jobs.

Despite the success and proliferation of EAPs and the use of traditional alcohol treatment approaches for the past 40 or more years, experts reviewing the empirical data agree that the vast majority of persons with mild or moderate alcohol problems are not being adequately identified or assisted in our healthcare settings, communities agencies, or work sites with our traditional ways of screening and treating clients. The IOM's report (1990) clearly summarized the current circumstances of American drinking problems:

> To put it simply, people who drink a lot have many problems, but few people drink a lot. People who only drink a little have fewer problems, but there are a great many people who drink a little. Therefore, the total number of problems experienced by those who drink a little is likely to be greater than the total number experienced by those who

drink a lot, simply because more people drink a little than a lot. If the alcohol problems experienced by the population are to be reduced significantly, the distribution of these problems in the population suggest that a principle focus of intervention should be on persons with mild to moderate alcohol problems. That such a focus may be advisable has been termed "the prevention paradox." (p. 215)

Here lies the challenge and the opportunity for EAPs: to understand the broader picture of the complexity and diversity of alcohol problems, to adopt newer and more innovative methods that will prevent serious alcohol problems from occurring, to reach far more at-risk employees sooner, and to offer clients a new choice they have not had before in our treatment approaches. These opportunities are consistent with EAP professional values and efforts to provide individualized treatment planning to clients as well as cost-effective and efficient services for the parent employer.

The Disease Model

The predominate model for intervening in alcohol problems in North America (but not internationally) since the 1930s, and which most EAP professionals have been taught, has been the "disease concept of alcoholism" based on the medical model. According to this model, certain persons have a vulnerability to a harmful level of alcohol consumption, which leads to negative and severe social, physical, and psychological consequences and, eventually, develops into an illness that inevitably progresses through stages until the drinker loses control over their alcohol use permanently. The alcoholic is then believed to suffer from a biogenetic and psychosocial condition that can be fatal.

Since the 1930s, the primary treatment for this addiction has been based on the Twelve Steps of Alcoholics Anonymous, including the Minnesota Model introduced in the 1950s. The goal of traditional approaches to treatment has been to help the person stop drinking entirely—lifelong abstinence. It is critical to remember that this approach was developed to treat chronic alcoholics, not problem drinkers, and has been the core of many EAP practitioners' knowledge about alcohol and chemical dependency. But the result has been a one-size-fits-all mentality, with abstinence as the only suitable aim, due to defining our clients as powerless over their consumption of alcohol. Many who have found abstinence an unreasonable goal and who have attempted to seek assistance from traditional programs have reported they felt the programs were provincial, dogmatic, and judgmental. This traditional approach to alcohol treatment services persists in most EAPs, despite the EAP industry's standard to assess clients based on specific criteria and then match the client to the appropriate level of care (EAPA, 1992).

Lastly, underlying the conventional treatment model is the strongly held belief, first asserted by E.M. Jellinek in 1946, that says that central to all alcohol problems is the notion that any problematic drinking is progressive and will worsen. In the classic text *Heavy Drinking—The Myth of Alcoholism as a Disease* (Fingarette, 1989), several researchers systematically showed the lack of empirical data to support Jellinek's notion. In fact, the belief in the progression theory is not universal and inevitable because most people can tell you about someone they personally know who once drank too much and learned to cut back to a social level of drinking on their own, without progressing to chronic alcoholism.

It is unfortunate that only one treatment approach is commonly accepted in EAPs for treating everyone, regardless of the severity of the alcohol problem. We find in the more progressive EAPs a matching process between severity and treatment intervention for all sorts of mental health problems. In other words, we assess the client's symptoms and prescribe no more treatment than needed. EAP practice has been conducted and based mostly on experiential, not scientific, knowledge. It is, however, understandable why the traditional approach persists within the EAP industry. Many professionals have come to EAPs out of their own personal recoveries and have a personal interest in supporting this approach. Others experienced substance abuse problems within their own families, which influenced their career choice. Hence, empirical data that drives treatment approaches, not personal experiences, should be the basis for professional practice.

If EAPs use approaches to treatment other than the traditional one, seek alternative models to the disease concept for drinking problems, or allow for other goals than abstinence, they risk being labeled *misled, dangerous,* or *in denial.* But EAP professionals need to step outside of the confines of this disease concept and challenge the conventional approach based on it if advances are to be made in reaching a broader scope of problem drinkers. EAPs have adapted to new conceptual models in substance abuse treatment; for example, just a decade ago, the status quo for addiction treatment was a standard 30-day inpatient stay for clients, whereas today, inpatient stays are reserved for only the most severe cases. This shift toward matching the level of care to the level of severity is at the center of accepting the concept of brief intervention. Scientific research supports the effectiveness of a broad array of approaches for different types of drinkers. We know that brief interventions are now available in many forms and have been extensively tested. We EAP professionals now need to argue that science supports the effectiveness of brief intervention approaches and that EAP clients expect and deserve the best practices and options available in healthcare as we begin to make changes in our assessment and treatment for problem drinkers.

CURRENT ASSESSMENT MODELS AND BARRIERS TO CHANGE

Our main focus in treating and intervening in alcohol problems in the United States has been primarily on those with the most severe drinking problems (i.e., chronic alcoholism or severe alcohol dependence). Often the assessment process is based on a self-report screening questionnaire, like the MAST or CAGE, or on a more extensive interview process interpreted according to standard diagnostic criteria listed in the *American Psychiatric Association: Diagnostic and Statistical Manual (DSM-III-R).* These criteria identify people with heavy alcohol consumption patterns that result in severe or substantial social, psychological, physical, occupational, or legal problems. As a group, heavy drinkers have received the lion's share of our attention and resources in both the EAP and alcohol treatment field. This group is likely to be the same one that has the most severe impact on the workplace and, usually, the most limited chances for overcoming problems because assistance came late when the condition was severe. We need to continue to identify better methods to improve recovery for severely dependent people, and we need to adopt early intervention approaches and to start working with problem drinkers because some unpredictable subset of problem drinkers will move on to heavy drinking and severe dependency. In order to prevent more serious problems and to have better outcome results in treating them, early identification and intervention using new models is necessary.

Screening and Defining Problem Drinkers

In their practice many EAPs have begun to standardize screening for alcohol problems using the MAST, CAGE, or a more sensitive instrument like the AUDIT. If, however, EAPs use a more sensitive screening instrument like the AUDIT, which can identify early-stage problem drinkers (Bohn, Babor, & Kranzler, 1995), or if they screen for consumption rates and other behaviors that place individuals at risk for a wider array of problems associated with elevated consumption, then EAPs will find problem drinkers among our clients who present with other conditions such as depression, stress, or grief. (An easily accessible and good description of screening problem drinkers and the background on the AUDIT, prepared by the U.S. Preventive Services Task Force by David Atkins, M.D., is available on the Internet at http://text.nlm.aih.gov/cpsi/www/cps.58.html.)

My experience in treating problem drinkers shows they often drink to cope with loneliness or boredom or they drink out of habit, such as after work or with friends, or they just drink in the wrong context, while driving or playing sports. These patterns can lead to such dire consequences as arrest, accidents, or injuries. Typically, problem drinkers have begun recently (usually within less than 5 years) to see their excessive-consumption patterns change; they become concerned about their increased use and want to do something to improve their health or to lower their risks. In general, they are not physically dependent on alcohol, are socially stable, function adequately at home and work, do not have long-standing histories of alcohol problems or suffer major consequences from alcohol use, and are not compulsive drinkers. They also do not view themselves as being out of control or powerless over alcohol. Instead, they are aware of having problems with their current consumption levels and of future risks if they do not change. Given this set of conditions, we can define *problem drinking* as any drinking that interferes with health, relationships, job performance, or other responsibilities. It is also any drinking that threatens personal safety. Early-stage problem drinkers are comprised of two groups: (1) hazardous drinkers who have not yet experienced alcohol-related problems yet consume alcohol in patterns that increase the risk of developing such difficulties, and (2) harmful drinkers who have experienced physical or mental harm from their drinking but are not alcohol-dependent.

Problem drinkers tend to have less severe problems with alcohol use and often have an internal locus of control (i.e., believe in being the master of their own destinies), which positively motivates them to initiate change. They often have prior experiences with such successful, healthful changes in their behavior as quitting smoking, eating healthier, or reducing other risky behaviors. When considering assistance options, they respond negatively to the suggestion of traditional alcohol services because they have fundamental philosophical differences with the assumptions of these services. Many have attended an AA meeting and have rejected the philosophy but understand the concept of needing ongoing support for severe alcohol problems. Hence, they avoid seeking the assistance they need or are dissatisfied with or reject help if they do seek it because alternative approaches are not available. Consequently, because EAPs are often the primary referral agent in the workplace for services, problem drinkers will view the EAP as having a limited range of services to meet their needs. This limitation becomes a major barrier to perceiving the EAP staff as approachable and concerned about providing secondary prevention to reduce the harmful effects of their consumption. To reach a far greater spectrum and number of employed people whose problems with alcohol vary, EAPs need to encompass more than the single disease-treatment model with which they have become identified and to adopt alternative conceptual models grounded in scientific knowledge, rather than untested beliefs and practices.

Several additional factors support the need to adopt alternative approaches. First, there has been an increased, national awareness of the wisdom of reducing risky behaviors like drinking among programs promoting health in the workplace and on campuses. Other professions, like nursing, have begun to question their approaches to alcohol abuse and to advocate adopting the brief intervention model (Minicucci, 1994). Major efforts by two leading groups of physicians—*Alcohol Risk Assessment and Intervention (ARAI)* by *The College of Family Physicians of Canada (CFPC)*, 1994; and *The Physicians Guide to Helping Patients with Alcohol Problems* by *NIAAA, 1995*—have been responsible for introducing the brief intervention model to those who deliver primary healthcare in the United States. Another research study conducted in the setting of an American primary-care health maintenance organization (HMO), using clinical randomized trials for at-risk drinkers, separated into a control group and an intervention group, confirmed that physicians who briefly advised patients help those patients reduce their drinking. Doing follow-ups after 12 months, researchers found that alcohol consumption dropped by 14% for males and by 29% for females, when physicians used brief protocols to change drinking behaviors and, in turn, improved their patients' health and reduced hospital days (Fleming, Barry, Manwell, Johnson, & London, 1997). Underlying the harm-reduction philosophy is the practical belief that any steps toward helping patients decrease their risk are ones being made in the right direction. Of course, if one wants to assume no risk with the use of alcohol, then zero consumption is the only option. Second, behaviorally managed care demands cost-efficient, effective approaches and services, including options that empower our clients to participate in the design of their own treatments. Third, overall annual rates of alcohol consumption are falling, but patterns of alcohol use are changing. For example, there have been increases in binge drinking by younger adults, especially on college campuses (Wechsler, Austin, & DeJong, 1993), who are at a higher risk for negative consequences and who present unique challenges to motivate or help. Fourth, population trends in the workplace show more women in the workforce with a higher risk for developing alcohol problems as they try to cope with the stress of their new roles.

Barriers and Beliefs to Nonabstinence Treatment Goals

Several beliefs have fueled the debate over brief interventions and have perpetuated the traditional focus on abstinence as the singular way to treat those with alcohol problems. These include: (1) the fear that moderation approaches will seduce individuals into giving up their sobriety, (2) the belief that alcohol problems are dichotomous, not multifaceted, (3) a distorted view of the scientific literature on goals for drinking for those who take a moderationist approach to treatment, (4) the belief that the traditional programs using the traditional approach have been able to define *success* in alcohol treatment as abstinence and to persuade others to accept this definition, and (5) the belief that all drinking problems are inevitably progressive. In EAP settings, certain other barriers arise to hinder alternative approaches: the feeling that EAP professionals are established experts and have already identified those populations they will treat; the sense that drug testing will identify problematic cases of alcohol use; the confidence that supervisors have been sufficiently trained to identify problematic cases for the EAP; the certainty that drinkers have to hit bottom before they are motivated to change; and the lack of formal training in such alternative approaches as motivational interviewing and brief interventions. To change these outdated beliefs and to remove these barriers, EAP professionals and others need to become more knowledgeable about scientific literature on treatments of problem drinkers and to take new approaches to helping them.

EMPIRICAL SUPPORT FOR BRIEF INTERVENTIONS

The first efforts to evaluate moderation programs for those with alcohol problems began in the early 1970s (see Hester, 1995, p. 155). A classic study of brief intervention to treat those addicted to tobacco described the "limited advice" British physicians offered early on to smokers (see Sobell & Sobell, 1993, p. 8). These physicians found that only a minimal amount of counseling and an educational brochure on how to quit smoking resulted in about 5% of patients quitting after one year. Researchers hypothesized that if all physicians used this approach, one highly cost-effective intervention would result in a large reduction in the number of smokers. The use of brief interventions with smoking has gained greater acceptability, even in the United States, because smoking has not been characterized as a disease. This has not been the case with alcohol moderation. Lacking knowledge of the effectiveness of brief interventions with drinkers, many professionals in substance abuse have resisted change in approaches to treatment; and market forces have failed to provide any incentives to support such a change. Two major researchers in the field of brief interventions, M. Sanchez-Craig and D. Wilkinson (1989), have noted that the impetus to brief treatment approaches are: (1) the rise of behavioral methods of treatment since the 1950s that emphasize problems rather than pathology, (2) the concept of a continuum of dependence, (3) the lack of research support for intensive treatments, (4) a shortage of healthcare resources, and (5) economic pressures for early identification of drinking problems as more cost-effective (pp. 234–235).

The definition of what is *brief* is often arbitrary, but it does emphasize that the intervention is minimal compared to intensive treatments. These interventions depend upon guidance and support in the process and are intended to reach broader populations than conventional approaches do. Brief interventions that conceptualize alcohol abuse and dependence as a learned habit can be divided into two basic approaches: (1) brief advice and (2) brief therapy.

Brief Advice

Brief advice is more often used in the healthcare setting in a single session when the clinical assessment identifies the client's alcohol use and alcohol-related problems. The professional (physician, nurse) then begins a brief, highly directive and prescriptive consultation to inform clients about the assessment results (e.g., elevated liver functions, physical complaints, work problems) and advises them to reduce or to eliminate their drinking. At a minimum, clients receive clear strategies and feedback on how to set goals, how to establish contracts for themselves, how to follow guidelines for drinking, and how to keep records on their consumption patterns so they can be reduced in the future. Typically, clients are expected to participate in a follow-up report to the health professional at which more intensive assistance can be offered if changes in drinking are not made. A well-designed study to test the application of this model in an EAP setting is needed to understand how it can be utilized.

Brief Therapy

Brief therapy is more than simple advice. It includes methods of self-management, bibliotherapy or self-help manuals that supplement the professional's level of involvement, and clear behavioral strategies for change. The professional role is to assess the biological, social, and psychological dimensions of the clients' drinking and to help clients understand the dynamics in changing drinking behavior. The professional must understand and possess advanced skills in therapeutic techniques in the types of behavioral-change strategies clients must use to gain self-control in using alcohol so they can meet their selected goals—strategies that are integral to the efficacy of the approach. The advanced skills necessary for professional behavioral-change approaches include key elements such as conducting a functional analysis of drinking situations; assisting clients in goal selection and goal setting; and teaching consumption-management techniques, self-monitoring, and alternative coping skills—all of which are conducted from a health-risk and health-education perspective.

Research Supporting the Effectiveness of Brief Interventions

International researchers have studied the methods and the effectiveness of brief interventions more extensively than any other intervention in both inpatient and outpatient settings. Their findings have shown that reduced alcohol use leads to improved health when compared with no intervention and that brief interventions can be as effective as more extended treatment protocols (see Bien, Miller, & Tonigan, 1993; Eighth Special Report, 1993, pp. 307–310; Hester & Miller, 1995, pp. 155–157; IOM, 1990, pp. 221–225, 459–461; Miller, 1992; Saunders & Aasland, 1987; Saunders & Foulds, 1992, pp. 224–229; Sobell & Sobell, 1993, pp. 1–36). Bien et al. (1993) best summarize the results of these studies: "To date, the literature includes at least a dozen randomized trials of brief referral or retention procedures, and 32 controlled drinking studies of brief interventions targeting drinking behavior, enrolling over 6,000 problem drinkers in both healthcare and treatment settings across 14 nations. These studies indicate that brief interventions are more effective than no counseling and often as effective as more extensive treatment."

There is encouraging evidence that the course of harmful alcohol use can be effectively altered by well-designed intervention strategies that are feasible within a relatively brief-contact context, such as primary care settings and employee assistance programs (Bien et al., p. 315).

M. Sanchez-Craig and colleagues (Sanchez-Craig, Spivak, & Davila, 1991) have also consistently found that women have better results when trained in behavioral self-control. Given the research results, it is fair to conclude that brief intervention programs have many advantages over more traditional programs. Brief interventions also can be applied to whole communities and to large populations with minimal resources. Because the focus of brief-intervention programs is on nondependent drinkers, these programs could affect an estimated 15 million to 20 million heavy drinkers in the United States (*Eighth Special Report,* September 1993, pp. 309–310).

BEST PRACTICES

I will summarize several of the best practices and models in brief intervention and moderation approaches currently available in the United States that are adaptable to EAP settings. Currently, several EAPs have adopted moderation programs within their organizations or utilize them in their referral networks. This summary is not an endorsement of any one approach or program, but, given the limited number of models and their potentially powerful impact as a intervention tool, each EAP setting or professional can learn from and explore the different programs and match them to each specific setting and population. Most of the material that provides a clinical and empirical understanding of this subject is printed in research publications and in government documents and is available at no cost. A few books and commercial products are also available at low cost. Some communities already have existing services and trained professionals that may be willing to learn and provide these types of services. For workforces that have widely diverse settings, it would be unreasonable to find accessible brief intervention services in all local communities, so national providers or other methods may be the solution. In this case, self-help publications can be mailed to problem drinkers seeking information. This type of intervention is supported in the research as being as effective as face-to-face services and may be more cost-effective.

EAP practitioners should know about and consider four types of brief intervention approaches currently available: (1) professionally led brief advice and brief therapy approaches, (2) computer-based, self-directed learning and Internet services, (3) mutual support or self-help approaches, and (4) bibliotherapy and public health educational materials.

Professional Programs

In just the past 4 to 5 years, brief advice programs for physicians and nurses have emerged in the United States and Canada. The first was the Alcohol Risk Assessment and Intervention (ARAI) project developed by The College of Family Physicians of Canada. This brief advice program, developed by an international group of consultants and researchers in addiction, includes a simple curriculum for training physicians and other health experts so they can identify, assess, and help with all at-risk patients. It includes a physician's manual, a workbook for patients, and other materials for training in family medicine residency programs. The materials are simple, concise, and easily incorporated into the daily practice of physicians. From this well-researched approach, EAP professionals can learn to use and adapt a simple triage system that separates problem drinkers from those who suffer from more severe alcohol problems. This material is well written and can be modified so it can appear in educational brochures on public health.

In November of 1995, the National Institute on Alcohol Abuse and Alcoholism released the second program: "The physicians guide to helping patients with alcohol problems, a step-by-step approach to aid primary care physicians during routine office visits identify and advise patients at risk for or experiencing alcohol problems during routine office visits." The 12-page manual incorporates brief screening and assessment instruments to help physicians advise two types of problem drinkers: (1) patients drinking above moderate levels who show no signs of dependence, and (2) patients who show evidence of alcohol dependence. For the first time in the United States, this guide sets a national standard and defines *moderate drinking limits* (based upon U.S. Dietary Guidelines, U.S. Department of Health and Human Services, 1990) as two standard drinks a day for men, one standard drink a day for women, and no more than one standard drink per day for persons over 65. In 1997 the NIAAA released the supplemental patient guide, which is also in the public domain and available for EAP use.

Currently, at least three different, professionally led brief intervention and moderation programs operate in the United States: (1) the DrinkWise program (www.med.umich.edu/drinkwise/) developed in Canada by Homewood Behavioural Health Corporation, (2) the DrinkLink program (www.drinklinkmoderation.com) in northern California, and (3) the Drinkers Risk Reduction Program at Rutgers Alcohol Studies Program in New Jersey.

DrinkWise

The DrinkWise program is a form of brief intervention that combines bibliotherapy, brief therapy, and specific, cognitive-behavioral approaches intended for behavioral self-control training. The aim of this program is to reduce or to eliminate alcohol consumption and the negative consequences that clients can experience from drinking. The program is delivered by a trained facilitator in individual, group, or telephone formats over a 7-week period of time. Current research supports the effectiveness of any one of the three formats (Sanchez-Craig, Wilkinson, & Davila, 1995).

DrinkWise is based on over 20 years of research conducted at the Addiction Research Foundation in Toronto. It has undergone several clinical trials and extensive testing and development. In Canada, DrinkWise services are available nationwide by phone, in private treatment, or in regional assessment centers. DrinkWise can be commercially purchased in the United States from HomeWood Behavioural Health Corporation located in Guelph, Ontario. The licensing to conduct the DrinkWise program includes intensive training for professionals. It has a well-developed, multistage evaluation system to track client outcomes for up to 1 year.

DrinkWise was first established in the United States in 1994 at the University of Michigan. Several offices operate in the United States, with a national telephone format program run at the University of Michigan. Its initial introduction and results received national media attention and refueled the acrimonious debate in the media over controlled drinking, pitting the moderation programs against more conventional addiction treatments. Initial results on over 200 individuals who have been seen at the program at the University of Michigan have been closely evaluated. For those who completed the DrinkWise program (N = 152), consumption dropped 73% on average, from 23 average drinks per week to 6.55 drinks per week, with clients being in full or partial remission, according to *DSM-III-R* criteria, at the 1-year mark (DrinkWise, 1996). Although the clinical trials with DrinkWise in Canada and the experience at the University of Michigan are similar, they are superior to the many clinical trials documented in published studies. Research results collectively show that people using behavioral self-control training respond favorably over extended periods and are comparable to those whose sole goal is abstinence.

The philosophy underlying DrinkWise, which we adopted, is that (1) people can take responsibility for changing their behavior; (2) excessive drinking is a learned habit that can be overcome; (3) if they participate, clients should be able to choose the type of program they want, the goals they want to reach, and the format for reaching them and to determine how private they want the contact with the counselor to be; and (4) only techniques clients rated as effective in reducing their drinking should be used. DrinkWise provides specific knowledge and guidelines, adjusted for both male and female clients' different needs, to reduce the risks of drinking too much and too often, in the wrong situations, and for the wrong reasons.

Most drinkers lack basic information on the content of alcoholic beverages and alcohol's impact on how drinkers act and think, so this information is emphasized early in the program. Then clients can better understand their own drinking patterns, when and where they are vulnerable to overdrinking, and develop an inventory of the consequences they experienced and those they desired to avoid. At the University of Michigan, we found attitudes about drinking changed for clients as they acquired new knowledge and understood the seriousness and undesirability of their alcohol use. Clients learned specific skills in setting realistic yet challenging goals, in adopting strategies for coping with change, in managing their consumption by selecting nonalcoholic beverages, in spacing their drinks, and in pacing themselves. They also learned how to recognize and to avoid situations where there was a high risk of overdrinking, how to monitor and keep coping diaries, and how to plan free time strategically.

Our experiences showed that a number of our faculty and other health and business professionals eagerly welcomed the opportunity to use the DrinkWise program, often with very favorable outcomes. As a group, clients were socially stable, successfully employed, and motivated for change. They liked the program's flexibility, the emphasis on improved health, its low cost, and their ability to choose goals. The brief therapy approach, in effect, offers a pathway to treatment and abstinence, if needed, for those individuals who would not otherwise have sought treatment.

DrinkLink

DrinkLink is a small program located in Santa Rosa and Mill Valley, California, that began in 1988 and is run by a professional therapist Donna Cornett, M.A. It was adopted from efforts made in England and adapted using Cornett's personal and treatment experience. Like DrinkWise, this counseling program teaches clients to identify triggers to overdrinking and is delivered on an individual, short-term basis over 7 weeks, using behavioral-cognitive approaches.

Drinkers Risk Reduction Program

At the Rutgers University Center for Alcohol Studies Consultation and Treatment Services, one of the oldest institutes in the United States dealing with alcohol problems, they have developed the Drinkers Risk Reduction Program (DRRP), an assessment model and brief intervention counseling program developed and led by staff psychologists. In the initial phase of this program, clients undergo two assessments to gauge their health and to determine if there is physical or social indicators of their abuse of or dependency on alcohol. Professional staff review the results of the assessments and conduct interviews with the clients to provide detailed feedback on the results according to the goals clients have set for themselves. Clients may then elect to enter into either one-on-one counseling or a self-change program to achieve their goals—either abstinence or moderate alcohol use. Follow-ups are conducted 6 months after completion.

DrinkChoice

The newest moderation program to enter the market, in 1997, is DrinkChoice, found on the Internet. DrinkChoice is a research-based program that replicates the efforts of several other moderation programs with an emphasis on helping the client select the appropriate treatment goal. It is available to clients over the telephone or through individual or group formats in the California area.

Other Treatments

For the professional therapist, the most recent breakthrough in self-learning and instruction is the *Guided Self-Change Treatment* developed by M. Sobell and L. Sobell in 1993. This book is based on years of empirical research and provides therapists with a structured, step-by-step clinical guide to working with problem drinkers and motivating them. It includes the program's procedures, handouts that can be photocopied for clients, and an excellent review of the literature and the research on brief interventions and problem drinkers.

For the individual wishing to learn moderation training and brief intervention approaches, M. Sanchez-Craig developed a standard manual that has been updated in its second edition. It is entitled *The Therapist's Manual: Secondary Prevention of Alcohol Problems* and can be obtained from ARF in Canada (1996).

Computer-Based Brief Interventions and Internet Services

Today a quick search on the Internet will produce a host of resources for problem drinkers with valuable information on brief intervention or moderation programs. For example, the web site for *Self-Help and Psychology* magazine (www.cybertowers.com /selfhelp) has articles on brief interventions and lists various professionals who provide moderation services in Canada and the United States. Another well-developed site that provides extensive information on alcohol moderation, habit change, addiction, and harm reduction is *Habit Smart* (www.cts.com/crash/habtsmrt/).

One of the most innovative models for moderate drinking is the "Behavioral Self-Control Program for Windows" (BSCPWIN). It was developed by Reid Hester, Ph.D., at the Alcohol Self-Control Program in Albuquerque, New Mexico. This is a personal, computer-based, interactive software, educational program for the Windows environment. BSCPWIN was supported by numerous controlled clinical trials (Hester & Miller, Chapter 9, 1995), which means we are seeing quality research applied to the field of addiction in very practical ways. The most recent publication by Hester and Delaney (1997) indicated positive outcomes using BSCPWIN in reducing drinking and other drug use at 12-month follow-up periods. The program consists of eight sessions over a period of 8 to 10 weeks. The program and manual assumes that supervising therapists have a working knowledge of Windows, but clients do not need it. Clients complete an on-screen assessment that scores their drinking patterns and provides information on risk levels. Clients also receive feedback on their individual rates of consumption as they try to moderate their drinking and on their progress toward their goals.

BSCPWIN is informative, well designed, and user friendly and has entertaining graphics. Each session is conducted with the therapist, and the material can be printed for home use. Clients also take home a computer disk to record their progress and consumption patterns that are reentered into the database later. This whole system is available for only a few hundred dollars, and its outcome results are impressive.

"Moderation Management" (MM) is a recovery program and national support group network for those wishing to reduce their alcohol use. MM has created a web site (http://www.moderation.org) that lists many of their services and support groups. The MM program is well developed and founded upon solid scientific principles. Its national e-mail group provides mutual support for members, with professional input, and provides a forum for healthy debate on the issues and struggles of those attempting to moderate their alcohol use. For an EAP professional new to the area of monitoring moderation, this debate is quite educational.

At the University of Michigan, we developed a computerized, alcohol screening instrument for our community. This anonymous, self-administered instrument is based on the AUDIT and CAGE and is suitable for faculty, staff, and students. The purpose of our instrument is to help clients determine if they have a drinking problem and if further evaluation at the EAP would help. The instrument is available on the University of Michigan's Faculty and Staff Assistance Program home page (www.umich.edu/~fasap), which also lists moderation guidelines published for our community.

Mutual Support Programs

As just mentioned, Moderation Management (MM) has been developing self-help support groups for those wishing to learn to moderate and to reduce their drinking. These efforts have single-handedly been conducted by A. Kishline, the author of *Moderate Drinking* (1994). Kishline is a classic homemaker who has taken the treatment community by the horns, dared to read and challenge conventional wisdom, and crafted her own nine-step program for recovery. All indications are that MM is growing both in the United States and abroad and will be a cutting-edge effort in the secondary prevention of harmful drinking. It is easy to set up a chapter meeting of MM in any town, and information can be obtained on the World Wide Web on MM. An EAP could sponsor this approach if it had the space and the initial professional support for establishing a work-site group.

In the best practices on prevention programs, responsible use, and moderating the drinking of younger adults, I recommend *Promising Practices: Campus Alcohol Strategies* (1996) by D. Anderson, Ph.D., and G. Milgram, Ed.D., produced at George Mason University, Fairfax, Virginia. Their handbook represents dozens of innovative approaches developed by college prevention experts and researchers.

Bibliotherapy and Public Health Educational Materials

One of the first classic texts to provide practical guidance on responsible drinking was *How to Control Your Drinking* by W. Miller and R. Munoz (1982). Dr. Miller, at the University of New Mexico and a leading figure in the field of alcohol studies, wrote his book early in his career but has since written a wide array of publications and worked on the development of different concepts and forms of intervention, including materials to train and to motivate substance abusers to address their problems. Miller's works are based on data from controlled studies and are presented as a well-thought-out manual, with many graphs and charts that show the behaviors needing change. For some, though, this manual may be too long or too detailed or may require too high a reading level; yet it does help clients decide whether moderation or abstinence is the more appropriate goal for them.

In 1993 M. Sanchez-Craig, Ph.D., a senior researcher at the Addictions Research Foundation (ARF) in Toronto, published *Saying When: How to Quit Drinking or Cut Down,* now issued by ARF as *DrinkWise: How to Quit Drinking or Cut Down* (1995). This book, based in social learning theory, is essential for anyone wanting to learn the basics of moderate drinking and is used by different moderation programs, expressing useful ideas in easily understandable terms. Without being falsely optimistic, this manual, grounded in sound medical and scientific research and widely field-tested, helps clients to understand their drinking and to decide whether they can control it and whether to seek professional assistance. It is a practical tool of bibliotherapy for EAP clients that contains information on self-assessment, setting goals, moderation limits, and simple diaries to use for coping with changes in drinking patterns, and it has become the basic text used in DrinkWise's telephone format.

Moderate Drinking: The Moderation Management Guide (1994), written by A. Kishline, the founder and president of Moderation Management Network, is the official handbook for her noncoercive, commonsense support group for people wanting to reduce their drinking. The book provides a detailed, nine-step program based on leading research and on professionals' advice for setting guidelines and ways to change. In addition, Kishline describes her own successful experiences in moderating her drinking.

Lastly, D.J. Cornett (1997) produced a self-help program in her book *7 Weeks to Safe Social Drinking: How to Effectively Moderate Your Alcohol Intake.* This simple-to-read text is based on years of experience and provides numerous practical examples and advice for those who want to change their drinking patterns, leading clients from a basic understanding of drinking problems through designing their own program and evaluating the results.

In January 1996, the U.S. Department of Agriculture (USDA) and Health and Human Services (HHS) released the fourth edition of their joint statement on federal dietary guidance policy for health promotion and chronic disease prevention. The guidelines provide basic public health education on moderation and specific guidelines on the amount and frequency of drinking. Specifically, the guidelines advise Americans to moderate their alcohol intake. In addition, the language of the guidelines has changed so that the statement that claims "drinking has no net health benefits" now reads that "moderate drinking is associated with a lower risk for coronary heart disease" and that "alcoholic beverages have been used to enhance the enjoyment of meals by many societies throughout human history" (U.S. Department of Agriculture, 1995). This change in language partly reflects the extensive research over two decades that reported an association between moderate alcohol consumption and a reduced risk for coronary heart disease, the leading cause of death among Americans. The Dietary Guidelines are anything but trivial. They have profound implications for health programs, in research, and, most importantly, in consumer choices of food and beverages. These guidelines appear in a public domain pamphlet entitled "Nutrition and Your Health: Dietary Guidelines for Americans," published by the USDA and HHS and a useful educational tool in EAPs.

CONCLUSIONS

The expectations and pressures on EAP professionals to stay current with developments in the clinical and prevention fields are great. The rate at which new approaches, research, and program materials develop each year is overwhelming and yet exciting for professional development and bringing new service to the work site. For all practical purposes, alcohol problems will remain a central function of EAP practice. Most EAPs already help employees to improve their health, to avoid missing work, and to decrease their health benefit claims—key measures of positive wellness outcomes that researchers have identified in the workplace.

In the future, EAPs could have the opportunity to integrate alcohol prevention programs into many already established wellness programs, a move that will reap benefits for employees and employers alike. The benefits are likely because it is widely believed that the best way to identify and to help employees who may be at risk is through programs that promote employee health and that first try to address non-alcohol-related health factors. Secondary prevention programs, which include brief intervention approaches for problem drinkers, are, in general, nonintrusive, are well-supported by research with positive outcomes, and are not likely to affect employee morale as drug-testing programs did in the 1980s. Further research to determine the short- and long-term effect of specific brief intervention approaches for problem drinkers conducted in EAP settings is warranted. Still, the evidence we now have suggests brief intervention programs are as effective as more traditional ones. The available models and theories for drinking also seem sufficient enough so that more EAP professionals can feasibly adapt the theories and research findings into viable practices at the work site and can provide their own evaluation results. We now need to begin doing just that!

REFERENCES

Anderson, D.S., & Milgram, G.G. (1996). *Promising practices: Campus alcohol strategies.* Fairfax, VA: George Mason University.

Anderson, P., Cremona, A., Paton, A., Turner, C., & Wallace, P. (1993). The risk of alcohol. *Addictions, 88,* 1493-1508.

Bien, T.H., Miller, W.R., & Tonigan, J.S. (1993). Brief interventions for alcohol problems: A review. *Addictions, 88,* 315–336.

Bohn, M.J., Babor, T.F., & Kranzler, H.R. (1995). The alcohol use disorders identification test (AUDIT): Validation of a screening instrument for use in medical settings. *Journal of Studies on Alcohol, 56*(4), 423–431.

Bradley, K.A., Donovan, D.M., & Larson, E.B. (1993). How much is too much? *Archives of Internal Medicine, 153,* 2734-2740.

Camargo C.A., Stampfer, J.M., Glynn, R.J., Gaziano, J.M., Manson, J.E., Goldhaber, S.Z., & Hennekens, C.H. (1997, February 4). Prospective study of moderate alcohol consumption and risk of peripheral arterial disease in US male physicians. *Circulation, 95,* 577–580.

Chou, S.P., Grant, B.F., & Dawson, D.A. (1996). Medical consequences of alcohol consumption—United States 1992. *Alcoholism, Clinical and Experimental Research, 20*(8), 1423–1429.

Cornett, D.J. (1997). *7 weeks to safe social drinking: How to effectively moderate your alcohol intake.* Secaucus, NY: Birch Lane Press.

DrinkWise. (1996). Client report #5. Health Promotion Division, University of Michigan Medical Center, Ann Arbor.

Employee Assistance Professionals Association. (1992) *EAPA standards for employee assistance programs, Part II: Professional guidelines* (p. 37). Arlington, VA.

Eighth special report to the U.S. congress on alcohol and health. (1993). *From the secretary of health and humans services* (NIH Publication No. 94-3699).

Figueredo, V.M. (1997). The effects of alcohol on the heart: Detrimental or beneficial? *Postgraduate Medicine, 101*(2), 165–168.

Fingarette, H. (1989). *Heavy drinking: The myth of alcoholism as a disease.* Berkeley: University of California Press.

Fleming, M., Barry, K., Manwell, L., Johnson, K., & London, R. (1997). A trial of early alcohol treatment (Project TrEAT): A randomized trial of brief physician advise in community-based primary care practices. *Journal of the American Medical Association, 277,* 1039-1045.

Hanna, E.Z., Chou, S.P., & Grant, B.F. (1977). The relationship between drinking and heart disease morbidity in the United States: Results from the national health interview survey. *Alcohol Clinical Experimental Research, 21*(1), 111–118.

Heather, N. (1995). Brief intervention strategies. In R.K. Hester & W.R. Miller (Eds.), *Handbook of alcoholism treatment approaches: Effective alternatives* (2nd ed., pp. 105–122). Needham Heights, MA: Allyn & Bacon.

Hester, R.K., & Delaney, H.D. (1997). Behavioral self-control for Windows: Results of a controlled clinical trial. *Journal of Consulting and Clinical Psychology, 65*(4).

Hester, R.K., & Miller, W.R. (1995). *Handbook of alcoholism treatment approaches: Effective alternatives* (2nd ed.). Needham Heights, MA: Allyn & Bacon.

Institute of Medicine. (1990) *Broadening the base of treatment for alcohol problems: A report of a study by a committee of the Institute of Medicine, Division of Mental Health and Behavioral Medicine.* Washington, DC: National Academy Press.

Kadden, R.M. (1994). Cognitive-behavioral approaches to alcoholism treatment. *Alcohol Health & Research World, 18*(4), 279–286.

Kessler, R.C., McGonagle, K.A., & Zhao, S. (1994). Lifetime and 12-month prevalence of *DSM-III-R* psychiatric disorders in the United States: Results from the national comorbidity survey. *Archives of General Psychiatry, 51,* 8–18.

Kishline, A. (1994). *Moderate drinking: The moderation management guide.* New York, NY: Crown Trade Paperbacks.

Miller, W.R. (1992). The effectiveness of treatment for substance abuse: Reasons for optimism. *Journal of Substance Abuse Treatment, 9,* 93–102.

Miller, W.R., & Munoz, R.F. (1982). *How to control your drinking* (Rev. Ed.). Albuquerque: University of New Mexico Press.

Minicucci, D.S. (1994). The challenge of change: Rethinking alcohol abuse. *Archives of Psychiatric Nursing, 8*(6), 373–380.

Michigan Department of Public Health. (1995). *Health risk behaviors 1993.* Lansing, MI: Author.

National Institute on Alcohol Abuse and Alcoholism. (1995). *Media advisory: NIAAA release physician's guide.* Washington, DC: U.S. Department of Health and Human Services, Public Health Service, National Institutes of Health.

Ontario Ministry of Health. (1993), *Partners in action: Ontario's substance abuse strategy.* Toronto, Ontario: Queen's Printer for Ontario.

Reiger, D.A., Farmer, M.E., Rae, D.S., Locke, B.Z., Keith, S.J., Judd, L.L., & Goodwin, F.K. (1990). Comorbidity of mental disorders with alcohol and other drug abuse. *Journal of the American Medical Association, 264*(19), 2511-2518.

Sanchez-Craig, M. (1995). *DrinkWise: How to quit drinking or cut down* (2nd ed.–Rev.). Toronto, Canada: Addiction Research Foundation.

Sanchez-Craig, M. (1996). *A therapist's manual: Secondary prevention of alcohol problems.* Toronto, Ontario: Addiction Research Foundation.

Sanchez-Craig, M., Wilkinson, D.A., & Davila, R. (1995). Empirically based guidelines for moderate drinking: 1-year results from three studies with problem drinkers. *American Journal of Public Health, 85*(6), 823–828.

Sanchez-Craig, M., & Wilkinson, D.A. (1993). Guidelines for advising on the goals of treatment: Abstinence or moderation. In B.-A.M. Howard, S. Harrison, V. Carver, & L. Lightfoot (Eds.), *Alcohol and drug problems: A practical guide* (pp. 127–141). Toronto: Addiction Research Foundation.

Sanchez-Craig, M., Spivak, K., & Davila, R. (1991). Superior outcome of females over males after brief treatment for the reduction of heavy drinking: Replication and report of therapist effects. *British Journal of Addiction, 86,* 867–876.

Sanchez-Craig, M., & Wilkinson, D.A. (1989). Brief treatments for alcohol and drug problems: Practice and methodological issues. In T. Loberg, W.R. Miller, P.E. Nathan, & G.A. Marlett (Eds.), *Addictive behaviors: Prevention and early intervention* (pp. 233–252). Amsterdam /Lisse, The Netherlands: Swets & Zeitlinger.

Saunders, J.B., & Aasland, O.G. (1987). *WHO collaborative project on identification and treatment of persons with harmful alcohol consumption. Report on phase I: Development of a screening instrument.* Geneva: World Health Organization.

Saunders, J.B., & Foulds, K. (1992). Brief and early intervention: Experience from studies of harmful drinking. *Australian and New Zealand Journal of Medicine, 22,* 224–230.

Single, E. (1996). Harm reduction as an alcohol-prevention strategy. *Alcohol Health & Research World, National Institute on Alcohol Abuse and Alcoholism, 20*(4).

Sobell, M.B., & Sobell L.C. (1993). *Problem drinkers: Guided self-change treatment* Addiction Research Foundation. New York: Guilford Press.

The College of Family Physicians of Canada. (1994). *Alcohol risk assessment and intervention project* (ARAI). Mississauga, Ontario

Turke, M. (1995, October 23). Personal business: For problem drinkers, a moderate proposal. *Business Week,* p. 136.

U.S. Department of Agriculture and U.S. Department of Health and Human Services. (1996). *Nutrition and your health: Dietary guidelines for Americans* (4th ed.) HG232. Washington, DC: USGPO.

U.S. Department of Health and Human Services. (1992). National institute on alcohol abuse and alcoholism: Moderate drinking. *Alcohol Alert* (No. 16), Ph 315. Washington, DC: U.S. Government Printing Office.

U.S. Department of Health and Human Services. (1995). *The physicians' guide to helping patients with alcohol problems.* NIH Publication No 95-3769. Washington, DC: U.S. Government Printing Office.

U.S. Department of Health and Human Services. (1990). *Nutrition and your health: Dietary guidelines for americans* (3rd ed.). Washington, DC: U.S. Government Printing Office.

University of Michigan Initiative on Alcohol and Other Drugs. (1993). *Survey regarding alcohol and other drugs* (Report to participants). Ann Arbor: University of Michigan.

University of Michigan Task Force on Alcohol and Other Drugs. (1991). *A university community approach to alcohol and other drugs, Phase one report: The "rollicking crew" revisited.* Ann Arbor: University of Michigan.

Wechsler, H., Austin, B., & DeJong, W. (1993). *Secondary effects of binge drinking on college campuses*. College Alcohol Study, Harvard School of Public Health, funded by Robert Wood Johnson Foundation.

Yen, L.T., Edington, D.W., & Witting, P. (1991). Association between health risk appraisal scores and employee medical claims cost in a manufacturing company. *American Journal of Health Promotion, 6*(1), 46–54.

Yuan, J.M., Ross, R.K, Gao, Y.T., Henderson, B.E., & Yu, M.D. (1977). Follow-up study of moderate alcohol intake and mortality among middle-age men in Shanghai, China. *British Medical Journal, 314*(7073), 18–34.

CHAPTER 13

Developing Clinical Tools for the Workplace: ORBIT*

DONALD L. OBERG

BACKGROUND

The Need for Tools Designed for the Workplace

Although the employee assistance program (EAP) has been in existence for approximately 50 years, very little has been produced by its practitioners in terms of tools for its use. If a comparison were to be made between the profession of employee assistance and professions such as psychology, psychiatry, counseling, and medicine, one would quickly begin to see that neither the employee assistance profession nor its practitioners have made significant contributions to the state of the art—much less to science.

For the most part, employee assistance has borrowed tools from other allied disciplines, particularly psychology and chemical dependence. This is not to say that there are not those creative individuals out there who have produced wonderful tools and systems for their own proprietary use—they do exist. But, taken as a whole, these have not been widely shared, much less put to the rigors of scientific scrutiny for the benefit of the profession, science, and, ultimately, those served by EAPs. Consequently, there is little to show—in terms of technology production—for the EAP's 50-year existence. The impact this lack of technology development has upon the profession of employee assistance (EA) is sizeable and significant.

From a professional identity perspective, having a hodgepodge of techniques borrowed from various sources dilutes the identity of the profession. This diluted identity serves in turn as a gateway for practitioners of any stripe to claim that they are EA practitioners simply because they have a "related" credential.

From the practitioners perspective, we fail to serve the best needs of our clients when we are constantly borrowing tools that are created for other populations and adapting them to our populations. More tools created expressly for the practice of employee assistance are needed. Oddly enough, a debt of gratitude is owed to the managed-care movement for helping us move in this direction.

By asking basic questions of providers such as: What do you do? When do you do it? How much do you do it? How do you know if what you do makes a difference? and Is this difference worth the price paid?, managed care has raised the bar on demonstrating efficacy and value.

---

*Occupational Resources Based Intervention Tool for Substance Abuse

By using its vast statistical savvy, managed care created a shift in employers' evaluation criteria, from a mixture of low-empirical/high-anecdotal-level evidence to a new world of the extremely highly empirical. Perhaps no area touched by this change was as hard hit as mental health because it traditionally was the least empirical of the lot.

Gone are the days when a patient simply submits their bill from their provider to the insurance company and awaits payment. Today, mental health practitioners, out of necessity, are better able to speak the statistical language of managed care. In order to have their services reimbursed, in today's environment, the provider must become involved with the insurance carrier even before services are rendered. Before benefits will be granted, many insurance plans require preauthorization: This requires the practitioner to submit extensive patient histories and exhaustive treatment plans for approval. In return, patients are allotted a certain number of visits, after which progress and treatment plans are reassessed. Consequently, practitioners have needed to modify the way they practice and to focus primarily on quantitatively measurable outcomes rather than qualitative clinical judgments.

As EAPs have largely followed a mental health model, they too have encountered this change in accountability. Suddenly, EAPs were being asked to account for what happened inside of the black box of their programs; and EAP conferences everywhere were abuzz with sessions on "data collection" and "developing outcome measures" and "marketing EAP services."

Managed care and its demands for data propelled many EAPs into the computer age. Today, EAPs have defined relevant outcomes and are better able to communicate these data to our payers. Our ability to do so is due, in no small part, to those EA practitioners who blended their computer skills with their EAP expertise to provide us the first tools created expressly for the field of employee assistance: computerized case-tracking systems. These people are owed a debt of gratitude. Due to their efforts, we are able to statistically demonstrate, primarily in terms of program utilization, the value of EA services. The time has now come for the creation of clinical tools created expressly for the workplace, that measure more than program utilization; and this is beginning to happen.

In 1994, the EAPI (Employee Assistance Program Inventory) was developed by William D. Anton, Ph.D., and James R. Reed, Ph.D. The EAPI was developed for EA professionals to use as part of their intake process as a generic screening tool for anxiety, depression, self-esteem problems, marital problems, external stressors, interpersonal conflict, work adjustment, problem minimization, and effects of substance abuse. The EAPI is described in the publisher's catalog as "the first clinical instrument specifically targeted for use in EAPs, as well as by all mental health professionals who provide counseling and other services to working adults."

The logical next step is to create instruments that go beyond the scope of the EAPI and that deal more specifically with the areas screened by the EAPI, such as substance abuse.

Substance abuse is a problem in the U.S. workforce; and no other area has been so clearly associated with EA work. Additionally, the linkages between substance abuse, the workplace, and EAP have been strengthened by two federal government initiatives: the Drug-Free Workplace Act of 1989 and the revised Department of Transportation (DOT) Drug and Alcohol Regulations (1996). The net result of both of these initiatives is greater involvement and responsibility for the EAP.

A Brief History of the Drug-Free Workplace Program (DFWP)

"Partially in response to evidence of drug use among employed individuals, public policy in the United States has influenced public- and private-sector employers to test prospective and current employees for evidence of drug use" (Blum, Fields, Milne, & Spell, 1992). Although there had been a federal drug abuse treatment-and-prevention effort for over 20 years, in 1989, this issue reached a critical mass resulting in the passage of the Drug Free Workplace Act. In order to meet the requirements of the Drug-Free Workplace (DFWP) Act, each federal agency had to develop a drug-free workplace plan. Even though each agency's plan differed, they all addressed the key components of deterrence, treatment, and prevention.

EAPs had typically been involved in the two latter components, treatment and prevention. However, although treatment, assessment, referral, and prevention through education had long been the domain of EAPs in regard to substance abuse, the level of responsibility for and the importance of these traditional functions were significantly increased under the DFWP.

DFWP and the Management Mandated Referral

Under the DFWP, a third type of referral to the EAP, the management-mandated referral (nonvoluntary), was added to the standard self-originated (voluntary) and management-suggested referrals of the past. The management-mandated referral in cases of substance abuse requires the employee to participate in the EAP and to comply with EAP directives. Employees that are subject to management-mandated referrals have either (1) self-identified their drug usage to management or (2) tested positive for drugs either in a random, a for-cause, or a postaccident drug screen.

A management-mandated referral differs from the management-suggested referral of the past in four very important ways:

1. Employees must accept the mandatory referral to the EAP or face termination.
2. Referral to the EAP under the DFWP represents a last-chance agreement because the penalty for noncompliance or treatment failure is termination.
3. For those individuals who occupy a testing designated position (TDP—those positions determined by management to be either safety or security sensitive), removal from this position is required.
4. A management decision to restore the employee to their TDP, based largely upon treatment data is required prior to treatment.

The Department of Transportation Regulations

Partly due to the increase in the number of accidents attributed to alcohol usage, the Department of Transportation expanded their Drug and Alcohol Testing Regulations to include testing for alcohol. Effective January 1, 1996, companies employing *even one* commercial motor vehicle driver were mandated to:

- Develop a comprehensive substance abuse policy.
- Educate and train supervisors.

- Test all employees with commercial driver's licenses for drugs and alcohol.
- Provide drug and alcohol information to all drivers.
- Identify a substance abuse professional (SAP).
- Comply with record-keeping and reporting requirements.

Accordingly, EA practitioners now, more than ever, are expected to make expert assessments, to refer to adequate treatment, to monitor client compliance and progress, and to interface with management in a straightforward way that has a direct impact on the client's employment.

RATIONALE FOR SERVICE INNOVATION

New Challenges for the EAP

Because a client's employment is directly linked to successful involvement with the EAP under the DFWP and DOT regulations, it is incumbent upon EA programs to fine-tune their operation so the client is afforded every opportunity for recovery. Therefore, EAPs must examine each stage of the EAP process—assessment, referral, and follow-up—to ensure adequacy regarding the demands created by the these new workplace initiatives. The black box approach, such as described by Walsh, Hingson, Merrigan, Levenson, Cupples, and Heeren (1992) in which "assessment and referral questions have been left for the individual counselors to work out as best they can," is clearly unsatisfactory for the following reasons:

- It presumes that all EAP counselors operate at the same level of competence and, therefore, assumes that assessment and referral will be comprehensive, adequate, and consistent.
- It cannot ensure equitable assessment/treatment across clients.
- The client cannot be evaluated relative to other similarly situated individuals.
- Counselors must defend their clinical judgment when it comes time to consider restoration of the client to a TDP.

The First Computerized Clinical Tool Designed Expressly for the EAP—*ORBIT*

In 1990 the National Aeronautics and Space Administration (NASA), in conjunction with COPE, Inc., the EAP provider for NASA Headquarters, recognized the need to address the aforementioned four reasons in a systematic way. An instrument that would serve as a standard treatment protocol was sought but not found. As a result the Occupational Resources Basic Intervention Tool *(ORBIT)* was created by this author to address this need. *ORBIT* is a computerized, easy-to-use instrument created expressly for EA programs that standardizes data collection and case management of substance abusing clients.

As a precursor to the development of *ORBIT,* a review of the literature was conducted to determine the form and substance of such an instrument. In general there is great support for such an undertaking:

Rioux and Van Meter (1990) advocated a multimodal approach to relapse prevention. Such an approach would include in their model: "relapse specific and interactive lectures, daily journal, frequent individual counseling, communication therapy groups, practice in cognitive mapping, stress reduction, training and development of individualized relapse-prevention plan, and fostering a specialized aftercare program."

Mackay and Marlatt (1990), in their review of determinants and predictors of relapse, supported the notion that the risk of relapse is determined by a combination of individual, situational, and physiological factors. Specifically cited were individual facts such as negative emotional states (frustration, anger, anxiety, depression or boredom, and coping skills), environmental and social factors, and physiological factors. Relapse-prevention efforts are designed to impart skill training, cognitive reframing, and lifestyle rebuilding. Such is the intent of *ORBIT*—being, however, workplace-based.

Carroll, Rounsaville, and Keller (1991) supported the integration of relapse-prevention techniques into a psychotherapeutic approach versus a purely psychoeducational approach in order to enhance treatment effectiveness with cocaine abusers.

Barber (1992) supported attempts to help drug addicted individuals modify their posttreatment environments.

Citing social learning theory for the development of behavioral skills, Rose-Colley and Cinelli (1992) outlined various techniques for a relapse model. General types of learning strategies were listed that may be used in developing instruction. Such techniques included lecture, self-monitoring, change contracting, problem-solving skills, and social skills. These and other strategies have been utilized in *ORBIT*.

Watson (1991), reviewing paradigms of recovery, argued that broad-based, long-term, holistic modalities appeared to be most promising. Furthermore, he believed that emphasis should be placed on empowerment of the individual through means of developing self-efficacy and spiritual meaning.

In their review of research and practice pertaining to relapse and recovery, Leukefeld and Tims (1989) cited the importance of identifying factors associated with relapse and incorporating this knowledge into the treatment process. Their recommendations support the development of treatment protocols, treatment contracts, and support systems that, among other things, focus on developing the client's skills in self-regulation and on increasing their commitment to abstinence. Furthermore Leukefeld and Tims cited the following as a summary of the predisposing/precipitating factors of relapse:

- Craving.
- Stress.
- False beliefs regarding risks.
- Lack of commitment to abstinence.
- Negative affective states.
- Social or environmental cues.
- Drug availability.
- Peer pressure.

They indicate the following as suitable treatments for recovery:

- Withdrawal maintenance.
- Aftercare.

- Appropriate medication as needed.
- Self-help to teach coping skills.
- Counseling.
- Cognitive therapy.
- Aftercare follow-up.
- Self-help in regulating behavior.
- Contingency management.
- Family counseling.
- Vocational rehabilitation.
- Employment services.
- Drug-testing service.

Guidance for weaving these predisposing factors and the suitable treatments into a complete assessment tool and treatment protocol, appropriate for the workplace was gleaned from Tarter's (1990) work within the adolescent community, wherein, he faced many of the same challenges faced by EAPs today. Tarter recognized that diagnostic evaluation and treatment for adolescents were not standardized and typically were not based upon empirically valid procedures. His goal was (1) to design an objective evaluation format, linking assessment to intervention; and (2) to improve objectivity, through standardization and accountability, so that maximum rehabilitation could be achieved.

To achieve his goals, Tarter created a structured interview that examines what he identified to be 10 basic domains. They are:

1. Substance-use behavior.
2. Behavior patterns.
3. Health status.
4. Psychiatric disorder.
5. Social skills.
6. Family systems.
7. School.
8. Work.
9. Peer relationships.
10. Leisure and recreation.

Tarter's work, thus, became the platform on which the development of an instrument appropriate for the workplace was based. The *ORBIT* was created by modifying the 10 basic domains and weaving them into a comprehensive four-part protocol for complete case management. These four component parts are:

Component I—Treatment History: Designed to maximize the information obtained from the treatment facility, and includes a comprehensive reporting of the client's medical history, social history, drug usage, and progress during treatment.

Component II—Assessment Tools: Designed to examine seven major areas identified as influencing recovery: family environment, coping skills, vocational adjustment, personality factors, stress level, codependence, and peer affiliation/leisure activities.

Component III—Client Tools: Involves working with the client on an ongoing basis to foster an understanding of the addiction-relapse-recovery process. Clients are provided with a *Recovery Guide and Handbook,* and, together with the EAP counselor, they monitor their progress in treatment.

Component IV—Workplace Tools: Is an individualized, outcomes-monitoring program, directly linked to workplace performance. It includes all necessary follow-up protocols and outlines the linkages among the client, the EAP counselor, and the workplace via the client's supervisor.

An integral design element of *ORBIT* is the quantification of data. All information collected is computer scored and results in a standard client profile. This is a critical advantage in that it:

- Allows counselors to track client progress in treatment in a quantifiable way.
- Assists in comparison of cases.
- Identifies variables directly related to outcome.
- Can profile various categories of client outcome (i.e., relapsed vs. abstinent).
- Supports counselor's recommendations regarding restoration to TDPs with comprehensive hard data, instead of relying solely upon clinical judgment.

A detailed analysis of each component, with supporting rationale, follows.

ORBIT Components

Component I—Treatment History

In the past, the exchange of information between a treatment provider and the EAP was little more than a report containing attendance and urinalysis results. To capitalize on the wealth of information routinely collected by a treatment provider, Component I is a structured interview completed by treatment providers. Areas covered are:

- Demographics, including treatment type [as defined by American Society of Addiction Medicine (ASAM)].
- Drug history.
- Legal history.
- Medical/psychiatric history.
- Present treatment history.
- Prognosis.

In constructing each category, emphasis is placed on capturing information that may portend the likelihood of relapse. For instance, Mulry and Stockhoff (1988) supported the medical/pharmacological questions found in this component relating to use of medications. These authors stated that "certain intoxicating drugs always will cause pharmacologic dependence. . . . Some non-intoxicating drugs that may affect mood may create a pre-relapse state." They further stated that illegal drugs, alcohol, sedatives, and narcotics virtually always cause relapse when used outside the hospital. These findings are incorporated into this component by inquiring about any medications taken and whether they have the potential for abuse.

Another example of the comprehensiveness of this component can be found in the Legal History section of the interview. In his work, Tarter (1988) examined the interplay of inherited behavioral propensities on temperaments with physical and social environmental factors that may predispose one to substance abuse. Factors that appear to correlate with the development of substance abuse (e.g., positive family history, impulsivity, and conduct disorders in childhood and adolescence) have been included in *ORBIT* in various components. Consequently, questions regarding a juvenile record are asked in the Legal section as a means of detecting the presence of a conduct disorder in childhood that may have resulted in a juvenile criminal offense.

In order to achieve maximum compliance, a referral letter to the treatment provider accompanies the client. The letter outlines what is required of the treatment program by accepting this person as a client and what the provider must agree to before accepting this person into treatment. All information is collected in a fixed format for statistical analysis and results in a composite score reflecting the significance of treatment findings.

Although Component I maximizes the information available from the treatment provider, it is clear that EA counselors also routinely obtain a wealth of information about their clients during an assessment. Yet beyond the standard intake information, most information is not systematically collected and analyzed in a standardized way to achieve a treatment recommendation. Rather, a treatment recommendation is made after the counselor, using clinical judgment, processes the information gleaned through his or her own particular set of filters, or black box. Component II seeks to eliminate the black box by defining these processes so that they may be consistently operationalized.

Component II—Assessment Tools

Development of this component began by asking the question: "What areas of a person's life are significant to recovery and the workplace?" Various studies such as Unnithan, Gossop, and Strang (1992), Wallace (1989), and Edwards, Brown, Oppenheimer, Sheehan, Taylor, and Duckitt (1988) all suggest multiple determinants of relapse. These are best summarized by Daley (1989), who identified relapse precipitants from a variety of perspectives. Related directly to the individual are the following variables:

Affective Variables:	Negative and positive mood states, depression, and anxiety.
Behavioral Variables:	Coping/refusal skills.
Cognitive Variables:	Attitude, self-efficacy, outcome expectancy, attribution of causality, decision making, and level of cognitive functioning.
Environmental and Relationship Variables:	Lack of social or family stability, living with another abuser, major life changes, lack of productive work/school roles, lack of quality leisure or recreational interests.
Physiological Variables:	Craving, diet, withdrawal, cues, brain chemistry, chronic illness, pain after medication.
Psychiatric Variables:	After addictive disorders, dual-diagnosed.
Spiritual Variables:	Belief system.

From these variables, seven basic screens were developed for use in assessing in the workplace the client's potential for relapse and recovery. These basic screens are:

1. Family Environment.
2. Coping Skills.
3. Vocational Adjustment.
4. Personality Style and Depression.
5. Stress and Anxiety Levels.
6. Codependence.
7. Peer Affiliation and Leisure Activities.

The purpose of the basic screens is to provide an indication of where additional exploration may be warranted. Accordingly, each screen was created to answer the basic question: "If one could only ask a few key questions to determine if this client has difficulty with this area of functioning, what would they be?" What follows is the rationale for each section.

Family Environment.   Various researchers have noted the importance of examining the family of origin and the present family settings in order to understand the addiction, recovery, and relapse processes. Finney and Moos (1992), in a 19-year follow-up study of 113 patients who received in-patient treatment and returned to their families, assessed 93 subjects at 2 years and at 10 years. Findings at this time revealed that "persons in less stressful life situations, in more cohesive and organized families, and who more frequently used active coping responses at the 2-year follow-up tended to function better at the 10-year follow-up." This suggests the importance of family and reinforces the spread of skills required for successful outcome.

Dawson, Harford, and Grant (1992), in a massive study of 23,152 drinkers age 18 or older, when adjusted for age, race, gender, and poverty and compared to persons without a family history of alcoholism, found that the odds of alcohol dependence were increased by 45% among persons with second- or third-degree relatives only, by 86% among those with first-degree relatives only, and 167% across all three degrees of relatives. Furthermore, they found that the effects of family history were the same among population subgroups as defined by race, age, gender, and poverty.

Pardeck, Callahan, Allgier, Fernandez, Green, Griffin, Herter, Underwood, Whitney, and Williams (1991), in a study of college students, found that the role of the dysfunctional family, and conflict contributed to the potential of alcoholism in college-age students.

Accordingly, questions regarding family functioning were incorporated into probe questions for this screen. The six questions comprising this screen address: genetic factors, historical factors, dysfunctional family dynamics, emotional timbre, reinforcement schemata, and relationships within the family.

Before continuing on with an analysis of the other six Basic Screens, it should be mentioned that for each screen, the counselor reads each question to the client, and the counselor is provided standard alternative questions to administer to the client in the event that the client is unable to understand the original question. Clients are asked to rate the strength of their responses on a Likert scale. Additional input is provided by the counselor as to their confidence in the client's ability to understand the question and in the truthfulness of the answers. These factors are then numerically combined to obtain a score for each screen.

Coping Skills.   Schonfeld, Rohrer, Dupree, and Thomas (1989) investigated the determinants of relapse and the antecedents of recent use for 30 substance abusers re-entering inpatient treatment. Findings revealed that alcohol was the most frequently used substance, both initially and subsequently, and that relapse occurred usually around 2 months following treatment. Regarding the antecedents of use, negative emotional states such as depression and loneliness were predominant among a mixture of inter- and intrapersonal events. The authors found that there was a dramatic shift to intrapersonal determinants such as depression, nervousness, or loneliness in recent use. They further suggested that "this might reflect alienation of friends or family or negative moods usually from continual substance use, implying greater need for teaching coping skills for such mood states to those re-entering treatment."

Unnithan, Gossop, and Strang (1992) investigated 42 opiate addicts in outpatient treatment. Subjects completed a questionnaire regarding social, psychological, and environmental circumstances. Forty percent had relapsed during the first 2 weeks of treatment. They found two sorts of factors to be linked with lapse to illicit opiate use: interpersonal factors and drug-related factors. Using self-report data, items relating to cues such as "I saw someone else use" or "I saw drugs and felt I had to use" and social items such as "I spent long periods of time alone" were found to be significant. This supports the work done in Component II—with questions specifically relating to cues, coping skills, and peer affiliation/leisure activities.

O'Brien, Childress, and McLellan (1991) cited that "relapse to drug use after detoxification is influenced by several factors both internal and external to the patient. To prevent relapse, all categories of relapse-producing factors should be addressed, including pharmacological, social, occupational, medical, legal, and family issues." Specifically, they cite four classes of relapse factors:

1. Psychiatric disorders (including depression) and anxiety disorders.
2. Social factors (e.g., employment opportunities) and social support network.
3. Protracted abstinence syndromes.
4. Conditioned responses.

Wells, Catalano, Plotnick, Hawkins, and Brattesani (1989), working with a group of 106 residential day-treatment clients, found that drug-specific skills such as drug and alcohol avoidance and relapse-coping consequential thinking were significant predictors of relapse, although the general skills of social, stress, coping, and problem solving were not predictors. This suggests the need to tailor such programs to the specific drug of choice and corresponding milieu.

Considering the findings of the studies mentioned in this section, five questions regarding coping skills were constructed to examine cue management, skills acquisition, triggers, contingency planning, and self-perception.

Vocational Adjustment.   Aside from the appropriateness including vocational factors in a workplace-based project, there is evidence that the vocational milieu is a significant factor in recovery.

DeSoto, O'Donnell, and DeSoto (1989) emphasized that full recovery is based on abstinence and time. Their research revealed that of employed subjects at the 4-year follow-up, 22% attained a higher status position, 70% remained the same, and 8% dropped to a lower status or became unemployed. The authors found that this validated the concept of "with confirmed abstinence comes increased employability."

O'Brien, Childress, and McLellan (1991) again cited that to prevent relapse, "all categories of relapse-producing factors should be addressed, including pharmacological, social, occupational, medical, legal, and family issues."

Factors investigated in the vocational screen are: premorbid level of job functioning, present level of job functioning, work situations likely to cause relapse, support of management for recovery program, empowerment, and importance of job retention to the client.

Personality.   Increasingly, a profile of who is likely to become substance abusing is emerging from the research. Glenn and Parsons (1991) examined the resumption of drinking in 58 male and 45 female alcoholics. They interviewed subjects immediately upon release from treatment and then on follow-up, 14 months later. Forty-one subjects (41%) relapsed. Considering five measures as predictor variables—depressive symptomology, attention deficit disorder, psychosocial adjustment, previous treatment history, and neuropsychological performance index—depressive symptomology was the best single predictor of relapse.

Miller (1991), in his work predicting relapse and recovery in alcoholism and addiction, examined neuropsychology, personality, and cognitive style. He found that relapsers were characterized by impulsivity, antisocial personality, and affective disorders, whereas nonrelapsers demonstrated future goal orientation, higher tolerance for frustration, and greater degrees of self-efficacy..

Again, O'Brien, Childress, and McLellan (1991) specifically cited psychiatric disorders, including depression and anxiety disorders, as one of the four classes of relapse factors.

Accordingly, the personality basic screen included questions regarding impulsivity, self-efficacy, obsessive-compulsive traits, depression, and other pathognomic indicators.

Stress.   Brown, Vik, McQuaid, Patterson, Irwin, and Grant (1990) used the Psychiatric Epidemiology Research Interview-Modified (PERI-M) as a structured diagnostic interview to gather information regarding the social, family, educational, alcohol, drug, medical, and psychiatric histories of 129 inpatient males. These researchers found that men who returned to drinking after receiving treatment reported more severe or highly threatening stress before their relapse than did their abstinent peers. These data then suggest that acute severe stress and highly threatening chronic difficulties may be connected with an increased risk of relapse.

Tiul'pin (1991) did an analysis on findings of a clinical psychological study of alcoholics for the purpose of predicating relapse using the Minnesota Multiphasic Personality Inventory (MMPI). The results indicated that the level of anxiety at the moment of discharge and the patient's personal anxiety had a definite role in the duration of remission.

Accordingly, questions on the Stress Screen examine negative coping behaviors, stress level, specific versus free-floating anxiety, somatic complaints, and sense of well-being.

Codependence.   Schonfeld, Rohrer, Dupree, and Thomas (1989) found that negative emotional states such as depression and loneliness were predominant among a mixture of inter- and intrapersonal events and found a dramatic shift toward these intrapersonal variables regarding recent use.

Gallant (1992) examined the generalizability of common predictors of abstinence and relapse among alcoholics and other drug abusers. In looking at both structural support (e.g., having a partner/spouse/significant other) and functional support (e.g., experienced helpfulness of others' behavior related to abstinence) among alcoholics, cigarette smokers, and opiate users, he found that there was a high correlation between abstinence-specific functional support and relapse risk, independent of the drug of choice. Consequently, he suggested integrating all possible structural support (including 12-step programs, partners, and aftercare alumni groups) into all treatment modalities. Given the interpersonal variable, the issue of codependence is suggested.

Therefore, this screen examines locus of control, self-defeating beliefs, self-esteem, and ego boundaries.

Peer Affiliation and Leisure Activities.   In his introduction to the *International Journal of Addictions,* Dr. Barry S. Brown (1990), Chief of the Community Research Branch of the National Institute of Drug Abuse (NIDA), addressed the need to involve service providers in changing the individual's environment, not just the individual. Brown suggested that such changes include:

- Working to change the role demand and expectations placed on the client by the family, school, or employer.
- Developing new and prosocial networks.
- Developing initiatives to help the exiting client structure his or her free-time activities to avoid relapse.

Additionally, the work of Gallant (1992) suggested the importance of one's peer group as well as incorporating them into the treatment milieu. As a result, questions regarding positive peer group, support networks, positive time management, and positive effects of lifestyle alteration are examined in this screen.

Component III—Client Tools

In order to facilitate the client's progress in treatment, Component III provides the EAP counselor with a 6-month set of practice guidelines regarding follow-up counseling sessions with substance abusing clients. After completing the basic screens in Component II, clients are provided two recovery tools: the *Recovery Guide* and the *Recovery Handbook.* The *Recovery Guide* consists of:

- A list of all basic screen questions.
- A graphical profile of the client's scores on the basic screens.
- A fill-in-the-blank Action Plan to address areas of weakness.
- A Recovery Calendar to track attendance at 12-step programs, work on the Action Plan, contacts with sponsor, counseling sessions, and various other treatment-related activities.

The *Recovery Handbook* is an explanation, in everyday language, of each question asked in the basic screens: why was it asked and what to do if this area is problematic. The *Recovery Handbook* is designed to be a practical reference for the client and also a guide for counselors for counseling session content.

This type of active participation is greatly supported in the literature. Annis and Davis (1991) cited the use of homework for skill acquisition. Five specific homework assignments are discussed:

1. Monitoring specific situations and cognition.
2. Anticipating problem situations.
3. Planning and rehearsing alternative responses.
4. Practicing new behavior.
5. Noting improved competence.

Annis and Davis (1991), following the need for specificity as related to drug-specific coping skills, outlined a procedure for working with alcoholic clients. Major aspects of their treatment paradigm are: identifying high-risk situations, assigning homework designed to reinforce desired changes, and developing client confidence and self-efficiency in coping with all areas of personal risk.

Monti, Abrams, Binkoff, Zwick, Liepman, Nirenberg, and Rohsenow et al. (1990), worked with 69 male alcoholics in a standard inpatient program. Three treatments were administered: communication-skills training (CST), family participation (CSTF), and cognitive behavioral mood management training group (CBMMT). CST and CSTF groups drank significantly less alcohol per drinking day during the 6-month follow-up than did CBMMT groups. All groups showed improvements in skill and anxiety with CST being most improved. This study supports skills development with addictive persons.

Hermalin, Husband, and Platt (1990) reviewed several intervention studies and found that training programs that emphasize cognitive problem solving and behavioral skills can be a useful and powerful adjustment to exiting programs. This article is especially important from a workplace perspective because it was written from the EAP point of view and examined cost-reduction strategies related to substance abuse.

Component IV—Workplace Tools

Component IV establishes appropriate linkages to the workplace for all treatment activities. Specifically, Component IV consists of:

- A *Return-to-Work Agreement,* negotiated with the client, the supervisor, and appropriate treatment personnel.
- A monthly *Client Tracking Form,* which monitors counselor contacts and specifics regarding the client's aftercare activities.
- A monthly *Return-to-Work Evaluation,* completed by the supervisor, to ensure that treatment gains are resulting in improved performance.

Component IV is an individualized, outcomes-monitoring program directly linked to the workplace. It includes all necessary follow-up protocols and outlines the linkages among the client, the EAP counselor, and the workplace. Treatment outcomes are measured in terms of absences, tardiness, accidents, disciplinary contacts, job performance, and compliance with treatment directives. Support for this type of integration of follow-up/support activities is cited in the literature.

Gallant (1992) examined the generalizability of common predictors of abstinence and relapse among alcoholics and other drug abusers. In looking at both structural support (e.g., having a partner/spouse/significant other) and functional support (e.g., experienced helpfulness of other's behavior related to abstinence) among alcoholics, cigarette smokers, and opiate users, he found that there was a high correlation between abstinence-specific functional support and relapse risk, independent of the drug of choice. Consequently he suggested integrating all possible structural support (including 12-step programs, partners, and aftercare alumni groups) into all treatment modalities.

Foote and Erfurt (1991) randomly assigned EAP clients assessed as substance abusing to a treatment group—"special follow-up"—or to a control group—"regular care." The treatment group received routine scheduled contact, whereas the control group received follow-up only as needed. Although this study was only partially implemented, it found marginally significant increase for the treatment group on three measures related to substance abuse.

Barriers to Change

Over the past three years, efforts to introduce *ORBIT* into EA practice have been underway and have met with mixed success. In general, it would appear that those practitioners who have the testing skills commonly taught in most Master's degree programs are more enthusiastic than those who do not. Resistance appears to be associated with three main variables: (1) level of formal training, (2) differences in practitioners' attitudes, and (3) differences in organizations.

Level of Formal Training

Most professions require a specific route of formal education before one can become a member of the profession. However, in the field of EAP, this argument is still unresolved, and the two professional associations for EA practitioners each take an opposing stand. EAPA (Employee Assistance Practitioners Association), the association with the largest membership, has no formal academic requirement as its criterion for entry into the profession. EASNA (Employee Assistance Society of North America) requires a minimum of a Master's degree. Consequently, there is wide variation among practitioners, ranging from individuals who acquired their skills set from their own personal recovery from substance abuse to those who have been formally academically training at the doctoral level. This lack of homogeneity of formal training tends to create a schism in the field in many ways, not the least of which is the use of tools and tests.

In most cases, those practitioners who have not received their training from master's and doctoral programs in the mental health disciplines have not received training in psychometrics. Understandably then, these individuals usually have neither an understanding of the value of psychometric tools, nor an appreciation for the intricacies of instrument development and utilization. Consequently these practitioners, and there are a number of them, are resistant to embrace any effort to incorporate formal clinical tools into their practice.

Practitioner Variables

In addition to the cited difficulties caused by differences in clinical background and training, when an instrument is computerized, an entirely different set of personal variables is introduced.

For the majority of present-day EA practitioners, computer skills were not included in their formal job training, no matter if they were academically or experientially trained. Most likely, computer skills have been acquired based on personal interest, need, availability of training, and availability of equipment. Here again, there is no common denominator from which all future efforts can proceed. Gaining computer skills can represent a significant threat for those individuals who have not yet become computer literate.

Additional individual perceptions also come into play. Concerns about greater accountability and increased workload are often barriers to the implementation of new protocols.

Organizational Variables

Just as individual practitioners vary, so do organizations. In general, organizations drive their technical departments toward computerization and then attend to the nontechnical ones, if funds permit. Of these nontechnical departments, it is not uncommon for the EAP to be at the bottom of the list for computer equipment and training. Consequently, many EAPs do not have the equipment to benefit from computerized tools, nor the funds to buy them.

Next Steps and Future Directions

ORBIT in its current state is a standardized clinical tool used for data collection and case management. As additional data become available from EA practitioners and independent researchers, future plans include determining the reliability and the validity of *ORBIT* as a psychometric instrument to predict relapse.

Regarding the future of employee assistance, the EA profession will have to move simultaneously along two levels: the organizational level (professional associations) and the individual level.

From an organizational level, EA professional associations must promulgate the standardization of the profession and its practices and practitioners. Standardization is essential if EA professionals are to have a place at the table alongside other recognized professions such as lawyers, doctors, and psychologists. Consequently, at an organizational level, practitioners must *universally:*

- Identify a body of knowledge and practice that is uniquely the domain of the profession.
- Determine the best method of acquiring this body of knowledge and the skills to practice it.
- Establish practice guidelines, or a standard of care, for each and every service that the profession provides.
- Require that ALL programs and practitioners subscribe to what results from the preceding three points in order to be included in the profession.

On an individual level, practitioners must:

- Work with their professional associations to develop a unified identity.
- Acquire new skills that will allow full and ethical practice within the scope of the EAP field.

- Create standardized tools that address challenges in EA practice and/or document practices that are known/believed to be effective, and expose them to scientific scrutiny.

Today, individuals who seek to make a contribution to the field must take on many tasks that are not really within the scope of their project, but rather are rightly the responsibility of others. As regards *ORBIT*, this has included training people in test construction, measurement techniques and statistics, and computer skills so that they can begin to use and evaluate the tool. Needless to say, this retards the development process and serves as a disincentive.

In the future, we must create an environment where those who seek to contribute will only face one challenge: proving the merit of their contribution. Coming to terms with the areas cited previously will undoubtedly be of great assistance.

SUMMARY

Although EAPs have been in existence for approximately 50 years, very little has been produced by this profession in terms of tools for its use. For the most part, employee assistance has borrowed tools from other allied disciplines, particularly psychology and chemical dependence. Managed care created a shift in employers' evaluation criteria from a mixture of low-empirical/high-anecdotal-level evidence to a new world of the extremely highly empirical. Managed care and its demands for data propelled many EAPs into the computer age. Today, EAPs have defined relevant outcomes and are able to statistically demonstrate, primarily in terms of program utilization, the value of EA services, thanks to computerized case-tracking systems.

The time has now come for the creation of clinical tools created expressly for the workplace. Unquestionably, substance abuse is a problem in the U.S. workforce, and no other area has been so clearly associated with EA work. Additionally, the linkages between substance abuse, the workplace, and EAPs have been strengthened by two federal government initiatives. The net result of both of these initiatives is greater involvement and responsibility for the EAP. Therefore, EAPs must examine each stage of the EAP process—assessment, referral, and follow-up—to ensure adequacy regarding the demands created by the these new workplace initiatives.

To address this need, *ORBIT* was created. *ORBIT* is a computerized, easy-to-use, instrument created by expressly for EA programs to standardize data collection and case management of substance abusing clients. Although this, in itself, is a great step forward, establishing *ORBIT*'s reliability and validity as a psychometric instrument for predicting relapse will result in even greater benefit. *ORBIT* consists of four components:

Component I—Treatment Tools is designed to maximize the information obtained from the treatment facility and includes a comprehensive reporting of the client's medical history, social history, drug usage, and progress during treatment.

Component II—Assessment Tools is designed to examine seven major areas identified as influencing recovery: family environment, coping skills, vocational adjustment, personality factors, stress level, codependence, and peer affiliation/leisure activities.

Component III—Client Tools involves working with the client on an ongoing basis to foster an understanding of the addiction and recovery process. Clients are provided a recovery guide and handbook; and in conjunction with an EAP counselor, they chart their progress in treatment.

Component IV—Workplace Tools is an individualized recovery program directly linked to the workplace. It includes all necessary follow-up protocols and outlines the linkages among the client, the EAP counselor, and the workplace. Treatment outcomes are measured in terms of absences, tardiness, accidents, disciplinary contacts, job performance, and compliance with treatment directives.

An integral design element of *ORBIT* is the quantification of data. All information collected is computer scored and results in a client profile. This is a critical advantage in that it:

- Permits counselors to track client progress in treatment in a quantifiable way.
- Assists in comparison across cases due to its standardized format.
- Identifies variables directly related to outcome.
- Can profile various categories of client outcome (i.e., relapsed vs. abstinent).
- Supports counselor recommendations regarding restoration to jobs with comprehensive hard data instead of relying solely upon clinical judgment.
- Shares with the client meaningful data geared specifically to their recovery.

In the future, we must create an environment where those who seek to contribute will only face one challenge: proving the merit of their contribution.

REFERENCES

Annis, H.M., & Davis, C.S. (1991). Relapse prevention. *Alcohol Health & Research World, 15*(3), 204–212.

Barber, J. (1992). Relapse prevention and the need for brief social interventions. *Journal of Substance Abuse Treatment, 9*(2), 157–158.

Blum, T.C., Fields, D.L., Milne, S.H., & Spell, C.H. (1992). Workplace drug testing programs: A review of research and a survey of worksites. *Journal of Employee Assistance, 1,* 315–349.

Brown, B.S. (1990). Relapse prevention in substance misuse: Introduction. *The International Journal of Addictions, 25*(9A &10A), 1081–1083.

Brown, S.A., Vik, P.W., McQuaid, J.R., Patterson, T.L., Irwin, M.R., & Grant, I. (1990). Severity of psycho-social stress and outcome of alcoholism treatment. *Journal of Abnormal Psychology, 99*(4), 344–348.

Carroll, K.R., Rounsaville, B., & Keller, D. (1991). Relapse prevention strategies for the treatment of cocaine abuse. *American Journal of Drug & Alcohol Abuse, 17*(3), 249–265.

Daley, D.C. (1989). Five perspectives on relapse in chemical dependency. Relapse: Conceptual, research and clinical perspectives [Special issue]. *Journal of Chemical Dependency Treatment, 2*(2), 3–26.

Dawson, D., Harford, T., & Grant, B. (1992). Family history as a predictor of alcohol dependence. *Alcoholism: Clinical & Experimental Research, 16*(3), 572–575.

DeSoto, C.B., O'Donnell, W.E., & DeSoto, J.L. (1989). Long-term recovery in alcoholics. *Alcoholism: Clinical & Experimental Research, 13*(5), 693–697.

Edwards, G., Brown, D., Oppenheimer, E., Sheehan, M., Taylor, C., & Duckitt, A. (1988). Long-term outcome for patients with drinking problems: The search for predictors. *British Journal of Addictions, 83*(8), 917–927.

Finney, J.W., & Moos, R.H. (1992). The long-term course of treated alcoholism: II. Predictors and correlates of 10-year functioning and mortality. *Journal of Studies on Alcohol, 53*(2), 142–153.

Foote, A., & Erfurt, J.C. (1991). Effects of EAP follow-up on prevention of relapse among substance abuse clients. *Journal of Studies on Alcohol, 52*(3), 241–248.

Gallant, D. (1992). Common predictors of abstinence and relapse among alcoholics and other drug abusers. *Alcoholism: Clinical and Experimental Research, 16*(4), 837.

Glenn, S.W., & Parsons, O.A. (1991). Prediction of resumption of drinking in post-treatment alcoholics. *International Journal of the Addictions, 26*(2), 237–254.

Hermalin, J., Husband, S.D., & Platt, J.J. (1990). Reducing costs of employee alcohol and drug abuse: Problem-solving and social skills training for relapse prevention. *Employee Assistance Quarterly, 6*(2), 11–25.

Leukefeld, C.G., & Tims, F.M. (1989). Relapse and recovery in drug abuse: Research and practice. *International Journal of the Addictions, 24*(3), 189–201.

Mackay, P., & Marlatt, G. (1991). Maintaining sobriety: Stopping is starting. Relapse prevention in substance misuse [Special issue]. *International Journal of the Addictions, 25*(9A–10A), 1257–1276.

Miller, L. (1991). Predicting relapse and recovery in alcoholism and addiction. *Journal of Substance Abuse Treatment, 8*(4), 277–291.

Monti, P.M., Abrams, D.B., Binkoff, J.A., Zwick, W.R., Liepman, M.R., Nirenberg, T. D., & Rohsenow, D.J. (1990). Communication skills training, communication skills training with family and cognitive behavioral mood management training for alcoholics. *Journal of Studies on Alcohol, 51*(3), 263–270.

Mulry, J.T., & Stockhoff, J. (1988). Drug use in the chemically dependent. How to avoid relapse to addiction. *Postgraduate Medicine, 83*(5), 279–280.

O'Brien, C.P., Childress, A.R., & McLellan, A.T. (1991). Conditioning factors may help to understand and prevent relapse in patients who are recovering from drug dependence. *NIDA Research Monograph, 106,* 293–312.

Pardeck, J., Callahan, D., Allgier, P., Fernandez, N., Green, R., Griffin, S., Herter, L., Underwood, S., Whitney, R., & Williams, C. (1991). Family dysfunction and the potential for alcoholism in college students. *College Student Journal, 25*(1), 556–559.

Rioux, D., & Van Meter, W. (1990). The ABC's of awareness: A multimodal approach to relapse prevention. *Alcoholism Treatment Quarterly, 7*(3), 77–89.

Rose-Colley, M., & Cinelli, B. (1992). Relapse prevention model of behavioral maintenance. *Journal of Alcohol & Drug Education, 37*(3), 85–96.

Schonfeld, L., Rohrer, G.E., Dupree, L.W., & Thomas, M. (1989). Antecedents of relapse and recent substance use. *Community Mental Health Journal, 23*(3), 245–249.

Tarter, R.E. (1990). Evaluation and treatment of adolescent substance abuse: A decision tree method. *American Journal of Drug and Alcohol Abuse, 16*(1 & 2), 1–46.

Tarter, R.E. (1988). Are there inherited behavioral traits that predispose to substance abuse? *Journal of Consulting & Clinical Psychology, 56*(2), 189–196.

Tiul'pin, I.G. (1991). Composite analysis of the findings of a clinical-psychological study for the purpose of predicting early relapse. *Soviet Neurology & Psychiatry, 24*(4), 61–68.

Unnithan, S., Gossop, M., & Strang, J. (1992). Factors associated with relapse among opiate addicts in an out-patient detoxification programme. *British Journal of Psychiatry, 161,* 654–657.

Wallace, B.C. (1989). Psychological and environmental determinants of relapse in crack cocaine smokers. *Journal of Substance Abuse Treatment, 6*(2), 95–106.

Walsh, D.C., Hingson, R.W., Merrigan, D.M., Levenson, S.M., Cupples, L.A., & Heeren, T. (1992). A randomized trial of alternative treatments for problem drinking employees: Study design, major findings and lessons learned for worksite research. *Journal of Employee Assistance, 1,* 112–147.

Watson, L. (1991). Paradigms of recovery: Theoretical implications for relapse prevention in alcoholics. *Journal of Drug Issues, 21*(4), 839–858.

Wells, E., Catalano, R., Plotnick, R., Hawkins, D., & Brattesani, K. (1989). General versus drug-specific coping skills and post-treatment drug use among adults. *Psychology of Addictive Behaviors, 3*(1), 8–21.

CHAPTER 14

EAPs and the Future of Work

T.J. ELLIOTT

Futurism—pronouncing what will definitely occur (or not)—is a tricky enterprise. Businesses, however, flourish or even survive in part by how well they respond to changes in the environment: how aligned they are with trends in their markets, the workplace, and their workers. Employee assistance programs (EAPs) as components of work organizations must also endeavor to determine the future. They must make decisions *now* about strategy, about the ways in which they will serve their customers—the managers, the supervisors, the human resource and benefits directors—within the host work organizations. EAPs must allocate resources to anticipate the demands of clients, whether they be workers or workers' family members. Yet how can they know the future? Much of this book reflects very recent innovations in response to phenomenal changes currently shaping the EAP environment. Ten years ago, one might have speculated as to the effects of the work environment upon EAPs and predicted some of those changes:

- The rise of external EAP providers as a by-product of business process re-engineering.
- The development of managed behavioral healthcare as an outgrowth of that trend and as a response to excessive and sometimes unjustified behavioral health treatment.
- The emergence of critical-incident-stress debriefing along with recognition of the effects of trauma upon workers' functioning.

However, 30 or 60 years ago, such predictions would have required the powers of Nostradamus. Would most observers have foreseen the cost of employee benefits increasing from 3% in 1929 to 38% in the 1990s (Mosca, 1997, p. 44)? Could they have predicted the shift of psychiatric and chemical-dependency treatment to for-profit enterprises or that more than 150 million people in the United States would be covered by managed behavioral healthcare organizations? Could they have conceived the recognition of a mind/body connection in employment law? The forces driving these examples of change in EAP services were not themselves fully formed. Employee assistance evolved from the original wartime programs into occupational alcoholism programs and, eventually, broad-brush employee assistance in the 1970s. Such a history is too short to provide multiple cycles for examination.

Additionally, the pace of change in organizations has quickened in recent years, constantly buffeting EAPs with new needs, new rules, and new competitors. This flux makes forecasters hesitant. Predictions that dare go beyond a decade or so may prove incautious. Saskia Sassen (1996) described the uncertainty of general predictions: "The nation state and their regulatory frameworks may disappear in the next century: then all bets are off . . . 2010 is about as far as you can go in the prediction business." Not unsurprisingly, *The Futurist* magazine in a retrospective found 32% of its forecasts wrong (Cornish, 1997).

Employee assistance (EA) workers, then, face a challenge in specifying the kinds of changes they expect to face, in assigning significance to these changes, and in charting the synergistic effects that may erupt. Choosing scenarios is not just a matter of asking for another cut of the tarot cards; established methods exist by which to seriously explore the future. The approach followed in this chapter is to examine some trends that were predicted using those methods—labor markets, structure, and business process (principally human resources for EA purposes)—that will greatly affect companies and, therefore, their EAPs. These areas are interdependent with broader spheres such as culture, learning, globalization, legislation, medicine, and technology, which we will also briefly consider. This will catalogue the various conjectures and the plausible implications of each area in the early years of the twenty-first century for the still relatively young and at times breathtakingly diverse field of employee assistance.

Employee assistance is a turbulent field. Although some good information exists from trusted sources, no one can state with absolute certainty how the future will unfold. The possible causes and effects described in the following discussion are not regarded by the author as desirable or undesirable, but only as possible components of the coming reality. The intent here is to offer a map of the future that spurs readers to action, to exploration, and to revision according to their own hopes and fears, experiences, and theories. "Thinking about the future is only useful and interesting," said James Robertson, a leading British expert on alternative futures, "if it affects what we do and how we live today" (Hancock and Bezold, 1994, p. 23).

Many individuals and communities possess a remarkable ability to resist, to slow, and to even incorporate a change so as to retain much of the characteristics of their previous life. EA workers seem to be among this group. Although they have seen dramatic movements in their own profession, most still describe their basic activities as they did a decade ago: assessment and referral of individuals with personal problems linked to performance.

EA workers can take the forecasts summarized here and guard against what Canadian futurist Norman Henchey called *the possible future* filled with "wildcards . . . those dramatic and seemingly implausible changes that can occur very swiftly" (Hancock & Bezold, 1994, p. 23), or they can use the data as background to their efforts to create *the preferable future:* the vision of the field that does not yet exist (p. 24).

LABOR MARKETS

Conjectures

EAPs' focus on employees guarantees an interest in the organization of the labor market. Will there be more or fewer jobs? What kinds will thrive? Three opinions (at least) dominate this discussion. First, Jeremy Rifkin (1995), author of *The End of Work,* emphatically states that there will not be enough jobs for the population. His reasoning is that global unemployment—800 million—driven by technological advances will cause work organizations to cut hours as they did in the 1930s. Rifkin believes that in their expanded spare time, workers will turn to community service jobs, thus holding the fabric of society together.

The second opinion finds ample jobs clustered at the bottom of a two-tier economy: 20% of the population will be knowledge workers with the attendant rewards, and 80% will fill low-paying service jobs with little upward mobility. A third view espoused by optimists such as Harry S. Dent (1993, pp. 2–43) is that new industries will more than replace any lost jobs. The driving forces will be a baby-boomer spending spree and technological revolution. Advances in training will allow those at the bottom to take on these new jobs. This view foresees a digitalized, dematerialized economy in which everyone is electronically connected to knowledge, services, and each other. This is the *Star Trek* option and unsupported by most data analyses.

Although data gathering by the United States may be flawed—geared to manufacturing, trailing movement to a service economy, unable to gauge the knowledge and information intensity of an enterprise, contradictory on measurements of productivity—Bureau of Labor Statistics projections into the years 2005 to 2010 offer the best picture of what the jobs situation will be:

- Massive growth in low capital-intensive and low knowledge-intensive service jobs with deteriorating conditions possible in both pay and benefits for this group; "almost two-thirds of the growth will be in occupations that require less than a college degree" (BLS, on-line, 1998).
- Three service industries—retail, health, and business services—will account for about 50% of all new job growth (BLS, on-line, 1998).

The occupational categories with the greatest projected increase in number of jobs (cited in Sassen, 1996) will be:

1. Retail sales.
2. Registered nurses (despite trend toward downgrading nurses).
3. Food-preparation workers.
4. Cashiers.
5. Truck drivers.
6. Waiters and waitresses.
7. Nursing aides.
8. Janitors.
9. Systems analysts.

From this group, only nurses and systems analysts fall under the "knowledge worker" category, with the remainder classified as low-capital-intensive and low-knowledge-intensive jobs. This list suggests a significant disparity with the majority on the downside of the gap struggling to survive. Some observers believe that the majority of new entrants to the workforce will be undereducated (Vann, 1996, p. 121).

It may be that although the numbers of knowledge workers do not increase exponentially, their power and influence do so. These workers are, in Peter Drucker's view, the "true 'capital equipment' . . . organizations need knowledge workers far more than knowledge workers need them" (1994, p. 71). Efforts to attract, retain, and even cater to this minority of the segment might translate into a demand for vastly enhanced services to them in contrast to the lower tier.

The popular notion that high-tech jobs are the wave of the future depends upon one's point of view. The high-technology industry employs more than 4 million workers today, having added 240,000 employees in 1996 alone (Minnesota Future of Work, 1997). However, a comparison of that increase to only 281,000 net new high-tech jobs from 1990 to 1996 provides a reality check. The current total amounts to just about 4% of all business jobs. And high-tech jobs are not spread evenly across the United States. California holds nearly 25% of the new jobs created, and just six states account for more than 50% of high-tech jobs.

On the other hand, the high-technology field, like other knowledge fields, may possess power far beyond its job numbers. It generated sales of $800 billion, comprising about 10% of the gross domestic product (GDP) in 1995. That kind of workers-to-revenues ratio ensures that high-tech start-ups will remain popular and that high-tech workers will continue to draw special attention.

High technology created almost four times as many jobs in 1996 as the manufacturing sector. Mass labor and mass production may be on the way out, but manufacturing has proved resilient with fewer workers in automated factories. Companies with smaller administrative teams in both sectors struggle to deal with the human resources (HR) issues posed by the rapid addition of complex new jobs (e.g., engineers, mathematicians, and physicists).

The numbers of best service jobs, such as accountants and lawyers, will also grow, however, they will comprise a small percentage of overall jobs. Thirty percent of jobs in the service sector are at the high end, but in the booming 1980s, only *9 million* were created. Some positions that required a college degree may decrease significantly in the near future because organizations are eliminating the middle management layer to which the degree granted access. Nevertheless, the nonintensive service area will still require supervisors. College-educated also-rans may find themselves in hybrid jobs that blend some administrative tasks with the actual performance of a service (e.g., store manager). The total number of job openings in blue-collar and relatively low-skilled white-collar positions will be high because of replacement needs as workers of the baby boom (and somewhat-less-educated) generation retire.

These changes in the makeup of the workforce will matter to EAPs. Wage pressures, if they continue, on middle-income and lower-income jobs will create new personal difficulties that work organizations may ask EAPs to address. New ways of measuring and enhancing job performance that arise from the shift will likely require changes in EAP methods. Technology and training will matter immensely, and EA workers must improve their own skills in both areas to stay relevant to the company. The opportunities produced by those forces will also rapidly produce obsolescence for some highly specialized workers, and EAPs must help those workers adapt to this change. As many EAPs in the 1990s found an opportunity to provide value by playing a role in downsizing and reengineering, so they may continue to deal with displaced employees whose skill set no longer matches a new company mission.

Implications

For EAPs the question of an excess labor pool as envisioned by Rifkin or mass shifts to contracting are not just theoretical. The number of people they serve in existing client companies would decline. They would face decreases in revenue that may threaten their existence.

Likewise low-paying service jobs dominating certain industries would threaten the existence of more varied EAPs. The diversity of EA approaches may widen in one respect: gold-card programs for the most well-paid occupations and telephone or Internet information or referrals for low-paying service jobs. The problems of serving the working poor that some EAPs have seen in recent years could become widespread in this labor market.

EAPs must go where both the jobs and the willingness to pay for the services exist. EAPs that can meet the needs of newer sectors, such as the high-tech industry, will serve themselves and the business community well. These EAPs must be willing to evolve, however they may not resemble today's internal or external EAPs.

INTERMEDIATES: AGENCIES AND NETWORKS

Conjectures

More intermediates in the labor market—employment agencies, headhunters, contingency employers, and networks—mean that firms are less and less involved in organizing their own labor. That organization included the provision of HR and benefits services such as EAPs. Contingency employees allow large companies (which still hire more workers than small businesses) to outsource such services or to eliminate them entirely.

A different and less-well-known aspect of intermediates in the labor market is networks. *Networks*—interconnected individuals with some commonality such as specialized knowledge (database design), education (alumni associations), or ethnic affiliation (Irish cops, Asian software code writers)—operate throughout the class structure. Workers now and in the future need networks to build or to borrow *social capital,* that is, favors, considerations, and information that allow them entry to certain industries and work organizations. Whether they are lawyers relying upon the referrals of neighbors or immigrants getting a job through a distant cousin, networks are vigorous.

Firms will increasingly desire workers' participation in networks because they offer access to people or knowledge in otherwise unreachable specialized areas. Knowledge changes so fast that the support afforded by a network is essential. The continuing dispersal of companies to remote sites also means that for many locations it is figuratively (and sometimes literally, as Sassen pointed out) a desert outside the workplace. Networks, either electronic or personal, provide emotional and intellectual sustenance for workers.

Networks address what Peiperl and Baruch characterized as "two fundamental forces—the basic human need for belonging and social support and the rapid globalization of communications and services" (1997, p. 13). The "support structures" they describe match up well with the networks pictured by others: agencies and consulting alliances, professional associations, and communities. Without such support, they worry that workers may develop problems both in work/life balance and in diminishing skills of interpersonal contact.

Intermediates are a parallel development to the waning of corporate career development and "jobs for life." Peiperl and Baruch described this change to postcorporate career by stating, "It seems that large organizations, having once developed vertical career paths (and then horizontal ones) for the purposes of motivating employees and providing for the future of the firm, may now be giving up on career management altogether. Put another way, it may be that careers, having existed for years predominantly within large organizations, have now started to move beyond them" (1997, p. 20).

The increase in *contingency workers*—workers whose careers operate outside any one corporation—seems to reinforce this view. The use of temps in the United States increased 240% in just the past decade. The breadth of the jobs involved—programmers, accountants, repairmen—is consistent with Charles Handy's prediction of the "withering of the 'employment organization' . . . [in which] a lot of us will become 'portfolio workers' selling our skills to a variety of clients. And all of us will be looking beyond work to find meaning and identity" (Ettorre, 1996, p. 15).

The workforce of 2005 may, however, resist such a uniform characterization; different needs will drive different profiles. Some jobs will allow for interchangeable workers; it will not matter much who does the work as long as the worker follows a procedure. *Some temp or contingency workers will fit into this group.* Other organizations will have an intense need for a worker to stay on the job but not for his or her entire work life. *Some contingent workers, such as turn-around experts, trainers, systems planners, and information officers, will also fit into this group.*

Contrary to Handy's elegant but sweeping predictions, not everyone will be a portfolio worker with skills portable to a new job every several years. Some firms gain from workers staying on the job. In fact, job tenure for men with four or more years of college actually increased by 9% between 1983 and 1991; overall job tenure, however, was down slightly in 1996 (U.S. Census Bureau, online report, 1997). Long-term research or knowledge of a complex customer is not always easily transferred.

Implications

When companies rely upon contingency workers or abandon long-term efforts to retain employees, EAPs have ample reason for concern. Traditionally, EAP programs were viewed as part of career management, helping employees to regain or maintain full productivity.

If companies rely upon intermediates to do much of their hiring, then the EA field might look to that same group for entry into new segments of the economy.

Approaches through professional organizations or regional economic groups may prove successful. EAPs might contract with a network rather than an employer in the twenty-first century. Consortia, although enjoying a mixed record of success in the past 20 years, may prove more successful in the high-tech area, where other kinds of cooperative arrangements, from benchmarking to shared services, already flourish.

The advantage a service such as an EAP poses is countered by the lure of a trimmer administration and flexibly composed workforce. The EAP field needs to promote itself accordingly. The customer who uses intermediates to hire, to teach, and to support no longer sees services for employees in the same way.

GENDER AND ETHNIC DEMOGRAPHICS

Conjectures

Women and minorities are strongly positioned for the future workplace. Seven of 10 new jobs in the 1980s were filled by women (women are more than half of job holders in New York City and some other urban centers). Eighty percent of women have jobs in service industries, compared to 55% of men. Thirty-four percent of these jobs held by women reside in the higher-earning information and capital-intensive service industries, compared to 25% for men; however, women still earn less than men.

Asian and Latino males will also enjoy greater job gains than black or white males. This diversity of the workforce will increase not as government fiat but as an outgrowth of the immigrant surge to the United States in the 1990s. These individuals will enter the workforce bringing different cultural and familial issues and requirements with them. For women, the group that emerges as the majority of the workforce will continue to increase in average age. Thus, new personal challenges may arise in the juggling of responsibilities.

Implications

EAPs who have already done much work in adjusting to gender and diversity issues in the workplace may find themselves facing extensions of those issues. The composition of EAP staffs must also change to reflect the aforementioned shifts.

AGE OF THE WORKFORCE

Conjectures

With some far-out predictions claiming that humans could live to the age of 200, the aging question is sometimes written off as science fiction. However, the massive shift of baby boomers into their fifties which started in 1995, is very real. Almost twice as many senior citizens will exist in the year 2025 as there were in 1995. Their readiness for retirement is certain: the savings rates among working adults are only 4.1% of personal income, down from 7.9% in 1980.

Implications

Population aging has genuine implications for the workforce and for EAPs. Presenting problems will change and so must EAP services, promotion, and case-finding. More subtly, the disparity between the age of frontline EA workers and the age of those whom they serve may widen. This may impede connections to some workers who will avoid situations where they have to speak to someone not of their generation. Although this disparity has existed at other times in EAPs, the bulge of the baby boomers may make it more prevalent.

LABOR

Conjectures

With new leadership and arguable recent successes, labor activism has reached a high point in this decade. Many observers still make much of the declining enrollment of labor but some trends, such as lagging wages of low-level service workers, may make membership more attractive. Labor's hope according to one opinion "lies in polls showing that approximately one-third of all nonunion workers say they would join a union if they had a chance. . . . Recent polls have also shown that two-thirds of Americans now hold a positive view of unionism and unions in general" (NYT, 1997, p. A26).

Labor unions will continue their efforts to organize temporary workers and contingents. In 1997, the AFL-CIO made a formal request to the Department of Labor (DOL) through the NLRB (National Labor Relations Board) for the right to organize temporaries. The AFL-CIO has argued before the NLRB that temporary workers should be allowed to join unions in the workplaces where they are assigned. Although current labor rules make such sign-up campaigns extremely difficult, the NLRB could decide (or a future congress could facilitate) rights for the unions to make temporary workers part of the same bargaining unit as the full-timers at unionized facilities (Reynolds, 1997). Business will fight fiercely, but the chance to secure health insurance benefits for these workers might persuade government.

Unions might renew their effort to gain advantages through helping workers deal with the challenges of automation. Downsizing is the most obvious effect, and unions have carefully fought over job security in many recent negotiations. The future, however, might see the success of one of the fledgling white-collar associations that have formed in the last few years. These associations might not bargain collectively; rather, they might follow the lead of interest groups, such as AARP (American Association of Retired Persons), and wage lobbying or public relations campaigns. Their causes could include worker displacement or a decrease in the number of hours worked per week. AT&T's reaction to popular pressure against its layoffs in the mid-1990s demonstrated the strength of such tactics even when informally applied.

Implications

In recent years the correlation and even connection between the benefit status of employees and their access to EAPs has grown. Of the 167 million people covered by behavioral health (BH) management companies, many have no differentiation between their BH provider and their EAP. If there is no benefit, there may not be any EAP. Additionally, the still irregular nature of providing services to temporaries for EAPs could become the norm.

Success in white-collar organizing might lead to an overlapping of EAPs—a membership assistance program (MAP) and a management sponsored program—as has already occurred in industries such as automobile and airlines. Both sides will need strategies to accomplish their objectives in such instances.

Negotiations over benefit packages (widespread in the 1980s and 1990s) could leave MAP out of the mix if no advocate for the service exists within the union. The consequences for EAPs might also include larger populations to be served, possibly at the same fees, as companies strive to control additional benefit costs.

STRUCTURE

What sort of work organization structures will sustain future employees? Certainly many organizations are moving further and further away from traditional hierarchical configurations. The government estimates that 86% of recent down-cycle unemployment was due to structural changes in organizations. In fact the companies responsible for some of the largest job cuts in the 1990s—AT&T, IBM, Boeing, Sears, and Xerox—reversed course and hired 63,800 employees in 1996. That figure was almost 40% more than they predicted in May of that year according to a Challenger, Gray, and Christmas report (Worsham, 1996, p. 20). These employees and the survivors find themselves amidst the trappings of new organizational structures: matrix models, team assignments, Total Quality Management (TQM) regimen, outsourced departments, leadership courses, and other staples of Dilbert cartoons.

More seriously, the image of the organization as a powerful force of understanding and defining work continues to evolve as described by Gareth Morgan (1986) and others. The old conception of company as machine or military unit gives way to metaphors of culture and controlled chaos. These changes carry ramifications for the workers of those organizations, for their processes, for their values, and, therefore, for EAPs.

FRACTAL, FEDERAL, AND FLATTER ORGANIZATIONS

Conjectures

Also known as decentralized or donut organizations, *fractals* (as termed by Hans-Jurgen Warnecke) are company units that act independently and that are responsible for their own organization and optimization. Their responsiveness and smaller span of control makes them attractive to other organizations seeking alliances. For example, AT&T buys goods and services from 100,000 small companies (Halal, 1996, p. 15). These fractals may or may not purchase services such as EAP or medical from the overall company. Expectations do often include some coherent culture that keeps the units connected in some way. According to some observers, fractals will proliferate, cutting drastically the number of employees in any given unit.

Theorists such as Drucker, Champy, and Hammer contend that successful information-based organizations will adopt these smaller, flatter, less hierarchical, and less control-oriented forms.

The shift of responsibility to teams has proceeded in fits and starts for the past decade. The new structures require substantial horizontal cooperation. What observers increasingly notice is that these teams throw together individuals who may or may not possess the interpersonal skills needed for the success of the unit.

From a different perspective, Charles Handy (1990) illuminated one of the realities of the new structures: fewer workers. In an interview, he laid out the formula he sees companies adopting: "half-by-two-by-three": half the workers, paid twice as well, producing three times as much. The other half [of those workers] will be outside the organization. And because there is a core on the inside working very hard to be paid twice as well, they will have short lives in the organization—20 or 30 years, instead of 50 years. Actually, it could be as short as 15 years (Ettorre, 1996, p. 22). Even if half-by-two-by-three occurs in a minority of work organizations, the effect will be to help many employees on their way—not to retain them.

Implications

How do EAPs fit fractals? EA workers may receive requests to help new team members gain communication skills or to coach teams through crises. Not every EA professional has the requisite knowledge or experience to respond to such requests. The reality, however, is that few EAPs will say no to an opportunity that might boldly demonstrate their value, particularly if Handy's prediction of fewer workers for these corporations proves accurate.

In examples like this one, EA workers may enjoy greater opportunities to help federal organizations that have unloaded administrative managers. They may find, however, that the virtual company—absent any player familiar with HR competencies—will not value or even know what EA offers.

The structure or container that Handy described is "decentralized and centralized. In some respects, an organization needs different bits . . . that do things more or less autonomously. But in some respects the organization needs to be centralized, doing things in the same way. For instance, purchasing should be centralized" (Ettorre, 1996, p. 18). Would the purchasing of EAPs work that way? Some chief executive officers (CEOs) have declared that the smaller units must make the decision of whether to buy services; other senior management teams hedge their liability bets by requiring what they consider to be an essential service. (Organizational consultants enjoy tremendous influence in this area, yet many EAPs have little awareness of their practices.)

EAPs are liable to side effects from such changes as facing narrowed economies of scale or an accelerated need to promote consortia approaches. In other words, external EAPs, rather than selling one program to a company with 5,000 employees, may have to sell 25 or 50 programs to fractal units or outsourced entities to equal the revenue.

Two other points from the new structures matter to EAPs: (1) fitting into organizations without hierarchy and (2) yielding of control. The first point is important because the EAP's provision of "expert consultation to supervisors, managers, and union stewards" (Roman, 1991, p. 8) evolved in hierarchical structures; EAP linkages and methods might need to change. The second is relevant in that new structures might desire an EAP that was less of an expert and more of a consultant service. An associated shift of status and alteration of attitude is required. The clinical authority fond of protocols may ill suit this structure; the flexible facilitator attentive to group needs might better fit the flatter organization.

TELECOMMUTING

Conjectures

One staple of futuristic workplace structure already occurring is telecommuting. Pushing likely expansion of this trend will be its documented decreased absenteeism, reduced commuting costs, increased productivity, improved morale, and other benefits. Futurist Joseph Coates estimated telecommuting or distributed work will increase from roughly 3% to more than 20% of all work by the year 2005 (McGoon, 1995, p. 18). Already companies create large networks of independent contractors to accomplish such diverse work as writing software code or abstracting newspaper articles.

Implications

Providing services such as EAPs to telecommuters requires novel approaches in program promotion, management referral, and follow-up. Telecommuters already report unique issues in establishing work/life boundaries. EAPs face multiple challenges identifying employee behavioral problems and responding to related organizational needs in this context.

INFORMATION TECHNOLOGY

Conjectures

The information technology structure of organizations will continue to transform as computers both grow in prevalence and in realized potential. Technology, such as intranets, video conferencing, and even desktop computers, provides a fraction of the power possible. The next 10 years will see an aggressive campaign to get more out of computers. Effects of greater integration might range from a reduction in face-to-face meetings to the use of artificial intelligence to analyze a company's human resources efforts.

May, Rajguru, Burns, Howes, and Matthews (1997) cited an example of this trend within companies as movement away from simply "more accurate methods of costing ... to a more scientific method of cost reduction ... culminat(ing) in an all-embracing advanced planning, monitoring, and control system." She predicted that such holistic systems that have previously focused almost exclusively on the financial side will now include correlations to dimensions such as "organization culture; staff competency; staff satisfaction; absence and staff turnover against workloads; costs of staff development against productivity improvements" (1997, p. 29). Data warehousing and Enterprise Information Systems will assure that performance measurement is pervasive. In many organizations, if an activity is not measured in some way, then it will not exist for the leaders of the company.

Implications

In this context, EAPs must consider at the least how their current methods are affected. For example, consultation would look very different in a world so tightly measured. EAPs who have ignored or even resisted the quantification of their roles in such valuable efforts as resolving conflicts, aiding work/life balance, or responding to psychological trauma may recoil at such systems. They may despair at how they will find the time to hook into these databases or to create parallel congruent ones. Larger external EAPs will carry a distinct advantage here. Yet many of those existing vendors lack a consistent or deep approach to such measurement.

As this shift toward measuring everything occurs, some companies will maintain relationships with unmeasured EAPs: The business scene is not uniform. The time-tested qualities of familiarity, integrity, and trust will serve some EAPs well. However, barring some pendulous shift in this current tendency of companies to measure more and more, EAPs will need to address this upshot of the technology of the future.

HUMAN RESOURCES AND BUSINESS PROCESS

Conjectures

Martin Leahy (1997, pp. 2–3) has said that companies possess four areas of activities to which they look when they change: (1) thinking, (2) communicating, (3) resourcing, or (4) organizing. The last of these has already seen rapid change in the past two decades: total quality; reengineering; the reemphasis upon mission, values, and strategy; emphasis upon high innovation in services; and the review of the role of management.

"Organizing and communicating are now increasingly associated with management as a way to make knowledge productive" (Drucker, 1994, p. 72). This would seem consistent with the core technology of EAPs, but the process through which EA has traditionally connected to the organization—human resources—is in the midst of momentous change. Although often considered as a separate department or silo, human resources in future may not constitute a separate piece of structure so much as a function woven into individual business units (Stewart, 1997).

This transformation will accelerate as reverse donut organizations proliferate, with small-core administrations in the middle supporting self-directed teams and units. Some organizations will come to resemble communities of practice, as suggested by Chris Turner of Xerox Business Systems (Webber, 1996, p. 113), where members concentrate on the sharing of learning and assistance for key processes. Leaders will contract out anything else. Some person may take responsibility for the traditional aspects of attracting, retaining, and motivating intellectual capital, but he or she is likely to do so only in a way that directly supports company mission and strategy.

As Yeung, Woolcock, and Sullivan point out (1996, p. 57) the "good old days" of HR functions have gone. "Simply possessing good social interaction skills is no longer sufficient for handling increasingly complex and challenging HR roles and responsibilities. . . . HR functions that focus on routine operational HR activities . . . simply will not survive for long. They may either be outsourced, automated, or eliminated altogether." HR is tied to forwarding strategy.

Significant movement in how HR competencies are pictured has already occurred as reported in a study published by the Society for Human Resource Management (Yeung, Woolcock, & Sullivan, 1996, p. 50). In that work, three HR competencies were "critical [for the future]: (1) solid knowledge of business or business acumen; (2) a capacity to facilitate and implement change; and (3) influencing skills." The HR leaders with whom EAPs interact and who are often crucial customers will need to demonstrate these abilities as well as leadership, organizational effectiveness, consultation/organizational development skills, and strategic/systemic thinking.

HR managers already recognize the variance with their old position. When asked the probable challenges or priorities faced in the twenty-first century, they look away from transactions to problem solving, to forwarding the business strategy, to consulting to managers of business units, to facing difficulties the workforce will have in achieving balance.

Implications

EA practice cannot remain the same in this new context; the new paradigm of HR will affect any interrelated domain. To stay influential with these customers, EAPs must convince HR that they can assist in addressing the issues. EAPs should expect requests to demonstrate the impact of their services upon the critical mission of a business.

GOVERNMENT AND OTHER SPECIAL SECTORS

Conjectures

Where structure and business process are concerned, some work organizations possess essential differences that may make for an altered future. For example, government does not operate according to the demands of the markets in the same way as other companies. Observers such as Osborne and Gabler called for the application of reengineering principles from the corporate environment to the public sector as an antidote to the "bankruptcy of bureaucracy" (1993, p. 12). A shift in power in both the executive and legislative branches around that same time brought these ideas into law at the federal level. Government agencies such as the Internal Revenue Service and the Commerce Department have experienced significant downsizing. Ironically, public demand for government services has increased at the same time as the public has sought to limit government spending (Osborne and Gabler, 1993, p. 4).

Sanders (1997), however, saw the future of bureaucracy more positively than many futurists and politicians. Bureaucrats are the intermediaries providing constancy and direction that many customers crave. It is bureaucrats who explain to both customers and workers (or producers) why they cannot have exactly what they want. As Sanders put it, "as long as there is unpleasant work to be delegated, there will be bureaucrats to delegate it to" (p. 49).

Sanders does not address, however, the likely application of technology to this sector. Further government downsizing is at least a possibility as network computers eliminate layers of processes and, therefore, workers.

Implications

Government EAPs might expect a troubled and tense future from these signs. Some EAPs have already played a role in downsizing and other cost-cutting ventures. Will the cost of EAPs induce governments to shift their operation to large vendors? Will service shrink or become more innovative? EA workers involved with government can seize the moment to suggest solutions to their customers in that sector, but they cannot likely avoid alteration.

LEARNING

Conjectures

Learning gives leverage to labor and structure and enjoys an unprecedented prominence in organizational considerations. Why? The shelf life of information keeps dropping; someone else can quickly replicate what you just invented and market it better. Information is at the core of knowledge-intensive and other service industries, and learning turns information into necessary intelligence.

The importance companies place upon learning is exemplified by organizational leader Hewlett-Packard, where lifelong learning is one of seven key cultural aspects. There is an expectation that the company will provide opportunities for continuous training (Johnson, 1997, p. 61). Thus both companies and their employees must reinvent themselves and grow more agile to compete globally.

Implications

This focus on learning may represent an opportunity for a group of professionals experienced in teaching and persuading: EA workers. Learning here, however, is very different from those familiar characteristics of organizational training: "personal development . . . separated from work development; . . . the deficit model, eliminating deficiencies in order to reach minimum competencies; . . . formal; classroom based" (Marsick in Chalofsky, 1996, p. 290). Learning in the workplace of the future is much broader: "how we actualize potential . . . an increased capacity to perform" (Gallwey, 1997, p. 2). EAPs can flourish here, given their training to recognize patterns, to powerfully engage and meaningfully instruct. A focus by practitioners solely on numbers and transactions or on separating encounters into separate clinical and business boxes, however, will preclude their customers from picturing them in this learning role. U.S. companies may honor such learning more in the breach (or in the bought but unread books on the subject) than in observance and adherence.

CULTURE

Conjectures

Organizational culture cannot be categorized in any catholic way. Many companies, however, are increasingly interested in the power of culture to accomplish their mission. Organizational expert Manfred Kets de Vries "believes an organization can (only) ensure long-term survival (through) cultural change" (Johnson, 1997, p. 60).

Some bedrock assumptions of business culture have shifted in the past decade. They are likely to slip even more with influences of unknown power such as technology—computer monitoring, group meeting support, and cyber isolation. Many observers in their attention to the digital future and global economy have overlooked the system of work, individual, family, and community that is still the foundation of culture. There is more than the digital space on the wires and chips that make up data networks; more than the home offices and catalogues of organizational knowledge; more than the strategies, roles, and responsibilities on color charts. Even the most digitized industry is partly embedded in and, therefore, dependent on material and mental structures, people and their minds. The future depends a great deal upon how organizations deal with that reality.

One challenge in new cultures is what Dr. Sassen (1996) called the "casualizing of the employment relationship" (lecture, 1996). This is not the same as casual jobs. Rather it describes people who make good money and have a changed attachment, a far less institutionalized relationship, with their firm. To some observers, this indicates the death of company loyalty. To others, the phenomenon simply requires work organizations to find new means to secure *some* satisfaction, dedication, and loyalty from their employees.

For either, the question is: How will an altered social contract (or the absence of one altogether) combine with marketplace elements to produce a way of working in the near future? In one recent survey, 11% of managers and 24% of nonmanagers said going to work each day was like, "going to prison." If, as Peter Drucker and Thomas Stewart opine, organizations need knowledge workers more than knowledge workers need them, the creation of a positive relationship or culture takes on tremendous importance.

What is unclear is whether organizations that contain the much larger numbers of workers will choose that direction. Because contingents make up a growing section of jobs and some organizations are able to relocate, they may forge cultures adaptable to frequent replacement of workers. Only time and bottom-line results will determine which cultural approach is more fruitful.

Organizational culture will also be thorny in non-knowledge-worker jobs. Their dominance in the United States coincides with a shrinking middle class. Workers lacking information skills will see a decline in real wages as they become cogs in the mass service organization. Half of all jobs for male workers pay less than $28,000 annually, a bare survival income for a family. This erosion of a group considered the bulwark of modern society raises concerns among the corporate and political elite, according to Sassen. Those leaders recognize that the values found in middle-class families provided the fabric of society in the twentieth century.

What effect does it have upon culture when, as Andrew Hacker (1997) put it, "The better off prosper while others are losing ground or standing still?" (1997, p. 25). Fears of aggression in the workplace grow out of this sense of rapidly changed organizational culture.

Culture is also present on a more immediate level in such diverse phenomena as the changing compositions of families, the rising average age of childbearing, the continued high rate of divorce, and the need for more extended caregiving to elderly dependents in the society at large.

Nevertheless, a 1995 study conducted for the Merck Fund by the Harwood Group found that 67% of people wanted to spend more time with their families. Focus on family can, however, pose problems in companies. The number of people who now say they constitute an alternative family is growing rapidly. Although much attention is paid to the large block of single-parent families, Coates estimated that, "for nearly 16% of children living with two parents in 1990, one of those parents is a stepparent." Competing trends exist in benefits design for this area: try to offer something to everyone; stay with existing tendencies, that is, the traditional idea of offering things to employees with minor dependents; or tie benefits much more closely to productivity.

Implications

Culture may prove the most essential sphere of concern for EAPs as they ponder the future. Culture is about people relating and communicating on the job, about the values they visibly and invisibly proclaim. EAPs may now enjoy the opportunity to be cultural messengers: possessing an overall awareness of the company from a people perspective and reinforcing the connection among employees and the other parts of a company. Their role in making workplaces attractive to prospective employees is already demonstrated by various surveys of the "Best Places" to work. The willingness to work "as long as it takes" often emerges as a commitment from ambitious mission statements alongside a workforce that includes many parents just starting families (Coates, 1996). The culture in such cases is characterized by contradictions of hurrying up to take time to learn, of embracing changes while appreciating constancy of purpose, of offering work/life programs to people who toil 12 hour days.

EA workers find themselves valued as representatives of a softer side of these cultures. However, they may endure the additional discomfort of being asked to operate within a culture while not commenting upon the pathological aspects of it. This conflict may constitute an important ethical question in the very near future.

It is in the area of work/life that EAPs have perhaps best anticipated the future. They formulated quick and innovative responses. The hope is that they will be able to do the same with the next generation of related effects: the maturity of children from these different family backgrounds, the increased stress on an even larger sandwich generation, and the shift in priorities to acquiring education before starting a family.

GLOBALIZATION

Conjectures

There is little doubt that the workers in all business are exposed to the effects of globalization. The sociologist Manuel Castells (in Barney, 1997) argued the downside of this trend: "What globalization means for a large proportion of humankind is that they are being disenfranchised politically and impoverished economically . . . they can never negotiate with their employers because their employers keep shifting places as much as they want, or outsourcing, or bringing workers or supplies from anywhere else." Even champions of globalization such as Vice-President Al Gore would have to admit to displacement in some workplaces and communities.

Globalization gives heightened power both to very large companies that can serve everywhere and to individual consumers who can use technology rather than going to their local markets. Slogans such as "the customer is always right" may hail from the past, but globalization heightens their emphasis because locality no longer binds the customer. Certainly the tensions created by a global process that must fit over various webs of national laws and regulations also create opportunities.

Implications

Unfortunately, only EAPs with certain capabilities can take advantage of those situations where companies need to negotiate the cultural differences, diverse geographic distribution, or the movement of a plant with large numbers of employees. As many smaller EAPs have discovered, regional strength or local familiarity handicapped them in serving distributed workforces *and* failed to offer them much preference with their neighborhood companies. As EA services evolved into more of a referral service and less of a management consulting resource in many environments, even midsize firms could choose to contract with EA providers headquartered halfway across the country.

These shifts make external EAP contracts less stable. Provider firms may be gobbled up by larger entities or disappear entirely. Their capacity is no longer relevant in a world where multinationals require coverage of a workforce that literally works 24 hours a day.

EAPs need to consider the effect of globalization not only on themselves but also on the employees and the companies that they serve. For example, workers may all come from a particular town in Mexico or India or Taiwan to a particular neighborhood in New York City because of a particular network enjoyed by a company. That requires a new approach by EA to serve them. Increasingly, EAPs will provide not only the translation and the culturally diverse services that some EAPs already furnish but also an understanding of the interplay of relationships emerging from these circumstances.

LEGISLATION

Conjectures

Legislation has proved a powerful force in EAP development. The Americans with Disabilities Act (ADA), the Drug-Free Workplace Act, the Drug-Free Schools and Communities Act, and the Department of Transportation and other governmental drug-testing regulations have all spurred the development of EAPs either directly or indirectly. Employee Retirement Income Security Act (ERISA) and various licensure and certification moves (such as designating Certified Employee Assistance Professionals (CEAPs) as substance abuse professionals (SAPs) federally) have also shaped the field. EAPs also operate within a culture responding to the requirements of the Family and Medical Leave Act.

The prediction problem here is that the passage of these laws was highly idiosyncratic. They depended on the presence of some committed and sometimes unexpected champions (such as George Bush with the ADA) or on a particular configuration of the legislative body and a judiciary that interprets them in broad or narrow fashion. An example of the influence of the judiciary is evident in the Supreme Court decisions on client confidentiality and sexual harassment. The former gave additional status to the EA position; the latter prompted many companies to reach out to their EAPs to help design preventive and reactive programs.

Implications

The passage of actual legislation is difficult to forecast, given the significant shifts seen in our national and state governments in the past dozen years. EA workers might best prepare for the future by thinking globally and acting locally. They need to concentrate on the legislative initiatives that possess the greatest capacity to affect their actual workings. These include those that involve their standing as an untaxed benefit to employees and companies or the often overlapping area of behavioral health.

HEALTH

Conjectures

Alvin Toffler and others have convincingly argued that the paradigms in health and other institutions are in the midst of extreme change. In this way of thinking,

"Healthcare becomes more sophisticated, more focused on and directed by the individual, and more concerned with community health . . . (or) even focuses more on greater use of our mental, emotional, and spiritual capacities in healing" (Hancock & Bezold, 1997, p. 29). The use of new psychopharmacological medications has already altered greatly the practice of psychiatry. Research continues to search for drugs that would control addictions, psychoses, anxieties, and much less significant behavior.

The initial findings here counsel using drugs in conjunction with the more traditional (but still relatively new) "talking therapies." However, the confluence of such powerful forces as managed care, technology, drug company influence, and cultural acceptance of "better living through chemistry" could produce several very different scenarios. Of course, they all depend to some extent on the position taken by governmental agencies in sanctioning or even requiring the use of certain therapies.

In another less traditional area for EAPs, emerging communicable diseases may play as great a role in the future as they have in the past two decades. The Ebola and HIV viruses are well known, but the return of "controlled" diseases such as tuberculosis and encephalitis may greatly affect the future with behavioral change and climate shifts possibly playing an additional role.

Implications

Although EAPs as defined by Roman and Blum's Core Technology (Roman, 1991, p. 8) do not provide treatment, they do "maintain a focus on employee alcohol and substance abuse problems." Their connection to behavioral health is still strong, although their focus has expanded in the direction of organizational development. An example of the abiding strength of this connection is the inevitable discovery of a drug that completely reduces craving for alcohol or that allows alcoholics to continue drinking with fewer side effects. That drug will change not only the role of the EAP but more importantly the perception of key organizational customers as to the very need for an EAP. Plague scenarios such as those mentioned previously are important to EAPs because they may represent instances in which the now refined skills of critical-incident response and critical-incident-stress debriefing are newly applied.

The trend in healthcare that may more immediately affect EAPs is and has been managed care. Many EAPs found themselves lumped in with overall cost-containment initiatives in the 1990s. The fortunes of managed care may suffer a reversal as governments investigate possible abuses by some of the largest entities in that realm and as market shake-outs imperil the already slim profit margins (Morris, 1997).

TECHNOLOGY

Conjectures

In a connection to the previous section, Michael Dertouzos (1996) of the Massachusetts Institute of Technology (MIT) predicts that in the near future each individual will possess an electronic medical history. It might reside on a smart card no bigger than a credit card. The implications for follow-up and for the aid such a system gives to managed care schemes is enormous. The speed of technological developments, however, threatens to baffle predictions.

Ironically, the future here will hold not only the expected slashes forward in hardware and software, but also the coming to terms with failures of technology, such as the ability of humans to catch up with the expected 100 times increase in microprocessor power.

A similar disenchantment with technology likely to play a part in the immediate future is the "productivity paradox": the disparity between the trillion-dollar investment in information technologies and the sluggish productivity growth both in the United States and Europe. One reason cited by observers such as Thomas Landauer is the failure of organizations to adapt to the possibilities of computers: they simply plug computers into old processes. Other reasons include the poor human/computer interface: the difficulties of people interacting with machines, disks, modems, and constant software upgrades.

If Zuboff is right and part of the problem is that management is unwilling to share real authority and power with frontline workers, then technology could be in for a rough time. If these problems are also the result of poor communication, destructive thinking, or human factors, then EAPs may find a colossal possibility.

Implications

Where technology is concerned, EAPs must first get up to speed before they can take advantage of some of the opportunities emerging. Are they using e-mail to communicate with clients and customers? Can they handle electronic newsletters, web pages, and Internet searches? Are their systems networked? Are they using relational databases to give customers the intelligence they need? Are their communication systems sufficient? Are they aware of diagnostic and screening software for such maladies as alcoholism and depression? Like surfing a wave, however, those who wish to take immediate advantage of technology need to be in position close to the edge as each crest finally comes. EA workers can ask themselves if that figuratively describes their own current technological position or if they are missing the wave.

WILDCARDS AND PENDULUMS

It is foolhardy to believe that one has thought of everything in assessing the future. Futurists themselves allow for wildcards: unexpected and consequential developments. EAPs could make their own list of wildcards: unusual designer drugs, cures for addiction, end of employer-sponsored health insurance, purchase of EAP units by large consulting firms, raising the retirement age to 70, or a long-lasting business depression. What would the result be of a persistent terrorist campaign extending effects such as those seen in Oklahoma City or at the World Trade center? The exercise diminishes complacency and encourages humility and practicality in predictions.

Some trends are pendulous; they regularly reverse because of powerful forces on both sides of the argument. A good example is the voting preferences of U.S. citizens from one party to the next. Perhaps more relevant to EA concerns, organizations may tire of HR and benefit initiatives. Executives who championed downsizing now attend conferences on "upsizing." Where lean and mean proliferated, values and even spirituality are now trumpeted. These cautions are not offered as mere hedges but as an invitation to gain insights from organizational history in which this oscillating effect is amply available. The certainty is that some trends are pendulous; the difficulty is ascertaining which ones will bounce back at us in the future.

WHAT WON'T LIKELY CHANGE

Charles Handy has written that, in the future, the real organizational resource will be people and their inherent knowledge and skills. The new organization will exist to make employees more effective. That fits the ideas of EAPs since their inception. One can sympathize with observers who say that there is much that will not change, that the future is where people will continue to work on themselves and on their ways of working together.

Human needs will stay the same to a great extent; one of the joys and the horrors of reading history is appreciating the great constancy of human needs. The manifestations may change but survival, relationships, self-esteem, and self-actualization will still figure prominently in the stories of those who come to EAPs.

Another likely immutable aspect will be those who will prosper in the organizations of the future. "They will be integrators and facilitators that support the other employees," said Charles M. Savage, author of *Fifth-Generation Management,* in a larger context, "individuals with the ability to see new patterns and capabilities, who can envision what could be, and who know how to seize opportunities" (in Ashley, 1997, p. 74). Those EAPs who fit that bill will likely thrive in whatever future arrives.

REFERENCES

Anonymous, (1997, September 1). What's ahead for labor. *New York Times,* A26.

Ashley, S. (1997). Manufacturing firms face the future. [on-line]. *Mechanical Engineering, 119*(6), 70–74.

Barney, C. (1997). Point of view: Manuel Castells. *Upside, X*(10), 108–111,114–115, 178–187.

Bureau of Labor Statistics. (1998). *Occupational handbook* [on-line]. http:\\stats.bls.gov.80.

Chalofsky, N.E. (1996). A new paradigm for learning in organizations. *Human Resource Development Quarterly, 7*(3), 287–293.

Coates, J.F. (1996, September/October). What's ahead for families: Five major forces of change. *The Futurist* [On-Line].

Cornish, E. (1997, March–April). Anticipations: The next 30 years. *The Futurist* [On-Line].

Dent, Jr., H. (1993). *The great boom ahead: Your comprehensive guide to personal and business profit in new era prosperity.* New York: Hyperion.

Dertouzo, M. (1996). *What will be: How the new world of information will change our "lives."* New York: HarperCollins.

Drucker, P. (1994, November). The age of social transformation. *Atlantic,* 53–80.

Ettorre, B. (1996). A conversation with Charles Handy: On the future of work and an end to the "century of the organization." *Organizational Dynamics, 25*(1), 15–26.

Gallwey, T. (1997). The inner game of work: building capability in the workplace. *The Systems Thinker, 8*(6), 1–5.

Hacker, A. (1997). *Money: Who has how much and why.* New York: Scribner.

Halal, W.E. (1996). The rise of the knowledge entrepreneur. *The Futurist, 30*(6), 13–16.

Hancock, T., & Bezold, C. (1994, March/April). Possible futures, preferable futures. *Healthcare Forum, 37*(2), 23–29.

Handy, C. (1990). *The age of unreason.* Boston: Harvard Business Press.

Johnson, M. (1997, July/August). HR: Tomorrow's strategic partner? *Management Review, 86*(7), 60–61.

Leahy, M. (1997) Farewell to organization [newsletter]. *Mind on the Job, 1*(2), 2–3. White Plains: Cavanaugh Leahy & Company.

May, M., Rajguru, A., Burns, L., Howes, M., & Matthews, G. (1997, February). Preparing organizations to manage the future. *Management Accounting-London, 75*(2), 28–32.

McGoon, C. (1995, January/February). 10 years from now. *Communication World, 12*(1), 18–22.

Minehan, M. (1997). The aging baby boomers. *HR Magazine, 42*(4), 208.

Minnesota Future of Work Web Site. (1997). [on-line compilation]. http://netco.tec.mn.us /~scanners/cardev.html.

Morgan, G. (1986). *Images of organization.* London: Sage.

Morris, K. (1997). Facing up to tomorrow's epidemics. *Lancet, 349*(9061), 1301–1303.

Mosca, J.B. (1997, March 1). Adjusting jobs for the year 2000. *Public Personnel Management, 26*(1), 43–59.

Naisbitt, J. (1984). *Megatrends: Ten new directions transforming our lives.* New York: Warner Books.

Negroponte, N. (1995). *Being digital* (p. 228). New York: Knopf.

Office Team. (1997, June). How to get through to Generation Xers. *Benefits and Compensation Solutions* [On-line].

Osborne, D., & Gabler, T. (1993). *Reinventing government.* New York: Plume.

Peiperl, M., & Baruch, Y. (1997). Back to square zero: The post-corporate career. *Organizational Dynamics, 25*(4), 6–22.

Petersen, J.L. (1997, July/August). The wild cards in our future: Preparing for the improbable [on-line]. *The Futurist.*

Pfeffer, J. (1994). *Competitive advantage through people: Unleashing the power of the work force.* Boston: Harvard Business School Press.

Piirto, R.H. (1996, July). The frontiers of psychographics. *American Demographics.*

Reynolds, L. (1997, April 23). Washington update. *HR Today.* http://www.jobfind.com/hrtoday/washington423.html.

Rifkin, J. (1995). *The end of work: The decline of the global labor force and the dawn of the post-market era.* New York: Putnam.

Roach, S. (1997, August 24). The worker backlash: News of the week in review. *New York Times,* p. A13.

Roman, P. (1991, June). Core technology clarification. *Employee Assistance,* pp. 8, 9.

Sanders, R.L. (1997). The future of bureaucracy. *Records Management Quarterly, 31*(1), 44–52.

Sassen, S. (1996, November 11). *Workforce implications of the 21st Century* [Seminar lecture—private audiotape].

Senge, P., Roberts, C., Ross, R.B., Smith, B.J., & Kleiner, A. (1993). *The fifth discipline fieldbook.* New York: Currency Doubleday.

Stewart, T.A. (1997). *Intellectual capital: The new wealth of organizations.* New York: Doubleday.

Sullivan, J. (1997). HRNET@cornell.edu [listserv]. http:ursus.jun.alaska.edu/archives /aom_arch.html.

Thornburg, L. (1995). HR in the year 2010. *HR Magazine, 40*(5), 62–70.

Toffler, A. (1984). *Future Shock.* New York: Bantam.

U.S. Census Bureau. (1997). On-line report.

Vann, B.A. (1996). Learning self-direction in a social and experiential context. *Human Resource Development Quarterly, 7*(2), 121–130.

Vogl, A.J. (1996). Memories of the future. *Across the Board, 34*(7), 39–43.

Webber, A. (1996, October/ November). XBS learns to grow. *Fast Company,* 113.

Wheatley, M. (1994). *Leadership and the new science.* San Francisco: Berrett Koehler.

Worsham, J. (1996). The flip side of downsizing (cover story). *Nation's Business, 84*(10), 18.

Yeung, A., Woolcock, P., & Sullivan, J. (1996) Identifying and developing HR competencies for the future: Keys to sustaining the transformation of HR functions. *Human Resource Planning, 19*(4), 48–58.

Zuboff, S. (1988). *In the age of the smart machine: The future of work and power.* New York: Basic Books.

EAP Programs and Services

PART TWO

EAP Programs and Services

CHAPTER 15

The Evolving Role of EAPs in Managed Behavioral Healthcare: A Case Study of DuPont

PAUL W. HECK

In 1997, approximately 95% of the Fortune 500 companies offered employee assistance (EA) services. Although the numbers change constantly in today's business environment, it is estimated that 90% of the existing employee assistance programs (EAPs) are *external,* meaning that these companies contract with a vendor to provide an EAP for employees. The remaining 10% are *internal* models, meaning that the EAP staff is employed by the host company.

These definitions are somewhat misleading, however, because very few EAPs meet them exactly. Over time, most programs have evolved into internal/external hybrids. Most external programs have at least one EAP professional on staff at the host company, and most internal programs have a few contractors involved in some way.

BACKGROUND AND HISTORY OF DuPONT

DuPont has been in continuous operation since its founder and namesake, Eleuthere I. du Pont, began making black gunpowder on the banks of the Brandywine River near Wilmington, Delaware in 1802. DuPont is the oldest company on the Fortune 500 list and one of the oldest industrial companies in the world. Its major product groups include chemicals, polymer fibers, petroleum products, and agricultural chemicals, which are made in about 175 plants around the world.

A Leader in Employee Benefits

Over the years, DuPont has operated within a very protective and paternalistic frame of reference. In the early 1800s, DuPont recognized the loss a family experienced if a worker was seriously hurt or killed (a not uncommon occurrence in the early days of making gunpowder), and records indicate that payments were made to compensate employees or families in these situations. This practice was unheard of in pre-Civil War America, but it was seen by E.I. du Pont as the "right thing to do."

Later, du Pont's descendants would establish additional employee benefits, such as a corporate medical department, health insurance, and housing, well ahead of other companies. One of those unique benefits was an alcohol abuse program that was created in part by one of the cofounders of Alcoholics Anonymous. A du Pont family member, Maurice du Pont Lee, met Bill W. while vacationing on Cape Cod and became intrigued with Bill's description of alcoholism and how AA was helping thousands of alcoholics. Out of those discussions came a formal alcoholism program that was launched in 1942 and made available to all DuPont employees. This early occupational alcoholism program was among the very first introduced by a major U.S. employer.

As mentioned earlier, there was a very strong commitment to employees from the first days of operation. However, this was not the only factor driving the development of these benefits. Safety has always been a major factor in everything DuPont does.

Safety, First and Foremost

DuPont's focus on safety is not difficult to understand, given its business and history. DuPont was founded as a black gunpowder manufacturing company in a very low-tech era. Manufacturing buildings E.I. du Pont used were made of fieldstone on three sides and timbers on the roof, with the fourth side facing the river. This design allowed the force of an explosion to be directed up or out over the river to minimize the threat to workers. Much of the work was done through openings in the walls of the buildings to shield employees as much as possible. Still, employees and du Pont family members were killed and hurt during explosions in these early days.

As the company grew and developed into the global chemical and energy producer it is today, it continued to make safety a priority. DuPont's devotion to safety is driven in large part by the products it produces. In order to be a solid corporate citizen, a responsible employer, a profitable business, and an attractive supplier, DuPont must be able to show communities, employees, investors, and customers that it is safe. In fact, DuPont has been so successful at turning safety into a science that it has a subsidiary business that sells its safety programs to other major global employers.

Corporate Work Environment

The DuPont company has experienced profound changes in its culture since 1991. The culture prior to the 1990s was that of a paternalistic giant with an unspoken expectation of a job for life, at least for those who came to work regularly and did not break a safety rule. Employees came to believe in the security of their jobs, and this sense of security was frequently shared with new employees as fact.

Independent Plant Management

This culture was enhanced by the autonomous nature of DuPont plants. DuPont production sites, whether they employed 100 people or 7,000 people, operated in a very independent style. The vast majority of employees worked "at the plant." Most plants provided direct services to employees on site, so there was little need for an employee to interact with "corporate." Services provided on site included a full medical department with at least one doctor, nurses, technicians, and support staff; benefits coordinators to help resolve claims problems or to compute retirement benefits; a cashier and credit union; a full-service cafeteria; and locker rooms with showers. In addition, many plants subsidized huge employee recreation areas that, in some sites, included fitness centers, ball fields, shooting ranges, or marinas. These services were very costly and redundant but were typical examples of the company's commitment to its employees.

In return, DuPont employees were fiercely loyal, and annual turnover was rarely more than 1%. It should be stated that this level of service to employees was not unique among large manufacturers in the post WWII era. However, the 1990s brought about a new business climate that changed this arrangement forever.

Downsizing in the 1990s

In 1991, chairman and CEO (chief executive officer) Ed Woolard announced a sweeping plan to reduce operating costs by $2 billion and to reengineer the way work was done in DuPont. Like so many other U.S. corporations, DuPont was being challenged to compete in a global economy where the financial realities were much different. As the impact of this fundamental change was beginning to affect the over 80,000 U.S. employees, DuPont's EAP was launched.

DuPont's EAP was a late entry into the field. Many employers had expanded their substance abuse programs into full EAPs years earlier. DuPont was able to benefit from the knowledge gained from other corporate experiences in many areas. But one issue was fairly new to mental health and substance abuse services: managed care.

EAPs and Managed Care

The concept of managed care, born out of the health maintenance organization (HMO) movement, was not prevalent among EAPs initially. Most companies considered the two as separate issues completely. There were early exceptions to this attitude, notably a computer service company, which used the EAP to manage all treatment and to process all claims internally, and a large retailer, which required EAP approval before its insurance carrier could pay mental health claims.

This use of the EAP as a gatekeeper and a claims processor was adapted by other employers in the late 1980s and early 1990s, but it never became a dominant model. More common was the separation of EAP services from benefit management. In fact, early attitudes among many in the EAP field supported this separation. The concern was that EAP staff would be pressured by employers to reduce treatment costs, thereby creating a conflict of interest. They felt that distancing themselves from the case management function by encouraging use of a third party could avoid this "catch 22." However, many EAP counselors found this was not a solution at all. Managed behavioral healthcare firms were in control of the benefits and were frequently denying care that had been recommended by a company's EAP staff.

The result was that a philosophical war of sorts developed, with frustrated EAP professionals believing that managed behavioral healthcare companies had no understanding of treatment needs and were only interested in short-term savings. Managed behavioral healthcare case managers viewed EAP counselors as out of touch with the cost pressures on employers related to benefit expenses and as too liberal with treatment referrals.

When each model was analyzed, the separation of the EAP from the benefit management function resulted in lower costs but higher rates of employee dissatisfaction than the integrated model in which the EAP controlled assessment, referral, and benefit authorization/case management.

EAP Structure at DuPont

Building and Development

Independent of the business issues being reviewed at the senior level within DuPont, a team of managers from both corporate and plant locations had been studying the idea of an EAP since 1988. The Occupational Alcoholism Program begun in 1942 had been expanded to cover all other drugs of abuse as well, but a full EAP had not been implemented. The six-person staff of DuPont's substance abuse program was finding it difficult to keep up with requests for assistance, and seven plants had already decided to contract for EAP services locally.

By 1990, DuPont began to develop an internal, integrated EAP that would include an enhanced substance abuse/mental health benefit (to become known as the "EAP Benefit"). Initial plans called for the total number of EAP staff to reach 64 by the time the program was fully implemented.

The first step for building the program involved assembling a management team. An experienced human resources (HR) manager was named EAP manager and teamed with the substance abuse program manager to begin an external search for experienced EAP professionals. Ultimately, a seven-member team was assembled by July 1991.

An EAP within Managed Care

The concept for the DuPont EAP was complex. The company was building a program that would incorporate the traditional care functions of an EAP within a managed care role. Four major components were developed simultaneously: (1) staffing, (2) preferred provider network, (3) customer relations, and (4) infrastructure.

Staffing

The decision to build an internal EAP required that a significant recruiting program be developed. DuPont had identified positions for 40 EA consultants within the new program, but only four current DuPont employees were qualified for these roles. Finding 36 EA professionals outside of the company with the minimum qualifications (Table 15.1) required would involve the review of hundreds of applications, dozens of interviews, and advertising in multiple publications. This task was further complicated by the fact that the requirements would necessitate a focus on midcareer professionals—people already employed and settled in EAP jobs elsewhere.

The staffing section of DuPont's HR organization assigned a full-time coordinator to this project, and working with the EAP leadership team, she created a comprehensive recruitment campaign and screening protocol that ultimately produced over 400 inquiries and 150 finalists. These final candidates were interviewed using a team approach, and by late 1992 all positions had been filled.

Preferred Provider Network

As daunting as the recruitment process seemed for professional staff, the task of developing a DuPont network of mental health and substance abuse treatment providers proved even more difficult. DuPont operated 129 plant sites in 1991 in the United States, and no outside managed care company could offer a prepackaged provider network. So, DuPont began building its own.

Table 15.1   DuPont Employee Assistance Consultant (EAC) Minimum Qualifications Required

1. *Education:* Master's Degree (one of the following):
   MS/MA in psychology (clinical, counseling, consulting), family counseling, employee assistance, addictions.
   MSW (master of social work) in clinical, employee assistance, addictions.
   MC (master of counseling).
   M.Ed. (master of education) in counseling.
   MRC (master of rehabilitation counseling).
   MPH (master of public health) in counseling, employee assistance, addictions.
   MSN (master of science in nursing) emphasis on psychiatric nursing.
   Other master's degrees that clearly have a counseling emphasis are acceptable. Preference will be given to candidates with doctoral degrees in clinical fields.
2. *Licensure:* Acceptable licenses include:
   Clinical Social Worker (ACSW, LCSW).
   Licensed Professional Counselor (LPC).
   Licensed Clinical or Counseling Psychologist.
   Licensed Marriage and Family Counselor (LMFCC).
3. *Certification:* Acceptable certifications include:
   Certified Alcohol and Drug Counselor (CADC).
   National Certified Counselor (NCC).
   American Association of Marriage and Family Counselors (AAMFT).
   Certified Employee Assistance Professional (CEAP).
4. *Experience:* A variety of experience is necessary for the employee assistance consultant, including a minimum of 5 years of professional clinical experience. This experience may come from several sectors and can overlap and must include at least:
   • 2 years of EAP professional experience.
   • 2 years of addiction experience.
   • 2 years of clinical experience.
   If the individual is in recovery, she or he must presently have a minimum of 5 years of continuous sobriety.

Working with the legal department, the EAP management team literally recruited providers one at a time, using local EA consultants who, themselves, were new to the company. The benefit design was flexible and would reimburse all levels of care. As providers agreed to join the network, each one received a contract from DuPont.

The steps of this enormous task include:

1. Identify standards.
2. Set fee schedules.
3. Develop contract language.
4. Review credentials.
5. Review applications.
6. Negotiate contracts.
7. Review of each contract by management.
8. Final signature of each contract by EAP regional manager.

The flow of paper and electronic information was huge and complex. The task was further complicated by the variety of providers being recruited—from individual practitioners in rural locations to huge healthcare corporations operating multiple hospitals. By the end of 1994, DuPont had contracted with more than 5,000 providers—and covered every state in the United States.

Customer Relations

As the first two components were developing, a third equally important task was being undertaken. DuPont had to "sell" the EAP to its customers—the plants. Because of the autonomy of the DuPont plants, described earlier, the fact that a corporate decision had been made to create an internal EAP did not immediately translate to an open door to the individual sites. In fact, the opposite could be true in some areas. A "road show" was developed, and each member of the leadership team began a tour of sites to introduce the concept of the EAP: its business value, structure, and return-on-investment projections. All 129 sites were visited or invited to group presentations, as were key leaders from corporate headquarters. There were some rocky times; but ultimately the concept was accepted, and each business and location signed on to the internal EAP.

Infrastructure

To support the work of the EAP, a sophisticated information system was required. An outside software developer was selected to work with DuPont's Information Systems Group to design the EAP Case Management Information System (ECMIS). This system included a unique decision grid designed by the DuPont EAP staff that was based upon Axis IV and Axis V of the *Diagnostic and Statistical Manual, Third Edition, Revised (DSM-III-R)* of the American Psychiatric Association. Although the final decision regarding level of care and duration was always the responsibility of the referring employee assistance consultant (EAC), this feature provided a quick reference. The ECMIS also held all client information, all provider information, client treatment histories, and staff information and was directly connected to the mental health carrier for immediate transfer of treatment authorizations. The DuPont EAP was organized around four regions, each with a regional manager and support staff in a regional office and EACs in individual plant sites. The four regions reported to the EAP manager in Wilmington, Delaware. As was true for the plants it served, the EAP regional managers operated with a high level of autonomy.

The EAP Benefit Plan

When considering the role of DuPont's EAP in the overall shift to managed care, one must recognize the critical importance of the mental health/substance abuse section of the DuPont Medical Benefit Plan. The plan design literally created the EAP role because it offered a significantly enhanced benefit to employees, pensioners, and eligible dependents only if they accessed care through the EAP, used a preferred provider (or exception provider if approved by the EAP), and agreed to have their care monitored and managed by the EAC. If these conditions were met, the client had access to the EAP Benefit, as it came to be known (although it was not "carved out" of the overall plan), which included the following characteristics:

- The coverage of all approved services was 90%, with no deductible (the benefit was available from the first dollar of treatment cost).
- All levels of care were covered (hospitals, residential treatment centers, halfway houses, day/evening treatment, outpatient, medication management).

- All recognized mental health/substance abuse professionals were covered (physicians, psychiatric nurses, social workers, psychologists, Christian counselors, master's level LPCs, certified substance abuse counselors, etc.).
- V codes were covered (marital counseling, adjustment disorders, etc.) up to a $1 million annual maximum; no lifetime maximum.
- It was available to all U.S. employees, regardless of their local benefit-plan selection.

The EAP benefit was only available by coming to an EAC for assessment and referral. Plant sites that did not wish to give up their contracted EAP services felt compelled to do so because only a DuPont-employed EAC would be authorized to provide this benefit—not a contractor. This generated initial conflict with these sites (9 out of 125 sites), but ultimately each location accepted the internal EAP. Without this benefit plan, it is questionable how quickly, if at all, the internal EAP would have achieved 100% participation.

Utilization Rates

Although the EAP benefit was unquestionably a major factor in the rapid acceptance of the internal EAP model, it also created a secondary consequence that was, and is, a major challenge. It drove the utilization rate (the number of cases expressed as a percentage of the total employee population) to unforeseen highs. Coupled with the ongoing restructuring at DuPont and reduction in force, the utilization rate was running well over 20% in many locations; for the entire system, it averaged 14% in 1991 and 1992. This high level of utilization added an additional dynamic to the already challenging set of tasks being implemented in the start-up phase. Staffing levels had been forecast and locked in at a 5 to 7% utilization level. Additional staffing was not an option in a downsizing environment. Yet the EAP mission within DuPont was clearly driven by the case management focus, which was the foundation of its work.

The site EACs were routinely working 50 to 70 hours per week, many of which were spent trying to resolve claim problems, negotiating with providers over treatment plans, addressing provider relations issues, and so forth. A 12-member support staff was involved in credentialing and recredentialing providers, processing certain types of claims, fielding 800-line calls (the 24-hour crisis line), and so on. The EAP was functioning like a behavioral healthcare management firm, but it lacked the time necessary to do more traditional and valued EAP functions. It needed more resources to handle the work volume, and because hiring was not an option, the EAP needed to partner with an outside vendor in the behavioral healthcare field.

EVOLUTION OF DuPONT'S EAP: RATIONALIZING CHANGE

The Need for Outside Managed Care Help

The need to seek a managed behavioral healthcare vendor was made even more acute by changes occurring in DuPont's administration of its benefit plans. As the pressure to control costs continued to increase, the decision was made to transition its benefit plans to a managed care model. This meant, among other things, that DuPont would shift its claims processing from two primary insurance carriers to eight. The enhanced EAP benefit was a dilemma because the ability to consistently apply it over eight different claims-processing operations was highly questionable. If it could centralize that administration under a managed behavioral healthcare vendor, DuPont believed consistent application of the benefit would be maximized.

The question facing DuPont at this stage of evolution was how to outsource work that did not add value to an internal model without diluting the EACs ability to authorize and control treatment services. The answer to this question was critical. Business pressures required that the overhead cost of the EAP to be reduced. However, these same business pressures also resulted in continuing demand and high value for the EAP's services.

EAP management, along with teams made up of all staff positions, studied the tasks currently being handled in-house. They needed to decide what tasks needed to stay in-house due to corporate culture of quality-of-care protection, and what could be outsourced.

DuPont's EAP staff was struggling to create the support structure necessary to manage its growing provider network efficiently, chronic cases were consuming disproportionate percentages of available staff time, and claims problems were increasing. The reality was that outsourcing certain functions would reduce costs and increase efficiency. This was painful because "reducing costs" translated into reducing personnel. Also, "increasing efficiency" did not necessarily mean that the same level of attention to detail and quick response times to claim issues could be maintained. But the business realities were clear: The cost of hiring additional staff could not be sustainable for the long term. Outsourcing was the only answer.

So, in early 1994, a request for proposals (RFP) was developed and sent out, and eight potential vendors were identified for evaluation. The initial services identified in the RFP were:

- Customer service, including eligibility verification; verification of benefits; and responding to requests for general EAP benefit information.
- Clinical services such as selected case management and clinical consultation for EAP consultants.
- Provider relations.
- Claims preprocessing for network and out-of-network claims.
- Coordination of benefits.
- Precertification, utilization review, and case management for out-of-network facility-based treatment.
- Case management services for certain treatment-resistant, chronic psychiatric patients referred by the EAP on a case-by-case basis.
- After-hours clinical triage.
- Communicating network-benefit authorizations to facilities, physicians, and plan members.

By late summer of 1994, a review process had been completed, and a vendor had been selected for these services. Teams were established to begin the transition of these tasks from the internal EAP staff to the vendor. One of the four EAP regional managers was named to manage the process, and each of the teams included a mix of EAP staff and vendor staff. Although conflicts were not uncommon in the early stages, a successful implementation was completed by early 1995.

DuPont learned valuable lessons with the use of these transition teams. Many key concepts about managed care were poorly understood by the EAP staff, and, likewise, many critical concerns of the EAP staff were unknown or misunderstood by the managed behavioral healthcare vendor. A key role of an EAP is its ability to provide confidential assistance for behavioral health problems while maintaining a work focus. In other words, the provision of mental health services occurs within the context of work. This allows the corporate culture to be included in the assessment and treatment experience, and the boundary between work and treatment is more permeable. By working in a plant environment, the EA professional can weave work options (such as shift changes to accommodate treatment, light work-duty alternatives to minimize lost time, and the like) into the treatment plans of employees. This role was not known or understood by the managed-care-vendor clinical staff. Likewise, the function of a managed care company was to reduce overall benefit costs by creating uniform treatment standards and practices that providers were required to follow. Also, only authorized or "preferred" providers under contract to the vendor were eligible for full benefit coverage.

This is an oversimplified description of the managed care concept. However, the point is that the use of uniform standards and practices was not rigidly followed in the EAP. Of course, clearly defined standards of care were in place for the EAP staff, but they had a high degree of autonomy to vary treatment using their clinical judgment. The EAP staff did not clearly understand how to consistently apply clinical practices across similar cases.

By creating the transition teams, DuPont and its vendor were able to develop a process for increasing understanding on both sides. As case after case was reviewed in the case management team, for example, the professionals from the EAP and the managed care vendor were exposed to real-life applications of the work focus of an EAP versus the standardized protocols of the vendor. Rather than working toward a win/lose scenario, it was agreed that the responsibility of both groups was to work toward a mutual goal: integration of both concepts. This is now an accepted part of the vendor relationship, and quarterly case management meetings still occur. Even though each group has learned and integrated the concepts of the other, it is understood that constant communication and case review is the only way to ensure this relationship is maintained.

EAP Survey, Study, and Review

As the vendor relationship was being defined and implemented, another significant project was also being undertaken that would have a dramatic impact on DuPont's EAP. A comprehensive study of the EAP was commissioned in 1995 to evaluate the overall effectiveness of the program. Three components were identified for review: (1) mental health and chemical-dependency claims analysis, (2) EAP costs and benchmarking with other companies, and (3) two surveys of customer satisfaction. A team of approximately 25 DuPont staff from EAP, human resources, benefits, and finance supervised the project.

The outcome of this study was generally positive, but it highlighted a philosophical discrepancy that would drive a dynamic change in the DuPont EAP: The highest value was attributed to strategic support of the businesses, not to the transactional services being performed to support the managed care functions. In general, the study (which was reported in January 1996) found that the DuPont EAP had attained nearly all of the financial and performance goals set in 1991 when it was originally established. These results included:

- Mental health and chemical-dependency claims rose through 1992 to $27.4 million and declined to $20 million by 1994. The percentage of benefit costs managed by EAP increased from 11% in 1992 to 82% in 1994, indicating that cost reductions coincided with EAP control over cases.

- The percentage of total healthcare benefits generated by mental health and chemical-dependency expenses declined from 7.5% in 1992 to 6.1% in 1994. The goal was 6%.

- The cost per covered life for mental health and chemical-dependency care declined from $130 in 1992 to $97 in 1994. Admissions per thousand for mental health dropped from 5.6 to 4.0 and for chemical dependency from 1.8 to 1.4.

- The ratio of inpatient mental health costs to total mental health costs for EAP cases declined from 53% in 1992 to 34% in 1994.

- By 1994, 66% of EAP mental health and 40% of EAP chemical-dependency costs were for outpatient services.

However, the survey that was directed to managers and supervisors found that they placed the highest value (87% to 96%) on services such as EAP training, critical-incident debriefings, and EAP consultations regarding workplace issues. The area of dissatisfaction most reported was with the ability to reach an EAC or to have a call promptly returned. A time study conducted as part of this survey added a significant insight: About 30% of the EAP staff time was spent on administration rather than on direct service. To maximize the value to the company, it was clear that a redesign of the EAP was needed.

EAP Renewal

During this time, the DuPont Integrated Health Care (IHC) organization was comprised of four primary components: (1) EAP, (2) Occupational Health, (3) Prevention and Wellness, and (4) Benefits Delivery Services. The intent was to formalize the working relationship among these healthcare-related services. The four EAP regional managers were complemented by counterparts from both the Occupational Health and the Prevention and Wellness competencies, meaning that each of the four regions had three Integrated Health Care managers. These 12 managers reported to the corporate manager of IHC, who in turn reported to a director. This system of management was difficult and slow to respond to business issues. When the EAP study results were added to the overall concerns about the management structure, a reorganization of management, as well as a change in the task focus of the EAP, was necessary.

The structural reorganization resulted in shifting the regional boundaries so that there were three regions instead of four. Each geographic region had only one manager, and each healthcare competency had one leader. Thus, instead of 12 managers there were 3, and a new position (competency leader) was created for each healthcare competency to provide functional guidance companywide.

A primary focus for the new management group was to address the EAP design. It was clear from the study that too much time was being spent in managed care activities and not enough time in other areas valued by the managers and the employees of DuPont. Likewise, access issues (ability to contact EACs or to receive immediate responses to inquiries) were developing due to the time spent on managed care tasks. However, the barriers to this change were formidable.

Change Barriers

In considering the brief history of the EAP up to this point, it may be difficult to fully appreciate the emotional aspects of the proposed change in service mix. First, one must consider that the majority of the staff had been hired in 1992 by regional managers who had significant authority over work assignments, pay, travel, and training. Each region was run autonomously, and loyalties to each regional manager and to one's regional team ran high. The 1996 management reorganization resulted in the loss of three of the four EAP regional managers. This was a traumatic experience for the entire staff. Shortly after the management reorganization, a downsizing of the IHC organization was announced, which included the loss of eight EAC positions and five support staff positions. However, the changes were not over.

From Case Managers to Strategic Consultants

To address the needs identified in the EAP study, it was decided that the EAP needed to get out of the managed care business. The managed care behavioral healthcare vendor was approached, and negotiations were begun to shift all of the preferred-provider network management and case management to the vendor. These changes raised difficult issues for the EAP staff:

- Having just experienced a traumatic change in leadership, many staff were still healing from the loss of their hiring manager and the only leader they had known while working in DuPont.
- All of the existing EACs had been hired when the case management function was considered a key role. Their personal interests, skills, and education were compatible with case management tasks. Conversely, duties such as management consultation, CISD, supervisor training, and so on were not emphasized initially and were considered secondary duties when each EAC was hired. Thus, EACs were required to shift their focus to more hands-on activities than they had engaged in previously.
- There was a general sense of mistrust of the managed care vendor's ability to adequately manage cases.
- There was additional concern of an unspoken intent by the company to outsource the entire EAP.

These issues and concerns were supported by continuous changes within the larger corporation. Many HR services were, in fact, being outsourced. Also, many joint ventures and divestitures were continuing, which contributed to a general sense of disruption within DuPont. Nonetheless, the refocusing of EAP work away from provider relations and case management was deemed necessary for the corporation. The changes going on within the company required support from the EAP for employees that could not be provided unless the EACs were freed from the time-intensive work associated with the case management process. In effect, the EAP needed to shift from a transactional focus to a strategic focus.

The Focus Shifts

An agreement was entered into with the behavioral healthcare carrier to take over management of the preferred-provider network as well as of case management for all pensioners, survivors, and dependents of employees. This agreement became effective in 1996 and included the expectation that employee cases would also transition to the carrier for case management once DuPont was confident that its protocols for treatment could be consistently applied by the vendor. Employee cases were then transitioned in late 1997.

The Structure Shifts

In addition to the changes in the program's primary task focus, an administrative shift was also occurring. As DuPont struggled to increase productivity and to enhance its ability to react swiftly to global business changes, senior management announced a plan to shift many corporate groups to the 19 strategic business units. All employees of Integrated Health Care were transferred from the corporate payroll to local-site payrolls. The three regions remaining were disbanded, the role of regional manager was eliminated, and the EACs went from reporting to a clinical manager to reporting, in most cases, to a site HR manager.

The benefits to this arrangement were that EACs were now firmly connected to the plants and businesses they served. They were "direct costs" for the sites and, therefore, had more influence on local programming and budgeting, and the sites could provide direct support services as needed.

Current Administration of the DuPont EAP

Administrative support is provided by the individual plant sites or businesses. The DuPont EAP is now a decentralized organization with a strategic focus. Core EAP services are provided along with specialized products such as critical-incident-stress debriefing, threat-of-violence consultation, substance abuse awareness training, executive consultation, disability case management, organizational consultation, professional resources for work environment improvement, and expatriate services. The staff size is now 34, down from a high of 64. Clinical and functional guidance is provided by the senior-consultant-global employee assistance services within the corporate HR group.

THE NEXT GENERATION

The EAP evolution at DuPont was not easy and did not happen overnight. Most of the EAP staff was hired with a focus on case management skills. However, the minimum qualifications required for the EAC position (see Table 15.1) were strictly followed during the buildup and resulted in a very well rounded staff. Internal training through various staff meetings were utilized. DuPont also created a clear vision of the future organization, and each EAC was encouraged to seek additional training based upon what she or he felt was most valued by the DuPont site that she or he served.

After two years in the new organizational structure, the DuPont EAP remains highly valued by the business leaders. Each EAC has successfully adapted to the new strategic role within the organization. Although direct services are still a core element of

DuPont's program (assessment/referral/follow-up, crisis intervention, etc.), the strategic role (management/organizational consultation, work environment, etc.) is growing in value and remains a key component of the program.

The future direction for DuPont's EAP suggests a global focus with emerging service needs in support of DuPont's international growth. EAP work will also include the developing challenges of creating work environments that truly embrace and empower a multicultural workforce. To be successful, the EAP must constantly modify its strategic contributions while continuing to provide the core services that define the EAP profession. Business demands in a global economy are far more complex than anything previously encountered. For example, as DuPont expands international operations into developing regions of the world, it will be necessary to assign trained managers, engineers, and other skilled professionals to these new facilities for 2 to 5 years or more. At one time, that might have meant a United States citizen going overseas. But today, and certainly in the future, the expatriate may come from any one of a dozen or more countries in which DuPont operates. These professionals' task will be to provide start-up expertise. The expatriate will then return to his or her home country after the initial assignment is over.

This process is not new. However, as international business opportunities expand at ever faster rates, they also introduce multiple cultural challenges to DuPont employees. The pace and the scale of global expansion will continue to increase. For the EAP, this represents a significant challenge. How do you support expatriated employees from multiple developed countries? Cultural norms are different, expectations are unique, and family structures may be very different; yet the issues faced in an undeveloped country will place very similar stressors on these families regardless of their country of origin. We know that the reason most frequently given for the failure of an international assignment is that the family could not adapt to the new culture. But how are potential candidates screened ethically and fairly? How can the EAP support expatriate families more consistently? How can the EAP effectively provide services to all DuPont employees?

These questions define the future challenge for DuPont's EAP. Several international regions have external EAPs in place currently. DuPont has EAP services in Canada, Mexico, Australia, Hong Kong, Taiwan, Singapore, and England. Conoco, DuPont's energy subsidiary, has extensive EAP services for expatriates in the Middle East and North Sea areas. Each vendor reports to an international region's medical director. These medical directors, in turn, form DuPont's Global Health Team, which is chaired by the company's chief medical officer. In March 1997, the senior consultant for global employee assistance services was added to the team and now serves as a resource to the regional medical directors. The goal is to maximize the benefits of each program by developing a global strategy for mental health. Services will be tailored for each region based upon cultural norms while focusing on the mental health strategy and its goals.

Of course, the need to create programs that recognize and incorporate regional norms requires a broad conceptual approach. "Americanizing" international EAPs will not work. Therefore, the senior consultant-global employee assistance services and the regional medical directors must think creatively as they plan for the expansion of EAP-like services. A process for evaluating the adaptability of an employee and his or her family for an overseas assignment has been added to the mandatory physical evaluation and is being implemented globally. This process will be monitored very closely and upgraded as DuPont's Global Health Team learns more about the evaluation techniques.

Evaluating and supporting expatriates is only one aspect of the EAP services being provided globally. DuPont will use this experience to build improved coordination into the delivery of EAP services internationally. By developing and implementing a global mental health strategy, DuPont will provide consistent services, modified to recognize unique cultural norms, across all of its international regions. Working in partnership with the Global Health Team, the DuPont EAP expects to see strong acceptance of EAP services by its international business leaders. EAP services will be targeted toward business needs such as improved expatriate services, coordinated prevention programming, management training/consultation, and critical-incident response. By actively sharing information about successful program modifications within the Global Health Team, DuPont will be in a position to transfer learning from one country or region to another.

Much remains to be done. In many regions of the world, it is difficult to identify qualified mental health professionals. Cultural differences regarding the use and abuse of alcohol vary dramatically. The roles of men and women in the family and in society differ markedly as well and will have a significant impact on how mental health services can be developed. Nonetheless, business needs will require the DuPont EAP to find answers to these and other challenges.

Employee assistance professionals can earn a place at the management-team table by demonstrating the value of their services and the influence they have on behavioral dynamics in the world of work. It truly is an exciting time as new opportunities develop for the EA profession.

CHAPTER 16

EAP and Wellness Collaboration

W. DENNIS DERR and GARRY M. LINDSAY

The value of building relationships and collaboration between employee assistance programs (EAPs) and wellness programs has been discussed in various professional journals in both the EAP and wellness/health promotion fields. These programs take different approaches to achieving similar objectives in lowering costs related to individual absenteeism, reduced productivity, healthcare cost, and unsafe work practices or behaviors among different target populations in the work site. Both the EAP and wellness/health promotion fields have published claims to the effectiveness of their programs in providing savings to the wise employer who encourages and supports the related activities.

In most organizations, EAP and wellness programs, whether provided internally or externally, operate as independent entities, competing for increasingly tight support dollars while claiming similar aspects of organizational effectiveness and impact. Health promotion activities tend to be more common in locations with established EAPs than in those without.

The wise external or internal provider of either of these programs will recognize the value of a business strategy that builds on collaborative efforts between two similarly focused programs. Because their approaches to the work-site population are similar, there are important gains to be made by the two programs working on linkages and coordinated activities.

This chapter examines the conceptual methodologies and practical advantages of collaborating or integrating wellness/health promotion programs and EAPs. Developing this common linkage provides both programs with expanded opportunities to increase their strategic value to employers. Designed as introductory in nature, this chapter provides a template for thought and actions to the EAP professional who would like to work more closely with an existing work-site wellness/health promotion program or who has been given the responsibility for arranging a wellness/health promotion program with their organizational responsibilities.

RESEARCH LINKAGE BETWEEN MENTAL AND PHYSICAL HEALTH

Key Literature Review

Mental health and physical health are linked. The old axiom of "sound body, sound mind" is based in fact. That is what many health professionals and people who exercise regularly felt subjectively. Over the past 10 years, the scientific literature describing the relationship between exercise and reduced reactivity to psychological stressors has increased. In the first Surgeon General's report on physical activity (U.S. Department of Health & Human Services, 1996), additional credence was placed on the relationship between physical and mental health.

People who read newspaper summaries of the report were surprised at the extent and the strength of the evidence linking physical activity to numerous health improvements. Most significantly, regular physical activity greatly reduces the risk of dying from coronary heart disease, the leading cause of death in the United States, and reduces the risk of developing diabetes, hypertension, and colon cancer. Physical activity also fosters healthy muscles, bones, and joints; and it helps maintain function and preserve independence in older adults.

The Mental Health section of the Surgeon General's report summarizes several studies of the effects of physical activity on mental health. The most frequently studied outcomes include mood (anxiety, depression, negative affect, and to a lesser extent, positive affect), self-esteem, self-efficacy and cognitive functioning. The literature reported in the Surgeon General's report supports a beneficial effect of physical activity on relieving symptoms of depression and anxiety and on improving mood. There is some evidence that physical activity may protect against the development of depression, although further research is needed to confirm these findings.

Physical activity appears to improve psychological well-being. Among people compromised by ill health, physical activity appears to improve their ability to perform activities of daily living.

Work-Site Wellness/Health Promotion Intervention Studies Linking EAP Techniques

The landmark research that provides a direct linkage to the EAP field from wellness/health promotion was conducted in the 1980s and early 1990s by the researchers at the University of Michigan Institute of Labor & Industrial Relations, Worker Health Program, under the direction of the late John (Jack) Erfurt and Andrea Foote.

Erfurt and Foote, as recognized and influential researchers in the EAP field, took many of the established core competencies of the EAP field (e.g., direct work-site intervention, supportive counseling, and systematic, directed follow-up) and applied them to traditional work-site health promotion and wellness activities (Erfurt & Foote, 1990). Their research, which was supported by grants from the National Institutes of Health and the Department of Health and Human Services and by major manufacturers such as General Motors and Ford Motor Company, and the affiliated United Auto Workers, laid the groundwork that linked collaboration of techniques and competencies already existing between the fields.

From an initial focus on controlling hypertension through work-site intervention and follow-up similar to EAP intervention techniques (Erfurt & Foote, 1984), their research expanded into examining the whole wellness/health promotion intervention model that provided intervention, linkage, and collaboration with the work-site EAP (Erfurt, Foote, Heirich, & Gregg, 1990).

In one of their last published papers, "Core Technologies of a Mega-Brush Program," Erfurt, Foote and Heirich (1992) laid the groundwork for the collaborative techniques and efforts that exist between EA and wellness/health promotion. They suggested that wellness programs should be structurally separate from EAPs, but organizationally linked, functionally coordinated, and effectively working together. Their research showed that EAPs should be staffed by EAP professionals and wellness/health promotion programs by wellness professionals trained and certified in their respective fields. The successful outcomes reported in their papers on this technique and on programmatic linkage noted continued successful interventions and benefit-cost containment and supported the need for collaboration and linkage. However, developing these collaborative linkages fully is still a challenge for both EAPs and wellness/health promotion professionals.

MARKETING, CREATING, AND UTILIZING LINKAGES BETWEEN EAP AND WELLNESS/HEALTH PROMOTION PROGRAMS

Joint EAP/Wellness Steering Committees

The use of employee steering committees to assist in promoting and operating a specific benefit function are not new. EAP labor-management steering committees are a critical part of the EAP history of success and destigmatization of seeking assistance in the workplace. Initially, EAP steering committees were often composed of interested employees who sought to promote the success of the EAP because of their own recovery process or that of someone close to them. This self-interest motivation provided the credibility and the energy for local-site EAP success. Some organizations have created health/wellness committees to act as a similar resource not only for benefit-plan design but also for wellness/health promotion activities.

There are advantages to linking these EAP and wellness steering committees formally or informally to better collaborate efforts through a single site-specific committee. Given variable credibility and general-population acceptance of each program, an integrated EAP and wellness/health promotion committee may create added acceptance into the company culture. Joint EAP/wellness steering committees may also link occupational health, safety, clinical services, training, and similar departments. Working together can help to identify and achieve common objectives with greater efficiency, with the result of lowering benefit health claim costs or improving program participation. An effective EAP sends a message to employees that the company cares. Combined EAP and wellness/health promotion activities can help increase overall program awareness and can market the caring perception of the employer among its employees. Some companies, including many Fortune 500 companies, have linked EAP and wellness programs by involving employees who participate on combined EAP/wellness steering committees. Moving to a singular committee broadens the focus of the activity and may be considered appropriate to achieving desired activity levels. These on-site planning committee can be used to plan and implement health promotion or wellness activities and local-site EAP programs.

Program Acceptance/Stigma Management

Management of stigmas associated with a work-site EAP intervention program is difficult. Often the EAP is stigmatized as a counseling program for people dealing with drug or alcohol or with other serious emotional problems. Employees who could benefit from brief behavioral interventions often do not take advantage of the EAP because of this perceived stigma. Wellness/health promotion activities are usually targeted to a larger population who are generally well but who have health risks that are likely to result in future serious illness or disability. Despite the grave results of unattended poor health behaviors, employees are more willing to involve themselves in health behavior change than in pure behavioral change. Offering wellness/health promotion linkage through the EAP or in conjunction with the EAP provides additional opportunities to market the EAP's behavioral change opportunities without the perceived stigmas. Linking wellness and the EAP can and does reinforce the holistic message to employees about health behavior and risk intervention. The linkage success is partially due to a growth in acceptance of viewing individual health, whether physical or mental, in a holistic manner. Articles in numerous popular magazines and newspapers link the overall benefits of exercise with health and mental well-being. Linking the EAP and wellness activities into this holistic acceptance removes the stigma thereby increasing employee acceptance.

"VALUE ADDED" BUSINESS APPROACH: ADDRESSING HEALTH RISK BEHAVIORS THROUGH MULTIPLE LINKAGES

The watch word for any program, process, or activity taking place in today's business world is *value*. Employers ask, "What is the value (or added value) of this activity?" Business scrutiny around value has increased with the rampant downsizing and restructuring that has taken place in industry. There are no longer any sacred cows in business. Every staff process or program must be able to demonstrate a strategic value to the employer. A process or a program with a demonstrated strategic value is likely to be retained. A process that cannot demonstrate strategic value will find itself under extreme pressure to be eliminated. EAPs and wellness/health promotion activities now are under the same strategic value scrutiny as is every other human resource (HR) or corporate activity.

Since the start of EAP and wellness/health promotion programs in the 1970s and 1980s, program managers have tried to find clear and unequivocal evidence for the cost-benefit of EAP or wellness/health promotion programs. Until fairly recently, the business or clinical literature documenting a clear guarantee of the cost justifiable nature of EAP or wellness/health promotion was hard to find.

The strategic linkage between the cost effectiveness of EAPs and wellness/health promotion has historically been difficult to demonstrate for many site-specific programs. Both programs have historically claimed benefit-cost-dollar savings. In search of demonstrating strategic value, both programs may find themselves competing for a limited budget.

The original McDonnell Douglas Aircraft Study (Alexander & Alexander, 1989) demonstrated the benefit cost of EAPs around benefit-cost reductions and provided the direction for much of the current managed behavioral care industry. The integration of EAP directly into or in partnership with managed behavioral care has created the central value-added aspect of EAPs. However, the more elusive strategic-value aspects of improved productivity, decreased absenteeism, and related "soft" measures continue to be more difficult to demonstrate consistently across industry.

Research into wellness/health promotion benefit-cost savings has paralleled that of EAP's indicating similar savings in benefit cost for those who engage in a managed and reasonable level of exercise and lifestyle change. A study of a large midwest manufacturer (Yen, Edington, & Witting, 1994) demonstrated dramatic benefit dollar savings when previously at-risk or high-risk employees began a moderate program of lifestyle health-behavior change and exercise.

In the 1970s and 1980s, business and clinical literature seldom reported clear and unequivocal evidence for the cost-effectiveness of work-site wellness. However, over the past several years, there is more than significant evidence for the value of wellness or health promotion programs and EAPs.

Larry Chapman (1996), on the health promotion side, in his book *Proof Positive: Analysis of the Cost-Effectiveness of Worksite Wellness,* performed a meta-evaluation of approximately 30 major evaluation studies of the economic benefit associated with work-site health promotion programs. Chapman stated that wellness programs, if done carefully and if based on sound program-design strategies, significantly impact health risks, help people use healthcare more wisely, and produce significant economic benefit to the organization involved. *The American Journal of Health Promotion* has provided a series of articles written by Dr. Kenneth R. Pelleka that summarize the results of numerous studies examining the impact of comprehensive health promotion programs on health and costs.

The Association for Worksite Health Promotion, in its publication *Economic Impact of Worksite Health Promotion,* provided a compendium of empirical and theoretical papers on important issues relating to the economic impact of work-site health promotion. Because benefit-cost savings is a direct value-added benefit, this is one of the areas on which both EAPs and wellness can collaborate to demonstrate combined value-added services through integrated functions and operations.

From combining resources at health fairs to cross-referring clients in a holistic approach to behavior change, working together or offering a combined product increases the viability of the service offered and allows for addressing of the strategic value. Some organizations are linking wellness/health promotion programs and EAP into short-term and long-term occupational and nonoccupational disability management and workers compensation. Workers-compensation-claims managers refer to the EAP staff to address the psychosocial aspect of an on-the-job injury, return to work, and family disruption. Professionally staffed on-site fitness centers at some work-sites are providing limited rehabilitative physical therapy that permits individuals to return to work earlier and to continue their rehabilitation while at the work site. This further integration increases the strategic value-added aspects of both programs and prevents the silo activities of separate functions that may be providing duplicative activities.

ELEMENTS FOR SUCCESSFUL COLLABORATION EAP/WELLNESS PROGRAMS

Understanding Professional Similarities and Differences and Leveraging for Success

To understand professional differences, EAP and wellness/health promotion professionals must understand commonalties and differences in marketing approaches and intervention techniques. This understanding will help both programs to leverage for collaborative success. The basic purpose of an employee wellness/health promotion program is to improve the health and productivity of employees and to reduce health-related costs for the company's business units. This goal mirrors that of EAPs in impacting healthcare cost through work-site intervention and counseling of employees regarding work-site behaviors, productivity, personal concerns, and the providing of consultation to supervisors, human resources managers, union representatives, and so on.

Program Development Constructs (Core Activities)

The goal of wellness/health promotion programs is to help change lifestyle health-behavior patterns and the behavioral choices of individuals in the group. The goal of an EAP is to help employees resolve personal problems through changes in personal lifestyle and behavioral choices.

A wellness/health promotion program targets general population health-risk factors associated with illness, disability, and/or early death. Health-risk factors targeted by most work-site wellness/health promotion programs include high cholesterol, cigarette smoking, high blood pressure, uncontrolled diabetic condition, obesity, lack of exercise or sedentary lifestyle patterns, and stress. EAPs target behavioral risk factors associated with substance abuse, depression, family dysfunction, stress, and related lifestyle difficulties. Because there are definite connections between the physical and mental health behaviors and the outcomes of poor health and or behavioral choices, EAP and wellness/health promotion professionals should be working together to strengthen the effectiveness of both programs on the impacting employee lifestyle.

EAP and wellness/health promotion programs have grown and become more sophisticated over the past decade. Employers offer wellness/health promotion programs to employees and their family members for many of the same reasons they offer EAP services: benefit-cost containment, employee retention, and increased employee morale.

Recognized experts in EAP and in work-site wellness/health promotion programs have categorized programs on different levels. These different levels or components are closely related to the likely impact on organizational and health goals of the program. Michael P. O'Donnell, Ph.D., M.B.A., M.P.H., coeditor of *Health Promotion in the Workplace, 2nd Edition,* and author of *Design of Workplace Health Promotion Programs.*

O'Donnell stated that within an organizational setting, most programs can be categorized in one of three levels:

Level I: Awareness.
Level II: Lifestyle Change.
Level III: Environmental Support.

Awareness programs increase participants' awareness or interest in the topic of the program (fitness, nutrition, stress management, etc.). However, awareness programs alone are unlikely to actually change a behavior or to improve health or lifestyle. Examples of awareness programs include pamphlets, brochures, flyers, health fairs, posters, and health or telephonic depression screening with feedback, referral, or follow-up.

Lifestyle change programs use a combination of health education, behavior modification, experience practice, and feedback. Lifestyle change programs must be allowed enough time over several sessions to produce the intended behavior change (e.g., quitting smoking, incorporating regular physical activity into one's daily schedule, managing stress, eating more nutritious foods, or losing weight). O'Donnell stated that the behavior-change process probably takes at least 12 weeks to start the lifestyle change.

If lifestyle-change programs are more likely to produce behavior change (a common outcome objective for EAPs and wellness/health promotion programs), why do many wellness/health promotion and EA professionals and programs focus on awareness programs alone? Part of the reason is that sending a pamphlet or presenting a lunch-and-learn, single-shot, educational program are much easier to plan and implement and cost less than full behavior- or lifestyle-change programs. The likely outcome of counseling a client only provided with a pamphlet through a general awareness program is poor!

O'Donnell stated that the goal of a *supportive environment program* is to create an environment within the work site that encourages an overall healthy lifestyle. It does not help an employee who learned about healthful eating and who cooks low-fat foods at home to be served only French fries and other fried foods in the cafeteria at work. A healthful environment includes providing, in addition to a broad-brush EAP, low-fat choices in vending machines, a smoke-free environment, lockers and shower area, and so on.

Building Program Collaboration from Scratch or Linking Separate Entities

The following process has been used successfully by the authors with health promotion planning committees alone and with combined EAP/wellness planning committees. The authors suggest that consultation from a health promotion professional who is experienced in developing EAP linkages be used when building or planning a comprehensive health promotion program from scratch. Subsequent renditions of the process can then be planned by the on-site committee and a qualified vendor providing selected services. The following tables provide guidelines for developing elements and the process necessary for establishing and linking health promotion and EAP programs at the work site. Table 16.1 provides a planning timetable for program-element implementation followed by a process flow.

Table 16.2 provides the 10 steps necessary for successful program implementation, and the following outline gives a more in-depth description of the step elements.

1. Announce program to employees, and describe program, emphasizing support of top management, by using:
   - E-mail or memo from site senior manager.
   - Personal letter to employees' homes.
   - Newsletter.
2. Recruit planning group (or charge planning to existing committee).
   - Broad cross section of the employee workforce including labor/management.
   - Selection of interested and enthusiastic employees (this is *Key*).
3. Plan and publicize overall program.
   - Determine aspects of program for local site.
   - Announce orientation session dates and times.

Table 16.1   Program Planning Timetable

Element	Approximate Time Required
Plan with on-site planning group and provide education on health promotion and EAP objectives.	3–6 weeks
Present program introduction to employees with link to EAP program.	30–60 minutes
Assess health risks (HRA/screening tests, depression in the workplace screening activities, etc.).	50–60 minutes
Interpret test results and provide feedback (health counseling and goal setting). • Group session. • Individual appointment.	 40 minutes 20 minutes
Provide risk reduction (group and/or self-help interventions).	4–6 hours (over several weeks)

Process Flow

Planning

↓

Introduction meetings

↓

Preparticipation screening (if fitness testing is included in program)

↓

Health-risk assessment/screening (elements determined by planning group)

↓

Interpretations session

↓

Risk reduction/Behavior change programs

↓

Evaluation

Table 16.2   Process for Establishing and Linking Health Promotion and EAP Programs at the Work Site

Step	Element
1.	Announce program to employees.
2.	Recruit planning group (or charge planning to existing EAP steering committee).
3.	Plan and publicize overall program.
4.	Present orientation to wellness in general and specifics of program at local site.
5.	Conduct screening (elements determined by the planning group).
6.	Interpret health-risk appraisal and screening-test results, and counsel individuals.
7.	Review aggregate report, and establish priorities for risk-reduction programs.
8.	Plan and publicize risk-reduction programs.
9.	Reassess risk factors with repeat of HRA and/or screening tests.
10.	Evaluate changes in risk factors.

4. Present orientation to wellness in general and specifics of program at local site.
   - Reasons for EA and wellness/health improvement programs (benefits to individual, employer, local site, shareholders).
   - Overview of the EAP and the wellness/health promotion program planned for local site.
   - Confidentiality in EAP and wellness/health promotion program.
   - Overview of various screening, interpretation, and risk-reduction elements of EAP and wellness/health promotion programs.
   - Sign-up for screening date/time.
5. Conduct screening (elements determined by the planning group).
   - Schedule and location of various or selected screening elements.
   - Full wellness screening, including HRA, blood work, and fitness testing (takes approximately 1 hour).
   - HRA; blood draw; determination of height, weight, blood pressure, frame size, etc.
6. Interpret health-risk appraisal and screening-test results and counsel individuals.
   - Appointment scheduled approximately two to three weeks after screening date.
   - Group interpretation session (approximately 40 minutes).
   - Individual counseling option (approximately 20 minutes).
   - Review of HRA, lab tests, and other test results.
   - Goal setting.
   - Interest survey.
7. Review aggregate report, and establish priorities for risk-reduction programs.
   - Planning-group review of HRA and screening data of entire group (no individuals identified) and interest survey.
8. Plan and publicize joint EAP/wellness/health promotion risk-reduction programs.
   - Plan/publicize risk-reduction programs to address risk factor that are both of high need and interest among participants.
9. Reassess risk factors with repeat of HRA and/or screening tests.
   - In 1 to 3 years, plan to reassess participants (possibly as part of surveillance exam in subsequent years).
10. Evaluate changes in risk factors.
   - Evaluate reduction of multiple health-risk factors and associate with lower healthcare costs and absenteeism rates.

BARRIERS TO SUCCESSFUL COLLABORATION

Competition for Shrinking Financial and Human Resources

EAPs and wellness/health promotion programs often find themselves in competition for shrinking financial and limited human resources. Successful collaboration requires developing shared objectives and goals that address the shrinking financial and human resources available while recognizing and validating the unique education and training required by EA and wellness/health promotion professionals. The ability to jointly create measurable objectives and to remove similar and competing activities eliminates the competition for funding. Today's financial scrutiny of business functions decries duplicity in functions, whether they are provided internally or through outsourced vendors. Erfurt, Foote, and Heirich (1992) foresaw the development of what they labeled the "mega-manager" to manage linked or collaborative programs like EA and wellness/health promotion under a single umbrella. The role of the mega-manager is to create an integrated team of distinct professionals who provide linked but separate activities that compliment or support the overall corporate objectives. The authors have found that such a role exists in various settings and is working to provide numerous opportunities for linkage and crossover activities. This combined program design captures the business requirement of scale and scope functional criteria to maintain a competitive advantage in a shrinking financial environment.

Misconceptions and Prejudices

Both EAPs and wellness/health promotion programs suffer from employees' prejudicial beliefs that may limit program success and collaborative efforts. These misconceptions often are supported by the providers of EAPs and wellness/health promotion programs due to a lack of understanding of where the synergistic opportunities exist between them and due to a desire to build a protective silo for the function. To link and build collaboration between these programs will move them beyond their own prejudices and sharing of responsibility and professional skills.

Professional (Ego) Competition

A large barrier for successful collaboration is often the professional egos involved. There are numerous activities or programmatic approaches and techniques that cross over and may create professional differences on approach and focus. Common crossover program differences may include approaches to programs for weight-reduction, stress management, and smoking cessation. For example, differences in approach may create internal disputes over how a smoking cessation program should be directed. The authors are aware of organizations in which differences in approach have pulled opportunities away from both EAPs and wellness/health promotion programs. EAP professionals may view smoking in terms of the addiction behaviors and the strong link between tobacco and alcohol abuse. A wellness/health promotion professional's approach may recognize the addictive nature, but focus on health behavior change rather than on the underlying clinical issues that drive addictive behaviors. By viewing these differences in approach as a need for collaboration and linkage, crossover activities could provide the best option for collaborative program design to create a concept of "cross-referral and support" between the two entities. Building the best of both takes the ability of the professionals involved, whether vendors or internal staff, to put aside personal ego desires for increased funding or profits and to recognize each other's skills that can make a collaborative effort succeed.

Business Focus on Short-Term versus Long-Term Pay Back

With a surging stock market and stockholder desire for greater shareholder return on investment, many business decisions are being driven toward immediate short-term gains rather than long-term payoff. Both EAP and wellness/health promotion programs face difficulty in showing immediate short-term payoff for program investments. Both programs are focused for providing long-term investment and payoff.

Although it is natural to want to conform to the current tenets of business by attempting to focus these programs on short-term rewards, that will do more to diminish the value of the programs than clearly focusing on the long-term gains of investment in collaborative efforts and removal of duplication. It has been the experience of the authors in various settings that clear understanding of long-term gains resulting from EAPs and wellness/health promotion activities is acceptable in businesses that for the most part seem short-term-gain focused. Long-term issues of employee morale, retention, and recruitment have been successfully included in creating investment into program activities.

FUTURE DIRECTIONS/OPPORTUNITIES

The business trend toward consolidation, outsourcing, and integration of functional activity across wider boundaries will be a significant driver toward greater collaborative activity between EAPs and wellness/health promotion providers. The few existing internal programs will find themselves under tremendous pressure to combine functions, budgets, and staffing to create greater return on investment. External providers of crossover activities will find greater scrutiny of what is being paid for under a contractual agreement, and they will notice pressure to consolidate the crossover activities to a single provider network. In their recent article entitled "Integration of Medical Care and Worksite Health Promotion" in the *Journal of the American Medical Association,* Stokols, Pelletier, and Fielding (1995) indicated that the future work-site health promotion services are likely to be more integrated with the EAP and medical surveillance programs. The integration of multiple examination facets as required as part of the Occupational Safety and Health Administration (OSHA) mandated tests will be used to reduce a diverse number of health risks and to capture benefit and health-cost-reduction opportunities. Employers will seek to purchase multiple behavioral-change services under a single contract. The following are some of the trends that are influencing this future behavior.

Influence of Managed Care/Mega-Healthcare Operation

Recent attempts to control all aspects of healthcare costs through various managed care actions has resulted in mega-provider organizations including HMOs (health maintenance organizations), hospital corporations, and benefit administration and management firms that can provide one-stop shopping for the employer seeking EAP, health promotion programs, and related employee-benefit services.

The managed behavioral care industry, for example, has consumed a substantial portion of the vendor-provided EAP services and continues its nonstop consolidation and merger with HMOs, benefit groups, and even large-scale venture-capital firms.

As managed behavioral care has grown the marketplace, many of the large providers have been purchased by larger Mega-healthcare operations like Value Health, Foundation Health, Columbia/HCA. This medical integration has also created a trend to expand services to include EAP and wellness/health promotion programs as part of a single medical-benefit purchased package.

Business Trends to External Contracting

As the availability of externally provided services has grown, businesses are exiting those internal services that do not meet their core activities. Traditional internal-staff functions, such as human resources, benefit administration, payroll, and training, are now being routinely provided by external contractors. As external contractors seek to maintain their current business partners, they are also expanding their offerings and encouraging cross-vendor linkage under a single contract. Few see any relief in the external contracting trend by business. Providers that can appropriately collaborate with other service providers under an integrated-vendor offering will continue to expand their business.

Expanded Academic Training and Certification

Academic training of graduate students in the behavioral science field and health education and promotion now includes crossover courses that provide a base learning on the collaborative opportunities within the two specialties. The linkage between physical condition and mental well-being has become a regular part of the curriculum.

As each profession's professional organization has moved into certification, opportunities for cross-certification and CEU (continuing education units) collection are becoming more common. Within the EAP field, there is nothing to stop a Masters in public health (MPH) health-education specialist from becoming a certified employee assistance professional (CEAP) provided the person can demonstrate both knowledge and experience in the EAP field and can pass a national examination. The Certified Health Education Specialist (CHES) Certification offered by the National Commission for Health Education Credentialing, Inc. is more restrictive in its certifying criteria. However, the walls separating these professional organizations are being broken down. Wellness/health promotion specialists have made well-received presentations at EAP professional conferences, and EAP professionals are not uncommon presenters at wellness/health promotion conferences. As these two programs become more strongly linked in the future through work-site collaboration, current perceived restrictions will diminish, thereby encouraging more cross-organizational development, training, and certification.

SUMMARY AND SUGGESTED READING RESOURCES

For many years, EAP and wellness/health promotion programs have developed along parallel but separate tracks. The separateness was justified on both sides by the different emphases and target populations for intervention and preventative strategies and by natural tension between the alternative but complimentary approaches. The current business trend is to consolidate processes and organizational operations with a high degree of leverage to influence healthcare costs. This encourages EAP and wellness/health promotion professionals to develop collaborative efforts. More businesses will be seeking to consolidate the number of external process providers under a single provider for all aspects of health and preventative programs. Whether internal or external, the synergy that can exist between these two health and behavior intervention efforts is being lost by duplicative or competitive efforts. Market-savvy healthcare and benefit providers will capitalize on these duplicative and competing efforts to capture market share. Strong evidence exists for employee assistance and wellness/health professionals to join together in collaborative and complimentary efforts to increase their role and influence in healthcare cost containment and prevention of death and disability.

For the EAP professional, there are a number of suggested readings in addition to texts cited in the footnotes that can provide greater insight into the similarity that exists between the objectives of wellness/health promotion programs and EAPs. The authors recommend that EAP professionals familiarize themselves with health promotion program planning by reviewing the following texts:

Design of Workplace Health Promotion Programs, Michael P. O' Donnell, *American Journal of Health Promotion,* 1992.

Health and Fitness in the Workplace (Health Education in Business Organizations), S.H. Klarreich (Ed.). New York: Praeger Press, 1987.

Health Promotion in the Workplace, 2nd Edition, Michael P. O' Donnell, Jeffrey J. Harris (Eds.). New York: Delmar Publishers Inc., 1994.

Planning Wellness: Getting Off to a Good Start, 2nd Edition, Larry S. Chapman. Summex Corporation Integrated Health Management Strategies, P.O. Box 55056, Seattle, WA 98155.

REFERENCES

Alexander & Alexander Consulting. (1989). *The financial impact of the "assist" managed behavioral health care program at McDonnel Douglas helicopter company.* Westport, CT: Alexander Consulting Group, Health Strategies Group.

Camacho, J.C., Toberts, R.E., Lazarus, N.B., Kaplan, G.A., & Cohen, E.D. (1991). Physical activity and depression: Evidence from the Alameda County study. *American Journal of Epidemiology, 134,* 220–231.

Center for Disease Control and Prevention, National Center for Chronic Disease Prevention and Health Promotion. (1996). *Physical activity and health: A report of the Surgeon General* (S/N017-023-00196-5). Washington, DC: U.S. Department of Health and Human Services.

Chapman, L.S. (1996). *Proof positive: Analysis of the cost-effectiveness of worksite wellness* (3rd ed.). Seattle, WA: Summex Corporation Integrated Health Management Strategies.

Doyne, E.J., Ossip-Klein, D.J., Bowman, E.D., Osborn, K.M., McDougal-Wilson, I.B., & Neimeyer, R.A. (1987). Running versus weight lifting in the treatment of depression. *Journal of Consulting and Clinical Psychology, 55,* 748–754.

Erfurt, J.C., & Foote, A. (1984). Cost effectiveness of worksite blood pressure control programs. *Journal of Occupational Medicine, 12,* 892–900.

Erfurt, J.C., & Foote, A. (1990, January). A healthy alliance: Ford Motor and the UAW endorse wellness program through their EAP. *Employee Assistance,* 41–44.

Erfurt, J.C., Foote, A., & Heirich, M.A. (1992). Integrating employee assistance and wellness: Current and future core technologies of a mega-brush program. *Journal of Employee Assistance Research, 1,* 1.

Erfurt, J.C., Foote, A., Heirich, M.A., & Gregg, W. (1990, March/April). Improving participation in worksite wellness programs: Comparing health education classes, a menu approach and follow-up counseling. *American Journal of Health Promotion.*

Prochaska, J.O., & DiClemente, C. (1986). Treating addictive behaviors. In W. Miller & N. Heather (Eds.), *Toward a comprehensive model of change.* New York: Plenum Press.

Stephens, T. (1988). Physical activity and mental health in the U.S. and Canada: Evidence from four population surveys. *Preventative Medicine, 17,* 35–47.

Stokols, D, Pelletier, K.R., & Fielding, J.E. (1995). Integration of medical care and worksite health promotion. *Journal of the American Medical Association, 273*(14), 1136–1142.

Yen, L.T., Edington, D.W., & Witting, M.A. (1994). Corporate medical claim cost distributions and factors associated with high-cost status. *Journal of Occupational Medicine, 35*(5), 505–515.

CHAPTER 17

Behavioral Health Disability Management

DANIEL J. CONTI and WAYNE N. BURTON

The total cost of illness to a corporation is a combination of direct and indirect costs (Berndt, Finkelstein, & Greenberg, 1995; Greenberg, Stiglin, Finkelstein, & Berndt, 1993). *Direct costs* are those associated with treating the illness. *Indirect costs* are those associated with the loss of productivity that accompanies the illness. Direct costs, usually represented by a corporation's medical plan claims, lend themselves more easily to definition, measurement, and control. Indirect costs have some ambiguity with regard to definition (Brady, Bass, Moser, Anstadt, Loeppke, & Leopold, 1997) and are correspondingly more difficult to quantify. Of the various components of indirect cost (e.g., short-term disability, decreased productivity, training time increases, reduced effectiveness of co-workers, increased overtime pay, and recruitment), those due to absenteeism are the most frequently measured (Walsh, Connor, Tracey, Goldberg, & Egdahl, 1989).

As some employee assistance programs (EAPs) have increased their role as key players in corporate behavioral risk management (Yandrick, 1996), they have expanded their responsibilities to better respond to the total cost of behavioral illness. With regard to managing direct costs, it has been established that EAPs may be effective in reducing medical-plan-claims costs for behavioral illness (Burton & Conti, 1992; Conti & Burton, 1994; McDonnell Douglas Corporation and Alexander Consulting Group, 1989). As more EAPs expand their domain into formal managed behavioral healthcare operations, further savings may be realized through combinations of EAP-centered precertification, utilization review, and network-management processes. Regarding the management of the indirect costs of behavioral illness, EAPs can be successfully employed to provide an oversight and certification function for employees receiving corporate-sponsored disability benefits for absence due to behavioral illness.

That a need exists to respond to the increasing costs associated with disability for behavioral illness is clear. In 1994, 23% of all disability claims in the United States were due to mental and nervous disorders (M&N), almost double that in 1982 (as cited in UNUM Life Insurance Corporation of America, 1996). In the workplace, stress is regarded as the second largest occupational disease after musculoskeletal disorders, and it accounts for 90 million lost working days annually (Jenkinson, 1996). UNUM Life Insurance Company of America ranks M&N as their fourth-fastest-growing cause of workplace disabilities, with a growth rate of 335% between 1989 and 1995. UNUM reports that M&N claims currently account for more than 11% of all new UNUM claims (UNUM Life Insurance Company of America, 1997). The *Global Burden of Disease* (Lopez, 1996), a report sponsored by the World Health Organization (WHO) and the

World Bank and produced by researchers at the Harvard School of Public Health, projects a steady rise in disability costs due to depression. According to the *Global Burden of Disease* (GBD), depression was the fourth-leading cause of long-lasting disability in the world in 1990. By 2020, the GBD predicts that depression will rank as the single leading cause.

The fact that corporate America has been experiencing significant change in terms of mergers, reorganizations, and layoffs seems to have increased psychiatric disability claims. A preliminary report of a survey sponsored by UNUM Life Insurance Company of America and conducted by researchers at Johns Hopkins University shows a clear correlation between layoffs and mergers and high M&N claims experience. For example, surveyed companies that had recently experienced mergers that led to layoffs reported a 33% higher M&N claim incidence (UNUM Life Insurance Company of America, 1997). A survey released by the American Management Association and CIGNA Corporation in 1996 showed that companies that eliminated jobs between 1990 and 1995 were more likely to report increases in seven of eight disability categories listed in the survey questionnaire than companies that did not eliminate jobs. The differential was greatest among disabilities related to psychiatric and substance abuse disorders. Furthermore, this survey showed a rise in disability claims not only among those who eventually lost their jobs, but also among the population of workers who kept their jobs (American Management Association, 1996).

Although corporate reorganizations play a significant role in increasing psychiatric disability claims, other factors also contribute. Increases in physician awareness and diagnosis of behavioral health disorders as a result of physician education programs (e.g., Pfizer's "Prime MD," 1995; U.S. Department of Health and Human Service's "Depression in Primary Care," 1993) have made it more likely that psychiatric diagnoses will be made when they occur. Public education campaigns, such as the Depression/Awareness Recognition & Treatment (D/ART) Program jointly sponsored by the Washington Business Group on Health and the National Institute of Mental Health (Regier, Hirschfeld, et al., 1988), have most likely increased self-referrals for mental health treatment. Demographic factors in the workforce have also influenced the trend, most notably the increased number of women in the workforce. The UNUM/Johns Hopkins Study (UNUM Life Insurance Company of America, 1997) noted that 72% of the M&N claimants were women; traditionally, women have shown higher prevalence of depressive disorders (Kessler, McGonagle, Swartz, Blazer, & Nelson, 1993; Regier, Boyd, et al., 1988), anxiety disorders (Emmelkamp & Van Oppen, 1994), and comorbid mental health disorders (Blazer, Kessler, McGonagle, & Swartz, 1994; Regier, Burke, & Burke, 1990).

The changing nature of work in corporate America may also increase the impact and the numbers of behavioral illness disability. Work in America is no longer dominated by manufacturing with its emphasis on manual labor. More and more jobs are dependent on information-processing skills and flexible interpersonal behavior. A prime example is the increase in customer service positions in which personnel are empowered to make decisions based on customer requests and complaints while examining computerized files on the customer or the transaction. The performance of these employees is rated not only on the correctness and cost-efficiency of their decisions but also on their speed and perceived "helpfulness" or "professionalism" to the customer. Given the fact that disorders such as depression and anxiety have as a chief component a disruption of optimal cognitive processes (e.g., slowed thinking, poor judgment, and high distractibility) and impaired social interaction (e.g., decreased frustration tolerance, social withdrawal, and increased irritability), it is understandable that these disorders provide interference with successful occupational functioning for jobs of this customer-service sort. In jobs in which manual labor is key, a musculoskeletal problem such as low-back pain may prevent the employee from performing required tasks. Although a depressive disorder may indeed limit this employee's performance, it would not seem to promote the same degree of disability as the loss of strength or range from the back disorder. On the other hand, jobs that stress cognitive and interpersonal skills with little if any physical strength or mobility demands would seem less disrupted by low-back pain but far more disrupted by depressive disorder (Finkelstein, 1996).

First Chicago NBD Corporation's (FCNBD) Experience

First Chicago NBD Corporation (FCNBD)

FCNBD is a major financial services corporation with headquarters in Chicago, Illinois. It employs approximately 38,000 people and is the parent company of the eighth-largest bank holding corporation in the United States, the fifth-largest credit card issuer in the United States, and numerous other financial service subsidiaries. FCNBD resulted from the merger of two large U.S. banking organizations, First Chicago Corporation and NBD Corporation, in December 1995.

With regard to medical benefit coverage, FCNBD offers its employees a choice between a self-insured medical plan and health maintenance organizations (HMOs). The corporation's medical plan offers an enhanced outpatient behavioral healthcare benefit that makes use of the corporation's EAP as a gateway to a network of behavioral healthcare providers. Employees accessing the network through the EAP are eligible for 85% reimbursement of their first 12 behavioral healthcare visits. The reimbursement decreases to 50% for visits after that point, provided that the regular medical plan deductible has been satisfied. Employees in the program also benefit from a reduced fee from providers in the network. Employees choosing to bypass the EAP and the provider network receive 50% reimbursement for outpatient behavioral healthcare following satisfaction of the $400 medical plan deductible. There are no separate yearly or lifetime limits of coverage for behavioral healthcare apart from the medical plan's $2 million lifetime limit. Inpatient behavioral healthcare claims are reimbursed at 85% following deductible, and FCNBD has offered the same reimbursement level for alternatives to inpatient stays (e.g., partial hospital programs, day treatment, and intensive outpatient programs) since 1984. This integrated behavioral healthcare management program has been shown to be cost-effective (Conti & Burton, 1992).

FCNBD's EAP operates within the corporation's Medical Services Unit and under the direction of the corporate medical director. FCNBD has medical departments in 10 corporate work sites across the country, which are staffed by occupational health nurses. The departments provide a variety of services, including treatment of employees who are ill or become injured on the job, wellness programs, short-term disability management, preemployment drug testing, and periodic health evaluations. Each medical department is also staffed by an EAP staff member. Employees who are employed at scattered small-office or retail-branch locations are served by EAP affiliates in the local community or by external EAP vendors.

In addition to serving as the gateway to outpatient behavioral healthcare, FCNBD's EAP also provides case management for major cases in the medical plan. Cases are designated as *major* on the basis of diagnosis or length of stay. In these situations, members of the internal EAP staff work in partnership with the Benefits Unit case manager to ensure clinical excellence.

FCNBD's Management of Psychiatric Short-Term Disability

At FCNBD, the EAP has managed psychiatric short-term disability (STD) since 1989. The STD program is a salary-continuation benefit for employees off work due to illness for more than five consecutive workdays. The duration of the benefit can be up to six months at full, half, or no salary, depending upon the tenure of the employee. The first five workdays leading to an STD event are considered scattered absence or illness days and are not counted in STD absenteeism statistics. FCNBD is self-insured for STD benefits. Long-term disability (LTD) benefits are administered by an insurance company, and eligibility begins after six months of continuous disability.

The goals of EAP involvement are the following: to assist psychiatrically disabled employees in receiving appropriate care, to manage the employee's return to work, and to provide follow-up support after the return to work. This last goal is common to the tradition of EAP services and is usually represented by continuing EAP counseling that reinforces newly developed coping strategies, encourages maintenance of the treatment regimen (e.g., attendance at AA, compliance with medication), and helps detect relapse tendencies. The first two goals of EAP involvement comprise the actual management functions. The EAP fulfills them through evaluative discussions with the employee, their treatment provider(s), and the employee's human resource manager and/or supervisor.

These management functions are triggered at FCNBD by the Medical Unit's receipt of a Notice of Absence form that is completed by the employee's supervisor on the sixth consecutive day of absence (Burton & Wilkinson, 1988). In turn, the Medical Unit sends the employee an STD Report Form that requires completion by the employee's healthcare provider. This form requests information regarding diagnosis, treatment, and possible length of disability and must be returned to the Medical Unit within 10 calendar days. An occupational health nurse who functions as the Disability Unit manager forwards returned reports that contain a psychiatric diagnosis to the EAP for management. Follow-up forms are sent to the disabled employee approximately once per month for the duration of the disability episode. Failure to return the STD Report Form can result in a cessation of the disability benefit. The benefit may be suspended at anytime by the Medical Director if there is insufficient proof of disability.

At FCNBD the mental health STD management function is centralized to one staff psychologist. This coordinator initiates contact with the employee and, when appropriate, their behavioral healthcare provider. Often these cases are already known to the EAP, and the disability event may have even been initiated by another EAP staff member. If unaware of existing EAP involvement, the coordinator can discover this information via the Medical Unit's integrated health-data-management computer system (nicknamed OMNI), which includes EAP and STD information (Burton & Hoy, 1993). In situations in which another EAP staff member is involved, the coordinator can discuss the case with him or her to learn of relevant background data.

In general, the coordinator reviews the information sent by the provider for concordance in diagnosis, treatment, and proposed length of disability. The coordinator also contacts the employee to explain the EAP's role during and after disability and to assess the employee's current functioning as well as his or her understanding of and satisfaction with treatment. In most cases, all gathered information converges in a positive and rational manner. It has been our experience that disabled employees are appreciative of the supportive role taken by the EAP in explaining the benefit, providing them with psychoeducational information regarding the nature of treatment, offering them guidance in returning to the workplace (e.g., what to tell co-workers regarding their disability period), and, when necessary, securing accommodations for their return to work.

Inspection of FCNBD's overall experience with psychiatric STD reveals that FCNBD has incurred an increase in behavioral health disabilities similar to that of the United States as a whole. Between 1989 and 1996 at FCNBD, behavioral illness rose from the sixth-leading cause of an STD event (excluding pregnancy and childbirth) to the third-leading cause. Examining the total number of STD days by major diagnostic category (MDC) of the *International Classification of Diseases, 9th Revision, Clinical Modification* (Jones, Brouch, Allen, & Aaron, 1993), behavioral illness ranked fourth in total STD days in 1989 (excluding pregnancy and childbirth) and second in total STD days in 1996.

In spite of this expansion in psychiatric STD, FCNBD's EAP can claim success in overall management. Figure 17.1 displays the number of psychiatric STD events per thousand employees from 1985 through 1996. The number of events per thousand employees increased from 2.5 in 1985 to 10 in 1996. What is most apparent is the rise in the number of events in the early 1990s. Figure 17.2 displays the average duration of psychiatric disability events for the same period, 1985 through 1996. Prior to EAP management in 1989, the trend in average duration was an increasing one. After EAP management, the trend stabilized.

Diagnostic Drivers of Psychiatric STD Duration and Recidivism

Further examination of FCNBD's psychiatric-disability data reveals differential aspects of various categories of behavioral illness. The major driver of psychiatric STD

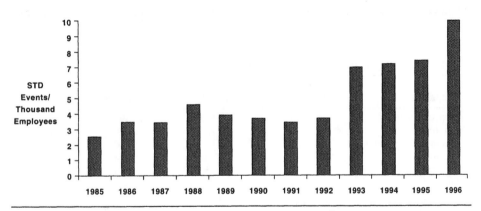

Figure 17.1   Psychiatric STD events per thousand employees, 1985–1996.

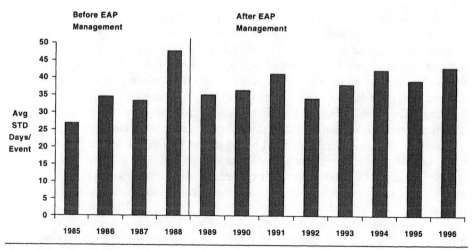

Figure 17.2   Average psychiatric STD event duration, 1985–1996.

for FCNBD is depressive illness. Table 17.1 illustrates that between 1989 and 1996, this illness accounted for 59% of the psychiatric STD events. In that same period, depressive illness accounted for 65% of the total psychiatric STD days. Given the fact that prevalence rates for depressive disorders hold a 2-to-1 ratio for females-to-males (Kessler, McGonagle, Swartz, Blazer, & Nelson, 1993; Regier, Boyd, et al., 1988) and that FCNBD's employee population is nearly two-thirds female, the number of events observed is not unexpected. In that same vein, the relatively low numbers of chemical dependency cases at FCNBD concurs with prevalence data that continues to show chemical dependency rates, particularly alcoholism, as occurring predominantly in males (Helzer, 1987). In addition, since 1988, FCNBD has conducted preemployment drug testing for drugs other than alcohol.

What might not be expected, as few published psychiatric-disability parameters exist, is the findings on average duration for different diagnostic groupings. Table 17.2 displays the average length of disability for selected psychiatric and medical-surgical diagnoses from 1989 to 1996. When the relatively long length (44 STD workdays) of the average STD event for depression is considered together with its frequency of occurrence, its significant impact on FCNBD's disability management efforts can be

Table 17.1   Psychiatric STD, 1989–1996

Diagnosis	STD Events	% of STD Events	STD Days*	% of STD Days
Depression	477	59	20,894	65
Anxiety	99	12	3,600	11
Chemical dependency	90	11	1,730	5
Bipolar	48	6	1,724	5
Psychosis	40	5	1,880	6
Other	57	7	2,483	8
Total	811	100	32,311	100

* Workdays lost not including the first 5 workdays lost leading to the STD event.

Table 17.2   STD: Average Days per Event, 1989–1996

	Diagnosis	Average STD Workdays/Event*
Psychiatric:		
	Psychosis	47
	Depression	44
	Bipolar	36
	Anxiety	36
	Chemical dependency	19
Medical-Surgical:		
	Heart disease	42
	Low-back pain	39
	High blood pressure	24
	Diabetes mellitus	22
	Asthma	21

*Workdays lost not including the first 5 workdays lost leading to the STD event.

understood. This impact, given the disorder's frequency and duration, can be compared to other common chronic medical-surgical disabilities as in previous studies (Conti & Burton, 1994; Wells et al., 1989). Once again, depression accounts for longer average disability duration than the comparison medical-surgical conditions.

Disability management also requires attention to the fact that certain illnesses have a stronger likelihood of recurrence and a return to disability. By definition, a condition deemed *chronic* will be present for a significant life period and will most likely wax and wane. But chronicity and recurrence of an illness are also due to factors beyond the illness itself, such as the environment and the nature and quality of treatment received. It is in this last factor that disability management may have some positive effect on chronic conditions—in the ability to influence a patient toward the most effective self- and provider-delivered treatment. Having information about the likelihood of recurrence or recidivism is a starting point for evaluating the effect of a disability management program and also for evaluating the necessity of or investment in a disease management program. Table 17.3 presents the percentage of individuals who returned

Table 17.3   STD: 12-Month Recidivism, 1989–1995

	Diagnosis	% of 12-Month Recidivism
Psychiatric:		
	Psychosis	35
	Bipolar	30
	Depression	20
	Chemical dependency	18
	Anxiety	11
Medical-Surgical:		
	Asthma	30
	Diabetes mellitus	21
	High blood pressure	10
	Heart disease	9
	Low-back pain	8

to disability status with the same diagnosis within 12 months of a disability period from 1989 to 1995. Once again, the comparison medical-surgical diagnoses are also presented.

These data on recidivism points out the chronicity and severity of behavioral illnesses, such as psychosis and bipolar illness. Although they affect a relatively small number of employees, their negative impact on life functioning is substantial. Effective treatment of these conditions is usually dependent on compliance with medication regimens. However, clinicians who serve patients with these diseases know the difficulty in keeping many of these patients compliant, particularly given the troublesome side effects of the antipsychotic and mood-stabilizing medications. Disability management activities provide a monitoring and reinforcing situation for these employees regarding the necessity of taking their medications. Disability management also offers the possibility of securing reasonable accommodations in the workplace for medication-produced problems.

In like manner, the recidivism data on depressive disorders demonstrate the necessity of attempting to intervene in a proactive manner to prevent or to attenuate recurrences of this disorder. Although the likelihood of recurrence of depression is not of the same magnitude as that for psychosis or bipolar illness, the relatively high prevalence of depressive disorders makes the recidivism situation a common one for the psychiatric disability manager. There is reason to believe that disease management programs may have a positive impact on recidivism with this disorder given the fact that effective treatments exist (i.e., psychotherapy and/or antidepressant medication) that have less-disturbing side effects than the antipsychotics or mood stabilizers and may increase treatment compliance.

EAP Management of "Complex" Cases

Whereas FCNBD's EAP manages psychiatric STDs, a team of Medical Unit members that include the Medical Director and occupational health nurses manages medical-surgical cases. Frequently, in their review, the team members encounter employees on STD with both medical and psychiatric problems. These cases may be a case of misdiagnosis (i.e., a physical medical diagnosis when a psychiatric diagnosis is more correct) or a case of comorbidity (i.e., the co-occurrence of physical and psychiatric diagnoses). Traditionally, these types of cases have been experienced by the STD management teams as difficult to manage with longer-than-average disability periods. From 1994 through 1995, these "complex" cases were examined in a more systematic manner, and data were collected regarding their course. Figure 17.3 illustrates that the perception of these cases as being difficult to manage with respect to length of disability is warranted.

Information as to the probability of psychiatric involvement in these cases may come from the original primary care physician or from discussions between the medical unit management team and the disabled employee. At times, a consultant psychiatrist is used to provide an additional independent medical evaluation. The EAP then contacts the employee and his or her physician to discuss a referral to a mental health specialist or for EAP counseling. In some cases, continuation of STD benefits is made contingent upon cooperation with the referral. Despite such leverage, a very small number of employees still elect to refuse mental health treatment.

EAP involvement in cases that are traditionally regarded as the domain of physical medicine represents a "carving-in" of mental health treatment and the realization that

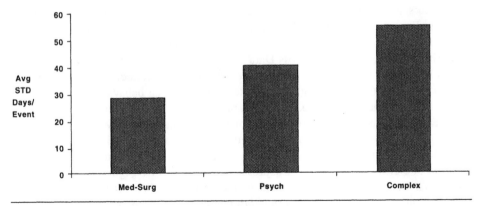

Figure 17.3   STD: average days per event, 1994–1995.

the whole patient merits treatment for the fastest recovery. The list of physical disorders that were recorded as "primary" encompassed a wide field and included asthma, Bell's Palsy, bronchitis, cancer, cardiac problems, carpal tunnel syndrome, chronic fatigue syndrome, corneal ulcer, diabetes, Epstein-Barr virus, gastritis, hemorrhoids, hernia, hypertension, irritable bowel syndrome, and migraine headache. It is interesting that the most common psychiatric diagnosis presenting for treatment with (or instead of) the physical disorder was depressive disorder (Figure 17.4).

ISSUES IN PSYCHIATRIC DISABILITY MANAGEMENT

The Education of Providers

As mentioned earlier, the EAP often contacts the disabled employee's provider during the course of the disability event. Usually, the discussion concerns one or more of three general areas: the length of the event, the elements of treatment, or a request for accommodation.

The Length of the Event

Our experience has been that the requested time away from work varies greatly within diagnosis and, problematically, seems only loosely correlated with symptom severity.

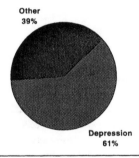

Figure 17.4   "Complex" STD cases, 1994–1995: Co-occurring psychiatric diagnoses.

Two factors seem to contribute to the wide variance in providers' proposed disability duration. First, as mentioned earlier, there is little published data on average duration of various behavioral health disabilities, especially in comparison to medical-surgical disabilities (Reed, 1994; Work-Loss Data Institute, 1996). The lack of available parameters is probably related to the fact that most corporations collect very limited, if any, data on disability (Watson Wyatt Worldwide, 1997) and that behavioral health disability has been a rather recent, albeit surging, phenomena. These factors have left behavioral health providers with few reference points for normal disability time frames.

At FCNBD, reference points are provided to behavioral health clinicians by sharing information from the disability data bank. For example, the median (50th percentile) duration of a disability episode for depression is 7 weeks (see Figure 17.5). Should an initial STD Report Form indicate that an employee will be absent for a longer period of time, 3 months, for instance (about the 75th percentile), the treatment provider can be asked about the factors in this case that cause it to significantly vary from the median length of disability (e.g., Are psychotic symptoms present? Is there moderate-to-high suicidal risk?). A Global Assessment of Functioning (GAF) score is requested on all behavioral health events, but both compliance and reliability have been a problem. As more data is gathered from more corporate settings, clinicians may find the data helpful in differentiating depressive illness from somatization phenomena and personality disorders, which occasionally present with depressive illness and cloud the disability picture. Again, most clinicians find it useful to be provided with some normative data when making their judgment.

The second factor that seems to contribute to the wide variance and relatively long duration of behavioral health disabilities may be connected to the nature of behavioral health treatment, specifically to psychotherapy. Although the relationship between the provider of treatment and the patient is important in any medical encounter, the relationship in psychotherapy is considered by many psychotherapy theorists to be the essential medium in which or by which any behavior change takes place. As such, behavioral health providers may be more uncomfortable with stressing the relationship by suggesting to their patient that it is time to return to work. Indeed, there is a very common answer when behavioral health providers are asked how they make the decision as to when a patient is ready to return to work. It is that the patient is ready when the patient says they are ready. Although it is only conjecture, it seems more common

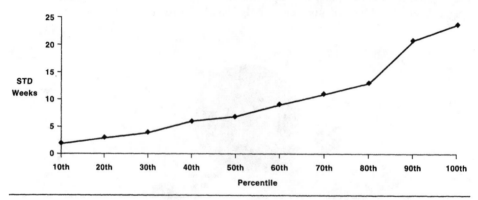

Figure 17.5   Percentile rank of depression STD length, 1989–1996.

for providers in other fields of treatment to play a more directive role in encouraging a patient's return to work.

The Elements of Treatment

With regard to the discussions held with providers about the elements of treatment, the natural demands of disability management place it in an advocacy role for more efficacious and higher quality treatment. FCNBD's integrated behavioral healthcare management program not only increases the likelihood of success for such advocacy but also builds in safeguards against wasteful overspending. This is accomplished through a system that empowers the Medical Unit and its EAP, in conjunction with FCNBD's Benefits Unit, to responsibly manage *total* healthcare costs, both direct and indirect. It is also accomplished as a result of being able to measure elements of both types of costs with the OMNI system. Consequently, recommendations for more-intense but higher-cost treatment are made with an understanding of the interdependence of direct and indirect costs; an increase in the cost of one may be offset by a greater savings in the other. Such recommendations are also later evaluated to test their validity.

The most frequent concerns discussed with providers about treatment includes timely access, the inclusion of either medication or psychotherapy, and the step up to a higher level of care. In general, these issues are less common for employees enrolled in the corporation's self-insured medical plan than for those enrolled in HMOs. Access issues have shown substantial improvement for FCNBD's HMO enrollees as a result of establishing liaison relationships between the EAP and a representative of the HMO's behavioral health department. Thus if an employee is off work due to behavioral illness and is awaiting an assessment appointment, a call to the HMO representative can move the appointment to the earliest possible time. The only type of HMO that has shown continued trouble in this area is the Independent Practitioner Association (IPA) type. This HMO arrangement seems to produce the greatest variance in quality of behavioral healthcare, depending on the primary care physician (PCP) and his or her view on behavioral healthcare. Some are lax to make a referral to a behavioral healthcare provider because of misdiagnosis or perceived monetary disincentives for doing so or simply because they don't know the referral process. On the other side of the coin, some IPA PCP groups represent the highest quality, cutting-edge understanding of the role that behavioral healthcare plays in the total healthcare of their patients and involve such treatment automatically.

The issue of the use of adjunct treatment, in this case psychotherapy, arises most commonly when a disabled employee is being treated by a nonpsychiatrist physician. Often in this case, the employee is given antidepressant medication and the recommendation to stay off work from 4 to 6 weeks, an average time for symptom relief with this medication. In this 4- to 6-week period, the employee may have no other therapeutic activities whatsoever; often depressed individuals have already significantly diminished any positive social contacts. During this unstructured time, misperceptions and work inhibitions may grow, making it even more difficult for the employee to return to work despite whatever symptom improvement occurred from the medication. Usually, no alterations in coping strategy, problem solving, or hardiness are being attempted. These changes can be especially important if the employee found the work situation to be a major aspect of the stress contributing to his or her illness. In these cases, the disability coordinator can suggest to both the provider and the employee that more permanent and positive change can take place with the addition of behavioral counseling.

The issue of stepping up the level of care represents a challenge to current treatment practice in general and perhaps to managed care specifically. Labeling a patient as disabled and unable to work necessarily implies a relatively high severity for the illness condition. Yet, FCNBD's experience has been that treatment intensity correlates negligibly, if at all, with this severity. The typical disabled employee continues to receive once-per-week psychotherapy, the same level of treatment provided for those experiencing mild, nondisabling psychological ills. Random checks of the behavioral-disability roster reveal that usually only 10% to 15% of these employees are receiving any treatment modality (e.g., inpatient hospitalization, partial hospital programs, or intensive outpatient programs) other than once-per-week outpatient counseling. Behavioral health treatment may represent the area of healthcare in which severity of illness is most loosely tied to treatment intensity.

That organized programs of higher therapeutic intensity may have a positive impact on disability durations may be found in FCNBD's data on chemical-dependency disability and depression disability. The changes that affected chemical-dependency treatment in the late 1980s are well known. Standard 21- and 28-day chemical-dependency inpatient-treatment units were replaced by variable-length, intensive, outpatient programs with multiple sessions per week. The majority of these programs also require attendance at 12-step Alcoholics Anonymous (AA) meetings during the same treatment week. Examining the percentile rankings of disability episode length for chemical dependency versus depressive disorder (see Figure 17.6) reveals a major difference in time spent away from work. Ninety percent of all chemical-dependency disability durations last less than 37 workdays. In contrast, only half of disability durations for depression end within approximately the same time frame. Certainly inherent differences exist in the recovery rates of the two illnesses. But employees disabled due to chemical dependency are not spending only one hour per week in treatment; such a condition would never be tolerated by a disability manager, a provider, or a managed care case manager. This massive difference in treatment style for the two illnesses must have some effect on the rate of recovery and on the return to work. The challenge to managed care is to design analogous, lifestyle-oriented programs for disorders such as depression and anxiety that will hasten recovery. This will allow managed care organizations (MCOs) to prove their interest in managing the *total* costs of behavioral illness.

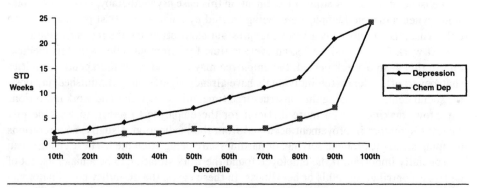

Figure 17.6   Percentile rank of depression and chemical dependency STD length, 1989–1996.

Requests for Accommodation

Accommodations are reasonable modifications in the job or the work environment that enable a worker to perform the essential features of the job. Accommodations in the work situation can represent a useful scenario for bringing disabled employees back to work in a therapeutic and timely manner. They also represent corporate compliance with the Americans with Disabilities Act (ADA), which calls for such modifications when a disability, as defined by the act, exists. The most common type of accommodations for psychiatric disabilities include part-time or adjusted work schedules, additional training, modifications in supervision, and job restructuring. At FCNBD, the disability coordinator can recommend to a line or human resource manager that an accommodation occur in order to bring an employee back to work earlier than if no accommodation existed. Such a modification is beneficial to the corporation in this era of lean, "right-sized" workforces in which worker redundancy has been significantly reduced; some employee is better than none at all. Bringing the employee back to work in this fashion can also serve a therapeutic purpose for the employee. The employee can return to work in a graduated fashion, increasing the likelihood of success at the job and providing him or her with feelings of increased mastery and control.

The request for an accommodation is frequently initiated by the treatment provider. However, a problem with many of these requested accommodations is that they do not meet the condition of *reasonable* as defined by the ADA or that they demand changes in the essential functions of the job. For example, it is not unusual to receive an accommodation request for a telephone customer-service representative that asks that the employee "no longer work on the phone" or "has minimal contact with demanding customers." Obviously, using the telephone is an essential function for a job of this sort, as is dealing with customers; eliminating these aspects of the job cannot be accomplished within the framework of the job. In like manner, ambiguous requests for accommodation are impossible to fulfill: Requests for a less stressful job are without operational definition and impossible to satisfy. Making these matters worse is the valence that disabled employees place in requests to their provider. Believing their provider to be omniscient and omnipotent, they are astonished and angered when the request is not accepted, and they turn on the employer with the entreaty, "But my doctor says . . ." The adversarial situation that follows can result in a delayed return to work, in a denial of further benefits, or even in job loss—unplanned stressful events that rarely are in the best interest of the employee. At the very least, such a disappointment can result in lowered expectations of success upon return to the job.

This problem can be avoided with discussion between the disability coordinator and the treatment provider. The disability coordinator can detail the job requirements for the provider and the spectrum of reasonable accommodations that are possible. For the most part, accommodations need to operate within a specific time frame. For example, an agreement to allow an employee to return to work with a reduced schedule will most likely be limited to a concrete time frame. Also, an employer is not required to lower or change work-performance standards as a form of reasonable accommodation. And although a job transfer may be desired and may be regarded as a reasonable accommodation, many corporations do not have vacant, equivalent positions available. In such a case, a position does not need to be created. The responsible treatment provider, therefore, investigates the parameters of reasonable accommodation, or supports, and encourages the patient to do so before "promising" the patient a change in the workplace.

Neglecting this research may result in disappointment for the patient and may represent either unfavorable passivity or a lack of knowledge about the corporate workplace on the part of the provider.

The Perception of Conflicting EAP Roles

A question that has followed EAPs since their origin has been whom they serve. Despite being paid for by the corporation and being legitimately charged with managing healthcare and disability costs and with improving worker productivity, EAPs are inherently positioned as employee-health advocates. The potential conflict between these two roles can erupt in the arena of disability management. The most common situation for such conflict takes place when the EAP denies the requested extension of an employee's disability benefit. The employee, angry at having a perceived entitlement taken away, may have no wish to work with the EAP in the future. Hence the potential positive effect of follow-up counseling is lost.

FCNBD's experience with such conflict was minimal prior to the major increase in psychiatric STD events in the mid-1990s. As the cases grew in number, so did events in which employees disagreed with the decision on disability duration. Even though these conflicts still represented a small minority, their negative impact was increasingly being felt by EAP staff. Additionally, the nature of disability management is that it requires a commitment of time in order that the EAP staff member will be available for calls returned by treatment providers and for appointments with disabled employees. Staff members found it difficult to apportion increasingly larger blocks of time for STD management at the expense of available time for EAP counseling appointments.

FCNBD's response to this growing staff-allocation and conflict issue was to centralize the STD management function to one staff member, a disability case coordinator. The follow-up counseling that occurs when the employee returns to work is handled by a different EAP staff member assigned to that employee's work area (often this EAP staff member is already known to the employee). Although such an arrangement may be criticized as encouraging the splitting of the EAP into a good service and a bad service in the perception of some employees, it is important to note the role of the disability case coordinator. Functioning first as a behavioral health clinician, the coordinator's role is to ensure that the employee/patient receives appropriate care and experiences the disability period as therapeutic and one that hopefully attenuates further disability periods. This requires more than simply acting as an adversary and counting days. It sets apart psychiatric disability management as a skilled function best performed by a behavioral health clinician with an understanding of psychodiagnostics, psychological treatment, and behavior change. The disability coordinator can structure his or her time in line with the demands of the task, which is different from the routine of traditional EAP service.

Behavioral Health Disability Management in the Era of Managed Care

The percentage of employees in managed care health plans has steadily increased from the late 1980s. A survey by A. Foster Higgins and Company (Umland, 1997) reported that membership in such managed care plans has increased from 52% in 1993 to 77% in 1996. At FCNBD in 1996, over 60% of employees who selected healthcare coverage enrolled in HMOs. As mentioned earlier, the FCNBD self-insured, traditional indemnity plan offers an enhanced behavioral healthcare option that uses the EAP as a gateway. This plan is also managed and includes utilization review, a preferred hospital network, and a preferred behavioral health outpatient network.

Given the reality of increasing membership in HMOs, corporate healthcare management requires new partnerships (Burton, Conti, & Hoy, 1995). With regard to the management of behavioral health disability, two aspects of the corporate-MCO partnership have been important to efficiency in the disability management process at FCNBD. The first has been to permit FCNBD EAP staff to directly refer to the behavioral health program of the MCO without a primary-care-physician referral. This has resulted in expedited treatment for employees and in a closer working relationship between the EAP and the MCO behavioral healthcare staff. The second aspect of the partnership that has been integral to success has been a benefits unit requirement that the MCO designate staff work specifically on disability. Thus when access issues occur, these MCO staff members can be contacted to decrease waiting times, to facilitate referrals, or to include treatment by a specialist.

A means of checking on the success of the partnership has been the annual MCO quality report that the Corporate Medical Director provides to the benefits unit for each MCO. STD absence information is an important component of this report, which is then shared with the MCO as a means of increasing quality in behavioral healthcare. Data regarding number of STD events per thousand covered employees, average length of disability event, recidivism rates, and other information are used to provide a comprehensive evaluation of the performance of the MCO's behavioral health program. For instance, Table 17.4 shows that in 1995, HMO "C" produced the shortest average duration of behavioral health disability event. On the other hand, their rate of 12-month recidivism was twice that of the next leading HMO. Thus, heavy-handed managed care operations may have been shortening stays but at the expense of returning individuals to work before they were ready.

SUMMARY

As behavioral health disability increases as a driver of indirect healthcare costs for corporations, the necessity of professional management of the disability event also increases. Disability management encompasses more than simply limiting durations of absences. It includes the assurance of appropriate care and the successful reintegration

Table 17.4 Sample Portion of Behavioral Health Program Quality Report for Managed Care Organization, 1995

HMO	Average STD Workdays/Events*	% of 12-Month STD Recidivism
HMO "A"	40	10
FCNBD Medical Plan	40	14
HMO "B"	34	15
HMO "C"	32	30

*Workdays lost not including the first 5 workdays lost leading to the STD event.

of the employee in the workplace. Without such professional management, the corporation will most likely incur further indirect healthcare costs, specifically, higher disability recidivism, lower productivity following return to work, and increased litigation costs. EAPs, particularly internal EAPs, seem to be in an excellent position to provide the total professional management required.

Although EAPs may have the best platform from which to work, their success is linked to three other variables. First, optimum disability management must be integrated into total corporate healthcare management. Stand-alone disability management, apart from occupational medicine, healthcare benefit administration, and human resources administration, could work at odds with these preferred partners. The goal of managing total healthcare costs, both direct and indirect, is dependent on being able to actively influence both types of costs. This is best accomplished by disability management empowered to act as full partners with other key players in corporate healthcare management.

Secondly, psychiatric disability management cannot be successful in an information vacuum. Outcome data from multiple corporate experiences are necessary to establish normative guidelines. This requires corporations that espouse total healthcare management to establish health data warehouse systems where such data are secure and are used by healthcare management professionals to guide decisions. These outcome data must be shared in order to establish benchmarks and in order to evaluate progress in behavioral healthcare in general and in the performance of MCOs specifically.

Finally, successful psychiatric disability management is incumbent upon a partnership with behavioral healthcare providers. As mentioned, disability managers must systematically collect more data on disability and share this with providers to decrease the ambiguity of the recovery period. On the other hand, providers must assume a more active role in realistic limit-setting for disability periods. When requesting accommodations for the disabled employee's return to work, providers need to be specific and reasonable. Behavioral health MCOs that can pioneer new, comprehensive approaches to behavioral health disability will demonstrate their allegiance to improving clinical outcomes rather than simply to limiting services and costs. Similarly, behavioral healthcare providers in an era of managed care need to recognize that employers are in large part the ultimate payer and are focusing on absenteeism and productivity as well as healthcare costs.

On the horizon for total corporate healthcare management are measurement techniques that establish the link between health and productivity (McCunney, Anstadt, Burton, & Greg, 1997; Yandrick, 1997). Disability is but one factor in measuring the indirect cost of behavioral illness to a corporation. As research is completed that can accurately capture the lost productivity of those who remain on the job but are impaired, new insights to behavioral health disability will be gained. Such research may lead to interventions that mitigate disability costs in the best manner possible: keeping the employee healthy.

REFERENCES

American Management Association. (1996). *Organizational staffing and disability claims.* New York: Author.

Berndt, E.R., Finkelstein, S.N., & Greenberg, P.E. (1995). Economic consequences of illness in the workplace. *Sloan Management Review, 36,* 26–38.

Blazer, D.G., Kessler, R.C., McGonagle, K.A., & Swartz, M.S. (1994). The prevalence and distribution of major depression in a national community sample: The national comorbidity survey. *American Journal of Psychiatry, 151,* 979–986.

Brady, W., Bass, J., Moser, Jr., R., Anstadt, G.W., Loeppke, R.R., & Leopold, R. (1997). Defining total corporate health and safety costs—significance and impact. *Journal of Occupational and Environmental Medicine, 39,* 224–231.

Burton, W.N., & Conti, D.J. (1992). Value-managed mental health benefits. In J.S. Harris, H.D. Belk, & L.W. Wood (Eds.), *Managing employee healthcare costs: Assuring quality and value* (pp. 151–154). Boston: OEM Press.

Burton, W.N., Conti, D.J., & Hoy, D.A. (1995). Making managed care partnerships work. *Managing Employee Health Benefits, 3,* 40–44.

Burton, W.N., & Hoy, D.A. (1993). First Chicago's integrated health data management computer system. In *Driving down health care costs: Assuring quality and value* (pp. 72–80). Boston: OEM Press.

Burton, W.N., & Wilkinson, F. (1988). Cost management of short-term disability. *American Academy of Occupational Health Nursing, 36,* 224–227.

Conti, D.J., & Burton, W.N. (1992). Swimming upstream: How First Chicago manages costs while expanding behavioral health benefits. *Behavioral Healthcare Tomorrow, 1,* 24–27.

Conti, D.J., & Burton, W.N. (1994). The economic impact of depression in a workplace. *Journal of Occupational and Environmental Medicine, 36,* 983–988.

Emmelkamp, P.M.G., & Van Oppen, P. (1994). Anxiety disorders. In V.B. Van Hasselt & M. Hersen (Eds.), *Advanced abnormal psychology.* New York: Plenum Press.

Finkelstein, S.N. (1996, November). *Mapping the landscape for workplace health and productivity.* Paper presented at the meeting of the Competitive Advantage of a Healthy Work Force, Naples, FL.

Greenberg, P.E., Stiglin, L.E., Finkelstein, S.N., & Berndt, E.R. (1993). The economic burden of depression in 1990. *Journal of Clinical Psychiatry, 54,* 405–418.

Helzer, J.E. (1987). Epidemiology of alcoholism. *Journal of Clinical and Consulting Psychology, 55,* 284–292.

Jenkinson, J. (1996, February). Stress—we can't live with it, we can't live without it—or can we? *Journal of Risk Management,* 10.

Jones, M.K., Brouch, K.L., Allen, M.M., & Aaron, W.S. (Eds.). (1993). *St. Anthony's color-coded ICD-9-CM.* Alexandria, VA: St. Anthony.

Kessler, R.C., McGonagle, K.A., Swartz, M., Blazer, D.G., & Nelson, C.B. (1993). Sex and depression in the national comorbidity survey: I. Lifetime prevalence, chronicity, and recurrence. *Journal of Affective Disorders, 29,* 85–96.

Lopez, A.D. (1996). In C.J. L. Murray (Ed.), *The global burden of disease: A comprehensive assessment of mortality and disability from diseases, injuries, and risk factors in 1990 and projected.* Cambridge, MA: Harvard School of Public Health.

McCunney, R.J., Anstadt, G., Burton, W.N., & Greg, D. (1997). The competitive advantage of a healthy work force: Opportunities for occupational medicine. *Journal of Occupational and Environmental Medicine, 39,* 1–3.

McDonnell Douglas Corporation and Alexander Consulting Group. (1989). *McDonnell Douglas Corporation employee assistance program financial offset study 1985–1989.* Bridgeton, MO: Author.

Pfizer, Inc. (1995). *Prime MD: Primary care evaluation of mental disorders.* USA: Author.

Reed, P. (1994). *The medical disability advisor* (2nd ed.). Horsham, PA: LRP Publications.

Regier, D.A., Boyd, J.H., Burke, J.D., Jr., Rae, D.S., Myers, J.K., Kramer, M., Robins, L.N., George, L.K., Karno, M., & Locke, B.Z. (1988). One-month prevalence of mental disorders in the United States: Based on five epidemiologic catchment area sites. *Archives of General Psychiatry, 45,* 977–986.

Regier, D.A., Burke, J.D., & Burke, K.C. (1990). Comorbidity of affective and anxiety disorders in the NIMH epidemiologic catchment area program. In J.D. Maser & C.R. Cloninger (Eds.), *Comorbidity of mood and anxiety disorders* (pp. 113–122). Washington, DC: American Psychiatric Press.

Regier, D.A., Hirschfeld, R.M.A., Goodwin, F.K., Burke, J.D., Lazar, J.B., & Judd, L.L. (1988). The NIMH depression awareness, recognition, and treatment program: Structure, aims, and scientific basis. *American Journal of Psychiatry, 145,* 1351–1357.

Umland, B. (1997). Foster Higgins national survey: Trends in behavioral benefits. *Behavioral Healthcare Tomorrow, 6,* 57–60.

U.S. Department of Health and Human Services. (1993). *Depression in primary care* (AHCPR Publication No. 93-0550). Rockville, MD: Author.

UNUM Life Insurance Corporation of America. (1996, July). Psychiatric disabilities: Studying the impact. *Perspective, 3,* 6.

UNUM Life Insurance Corporation of America. (1997). *UNUM's long-term disability database.* Portland, ME: Author.

Walsh, D.C., Connor, E., Tracey, L.V., Goldberg, G.A., & Egdahl, R.H. (1989). Posthospital convalescence and return to work. *Health Affairs, 8,* 76–90.

Watson Wyatt Worldwide. (1997). *Staying @ work.* Bethesda, MD: Author.

Wells, K.B., Stewart, A., Hays, R.D., Burnam, A., Rogers, W., Daniel, M., Berry, S., Greenfield, S., & Ware, J. (1989). The functioning and well-being of depressed patients: Results from the medical outcomes study. *Journal of the American Medical Association, 262,* 914–919.

Work-Loss Data Institute. (1996). *Official disability guidelines 1997* (2nd ed.). Riverside, CT: Author.

Yandrick, R.M. (1996). *Behavioral risk management.* San Francisco, CA: Jossey-Bass.

Yandrick, R.M. (1997). High demand, low-control jobs reduce productivity and increase workplace disability costs. *Behavioral Healthcare Tomorrow, 6,* 41–44.

CHAPTER 18

EAP Intervention with Workers' Compensation and Disability Management

GEOFFRY B. SMITH and TED ROONEY

This chapter will review the experience at L.L. Bean, Inc., integrating employee assistance (EA) expertise and services with on-site medical treatment and disability management services for workers' compensation and short-term disability injuries and illnesses. Following its inception, the employee assistance program (EAP) became the facilitator for addressing the psychosocial issues that are so often involved in the treatment of employees with disabilities. Through facilitating a collaborative process with the medical care providers, the EAP has been able to become a full partner in treatment at the earliest stages.

We begin by offering a brief description of L.L. Bean as a company and by describing the evolution and structure of the L.L. Bean EAP. We then outline the purpose and function of workers' compensation and other disability programs and describe the factors specific to L.L. Bean's regulatory and corporate environment. Because workers' compensation statutes are written at the state level, significant variation exists within the United States regarding coverage and employer responsibilities. Knowledge of the specific context within which L.L. Bean designs and operates its programs will help the reader to extract from our solutions those aspects most applicable to their own circumstances.

We then review the research from experts in the medical and workers' compensation field on injuries and disability and describe L.L. Bean's pre-EAP injury management system. The research, which emphasizes the importance of psychological and social factors in disabilities, demonstrates why EA services are a key aspect of any comprehensive injury management program. We continue by describing the components and functioning of L.L. Bean's current integrated system of employee assistance and disability management, discussing psychological trauma and other clinical issues and conclude by outlining some of the challenges we see for the future.

L.L. BEAN: THE COMPANY

L.L. Bean, Inc., is a catalogue retailer founded in 1912 and based in Freeport, Maine. It specializes in outdoor clothing, products, and services and is known for its emphasis on quality and customer service. L.L. Bean is privately held. It has annual sales of over $1 billion.

L.L. Bean employs approximately 4,000 employees year-round and adds an additional 6,000 seasonal employees in the fall. Depending on the season, the company employs 1,500 to 4,000 employees in telemarketing, 1,000 to 3,000 in warehousing and distribution, 500 to 1,000 in retail, 500 in manufacturing, and the rest in office environments. Employee relations are generally very good, work environments clean, and supervisors well trained. The workforce is geographically concentrated, with most employees working in central midcoast Maine.

THE EVOLUTION OF THE L.L. BEAN EMPLOYEE ASSISTANCE PROGRAM

Prior to 1995, L.L. Bean's EA services utilized human resources (HR) staff as referral agents. In this role, they would elicit basic presenting problem information from a troubled employee and refer the employee to a community resource. Although the HR staff strongly supported the need for such services, this was an add-on responsibility to their regular duties, and one for which they felt ill-trained. Assessment was rudimentary, and follow-up was inconsistent. HR staff members were frequently anxious that they had missed something about a case and were at times overwhelmed by the difficult material and complex problems with which they were presented.

The HR staff was also acutely concerned about potential role conflicts (e.g., assisting an employee with personal problems while advising the employee's supervisor on disciplinary procedures). Not surprisingly, they were key lobbyists for professional EA staff and services.

L.L. Bean instituted a formal EAP in 1995. EAPs have often been funded on the expectation that, through careful assessment, treatment planning, and follow-up, they will reduce the mental health and substance abuse (MHSA) component of group health costs. This did not seem probable at L.L. Bean. Even though L.L. Bean did not offer a managed care plan to its employees until 1995, MHSA spending under the indemnity plan in 1993 and 1994 comprised only 5% of annual group health plan expenditures, and there was little likelihood of future EAP-related reductions in this area. In fact, there was some discussion that the low expenditure for behavioral healthcare indicated that employees were being undertreated. It was suggested that the introduction of an EAP (with the corresponding increase in visibility regarding emotional-health issues) and managed care (with a $15 copayment, rather than the 50% copayment required under the indemnity plan) would increase MHSA costs. This caused some concern, which was tempered by the expectation that any such increases would be modest and that they could reasonably be seen as investments in employee health and productivity. (MHSA costs did in fact increase modestly between 1995 and 1997.)

Workers' compensation costs presented greater opportunity for reductions. These represented a significant part of the health budget, and, as will be seen later, there was a growing awareness that psychological and social factors played a major role in delaying recovery and return to work. The EAP was cost-justified through the expectation that it would reduce the expenses associated with medical and lost-time costs of injured employees.

Design Aspects of the L.L. Bean EAP

A full-time external consultant (GBS) was hired to design and deliver services. The consultant reported to the Manager of Employee Health (TR), who was responsible for all group health, disability, and wellness programs at the company. EAP office space was allocated in or near the four major L.L. Bean work locations in the state. The company was very responsive to the EAP, and close working relationships were easily established with HR supervisors, and members of the injury-management system.

From its start, the scope of the L.L. Bean EAP has been broad-brush, with additional responsibilities in injury management, as will be described. The basic services of the EAP core technology (Roman and Blum, 1985) are offered, including training and consultation for supervisors and HR staff, employee orientation, and assessment, referral, brief treatment, and follow-up services.

The program is voluntary, except in cases where there is a potential threat of violence or when an employee shows indications of being under the influence of drugs or alcohol while on the job. At the time of program inception, drug testing was not a major issue at L.L. Bean. There were a small number of interstate drivers who were subject to testing under Department of Transportation regulations. During 1998, there was active consideration of broadening drug testing to include those employees who work in safety-sensitive positions (e.g., equipment operators), but this matter is still in the analysis stage.

EAP services are offered to employees, family members, and retirees. The fact that the employee population more than doubles for 3 months in the autumn poses a special set of EAP staffing issues. All EA services are offered to seasonal employees, most of whom do not have health insurance. The EAP has been able to provide service to them, including short- and intermediate-term individual counseling, by using master's level counseling and social work interns.

In addition to providing broad-brush services, the EAP has been responsible for developing interventions to address the various psychological factors that could delay the recovery of injured workers. Before describing this aspect of the L.L. Bean EAP, we will discuss the workers' compensation system and the science behind musculoskeletal disorders and describe the initial development of L.L. Bean's injury-management system.

Workers' Compensation and Short- and Long-Term Disability

Most companies' disability programs comprise three separate but related programs: (1) workers' compensation, (2) short-term disability, and (3) long-term disability. Workers' compensation programs are typically managed by a company's finance or risk-management department, whereas HR typically manages short- and long-term disability programs. Departments rarely have coordinated efforts, so workers' compensation may claim a savings when a claim is found to be non-work-related, whereas HR often pays out those same benefits in the form of short- or long-term disability payments, thereby canceling out any potential savings for the company. In fact, a company may wind up with a higher total payout when the costs of investigating the claim are taken into account.

Companies began paying more attention to these programs as they grew more costly. During the 1980s and 1990s, costs rose as more employees began filing claims and staying out of work longer on the claims they did file. At the same time, business became more competitive, and companies found that it was increasingly important for them to manage all their costs. Corporate officials realized their companies could become more operationally and financially efficient by coordinating their various disability services (Tortarolo & Polakoff, 1996).

As companies started to integrate the management of their various disability programs and to seek ways to increase their effectiveness and efficiency, they recognized the enormous impact that psychosocial factors played in the onset and the continuation of disabilities. There is almost always a behavioral health component in disability claims, especially for long-standing and costly ones. When employees develop chronic pain syndrome or other psychosocial conditions along with their physical problems, it becomes difficult to help them improve with a traditional medical model. Behavioral health interventions help employees to deal with the psychosocial issues that are impeding the healing process and the return to work. With its knowledge both of the individual and of his or her health problems, as well as of a company's work processes and culture, an EAP can play an important role.

To understand the features of disability programs, it is useful to understand their evolution. Workers' compensation and short- and long-term disability programs grew out of two different backgrounds: (1) statutory requirements and (2) the need to attract and to retain quality employees. One was legally mandated; the other was offered as a voluntary benefit.

Workers' Compensation

Workers' compensation is a state-mandated disability program that originated in 1911 to cover work-related injuries and illnesses (Owens, 1997; Worrall, 1992). Before workers' compensation laws, an employee hurt at work had to sue the employer for benefits. This was a hardship on both employees and employers. Workers' compensation was created as a fair means of providing payment of medical bills and lost wages for employees, while also protecting employers from infrequent but expensive liability suits. By its nature, workers' compensation is *no-fault*—an employer cannot deny payment because an employee's behavior contributed to the injury (except in cases of overt horseplay where company rules are clearly violated), nor can an employee sue the employer for assumed negligence concerning workplace conditions. (For example, employees suffering ill effects from asbestos exposure in the past sued the asbestos manufacturer for compensatory damages, that is, awards for pain and suffering. Under the terms of workers' compensation, they cannot sue their employer.) Workers' compensation is an "exclusive remedy" for workplace exposure.

Each state's workers' compensation programs have similarities and differences. Much of the difference is in the amount of payment, the extent and comprehensiveness of coverage, and the length of the coverage period. For example, all states cover accidents occurring at work (e.g., broken legs), but states vary on how much of a gradual-onset injury (e.g., chronic back pain) must be work-related to qualify for coverage. States also differ in the extent to which they will cover work-related "mental stress" claims. (In Maine, for example, the regulations are written in such a way as to make mental stress claims extremely rare. This means that employees leaving work because of stress are dealt with through the nonoccupational disability plans and group health insurance.) Finally, there are large differences among states in how much workers can be compensated for the same injuries. For example, in 1995 an employee with a temporary total disability, such as a back strain, was eligible for a maximum of $797 per week for the length of the disability in Iowa, $444 per week for a limit of 104 weeks in Florida, and a maximum of $250 per week for a limit of 450 weeks in Mississippi.

Historically, workers' compensation was viewed within a company as accident insurance and was managed like other property and casualty insurance. Fire, theft, auto, product liability, and workers' compensation were usually administered by the risk management (RM) department. The RM culture was legalistic and loss-oriented; claims were "managed," and losses or "damages" from claims were minimized. As with any insurance based on accidents, the goal was to prevent them from occurring and to minimize losses when they did occur. Thus, companies focused on traditional safety programs, and many made much progress in reducing traumatic injuries.

Until the 1980s and the increase in gradual-onset injuries such as tendonitis, carpal tunnel syndrome, and cumulative back strain, workers' compensation was not very expensive. Claims were typically paid out for accidents in which the cause of the injury (e.g., slipped on wet floor), diagnosis (e.g., broken leg), and the prognosis (e.g., 8 weeks on crutches, then return to work with minimal limitation) were straightforward. However, when faced with less clear-cut injuries and illnesses (e.g., back injuries, cumulative trauma disorders, or repetitive strain injuries), problems occurred. Injuries were less easy to define, more difficult to manage and predict, and more complicated by psychological and social factors. Employees stayed out of work longer, and costs increased.

Short- and Long-Term Disability

In contrast to workers' compensation, short- and long-term disability programs arose from an entirely different background in most companies—the benefits department. Whereas risk management (which usually handled workers' compensation) typically reported to the finance department and was primarily focused on saving money, the benefits department was part of human resources, which focused on attracting, retaining, and motivating high-quality employees. Vacation, holidays, medical insurance, pension, savings, and short- and long-term disability programs were all part of the benefits packages companies offered (Hallman, 1992; Rosenbloom, 1992).

A second difference between workers' compensation and disability insurance concerns coverage. For work-related injuries, workers' compensation covers both medical and lost-time payments, whereas non-work-related injuries are covered separately. In such cases, an employee's medical insurance pays for medical bills, and short- and long-term disability programs pay for lost wages. Short-term disability typically lasts for 6 to 12 months, after which the long-term disability program commences. (The short-term disability and long-term disability programs are typically different insurance policies and are often insured by different companies.) Although short- and long-term programs are broadly similar throughout the country, differences among companies do exist (e.g., whether both programs are offered, which employees receive disability coverage [e.g., salaried versus hourly, full-time versus part-time], and the percentage of the employee's wages that are replaced [e.g., 67% or 75% is typical] (Doudna, 1992).)

Table 18.1   Comparing Workers' Compensation and Short- and Long-Term Disability Programs

Workers' Compensation	Short- and Long-Term Disability
State mandated.	Voluntary (except CA, HI, NJ, NY, RI).
Covers all permanent and seasonal employees.	Covers selected employees.
Benefits and covered conditions are the same in companies within each state.	Benefits and covered conditions are different among companies within each state.
Benefits and covered conditions vary widely among states, even in the same companies.	Benefits and covered conditions are the same within companies with operations in different states.
Pays both medical and lost-time benefits.	Pays lost-time benefits only (medical benefits included in medical plan).
Employee choice of provider is the same within each state, but ranges among states from employer choice to employee choice, with variations in between.	Employee choice of provider dictated by medical plan design (e.g., managed care or fee for service). Typically is the same within a company, even across states.
Fully funded by employer.	Funding ranges from 100% employer to 100% employee, with infinite variations.

Table 18.1 summarizes the differences between worker's compensation and short- and long-term disability.

Evolution of Disability Management

For much of the 1980s, the rising costs of medical insurance occupied companies' attention. Medical insurance costs rose by double digits each year and reached 10% to 15% of payroll. Companies experimented with different strategies to reduce costs, including utilization review, second surgical opinions, case management, restricted provider networks, and other variations of managed care. In reality, these early efforts were mostly "managed cost" programs. The current trend among progressive employers is to use comprehensive managed care plans that focus on quality and employee satisfaction, as well as cost.

In the early 1990s, many companies also began to pay more attention to their disability costs. Researchers estimate that the full cost of disability averages 8% of payroll for most companies (Berkowitz, 1996). The direct cost of workers' compensation and short- and long-term disability insurance is 4%; the cost of lost productivity and other indirect costs is 3%; and the cost of administering the program is 1%. With business becoming more competitive, reducing these figures became attractive.

During the early 1990s, two other forces propelled companies to focus attention on their disability programs: One was corporate downsizing; the other was the changing nature of disability claims. As companies restructured and downsized to reduce costs and to stay competitive in a global economy, fewer people remained to manage programs within corporations. To achieve greater efficiency, it made sense to combine efforts in disability management.

Depending on any given company's benefit-plan richness and on the state in which it does business, either workers' compensation or short-term disability will be a larger problem. As noted earlier, benefit levels differ among companies for short- and long-term disability plans and among states for workers' compensation. In a company with rich benefit plans and low state workers' compensation costs, employees are incented to file for short-term disability benefits for injuries that could be either work- or non-work-related (e.g., gradual-onset back strain). On the other hand, in companies with less rich benefit plans in states with high workers' compensation costs, the financial incentive is to file for workers' compensation benefits. Thus, it is important to know the benefit levels and the workers' compensation costs for a given company in determining the scope of a disability problem and the best ways to address the problem.

L.L. Bean at first focused its efforts on workers' compensation disabilities because of their greater prevalence and costs. More recently, attention was given to non-work-related disabilities because their prevalence and costs increased as well. It also became increasingly difficult to explicitly determine whether or not an injury was work-related. Many disability claims result from musculoskeletal injuries. As science and medical research indicate, many back and upper-extremity conditions are caused by multiple factors over time. For someone who was a material handler at work and who cut wood and was active in the outdoors in their personal lives, it was very difficult to determine just what caused a gradual-onset back injury. However, it was easy to determine that either way, the injury would be costly to both the individual in regard to life disruption and to the company in regard to lost productivity and financial costs. As companies began to pay more attention to chronic or long-term disabilities, it became clear that a more holistic approach to managing disability claims was needed (Rooney, 1997).

Over the past few years, L.L. Bean helped return employees with nonoccupational injuries to work safely. However, the company was slow to aggressively manage these cases because employees often thought of their short- and long-term disability benefits as they did their vacation (i.e., something to which they were entitled). The company is slowly increasing its management of non-work-related disabilities so that within a year, the differences in injury management will likely all but disappear.

SCIENCE BEHIND GRADUAL-ONSET MUSCULOSKELETAL INJURIES

During the 1980s, some good science was produced to help guide the evolution of disability management programs.

Silverstein (1985, 1986, 1987), Snook, Campnelli, and Hart (1978), Armstrong (1983; Armstrong et al., 1987), Rodgers (1987), Garg and Moore (1992), and others produced the foremost research on gradual-onset musculoskeletal disorders, commonly called *cumulative trauma disorders* (CTDs). These researchers linked the physical demands and the ergonomics of the workplace to the incidence of CTDs of the upper extremity and back.

In a 1992 article in the *Journal of Occupational Medicine,* Nortin Hadler offered evidence that CTDs were related to significantly more than the physical demands of the workplace. In an analysis of one company's (U.S. West) experience with CTDs, Hadler concluded that the six-to-eight-fold differences in the number of cases of CTDs among plants in different states was due to a complex set of factors. Among these were:

- Labor management relationships at the plants.
- The responses of the local medical communities to employees reporting arm pain.

Hadler also believed that biomechanical factors were not the major cause of this variance because all the workplaces were ergonomically similar. In a subsequent report on U.S. West's experiences with CTDs, the National Institute of Occupational Safety and Health found that psychosocial factors were as important as ergonomic factors in U.S. West's increased incidence of CTDs. This was a view also expressed by the Communication Workers of America, the union that represented U.S. West's employees (Bureau of National Affairs, 7/22/92).

In a study of workers at Boeing (Bigos, et al., 1986, 1991), Bigos and colleagues found that the factors most likely to predict disability from low-back pain were worker dissatisfaction and disciplinary actions by the employer prior to the low-back-pain episode. Nachemson (1992) concluded after years of studying the causes of low-back pain:

> Most case control studies of cross-sectional design that have addressed the mechanical and psychosocial factors influencing LBP (low back pain), including job satisfaction, have concluded that the latter play a more important role than the extensively studied, mechanical factors. This applies in particular to those 5–10% of patients who are disabled for more than three months and who account for 75–90% of the costs.

These studies demonstrate that the origin and management of CTDs in a company were complex. Narrowly focusing on the physical demands of the job or on the treatment of physical injuries alone would not resolve the problem. Multidisciplinary, multifactorial solutions that addressed psychosocial concerns were needed. The EAP was a natural ally to help address the problem.

L.L. BEAN AND QUALITY

Although traditionally focused on quality, L.L. Bean renewed this emphasis by implementing a total quality management (TQM) program in 1989. Part of the TQM effort was on improving the effectiveness and efficiency of all company operations, including disability programs, and on reducing failure costs (i.e., those costs that do not add value to any part of the system). The health sector viewed disability costs as failure costs. Although wage replacement is a very important factor for employees who could not work due to injury or illness, there is no inherent value in a disability payment. It is much better to have the employee on the job, even in a limited capacity. Medical payments do potentially have value, though, if they help to improve the employee's overall health and productivity. L.L. Bean thus viewed medical payments as investments that should be maximized.

One method of operationalizing this investment strategy is to focus on *value,* which is being defined as:

$$\text{Value} = \frac{\text{Change in health status and Employee satisfaction}}{\text{Cost}}$$

In this way, medial payments should result in the maximum change in health status (e.g., increased functionality and reduced lost time) and in the most employee satisfaction for the funds spent. This is an approach adopted by many companies for their group health plans, and, in this case, it was applied to disability management.

THE INJURY MANAGEMENT SYSTEM

Changes to the Maine workers' compensation law in 1993 allowed the employer to choose the medical provider for employees within the first 10 days of an injury. After that, the employee could request up to two other medical providers, to which the employer could object. However, L.L. Bean found that if quality on-site healthcare was provided in a respectful manner, 90+% of employees stayed with on-site care. Anecdotal contacts with other companies supported this finding.

L.L. Bean chose to steer employees to on-site clinics staffed by independent contractors, including physical therapists, nurse practitioners, physicians, and rehabilitation counselors. If the employee then wanted to see an outside provider, a relationship had been started in which the on-site provider could at least monitor the employee's care. This was important because outside providers would often unnecessarily disable employees rather than help them cope with their injuries and partial disabilities.

Research supported the view that medical providers could have a profound effect on disability rates. Hadler (1992) identified the medical community's response to CTDs as one of the major determinants in the extent of a company's CTD problem. Medical providers needed to address the whole person, not just the injured part. They needed to understand the function of work in the patient's life and the nature of specific jobs and work settings. Medical care needed to comprehensively focus on restoring maximal function outside of work as well as on returning the employee to maximal capacity on the job. By locating services on-site, barriers to treatment (e.g., transportation and scheduling problems) were reduced, supervisors and employees could become familiar with providers, and providers were in a position to understand the company's work environment, culture(s), and processes. However, quality healthcare and credibility with employees required that providers be objective and independent of the company. They must be *in* the company, but not *of* it.

During the early 1990s, L.L. Bean contracted with independent providers for clinical services. Long-term arrangements were developed with physical therapists, physicians, rehabilitation providers, and mental health professionals, although the last were contracted on an as-needed basis. All the consultants worked very closely with L.L. Bean to provide needed services, but they emphasized physical care and the general psychosocial support that good generalist physicians, physical therapists, rehabilitation providers, nurses, and health and fitness personnel could provide. However, the company at this time did not have an EAP, and the on-site services lacked a focused psychosocial approach.

The official goals of L.L. Bean's on-site health services were to provide injured employees with a system of healthcare that would:

- Promote healing.
- Improve employee level of functioning both at home and at work.
- Empower employees to manage their health and to prevent further injury/illness.

The health services group recognized that the most effective way to return employees to productive work was to help them improve functioning in all aspects of their lives and to help employees assume and maintain responsibility for their own health and well-being.

In 1993, L.L. Bean's primary health team (occupational health nurses, physical therapists, physicians, rehabilitation providers, and consultant psychologist) spent 6 months using continuous quality-improvement techniques to establish protocols, relationships, and approaches to treating employees. The team spent significant time on how to identify and effectively treat the most complicated disability cases—those in which there was more than just a physical problem involved. Health and fitness specialists were added later to the team to broaden the focus on health improvement and prevention.

The team also paid special attention to those areas where employee transitions from one discipline to another were necessary (e.g., physical therapist to physician to specialist to rehabilitation provider). Typically, each discipline focuses well on its own processes but does not interface smoothly with the other disciplines because of lack of interest, time available, relationships, physical location, communication methods, and many other factors. Quality theory suggests that in an organization, the processes with the greatest potential for improvement are often found in those areas where different disciplines or functions interface (Rummler & Brache, 1991). This holds true for case transitions from one discipline to another within the injury management system.

Another major theme in improving the injury management system was the progressive physical rehabilitation of employees within a supportive psychosocial environment. A team approach combining physical and behavioral therapeutic interventions helps to restore functioning and to return employees to work more quickly than does a physical approach alone (Lindstrom, et al., 1992; Waddell, 1987).

Chronic disability can be avoided by ensuring that employees work in a job they can safely perform. The primary health team believed it was critical to provide jobs that a conservative physician could approve as safe, even if the employee was highly inclined to be out of work (e.g., an employee who wanted to remain out of work due to psychological or personal issues but who could physically perform appropriate work). Although most L.L. Bean employees did want to return to work, the system had to address those who did not. No research existed that showed an employee's overall health was reduced by returning to a job fitting within their restrictions or abilities. On the other hand, numerous references reported the positive effects of returning partially disabled employees to work (Aronoff, 1991; Derebery & Tullis, 1983; Haig, 1992; Hazzard et al., 1989; Lindstrom et al., 1992; Matheson, 1993; Waddell, 1987).

To this end, vocational rehabilitation counselors and other members of the disability management team worked with supervisors to develop *transitional work:* jobs that are not regularly funded positions, but that are required to add value to the overall operation. They involve light physical duty and are, therefore, well-suited to workers with physical injuries. They are counterregressive in that they help keep employees in the workplace doing useful tasks. But because L.L. Bean's goal is to return injured employees to their original jobs or to other regular positions, these transitional jobs also have built-in disadvantages (e.g., no pay raises), which keep them from being attractive to employees as long-term solutions.

PREVENTION PROGRAMS

Total quality management stresses the importance of preventing problems first, then finding problems early through an inspection process, and lastly focusing on minimizing the failure costs if a problem, or in this case an injury, does occur. Because of the theme of this chapter, much of what has been described so far has focused on inspection and failure. Finding employees with injuries early, obtaining active aggressive treatment, and modifying jobs so injured employees can safely perform them are all part of the inspection process. Once people are out of work, assigning rehabilitation, creating transitional-work opportunities, minimizing litigation, and other measures are attempts to minimize the failure costs. In reality, though, much attention is focused on preventing problems or injuries from occurring at all.

The company takes and aggressive approach to preventing work-related injuries from occurring. Programs include:

- Ergonomic design of work processes and work stations.
- Health and safety education and training.
- Work-site stretching programs.
- Health screenings at date of hire and during employment.
- Health and fitness programs focused on physical, mental, and emotional well-being.
- Depression screenings and other EAP related interventions.

A comprehensive program requires prevention, inspection, and failure-cost management. In a company shifting toward a prevention-and-inspection mode, employees will be more productive, their quality of life will be better, and company programs will be more cost-effective.

In summary, throughout the early 1990s, L.L. Bean implemented innovative disability management programs. The company employed on-site physical therapists, physicians, rehabilitation therapists, and claims managers. It also implemented on-site fitness programs and adopted an athletic training model. L.L. Bean emphasized workforce involvement in preventing and treating injuries, and hourly employees were trained in how to apply ice to sore arms, to make basic work-station changes, and to make referrals to the physical therapy and medical clinic.

The medical team valued behavioral health services, but the company did not have a formal EAP program. It was, therefore, difficult to get early intervention for behavioral health because it required an outside referral. The medical team did have access to a consulting neuropsychologist who specialized in chronic pain. He became involved in some of the more complex cases and was available for job-site visits and for on-site medical-team meetings. He also saw some employees in his off-site office for assessment and therapy.

Unfortunately, his expertise and perspective were not integrated into the injury-management-program processes in a way that made them available on a day-to-day basis. Consequently, but the time L.L. Bean's on-site team referred employees to him (in some instances, 2 years after their date of injury), their chronic pain had become entrenched. It became clear that adding EAP services to the disability management team would enable earlier intervention for behavioral health. This would considerably broaden the team's impact, especially in the long-term and more expensive cases. This process began to occur in 1995, when L.L. Bean instituted a formal EAP program.

REVAMPING THE INJURY MANAGEMENT SYSTEM

Most of L.L. Bean's injured employees recovered within several weeks and returned to full work duties uneventfully. Those who did not challenged the company to improve its system. In early 1995 a team composed of the manager of L.L. Bean health programs, the EAP consultant, a senior physical therapist, the workers' compensation claims administrator, an occupational health nurse, a vocational rehabilitation counselor and one of our on-site physicians began a series of process redesign meetings.

The team visited a research site for the treatment of low-back injuries funded by the National Institute of Safety and Health (NIOSH). The NIOSH-funded clinic had discovered that six weeks was a key point in the trajectory of injury recovery. If an employee's condition was improving in a relatively steady fashion at this point, clinical experience indicated that the injury would successfully resolve. If the employee's condition was deteriorating, or had stalled, it was likely that there were unidentified factors operating to delay recovery. These factors might be medical, psychological, financial, social, or job-related in nature. At this point, the risk of chronicity increased, and it was important to take steps to identify and address these recovery-opposing factors.

A review of L.L. Bean's cases supported these findings. Eighty percent of employees were on their way to recovery six weeks after their injuries had occurred. The remaining 20% required more care, and a subset of this group later developed chronic problems. This realization helped the company develop a case management process for disability claims that focused on early identification and intervention for employees at risk for chronicity.

Each on-site clinic now holds a case conference every two weeks. The purpose is to identify and intervene in "slow-to-recover" cases and to coordinate care for all injured employees. Attendees include a physical therapist, an occupational health nurse, a nurse practitioner or physician, a vocational rehabilitation counselor, a fitness specialist, and the EAP consultant. The physical therapists, as experts in musculoskeletal disorders and nurse practitioners are the "primary care" professionals of our system. Since they work on site, they are familiar with job requirements, know the resources, and have built relationships with supervisory personnel. They are in a position both to treat the patient and to respond in a timely and direct fashion to the concerns and questions of supervisors.

Recognizing the need to manage case-conference data and to provide continuity of care, L.L. Bean's team designed and built a networked database system that could track and employee's movement through the medical management system. This enabled the company to more effectively follow up on referrals, to sort and manage subpopulations and individual employees, and, most importantly, to keep people from falling through the cracks.

The case conferences have four main foci: (1) slow-to-recover cases; (2) early red flags, or warning signs; (3) long-term or chronic patients; and (4) systems issues.

The Slow-to-Recover and Red Flag Patients

At the biweekly meetings, the physical therapists present the cases of those injured employees who are approaching 6 weeks of treatment and about whom they are concerned regarding the pace of quality of recovery. Physical therapists also discuss any patients who present with red flag (i.e., signs of factors that may negatively impact recovery). The 6-week rule does not apply for these cases (i.e., these cases are discussed at whatever point in treatment the red flags become apparent). Red flags include these situations:

- Employee complains of job dissatisfaction.
- Employee complains of problems with supervisor.
- Employee complains of stress, either at home or at work, or the physical therapist is aware of multiple stressors in the employee's life.
- Provider is concerned about a possible substance abuse problem.
- Provider is concerned about a possible psychological disorder (e.g., panic attacks or clinical depression).
- Employee shows evidence of symptom magnification and other chronic-pain-syndrome behaviors.
- Employee is noncompliant with treatment, complains inappropriately about the treatment, or expresses undue pessimism or hopelessness about treatment.
- Provider finds clinical picture to be anomalous or contradictory.
- A member of the team receives information from the employee's supervisor indicating attitudinal or behavioral difficulties.

When an employee is slow to recover or when red flags are noted, several options are available. In many cases, the team will have a suggestion or an insight that the treatment provider can use in treatment. When a more extensive medical workup is needed, the team will recommend a referral to an on-site physician or nurse practitioner or to an external medical professional (e.g., a hand specialist or a neurologist).

As can be seen from the list of red flags, L.L. Bean's case management team is especially alert for psychosocial factors that can prevent or limit recovery. For example, an agitated employee may discuss recent staff departures and an increased workload or may reveal that she has just filed a restraining order against her alcoholic, abusive husband. If factors such as these are present, the team discusses the best approach for further assessment and intervention. Depending on the issue, the next step will often involve a referral to the EAP consultant, fitness specialist, or vocational rehabilitation counselor. As will be discussed later, confidentiality is a central concern, and any disclosures to other caregivers are first cleared with the patient.

Because employees are presenting with concrete physical problems (e.g., "my neck hurts and it isn't getting better"), a psychosocial referral must be presented in a way that makes sense to the employee. The physical therapist or nurse practitioner must also avoid leaving the employee with the impression that the caregiver is saying that the injury is "all in your head." Talking with the patient about the stresses of having an injury and discussing the mind-body connection are two common approaches to introducing employees to this type of help. These "preparation for referral" statements cannot be presented glibly or by rote. They often require considerable explanation, with examples drawn from life experiences that will be readily understandable to that particular patient. The employee with the chronically sore neck may have mentioned, for example, that he gets a "nervous stomach" before giving weekly production reports to his management chain. With coaching from the EAP, the alert physical therapist can draw apt parallels between bodily systems (neck, stomach), psychological factors (unrecognized stress, performance anxiety), and the interplay between the two (delayed healing, a poor presentation).

The EAP and vocational rehabilitation counselors are important and obvious resources for psychosocial issues. Although at first glance the health-and-fitness specialist may seem less relevant to recovery, this person adds a key dimension to L.L. Bean's comprehensive health services. She is visible among line employees, possesses strong interpersonal skills, and is well liked. She has a background as an athletic trainer and is in a graduate counseling program. Employees who are reluctant to involve themselves with mental health professionals will frequently accept a referral to "see Karen" for help with nutrition, cardiovascular conditioning, weight loss, stress reduction, or smoking cessation. While engaged in a fitness program, they often share their personal concerns. A referral to the EAP or to other behavioral health resources can follow naturally from such a conversation.

Fortunately, fitness, health, wellness, and outdoor activities are a core part of the L.L. Bean culture. The company's customer-service philosophy encourages employees to be active. For example, L.L. Bean would like the employee taking a telephone order for boating equipment to have actually spent some time in a canoe or a kayak. Thus, suggesting involvement in a fitness program is a psychologically easy connection, even for employees who do not habitually exercise.

The company has found that the positive experience of becoming physically fit, as well as of taking control of a sector of one's behavior and life, is a major and powerful step for employees who have had little experience with self-efficacy. In addition, many of L.L. Bean's wellness programs are conducted in groups, and, therefore, they have potential for reducing social isolation and for increasing interpersonal skills. A referral to the fitness program may look like "only a fitness intervention," but from the treatment team's perspective, it is also a stealth behavioral health strategy. The team finds that successful engagement in such a program can be an important building block for growth in other areas. L.L. Bean provides incentives for injured employees to participate in fitness programs by allowing them to attend these activities on company time (i.e., the company pays them to exercise for up to 6 months), just as they would their physical therapy or EAP visit.

Long-Term or Chronic Cases

The case management team also periodically discusses chronic or relapsing cases. In the first several months of using the case-conference format, the team discussed these patients at the beginning of the meeting but found that there was often no time left to discuss new patients. The team realized that countertransference (i.e., the frustration inherent in these difficult cases) rather than cost-effectiveness was driving the process, so chronic cases are now discussed at the end of the meeting.

There are at least two subcategories within this group of chronic cases: (1) those with emotional and vocational difficulties adapting to intractable or severe injuries and (2) those with chronic pain syndrome (i.e., the patient's thoughts, behaviors, self-concept, relationships, and activities have become organized around the pain associated with an injury or illness).

To assist these employees, L.L. Bean offers on-site chronic pain ("Injury and Stress") groups. Membership is usually drawn from both of these subcategories. The groups run for 12 weeks and contain two components: The first is a weekly 90-minute "talk" session that focuses on goal-setting, pain management, attitude management, active coping strategies, and meditation and visualization techniques. The second component is a group-based exercise program that meets twice weekly for one hour in one of the company's on-site fitness centers. The fitness center is closed to other employees during this time, and each member does his or her own custom-designed fitness program.

L.L. Bean also refers a number of its long-term injured employees to the EAP, as well as to external provider-specialists. Often these employees suffer from clinical depression or substance abuse disorders that may be antecedent or secondary to the chronic impairment. In either event, these problems must be properly identified and treated in order for physical and functional recovery to occur. Furthermore, family and social systems may reorganize around the injured employee to create a new, injury-centered homeostasis that is hard to disrupt.

Once this occurs, even the best efforts may yield only partial success. In one example, an employee who had minimal objective evidence of physical impairment baffled the treatment team. She seemed well but was unable to increase her time at work beyond 4 hours a day without expressing great physical distress. Exploration during a team meeting with the patient and several members of the injury management system revealed that the employee's spouse was relying on her to stuff bait sacks for his fishing business and that a paraplegic sister had recruited her to run errands three or four afternoons a week. With the family relying on her for so much, it was not possible to get her back to work for more than 30 hours a week.

A Note on Psychological Trauma and Chronic Injuries

The treatment team has found that many chronic or long-term cases involve employees who have histories of early trauma. The role of trauma and neglect in these cases is not always clear, but some of the following factors are relevant:

- A physical injury in the present may reawaken anxieties associated with past traumatic experiences (e.g., body integrity).
- The experience of diminished autonomy, competence, and self-control associated with injury may activate trauma-linked ego states and affects that flood the patient. Self-esteem may begin to disintegrate in employees who found mastery of their jobs to be an essential component of stabilizing a vulnerable self-organization.
- The resources and accommodations available to injured employees (e.g., attention, medical staff concern, restricted work schedules) may activate regressive passive longings. L.L. Bean's "athletic training model" approach to physical therapy is deliberately counterregressive, as is its strategy of keeping people at work in jobs appropriate to their physical capacity. Nevertheless, the lures of the injured status can be powerful for those who have never had their dependent needs met in a consistent and appropriate fashion.

- The internal objects or deep cognitive schema related to the victim-persecutor aspects of early trauma can be reactivated, with the company or its contracted healthcare providers potentially being case in the "bad object" role (e.g., the patient for whom there is no good clinical reason to schedule an MRI but who feels the company is pinching pennies to deny needed care—as his or her parents may have done in the past). Feelings of neglect, entitlement, and rage are likely to result, with attendant strain on the therapeutic relationship.

In some cases, employees can make connections between what happened then and what is happening now. They are able to see that the unacknowledged affects, cognitions, and coping styles of their earlier years are impacting their ability to get and stay well. They may also be able to see that needs that were disowned or split off are now being gratified in dysfunctional ways by the circumstances of their injuries.

Other employees may resist such insights and steadfastly hold on to their injury. The caregivers then become frustrated, and an impasse is reached. This dynamic can be powerfully reinforced if the employee finds an external caregiver who reinforces the employee's sense of victimization and who shares a perception of the company as a persecutor. The addition of such a rescuer to the equation can cement a case in chronicity. For this reason, work with external providers is an important part of L.L. Bean's injury management program.

Vocational rehabilitation counseling and associated case management services are central in the treatment plans of employees with long-standing injuries. The focus is on helping employees to help themselves rather than on "getting them a job." The counselors are knowledgeable about the workers' compensation system, as well as about the L.L. Bean culture and job types. They serve as case managers for many injured employees and work closely with the EAP if there are behavioral health problems. Vocational rehabilitation counselors function as career counselors (e.g., resume writing and interviewing skills), coaches (e.g., attitude support), and advocates for employees who are unlikely to return to their preinjury jobs. Through such interventions and their company-wide networks of supervisors, the rehabilitation counselors are able to help some employees make significant career shifts. For example, an employee originally hired to take telephone customer orders successfully made a career change into the information technology field after suffering upper extremity injuries.

Systemic Issues

In addition to issues specific to individual employees, members of the case-conference team remain alert for evidence of systemic problems and opportunities. The team looks for trends and may notice, for example, that the employees of a particular operational area are below the norm in treatment compliance (e.g., they may miss a lot of physical therapy appointments). The matter is flagged for further investigation and, perhaps, intervention. In the example given, the case-conference team may discover that a new team leader has not been fully briefed on policy regarding injured employees and is discouraging them from leaving a busy loading dock when they have medical appointments.

The case-conference team also looks for situations that can be generalized; that is, if one employee is having a particular difficulty, others may as well. If this is the case, a group-based intervention may be more efficient and powerful. For example, a recent case-conference discussion centered on an employee with wrist injuries who had been work-restricted from computer keyboards and was now using L.L. Bean's Voice Input Computer Center (VICC). Difficulties arose when various managers asked her to do work that required keying. She would comply and aggravate her injury. The group's first recommendation was to offer the employee training in assertiveness skills to assist in setting appropriate limits with her managers. Although some consideration was given to having a team member talk with the employee's manager, the team decided the most empowering response would be to assist the injured employee in addressing the issue herself. Further exploration then revealed that the other dozen employees in the VICC area often had similar problems saying no. After discussing the dynamics involved (e.g., guilt at being injured), we decided that group discussion plus assertiveness training for all members of VICC would help build skills on an individual level, would help increase team support, and would help modify the norms of the whole group.

In another instance, the team decided that they themselves needed intervention. At times, a frustrated physical therapist or other team member would report a situation like the following: "I assessed the patient's arm, explained that he had a tendonitis, discussed ergonomic adjustments, and prescribed physical therapy three times a week, with stretching and strengthening exercises for homework. Compliance was at best minimal." The team would then discuss psychosocial factors and secondary gain but discover nothing to explain the employee's behavior. After several cases like this, the team members decided that they were pretty good at talking with employees about their injuries but that they needed some work on talking with them about their concerns, hopes, fears, and ideas about treatment and goals. The team concluded that they were probably making unfounded assumptions about these issues. The EAP suggested that training in motivational interviewing and the stages of change (Prochaska, DiClemente, & Norcross, 1992) would help the team to listen more effectively to patients and to align team goals with the employees' goals. The team worked with a physician who is an expert in motivational interviewing to adapt the concepts to workplace injury issues and contracted with him for two workshops and videotaped practice sessions. To keep the learning alive, part of the follow-up commitment was to make sure that team members asked each other such questions as, "So, what does the patient want?" If the team were better able to understand the patient's perspective, it would be much more likely to develop a treatment relationship that facilitated change.

THE ROLE OF CONFIDENTIALITY

In the workers' compensation system, medical information is not normally considered confidential. It is available to attorneys, claims adjusters, employers, and others. When employees meet with physical therapists or vocational rehabilitation counselors, this is explained to them. As L.L. Bean integrated its EAP into the injury management system, it was important to maintain the traditional EAP standards of confidentiality. Specifically, there could not be one set of confidentiality standards for injured employees and another set for traditional broad-brush EAP clients. When EAP staff meet with injured employees, they explain that discussions are confidential, and information from the discussions will not be placed in company personnel or medical records. The EAP professional outlines the exceptions to this policy (i.e., imminent danger to self or others, mandated reporting of child or elder abuse) and asks if he or she may speak, in a limited way, with supervisors and healthcare providers. Most employees are willing to allow such contact. If they are not, EAP staff respect their wishes, with the option to revisit the issue at a later time. When employees refuse to give consent, it is often because of mistrust of some aspect of the system. EAP providers focus their efforts on understanding this concern, on troubleshooting, and on coaching. In these instances, the case may lose some degree of clinical care integration, but the important strategic value of workforce trust in the integrity of the EAP is protected.

INTEGRATING EXTERNAL PROVIDERS

A central objective of L.L. Bean's injury management program is to ensure that physical therapists, physicians, nurse practitioners, EAP professionals, and fitness and vocational rehabilitation counselors are connected and communicating in an optimal manner. This effort to integrate all caregivers extends to external providers. The EAP has developed a small network of psychotherapists to work with its disabled employees. Because clinicians with experience in injury management were rare in the company's geographical area, L.L. Bean recruited senior clinicians interested in treating injured employees and worked with them to develop a training program.

Since 1995, a group of approximately 10 clinicians with master's- or doctoral-level degrees in psychology, social work, counseling, or nursing have come to L.L. Bean every other week for training and case consultation. The company had three goals: (1) to help clinicians develop the understanding and skills to work with injured employees, (2) to form a strong working relationship between internal and external caregivers, and (3) to develop a group of clinicians who would know the company well and be available to work with the EAP on a variety of other projects.

In the first year, the EAP contracted with a neuropsychologist who was an expert on injury management and chronic pain. He taught six 2-hour classes on chronic pain and associated topics. These sessions alternated with training provided by the EAP consultant that focused on hypnotherapy, relaxation techniques, and guided imagery. Given the opportunity for continuing education in topics that interested them, as well as for a deeper working relationship with a major employer, the therapists were willing to attend on their own time.

In an effort to foster relationships between external psychotherapists and members of L.L. Bean's injury management system, the classes on chronic pain were open to and attended by the company's on-site physical therapists, vocational rehabilitation counselors, fitness instructors, occupational health nurses, and workers' compensation claims administrator. This proved to be a positive experience for all participants and was especially useful for the external clinicians. These psychotherapists arrived at a more nuanced understanding of the work world. They also saw first-hand L.L. Bean's commitment to providing top-quality care to its employees. The workers' compensation system can be tinged with a negative aura in the minds of therapists, who often hear only the worst from patients who are frustrated with the system. In these meetings, the therapists saw how members of the L.L. Bean injury care system worked to provide employees the best possible service. This helped them to better manage patient distortions, splitting, and projections.

In order to maintain, strengthen, and leverage the relationships with external clinicians, the on-site team involved the clinicians in conjoint projects whenever possible (e.g., the motivational interviewing workshops). Several of these clinicians also served as trainers in a recent company-wide depression-education program, and others are currently involved in projects dealing with outcomes measurement, collaborative healthcare, and nonoccupational disability management.

STRENGTHENING THE ROLE OF SUPERVISORS

From the beginning, EAPs have emphasized the importance of supervisors. Training supervisors in the effective use of EA services is a routine activity in successful programs, and establishing solid relationships with "people leaders" has been central to the effectiveness of the L.L. Bean EAP. Frontline leaders are taught to manage performance, to use "constructive confrontation" when appropriate, and to stay involved with the employee in an alliance based on support, respect, role clarity, and accountability. Ongoing consultation with the EAP and human resources staff helps support the supervisor in handling challenging situations and in developing a proactive attitude toward employee problems.

In some areas of the company, the treatment of injured employees was often an exception to this principle of management involvement. Supervisors might hand off the employee to the on-site system of care, after which the employee would move out to the periphery of the supervisor's attention. Following injury, an employee would be likely to have more contact with his or her physical therapist and occupational health nurse than with the supervisor. If the employee were work-restricted, this loss of connection would be increased. An employee could feel forgotten by his or her work group, while receiving good care and attention for the injury. This unintentional but dysfunctional estrangement was primarily the product of supervisor uncertainty of discomfort about dealing with injured or work-restricted employees. It had the potential effect of maintaining disability.

In recent months, the on-site team has attempted to put the employee/supervisor relationship back in a central position. In order to do this, the team has developed stronger links and more direct contact between physical therapists and supervisors and moved the occupational health nurses out of their position as liaison between physical therapist, patient, and management. In current practice, the supervisor will consult directly with the physical therapist about such matters as work restrictions and accommodations and with the EAP and HR staff about behavioral health and job performance issues.

RESULTS

During the years (1990–1997) in which the disability management programs were instituted, L.L. Bean experienced positive results. The areas measured were reduction in days lost, costs, satisfaction, and placement rates of employees with disabilities into their own or other positions.

From 1990 to 1997, L.L. Bean experienced a 47% reduction in work-related lost-time injuries, and an 85% reduction in injuries for which 3 or more weeks of work are lost. This latter measure is especially significant because the injury management system is targeted at minimizing disability once employees experience a health-related problem. From 1994 to 1997, there was a major expansion in operating areas. The injury rate went up slightly, but there was a 41% reduction in injuries causing 3 or more weeks of lost work. During this time period workers compensation costs as a percent of payroll declined 57%, while short-term disability costs stayed flat. This reduction in injuries of 3 weeks or more attests to the effectiveness of the integrated disability management system. L.L. Bean sees the contribution of the EAP, with its focus on behavioral healthcare, as a major contributor to these reductions.

Equally important is how satisfied employees are with the on-site disability management services. For employees to buy in and support efforts to keep them at work, the company feels it is critical that they are satisfied with the services they receive. In 1995 and 1997, a sample of several hundred employees who utilized on-site services were surveyed using an instrument rigorously developed with a student in a master's program at a leading medical school. Results were very positive:

	1995	1997
Overall satisfaction	96%	91%
Quality	90%	91%
Convenience	97%	91%

In addition, for a pilot group of employees in L.L. Bean's focused behavioral health and fitness program, progress in returning to their own or other positions was measured. The program focused on employees with chronic injuries and on improving their overall physical, mental, and emotional well-being. Over a 1-year period, the following results were obtained for 33 employees who went through the program. Only one employee did not make progress or hold his or her own, a significant accomplishment for this group of employees.

Employee Category	Number of Employees
Working full-time job who maintained status.	10
Working full-time job with restrictions who progressed to working full-time job without restrictions.	2
Progressed from transitional work job to own job.	7
Working partial job who increased hours.	3
Working partial job who maintained hours.	8
Working partial job who decreased hours.	1
Retired	2

Another indicator of program effectiveness was the sharply reduced demand for Injury and Stress Groups in 1997 as compared to 1996. There were fewer employees with chronic injuries and, therefore, less need for this type of intervention.

As the program continues to mature, more sophisticated measures will be employed to help improve overall programs success. However, with the measures currently available, the company is very pleased with results to date.

FUTURE CHALLENGES IN DISABILITY MANAGEMENT AT L.L. BEAN

In addition to making incremental improvements in the management of occupational injuries, the disability management team is now focusing on improving the effectiveness and integration of the processes relating to short- and long-term nonoccupational disabilities. Some of the issues that need to be addressed are:

- Employees see short- and long-term disability programs as benefits to which they are entitled. HAving this benefit managed is against tradition and expectations.
- Educating and working with a large number of external providers present logistical challenges. Most injured employees seek their service on site, from providers who are oriented toward helping employees function in their jobs. Employees with nonoccupational disabilities seek their services off site, from an array of medical and behavioral health caregivers. Some of these caregivers are quick to disable and slow to collaborate with work-site resources.
- The incentives of managed care companies must be brought into alignment with the needs of employees for prompt and effective treatment. It is in the interests of both the company and the employee that medical care be delivered as rapidly and comprehensively as possible. This need can, depending on the structuring of contracts, be contrary to the financial interests of the managed care company, which may wish to take a more gradual approach to the delivery of treatment.
- A relatively small number of employees drives a large portion of medical, behavioral health, and disability costs. Identifying these so-called "thick chart" patients and engaging them in collaborative relationships to improve health and to increase function have occupied the attention of the injury management system. The group health plan and the nonoccupational disability programs face the same challenge.

CONCLUSION

The EAP arrived at L.L. Bean with a highly developed injury management system already in place. Although there was a growing awareness of the importance of behavioral health issues, the system was not designed with these types of problems in mind and, therefore, did not easily manage them. The ready availability of on-site EAP services added a new capacity to the system, but it was equally important to redesign parts of the system so that this capacity would be fully integrated. Getting "everyone (i.e., all the caregiver specialties) into the same room at the same time" was an important change in the way L.L. Bean's injury management system worked, and this large meeting was made more productive by the development of patient flow algorithms and tracking software. Team members were encouraged to pay attention to the overall system of care, as well as to their own roles and functions.

Concurrent with improving the internal care-delivery process and components, the team also works to continuously integrate and enhance the functioning of supervisors and external providers. Supervisors, while keeping their focus on job performance, are learning more about biopsychosocial factors and disability management. Psychotherapists are grasping the necessities and complexities of the world of work at a company that is dedicated to being a "great place to work." This close connection to L.L. Bean, initially through the injury management system, has given providers an insight that makes them more effective broad-brush therapists as well as willing allies for other behavioral-health-improvements efforts.

L.L. Bean has found its expansion of EAP services into the disability management arena to be a logical extension of EAP practice and values. From the beginning, L.L. Bean's fundamental rationale and underlying assumption for employee assistance has been that good management of employee performance is not, by itself, sufficient. If an employee has a personal problem, such as alcoholism or untreated clinical depression, even the most skilled supervisor will not likely be able to singlehandedly manage the situation to a successful resolution. The employee's job performance needs to be managed, but there must also be a process and system by which the employee can be talked with, referred, evaluated, treated, and followed until a stable state of restored or higher functioning is reached.

It is no different in the world of disability management. If an injured employee has an undetected and untreated problem with alcohol, clinical depression, or chronic pain syndrome, even the most sophisticated constellation of medical management specialists will, in most cases, be unable to effect a successful recovery and return to work.

In both instances, employee assistance intervention, when properly integrated, provides a means to identify, educate, and treat employees who may have any of a broad range of psychological-social problems—problems that, if left unaddressed, will limit or prevent their recovery.

REFERENCES

Armstrong, T.J. (1983). *An ergonomic guide to carpal tunnel syndrome.* Akron, OH: American Industrial Hygiene Association.

Armstrong, T.J., Fine, L.J., Goldstein, S.A., et al. (1987). Ergonomic considerations in hand and wrist tendinitis. *Journal of Hand Surgery, 12A*(2 pt. 2), 830–837.

Aronoff, G.M. (1991). Chronic pain and the disability epidemic. *Clinical Journal of Pain, 7*(4), 330–338.

Berkowitz, M. (1996). Full cost of disability: Results, trends, and assessment. *Insight, 3*(2).

Bigos, S.J., Battie, M.C., Spengler, D.M., Fisher, L.D., Fordyce, W.E., Hansson, T.H., Nachemson, A.L., & Wortley, M.D. (1991). A prospective study of work perceptions and psychosocial factors affecting the report of back injury. *Spine, 16*(6), 688.

Bureau of National Affairs. (1992, July 22). *Occupational safety and health reporter.* Washington, DC: Author.

Derebery, V.J., & Tullis, W.H. (1983). Delayed recovery in the patient with a work compensable injury. *Journal of Occupational Medicine, 25*(11), 829–835.

Doudna, D.J. (1992). Group disability income benefits. In J.S. Rosenbloom (Ed.), *The handbook of employee benefits* (3rd ed., pp. 429–444). New York: Irwin.

Garg, A., & Moore, J.S. (1992). Epidemiology of low-back pain in industry. In J.S. Moore & A. Garg (Eds.), *Occupational medicine: State of the are reviews (Ergonomics),* (Vol. 7, No. 4, 593–609). Philadelphia: Haley and Belfus.

Hadler, N.J. (1992). Arm pain in the workplace: A small area analysis. *Journal of Occupational Medicine, 34*(2), 113–119.

Haig, A.J. (1992). Diagnosis and treatment options in occupational low-back pain. In J.S. Moore & A. Garg (Eds.), *Occupational medicine: State of the are reviews (Ergonomics)* (Vol. 7, No. 4, pp. 641–653). Philadelphia: Haley and Belfus.

Hallman III, G. V. (1992). Functional approach to employee benefits. In J.S. Rosenbloom (Ed.), *The handbook of employee benefits* (3rd ed., pp. 15–38). New York: Irwin.

Hayes, W.L. (1992). Disability income benefits. In J.S Rosenbloom (Ed.), *The handbook of employee benefits* (3rd ed., pp. 445–460). New York: Irwin.

Hazzard, R.G., Fenwick, J.W., Kalisch, S.M., et al. (1989). Functional restoration in industrial low back pain. *Spine, 14,* 157–161.

Lindstrom, I., Ohlund, C., Eek, C., et al. (1992). The effect of graded activity on patients with subacute low back pain. *Physical Therapy, 72*(4), 279–293.

Matheson, L.N. (1993, September). Work hardening for patients with low back pain. *Journal of Musculoskeletal Medicine,* 53–63.

Nachemson, A.L. (1992). Newest knowledge of low back pain: A critical look. *Clinical Orthopaedics and Related Research, 279,* 8–20.

Owens, P. (1997). The world of work. *Insight, 4*(2).

Prochaska, J., DiClemente, C., & Norcross, J. (1992). In search of how people change: Applications to addictive behaviors. *American Psychologist, 47*(9), 1102–1114.

Rodgers, S.H. (1987). Recovery time needs for repetitive work. *Seminars in Occupational Medicine, 2*(19).

Roman, P., & Blum, T. (1985, March). The core technology of employee assistance programs. *The ALMACAN,* 8–19.

Rooney, T. (1997). Cumulative trauma disorder programs in industry: L.L. Bean. In M. Erdil & O.B. Dickerson (Eds.), *Cumulative trauma disorders, prevention, evaluation, and treatment* (pp. 359–384). New York: Van Nostrand Reinhold.

Rosenbloom, J.S. (1992). The environment of employee benefit plans. In J.S. Rosenbloom (Ed.), *The handbook of employee benefits* (3rd ed., pp. 15–38). New York: Irwin.

Rummler, G.A., & Brache, A.P. (1991, January). Managing the white space. *Training,* 55–70.

Silverstein, B.A. (1985). *The prevalence of upper extremity cumulative trauma disorders in industry.* PhD dissertation, Ann Arbor, University of Michigan.

Silverstein, B.A., Fine, L.J., & Armstrong, T.J. (1986). Carpal tunnel syndrome: Causes and a preventative strategy. *Seminars in Occupational Medicine, 1,* 213–221.

Silverstein, B.A., Fine, L.J., & Armstrong, T.J. (1987). Occupational factors and carpal tunnel syndrome. *American Journal of Industrial Medicine, 11,* 343.

Snook, S.H., Campanelli, R.A., & Hart, J.W. (1978). A study of three preventive approaches to low-back injury. *Journal of Occupational Medicine, 20,* 478–481.

Tortarolo, J.S., & Polakoff, P.L. (1995). The future of disability management is integration. *Benefits Quarterly,* (Third Quarter), pp. 49–55.

Waddell, G. (1987). A new clinical model for the treatment of low-back pain. *Spine, 12*(7), 632–644.

Worrall, J.D. (1992). Workers' compensation insurance. In J.S. Rosenbloom (Ed.), *The handbook of employee benefits,* (3rd ed., pp. 107–120). New York: Irwin.

CHAPTER 19

Innovative Stress Management for Financial Service Organizations

DAVID CAMBRONNE, JERRY SHIH, and KATE HARRI

Costs of Occupational Stress

High levels of employee stress are costly to organizations, reducing worker productivity and effectiveness and depleting financial and other organizational resources. According to the U.S. Department of Commerce (1990), workers' compensation payments are expected to exceed $90 billion by the end of the twentieth century. According to a study by the National Council on Compensation Insurance (1985), claims for "gradual mental stress" account for about 11% of all claims for occupational disease.

High levels of employee stress are associated not only with increases in workers' compensation costs, but also with decreases in employee productivity and morale and with increases in employee absenteeism and turnover. All of these represent significant costs to organizations. Industrial and organizational psychologists estimate that many billions of dollars are lost annually in the United States due to occupational stress (e.g., Beehr & Bhagat, 1985). Although no precise estimates are available, it is clear that the costs of occupational stress to individuals, organizations, and society are substantial. Consequently, the development and implementation of effective strategies and interventions to reduce and manage occupational stress are critically important to the effectiveness and health of an organization and its employees.

Although the exact cost of occupational stress is difficult to measure, mental health and substance abuse claims (often listing stress as a symptom or cause) have much clearer statistics pointing to the need for preventive strategies. In a recent article by the *Minneapolis Star Tribune,* some staggering statistics about mental illness in the work place were listed. It is estimated that 52 million American adults, "experience significant mental health or substance abuse disorders each year" (June 9, 1997). Emotional and psychological disorders rank second to back injuries as the prominent cause for lost work productivity. Disability claims relating to psychological or emotional problems have increased 200% in the past 5 years, and depression alone is responsible for $17 billion in lost productivity on a yearly basis (Tevlin, 1997). It is estimated that stress-related claims can cost, per case, anywhere from $8,000 (Warshaw, 1988) to $15,000 (Kottage, 1992).

WHAT IS STRESS?

The stress process begins with a life event that a person perceives as being beyond his or her control physically, mentally, and/or spiritually. This perception leads to emotional arousal, such as fear, anxiety, and anger, which in turn leads to physical arousal, such as elevated heart rate, elevated blood pressure, and increased perspiration. Since the beginning of human existence, traumatic experiences in particular have altered humankind's ability to cope with the manifestations of stress. Whether dealing with a natural disaster or experiencing a human created trauma (i.e., war, sexual assault, robberies) human beings react to these events both physiologically and psychologically. It is only within the past 100 years that people have sought to understand the complex relationship between biological and emotional influences, if one even recognizes a difference between the two. Until the 1970s, most of the research on traumatic stress revolved around war, specifically the World Wars and the Vietnam War. Very little attention was paid to stress in the workplace, and workers' compensation claims resulting from stress were nonexistent. It was in World War I that attention was paid to soldiers who were said to be experiencing "shell shock" (Goodwin, 1987; Schlenger et al., 1993; Ursano, Fullerton, & Norwood, 1995). In World War II and the Korean War, observations were made on the number of mental health cases related to the stress of combat. Goodwin (1987) reported that the President's Commission on Mental Health observed that as the Vietnam War was winding down, psychiatric disorders with the American military population began to increase. In addition to this activity, civilian populations were also experiencing traumatic experiences that drew the attention of the media and the mental health profession (Fairbanks, Schlenger, Caddell, & Woods, 1993; Goodwin, 1987; van der Kolk, B., & van der Hart, O., 1989). As indicated in van der Kolk and van der Hart, "This recognition was reflected in the formulation of the formal diagnoses of posttraumatic stress disorder and the dissociative disorders in the *Diagnostic and Statistical Manual of Mental Disorders, Third Edition (DSM-III),* in 1980" (1989, p. 1531, 1989). At this point in the history of stress, the mental health field began to recognize the impact of unmanageable stress in the workplace. Examples of some of the most common negative consequences in the workplace are absenteeism, disability, turnover, and deterioration of morale, job satisfaction, and job performance.

SOURCES OF OCCUPATIONAL STRESS

The sources of occupational stress are many and varied. In today's business climate, organizational change is one of the major sources of occupational stress. Examples of organizational change include reorganizations, mergers, acquisitions, and reductions in force. Although organizational change is prevalent in all industries, in recent years, organizational change in the financial service industry has been particularly rapid and intense. In the 1980s and early 1990s, after a period of high inflation and interest rates, many financial service organizations went bankrupt or reduced their workforces in order to survive (MacLennan, 1992). Forced by external pressures to become more competitive and efficient, financial institutions began to actively market their products and services. In the past few years, external pressures to maximize organizational effectiveness and efficiency have continued to increase. Consequently, financial service organizations today are extremely fast-paced environments characterized by rapid and intense change. Acquisitions and reductions in workforce are a common occurrence.

ACUTE VERSUS CHRONIC STRESS

There are numerous definitions of *stress,* but most generally agree that stress is a *reaction* to something. Leon Warshaw (1988) described stress as, "inherently a process—physical, chemical, physiological, psychological, emotional, even metaphysical—through which the individual responds to an ever-changing combination of stressors. They may arise in the physical environment or in the thoughts and feelings generated by elements in the psychic and social environment" (p. 588). Another article succinctly stated that, "Psychological disturbances are considered an imbalance between the individual and the environment . . ." (Sauter, Murphy, & Harrell, 1990, p. 1149). Generally the EAP counselor is faced with two different manifestations of stress: acute or chronic. Again, research abounds with statements to the effect that everyone deals with stress differently. In the coming sections dealing with different and possible sources of stress, a general philosophy about successfully dealing with all types of stress will emerge.

Most stress is successfully managed by working with clients around a few key factors. Regardless of whether stress is acute or chronic, the employee assistance program (EAP) counselor must, first and foremost, help the client to recognize that options exist. *Options* are considered external, environmental, and continually present regardless of a client's internal reactions to a specific event. Second, with respect to dealing with the client's internal reactions, the EAP counselor can also assist the stressed individual in seeing that he or she has choices. *Choices* are defined as an individual's intrinsic ability to select from the options of which he or she is made aware. Third, EAP counselors can assist individuals in managing stress by helping them identify and utilize their naturally occurring supports. Following a traumatic event, it is not uncommon for people to underestimate the value of talking with friends, family, and community resources. Normal reactions such as feelings of isolation and an acute sense of one's own vulnerability may lead an individual to wonder what benefits can be derived from simply retelling others about the traumatic experience. EAP counselors can help individuals see the healing cathartic properties inherent in talking with those closest to them. The fourth and final factor in assisting an individual to manage their stress is normalizing. The process of normalizing is perhaps the single most important element in helping an individual recognize that stress responses are temporary and manageable.

It is important to note that all four factors—identifying options, recognizing choices, utilizing supports, and normalizing—are psychological tools that are just as useful prior to the occurrence of a stressful event as they are following one. A consistently used stress-inoculation curriculum in the corporate setting containing these four factors can be instrumental in promoting a healthier workforce, less traumatized by stressful events. This type of curriculum can also aid employees in moving past unpleasant stress reactions more quickly. It is crucial that EAP counselors recognize the importance of keeping the stress-inoculation process simple and straightforward. Likewise, stress debriefings following a traumatic event are most successful when they follow a basic and consistent outline incorporating the four factors mentioned earlier. EAPs utilize a straightforward and consistent approach that is usually successful in teasing out whether an individual's stress is acute or chronic. If stress symptoms persist, a referral for additional counseling is usually appropriate.

For the purposes of this chapter, the variety of therapeutic techniques available that are designed to mitigate chronic and persistent stress symptoms will not be covered at length. Rather, the focus will be on the common situations in the workplace in which stress predictably occurs and on how the EAP counselor can take a proactive role in facilitating stress reduction. Before moving into different areas of stress, we present a brief case example of how acute stress and chronic stress can interact.

Case Example: The Interplay between Acute and Chronic Stress

In one situation, a former teller of a financial institution called her EAP counselor 6 months after a robbery had occurred in which she had been the affected teller. The teller believed that she was continuing to feel stress reactions directly related to the experience of having a gun pointed at her. This individual was concerned about what long-term effects this robbery might have had on her. Symptoms that the woman talked about included nightmares, insomnia, anxiety, and general tension around anything too unfamiliar. At first glance, the EAP counselor's primary concern was chronic stress. After spending some time talking with the individual, a number of details were revealed to suggest otherwise. In particular, this individual stated that she had made a number of major changes in her life since the robbery occurred. The individual stated that she had moved out of state for a time and then had moved back again. She also indicated that she had recently ended a significant relationship and that she had also purchased a small business that she was in the process of learning how to run. As the EAP counselor worked with her, the individual began to realize that many of her stress-related symptoms were acute and connected to more recent significant events in her life. The individual began to see that her thoughts about the robbery weren't as much chronic stress responses as they were her body's way of saying that she had not allowed herself the time to process this experience. This realization alone provided the individual with a reduction in stress symptoms around the robbery, and it allowed her to work on managing her most immediate stressors connected to changes in career and in her relationships.

TYPES OF STRESS

Regardless of the type of organization, financial or otherwise, stress in the individual employee can take on a variety of forms dependent on both internal and external factors.

Reorganization

Stress can manifest itself through tension resulting from a time lag between the announcement of layoffs and the actual event. It is not uncommon in the deadline-driven corporate environment to ask employees to "stay aboard" through the completion of a specific project following the announcement that their jobs will be eliminated once that project is finished. Frustration, anger, resentment, and a sense of betrayal in the face of company loyalty can all be present and very real reactions to this type of situation. EA professionals can play an important role in helping organizations to plan and implement organizational change in such a way as to minimize negative affects on employees, and they can help employees to understand, prepare for, and cope effectively with all different kinds of organizational change, including the types of change just discussed. For example, when a department or division anticipates restructuring (as opposed to layoffs), the EAP can be called in to work with management and with the employees. Dialogue in group meetings can help employees identify ways to address the change while remaining productive during the transition.

Interpersonal Relationships

Another major source of occupational stress is interpersonal relationships. In a recent study of employee stress and coping strategies, Smith and Sulsky (1995) found that nearly 25% of subjects identified a job-related stressor involving a co-worker or a supervisor as the most troublesome. This finding, they claimed, suggested a clear need to investigate stressors other than the commonly studied work-role stressors, such as role conflict and ambiguity. As indicated earlier, the current corporate environment is in a constant state of flux due to such factors as restructuring and downsizing. In this climate, employees can quickly find themselves managing or being managed by another employee who previously was their equal. Understandably, this can cause employee-relations issues that can impact an entire work group. When this occurs, the EAP can provide support and guidance during this time of transition.

Winnubst and Schabracq (1996) likewise pointed to a growing body of research in which interaction with others is a main contributor to employee strain responses. It is not uncommon to hear employees state that they are uncomfortable about having to provide direction to subordinates who yesterday were co-workers. Likewise, such change can frequently make individuals evaluate their own career path and question "why they weren't the ones to get the promotion." EA professionals can play an important role in reducing occupational stress resulting from interpersonal relationships by developing and implementing strategies to enhance communication and interaction among employees at all levels of an organization. Rather than using any one type of stress therapy, the EAP counselor can work with individuals so they recognize that they have choices and options about how they want to interact with others or what decisions they may wish to make with respect to managing their own career.

Case Example: Reframing Stressful Events

In one case example a manager of a small bank that was recently acquired by a larger bank was moved into a position of less authority and more contact with customers. This individual initially called her EAP counselor over grief and loss issues around the loss of her authority. She was also stressed over having to take orders from someone in a position that used to be hers. In this situation, the individual's pay was not decreased, and she was told that once she had gained some experience with the new company's way of doing business, she would probably be moved back into a management position. In this situation, the EAP counselor was able to help her with her stress over change by getting her to recognize the choices she could still make about whether or not she wanted to remain with the new company. The EAP counselor was able to also help her see that her feelings of grief and anxiety over change were normal. In talking through some of these issues, the client was able to recognize that one of the things she had missed while being a manager was the customer interaction. The client was then able to "reframe" her current (and in her mind, temporary) situation as an opportunity to get back to one of the things she loved most about banking. Where in one moment change had been stressful, it had become an opportunity for growth and even joy.

Critical Incidents

Yet another major source of occupational stress is workplace critical incidents. Mitchell (1986) defined a *critical incident* as a significant emotional event that, due to its nature or the circumstances in which it occurs, can cause unusual psychological distress in healthy, normal people. Examples of critical incidents are instances of workplace violence, which, according to the Society for Human Resource Management (1996), are common and have increased in recent years. In a survey conducted in 1996, 25% more human resource managers reported a violent incident or a threat than in a similar survey conducted in 1993. Financial service organizations experience a wide range of critical incidents, including various forms of workplace violence (bank robberies being perhaps the most common), natural disasters, and other unexpected traumatic events.

Imagine a scenario in which the work day is coming to an end and the bank is about to close. The tellers, who having been serving customers all day, are ready to go home, relax, and be with their families. An unassuming individual walks up to the teller window nearest the door and proceeds to pull out a gun. In a loud, uncertain voice he warns everyone to stay put or they will get hurt. He then points the gun directly at the teller in front of him and tells the employee to deposit his till into the bag now being thrown across the counter. The robber then whispers to the teller that if he feels that the teller is stalling he will be shot. The teller complies with the wishes of the armed assailant and hands the bag, now filled with money, back to him. The robber smiles and then says to the employee that this must be his lucky day because he gets to live. The robber runs out of the building leaving the bank employees and remaining customers stunned and in disbelief.

The situation described could be a brief scene on a crime drama showing any night of the week. What these weekly crime shows don't often reveal is the impact this type of situation can have on those affected in the bank. In an EA service dealing with traumatic events like this one, it is not uncommon to hear similar stories. This situation is just the beginning for the impacted employees. Perhaps the employee held at gun point and the teller next to him are the most dramatically impacted. Perhaps other employees start to question whether they can continue to work in an environment like this or whether they would have been able to handle the situation as well, had the gun been pointed at them. Feelings of anxiety and stress increase, causing negative repercussions for both the individuals and the bank as a whole. This is where critical-incident stress management (CISM) plays a crucial role in preventing unmanageable and escalating stress. It is generally believed that support services are enhanced by providers who know the culture. Intimate knowledge of culture provides structure and understanding. As the EAP counselors know the business, they can more quickly assess how and where to intervene. They know who are the key people for problem resolution. They see the organizational dynamics and know the boundaries and options available for intervention. Gerald Lewis (1994), in an article for EAPA exchange stated, "As more EA programs offer crisis/trauma interventions, there is a growing awareness that a debriefing is not the total intervention, but rather part of an ongoing recovery process. And, this process requires close attention to organization, planning, and follow-up" (p. 32).

In reviewing the literature, one can see that there are many individuals who believe in this process. One article, citing an example of a company that eventually closed its doors after an extremely violent event that left nine people dead, six wounded, and hundreds forever impacted, stated that such a debriefing is "critical to the overall functioning and well-being of the organization. By not doing so, both the organization and its employees will pay a very high price, and may never return to pre-event levels of being" (Lambert, 1996, p. 14).

In the same week that this chapter section was written, a traumatic bank robbery occurred. In this robbery, a customer was shot in the back, and the robber was shot in the head. Bank staff and customers survived 12 to 14 rounds of gunfire flying above their heads. During this same time period, the evening news relayed a story of a robbery in Detroit that led to a fierce gun battle and the deaths of the two robbers in front of several horrified onlookers.

In all of these situations normal people are put through extremely *abnormal* events. In the case of EA services that provide posttrauma support (modeling the work of Mitchell), the goals of conducting CISM and stress training serve to lessen the impact of a horrible event and to "accelerate normal recovery processes in normal people who are experiencing normal reactions to totally abnormal events" (Mitchell & Everly, 1995, p. 47). The final goal of debriefings is to identify individuals who need long-term supports and to assist them in securing those supports (Wollman, 1993). Some EAPs currently make themselves responsible for follow-up counseling sessions over the phone or in person and for assisting the employee in coordinating local support services. As Michael Davis, an officer with the New York State Department of Correctional Services, stated in regard to who should be involved in the CISM process, "An EA person is an ideal team member should the employee require professional treatment" (Davis, 1995, p. 2). The goals outlined previously are not unlike the central parameter and goal of the disaster mental health (DMH) model used by organizations such as the Red Cross: "the target population primarily consists of normal people who have been through an abnormally stressful disaster/emergency situation . . . victims become survivors by doing whatever can be done to prevent long-term, negative consequences of the psychological trauma" (Weaver, 1995, p. 1). EA professionals can play an important role in reducing and minimizing the negative effects of robberies and other critical incidents by offering effective interventions both before and after these incidents occur.

THE EVOLVING ROLE OF THE INTERNAL EAP

The EAP plays an important role as corporations change and employees face new and different stressors. As these corporate changes affect individuals, work groups, and entire business divisions, many problems arise. Faltering productivity, illness, absence, and disability increase; communication suffers; and interpersonal work relationships become strained. EA professionals can help an organization and its employees to become better prepared for these incidences as well as critical incidents; and they can offer a wide range of services after a critical incident to help the organization and its employees recover more quickly.

In the past, the EAP was typically viewed as a last resort, to be used only in a crisis (e.g., if an employee on the verge of decompensation or suicide required treatment or hospitalization). The program was known for its ability to come to the rescue "at the eleventh hour" and was used for that purpose. Corporate management typically developed and implemented game plans and strategies, and then the EAP was called to help when problems arose. EA professionals were accustomed to reacting to crisis after crisis. Attention to prevention was mostly an afterthought.

Today, the EAPs are no longer just for crisis work. They have evolved to meet the dynamic and challenging corporate environment by offering both short-term support (crisis management) and long-term solutions (prevention). EAPs have been moving away from crisis response toward prevention as the most important service. The underlying philosophy is that an emphasis on prevention and on improving the health and safety of employees will improve both the return on investment in the EAP and the bottom line for the corporation. Documentation is plentiful around this point. Consider employee stress. During periods of downsizing, employee stress increases resulting in increased absences, short-term disability claims, workers' compensation claims, and interpersonal difficulties on the job. In these situations, a strong EAP presence plus group and individual interventions give employees the opportunity to vent in a safe way and in a safe place. Employees also have the opportunity to problem solve and to refocus, enabling them to see their options. Under these conditions, the stress levels are likely to decrease, and the employee's ability to move forward increases. A well-integrated EAP is also able to gather data so that program staff can spot changes and trends in the business that may affect employee well-being and can offer recommendations of a preventive nature to management and human resources. For example, as a particular business consolidates and merges some of its internal functions, a baseline of data can be gathered before the change occurs through calls to the EAP. This includes problem categories and issues for that business. Early into the change, data is collected again using the same categories addressed in those early calls to the EAP. Trends that occur, such as increases in chemical abuse, marital distress, and emotional distress, are noted and discussed with the head of that business. Strategies for intervention with that group are also suggested, such as an increased presence of the EAP on site, presentations, group dialogs on stress/changes, and meetings with management on how they can support employees through the time of change. When implemented, these recommendations can help to change undesirable trends and to avert crisis situations.

The change in the way corporate acquisitions are handled illustrates the EAP's movement away from crisis response toward prevention. In the past, the program was notified of acquisitions after the close date when new employees were already on board with the company. EA staff would go into crisis-response mode, calling the acquired business, arranging a site visit, and distributing information intended to help employees cope with the transition. The most common response was, "Where were you three months ago when we really could have used your support?" Consequently, the program switched to a more preventive approach. Today, EA staff are involved in the advance planning when a new business will be acquired. During the planning phase, discussions are held with the human resources representative and the business head of the new group. Important relationships are established and developed early. At an early stage, EA staff ascertain the needs of the new group based on the business conducted and through discussions with human resources and the business head. Strategies are discussed and implemented to help employees deal effectively with the transition. As a result, employees have reported they felt supported during the changes. They also often indicated a feeling of positive regard for the acquiring company. In follow-up discussions with employees coming into a new corporate climate through an acquisition, the employees often reported feeling it was easier to "get on board" and support *their* new company vision and goals.

Close partnering with other company resources and departments is viewed as a critical EA activity. This enhances the EAP's effectiveness and utilization. In the past, the program was perceived as somewhat isolated, secretive, and silent. Today, program staff are highly visible in the company, working closely with representatives of many other departments. Without compromising their professional integrity, confidentiality, or unique EA perspective, program staff work closely with others to ensure the success of the company by promoting a healthy and resilient workforce. They partner with human resources, management, disability, benefits, legal, security, and others to resolve employee issues. For example, when large-scale change is planned, program staff participate in the planning activity, making recommendations about ways to minimize the negative impact on employees. The EAP meets with the HR function of that group and the business head in a consultative role. Strategies are suggested to implement consistent organizational development and group theories that will help to reduce stress and to increase communication and cooperation. During times of change, it is crucial that management communicate—almost to the point of over communication. The EAP has suggested daily and weekly communication in multiple formats (verbal, written, staff meetings, one-on-one). Managers report that when they communicate, daily and weekly, their goals, reasons for change, and vision, employees are better able to get their work done. Although one would expect management to understand and to do this, they are experiencing stress due to the changes and tend to forget the basics as they become overwhelmed with the multiple tasks and issues confronting them. The EAP serves as one who can facilitate the business's ability to stay focused and on track with its attention to the "people issues."

STRESS MANAGEMENT INTERVENTIONS

As discussed earlier, the costs of occupational stress to individuals, organizations, and society are substantial, and the sources of occupational stress are many and varied. To reduce the negative effects of occupational stress, the EAP offers a wide range of stress management interventions that reflect a combination of crisis response and prevention. The services offered by the EAP related to workplace critical incidents exemplify this dual emphasis on crisis response and prevention.

The devastating effects of workplace critical-incident stress on employees are well documented. As indicated in the *DSM-IV* and in much of the literature on increased stress responses, the three main symptom categories are intrusions, avoidance, and increased states of arousal. It becomes important to note that these symptoms, to some degree, are useful, and only when they become problematic do we look at them as possibly making up a disorder. In some cases these types of symptoms may have initially come about to help people identify and avoid similar dangerous situations that could potentially threaten their safety or even their lives. Donald Meichenbaum, at a workshop called "Treating Patients with Post-Traumatic Stress Disorder (PTSD)," stated, "To become vigilant and to overrespond after exposure to a trauma can be adaptive initially.

But what happens to the people who have difficulty recovering is that they continue to behave in ways that may be no longer 'necessary'" (Levin, 1995).

An *intrusion* is one way in which an individual may be demonstrating an increased-stress response. These intrusions often take the form of flashbacks, nightmares, occasional hallucinations, and/or other perceptions. One could postulate that intrusions, being a function of memory, could serve the purpose of reminding an individual how to act/react in a threatening environment. *Avoidance,* another potential posttrauma stress symptom, could be beneficial in preserving one's safety by staying away from the threatening environment. Avoidance becomes a danger when it leads to unnecessary isolation or to rituals/traits not conducive to present circumstances. Finally, *increased states of arousal,* or hyperarousal, may have been a necessary evolutionary adaptation in order to avoid hungry predators. In present-day terms, an increased state of arousal may also serve to benefit a soldier in hostile territory. However, this heightened sense of arousal may cause distress when the same soldier is out of the war zone and at home where an inability to sleep or an easily triggered startle reaction no longer serves a purpose. In the workplace, traumatic experiences may cause employees to become agitated or anxious about things that were previously commonplace. In robbery follow-ups, for example, it is not uncommon to hear a teller state that she is nervous around customers that vaguely "look" or "sound" like the robber.

Research would seem to suggest that lingering and unmanageable stress symptoms are not always inevitable when an individual experiences a traumatic event. If one accepts this notion, then it is not a significant leap to suggest that there would be ways to help prevent the onset of a potentially costly disorder. An employment setting is no different than the other examples described. Traumatic employment events may include accidents, robberies, hostile customers, and so on. Here again typical responses to traumatic stress include physical, cognitive, and emotional stress reactions. Even though such reactions are normal, employees often consider them to be abnormal and commonly blame themselves for having them. If EA counselors or other mental health professionals do not intervene, these acute-stress reactions can become chronic, leading to serious and costly consequences for both the organization and its employees. For example, following a workplace critical incident, employees often experience severe anxiety reactions. If these employees are not able to put these reactions into context, several negative consequences are possible. They may quit, necessitating the hiring and training of new staff. They may start to avoid the work setting and may develop a problem with absenteeism. Their symptoms may get worse, possibly to the point of requiring a disability leave or filing a workers' compensation claim; or their levels of morale and job satisfaction may suffer, ultimately affecting job performance.

MINIMIZING POSTTRAUMATIC STRESS SYMPTOMS

Based on the stress model (Figure 19.1), mental health professionals have attempted to minimize the negative consequences and the costs of traumatic incidents by setting up roadblocks at various points throughout the stress process to minimize or to reduce the negative impacts at each stage. Understanding, treating, and preventing deleterious posttrauma stress presents some unique challenges leading most researchers to conclude that more studies are needed. As one article indicated, issues around predictability and controllability make investigating and, subsequently, researching stress levels following

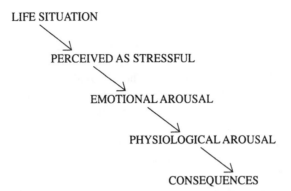

LIFE SITUATION

PERCEIVED AS STRESSFUL

EMOTIONAL AROUSAL

PHYSIOLOGICAL AROUSAL

CONSEQUENCES

Figure 19.1   Stress model.

a traumatic event an arduous task (van der Heart, van der Kolk, & Burbridge, 1986). In another study done, John Reid reported that, "Much of our knowledge of the short- and long-term effects of traumatic stress and disasters has been developed through the study of victims and control subjects after the event has happened. A number of problems inherent in such post-hoc research strategies make it difficult to isolate the specific contributions of the severe stressor itself to subsequent adjustment" (Reid, 1990, p. 1695). Reid (1990) went on to discuss the difficulties with trauma-related stress research. He stated that the primary difficulty is often due to not having an accurate sense of pre-event adjustment in the individual impacted. This can be problematic for several different reasons. First, it decreases the likelihood of assembling a control group that will match the group impacted by the event. Second, the researcher may be unaware of how the traumatic event being examined has caused past unresolved traumas to surface and impact the individual's ability to cope with the present situation (Baldwin, 1995). Another issue confronting trauma research is that many survivors are not interested in participating in research that will ask them to continually focus on the traumatic event (Reid, 1990). Flannery, Perry, and Harvey (1993) looked at these issues as well as issues concerning an individual's sense of safety and degree of acute symptoms to highlight other problem areas associated with exploring the efficacy of trauma research. Although research with veterans has been invaluable, much work still needs to be done with the general public, particularly in the area of prevention.

In recent years, the diagnosis for PTSD has become more common. In a report done in the late 1980s, a prevalence of 1% to 2% of the general population was diagnosed with PTSD (Helzer, Robins, & McEvoy, 1987). Another study reported statistics suggesting that 6% to 7% of individuals living within the United States are exposed to some type of trauma each year (Ursano, Fullerton & Norwood, 1995). It is due to numbers like these, that individuals such as Jeffrey Mitchell began to examine ways to prevent chronic trauma-induced stress. As indicated by Mitchell, "there is no generally agreed-on treatment of choice for PTSD. The severity, prevalence, and lack of generally agreed-upon therapeutic interventions argue strongly for the development of a program to prevent the onset of chronic trauma-related stress, especially in high-risk populations such as among emergency service personnel and individuals working in financial institutions such as banks." One such program used for setting up roadblocks in the stress process is the common practice of conducting a critical-incident stress debriefing (CISD) following a traumatic event. A CISD is an example of a roadblock following the physiological arousal stage. An article written by Mitchell and George Everly stated, "CISD appears to be the most widely used group-intervention technique in the world for the prevention of work-related PTSD . . . There are more than 360 quick-response CISD teams around the world" (Everly & Mitchell, 1995, p. 173). The CISD takes place within 72 hours after the traumatic event has occurred and after employees have already reacted emotionally and physiologically to the event. In recent years, financial institutions, factories, school systems, the military, and clergy have used the CISD more (Everly & Mitchell, 1995). Essentially, this has applications to any group that may experience a work-related trauma. "CISD and defusing protocols have been estimated to have been used in more than 20,000 group sessions during the past 12 years in a variety of settings" (Everly & Mitchell, 1995, p. 174). The goal of a CISD is to help employees cope with the reactions after the event, to normalize their experiences, to provide emotional support, and to give them information about coping strategies and available resources.

In talking about the posttrauma support, one author indicated that the "CISD represents an important and relatively recent innovation of support services to work systems exposed to traumatic events" (Wollman, 1993, p. 72). This author cited an example of individuals involved in a convenience-store robbery and then later in a debriefing. Follow-up with this group 2 weeks after the debriefing revealed that these individuals' feelings of stress about the situation were less "disruptive" and less "intense" (Wollman, 1993, p. 81). Kenardy et al. (1996) stated that stress debriefings have "gained popularity as a desirable intervention following trauma, probably due largely to increased recognition of the psychological effects of trauma" (p. 37). Although the psychological field in the past several years has begun to recognize the possible significant impact trauma can have on a person, an individual affected may not seek out the necessary supports. Indeed, many are able to handle the stress stemming from the traumatic event, but others without necessary supports may develop a host of symptoms that could potentially lead to depression, confusion, and frustration. These individuals may not be aware that many of the things they are thinking and feeling are thoughts and emotions with which others are dealing as well. Maggio and Terenzi (1993), who utilize debriefings in a federal probation environment, stated, "Debriefings are group meetings that are designed to allow participants an opportunity to discuss their thoughts and emotions about a distressing event . . . and to understand that they (the participants) are not alone in their reactions but that many others share similar, if not the same, reactions" (p. 14). Because these individuals may not reach out for the supports they need, it follows that those supports may need to go to these individuals (Ursano et al., 1995). It was this general belief that led to much of Jeffrey Mitchell's work.

In the late 1970s and early 1980s, Mitchell began to see a corollary between soldiers' experiences and emergency personnel's experiences. He noticed that these professionals needed a safe place to vent emotions and reduce the stress that had developed from working in one traumatic situation after another. Mitchell's early writings on this subject were generally well received due partially to PTSD being considered an official diagnosis in 1980. Since this time, the CISD model has been widely used in many different settings, Mitchell became one of the early shareholders in the International Critical Incident Stress Foundation (ICISF). Mitchell and his frequent business partner George Everly went on to start the Chevron Publishing Company, a publication house that focuses on CISM and CISD materials.

The CISD Model

The model outlined by Mitchell has seven stages (Mitchell & Everly, 1995): Stage 1 is the introduction and allows facilitators to establish the process and to set expectations. Stage 2, the fact stage, asks participants to talk about the trauma on a cognitive level. Stage 3, the thought stage, engages participants in describing their cognitive reactions and allows them to transition to the next stage, which deals more with emotions. Stage 3 is crucial in creating an atmosphere in which participants can feel safe sharing their feelings. Stage 4, the reaction stage, asks for participants to voluntarily talk about what aspect of the trauma was most difficult for them emotionally. Stage 5 is the symptom stage. At this point participants talk about personal (and often physical) symptoms of distress such as stomachaches or headaches. Stage 6 is referred to as the teaching stage. The facilitator assumes a more active role by talking about stress management. Stage 6 assists individuals in making the transition back to a cognitive level. Normalizing symptoms is also crucial. Stage 7 is the re-entry stage, when closure of the CISD takes place.

Although the seven stages of the CISD make up a group process whereby individuals are able to discuss thoughts and feelings, Mitchell is careful to point out that this process is not therapy. There are a number of factors that differentiate Mitchell's CISD model from psychotherapy. Counseling and communication skills are used in the debriefing. However, unlike therapy, the CISD process has a high level of structure, which the facilitator controls. Facilitators also do not "interpret or challenge the underlying 'meaning' of the behaviors, thoughts, or feelings" of the individuals involved in the process (Tehrani & Westlake, 1994, p. 254). Perhaps the most significant difference is that the debriefing is an isolated intervention and not part of an ongoing therapy process. The CISD process is geared toward either preventing the need for long-term therapeutic supports or identifying that need in specific individuals who may be experiencing increased distress resulting from a previous traumatic experience or as a result of inadequate coping mechanisms.

Conducting a Stress Debriefing

How a debriefing should be done and who should do the debriefing are questions that a number of individuals within the trauma field have experienced. The primary differences in debriefing models have to do with where the emphasis is placed. Whether one looks at John Weaver's Disaster Mental Health model, Dyregrov's model of disaster management, or Mitchell's model of CISD work, all models contain some aspect of asking those involved to examine their experience from cognitive and emotional perspectives (Mitchell & Everly, 1995; Tehrani & Westlake, 1994; Weaver, 1995). In all models, normalizing these cognitive and emotional reactions becomes a high priority.

Whether emphasis is placed more highly on cognition or emotions, most models focus on preventing pathology and agree that catharsis of some kind is paramount to recovery. Although there is some controversy over the use of a CISD, perhaps it is the issue of catharsis that becomes most perplexing. Although more research is usually a beneficial pursuit, a more thorough examination of existing literature on the value of catharsis might also lend support to the continued use of posttrauma debriefings. If anything, this type of examination could assist in improving on existing debriefing models.

Literature on the benefits of talking about traumatic events is plentiful. It is generally accepted in the field of psychology that the group process is an area where pathology prevention and reduction occur in many settings. Much of the benefits of group work has been talked about and examined by Irvin Yalom (1995). His work on the subject has influenced not only group therapy, but also much of what we know about facilitating an effective CISD group. Exploring the various ways that the helping profession can assist individuals in decreasing the potential long-term negative impact of a traumatic event is a pursuit that seems well-suited to employee assistance programs.

Although there is limited research on using stress debriefings, the research supports the belief that EA services and similar support facilities should strongly consider using the CISD model in preventing and dealing with trauma-related stress. A study cited by Mitchell and carried out by Leeman-Conley in 1990 concerned a population of bank employees. Leeman-Conley gathered data on sick leave and benefits both before and after a CISM program was put in place. As stated by Mitchell, "Her results indicated that the CISM program yielded a 60 percent decline in sick leave and a 68 percent decline in compensation benefits" (Mitchell & Everly, 1997, p. 90). What is ultimately useful in Leeman-Conley's study is that bank robberies actually went up while measured negative impact went down following the implementation of a CISM program, which included CISDs.

Mitchell also defends his CISD model against a great deal of criticism on the basis that much of the research that has shown no effect or an adverse effect following a debriefing has not been on the CISD model. Rather, this research has been on some other form of debriefing. Mitchell also counters criticisms arising from longitudinal studies stating, "It is not a legitimate research method to perform long-term studies on short-term interventions" (Mitchell & Everly, 1997, p. 88). Perhaps one of the longitudinal studies to which Mitchell may be referring is one reported in a British medical journal in 1995. The authors of this article reported a longitudinal study involving 195 people following an earthquake. Sixty-two of these individuals received a debriefing, whereas 133 did not. Assessing for various trauma-related symptoms, the researchers found "a general decrease in symptoms, with less improvement over time among those who had been debriefed . . . " (Raphael, Meldrum, & McFarlane, 1995, p. 1479). What is curious about this study is that 80% of those debriefed reported that the debriefing was helpful. Another study in this same article reported that 167 men and women involved in welfare work and emergency services indicated that 2 weeks after a debriefing they reported that it had been helpful (Raphael et al., 1995).

Two final studies done by Mitchell and his colleagues support the CISD model. In one research study done, the records of two plane crashes were examined, one from a 1978 crash in San Diego and another from a 1986 crash in Cerritos, California (Mitchell & Everly, 1995). More than 300 emergency service individuals were involved in each crash, and more than 10,000 body parts were recovered. In San Diego, crisis intervention teams were used on site. In Cerritos, 12 CISDs and a telephone hotline were used in addition to on-site crisis interventions. The results of the research found that within 1 year of each crash, San Diego had lost 7 fire personnel, 5 law enforcement officers, and 15 paramedics. Cerritos lost only 1 paramedic. In addition, mental health utilization went up 31% in San Diego within a year, while utilization appears to have only increased 1% in Cerritos (Everly & Mitchell, 1995).

In another study, Mitchell and Robinson looked at the impact of CISD work on 172 emergency service, welfare, and hospital staff in Australia (Robinson & Mitchell, 1993). For this study, a questionnaire with both rating scales and open-ended questions was used to obtain the opinion of those who had participated in a debriefing. In addition, a 5-point scale was given to each of the participants in order to rate their perception of the impact the critical incident had on each of them. Mitchell and Robinson reported that "96% of emergency service personnel and 77% of the welfare/hospital staff who experienced a reduction of stress symptoms, which they attributed, at least in part, to the debriefing" (Robinson & Mitchell, 1993, p. 376). Numerous articles have been written in recent years that point to the increased use of the CISD model in the financial field. As previously indicated, however, a minimal amount of research dealing with CISD work done within this specific area has been done.

Stress Inoculation

Sometimes used as a complement to CISD, the intervention called *stress inoculation* has also shown to be effective in reducing and minimizing the negative consequences of traumatic events and critical incidents. Essentially, stress inoculations provide employees with a level of awareness about how to manage stress in the face of difficult situations they might encounter on the job. Resources and tools are given on the subject of stress. The idea is that this information will become more integrated into the employee's style of processing. This, in turn, will bring a greater level of awareness to the presence of choices, options, and support even under the most difficult of traumatic situations. General research into the area of stress inoculation training in the workplace has been promising, particularly with groups that may already be experiencing some level of anxiety as a result of their work environment (Sauders, Driskell, Johnston, & Salas, 1996). Stress inoculation takes place before a traumatic event occurs. As its name implies, the intervention is intended to inoculate employees against stress reactions (i.e., to make them less vulnerable to the negative consequences of a traumatic incident).

In terms of the stress model, the hypothesis is that after receiving stress inoculation, an employee's reactions to a future critical incident will be less severe than if they had not received the inoculation. The goal is to prepare employees so that if a critical incident does occur, they will have the information, tools, and resources to cope effectively. Proponents of stress inoculation contend that it can affect employees' perceptions of a critical incident so that they will tend to regard the incident as an unpleasant (or negative) but survivable event, as opposed to a terrible, earth-shattering trauma. With a more moderate perception of the event, the levels of emotional and physiological arousal immediately following the event are likely to be lower.

While CISD represents a crisis-response approach, stress inoculation represents a preventive approach. In the recent past, EAPs offered CISD services only following workplace critical incidents, such as bank robberies. With the increasing emphasis on prevention, however, the program began to consider stress inoculation as a preventive approach to minimize employee stress reactions to workplace critical incidents. Additionally, based on the previously cited research, some EAP services have anticipated that this preventive approach could keep an acute incident of normal stress reactions from becoming chronic.

For example, when bank robberies in one geographical location began to increase in frequency and severity, program staff decided to introduce stress preventive interventions to supplement the crisis-response interventions. A stress inoculation pilot project was presented to corporate management and human resources. It was proposed that EA staff would conduct stress inoculation training for tellers and other bank employees in selected geographical locations. The training module was to include information about a variety of critical incidents that can occur in the workplace and in an employee's personal life. The module was also designed to contain descriptions of typical physical, cognitive, and emotional reactions to such incidents, instruction in various coping techniques and strategies, and information about internal and external resources available to employees in the event of a critical incident.

In their proposal to corporate management and human resources, EA staff described the anticipated benefits of stress inoculation. Program staff hypothesized that after receiving stress inoculation training, employees would be predisposed to respond more effectively to a critical incident and to exhibit fewer and less severe negative symptoms. They also claimed that stress inoculation and CISD would reinforce each other (i.e., if a CISD is conducted following a critical incident, it will reinforce what employees have already learned in the stress inoculation training and will remind them about the coping techniques and strategies and the resources to which they were introduced previously). EA staff proposed that the implementation of stress inoculation would result in less employee turnover, less absenteeism, fewer disability claims, higher morale and job satisfaction, and higher levels of employee performance.

After corporate management and human resources approved the proposal, the stress inoculation pilot project was developed and implemented in three selected geographical locations. Preliminary research was conducted to assess the effectiveness of this project. The subjects of this research were 87 branch employees of banks in Tucson, Arizona, and Fort Wayne, Indiana. Subjects were given the same five-question evaluation before and after the training (Table 19.1). The stress inoculation training consisted of lecture, group exercises, individual reflection, and handouts. The handouts given dealt with the stress model similar to that described earlier in this chapter (Figure 19.1). These included a personal-reflection worksheet on assessing one's own stress level (Figure 19.2), a continuum of stress model diagram (Figure 19.3), worksheets on stress management strategies (Figures 19.4–19.8), group exercise worksheet on identifying support systems (Figure 19.9), and information on normal reactions following a CISD (Table 19.2). Pretest and posttest information was compiled, and a dependent *t*-test was run to test the null hypothesis, the *null* being defined here as "no difference between pretest and posttest scores" or "no increased awareness of stress prevention following the training." In this initial testing, we were able to reject the null hypothesis at $p < 0.001$, with a mean difference $= -4.379$, a standard deviation $= 2.476$, and an obtained *t*-value $= 14.875$. Furthermore, positive comments from employees who attended the training, their supervisors and managers, and human resources staff provided additional anecdotal evidence of the effectiveness of the stress inoculation intervention. Based on the data collected and on the feedback received from various sources, the EA staff concluded that the training was effective in increasing employees' understanding

Table 19.1   Pre- and Posttraining Assessment

	Not at all			A lot	
1. I understand stress and how it affects people.	1	2	3	4	5
2. I know what the common stress reactions are.	1	2	3	4	5
3. I am aware of my own stress levels and reactions.	1	2	3	4	5
4. I am familiar with strategies for dealing with stress.	1	2	3	4	5
5. I am aware of resources that can help me cope with stress.	1	2	3	4	5

In times of stress, what do I feel like physically?

_____

_____

_____

In times of stress, what do I feel like emotionally?

_____

_____

_____

In times of stress, what kind of thoughts do I have?

_____

_____

_____

_____

What are some clues that I am feeling stressed?

_____

_____

_____

_____

How do I know that my stress level is within normal limits for me?

_____

_____

_____

_____

How can I tell that my stress level is becoming excessive for me and that I can use some extra help?

_____

_____

_____

_____

Figure 19.2   Assessing my stress level.

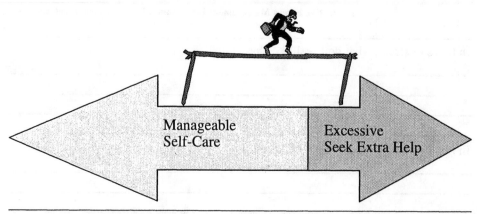

Figure 19.3 Continuum of stress.

Two important aspects of health management are nutrition and exercise.

Nutrition

Good nutrition can be an effective way to combat stress and tension. Some guidelines for good nutrition are:

- Eat a variety of foods, making selections from each of the major food groups (vegetables and fruits; cereals and grains; dairy products; protein foods).
- Practice good eating habits: eat slowly, eat regularly, avoid eating when you're emotionally upset, eat small portions, and don't engage in other activities while you are eating.
- Avoid fats, sugar, sodium, alcohol, and caffeine.
- Eat more whole foods.
- Take vitamin and mineral supplements.

Exercise

Exercise is a very effective way to reduce stress and tension. There are two major types of exercise:

- Aerobic exercise involves sustained, rhythmic activity of the large muscle groups. Examples are running, swimming, bicycling, and dancing. Aerobic exercise can improve cardiovascular efficiency and metabolism.
- Low-intensity exercise includes everyday activities, calisthenics (for example, stretching exercises), and isotonics (for example, weight training). Low-intensity exercise can increase muscle strength, flexibility, and joint mobility.

Some suggestions for exercising:

- Consult with a physician to develop an exercise program that is suitable for you.
- Avoid injury by using proper equipment and clothing.
- Take a gradual approach. Be aware and respectful of your body's limits.
- Keep records of your activity and progress.
- Focus on the rewards of exercise.
- Congratulate and reward yourself for your accomplishments.
- Get support from friends and family members.

Figure 19.4 Health management.

Your imagination is a very powerful tool that can be used to reduce stress. By consciously visualizing or imagining relaxing images, you can achieve a feeling of relaxation. In addition, by consciously revisualizing a stressful experience or situation, you can reduce the intensity of your stress reactions.

Some suggestions for visualization:

- In your imagination, create images that involve all the senses. You can imagine soothing sights, sounds, touches, tastes, and smells.
- Visualize an image representing stress, and then replace it with an image representing relaxation. For example, you can visualize a harsh red color turning into a soft blue.
- Visualize a special place in which you feel safe and comfortable. Let your imagination fill in as many details as possible.
- Combine visualization with physical relaxation. Relax your muscles as you visualize.
- Combine visualization with affirmations. As you visualize, repeat short, positive statements, such as "I am releasing tension."
- Listen to soft, relaxing music as you visualize.

Figure 19.5   Visualization.

What we say to ourselves in response to a particular situation can affect our mood and feelings. Consider, for example, two people reacting to the same unpleasant event. Suppose Betty thinks, "This is a catastrophe, and I'll never be able to deal with it," while Mary thinks, "This is unpleasant, but I have some skills and resources to cope with it." Mary is likely to experience significantly less tension, anxiety, and stress than Betty.

The following self-talk guidelines can be effective in reducing anxiety, tension, and fatigue:

1. The first step is to become aware that you are engaging in negative self-talk. Often uncomfortable feelings, such as anxiety or guilt, are clues that a person is engaging in negative self-talk.
2. Try to identify some of the negative statements you have been saying to yourself. It is sometimes helpful to ask, "What am I telling myself that is making me feel this way?" You might first ask, "What have I been feeling?" Then ask, "What thoughts were going through my mind to cause me to feel that way?"
3. Do some "rational questioning" to try to discover logical errors in your negative statements. For example, ask the following questions: "What is the evidence for this?" "Am I looking at the whole picture?" "Am I being fully objective?"
4. Try to come up with positive, supportive statements to counter the negative statements. Repeat the positive statements or affirmations over and over again. Examples of affirmations are, "I have skills and resources to help me handle this situation," and "I have survived more difficult events in the past, and I will survive this one."

Figure 19.6   Self-talk.

Breathing properly is an antidote to stress. People often breathe with their chest muscles, which results in shallow, jerky, and irregular breathing. The proper way to breathe is with the diaphragm, which results in even, smooth, and deep breathing. The diaphragm is a sheetlike muscle that separates the chest from the abdomen. When you breathe with the diaphragm, air is drawn into the lungs as the diaphragm contracts and lowers. The air is expelled as the diaphragm relaxes and comes back up.

The following breathing exercises can be effective in reducing anxiety, tension, and fatigue.

Learning to Breathe Deeply with the Diaphragm

1. Lie on your back on a comfortable surface. Place one hand just above the navel, where the abdomen begins.
2. Imagine that your belly is a balloon. As you inhale slowly through your nose, the balloon fills with air; as you exhale, the balloon deflates. As you inhale, your hand rises; as you exhale, your hand falls.
3. Try to make the inhalation the same length as the exhalation. Continue breathing deeply for 5 to 10 minutes.

Once you have learned to relax by breathing deeply with the diaphragm, practice it whenever you feel tense or anxious.

Counting Breaths

Counting breaths can be an effective way to reduce anxiety and tension. Exhale and count "one," inhale "two," exhale "three," and continue to count with each breath. Let the sound of each number in your mind fill the entire length of the breath. Then go on to the next breath and number. Try counting to five and then back to one over and over. Or count to fifty, or even to one hundred.

Intentional, Relaxing Sighs

Sighing and yawning are the body's natural responses to a lack of oxygen. Intentional sighing can be practiced as a means of relaxing and reducing tension and fatigue:

1. Sit or stand with the spine straight.
2. Expel the air from the lungs all at one, letting out a deep sigh.
3. Don't focus on inhaling, but just let the air come in naturally.
4. Repeat the procedure several times as needed.

Figure 19.7   Breathing.

Progressive relaxation of the muscles in the body is an excellent way to reduce stress, tension, and anxiety. It can be practiced lying down or sitting in a chair. The basic procedure is to focus attention on four major muscle groups:

• Hands, forearms, and biceps.
• Head, neck, and shoulders.
• Chest, stomach, lower back, and abdomen.
• Thighs, buttocks, calves, and feet.

To practice progressive relaxation, focus attention on each muscle group, tensing it for a few seconds, and then relaxing it for a bit longer. When finished with one muscle group, proceed to the next.

Some people find audiotapes useful to practice progressive relaxation. You can make your own relaxation tape or buy one in a bookstore.

Figure 19.8   Progressive relaxation.

of stress and its effects, their awareness of stress management strategies, and their sense of self-efficacy in coping with stressful events and situations.

In the near future, the EAP plans to extend and replicate these preliminary findings and to conduct a more in-depth and systematic evaluation of the stress inoculation intervention. This effort should include the use of more objective measures and less reliance on employee self-report. Supervisor and manager ratings, in addition to other measures of employee performance, attendance, morale, and so forth, would provide more valuable information about the effectiveness of the stress inoculation intervention. Ideally, comparisons on such measures will be conducted between sites that received the stress inoculation training and sites that did not receive it. If these evaluation efforts indicate that the stress inoculation intervention is effective, the next step will be to propose that the training be delivered to all bank employees throughout the company. In addition, it will be proposed that stress inoculation training be included as an integral part of the standard training for all new bank employees. The EAP implementing this form of training has also begun to expand its scope and range beyond robbery situations. This expansion of the stress inoculation curricula would consider hostile customer interactions as a potential traumatic event. Descriptions of potentially difficult customer interactions would be given as well as strategies for diffusing hostile or tense situations.

Challenges in Communication and Education

Developing and delivering innovative stress management interventions in a financial service organization can be a challenging process. EA professionals commonly encounter resistance in various forms. There is often misunderstanding of the EA function within an organization. For example, some individuals perceive that the EA role is limited to crisis response and does not include prevention. In addition, some corporate functions, such as human resources or training and development, may respond to EA innovations as threats, perceiving them as potential incursions into their areas of

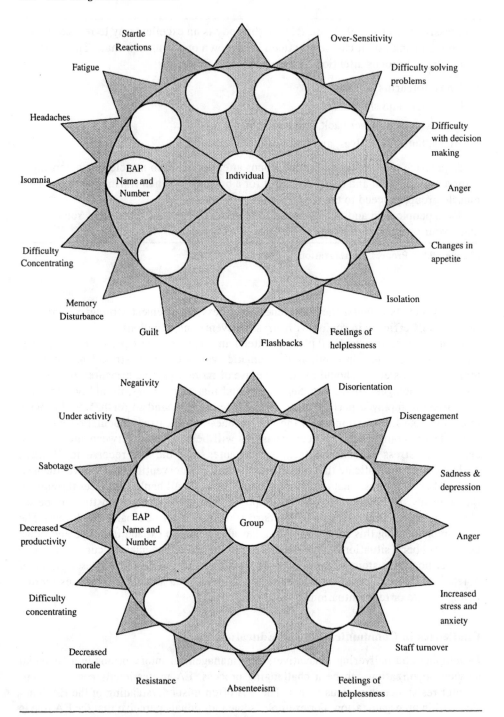

Figure 19.9   S.H.I.E.L.D (<u>S</u>upport & <u>H</u>elp <u>I</u>n <u>EL</u>evated <u>D</u>oses).

Table 19.2   Common Stress Reactions

Thoughts		
Difficulty concentrating		Difficulty solving problems
Difficulty making decisions		Asking yourself "What if" questions
Flashbacks		Memory disturbance
	Isolation	

Feelings		
Fear	Guilt	Anxiousness
Feelings of depression	Feelings of helplessness	
Emotional numbing	Over-sensitivity	Feeling shocked
	Anger which may manifest by scapegoating, irritability, frustration with bureaucracy, violent fantasies	

Physical		
Fatigue	Digestion problems	Insomnia
Exhaustion	Hypersomnia	Hyperactivity
Underactivity	Startle reactions	Headaches
Nightmares		Changes in appetite

expertise. Another common form of resistance is management reluctance to report or to acknowledge the existence of problems in the workplace. Some managers and supervisors appear to hold the belief that disclosing or admitting to problems will have negative impacts on one's career. For example, following a critical incident, a supervisor and a manager may be quick to reassure others that everything is back to normal, when in fact employees continue to experience significant distress.

Continual and consistent communication and education efforts, characterized by adherence to professional integrity and ethics as well as to the EA perspective, overcomes resistance and breaks down barriers over time. In this service organization, EA staff communicate continually and consistently about the importance and effectiveness of stress management interventions and the role of the EAP. This communication takes various forms: formal presentations to groups of employees, supervisors and managers, and human resources professionals; counseling of individual employees; consultation with supervisors, managers, and human resources staff; and printed literature about a wide range of topics. Communicating the EA message in multiple forms has proven to be an effective way of enhancing employees' accurate understanding and effective utilization of the program. For example, following a bank robbery or other workplace critical incident, an EA professional contacts the bank manager to offer support, to assess the situation, and to discuss the options of various stress management interventions, including CISD. The EA professional also provides printed information about recommended interventions and responds to any questions or concerns the bank manager may have. Consequently, the bank manager is likely to make an appropriate, informed decision about how to best respond to the critical incident, and the employees are likely to get the services they need to facilitate recovery from the critical incident.

SUMMARY

Over the past hundred years, we have gained a great deal of information about what stress following a trauma looks like externally, and internally, and yet we have very little information around how to prevent it. This may be in part due to how we empirically do research, and how difficult it is to measure prevention without a tangible baseline. It is also possibly due to our lack of understanding around what coping tools and environmental support human beings need to physically and mentally survive a traumatic event. In most cases, we are left to measure our successes by the self-reports of those who survive a critical incident. It is largely due to these self-reports of what works and what does not work that the CISD model was developed and has endured. In the face of measured reductions in anxiety and stress following a traumatic event, the CISD model continues to receive criticism around its efficacy. These criticisms have been countered by research displaying positive results and editorials clarifying the role of a CISD and its limitations. In the midst of the literature for and against CISD work, the task of refining and improving how we presently support individuals involved in critical incidents has begun. The stress inoculation training is one example of how current beliefs around stress management are being put into action. With the increased use of the CISD model in the corporate and private sectors, it would seem that the mental health field and the EA arena are well poised to gain a better understanding of trauma-related stress prevention.

REFERENCES

American Psychiatric Association. (1994). *Diagnostic and statistical manual of mental disorders* (4th ed.). Washington, DC: Author.

Baldwin, D. (1995). *Issues in trauma treatment & outcome research* [On-line]. Available: http://gladstone.uoregon.edu/~dvb/issues.htm.

Beehr, T.A., & Bhagat, R.S. (1985). Introduction to human stress and cognition in organizations. In T.A. Beehr & R.S. Bhagat (Eds.), *Human stress and cognition in organizations* (pp. 3–19). New York: Wiley.

Davis, M. (1995). Critical incident stress debriefing: The case for corrections. *The Keepers' Voice*. Available: http://www.acsp.uic.edu/iaco/kv160145.htm [1997, January].

Everly, G., & Mitchell, T. (1995). Prevention of work-related posttraumatic stress: The critical incident stress debriefing process. In L. Murphy, J. Hurrell, S. Sauter, & G. Keita (Eds.), *Job stress interventions*. Washington, DC: American Psychological Association.

Fairbank, J., Schlenger, W., Caddell, J., & Woods, M. (1993). Post-traumatic stress disorder. In P. Sutker & H. Adams (Eds.), *Comprehensive handbook of psychopathology* (2nd ed.). New York: Plenum Press.

Flannery, R., Perry, J., & Harvey, M. (1993). A structured stress-reduction group approach modified for victims of psychological trauma. *Psychotherapy, 30*(4), 646–650.

Goodwin, J. (1987). The etiology of combat-related post-traumatic stress disorders. In T. Williams (Ed.), *Post-traumatic stress disorders: A handbook for clinicians*. OH: Disabled American Veterans.

Helzer, J., Robins, L., & McEvoy, L. (1987). Post-traumatic stress disorder in the general population. *New England Journal of Medicine, 317,* 1630–1634.

Kenardy, J., Webster, R., Lewin, T., Carr, V., Hazell, P., & Carter, G. (1996). Stress debriefing and patterns of recovery following a natural disaster. *Journal of Traumatic Stress, 9*(1), 37–49.

Kottage, B. (1992). Stress in the Workplace. *Professsional/Safety.* (August) 24–26.

Lambert, B. (1996). Long-term effects of workplace violence: Under estimating needs for follow-up creates new casualties. *Employee Assistance, 8*(6), 12–15.

Levin, G. (Ed.). (1995). A conversation with Donald Meichenbaum *[Behavior Online]*. Available: http://www.behavior.net [1997, February].

Lewis, G. (1994, November). Above and beyond trauma debriefings: Strategies for pre-intervention planning and post-intervention follow-up. *EAPA Exchange,* 32–33.

MacLennan, B.W. (1992). Stressor reduction: An organizational alternative to individual stress management. In J.C. Quick, L.R. Murphy, & J.J. Hurrell, Jr. (Eds.), *Stress and well-being at work* (pp. 79–95). Washington, DC: American Psychological Association.

Maggio, M., & Terenzi, E. (1993). The impact of critical incident stress: Is your office prepared to respond? *Federal Probation, 57*(4), 10–16.

Mitchell, J., & Everly, G. (1995). *Critical incident stress management: The basic course workbook.* Baltimore, Maryland: International Critical Incident Stress Foundation.

Mitchell, J., & Everly, G. (1997). The scientific evidence for critical incident stress management. *Journal of Emergency Medical Services, 22*(1), 86–93.

Mitchell, J.T. (1986). Assessing and managing the psychological impact of terrorism, civil disorder, disasters, and mass casualties. *Emergency Care Quarterly, 2,* 51–58.

National Council on Compensation Insurance. (1985). *Emotional stress in the workplace: New legal rights in the eighties.* New York: Author.

NEAR. (1997). *Critical incident support services for northwest businesses* [Brochure]. Harri, K: Author.

Raphael, B., Meldrum, L., & McFarlane, A. (1995). Does debriefing after a psychological trauma work? *British Medical Journal, 310*(6993), 1479–1480.

Reid, J. (1990). A role for prospective longitudinal investigations in the study of traumatic stress and disasters. *Journal of Applied Social Psychology, 20*(20), 1695–1703.

Robinson, R., & Mitchell, J. (1993). Evaluation of psychological debriefings. *Journal of Traumatic Stress, 6*(3), 367–382.

Saunders, T., Driskell, J., Johnston, J., & Salas, E. (1996). The effect of stress inoculation training on anxiety and performance. *Journal of Occupational Psychology, 1*(2), 170–186.

Sauter, S., Murphy, L., & Hurrell, J. (1990). Prevention of work-related psychological disorders. *American Psychologist, 45*(10), 1146–1158.

Smith, C.S., & Sulsky, L.M. (1995). An investigation of job-related coping strategies across multiple stressors and samples. In L.R. Murphy, J.J. Hurrell, Jr., S.L. Sauter, & G.P. Keita (Eds.), *Job stress interventions* (pp. 109–123). Washington, DC: American Psychological Association.

Society for Human Resource Management. (1996). *1996 workplace violence survey.* Alexandria, VA: Author.

Tehrani, N., & Westlake, R. (1994). Debriefing individuals affected by violence. *Counseling Psychology Quarterly, 7*(3), 251–259.

Tevlin, J. (1997, June 9). Mental illness at work. *Minneapolis Star Tribune,* Section D, 1, 4.

Ursano, R., Fullerton, C., & Norwood, A. (1995). Psychiatric dimensions of disaster: Patient care, community consultation, and preventive medicine. *Harvard Review of Psychiatry, 3*(4), 196–206.

U.S. Department of Commerce, Bureau of the Census. (1990). *Statistical abstract of the United States* (110th ed., p. 363). Washington, DC: Author.

van der Hart, O., van der Kolk, B., & Burbridge, J. (1986). Approaches to the treatment of PTSD. In M. de Vries & S. Hobfoll (Eds.), *Stress, social support and women*. Washington, DC: Hemisphere.

van der Kolk, B., & van der Hart, O. (1989). Pierre Janet and the breakdown of adaptation in psychological trauma. *American Journal of Psychiatry, 146*(12), 1530–1538.

Warshaw, L. (1988). Occupational stress. *Occupational Medicine, 3*(4), 587–593.

Weaver, J. (1995). *Disaster mental health: Detailed information* [On-Line]. Available: http://ourworld.compuserve.com/homepages/johndweaver/dmhi.htm [1997, March].

Winnubst, J.A.M., & Schabracq, M.J. (1996). Social support, stress and organization: Towards optimal matching. In M.J. Schabracq, J.A.M. Winnubst, & C.L. Cooper (Eds.), *Handbook of work and health psychology* (pp. 87–102). New York: Wiley.

Wollman, D. (1993). Critical incident stress debriefing and crisis groups: A review of the literature. *Group, 17*(2), 70–81.

Yalom, I. (1995). *The theory and practice of group psychotherapy* (4th ed.). New York: Basic Books.

CHAPTER 20

Workplace Safety, Drug Testing, and the Role of the EAP Professional

KENNETH R. COLLINS

INTRODUCTION

This chapter will examine the role of the employee assistance program (EAP) professional with respect to drug testing. The role of the EAP professional can best be understood by first examining how the background of the workplace sets the priorities with which the EAP must align in order to be accepted. This chapter will discuss current EAP practices and, using outcome and safety data from an internally staffed corporate EAP, present a rationale for EAP service innovation. This chapter will also consider those factors that stand in the way of service innovation. Finally, this chapter will present some recommendations for the EAP field to overcome some of the barriers to change and to identify next steps for bringing the future of EAP service delivery closer to realization.

THE BACKGROUND OF THE WORKPLACE

Workplace Safety

Although there have been many studies over the past decade confirming the relationship between substance abuse and workplace accidents, the EAP's relationship to drug testing may be influenced more by the values of the company and of the EAP practitioner than by the type of industry in which the EAP practices.

The Bureau of Labor Statistics reports that one out of eight workers who dies on the job had recently consumed alcohol or illicit drugs ("The Alcoholism Report," 1995). Nearly a quarter of commercial drivers who die on the job have elevated blood-alcohol levels (Transportation Research Board, 1987). In a 1991 study of fatal railroad accidents, 40% of the time, at least one employee tested positive for illicit drugs or alcohol (Moody et al., 1991). A study of 1,325 municipal workers showed that drug use was the best predictor of accidents for high-risk jobs and, conversely, that employees in high-risk jobs were more likely to use drugs and to drink frequently. A National Health Institute survey of nearly 30,000 employees showed a clear relationship between heavy drinking and occupational injury (Dawson, 1994). A study of postal employees demonstrated that preemployment positives for marijuana or cocaine increased the probability for on-the-job accidents by 55% and for on-the-job injuries by

85% (Zwerling, Ryan, & Orav, 1990). Studies done at Stanford University established that smoking a single marijuana cigarette impaired the performance of pilots for up to 24 hours, even though the pilots, hours after smoking, were unaware of any continuing effects (Leirer, Yesavage, & Morrow, 1991). A study in Washington State showed that alcohol and/or drugs were present in more than half of fatally injured drivers and that alcohol contributed to 61% of the single-vehicle fatalities (Logan & Schwilke, 1996). The evidence just cited is only a sampling of the available studies that link substance abuse to workplace accidents.

Company Values

It is a curious fact that the manufacturing, petrochemical, aerospace, and public utilities industries vary widely in their definitions of *safety-sensitive jobs* and in their application of random testing, apart from those positions for which the federal government has mandated testing. A large manufacturer of communications technology and computer chips decides that all positions within the company should be subject to random testing, while other high-tech manufacturing companies elect a far more limited approach to the same problem. One oil company defines 70% of their positions to be "safety sensitive" and subject to random testing. Yet another oil company determines that only employees who work in command positions or who work independent of direct management supervision are "safety sensitive," subjecting less than 15% of its workforce to random testing. Labor negotiations with management can lead to counterintuitive definitions of *safety sensitive*. As a result of union negotiations, a major metropolitan rapid transit company does not define the job of electrician as safety sensitive because the power is off (hopefully) when the electrician is working. Court cases and state laws set other boundaries as to what positions can and cannot be randomly tested. Thus the same petrochemical company can test an office worker in Texas and Louisiana, but not in Iowa or California.

EAP Values

How the EAP chooses to position itself with respect to substance abuse, drug testing, and safety-sensitive employees is a product of EAP values and the EAP's intention to integrate with management processes. EAP values develop from personal experiences that influence the choice of profession and are reinforced by professional training. Across all industries, the role of the EAP professional requires a careful balancing of the needs of the employee as client and the needs of the employer as client. In the context of workplace safety and drug testing, the EAP practitioner may perceive these needs as being in sharp opposition to each other, presenting a major ethical, philosophical, and functional dilemma. Some EAP managers have chosen to distance themselves from workplace drug testing in an effort to retain the unblemished mantle of the "helping professional" and to avoid the stigma of the workplace "drug cop." One internally staffed municipal EAP is not involved with substance abuse training, drug testing, or the rehabilitation of substance abusers, which is all handled through an external provider. Other EAPs position themselves much closer to drug testing as part of their corporate mandate. These EAPs believe that providing consultation on substance abuse policy, training supervisors, doing employee substance-abuse-awareness sessions, and offering help to individuals with substance abuse problems allows the EAP to represent itself to management as making an important contribution to workplace safety.

RATIONALE FOR SERVICE INNOVATION AND BARRIERS TO CHANGE

The delivery of EAP services in companies having significant numbers of employees who are subject to random and for-cause drug screening can best be understood as a subset of roles that the EAP must learn in order to maximize the program's effectiveness. The success with which the EAP professional functions as drug-and-alcohol-policy consultant, management trainer, and substance abuse clinician is not dependent on whether the EAP is an internal or an external program. EAP effectiveness is much more a function of the organizational model guiding the delivery of EAP services and the clinical model informing the evaluation, referral, and follow-up for drug and alcohol cases.

EAP Integration

Corporate cultures vary widely, as do company histories of successful or acrimonious labor relations. Therefore, no universal answers apply to the question of whether it is appropriate for the EAP to be heavily involved with workplace drug testing or whether the program will be compromised by close identification with management's efforts to identify and mitigate the risks associated with employee substance abusers. Whatever choice the EAP professional makes will likely have some negative consequences in terms of either management or employee perceptions. For the EAP that elects to distance itself from the company drug testing program, the trade-off will be integration with management and the ability to influence company policy as a stakeholder and subject-matter expert. For the EAP that chooses integration with the company's substance abuse control procedures, there will be an impact on employee perceptions and employee utilization rates, depending on the broader context of management and labor relations and on how employees perceive the intentions of corporate and local management. One reason that employee trust frequently declines when the EAP is well integrated with the company's drug testing program is that some 10% to 15% of employees have intense personal biases against drug testing. Because drug testing holds employees accountable for an off-the-job behavior, it is always an emotional and divisive issue. The labor climate of a particular workplace determines whether the union(s) will label the EAP as a "management tool" and will warn employee to "use at your own risk." The fact that the EAP receives a significant number of supervisory referrals does not have the same perceptual impact on employees as its being aligned with the company's drug testing program.

Whether EAP integration with management in addressing workplace substance abuse will have a large or a small negative impact also depends on how assertively the EAP delineates its role for the general employee population. Highly visible EAP professionals can define their roles and their success records for the bulk of employees who are willing to listen. Where the labor climate is less adversarial, it is often possible and desirable to open a dialogue with union representatives. It is especially useful to identify union leaders who personally benefited from substance abuse treatment. Recovering shop stewards and union officers can become the EAP's political allies and a significant source of employee referrals. Through substance-abuse-awareness sessions, the EAP can educate employees about the hazards that substance abuse creates in the workplace and can explain how weekend drug or alcohol abuse impacts Monday's job performance.

The EAP as Substance-Abuse-Policy Consultant

Corporate policies and procedures embody the values and strongly held beliefs of corporate executives. Excessive drinking and the use of illicit substances are emotional issues for many people, including those who hold senior management positions in corporate America. To be effective in the role of drug-and-alcohol policy consultant, the EAP professional must first be credible as a subject-matter expert. The EAP professional will need to skillfully communicate, negotiate, educate, and advocate for an approach based on knowledge, research, and sound behavioral principles. In every company, there are managers who view the EAP as too much of an employee advocate and/or too distant from the realities of the industrial environment to be of value at the policy-making table. Even being invited to the table does not guarantee that the EAP professional will be able to overcome personal biases and conflicting professional objectives. Some line managers view substance abusers as social deviants who have no business in the workforce. Company attorneys are paid to focus on minimizing corporate legal exposure. Human resource managers today typically feel compelled to find expedient solutions to complex problems.

To be effective as a substance-abuse-policy consultant, the EAP professional must be sensitive to the tendency of others to stereotype the EAP as an overly idealist helper. The best approach is to ground one's recommendations in available research, knowledge of industry practices, and a clear understanding of company objectives. The challenge is to demonstrate how humane policies are also the best approaches to ensuring a safe and sane work environment. The EAP professional consulting on substance abuse policy has the opportunity to influence management toward the development of a comprehensive program based on education and rehabilitation, along with the identification of chemically dependent employees. Providing employee education about substance abuse and the company's rehabilitation program acts as a preventative measure in discouraging the occasional user who can be influenced by an educational program and in encouraging the more frequent user to get help sooner rather than later. A very basic policy question that the EAP professional must identify and make explicit is the underlying purpose of the random-testing program. The EAP professional must determine whether the executive strategy is to "cleanse" the workplace of substance-abusing employees or to salvage employees through outreach and rehabilitation. Some companies have implemented random-testing policies that mandate firing employees who test positive on the first offense. The theory behind this policy is that employees who have alcohol or drug problems will step forward and ask for help, rather than risk losing their jobs by being caught in a random drug or alcohol test.

The EAP professional as subject-matter expert must constructively point out the fallacy of that theory. First, it runs counter to behavioral psychology, as it applies to the substance abuser. The EAP professional who has worked with chemically dependent people knows the extent to which the substance abuser will rationalize his or her dependency. Virtually all habituated behaviors require that the impulse-driven person deny the probability of future negative consequences, however serious they may be, in the pursuit of immediate gratification. Company managers who advocate firing on the first offense typically overestimate the ability of most random-testing programs to identify substance abusers. These managers also underestimate the ingenuity of the substance abuser. It is common knowledge among pot smokers that drinking a lot of water prior to a urine drug screen sharply reduces the chances of coming up positive. According to an Institute for Behavior and Health study, a random program testing half the employee population on a yearly basis requires over 2 years to identify all of the daily users. The same testing program requires more than 10 years to identify all of the monthly users and at least a century to identify employees who use only once a year (DuPont, Griffin, Siskin, Shiraki, & Katze, 1995). Depending on the screening technology used in the initial test, these probabilities may, in fact, be overly optimistic. Studies of testing accuracy (Cone & Huestis, 1993; Schwartz et al., 1991; Wells, Halperin, & Thun, 1988) suggested that marijuana is detectable in the body for shorter periods of time than is generally assumed, even among clinicians who work in the substance abuse field. To overcome technical and statistical limitations and to accomplish a comprehensive detection function, the company would need to test the entire employee population at a rate of 300% per year. This testing frequency is universally unacceptable in private industry for both financial and social reasons.

The EAP professional should point out that the standard random-testing program, while less than perfect, will identify habitual users and will also deter some users whose involvement with drugs is casual rather than compulsive. The EAP professional as substance-abuse-policy consultant should remind management that the cost of replacing a fully trained, technically skilled employee, such as a refinery or chemical plant worker, is about $50,000. At the same time, it should be stated that the total cost of rehabilitating the same skilled worker today is typically well under $10,000, including treatment, follow-up testing, EAP time, time off the job, and so on. For companies with skilled employees, it is five times more expensive to terminate than rehabilitate employees with substance abuse problems. Highly punitive policies tend to reduce self-identification and to drive the problem underground, thereby increasing the risks presented by drugs and alcohol in the workplace. The Chevron Corporation EAP found substantial differences in self-referral rates between refineries having more lenient and more punitive policies and within the same refineries over time, when policies changed.

The EAP professional should be prepared to advise management on how to manage the risk of offering rehabilitation to employees with drug and alcohol problems. The EAP professional should acknowledge the legal exposure created when a company knows that an employee has a substance abuse problem and allows the employee to reassume safety-sensitive responsibilities following treatment. This exposure can be managed if the EAP provides tightly structured follow-up and if the company clearly defines and enforces the consequences for being out of compliance with EAP recommendations.

Managing the risk associated with rehabilitating substance-abusing employees in safety-sensitive jobs continues to be a controversial issue within comparable industries. Some companies' attorneys advise using a contracted EAP and keeping the EAP "at arm's length" from the corporation. These attorneys believe that the company cannot then be held responsible if a particular employee with a substance abuse problem known only to the EAP causes a serious, substance-related accident. Other companies provide an extra chance for employees who self-refer. This practice increases the number of self-referrals, but it also increases the possibility that an employee may risk a return to usage, knowing that he or she will be given a second chance. Although policies on self-referral vary, it is a common practice to terminate employees identified by random testing if they come up positive in a postrehabilitation drug test. When the EAP professional advocates either for offering rehabilitation to employees caught for the first time in a random screen or for giving self-referred employees a second chance, it is critically important that the EAP provide a rigorous follow-up program. Managing the risk created by returning employees treated for substance abuse to safety-sensitive jobs requires weekly testing for at least the first year. Weekly testing for recovering employees in safety-sensitive positions is far from being an industry standard, even in companies with a decade of drug testing experience. As documented by the National Research Council/Institute of Medicine study (Normand, Lempert, & O'Brien, 1994), there are wide variations in EAP practices. This study criticized the EAP field in general for placing far greater emphasis on case finding and the documentation of utilization rates than on case management and the documentation of recovery rates. The general lack of attention to collecting treatment-outcome information even within industries with formidable safety issues contributes to the lack of understanding about how follow-up testing should be structured. This same lack of understanding also results from a lack of guidance from the federal government, which sets standards as to how long an employee in a federally regulated position can be tested, but not as to how frequently the employee *ought* to be tested.

The EAP professional functioning as a substance-abuse-policy consultant needs to understand from other EAP professionals what are industry "best practices" and what data is available that confirms a best practice. The EAP professional must also be a champion for documenting success in treating substance-abusing employees. Subject-matter expertise based on knowledge of EAP best practices is critical in providing advice to companies about managing risk related to employee substance abuse. Legal precedents are not numerous nor is jury behavior highly predictable, but juries do consider whether the company's drug and alcohol policies and procedures meet current industry standards. Dr. David Smith, former president of the American Society of Addiction Medicine, has reported that the reason that the Exxon corporation was found negligent in the Exxon *Valdez* incident and subject to a multi-billion-dollar penalty was that Exxon management knew that Captain Hazelwood had an active drinking problem and failed to take appropriate action. There are a number of legal precedents (Chinski & Vinson, 1993) for holding employers liable for knowingly permitting employees to drive after consuming large quantities of alcohol and even for unknowingly having intoxicated employees in company vehicles on company business cause third-party accidents and injuries.

The EAP as Trainer

The EAP professional, acting as a management consultant, should emphasize the preventative value of having an EAP that is accessible, visible, and credible. Some EAP professionals feel strongly that the EAP should not participate in programs that management uses to articulate company policy on substance abuse or to "roll out" a random-testing program. Other EAP managers and consultants believe that EAP participation in such programs enhances the value of the EAP in management's eyes and allows the EAP to reinforce its position as a knowledgeable, helping resource for the employee audience. To deter the casual user who can be influenced by education, the EAP provides information about substance abuse and on-the-job accidents, deflates the myths about what constitutes a substance abuse problem, underscores EAP availability and confidentiality, delineates exceptions to EAP confidentiality, and educates employees about the far greater probability for success in seeking rehabilitative services through the EAP, than with going on your own. The CATOR study (Hoffman & Miller, 1993) reported that 63% of patients who had completed aftercare had achieved a year of abstinence, but patients who completed aftercare represented less than half of the treated population. Thus, the total recovery rate, taking the most conservative approach to those who did not complete aftercare, would be about 35%. Such a conservative approach is warranted, based on studies (Simpson, Joe, & Rowan-Szal, 1997) that show that patients who drop out of aftercare have a recovery rate equal to 20% of those who continue with aftercare, over the course of a year.

It is worth the time and effort required for the EAP professional to convince management of the continuing importance of supervisor training on how and when to refer employees to the program. Following the corporate reengineering and downsizing of the past few years and the implementation of self-managed work teams, getting management to commit scarce supervisory time for such training can be a very challenging task. Nonetheless, supervisors need to understand that they cannot rely on random testing as a substitute for addressing substandard employee job performance. Comparison by the Chevron EAP of nearly a thousand employee job-performance profiles revealed that drug-abusing employees, the majority of whom had been identified by random testing, had more serious job-performance problems than alcohol-dependent employees or employees with no substance abuse problems. Of further interest is the fact that the particular job-performance problems evidenced by drug-abusing employees were in areas of "roles and responsibilities" and "relationship with supervisor." In contrast, alcohol-dependent employees' most prominent problem tended to be absenteeism. This suggests that the reason supervisors are reluctant to refer drug-abusing employees to the EAP for job performance is that they fear that confronting such an employee will worsen an already strained relationship.

The EAP as Chemical Dependency Clinician

One of the fascinating things about working as an EAP professional in an industrial setting having a random-testing program is how often one encounters employees who are "visited by old college roommates." Employees also explain a random positive drug screen by claiming that someone surreptitiously "put substances in their beverage" at a party. Other employees emphatically state that they have no idea why a urine sample, which they witnessed being sealed and sent to the testing laboratory, should come back with traces of marijuana, cocaine, or other illicit contents. Equally impressive is how, for some people, recollection of years of regular substance usage returns within weeks following initiation of treatment. Other employees never acknowledge the use of drugs, even when confronted with one or more subsequent positive drug screens. In the face of profound denial and both covert and overt intimidation, it can be very difficult for the EAP professional to steadfastly insist that the employee participate in a treatment program, accept a return-to-work contract, agree to EAP monitoring, and submit to ongoing testing as a condition for being permitted to return to work.

One of the mistakes that inexperienced EAP counselors make is to agree to a subsequent "diagnostic" drug screen following a positive random test. Although it may be very useful to know how quickly the level of, for example, THC in the employee's system is dissipating, a negative result based on a test occurring more than 48 hours after the earlier positive should never be taken as proof that the first test was invalid due to the rapid rate at which most substances are metabolized by the body. Rather than interminably arguing the point of whether the employee used or not, the EAP professional should restate company policy on positive drug screens and volunteer that there is no available means to discriminate between employees who may be honest in denying that they used drugs and those who are not. On the other hand, the EAP professional can assert that the testing technology of gas chromatography/mass spectroscopy has a very high rate of scientific reliability and has also proven consistently resistant to court challenges, as have the chain of custody procedures provided by National Institute on Drug Abuse (NIDA) certified laboratories.

The assessment provided by the EAP professional needs to be comprehensive. Information should be sought from the supervisor and from significant others, providing that the employee is willing to sign appropriate release-of-information forms, as required by law and company policy. The evaluation should identify how long the employee has been involved with what particular substances and in what quantities. The EAP should inquire as to whether the employee has ever tried to stop using drugs or alcohol on his or her own and what the results were of such efforts. Equally significant is whether the employee's use of substances has created problems on the job or with personal relationships or has led to encounters with the legal system. It is simple enough to tell an employee who has been caught in a random-testing program that any repeated use of illicit substances will put his or her job at risk. It is anything but simple to convince the same employee that the use of alcohol as well will have the same effect on his or her employment status. It is common knowledge among substance abuse clinicians that cocaine users are far more dependent on alcohol than they are likely to recognize and that relapse to cocaine and other drugs frequently occurs under the influence of alcohol. Although a policy of requiring total abstinence from drugs and alcohol makes good clinical sense and offers maximum protection for the company against a treated substance-abusing employee causing an industrial accident as a result of alcohol or drug usage, this policy is, admittedly, challenging to administer.

The fact that the employee is reasonably open about substance usage and appears to recognize its negative impact during the assessment phase is not in itself highly predictive of treatment outcome. The lack of relative denial certainly makes the employee an easier one for the EAP professional to work with, but the only reliable predictor of eventual success in recovery is initial success in recovery. Analysis of data from the Chevron EAP demonstrated that employees were most vulnerable for relapse in the first 3 months following treatment and that relapse rates sharply declined thereafter. Of employees who had maintained abstinence for a period of 12 months, 96% were able to complete the second 12 months of follow-up without incident. It is worth noting that encountering angry, resistant, and frankly hostile employees may be emotionally punishing for the EAP counselor who not only genuinely wants to help, but also may have a strong personal need to be seen by others as a helping person. Therefore, it remains good practice for companies to hire EAP professionals who have worked in chemical-dependency treatment programs and for EAP vendors to provide such experienced individuals to their corporate clients. Although the initiation of substance abuse treatment can be upsetting for both the employee and the EAP counselor, the rewards of success should not be understated. Witnessing both the subtle and the dramatic changes in attitude that often accompany successful employee rehabilitation is a highly gratifying and rewarding experience and remains so even for the well-seasoned EAP professional. Research has verified not only that attitudes change when employees are successful in treatment (Freedberg & Johnston, 1979), but also that employees who enter treatment involuntarily do just as well as those who self-refer (Chopra, Preston, & Gerson, 1979; Freedberg & Johnston, 1980).

Standard practices for EAP professionals in referring employees for substance abuse treatment have changed dramatically over the past decade, as a result both of changing philosophies of clinical practice and of the nearly complete conversion from indemnity coverage to managed care for the nation's employed population. Effectively, the "21-day standard" of inpatient or even residential treatment has been replaced by a wide range of options. In working with employees in safety-sensitive jobs, it is essential to remove the employee from work until the individual can provide one or more negative drug/alcohol screens. Residential care is still appropriate for the employee at high risk for relapse due to a history of intensive substance abuse or at risk to self or others while under the influence. Environmental factors, such as whether the employee is regularly exposed to substance-abusing family members, roommates, friends, and acquaintances, should also be taken into consideration. Inpatient care, of course, remains appropriate for employees with medical issues related to their usage. In taking employees off the job, the EAP professional should strongly consider the use of day treatment programs. Day treatment provides a more compact version of outpatient treatment in a far shorter period of time. Sound clinical practice avoids providing large blocks of unstructured time to an individual struggling to resist both emotional and psychochemical inducements to return to usage.

Referring the employee identified by random screening is often problematic due to anger, resistance, and denial. Although the temptation may be to take the course of least resistance and not impose an intensive and restrictive experience on an individual who ardently denies usage and is adamantly opposed to treatment, there are two rules that experience has shown deserve to be consistently observed: (1) Under no circumstance should an employee be returned untreated to a safety-sensitive job when the individual has been identified by a random or for-cause drug or alcohol test. Breaking this rule will more than likely result in the employee's failure to remain abstinent and increase the probability of subsequent loss of employment. Failure to test an identified safety-sensitive employee also exposes the company to substantial and unnecessary legal risk in the event of an on-the-job accident. (2) All employees involved with day treatment and outpatient programs should be subject to company standard drug screening on a weekly basis during treatment. Employees should understand (from a written agreement or written policy statement for which they are required to sign a statement acknowledging that they have read and understood the conditions) that continuing usage while they are in treatment will not be tolerated.

Economic Constraints

The current economic environment governing both internal and external programs makes delivery of best practice EAP case management the exception rather than the rule. Best practice EAP case management of a safety-sensitive employee with a substance abuse problem requires 10 to 15 hours for evaluation, referral, treatment, return-to-work coordination, and follow-up in the first year and 6 to 10 hours for each subsequent year of

EAP monitoring. Internally staffed EAPs have been under intense scrutiny the past few years in having to justify their existence and to fight for adequate budgets in an era of downsizing and outsourcing. Externally staffed EAPs have long faced severe price competition in the pursuit of contracts. Market forces have substantially reduced profit margins and have limited the number of times the EAP can see the average employee client, regardless of whether the EAP model allows three, five, or eight sessions. Such financial constraints have led many EAPs to place far more emphasis on the number of cases opened than on the delivery of optimal case management and the demonstration of positive treatment outcome for substance abuse cases or, for that matter, supervisor referrals (Normand et al., 1994).

The Chevron Study

In the face of formidable economic pressures, it may still be possible to argue effectively for a best practice EAP. This study of Chevron's internally staffed EAP demonstrates how the EAP professional can effectively play the roles of policy consultant, trainer, and clinician. The data collected by the EAP was successfully used to convince company executives that treated employees who are effectively followed-up have no more accidents than the general employee population. The data also served to dissuade management from adopting approaches that would penalize self-referral, accepting the argument that doing so would increase rather than reduce the probability of substance-related accidents.

Background for Drug and Alcohol Safety Study

When I became EAP manager at Chevron in 1989, the manager's position had not been filled for 3 years, and the company perceived itself to be in a crisis related to substance-abusing employees. A few years earlier, the company had conducted a study of employee drug usage by covertly testing for drugs when employees came in for their periodic, company-sponsored, health evaluations (which have since been discontinued). The test results were processed anonymously, and there was no matching of individual findings with specific employees. However, the company was distressed to learn that nearly a third of its safety-sensitive employees who worked as refinery operators in major metropolitan areas were coming up positive for marijuana and cocaine. The company responded by swiftly implementing a program of preemployment drug testing and embarking on a campaign to train all of its supervisors to recognize the signs and symptoms of substance abuse and to refer suspected employees for mandatory testing. At the time this program was initiated, Chevron's domestic employee population was about 50,000. The first year following supervisor training on for-cause referrals, there were 17 referrals. The next year, there were 24. These results convinced senior management to not place their faith in supervisor for-cause referral to identify substance-abusing employees, but instead to make all domestic safety-sensitive positions subject to random testing.

Benefit Design Issues

In 1988, Chevron's EAP provided critical input on the design of the company's substance abuse benefit. During the mid-1980s, Chevron's EAP examined treatment outcome for employees who had HMO coverage and for those who were covered by the indemnity plan. This study revealed that the recovery rate was twice as high for the indemnity insurance cases. This finding, coupled with the frustration that the EAP was experiencing in not being able to get sufficiently intensive care for employees with serious substance abuse problems led the EAP to recommend to the company Benefits Analyst that Chevron consider a behavioral healthcare carveout. The advantage of the carveout, from an EAP perspective, was that all employees would have the same, company-paid benefit for substance abuse treatment. The EAP further recommended that management of employee substance abuse cases be left in the hands of the internal EAP counselors. As a result of EAP consultation, Chevron structured the employee substance abuse benefit with strong financial differentials to encourage self-referral through the EAP. This was accomplished by the company providing a lifetime benefit of $20,000 for employees seeking treatment through the EAP, which paid the first $5,000 of treatment costs at 100% and the remaining treatment costs at 80%, up to the benefit maximum. If the employee chose to enter treatment independent of the EAP, there was a $5,000 lifetime benefit, which was paid at 50% of treatment costs. The compelling rationale that the EAP provided to management resulting in these benefits design changes was that they would motivate employees to seek help through the EAP and, if in safety-sensitive jobs, the employees would be closely followed by the EAP after treatment.

EAP Follow-Up Testing

Beginning midyear in 1989, Chevron's EAP adopted the standard of weekly drug-and-alcohol screening for all employees in safety-sensitive jobs for the first year following treatment and biweekly screening for the second year. This change from a prior practice of less structured and far less frequent random testing was based on both a political and a clinical realization. The political reality was that refinery managers in 1989 adamantly believed that their facilities were being placed in jeopardy by employees with substance abuse problems and they had little confidence that treated employees could be counted on to remain abstinent and to perform their jobs safely. A 1989 analysis of 3 years of data on treated employees seemed to confirm management's worst fears. More than half the drug cases were terminated for coming up positive in locations that had the highest frequency of follow-up testing, typically once or twice monthly. More remote locations would allow employees to go for several months between follow-up tests. EAP persuaded management that frequent follow-up testing would ensure workplace safety by identifying safety-sensitive employees who go back to using alcohol or drugs sooner rather than later. The EAP also argued, on the basis of behavioral psychology, that more frequent follow-up testing would significantly reduce the likelihood of recidivism. Weekly testing would act as a powerful disincentive, linking usage to highly probable detection to certain job loss.

Rationale for the Study

Because the risks for both human and environmental catastrophe within the petroleum industry are so enormous, there continued to be an ongoing debate within the company as to the best policy on employees who abused alcohol and drugs. The EAP demonstrated a high level of success in retaining employees after treatment through the use of a highly structured follow-up program. But the controversy continued as to whether employees who tested positive should be given any chance for rehabilitation and whether employees should be permitted to self-refer and be given treatment more than a single time. The pivotal point in the argument was reached when the EAP was able to cite a couple of studies done in other industrial settings that showed that treated employees were no more a risk for accidents than the rest of the population. Because past experience had shown that the policy controversy tended to resurface on a regular basis and that the research literature contained only a couple of studies, it was decided that, in spite of limited resources, it would be valuable to analyze Chevron data.

Outcomes

Annual outcomes analysis showed that Chevron employees who were subject to weekly follow-up testing, beginning midyear 1989, were more likely to be employed 2 years after treatment than Chevron employees who were followed by less intensive, random testing prior to midyear 1989, as seen in Figure 20.1. In this analysis, all treated employees who were terminated for any performance issue or who voluntarily resigned were counted as program failures. Employees who retired and who lost their jobs due to downsizing were not counted as treatment failures. This conservative approach to outcome calculation is based on the fact that the number of resignations, which were actually treatment failures, is unknowable. The ratio between for-cause terminations and resignations was virtually one to one. An interesting footnote to the data is the fact that the number of rehabilitation successes began to decline at the same time the company began downsizing. According to behavioral psychology principles, if the positive reward for not using drugs or alcohol becomes less certain, then its potency as a behavioral reinforcement is proportionately diminished.

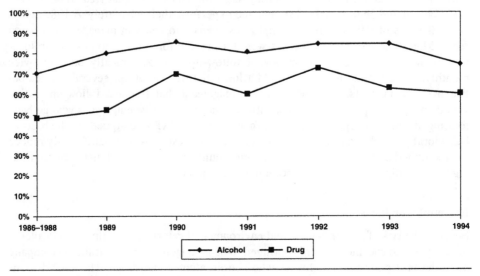

Figure 20.1   Employee retention 2 years after treatment.

Additional Policy Challenges

At Chevron, the question of whether to include white-collar employees in a random-testing program was debated for years. Whereas some states, like California, limit random testing to employees in safety-sensitive jobs, many other states where the company conducted business had no such restrictions. In states that had more liberal policies on random testing, the company had to choose between raising equity issues if only blue-collar employees were subject to random testing or raising morale issues if all employees were included in the random-testing pool. Some Chevron facilities gave employees the opportunity to vote on whether to make the random-testing program all-inclusive. Those facilities that solicited employee opinion found that their programs were met with far less resistance and anger than programs at facilities that implemented such policies solely on the basis of a management decision.

The Chevron Accident Study

The purpose of the study was to compare the occupational and nonoccupational injury rates of employees treated for drug and alcohol abuse with the rate of employees in the general company population. In order to accomplish this study in the most cost-effective manner, it was assumed that the case had already been proven that alcohol- and drug-abusing employees were more at risk for on-the-job and off-the-job injuries (as the studies mentioned at the beginning of this chapter). Therefore, the scope of the study did not include a comparison of the treated employees' injury rates prior to treatment. A total of 637 employees were treated for substance abuse problems by the EAP from 1991 through 1994. The on-the-job and off-the-job injury rates of these treated employees were examined in the year following treatment and compared with the rest of the Chevron employee population.

Study Results

Out of the 637 cases, seventeen having significant amounts of lost time were examined in detail to determine if the absences resulted from accidents that preceded treatment and carried over into the study period. Six of these seventeen cases were excluded as a result of pretreatment injuries. Figure 20.2 shows the percentage of rehabilitated employees who lost workdays the year following treatment due to an on-the-job or off-the-job

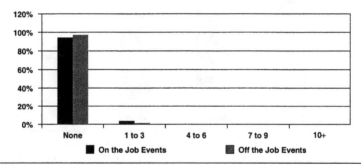

Figure 20.2   Accident rates for rehabilitated employees one year after treatment N = 637.

accident. Out of the 637 cases, 95% had no lost time due to on-the-job accidents, and 97% had no lost time due to off-the-job accidents.

Figure 20.3 shows lost-time rates for both occupational (OCC) and nonoccupational (NONOCC) injuries to the rehabilitation cases compared to the regular employee population for the years 1992 through 1995. Due to the relatively small number of treated employees per year, as compared with the much greater number of nontreated employees, a single event will move the percentage for the treated employee population by a full percentage point. Comparison of the posttreatment EAP cases with the rest of the company population shows no significant differences in on-the-job or off-the-job injury rates.

The experience of Chevron and other companies has demonstrated that it is possible to achieve a high rate of treatment success and to save the company approximately $50,000 for each employee who does not have to be replaced. The use of a highly structured follow-up program, involving weekly drug screening for the first year and biweekly for the second year, ensures that employees who have gone through treatment and are returned to safety-sensitive jobs are no more likely to have on-the-job or off-the-job accidents than any other employees working for the company. In addition to frequent follow-up testing, the Chevron return-to-work contract provides clear expectations about 12-step meeting attendance, completion of 6 to 12 months of aftercare, and biweekly EAP contact for the first 3 months, followed by monthly contact for the next 21 months.

NEXT STEPS AND FUTURE DIRECTIONS FOR EAP SERVICE DELIVERY

It is not surprising that the issue of substance-abusing employees that led to the development of the EAP profession comprises, decades later, one of the best rationales for EAP services. It *is* surprising that in the intervening time since the inception of the first EAPs the competition among external providers and the budgetary constraints placed on internal program have resulted in severely limiting the number of EAPs providing intensive case management and documentation of treatment outcomes.

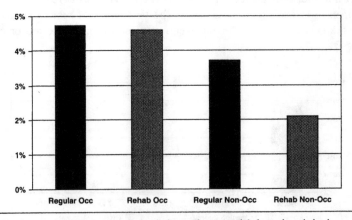

Figure 20.3   Percentage of regular and rehab employees with lost time injuries.

One next step the EAP professional can take is to appreciate the fact that successful integration with management is the key to effectively serving employees with substance abuse problems. This step depends on the EAP professional educating the customer and company management on the role he or she needs to play in managing substance-abusing employees in safety-sensitive jobs. Although there is great value in helping companies think rationally, rather than emotionally, about workplace substance abuse, this is politically hazardous territory. Being effective in the role of chemical-dependency policy consultant to the corporation typically means playing against type to overcome management stereotyping of the EAP counselor as an ineffectual, ingenuous do-gooder. Such projections serve as a defense against feelings of compassion for employees who inexplicably drink too much or say yes to drugs. Rather than offer a psychodynamic interpretation of management perceptions (which they will assuredly not appreciate), it is far wiser to sidestep the issue by tying one's recommendations to company-generated data, comparable industry studies, and comparable industry practices and to offer strategies that align with the company's commitment to safety and productivity. It may be useful to point to the experience of Chevron and other companies in demonstrating that high rates of treatment success can be achieved. In an environment where the customer is sensitive to either provider costs or internal program budgets, the EAP professional can make a compelling argument that a well-structured EAP saves approximately $50,000 for every skilled employee who does not have to be replaced. In a workplace with prominent safety issues, the EAP professional can cite research data demonstrating that highly structured follow-up programs ensure that treated employees are no more likely to have on-the-job or off-the-job accidents than any other employees.

Future Directions

Drug testing can be a powerful tool to prevent workplace accidents related to employee drug and alcohol problems. The EAP professional should help companies understand how to use this tool effectively. The consulting role of the EAP professional should include advising companies who too narrowly limit random testing to those positions covered by federal regulations and who exclude large numbers of employees in other safety-sensitive positions. The EAP professional should also advise companies not to overestimate the potency of random testing to identify and/or deter substance abusers. Central to the EAP mission is helping companies effectively utilize follow-up testing to deter and detect relapse.

An additional challenge for the EAP professional is to encourage companies to implement comprehensive programs, which include education and rehabilitation, along with identification of employees with substance abuse problems. The EAP professional acting as a policy consultant must employ multiple strategies. These include advising the company on benefit designs to encourage self-referrals. Another strategy is educating the supervisory on when to refer an employee with job-performance problems and providing consultation on how to refer a particular employee, regardless of when the need becomes acute. One of the lessons learned in the Chevron experience was that supervisors do refer to an EAP that maintains a high level of staff continuity and a visible workplace presence.

Conclusion

In researching this chapter, it became apparent how few studies had been published on using EAPs to improve employee productivity, to achieve positive treatment outcomes, and to prevent workplace accidents. Even though corporate competition for funds has probably never been more intense than it is today, there are ways of demonstrating that EAPs provide a significant return on investment, several times greater than what the program costs. Internal and external programs alike need to prioritize treatment outcomes. The issue is systemic and cyclical: Inadequate funding impedes best practice case management, which impedes outcome studies and positive results that could be used to compellingly argue for adequate budgets for internal programs and against commodity price competition faced by external providers.

To break the cycle, internal EAPs need to be more cognizant of published research and willing to use available industry experts to make a case for adequate funding. Where the case management structure is rigorous but the research technology is not available, EAPs should consider a partnership with university-based researchers to document results. External EAP vendors must differentiate themselves in the marketplace. External vendors must recognize various market segments and provide safety-sensitive-jobs industries with programs that are priced to reflect the more intensive needs of substance abuse cases, supervisor referrals, and clinically complex clientele.

The role of the EAP professional has never been easy. Employees identified by supervisor referral or by random testing are often angry and in deep denial, making an accurate assessment nearly impossible. There are many mistakes that the EAP novice can make that undercut treatment effectiveness and undermine workplace safety. EAP professionals wherever possible and when appropriately authorized should collect collateral information from a supervisor or a spouse. Without collateral information and with only a positive drug screen in the face of strident employee denial, it is still a bad practice to send an employee back to a safety-sensitive job untreated. A properly structured program is capable of fostering successful recovery in 75% of employees. Seeing the majority of employees retain their jobs 1 and 2 years after treatment compensates the EAP professional for the initial resistances of both employees and management. Ultimately, the most important results of a well-run EAP do not fit into a cost/benefit analysis. There are no formulas to set a dollar value on accidents that did not happen, on careers that were not destroyed, or on the emotional impact of an employee saying to you, "Thank you, you saved my life."

REFERENCES

Bureau of Labor Statistics. (1995, March). *Alcoholism Report, 23*(3).

Chinski, A., & Vinson, K. (1993). *Drug and alcohol issues in the workplace.* Los Angeles: Institute of Business Law, California State University.

Chopra, K.S., Preston, D.A., & Gerson, L.W. (1979, November). The effect of constructive coercion on the rehabilitative process: A study of the employed alcoholics in an alcoholism treatment program. *Journal of Occupational Medicine, 21*(11), 749–752.

Cone, E.J., & Huestis, M.A. (1993, December). Relating blood concentrations of tetrahydrocannabinol and metabolites to pharmacologic effects and time of marijuana usage. *Therapeutic Drug Monitor, 15*(6), 527–532.

Dawson, D.A. (1994, October). Heavy drinking and the risk of occupational injury. *Accident Analysis & Prevention, 26*(5), 655–665.

DuPont, R.L., Griffin, D.W., Siskin, B.R., Shiraki, S., & Katze, E. (1995). Random drug tests at work: The probability of identifying frequent and infrequent users of illicit drugs. *Journal of Addictive Diseases, 14*(3), 1–17.

Freedberg, E.J., & Johnston, W.E. (1979, August). Changes in feelings of job satisfaction among alcoholics induced by their employer to seek treatment. *Journal of Occupational Medicine, 21*(8), 549–552.

Freedberg, E.J., & Johnston, W.E. (1980, February). Outcome with alcoholics seeking treatment voluntarily or after confrontation by their employer. *Journal of Occupational Medicine, 22*(2), 83–86.

Hoffmann, N.G., & Miller, N.S. (1993, March). Perspectives of effective treatment for alcohol and drug disorders. *Psychiatric Clinics of North American, 16*(1), 127–140.

Holcom, M.L., Lehman, W.E.K., & Simpson, D.D. (   ). Influence of personal characteristics, job characteristics and substance abuse. *Journal of Safety Research.*

Leirer, V.O., Yesavage, J.E., & Morrow, D.G. (1991, March). Marijuana carry-over effects on aircraft pilot performance. *Aviation Space & Environmental Medicine, 62*(3), 221–227.

Logan, B.K., & Schwilke, E.W. (1996, May). Drug and alcohol use in fatally injured drivers in Washington state. *Journal of Forensic Science, 41*(3), 505–510.

Moody, D.E., Crouch, D.J., Smith, R.P., Cresalia, C.W., Francom, P., Wilkins, D.G., & Rollins, D.E. (1991, September). Drug and alcohol involvement in railroad accidents. *Journal of Forensic Science, 36*(5), 1474–1484.

Normand, J., Lempert, R.O., & O'Brien, C.P. (1994). *Under the influence? Drugs and the American work force* (pp. 241–268). Washington, DC: National Research Council/Institute of Medicine, National Academy Press.

Schwartz, J.G., Zollars, P.R., Okorodudu, A.O., Carnahan, J.J., Wallace, J.E., & Briggs, J.E. (1991, March). Accuracy of common drug screen tests. *American Journal of Emergency Medicine, 9*(2), 166–170

Simpson, D.D., Joe, G.W., & Rowan-Szal, G.A. (1997, September 25). Drug abuse treatment retention and process effects on follow-up outcomes. *Drug & Alcohol Dependencies, 47*(3), 227–235.

Wells, V.E., Halperin, W., & Thun, M. (1988, July). The estimated predictive value of screening for illicit drugs in the workplace. *American Journal of Public Health, 78*(7), 817–819.

Zero Alcohol and Other Options: Limits for Truck and Bus Drivers. Special Report 216, Transportation Research Board, National Research Council.

Zwerling, C., Ryan, J., & Orav, E.J. (1990, November 28). The efficacy of pre-employment drug screening for marijuana and cocaine in predicting employment outcome. *Journal of the American Medical Association, 264*(20), 2639–2643.

CHAPTER 21

The EAP and the Work-Family Connection

BRUCE N. DAVIDSON and PATRICIA A. HERLIHY

Over the past 20 years, an employee-service parallel to traditional employee assistance programs (EAPs), Work-Family Programs, has developed in corporate America. Work-Family initiatives began to evolve in the early 1970s, initially in response to day-care shortages due to the increased entry of women into the workplace. In contrast, EAPs emerged during World War II when there was a shortage of available males in the labor force. As a result of the workforce shortage, occupational alcoholism programs (the early precursor to EAPs) were developed to rehabilitate alcoholics and quickly return them to work. This chapter explores the similarities in these programs' underpinnings while also acknowledging their different historical beginnings and ideological frameworks. Each program model is explored from its historical evolutions to the current debate over whether these programs should merge in some way. Trends in healthcare delivery and their influences on the purchasers of both EAPs and Work-Family services are also discussed. It is important to note that this chapter is being prepared in the midst of dramatic change in healthcare and the EAP fields. Current program models and delivery systems are evolving, some out of necessity for survival and cost pressures versus a strategic and planned process.

OVERVIEW OF THE CURRENT STATE

A variety of forces are influencing both EAPs and Work-Family services providers. Over the past decade, Work-Family services have been filling voids left behind by many EAPs as a result of managed care and the differences in each program's approach to the population it serves. EAPs' roots were in the alcohol-rehabilitation field, and the programs expanded to include personal and family difficulties. A service-delivery design using a problem-focused paradigm has been the main focus of most EAPs. Historically, EAPs have not been prepared to address the notion of "family" difficulties, commonly referenced in program brochures as hurdles of "normal" living. Lifecycle issues such as finding child care, identifying the services needed by an elder parent, trying to adopt a child, and helping a child navigate through secondary school or selecting a college are the arenas that Work-Family services have carved out for themselves. Though most EAP program models identify prevention as a core competency, most preventative efforts are minor at best and narrow in focus—and continue to be problem-focused. Most practitioners in the EAP field are well schooled in the "troubled employee," or illness model. Further complicating the equation is the evolution of many EAPs as gatekeepers to a managed care behavioral health benefit.

Work-Family services, on the other hand, evolved from their initial response to the influx of working women. Employers, responding to the expressed needs of employees, began looking for solutions to support normal work-and-family issues. As mentioned earlier, Work-Family services address the normal lifecycle needs of working individuals. These are addressed not as problems requiring treatment but as life events requiring resources, information, and skills for proper management.

In response to the growth of the Work-Family field, many EAP consultants are trying to shift from a problem-focused model to a more normalized focus. They are also expanding services as well as methods of delivery in order to remain competitive. Some EAPs are developing strategic alliances with Work-Family service providers while others are merging with this new service industry to create an integrated delivery model. Models are emerging that look at the lifecycle of employees and their families, thereby positioning services to meet a broad spectrum of needs.

In an effort to gain efficiencies, purchasers continue to measure the value of the programs they are offering internally, as well as all noncore work that is outsourced. As the twenty-first century approaches, the paradigm for EAP practice will likely need to change in order to survive. Had EAPs studied industrial social welfare history, adult learning theory, changing demographics, and the resultant shift in the purchaser's needs, the industry would be naturally evolving rather than being forced into dramatic change by the shifting marketplace. This chapter considers some of the historical factors and research trends that point to the reevolution of the EAP model, addresses purchasers' business agendas, and explores future challenges.

HISTORICAL EVOLUTION OF THE EAP

The historical antecedents of EAPs offer an interesting perspective. In the first half of the nineteenth century, drinking alcohol was common on the job. In the South, men would take off work for an "elevener," the whiskey-and-brandy version of the coffee break (Jansen, 1935). During the mid-1800s, a group calling themselves the "Washingtonians" began voicing concerns about on-the-job drinking (Fehlandt, 1904). Around 1880, a group of farmers attempted to ban alcohol from the workplace in an effort to ensure the availability of a dependable and predictable workforce (Guttmen, 1977). The Temperance movement also came into prominence at the turn of the century, advocating for the removal of alcohol from the workplace. The steel and railroad industries were among the first to adopt no-alcohol measures at the turn of the century.

In the 1920s, two theoretical claims arose that impacted the acceptance of alcoholism in the workplace. The gospel of efficiency and the workmen's compensation movement added further economic and legal motivation to the bans on alcohol in the workplace. These two movements focused on unproductive workers and on concerns over the incidences of injury on the job due to alcohol impairment.

It was during this same period that the influence of psychological factors on productivity emerged as the result of the famous Hawthorne studies. The research considered the problematic behavior of workers in a bank's wiring room. Human relationist Elton Mayo, in 1923, suggested that employees' irrational sentiments, such as unionization efforts, work slow downs, and strikes, prevented them from cooperating with management. Mayo suggested that companies establish psychiatric clinics to eliminate these "eccentricities" from "normal" employees. He further postulated that by management demonstrating concern for workers, morale would improve along with productivity.

It was during the late 1930s and 1940s that the early forces shaping the EAP workplace model emerged. The rapid growth of AA (Alcoholics Anonymous) groups in the United States and Canada in the early 1940s set the stage for emerging champions to address the problem of alcoholism in the workplace. Trice and Schonbrunn (1981), in a historical overview of Occupational Alcohol Programs (OAP), cited Dr. Daniel Lynch from New England Telephone as the first to establish a corporate program for alcoholics in the mid-1930s. Likewise, Dr. James Roberts from New England Electric reportedly recruited from employment agencies in the Bowery area of New York City. With many employees at the "skid row" level, the need for good rehabilitation programs became a matter of necessity rather than benevolence.

Following World War II, the Yale Center for Alcohol Studies promoted the notion of Occupational Alcohol Programs (OAP) in the labor market. Though slow to catch on, the National Council on Alcoholism (NCA) joined Yale in recommending OAPs. In the mid-1960s, Mayo's earlier notion of the workplace psychiatric clinic was merged with recommendations from Louis Presnall, an NCA consultant, who advocated the development of broad-brush programs that would assist all troubled employees. The concept of reaching the troubled employee meant that alcoholics would be diagnosed earlier in the disease process when family/relationship problems and job-performance problems were emerging. Employers appeared to be more willing to implement a broad-brush model because it met a wider spectrum of employee needs. The model enabled employers to distance themselves, and more specifically the supervisor, from diagnosing the problem or labeling the employee by virtue of a performance intervention and referral. From this point forward, EAPs evolved from the original OAP model and adopted the focus on the "troubled" employee.

In the early 1970s, the National Institute of Alcoholism and Alcohol Abuse funded 100 positions across the United States to work in each state as occupational program consultants. Their mission was to influence the evolution of EAPs throughout the United States. By the mid-1970s, private EAP consulting firms emerged, selling services to public and private employers. Most firms were local or regional. Around the same time the Association for Labor-Management Administrators and Consultants on Alcoholism was formed. It was during this period that a small group of regional consultant firms grew to become the first national consulting firms. Human Affairs International and Personnel Performance Consultants are two worthy of mention. Each developed a network of offices and subcontractors in response to major corporations contracting for services across their U.S. workforce.

The number of EAPs continued to grow into the 1980s. Following a parallel course was the growing acceptance of alcoholism as a treatable disease. Corporations expanded their benefit designs to include alcohol rehabilitation. Private and nonprofit treatment centers grew rapidly in response to this flow of benefit dollars and patients generated by EAPs. Research and subsequent publication of the virtue of EAPs fueled their expansion.

By the late 1980s and early 1990s, the broad-brush model embraced all mental health categories resulting in a shift in the competency model for staffing EAPs. Ideological struggles existed between the recovering alcoholic community, the original staffers of OAPs and early EAPs, and general mental health practitioners, who began staffing the broad-brush EAPs during this period. The debate was whether EAPs had lost their core mission (identifying alcoholics early in the disease process) as a result of staffing with professionals whose experience and skill in the alcohol field was suspect. Despite these evolutionary struggles, the EA professional certificate is emerging as a credential of competency that differentiates the special skills required by EA professionals above and beyond substance abuse or general mental health training and experience.

During the late 1980s, two divergent forces emerged that continue to impact the EAP field today: (1) the move toward drug testing by public and private employers and (2) escalating medical costs. Mandated drug testing recognized the value of EAPs as a means of identifying substance abusers through work-site testing. Government regulations required EAP-type programs to exist in the workplace to meet compliance. At the same time, medical costs were escalating at alarming rates. Purchasers who spent years expanding benefit coverage now looked for ways to curb costs without necessarily cutting benefits. Alcoholism and psychiatric treatment were identified as major contributors to the escalating healthcare cost. The efficiencies of the treatment models being used were questioned. Issues of accountability and appropriateness of extended inpatient care led to the emergence of managed care and protocols to differentiate the needed level of care. Conflicts evolved within companies between the EAP and the benefits organizations, generally complicated by distinctly different organizational reporting relationships. Benefit design changes did not take into consideration the impact on the EAP's role and the linkages with their treatment networks. As a result of these conflicts, new models have evolved placing the EAP as a gatekeeper into the treatment-delivery model. In some corporations, the only way to access care today is through the EAP, thus, the emergence of a single-vendor EAP-managed care-delivery model.

Essentially these changes represent a structural shift of the EAP from being internal to one of being more external to the workplace, as well as one frequently linked directly with the behavioral-health-benefit delivery system. As a result of these shifts, the EAP work associated with prevention, education, and early intervention has diminished in importance. These factors are likely to significantly influence the role of the EAP professional and the model for EAPs into the future.

HISTORICAL EVOLUTION OF WORK-FAMILY SERVICES

The concept of *work and family* initiatives is an evolving one. During the Colonial Era, when agriculture was the primary industry, work and family were inseparable. The family represented the primary economic unit. Family life and work life were intertwined, and any conflict concerning conflict was essentially a family conflict. During the mid-1800s, as the Industrial Era began to evolve and the number of nonfarm workers rose from 28% to 41%, the family as a self-sufficient unit began to disappear (Kett, 1983). Some historians suggested that the role of the woman as the child rearer and homemaker began to take shape during this period (Deyler, 1980; Mintz, 1988). At the same time, with the onset of the Civil War, female workers were needed in the factories. It is reported that one manufacturer of soldier's clothing began an on-site child-care center during this period in order to facilitate getting women into its factory positions (Friedman, 1990).

From the late 1800s to the early 1900s, the United States became a world-class manufacturing leader. The new working class was fueled by the influx of close to 9 million immigrants. Businesses found that wages were not sufficient to maintain their workforce. Workers needed to be housed and fed, in-culturated, properly trained, and educated for the industrial society. Companies established company towns, owned housing, and established schools, restaurants, and stores. These practices became known as "Welfare

Capitalism" (Brandes, 1976). Yet the practice was criticized as businesses' attempt to co-opt the employee and his family into believing this was one "big happy family."

The Depression seems to be the demarcation point of the demise of Welfare Capitalism. The symbiosis no longer applied. Jobs were scarce, and women were relegated to the home to care for the children, as men looked for any available work.

It was not until the resurrection of the manufacturing force to meet the demands of World War II that one sees a resurgence of work-and-family services. Women were welcomed back into the workplace. In fact, close to half the women in the United States worked outside of the home (Sidel, 1986). Nearly 3,000 child-care centers opened, most at or near manufacturing plants (Friedman,1990). Some centers were reportedly open 24 hours a day, 365 days per year to accommodate the round-the-clock work shifts supporting the war machine.

After World War II, the men returned to the jobs and women to the homes. After recovering from the Depression and the War years, the 1950s represented a period of introspection for the family. Birthrates were high, and a separation of work and family evolved. As the family moved to the suburbs, husbands commuted to work, leaving the home except for brief nighttime and weekends visits. Due to this absence, mothers managed both the households and the majority of child rearing. Corporate America promoted the family's role as that of supporting the breadwinner. One form of support was the transfer. An informal survey from Atlas Van Lines stated that the typical corporate manager, during this era, relocated an average of 14 times for the company (Mintz, 1988).

Television emerged during this period as one of the key foci of communication. Some would say that the television images and family systems did not just reflect the culture of the time but influenced the culture. Remnants of this influence are still present today. A generational dichotomy evolved between parents and their dual-earner adult children's lifestyle.

During the Great Society of the 1960s, the federal government sponsored the formation of county-based "child-care coordinating councils." These programs were designed to coordinated child-care resources for preschool children as part of the Head Start program. These councils became the foundation on which child-care resource and referral services were created in the early 1980s (Burud, 1984). These Councils created a visibility for the shortages of care, which resulted as women entered the workforce at unprecedented levels during the 1960s and 1970s.

By the early 1980s, there was a significant increase in the number of on-site day-care centers, particularly in hospitals. In 1982, a national survey documented the existence of 152 hospital-base child-care centers and 42 industry-based ones (Burud, 1984). However, it was the creation of employer-sponsored child-care resource and referral (R&R) services in the early 1980s that is credited for the beginnings of Work-Family and subsequently the work/life industry. Regional networks linking county-based R&Rs quickly became national networks. By 1985, there were several private companies administering R&R networks for large multisite employers (Phillips, 1997). By offering to assist employees in finding and managing their child-care arrangements, employers validated this agenda and created a new function for their human resource departments. Once this agenda was validated as a business issue, employees were able to voice their needs and concerns more openly.

Women of the baby-boom era were completing their secondary education in greater numbers with many completing college. The economy was growing, and so were the needs for labor. In 1981, Federal legislation initiated Dependent Care Assistance Plans providing tax credits for child-care expenses. Dependent Care Assistance Plans (DCAP) providing pretax deductions for anticipated child-care expenses were instituted by employers and continue to be a popular Work-Family benefit. The economy, affirmative action programs, and the demands put forth by women led to a shifting in the cultural paradigm.

The demographic makeup of the workforce no longer featured the male as the chief breadwinner with the woman relegated to the child-rearing role. The proportion of married employees living in dual-earner households increased from 66% in the mid-1970s to 78% in the mid-1990s (Bond, 1998). Dual-earner couples with and without children, single parents, and singles (never married) represent the majority of the workforce of the 1990s.

The parents of the current worker generation, young parents in late 1940s and 1950s, are now retired and aging. Workers are finding themselves in conflict with their career or job responsibilities and the responsibilities of being a parent and having aging and increasingly dependent parents. In response to this conflict and their need for talent and labor, employers turned to Work-Family services to assist employees in managing these multiple demands.

By the mid-1990s, an entirely new service industry evolved. These services are focused on helping today's workers deal with the demands of their careers, the care of their children, and the care of their dependent parents. Work-Family services assist employees in finding and selecting quality child care, making decisions regarding adoption, negotiating and communicating with an employee's children's teachers, making vocational or college choices, and orchestrating the necessary resources an employee's older adult parents may require within their communities necessary to maintain normal functioning. These service providers use articles, tip-sheets, seminars, and coaching extensively as a means of providing employees with the information and subsequently the skills necessary to be successful in managing lifecycle events.

In 1993, the government changed its hands-off posture regarding work and family when it passed the Family and Medical Leave Act. This represented government's first intervention in response to the role complexities of 1980s/1990s workers. The Clinton-Gore administration sponsored a number of similar initiatives including, a July 1996 White House Conference entitled "Family Reunion V: Family and Work." The conference focused on how work interferes with optimal family functioning and what steps could be taken to remedy such impacts. With the public sector attempting to influence Work-Family balance, employers started to also adjust policies and practices to be more responsive to the changing nature of how and where work is performed and the changing needs of the worker.

THE CHANGING WORKFORCE AND THE NATURE OF WORK

By the mid-1990s, 65% of employees were married or living with a partner. Of employed workers, 46% had children under the age of 18, 35% had children under the age of 13, and 19% had children under the age of 6. And 19% of working parents were single, with one quarter of these being men (Bond, 1998). As many as 10% of full-time employees were caretakers for elderly relatives, and an additional 2% to 3% were caretakers for dependent adults (Galinsky, 1992). Many of these caretakers were sandwiched between caring for their children and their elder parents. The realities of these demographics place increasing pressures on employer-benefit programs and practices that were initially developed in the period from the 1950s to the 1970s, when family structures were different.

In addition to the changing workforce, the nature of work has been altered. The United States began transitioning from a production-based economy to a service economy in the 1980s. The early 1990s marked an era of dramatic reorganization within major corporations. Downsizing, reengineering, work redesign, quality and efficiency, and core competency are all labels used during this transition. There is no longer any "bench" strength to pick up the work when a worker is absent or disabled or is experiencing a period of reduced productivity. Workers are asked to do more. They struggle to find the time to keep pace with the changing technologies.

Employers, in turn, struggle to provide the necessary technical training. Worldwide, computers have redefined where people are when they work. Project teams can exist across the globe, each handing off their work to the next team across time zones resulting in a virtual 24-hour shift. Benefit programs and practices struggle to keep pace with the changing nature of work, demographic shifts, and resultant worker needs. Evolving almost as quickly is the healthcare system. The question remains whether EAPs have been able to keep pace with these transitions.

THE ORGANIZATIONAL CONVERGENCE OF EAP AND WORK-FAMILY SERVICES WITHIN CORPORATIONS

Organizationally, EAPs and Work-Family services have evolved differently within corporations. The sponsors, purchasers, or hosts for EAPs in the 1970s and 1980s were medical departments and employee/industrial relations or risk-management groups. In the late 1980s, the organizational owner shifted for many EAPs to the benefits organization, with the services of EAPs considered aligned with the evolving medical-benefit agenda. In contrast, Work-Family services evolved in different organizational departments, such as generic human resources services groups, diversity organizations, or employee relations. By the mid-1990s, in response to a refocus of some companies' benefits strategies, Work-Family services could be seen moving to or being initiated under the benefits organization.

Companies are questioning the number of vendors and freestanding programs being offered to employees and the efforts necessary to manage multiple vendors. Employers are starting to ask how many 800 numbers they need to have to meet their employees' needs. Ultimately the purchasers define the way services will be delivered within their respective companies and, as a result, will influence the service models.

THE RATIONALE FOR THE MERGING OF EAP AND WORK-FAMILY SERVICE MODELS

Employers are looking for services that meet employees' needs, that are efficient, and that contribute to their business success. From the purchaser's point of view, the business case for EAPs and the business case for Work-Family services generally include very similar rationales:

Decreased employee stress.

Decreased absenteeism/tardiness.

Improved retention and attraction of employees.

Improved morale.

Increased productivity.

Enhanced company image.

Recognizably the EAP and the Work-Family service managers will differ in what they emphasize in marketing the benefits of their service. The services provided by EAPs and Work-Family service providers differ in many respects and overlap in many others. These differences center around different worker skill sets and community resource databases. Yet, the internal operational processes employed to deliver the services are quite similar. Table 21.1 provides a partial list of program components for EAP and Work-Family services.

When breaking the services down in a process flow chart, the similarities become evident. Each service requires a system of access. In larger EAP and Work-Family service systems, this is generally performed by an intake screening system of trained telephone workers who initially screen and direct calls to the appropriate service provider. Each system has a means to back up these workers with professionally trained staff. The selected service provider is generally an individual with more advanced training in the specialty determined to be needed for the caller. With most EAP delivery systems, the service provider is a mental health or substance abuse counselor who sees the client for a face-to-face meeting. The family resource specialist, on the other hand, who may specialize in childcare, eldercare, adoption, or school guidance, more frequently provides the service over the telephone. Each service provider will follow up with the service recipient, measure satisfaction, and ascertain perceived value. EAP and Work-Family service professionals provide similar and overlapping prevention and educational materials and information. Work-Family service providers commonly use cognitive and psychoeducational techniques, whereas EAP service providers focus on symptom recognition and solutions to problems. Each purchaser develops brochures, booklets or tips sheets, books, videos, and audiotapes as mechanisms of delivering informational and educational services. Work-Family and EAP providers are looking to the Internet as a new means to deliver information and resource information. Each also uses seminars as a delivery mechanism using experienced trainers or subject matter experts. EAP and Work-Family service providers maintain databases of qualified community resources, whether a list of therapists organized by specialty and location or of child-care centers organized by type, size, and location. There is a credentialing process for community resources based on state licensing as well as on national quality standards for providers.

EAP and Work-Family professionals utilize the same core consultation skills when working with managers and supervisors around employee performance problems. Organizational consulting is dependent upon the business question being posed. The purchaser will seek consultation services from the consultant and/or organization that they perceive to have the subject-matter expertise. For example, the initiation or management of a day-care center requires different knowledge than the establishment of a system to respond to threats of violence. When the operational processes of EAP and

Table 21.1   Program Components of EAPs and Work-Family Services

Core Service Provided	EAP	Work-Family	Differences in Staff Competency
Intake: Issue/Problem Assessment	X	X	Work-Family intake workers may not be trained to screen for severe mental health issues.
Identification of alcohol or mental health issues plus referral or brief treatment	X		Work-Family staff may lack professional training and skills required.
Childcare/eldercare/adoption—coaching/counseling	X		EAPs may lack special training and skills required in each subject area.
Childcare/eldercare/adoption Resource and Referral	X Requires resource database	X Requires resource database	Requires subject mater expertise to assemble initial database.
Identification/referral for other life issues as legal or financial	X With adequate database	X With adequate database	Some subject matter competencies enhance quality of service.
Prevention-Education materials	X	X	Can be purchased through expert sources
Management consultation on performance problems	X	X (not always identified as a core service)	Though causes of performance problems may differ, core performance consultation is the same and can be learned by EAP or Work-Life staff.
Service follow-up/quality assurance, return-on-investment/value analysis and management reports	X	X	Management skills needed by EAP and Work-Family staff
General consultation	X	X	Consultation skills needed by EAP and Work-Family staff; subject matter expertise differentiates who delivers what.

Work-Family services are compared, the major difference is the subject-matter expertise of the staff.

From a business point of view, there appears to be strong similarities in the infrastructures required to support each of the service delivery models. For example, each system implements its own communication strategy, brochure, and related program materials designed to entice the employee to access service. When compared, brochures for each program seem quite similar, only differentiated by the life-cycle issue addressed by each. The method of access and subsequent contact with a counselor or a consultant is essentially the same. From the employee's perspective, the differentiation between the service providers may not be that clear, lending to some confusion when selecting which service provider to contact. With these service industries having such similar infrastructures and less differentiation between the services offered, competitive pressures may lead to the strategic partnering or merger between EAP and Work-Family service providers.

EAP FIELD IN TRANSITION

In light of the changing competitive climate and purchaser expectations, how does the EAP field perceive itself in relation to Work-Family services? In 1994, Boston University's Center on Work and Family conducted the National Survey of EAP and Work-Family Programs. This research hinted at a transition in both the EAP and the Work-Family fields.

This national descriptive survey focused on the relationship and the linkages between EAPs and Work-Family programs of companies with more than 1,000 employees. The Work-Family manager and EAP director of 127 companies were approached to participate in the survey. A total of 96 companies responded from either the EAPs or Work-Family programs, giving the study an overall response rate of 76%.

One of the key findings of this study was that EAPs and Work-Family programs viewed themselves as "separate programs" for the most part and were not interested in integrating their services, at least at the time of data collection (1994). The two areas that highlighted these results were the questions regarding the extent of integration of EAPs and Work-Family programs and the rationale for keeping these programs as separate entities.

INTEGRATION BETWEEN EAPs AND WORK-FAMILY PROGRAMS

Survey respondents were asked the following three questions about integration:

1. Is there any interface/linkage between the EAP department and the Work-Family program in your company?
2. Are there any current plans to integrate the Work-Family program and EAP in the company?
3. Have you had any discussions with your external vendor about the integration of EAPs and Work-Family programs?

The results of these questions are summarized in Table 21.2. It is interesting that 76% of the EAP and 71% of the Work-Family program respondents answered positively to the question about the existence of linkages between the two programs. However, when asked about whether they had any plans to integrate, only 28% of EAP and 26% of the Work-Family program answered in the affirmative. These results were surprising in that both programs seemed to understand a need to collaborate on some level, but they were not interested in actually integrating their services. It is also noteworthy that more Work-Family respondents had gone as far as asking their vendor about the issue of integration.

At the time of the research in 1994, only one national vendor was marketing a combined EAP and Work-Life service model. Several vendors were evolving some strategic alliances between service companies to jointly market or to submit proposals for linked-service delivery but only when purchasers requested it. Most major EAP national vendors focused their attention on expanding into managed behavioral healthcare. This focus on the part of EAP vendors resulted in a closer alignment with mental health and addiction-related treatment-service delivery and an "illness." At the same time, Work-Family service vendors continued to evolve their model, expanding beyond information-and-referral services to include coaching and counseling around day-to-day issues of living, such as parenting, adoption, child rearing, school selection, and role changes associated with supporting aging parents. Also included were the personal stress and strains people experience in performing these everyday life roles. Educational materials and seminars reflected this life-cycle approach.

In 1995 and 1996, the first significant signal of change emerged. Predictably, through either a business merger or an acquisition, a melded delivery model between an EAP and Work-Life service providers was obtainable. Ceridian, a large national

Table 21.2   Integration Questions

Integration	
No	
Yes	
Already Integrated	
EAP	W/F
EAP	W/F
EAP	W/F
Linkages between EAP and W/F	
24%	29%
76%	71%
—	—
Plans to integrate	
72	74
16	11
12	15
Discussions with external vendors	
62	55
25	45
—	—

EAP firm, acquired the second-largest Work-Family service provider, the Partnership Group. Around the same period, the largest Work-Family service provider, Work/Family Directions, began expanding their service options to include EAP-like services at the request of some of its clients. Each firm's goal was to devise a one-stop-shopping product. Companies and their employees need only dial a single telephone number to obtain service across a broad array of life issues. The callers' needs are assessed by an intake worker who then directs the call to the appropriate staff member with subject-matter expertise.

Artificially, purchasers, like Digital Equipment Corporation, began to integrate their service models, not by purchasing from a single-source vendor, but by merging the program branding. DIGITAL, for example, created a branding they called Work-Life Connections. Under this title, they revamped their employee communications, creating one brochure for both service delivery models. They brought their service vendors together to define cooperative delivery arrangements with the goal of achieving a seamless service system.

BARRIERS AND CHALLENGES FOR CHANGE

Herlihy's research (1997) also addressed the issue of why companies chose to keep their EAP and Work-Family program separate. Specifically, survey respondents were asked: "If there is a separation between the EAP and the Work-Family initiatives in your company, which of the following reasons most accurately describes the rationale for that policy?" The overwhelming response, as can be seen in Figure 21.1, was that EAPs and Work-Family programs were historically developed as different programs (81% EAP and 69% Work-Family).

These differences in how EAPs and Work-Family programs originated and evolved impacted the program focus. As shown in Figure 21.1, different foci were the second most frequent response reported by 44% of EAP and 44% of Work-Family. In addition to the specific initial foci of alcoholism and child care, respectively, both programs have continued along slightly different paths. EAPs have remained more problem oriented and are staffed, for the most part, by clinicians. Work-Family programs have taken a more solutions approach and tend to provide more consultative, informational, and referral services.

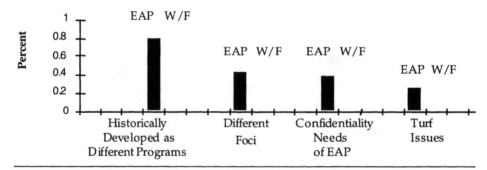

Figure 21.1   Separation of EAP and work/family.

The fact that these two programs were developed in different time periods and emerged with a different focus is only a partial explanation of the lack of integration. Many respondents to the survey wrote comments or verbally communicated that the real problem with integration between these programs was confidentiality of case information (40% EAP and 41% Work-Family). EAP professionals were more likely to see confidentiality as a barrier.

The second most stated reason for separating EAP and Work-Family programs was that of social stigma. Work-Family respondents claimed that they did not want to be associated or "pulled down" by EAP's negative stigma. They viewed their agenda as addressing the normal adaptational coping issues of the everyday employee. Even though quantitatively the issue of stigma was ranked fifth (10% EAP and 14% Work-Family) in this survey, the open-ended comments indicated that the issue of EAP stigma was deeply rooted and created a serious stumbling block to integration of these two programs.

Turf issues were ranked fourth and reported to be a reason for separate service delivery by 27% of the Work-Family respondents and 19% of the EAP respondents. Although few respondents were comfortable talking about the specifics of these turf issues, many alluded to problems in this area. One EAP respondent stated that he was just too busy to even think about integration of services and that "EAP needed more basic control over EAP before reaching out." With reorganization, downsizing, and layoffs being prominent in the work world, everyone is wondering about the security of his or her own job. Given this corporate climate, the idea of collaborating or perhaps giving up a piece of one's job may impact an individual's openness to the question of integrating services.

EAP's broad-brush model, a concept that had its roots in the notion of identifying alcoholics earlier in their disease process, has, by default, distanced itself from the notion of normal lifecycle challenges of living. Most employees choose not want to see themselves as being "ill," and many associate EAP with illness, performance issues, "those kinds of problems," mental illness, positive drug screens, and substance abuse. Though this has not been intentional, it is the by-product of the model. However, normal lifecycle problems of living are the very areas on which Work-Family service providers have focused their attention. Work-Family services have positioned themselves as providing solutions to the daily challenges of life. Though some of these daily life challenges do negatively impact performance, these services have managed to keep a safe distance from the performance disciplinary process and the medical system. Whereas EAPs main marketing thrust is the recovery of performance/problem employees, Work-Family services market improved productivity through the more timely and efficient delivery of information and solutions that enable employees to manage daily life events.

Therein lies the challenge for EAPs. Just as EAPs evolved from OAPs, encompassing broader issues, Work-Family services have evolved from an even wider framework, attracting employees through normalizing lifecycle events.

THE FUTURE OF EAPS

Ultimately employers, the purchaser of services, will define the models of service delivery. What is likely to emerge are designs across a continuum. For organizations that utilize the EAP model as a gate to managed care, a critical step in managing workplace performance and behavior, and/or a key component of their drug-testing program, little will change. In these instances, the EAP managers are best to consider partnering with Work-Family service initiatives as they exist within the company. In instances where the EAP has no distinct role in determining an employee's fitness for work, the purchaser may resolve any organizational conflicts or vendor-service overlaps by merging its program strategies. Subsequently, the purchaser may either solicit a seamless product from a single source or force a partnership between vendors. The likelihood of this occurring increases either if the services report into the same department or if the employer is searching for cost efficiencies and greater clarity in the benefits it offers its employees. The recent emergence of single-source vendors creates a new force in the evolutionary process of EAPs. Future writings will look back at these evolutionary forces and debate whether EAPs actually lose their distinct identity and their link to performance and substance abuse in favor of a more normalized, lifecycle, Work-Family service model.

EAPs have the opportunity to assess their current position and to proactively plan their future direction. Internal programs can initiate an organizational review to establish a long-range plan that takes into account the factors described in this chapter. External EAPs, not already wrestling with these issues, are likely to in the near future as the result of market forces and purchaser requirements. EAPs are not likely to become extinct. However, it is likely that some larger EAPs will shift from partnership arrangements with Work-Family service providers and purchase them in an effort to have a broader portfolio of products. Smaller consulting firms are likely to explore mergers in order to stay competitive. Employers of all sizes will continue to have different needs and agendas. As a result, market forces will define the landscape. What is likely is that the services provided by many EAPs will continue to exist, but as services absorbed under other program names, models, and structures influenced by a broader purchaser agenda that are less stigmatic and more inviting to a broader number of employees. The success of these new models rests with their ability to meet the needs of the purchaser and the employee and are ultimately able to demonstrate their value.

REFERENCES

Brandes, S. (1976). *American welfare capitalism 1880–1940.* Chicago: University of Chicago Press.

Burud, S., Aschbacher, P., & Miecroskey, J. (1984). *Employer supported child care: Investing in human resource.* Dover, MA: Auburn House.

Fehlandt, A. (1904). *A century of drink reform in the US.* Cincinnati: Jennings and Graham.

Friedman, D. (1990). Work and family: The new strategic plan. *Human Resource Planning, 13*(2), 79–90.

Galinsky, E., Bond, T., & Swanberg, J. (1998). *The 1997 national study of the changing workforce.* New York: Families and Work Institute.

Gutman, H. (1977). *Work, culture and society in industrializing America.* New York: Vintage Books.

Herlihy, P. (1997, Spring). Employee assistance programs and work-family programs: Obstacles and opportunities for organizational integration. *Compensation and Benefits Management, 13*(2), 22–30.

Janson, C. (1935). *The stranger in America 1793–1806.* New York: Press of the Pioneers.

Kett, J. (1983). The stages of life, 1790–1840. In M. Gordon (Ed.), *The American family in social historical perspective* (3rd ed.). New York: St Martin's Press.

Mintz, S., & Kellogg, S. (1988). *Domestic revolution: A social history of the American family life*. New York: Free Press.

Philips, T. (1995, Winter). Employee assistance programs and worklife initiative. *Dependent Care Quarterly, 9*(4), 1–2.

Trice, H., & Schonbrunn, W. (1981, Spring). A history of job-based alcoholism programs: 1900–1955. *Journal of Drug Issues,* 171–198.

CHAPTER 22

The Alignment of EAP and
Business Unit Goals

REGINA SCHAAF DICKENS

Employee assistance programs (EAPs), whether internal or external, face the issue of identifying needs and developing effective interventions to satisfy those needs for various systems throughout the organizations they serve. Understanding the various client populations, including individual employees and their families, front-line supervisors and their natural work teams, and middle and upper management, is critical. This issue is particularly challenging in large, highly decentralized companies because each location may have its own culture, business issues, management style, and problem-solving approach. This chapter addresses the need for creating strategic business alliances to maximize EAP efforts in such environments. Productivity and profitability are bottom-line issues for management and union leadership. For this reason, EAPs have been positioned to demonstrate the impact of employee performance on shareholder value. The EAP has for years documented the return on corporate dollars spent for its programs and has enjoyed some level of acceptance in business and industry (Employee Assistance Professionals Association [EAPA], 1996, p. 9). The next steps for future growth require the profession to demonstrate its value by defining and measuring concrete outcomes. This chapter provides an approach for developing these outcome measures, for selling the concepts to relevant partners within business units, and for integrating the EAP into a company's day-to-day functioning. It is developed from the author's experience as an external consultant and internal manager of EAPs and is greatly influenced by the joint development of an integrated Health and Family Services model at one corporation.

"What Business Are We In?"

In reviewing the 25th Anniversary Commemorative Journal of the Employee Assistance Professionals Association (1996), one finds the historical overview of a growing profession with a definition of purpose, core technologies, a code of ethics, and clear documentation of cost savings. The EAPA defined *employee assistance* as: "a worksite-focused program designed to assist (1) work organizations in addressing productivity issues and (2) employee clients in identifying and resolving personal concerns . . . which may affect job performance" (EAPA, p. 4). Service components include: "(1) consultation and training for work organization leadership and outreach to employees and families, (2) confidential and timely assessment, (3) confrontation, motivation and short-term intervention to deal with job performance issues, (4) referral and follow-up for diagnosis and treatment, (5) management of provider contracts of outside managed care entities, (6) consultation to the organization around benefit design and (7) quality assurance around EAP effectiveness" (EAPA, p. 4).

Amaral and Harlow (1996) discussed the future of the EAP as a part of an integrated occupational health system. They focused upon developing an integrated, systems approach with the EAP taking the leadership role. Communicating the value of the EAP is viewed as crucial along with a commitment to continuous improvement based on identifiable key performance indicators. Further specialization is recommended in the areas of training, prevention, benefits, crisis and risk management, program evaluation, and organizational/management skills (pp. 42).

For the most part, EAPs have to date offered the greatest return on investment in the area of increased employee productivity and performance. The majority of large corporations offer behavioral health benefits, EAPs, and wellness initiatives because they know these programs impact employee health and safety, thus allowing employees to be at work and producing. Assessment, referral, and follow-up; provider networking and gatekeeping; maintenance of individual confidentiality while serving as a client advocate; and intervention into problematic job performance are components of the successful EAP. What are future opportunities? How does successful integration occur? Where are new markets opening? Where does the core technology lead with regard to organizational health?

THE WORKPLACE

A large, multisite, decentralized company may be comprised of a number of large or small locations with numerous product lines. This defining characteristic is typical across business and industry. The EAP is viewed as a corporate-driven programming effort that local sites must incorporate into their cultures individually. Philosophy, guiding principles, functional responsibilities, protocols, and procedures may be set at the corporate level; however, funding and implementation are often local decisions with varying degrees of commitment at each site. Local implementation may be achieved by a combination of in-house or outsourced employee assistance (EA) professionals and services. The EAP may function as a part of human resources, medical, benefits, or environmental health and safety departments. The reporting structure is less important than the priority and resources it receives from the department head where it is located.

The variation of EAP implementation, reporting structure, and commitment at each site sets the stage for the challenge in obtaining resources at the location level. Past experience with a successful EAP may dictate a manager's level of future support. Perceived success will more often be tied to bottom-line implications than to an employee-friendly orientation of "doing the right thing"—the current business climate may directly affect capital available to support programming efforts. Changes in benefit packages negotiated with unions may also impact treatment options available to consumers of EAP services. Many factors set the stage for the initiatives offered at a particular location. Unfortunately these factors are often not the influences the EA professional would like to utilize in program planning.

PAST APPROACHES TO PROGRAM PLANNING

In the past, the EAP was introduced to employees and their dependents through meetings and multimedia campaigns. An effective program continually promoted itself through posters, brochures, home mailings, safety meeting presentations, and supervisory training efforts. Consultations were offered to managers and to union officials. The EAP focused on the broad range of issues that confront employees and family members attempting to balance work and personal life.

Some locations may have developed joint management/union advisory teams to guide the direction of the EAP's program. These teams would provide feedback to the EA professional on the program's perceived status and would participate in developing the annual program plan. The combination of formal and informal satisfaction results, coupled with utilization data from past years' EAP experience, were used in program planning. Community concerns and awareness campaigns often drove the EAP's annual activities. Traditionally, EAPs focused on specific program development and promotion and possessed sound justification for the efforts to be funded in the coming year. As a result, the advisory groups were usually enthusiastic, and many would actually spearhead some of the efforts.

Success would be measured by the number of programs offered, the level of participation, and customer satisfaction. Usually these factors would measure what has succeeded in the past and would reinforce maintaining the status quo while possibly adding new initiatives.

A NEW WAY OF DOING BUSINESS

The basic core technology can be conceptualized in traditional prevention terminology. Primary, secondary, and tertiary levels of prevention are what EAPs are about. In the past, the vast majority of resources have been targeted at tertiary care. Problem identification, assessment and referral, treatment and follow-up, and the development and maintenance of the provider network took a great deal of time and capital. In highly decentralized companies, each location's resource and referral systems had to be developed. Program installation and maintenance was to be balanced with more proactive educational efforts. Often it was difficult to compete with other training events for time to provide managers and union stewards with skills for recognizing and referring employees with performance issues. Awareness efforts had to be sandwiched into safety meetings, many of which had to meet Occupational Safety and Health Administration (OSHA) requirements and left little time for other human-service messages to be delivered.

The EAP rarely has been a priority for the business unit primarily because of its past emphasis upon reactive, tertiary care. Safety, reengineering of the workforce (training), and quality improvement have been the favored areas for more generous funding in recent years. An important question then is how can the EAP capitalize on the current corporate concerns and activities?

Today's EAP Professional

A significant change in the function of the EAP began with the advent of managed behavioral healthcare. Companies are choosing to partner with outside vendors to provide not only gatekeeping but also case management services to ensure appropriate assessment and treatment for medically necessary interventions. In the past, this was viewed as the primary role of the EA professional. This person would:

- Identify and credential providers.
- Screen and refer consumers of counseling services.
- Monitor and pay bills.
- Evaluate satisfaction.
- Recredential competent providers.

In the new scenario, EA professionals become vendor managers. They can act as:

- Facilitators by sharing their existing provider networks with vendors.
- Partners by continuing to provide work-site liaison and community contact for provider recruitment and evaluation.
- Evaluators by setting and monitoring key performance indicators with the vendor ensuring clear expectations and quality measures.

Vendor management and benefits coordination may become the focus of the EAP as the shift of tertiary interventions moves more to the outsourced managed care system.

The new EA professional may work with the benefits department to define the EAP's philosophy and to set parameters to support behavioral health interventions. For example, assuring appropriate annualized and lifetime insurance maximums for an array of mental health and chemical dependency services is crucial if a company believes that appropriate, medically necessary treatment ultimately results in cost-savings. Educating the benefits staff may be required to help them understand the phenomenon of cost-shifting that occurs among employees and family members when necessary psychiatric and chemical dependency treatment is withheld.

These parameters provide the ground rules for contracting with outside vendors who share a philosophy of matching clients with appropriate levels of care. Specific contracting must address such issues as provider network development, access to services, availability of managed care case managers and treatment providers, claims-payment accuracy and timeliness, appeals processes, and a clear understanding of the company's responsibility as a purchaser of managed care services. The EA professional must maintain a high profile in the workplace to promote outsourced services and in the community to aid in monitoring and recruiting qualified service providers. Direct care is no longer the highest priority. The EA's shift of focus from that of gatekeeper to vendor management must ensure the availability of appropriate, quality, direct service.

A CONTINUUM OF WELLNESS

A close examination of EAPs shows that potential customers fall somewhere along a continuum of health. At any given time, people can be healthy (one end of the continuum), they can be at risk for a problem, or they can be disabled by an illness, accident, or other psychosocial concern (the other end of the continuum). This concept is directly related to the primary, secondary, and tertiary levels of care referenced earlier. If EAPs are to be responsive to the needs of individuals and families, interventions must be designed to correlate with the points of the continuum (Figure 22.1).

A responsive service-delivery system will provide interventions at the earliest stages of problem development. Early interventions are most effective and are far less costly to individuals, families, and the company when offered before disability occurs. Employees, family members, and work groups who are well can benefit from *prevention efforts*. Likewise, someone at risk for accidents, injuries, or psychosocial stressors can benefit from *early intervention initiatives*. A person who has become ill or injured, on the other hand, is in need of *rehabilitation and disability case management*. A description of the three components of this model follows.

Prevention

Preventive activities educate employees and their families on how to avoid problems and how to recognize potential behavioral characteristics that can lead to long-term dysfunction. Programs could include health education and awareness seminars on topics such as parenting, couple's communication, learning problems of children, substance use and abuse, dual-career families, aging issues, and advanced directives. Safety meetings or departmental training on the effects of stress, the importance of trauma response, and the avoidance of workplace violence are also effective prevention efforts.

Early Intervention

Early intervention activities and services help employees and families to recognize problems and to seek help at an early stage. These services also help supervisors and union stewards recognize warning signals for potentially serious performance problems. Examples include job-performance referral training, trauma-response intervention or screening and referral for early identification of personal problems.

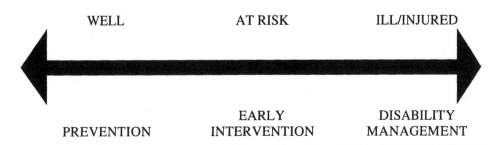

Figure 22.1   Wellness continuum.

Disability Management

The EAP continues to provide services to people experiencing significant problems that interfere with personal and job performance. This level of intervention could include screening and referral for appropriate treatment, return-to-work planning, or impaired-employee intervention.

In the past, EAPs focused the majority of resources on disability management. Individuals and families were most likely to access services after typical coping mechanisms broke down. The EAP's services were used to return the person to full and productive life and work as quickly and as safely as possible.

STRATEGIC SHIFT

How can an effective EAP manage resource allocations in order to drive activities into prevention and early intervention efforts while maintaining appropriate attention on disability management services? The following sections provide a blueprint for executing such a strategic shift.

Key Operating Principles

It is imperative that basic philosophical principles be established to guide the strategic shift in thinking and program conceptualization and to provide for appropriate resource allocation. The EA staff can develop these principles; however, it is more effective to include key constituents who may be essential future partners. Obvious natural alliances occur within human resource departments and among such departments as wellness, medical, benefits, workers' compensation, environmental-health-safety, and organizational development and training. The most logical partnership on a wellness continuum is between the EAP and those who touch employees from a biopsychosocial standpoint.

Resource Allocation

The key players should identify the primary components of the services that each one offers and should categorize them according to where the service falls on the wellness continuum (prevention, early intervention, or disability management). The next step is to estimate where the bulk of each one's time and resources have traditionally been allocated. *Resources* are defined as actual dollars spent on program initiatives as well as staff time devoted to specific activities. Numbers of volunteers involved in program development and services delivery should be included in staff-time calculation to accurately reflect time-resource allocations. Is there an underutilization of expenditures in specific areas?

Questions regarding the actual mission of each department should be explored. For instance, it may be determined that the EAP needs to continue to focus a larger percentage of resource allocation upon disability management at the current stage of business planning; however, a concerted effort to begin developing the weaker end of the wellness continuum may be identified. Likewise, wellness initiatives that have been primarily prevention focused may need to be expanded to opportunities for disability management, such as on-site physical therapy for people returning to work. A wholesale redistribution of resources may not be warranted. Strategic allocation of resources should be based on a business planning process that meets individual and organizational needs.

Program Evaluation

After defining the program components and the levels of services, it is important to evaluate how they are functioning. Are there elements of the business that are so entrenched and well run that they may require little attention from a program manager? Are there other areas that with a slight increase in resource allocation can become new "winners" and support the concept of a more fully developed continuum? Are there efforts that are producing poor results and that should be terminated or shifted to another department within the organization? These questions need to be revisited over time as programming needs and workplace conditions change.

This exercise allows the EAP and its partners to remove the functional barriers that inhibit good collaboration and improve resource allocation. It paves the way for joint endeavors and, at the same time, allows the development of specialization among the key players who most directly impact employees' support services.

A Holistic Approach to Service Delivery

Collaborative thinking sets the stage for developing a holistic approach to service delivery. A true biopsychosocial continuum will develop with fewer overlapping services and less duplication of effort. The potential for improved performance of each program component is illustrated by an individual case history: An employee sustains a fall at work that results in a serious sprain. During the course of his medical evaluation, he relates symptoms of weakness, dizziness, and recent weight loss. It is discovered that he is diabetic. The workers' compensation case manager develops a plan that includes a referral to the EAP to ensure that appropriate support services are available to the employee and the family to help them deal with a member who is facing a chronic illness. The health services staff provides on-site physical therapy as a part of the return-to-work plan. The workers' compensation case manager coordinates with the medical department to accommodate work restrictions and to allow the employee to return as soon as possible. The employee continues follow-up on diabetes management with the health services staff.

This more fully integrated approach to wellness reflects a biopsychosocial focus. This concept addresses the psychological aspects of interventions needed for persons with acute or chronic diseases and support for families during times of crisis and behavioral change. At times, medical and physical interventions are needed for some mental health and substance abuse treatment plans. By integrating efforts, the individual's and the family's needs are met in a holistic effort that allows for referrals among various departments. This empowers the employee to choose services viewed as desirable. Confidentiality is maintained as information is shared only on a need-to-know basis and is subject to informed consent.

Return to Health versus Return to Work

The preceding case history introduces an additional concept associated with the wellness continuum—the idea of "return to health" as opposed to a simple return to work.

Frequently people return to work before becoming completely rehabilitated and remain at risk for relapse or reinjury. A total case management approach is necessary to ensure the long-term health and well-being of consumers. Support services are reintroduced at a second at-risk stage in the continuum because people are vulnerable as they begin the progression to a return to health. Certainly the fields of chemical dependency and mental health have focused on after-care planning and follow-up as a crucial part of treatment. The same care and concern for disability management is true for acute and chronic medical conditions. Figure 22.2 depicts the cyclical nature of the return to health concept.

Developing a Business Plan

The philosophy of providing EA services and initiatives along the wellness continuum allows the development of an array of interventions that will benefit all potential consumers. The type and intensity of services is driven by location-specific needs. How to determine "what will sell" to all levels of the EA constituency is the greatest challenge to the professional. Adding value for management is a key. Providing necessary services to employees is crucial to union leadership. Targeting relevant issues is most important at the direct consumer level. Marketing is the key to successful business plan implementation, and knowing the audience is critical.

The first step in identifying location-specific needs is understanding what is driving the business. The EA professional must ask several questions of the organization.

- What has the management team set as its business targets?
- What issues has the team identified that require strategic planning?

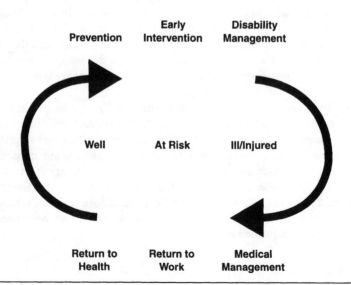

Figure 22.2   Total health strategic model.

- What EA or other human service initiatives will impact these issues?
- How does the EAP specifically set strategies that tie into the management plan?

The following case example describes the business planning process:

Positioning the Business Plan

Company X has 14 production sites scattered along the East Coast. Each plant produces specific products designed to meet a particular market niche. The oldest plant is experiencing problems with equipment repair, inventory shortages, and lack of increases in product pricing. The cost of production per employee has risen due to market issues as well as to an aging workforce whose medical claims and absentee rate has increased significantly in the past 2 years. The management team is faced with considering changing the product line and restructuring the workforce. Early retirement packages may be offered to 10% of the workforce within the next 9 months. Stress levels are reported to be high, and employee morale is low. Training for empowerment of work teams has been ongoing for 5 years, and there are pockets of success where restructuring has made a difference in productivity.

The management team has identified production costs as a target for reduction in the current fiscal year. Every department is developing goals and strategies that will impact per capita expenditures.

The human resources (HR) manager has set specific targets around cost containment for medical claims over the next 2 years. The EA professional begins collecting available data to determine potential areas for strategic planning that will directly impact healthcare costs.

Data Gathering

The goal of the management team and the HR department is the first piece of data necessary for beginning the business planning process. Next steps include collaborating with other departments to determine what additional information is available or needed to develop specific strategies. Data collection should include medical claims data on levels of payment by diagnostic categories, workers' compensation claims, accident and injury rates, demographics, absentee information, aggregate health-risk appraisal data, and past EA utilization rates by categories of presenting problems.

Equally valid data points include employee feedback through formal and informal mechanisms including satisfaction surveys, interest surveys, and focus-group results. Surveys conducted by other departments may also provide useful information on perceived needs. Advisory council members who have been promoting EA activities should have anecdotal data that is helpful in understanding how programming efforts are received and how they are really working.

After collecting relevant data, the EAP staff should evaluate the findings. This is best done jointly with all departments supplying the information so trends can be tracked and findings can be appropriately analyzed. Data should be collected for multiple years to avoid overinterpretation of immediate trends. For instance, a significant rise in chemical dependency cost from one year to another could indicate a successful awareness campaign that resulted in increasing self-referrals. It could also reflect supervisory training that resulted in spotting and referring troubled employees. It could also simply mean that there were no referrals for in-patient treatment one year. Caution should be exercised when comparative data is limited to a short period of time.

To develop specific goals and strategies, the EA professional will need to collect and review the strategic plans of other key departments such as: Wellness, Loss Prevention, Training, and Benefits. Vying for limited resources, training time, and the interest of various teams and work groups can cast potential partners in a competitive position. Partnering in strategy development is an evolutionary process and often follows the cycle of the EA professional first communicating the proposed EAP plan and asking other key players for information on their planned activities for the coming year. The next phase is seen as more collaborative when the data sharing and analysis leads to a better understanding of what each department has to offer. Avoidance of duplicating efforts or sending conflicting messages is an important by-product of collaboration. The most mature stage of partnering occurs when departments begin to integrate their planning efforts by jointly offering services and programs or by identifying the best positioned group to provide leadership for a given initiative. For example, the EAP and wellness services at an organization may both offer stress reduction initiatives. There may be overlapping messages regarding awareness and techniques for coping with stress. The Advisory Council members of each department recognize the redundancy as they are offered by both programs. The next year, the departments collaborate to offer a psychosocial approach through the EAP and a physical intervention through Wellness. When the departments integrate their business plans, mutually agreed upon targets, such as reduced cardiovascular costs, emerge. A single approach is developed with multiple strategies that reflect expertise of their own and other relevant departments. Overlapping services are reduced, and multiple approaches are offered that may result in a wider penetration of the targeted employees and families.

Training

Training is an example of true integration opportunities in an organization. When training efforts are being designed, it is incumbent upon the EAP to provide information that other departments may deliver. Marketing from within the EAP can be viewed as self-serving and promotional. If other departments include EAP messages in their training efforts, the EAP begins to be institutionalized into the fabric of the business's daily operations.

For example, when frontline supervisors and union stewards conduct training on early recognition and referral of troubled employees, addressing enabling behaviors in work groups and asking for work/personal life programs, then true early intervention has begun. If the EAP must continue to make formal presentations to supervisors and to employees representing service availability, little has happened to reflect the program's acceptance. As a result, the EAP's impact is questioned. When the EA message is delivered in regular training for supervisory skill building or is referenced in benefits enrollment meetings, then EAP is no longer an add-on, specialized service, but a part of the organizational structure or the benefit design.

Strategic Partnering

Who are strategic partners? Generally, strategic partners are the departments most closely aligned with the EAP through current organizational structures. For example, if reporting relationships exist that compliment one another in Human Resources, capitalize on them first. Health/Wellness Services, Medical, Benefits, Loss Prevention, Training, and Organizational Development are each strong partners who may be developing and delivering overlapping services and programs.

After collaborating or integrating with strategic partners, it is time to develop clear, measurable goals with specific key performance indicators that can be tracked. Expected outcomes should be stated with target dates for benchmarking progress. Assignment of responsibility may be included as well as identifying the potential partners for collaborative efforts. Strategies should reflect an effort to meet consumer needs at each point of the wellness continuum. Therefore, (1) a goal is clearly stated, (2) strategies identified, (3) key performance indicators set, and (4) evaluation criteria and time frames are developed.

Documentation

The following sample plan would be appropriate for the scenario of Company X developed earlier. The HR department has targeted healthcare cost containment for 2 years. Additional health-related cost data is collected and analyzed. The EAP determines that collaborating with the wellness and loss prevention groups will result in a leveraging of resources and a greater potential impact upon healthcare costs. A goal is set that reflects the need to reduce risk factors associated with lifestyle behaviors and work/life stress-related claims. A rationale statement provides the specific data that leads to the development of the strategic components of the plan. Evaluation criteria are set to measure success. The targeted outcomes may remain constant for a 2- to 3-year period, with strategies changing annually or less often as new initiatives replace what may not be working well. Table 22.1 represents a way of documenting the strategic business plan.

This outcomes-oriented business plan shows the management team how the EAP contributes to their efforts to impact the bottom line. The evaluation of success is based on real data and progress toward goals as opposed to utilization rates in the past. It has the potential of measuring what is being done *right* versus what has been done *well*. Ultimately this data-driven, outcomes-oriented planning requires innovation, rather than institutionalization of old programs.

The Business Plan as a Marketing Tool

Once the business plan has been completed, it is an excellent tool for marketing to key players throughout the organization. It should be shared with the local management team and union leadership, some of whom may have been involved in developing the plan. If the plan is shared early in the year, it should be reviewed for progress regularly with HR management and twice a year with the management team.

This sharing serves the dual purpose of obtaining management and business-unit approval and of keeping the EAP issues in front of these potential program advocates. It encourages their input and allows them to monitor the key performance indicators. Although reaching the goal may be far in the future, the incremental steps toward meeting the goal confirms the work being accomplished.

The business plan becomes the road map for the EAP staff and for the Advisory Council. Changing circumstances at a specific location present new or additional opportunities for immediate intervention, such as critical incident stress management (CISM)

Table 22.1   Key Performance Indicators

PREVENTION		
Objectives	Programs/Services/Initiatives	Key Performance Indicators
• To reduce the risk of heart attacks and heart failure.	*Health Services*	
	• Exercise Initiatives	• Exercise Program: 45% headcount completion
• To reduce risk of stress relating to work/life issues.	• Preventive Care Services	• Preventive Care: 83% headcount
	• Nutrition Awareness	• Nutrition: Promote consultations (2–3 articles)
• To reduce the risk factors associated with birth complications.	• Prenatal Program	• Prenatal Program: 85% of eligible enrolled
• To increase awareness of the effects and treatment options for substance abuse.	*EAP*	
	• Education & Awareness	• EAP: Articles in local publications quarterly
	• Work/Life Program	• Work/Life Program: 3 workshops by Dec. 31, with quarterly publicity
	• Substance Abuse: Awareness & Education	• Substance Abuse Awareness: SA Red Ribbon Day, Break Room information distribution bimonthly
	Health Services & EAP	
	• Joint News Articles	
	• Smoking Cessation	• Smoking Cessation: Information distributed by June 30

EARLY INTERVENTION		
Objectives	Programs/Services/Initiatives	Key Performance Indicators
• To manage high blood pressure and cholesterol levels.	*Health Services*	
	• Nutrition: One-on-one consultations	• Nutrition: Document one-on-one consultations
• To assist people with problems before they reach crisis proportions through EAP Work/Life.	• Preventive Care Services	• Preventative Care: 83% headcount
	• Cholesterol Education	• Follow-up at-risk cholesterol with letter to the home.
	• Exercise Activities	• Exercise: 22% employees participate
• To facilitate follow-up of at-risk people through preventative care strategies.	*EAP*	
	• Work/Life: Training	• Work/Life: 10% employees referrals
	• Peer Referral: Training	• Peer Referral: Plan in place in December '96.
	• Resource & Referral	• EAP: 200 referrals*
	• Impaired Worker Training	• Impaired Worker: Supervisory Training by December '96.
	• Drug-free Workplace Training	• Drug-free Training in 3rd quarter 1996
	EAP & Loss Prevention	
	• Crisis Intervention: Consultation & Planning	• Crisis Intervention: plan in place by 1st quarter

Table 22.1   (Continued)

	DISABILITY MANAGEMENT	
Objectives	Programs/Services/Initiatives	Key Performance Indicators
• To assist ill and injured employees to return to daily functions and activities of daily living. • To help keep them at work, focused, and healthy.	*Health Services* • Cardiac Rehabilitation • Physical Therapy: Back to work *EAP* • EAP: Back to work *EAP & Loss Prevention* • Disability Management	• Cardiac Rehabilitation: Contacted within 2 weeks of incident/ notification • Physical Therapy: Maintain costs below $30 per treatment visit • EAP: 2% increase in performance referrals • Disability Management: Contacted within 2 weeks of incident/notification; collaborate with Loss Prevention

*Includes Work/Life referrals

opportunities or benefit-redesign committee development. The EAP should be ready to provide crisis intervention or professional consultation when opportunities arise. However, the business plan should guide daily operations for the most part, rather than relying on one-time, hit-or-miss initiatives.

Sharing the plan and progress throughout the year with other departments and frontline managers allows them to identify opportunities for their departments to participate and to aid in the overall goal attainment, and it reminds them of the EAP's ability to consult with them on a variety of issues. This sharing allows more sources of feedback to the EAP on perceived future needs and actual performance. It also continues the evolution of collaboration to integration. For example, if labor relations is about to begin contract negotiations in a specific location, benefit-design issues go onto the bargaining table. If downsizing is being considered, the need for a strong behavioral health component is increased. Advocating for richer benefits may result in an overall reduction in medical claims in the future if early intervention is offered through an EAP/wellness/loss prevention/labor relations effort. Outplacement counseling, support for job training, "survivor" support, ergonomic evaluation and work hardening, coping with stress seminars, and other integrated efforts can impact grievances and performance problems before they begin.

The plan may also be effectively shared with external partners, such as behavioral health vendors, and with employees. This helps them understand why and how programming may be changing in the future. It acquaints them with the new philosophy and allows for more valuable input from their perspectives.

BARRIERS TO CHANGE

Outcomes Orientation versus Program Promotion

Effective business planning is a skill-building process based on a combination of training, experience, feedback, and reinforcement through goal attainment. Training human service staff to become outcome-driven versus program-promotion-driven is difficult. One company set aside three days of joint training for the EAP and health services staff to simulate the business-planning process. Scenarios were developed for several teams. Corporate staff role-played key partners who possessed valuable information necessary for developing an integrated business plan. The data was available, but the team had to identify the sources of data and collect it. They had to collaborate on analyzing the information, developing a rationale, and identifying measurable goals and targets. The staff struggled with developing plans that supported programs they wanted to continue because they had worked in the past or because they were state-of-the-art and made sense. The training focused on data collection and outcomes measures that would impact business efficiency and show true value added. When the frontline staff returned to their locations, they were prepared to try out the new planning process.

The first year after the training, the corporate staff reviewed the local plans and provided feedback designed to address both content and style. A Quality Control Checklist was designed to set the agenda for feedback sessions. These sessions included all EAP and health services staff members who participated in developing the plan. Future feedback sessions will include other stakeholders who become planning partners.

The following questions guided the feedback sessions:

- Are goals aligned with company objectives?
- Are goals aligned with department objectives?
- Are goals outcome-oriented?
- Are strategies consistent with outcomes desired?
- Is there balance among prevention, early intervention, and disability management?
- Is there alignment between outcomes and activities?
- Is the plan succinct?

The following two questions forced the EAP and health services staff to think about the implications of the planning process and reinforced the need to take ownership of the plan, rather than viewing it as a paper exercise for the corporate staff:

- How will you use the business plan?
- How can we at the corporate level help you continue to utilize business planning strategically?

By the second planning cycle, the targets were more realistic and desired outcomes were more clearly articulated.

Time

Time poses a problem when collaboration is a key ingredient of the planning process. Every department is busy, and this process has to become valuable to each player in order to be successful. Meetings should have clear, expected outcomes with next steps delineated, including realistic timelines and assignment of leadership responsibilities.

Key players emerge with a sense of commitment to the plan and an awareness of the potential related to becoming a team player. Leveraging resources to maximize the impact on the bottom line must be a mutually accepted goal.

Functional Silo Syndrome

Functional silo syndrome continues to exist in most large, decentralized companies. It occurs when departments plan and deliver services in traditional ways, focusing only on input from immediate consumers and internal staff. Old ways of doing business can change when territoriality and turf issues are addressed directly. A commitment to modeling a collaborative approach by seeking input and help in service delivery from other groups challenges the EAP's own way of thinking. The EAP may need to serve as a catalyst to breaking down existing walls around its own shop. For instance:

- Does the EAP need to head the critical incident management effort, or would critical incident debriefing better fit the mandate of the emergency response team with backup from the EAP?
- Could a health resource library house EAP and work/family materials?
- Should smoking cessation efforts be part of medical?
- Can recognizing troubled employee training be entrusted to the organizational development department?

Giving up direct responsibility and delegating tasks can strengthen programs perceived to be jointly sponsored.

Fear of Unknown

Fear of the unknown or of failure can keep people from trying new approaches. Concerns about documenting desired outcomes and about not hitting the mark may interfere with initially setting realistic goals that stretch resources. Initially, goals may need to be modest. Key performance indicators should be attainable, and a feedback mechanism should be built in that allows for the explanation of both progress or lack of progress toward the targets. The key performance indicators should be negotiable with no significant penalty for risk taking. They are not the ultimate indicators of success.

Sacred Cows

Being aware of "sacred cows" is very important. In one instance, a well-documented, well-informed decision was made to discontinue a particular initiative, replacing it with a much improved product. The plan was communicated well to upward levels of the organization, and management approved the change. But the employees were informed of the change just prior to the typical implementation date of the old program. The level of the ground swell of resistance to change was unexpected.

Communication throughout the organization is critical, and change is a process. It may be appropriate to make a significant change in one location quickly and cleanly. In another location, a strategic, well-planned approach may be more desirable. Employee and union approval will help EAP and wellness staff to not move too quickly in giving up something that is both working well and "doing the right thing" from the customer's perspective.

Communicating the Big Picture

Helping the key players see the big picture takes time and the ability to get their attention. These efforts should be carefully planned and orchestrated with the EAP champion within the corporation and at the specific location. The EAP should maximize the time available by delivering clear messages. Corporate staff should develop a good communication tool that can be customized for location-specific delivery. A common, consistent message is crucial in reinforcing the belief that the EAP is outcomes-oriented and ready to deliver services that impact the bottom line. The communication plan can be incremental in presentation, or it can be a full-blown approach to acquainting key constituencies with the changing philosophies that drive program planning.

The key elements described earlier in the chapter should be the focus of the communication tool. For example, primary, secondary, and tertiary prevention should be defined and coupled with the wellness continuum. A holistic approach clarifying biopsychosocial elements should be explained. The efficiency of integration of departmental efforts should be highlighted. The "return to health" concept as opposed to a simple "return to work" ethic should be developed. Outcomes orientation based on location-specific needs identified through various modalities of data collection should be emphasized. Overheads or handouts for a 10-to-15 minute presentation should be developed so the message can be delivered one-on-one in a senior manager's office or to the entire HR staff at a specific location.

FUTURE IMPLICATIONS FOR EAP/STRATEGIC BUSINESS UNIT ALIGNMENT

The integrated approach to EAP planning has great potential power in planning and delivering services that impact overall organizational health. As companies recognize the need to compete in a global market, the stress associated with continuous improvement and change never abates. Transitions are a way of life that, even when welcomed, impact the health and well-being of individuals throughout the organization. Productivity and profitability are directly related to the care and maintenance of human capital as well as of machines and technology. The EAP is a critical partner in developing approaches for identifying and handling stress associated with organizational change. Let's return to the case of Company X.

Company X is spending 1 year examining its product line, evaluating its viability in the global market, questioning its current management structure, and readying itself for future opportunities for mergers or buyouts. Several production sites have shown low profitability for several years and have been targeted for significant change. The plant facilities are older and require a high level of maintenance. Many employees have 20 years of longevity and if retirement packages are offered, those employees will be willing to leave. What can an integrated total health service offer this organization?

A heightened awareness of traditional EAP, health services, and organizational development interventions should be given to managers, union leadership, frontline supervisors, union stewards, employees, and family members. Promotion of stress-reduction programs, the benefits of exercise, and the proactive management of chronic disease are important strategies to be offered. Team building and empowerment training have probably already been in place and efforts are likely to increase around redesigning workflow. Workplace violence policies and procedures should be reviewed, and action plans should be put in place should an incident occur. Work/personal-life-balance programming should be in place and promoted in anticipation of life events that add to work stress. Benefit packages should be prepared and out-placement services developed to aid employees in transition.

These initiatives can be offered by individual departments and coordinated by a HR manager. They also could be offered collaboratively with an additional focus on what happens with the survivors of the restructuring process. Prevention and early intervention efforts are crucial if productivity is to increase in the midst of significant transitions. Early retirements often result in loss of expertise, overwork for those who are left, anticipation of the next change, and increase in medical claims due to accidents and injuries or stress.

An integrated team will step forward with a plan for coping with the continual change. Possible actions include developing working relationships so that cross-functional teams become consultants for individual work groups, helping the group anticipate and prepare for the stresses the transitions are bringing. EAP, health services, organizational development, and other HR staff people are trained to lead focus groups to address the change process. The individual work group is trained to recognize that resistance to change is normal and to evaluate where it stands in the change process. The group develops a strategy and an accepting culture that allows for expression of feelings while moving the process forward. Steps for change are developed with target dates and clear assignment of responsibility.

As people are assigned new jobs, their individual training needs are identified and a plan developed for skill building necessary for success. People moving from more sedentary jobs to ones requiring increased physical activities may need an ergonomic assessment of their work station or work hardening to prepare them for increased physical strain. What are the new job requirements? What are the new employee's abilities or limitations? Should the work area be redesigned? Does a work-hardening intervention need to be offered?

Psychologically, are the individuals in the work group ready to move forward? Any change process produces anxiety, and grieving over the loss of the old way of doing business must occur. Is the supervisor ready? Does more team building need to occur? Are any team members showing signs of stress that is interfering with their performance at work or in their personal life? Should the EAP be suggested, or is a job-performance referral warranted?

Who needs to be a resource to the work group to clarify management expectations or union contract language? Who is an advocate for proactive approaches to coping with change? Who is responsible for communication, and who is responsible for action?

An integrated organizational health team is the catalyst for identifying problems and for developing strategic interventions that move the change process positively, rapidly, and safely. The EA professional brings a strong skill set to a cross-functional team, which is crucial for the survival and the ongoing success of the work site specifically and of the company as a whole. Reflective listening, brief problem-resolution approaches, evaluation and intervention around entrenched behavioral patterns, constructive confrontation, goal setting, and monitoring goals are part of the EAP arsenal that can be applied in the organizational development effort of a company facing significant change.

Outcomes-oriented planning will result in positive results for individuals, for naturally occurring work groups, and for the company as a whole. Individuals will see an improvement in health, an enhanced sense of well-being, and a reduction in healthcare costs. Work teams will function at a higher level with improved morale, better decision making, and decreased productivity costs. The company will experience improved productivity and increased profitability.

REFERENCES

Amaral, T., & Harlow, K. (1996). The future of employee assistance: Integrated occupational health systems. *Many Parts One Purpose,* 42–43.

Employee Assistance Professionals Association, Inc. (1996). *Many Parts One Purpose* (25th Anniversary Commemorative Journal). Arlington, VA: EAP Association.

CHAPTER 23

Organizational Counseling and the Delivery of Integrated Human Services in the Workplace: An Evolving Model for Employee Assistance Theory and Practice

MARK R. GINSBERG, RICHARD R. KILBURG, and PAULA G. GOMES

The Sultan Corporation (a fictitious company) is a large, diversified, and decentralized manufacturing and service company. Sultan employs 6,000 people, many of whom have been with the company for at least 10 years. Historically, loyalty to the company was high, and many of the employees had parents who worked for Sultan when it was a small manufacturing firm making replacement parts for the secondary automobile market. Eight years ago, the company merged with a larger firm, and Sultan began to serve multiple markets and to manufacture products for automobiles and mechanical parts for other engines. They also purchased a network of service centers in nine western states. Its management team moved the company's central headquarters to another state. A vice-president was brought in to run the new Sultan "Division," and the former Sultan managers were terminated. To be sure, the culture of the company changed, as did the management structure and corporate philosophy.

A manufacturing unit of Sultan that employs 500 people had been a stable part of the company for many years. The unit was profitable because it manufactured an important component part for a particular kind of automobile engine. Competition had recently sprung up, and newer engines required fewer replacement parts. The profits of the unit declined, and with diminished profits came more pressure from Sultan Management to develop new markets and new products. There was a rumor that the unit would soon be downsized and that most of the manufacturing jobs would be moved to another state to be blended into a new plant recently acquired by the company. The unit manager, who had been with Sultan for 26 years, left the company with a buyout plan. Some managers and line staff believed that he was forced out. One unit manager recently was divorced, and another senior supervisor frequently has been absent from work. Several months ago, a rumor circulated throughout the unit that he had a drinking problem and would be out of work for about a month. Many plant workers reported feeling stressed, absenteeism was rampant, and the talk among most concerned how to find a new job before the "other shoe drops" and there were layoffs. Everyone was scared, and the stress level in the plant was very high. Morale had never been this bad.

One of the Sultan managers contacted the employee assistance program (EAP) for a consultation on how to deal with the multilevel issues that were emerging throughout the new plant. The manager was alarmed about the problems that were developing for individuals, work teams, and the entire organization.

INTRODUCTION

Sultan, although a fictitious company, is not unique. Many organizations today are in the midst of similar types of major corporate change. The issues facing Sultan and the impact of changes made by its leadership team affected corporate philosophy and culture, as well as all of its employees. In this example, the impact of change on Sultan and its employees is both dramatic and traumatic.

In many corporations like Sultan, EAPs have been available to assist troubled employees and often their families. However, like many industries and corporations, the employee assistance (EA) field also is in the midst of major change. Historically, EAPs have been linked to health benefit structures and to the overall human resources functions of sponsoring organizations. Although the EA field has continued to evolve, and most large and many smaller organizations now have programs as a component of their health benefits or human resources operations, EAPs today are in the process of significant change. As the healthcare delivery system has been transformed and as the human resources development function in many organizations in which they are embedded has evolved and changed, EAPs have started to redefine and expand their purpose, operating philosophy, and service-delivery model.

In recent years, with the recognition and experience of cases like the Sultan Company, the EA field has evolved from its historical emphasis on individual impairment to a broader focus on promoting both the health of the workforce and the productivity of the workplace. Consequently, the roles and functions of EA professionals have evolved from an individual focus to a more systemic view. This shift and the resulting conceptual changes that many EA professionals have adopted are consistent with the use of a systems model for understanding the behavioral challenges faced by organizations. In light of this shift, the EA field now must become more closely aligned with the theory and practice of organizational development. This evolution in EA is identified as *organizational counseling* (OC) and can be viewed as a new service component of the core technology in a fully functional EAP program. OC is a framework for behavioral interventions that are directed to individuals and groups within the workplace. The goals of the OC approach are to restore or to enhance the emotional and interpersonal functioning of members of the workforce, and their families and significant others, as a means to assist employees in performing their jobs and to strengthen the enterprise by facilitating organizational development.

ORGANIZATIONAL COUNSELING: A CONTEMPORARY MODEL FOR EMPLOYEE ASSISTANCE PRACTICE

Organizational counseling, as an expansion of the core technology of EAPs, embraces the traditional broad-brush approach of most programs with its emphasis on the identification, assessment, and referral for treatment of individuals and family members with mental health and substance abuse/chemical dependency problems. OC integrates within this traditional model for EA practice an increased emphasis on understanding the dynamics and ecology of an organization. Through this OC perspective, the organization itself becomes a client, understood through the application of organizational and systems theories, while the core EA technologies that emphasize working directly and confidentially with employees and their families are also maintained.

The purposes of this chapter are to describe the developing model for OC and the integrated human services system that has been established at The Johns Hopkins University and Hospital. The chapter summarizes some of the salient concepts from the field of organizational development that are integral to this model, provides several case examples to illustrate this approach, and offers suggestions with respect to the ongoing development of this area of practice by EA professionals.

THEORETICAL OVERVIEW

Today's large organizations are complex, rapidly changing, and multifaceted institutions. High-performing enterprises have been characterized as those that recognize that their effectiveness is enhanced by promoting the development of the organization, in part, by assisting its members to confront and manage successfully both personal and professional challenges. In our OC model, organizational counselors can be viewed as primary providers of services within an organization who focus on helping employees to succeed. The well-prepared organizational counselor can focus both on issues that challenge individuals within an enterprise and on the organization itself. These may include personal issues such as depression, anxiety, family conflict, and chemical dependency, as well as workplace challenges such as the impact on employees of a reorganization, interpersonal conflict, or the changes that result from a shift in management philosophy. The EA professional practicing within the enhanced OC core technology may intervene with the individual and may also participate in an intervention directed to an organization or a unit in trouble. In smaller organizations, properly trained EA professionals working from the expanded core technology may well provide a broad spectrum of individual and organizational interventions. In larger organizations, EA professionals will most frequently collaborate with specialists from fields such as organizational development, training, or human resources to provide an expanded, multidisciplinary, team-based range of services. The metaphor is that in some settings the EA professional may need to function like a small town, family doctor or a traditional general practitioner, whereas in larger organizations the EA professional often will be the point of entry to a multidisciplinary team of colleagues.

The OC model is consistent with the suggestion by Maloof, Governale, and Berman (1997) that many contemporary EAPs are struggling to find their identity within the changing realm of behavioral health practice and within the rapidly changing organizational schema to which they are linked. Maloof et al. suggest recasting the EAP as a corporate assistance program (CAP). A sampling of the roles and functions of their newly defined corporate assistance program professional (CAPP) includes organizational conflict management and resolution, team building, design of work/family-related programs, benefits review, and more general community development activities within the institution and between the enterprise and its community partners.

The OC model applies a systems approach (Von Bertalanffy, 1950) in seeking to understand the many parts of an organization as well as the interrelationship of the parts. The emphasis of the OC model has been on working to enhance the functioning of the parts while acknowledging that "the whole is greater than the sum of its parts." This approach is embedded in a developmental model, which is compatible with our systemic perspective. This approach follows the general tenets of, and borrows generously from, a life-development model (Danish, D'Augelli, & Ginsberg, 1984). This model:

- Incorporates statements about desirable goals.
- Focuses on sequential change.
- Provides remediative assistance as necessary, while emphasizing approaches that promote individuals and organizational development.
- Considers the challenges identified within their context.
- Views the context as part of an ever-changing organizational entity.

The OC approach springs from the traditional core technology of EA practice but now joins to it the theory and practice of organizational behavior and development. Table 23.1 provides an illustration of the blending of the principles and practices of both EAP and OC.

EMPLOYEE ASSISTANCE PRACTICE AND ORGANIZATIONAL DEVELOPMENT: AN IMPORTANT STRATEGIC ALLIANCE

Smither, Houston, and McIntire (1996) defined *organizational development* (OD) as the theory and practice of bringing planned change to organizations. They further suggest that OD is "concerned with improving organizational effectiveness, developing new approaches to organizational problems, and providing for the psychological well-being of organizational members" (p. 6). Historically, OD practitioners also have

Table 23.1   A Model for Organizational Counseling That Blends Traditional Elements of EA Practice with an Added Emphasis of the Organization as a Client

Employee Assistance Practice	Organizational Counseling Practice
Emphasis on the individual and family	Emphasis on the organization and in organizational units
Mental health interventions	Organizational change
Chemical dependency/substance abuse treatment	Personal growth of organizational members
Assessment, triage, and referral	Organizational assessment
Psychological counseling	Organizational consultation and coaching
Prevention and promotion of human development	Team building with focus on organizational health
Crisis intervention	Change management
Benefits consultation	Managerial training
Disability and care management	Performance monitoring and appraisal
Work/family interface	Supervisor/supervisee interface
Personal relationship enhancement	Workplace communication enhancement

drawn upon psychological principles of human development and the intrinsic need that individuals have for growth. The OD model has also been extended to include the needs that organizations have for growth that parallel the needs of the individuals that comprise the enterprise. From an earlier era with its emphasis on T-groups and focus on communication and relationships, to its current emphasis on the issues of organizational culture and climate, social and behavioral science have been fundamental to the OD field.

A basic characteristic for both OC and OD is the belief that the people who comprise the organization are the most important predictors of organizational success and of how an organization functions. This basic characteristic does not suggest that organizational structures or processes are unimportant; rather it affirms the significance of the workforce as the primary ingredient of all organizational operations. Consequently, many OD professionals focus on the interface between individual roles and functions and the structure and processes of the organization itself. In our revised OC model, the organizational counselor must be prepared to understand and to intervene at multiple levels and with subsystems of the organization in which they are working. This perspective is similar to the cybernetic model for transforming organizations recently postulated by Espejo, Schuhmann, Schwaninger, and Bilello (1996). Their model, also reliant on systems theory as an orienting construct, shifts thinking about organizational functioning from linear explanations to systemic formulations and the principle of circular causality. They suggested that actions have reactions and consequences that produce change. They also suggested, consistent with systems theory, that effective organizations "develop the cohesion of the whole and the autonomy of individual participants" (p. 105), which they view as synergistic.

Our work at The Johns Hopkins University and Hospital suggests that there is a powerful and positive correlation between human development, as experienced by individuals and their families, and organizational development, as experienced in an enterprise. Recently, members of our research team developed a new model of organizational regression that is useful for describing the levels of functioning of organizations or subunits and for determining when OC interventions may be useful (Kilburg, Stokes, & Kuruvilla, 1997). This model, which integrates psychodynamic and systems theories, suggests that organizations must manage both internal and external regressive forces by creating or using internal balancing forces in order to prevent dysfunctional regression that can dramatically and adversely influence performance. *Internal regressive forces* include individual needs, the dynamics of the individual and of their family systems, group dynamics of the organization, leadership and followership issues, the physical and mental health of the persons within the organization, and the meta issue of organizational health. *External regressive forces* include the pressures of the marketplace, resource issues, issues of technology, and the economics and demographics of the industry of which the organization is a part. *Balancing forces* include the interpersonal and emotional maturity of leaders and staff; managerial competency; clarity of vision, mission, and values; and effective organizational structures and processes.

There are six identifiable stages in this model, ranging from Phase I, superresiliency, to Phase VI, the dying organization. Table 23.2 provides a description of each of the six phases that can characterize organizations within this model. When an organization experiences regression, a wide variety of efforts may be made to ameliorate its effects. In superresilient and normal organizations, these efforts are sufficient to prevent the organization from further decline. However, when efforts to enhance organizational coping or to ameliorate regression are unsuccessful and the enterprise slips

Table 23.2   Characteristics and Phases of Organizational Regression

Characteristics of the Organization	Phase I Superresiliency	Phase II Normal Operations	Phase III Regressive Oscillations	Phase IV Visible Regressive Patterns	Phase V Chaotic Organization	Phase VI Dying Organization
1. Organizational problems	Growth and adaptation Internal integration External adaptation	Growth Adaptive problems Internal integration External adaptation	Adaptive problems and some recurrent problems	Adaptive, recurrent, and permanent problems	Permanent problems Organizationally threatening	Permanent problems Organizationally threatening
2. Behavioral symptoms	Problem solving Creativity Communication Trust Humor Curiosity Sublimation Love	Transient effects Behavioral colds	Transient effects and symptoms Patterns of symptoms appear for periods of time and then disappear	Quasi-permanent and visibly maladaptive symptoms	Permanent and visible maladaptive symptoms	Flagrant and out-of-control maladaptive symptoms
3. Coping methods	Individual and organization development and enhancement Fix the problem not the blame.	Sufficient internal coping and regulation Some development and enhancement	Internal coping breakdowns Recurring injuries Equilibrium mostly reestablished	Internal coping failures Permanent injuries Equilibrium Failures in some areas	Regular failures of coping efforts Permanent visible injuries Visible equilibrium failures	Most coping efforts have ceased
4. Organizational performance	Excellent Goals achieved A healthful place to work	Goals typically achieved Mostly a healthful place to work	Goals reached with strains and lapses Some real problems Unhappy people	Goals are hard to attain Ill people Low morale Real achievement problems	Chronic underperformance Very low morale Acting out Turnover Organization's future is threatened	Goals are not attained High turnover of best people Acting out among those that remain Organization dying
5. Organizational consequences	Healthy returns Effective organization Normal stresses and strains	Solid returns Effective organization Stresses and strains No permanent consequences	In the black, but often shaky Periodic failures Periodic identifiable consequences	Periodic deficits Unpredictably predictable failures Permanent identifiable consequences (loss of market share)	Chronic deficits Predictable failures Permanent identifiable consequences (loss of market share; lack of innovation)	Death, dismemberment, and imminent liquidation
6. Restoration/enhancement approaches	Reflective Dialogue and metalogue development Strategic vision Cognitive complexity	Reflection Dialogue and metalogue Crisis management development Vision Cognitive complexity	Crisis management Fire fighting Some development and planning efforts Attempts at dialogue	Chronic crisis management and fire fighting Episodic flights into health Islands of sanity in the organization	Fire fighting Infighting Lifeboat behavior Heroic measures	Heroic measures fail Too little, too late
7. Descriptive metaphor	Radiant sunlight	Solar flares	Sun spots	Jupiter storms	Dying planets and stars	Black holes

or jumps into Phase III, IV, or V level functioning, they become candidates for OC interventions. These approaches can be used to restore equilibrium, to enhance operations, and to return the unit to normal levels of function in which more traditional OD or training interventions can be successful. The regression model is helpful to practitioners for making this crucial determination, because if an organizational unit has slipped into Phase IV or V level regression, OC techniques are necessary before other methods are applied (Kilburg, Ginsberg, & Gomes, 1997). The case examples and methods presented at the end of this chapter provide descriptions of the types of activities to include in OC interventions.

The OD field is a large and diverse domain. There are a multitude of theories, training programs, and suggested models for practice; however, OD has now become an important partner for the EA field. Without an ability to stretch beyond its traditional boundaries, an EAP will forever be constrained to deal with the consequences of organizational regression by helping individual members of the workforce cope with their symptoms but will not be able to change some of the most rudimentary causes of these problems. EAPs are strengthened by capitalizing on this suggested alliance, both through the deployment of the expanded core technology of OC as a valuable and powerful framework for EA practice and through increasing collaboration among EA professionals and professionals from other related human service fields. The Johns Hopkins University and Hospital has developed internal human service and EAPs within this evolving perspective.

THE JOHNS HOPKINS MODEL FOR INTEGRATED HUMAN SERVICE DELIVERY IN THE WORKPLACE

The Johns Hopkins model for integrated human service delivery in the workplace is consistent with the rubric for OC. The Office of Human Services contains Career Management, WorkLife, Training and Education, Organization Development and Diversity, and EAPs. Through the multidisciplinary, collaborative efforts of the talented members of its staff, a broad array of services have been developed and implemented with the goal of enhancing the resiliency and effectiveness of the Hopkins institutions and the individual members of its community. In addition, the office strives to prevent organizational dysfunction and its potentially lethal effects, and it works hard toward improving the capacity of its people to do their jobs and to live productive, healthy, and fulfilling lives. In its integrated human service model, the enhanced, OC-oriented, core technology of the Johns Hopkins EAP is often blended with the consultative strategies of organizational development and expanded collaboration with professionals from the training, career management, and WorkLife staff members. This integrated human services model provides a platform through which OC interventions can be successfully implemented. This approach blends the more action-centered, OC-enhanced EAP with other service-delivery units to focus on individual, family, and organizational development.

ORGANIZATIONAL MAKEUP

Johns Hopkins is a large, urban, decentralized, and diverse organization that includes eight academic divisions and the Applied Physics Laboratory within the university system. Two large hospitals and a set of interrelated healthcare enterprises make up its health system. A number of other interdependent organizations also operate under the umbrella of Johns Hopkins. The institution is the largest private employer in Maryland and one of the largest organizations in the Middle Atlantic region. The collective organizations employ approximately 25,000 people. The units of the institution are spread across a relatively large geographic region in the Baltimore, Maryland/Washington, DC, metropolitan areas, with a number of satellite units in other states and countries. The individual units of the organization can range in size from less than 10 to nearly 10,000 employees, depending on how they are defined within the structure, and each has its own subculture. The university's experience, over the past twelve years, has been that the unique ecology of the components of the organization must be considered in the design and delivery of services to any of its organizational components. In addition, like most organizations, Johns Hopkins continues to evolve and change at a rapid rate. Consequently, the intervention activities of the integrated human services programs must remain sensitive to the context within which its units operate and to the ever-changing nature of the structures and people that comprise the institutions.

EARLY EAP EFFORTS

In 1986, an EAP was developed across most of the Johns Hopkins system. The original model for the Johns Hopkins Faculty and Staff Assistance Program (FASAP), the blended institutional EAP, was founded on the assumption that a broad-brush program could serve the needs of the employees who comprise the institution as well as their families. FASAP continues as one of the core programs that comprise our integrated human services delivery system. FASAP staff provide assessment, triage and referral services, brief counseling, crisis intervention and critical-incident-stress-related services, and consultation about the management of both mental health/chemical dependency services and behavioral/interpersonal issues. FASAP staff also frequently collaborate with staff from other programs as part of multidisciplinary project teams. FASAP staff provide direct services annually to more than 1,500 individuals and numerous consultations to management and supervisory staff on employee-related issues. FASAP staff also are involved with benefits design and other human resources policy issues. The staff of the FASAP include three doctoral-level psychologists, including the Director and Associate Director; six master's-prepared counselors or social workers; three part-time, medical consultants; three administrative staff; and a research assistant. The FASAP program operates from three clinical sites convenient to the major institutional campus settings. In 1992, the broad-brush EAP model for the FASAP was integrated within a larger structure that was formed and identified as the Office of Human Services (OHS) (Ginsberg, Kilburg, & Gomes, 1994). OHS (outlined in the earlier discussion of the Johns Hopkins model) is the institutional structure within the central human resources division of the university that serves as the hub for the development and coordination of human services programs for employees and their families. Each of the other four OHS programs are described briefly.

JHU WorkLife Program

The JHU WorkLife Program provides information and referral services regarding family issues such as child care, elder care, and other developmental and critical-event issues faced by the families of Johns Hopkins employees. This program's focus is assisting employees in creating a comfortable balance between the demands of the workplace and the challenges of personal life. The program operates a statewide database for child-care and elder-care referrals, sponsors a wide array of educational programs and support groups, and serves as an institutional clearinghouse for matters pertinent to family development. Although similar to other such programs that have been developed in industry, this program was one of the earliest such programs within a higher education setting. There are five members of this staff, including one administrative support person and four professionals, including one master's-level social worker and a doctorate in social work who is the program's director.

Organizational Development and Diversity Program

The Organizational Development and Diversity Program provides to institutional managers and supervisors an array of consultative services, such as leadership coaching, organizational assessment, diversity and process consultation, sociotechnical systems interventions, retreat design and facilitation, strategic planning, and crisis intervention. This program employs four experienced OD consultants and is a well-respected unit within the organization, which routinely is consulted about a wide range of organizational challenges and problems. The program also emphasizes facilitating a greater understanding and integration of diversity initiatives within the institution. This unit has grown in 4 years from a single staff person to the current four-person professional staff of internal OD consultants. Three of the consultants have doctoral degrees and the fourth has two master's degrees. Two administrative support people provide assistance to this program.

The Education and Training Center

The Education and Training Center was designed as a university-wide program to coordinate and offer training programs for faculty and staff. More than 200 courses are held annually, including training with respect to administrative procedures, finance, management, supervision, interpersonal skills, team development, leadership development, and laboratory procedures. The center operates from a modern training facility, and staff also conduct on-site training programs across the university. The director has a doctoral degree in education with a concentration in adult learning and training.

The JHU Career Management Program

The JHU Career Management Program for faculty and staff offers a variety of career-centered services. Like the other programs within the OHS, employees are able to participate in the activities of this center without fee. Services include career assessments, career planning, job-search coaching, and, when indicated and necessary, informal outplacement, dual-career assistance, and mentoring. The staff of this unit is comprised of three master's-level career counselors and two administrative people.

OHS Collaboration

The five programs within the OHS work in collaboration with each other, that is, staff from these programs frequently form interprogram teams to offer assistance both to individuals within the workplace and to organizational units of the workplace. The working style fosters cooperation among team members and results in value-added opportunities for human service delivery within the organization. As a group, these five, interrelated, service-delivery centers provide the foundation for an integrative approach to human services delivery in the workplace.

Collaboration must take place on several levels. First, a multidisciplinary team is considered as a powerful grouping of professionals to implement a highly effective intervention. Our collaborative teams are comprised of psychologists or other mental health personnel, OD specialists, career counselors, HR professionals, and other individuals who can contribute to the overall project (Stokes, 1997). Second, relationship development among team members and project management is essential to ensuring a high level of team functioning. It is imperative that time and attention be devoted to establishing a high-performing project team. Key factors that are useful for establishing these teams include:

- The development of appropriate and successful communication mechanisms among the consultation team.
- The establishment of mechanisms for managing conflict on the consultation team.
- Opportunities for discussion concerning each team member's strengths, challenges, and skill areas for coordinating the implementation of the intervention.
- Scheduling regular debriefing and feedback meetings.

Attention to each of these identified components is necessary to ensure the success of multiprogram projects.

There a number of interrelated steps to design and implement a collaborative project. At JHU, an individual client usually calls on one of the programs to provide services. In that process, the staff member can identify that there may be a need for other services to be deployed. That staff member may call for a collaborative project with other component programs within OHS via a written request, which may be sent over e-mail. Next, a project team assembles, compares information, and develops a preliminary plan for the approaching intervention. When working with institutional subsystems, this stage of the project is an opportunity to develop a strategy for entering the organizational system. After entering the system and considering the understanding of the challenge or problem from a more systemic perspective, the process of intervention design can begin. The intervention design process, like the assessment phase, also relies on a foundation of collaboration with the client system.

The actual intervention processes take different forms. The range of intervention options includes counseling with individuals and/or groups, consistent with traditional EA practices; career counseling; managerial and executive coaching; technical consultation about issues such as human resources policies; other OD interventions; and educational interventions such as seminars and workshops. Frequently, several modalities are applied concurrently. For example, one member of a project team may work with a supervisor or a manager using an executive coaching approach. Another team member helps to identify and establish a personal-intervention program for an employee experiencing a specific stressful life event, while several other team members may be collaborating in conducting a group process intervention with a small group of employees experiencing interpersonal conflict. A fourth team member is providing technical information to the unit administrator about a specific human resource policy, while the training team members are collaborating in the delivery of a workshop on interpersonal relationships in the workplace. In complex, conflict-ridden subunits, OC interventions are most often used early in an effort to move the organization to a higher level of functioning in which other services can prove useful. This approach is multimodal and often is characterized by a series of concurrent initiatives.

Throughout an intervention, a variety of communication and decision-making processes are used to help keep the members of the team co-oriented in their efforts and to prevent them from working at cross purposes. Finally, although the critical component of our activities is intervention design and delivery, program evaluation is essential. Whenever possible, evaluations should consider both formative and summative issues, as well as utilization patterns including resource allocation, cost-effectiveness, and other related issues and factors. Johns Hopkins programs seek to identify collaboratively with its clients benchmarks for evaluating the success of the interventions. In this way, the responsibility for success is shared among all parties to the assessment and the interventions, including both consultants and clients.

CASE EXAMPLES

The next section of this chapter offers several case studies that serve as examples of Johns Hopkins's integrated and collaborative approach to human services delivery in the workplace. The case studies provide descriptive reviews of the specific projects and the client systems; an overview of the approach used for assessment and goal setting, which focuses on strengths and challenges; a review of the actual interventions; and a report with respect to the evaluation of outcome variables.

Example 1

Definition of the Problem

The first example involves a medium-sized organization within the university. It is both an applied unit and a highly respected research center. The organization, directed by a world-renown research scientist, is comprised of about 300 people and is divided into approximately 20 research laboratory and service centers. Its staff is diverse with respect to age, gender, and ethnicity. The director, a caucasian male, has a generally passive management style and frequently is absent for more than a month at a time. Historically, he is known for taking strong positions on issues for which he has a personal interest. Although well liked, he also is feared by some as a powerful and reasonably unpredictable leader.

Several issues emerged that created an organizational crisis and resulted in organizational chaos. Much of the difficulty initially was confined to a single laboratory. Over time, however, the problems spread to other parts of the organization and ultimately to other parts of the university.

The leader of the organization contacted a senior organization development specialist (OS) for assistance. The presenting problem, initially, was that a number of research grants were up for renewal and were not likely to be re-funded. This lack of fiscal support could result in a reduction in work for the lab and in the need to terminate a number of technical staff. The OS was asked to assist the leader in navigating the transitions that would need to occur with the likely reduction in force (RIF).

During the initial assessment, it was learned that the funding crisis actually stemmed from one laboratory director's personal crisis. He had been out of work for several long periods of time over the past few years, which left him unable to seek renewals to several major grants. This person was a well-regarded senior scientist with a long, successful track record for grant development, and he supervised a staff of about 20 people. During periods of his absence, he left a senior associate in charge of the operations, yet did so without announcement about the interim leadership arrangements. This left the associate unable to act decisively with respect to funding or personnel issues. It also resulted in a vacuum in leadership and in a sense of urgency driven by funding anxiety. Historically, the unit's leader had little contact with the laboratory director and permitted him to operate as if he were a lone entrepreneur within a facility-based cooperative. (Parenthetically, this relational style characterizes many university research centers.)

As the OS continued the assessment, interviews were conducted with the key leaders, which illuminated significant conflict among several of the senior associates of the laboratory. The catalyst for the conflict was the ambiguity in the leadership-succession issues during the time of the laboratory director's absence, and the conflict was being fueled by the anxiety of the funding crisis, which was known by all, yet never discussed in any formal or sanctioned way. Furthermore, there were significant differences in interpersonal and work styles among the three people most in conflict. The dynamic seemed, at first, to be a two-versus-one situation. Later this shifted, and there was no longer an affiliation or a collusion. This conflict had become dysfunctional to the system, with others in the lab choosing sides.

The model for understanding regression in organizations (Kilburg, Stokes, & Kuruvilla, 1997) provides a useful perspective for understanding the challenges and the levels of function and dysfunction of the unit. The regressive elements of this unit predict the symptoms identified through the early part of the assessment process. Although functional, as evidenced by the unit's ability to continue operating despite the wealth of problems, the coping success of the unit was believed to be a consequence of the relative autonomy and differentiation of several reasonably high-functioning individuals within the unit. Overall, the organizational health of the unit and the dynamics of organizational regression were hypothesized to be negatively influenced by a series of issues concerning leadership, financial struggles driven by external factors as well as by internal performance-based issues, poor patterns of communication characterized by indirect communication mechanisms and imprecise use of language, and interpersonal conflicts among individuals with several factions forming and then competing for power, influence, and control. Although not yet "dying" in organizational-regression terms identified by Kilburg, Stokes, and Kuruvilla (1997), this unit is exhibiting patterns of behavior consistent with Phase V organizational regression and chaos.

The OS understood the complexity and the gravity of the presenting problems and systemic challenges and requested collaborative partnership with the EAP to assist with the assessment and in planning a possible intervention. In addition, a senior human resources staff member was asked to join the team to provide information about transitions and services available during a RIF. After a series of meetings with the lab as a group and with nearly all of the individual members of the lab, the OS and a psychologist working as an EAP met with the two leaders to begin an intervention planning process.

Implementing the Intervention

The team decided to proceed on several tracts concurrently, including (1) an intervention with the lab group to discuss the reality of the fiscal situation—what was needed to be done to generate additional funds—and also to begin developing, in concert with the Departmental Administration, contingency plans for bridging the looming fiscal crisis; (2) an OC intervention to assist the conflicting parties to negotiate with each other mechanisms for reducing the conflict, including group sessions and individual meetings, as necessary; (3) an intervention with the organizational leaders to assist them in reshaping their relationship as a collaborative partnership; and (4) an executive-coaching intervention by the OS with the laboratory leader. The executive-coaching process involved issues with respect to leadership as well as this person's relationships with his subordinates and the larger university system. The overall goal of this multimodal intervention was to address the major components of organizational functioning that, based on the assessment, were contributing to organizational regression and the experience of organizational dysfunction and resulting chaos.

Over time, a number of related intervention components were added. These included a long-term, EAP-managed, clinical intervention, with one of the participants in the conflict-reduction intervention. The other parties to this intervention were also offered adjunctive clinical services. In addition, other career management and EA staff became involved in assisting lab staff to consider individual career issues within the context of transitions that could occur with a RIF. Workshop formats also were used with respect to organizational change processes and more general team-building models.

This human services project took place over a year's time. The members of the multidisciplinary team worked actively to ensure that the goals and objectives defined were met. The intervention process assisted all parties by developing a more sophisticated understanding of the issues and challenges and helped them to move from a sense of powerlessness and inertia to a more empowered position allowing change. The dynamics of leadership and consultation regarding leadership issues with both leaders were critical components of the intervention. Similarly, the educational workshops directed to issues of career development and organizational change and the OC process and individual counseling sessions with the participants in the conflict were critical to ensuring both behavior change and changes in the organizational functioning of the system. The executive-coaching components of the intervention plan continue; however, other components of the intervention have concluded. The work was well received and had a positive impact.

Example 2

Definition of the Problem

The second example involves a small unit within the university. The organization is directed by a nationally and internationally recognized researcher, and the staff is comprised of approximately 20 people. The leadership is predominately caucasian and male and also includes one caucasian female. The unit is diverse with respect to gender, ethnicity, educational status, and sexual orientation. The leader has an authoritarian style of management that generates a mixture of responsiveness, frustration, and, at times, fear among the staff. Similar to many units at Johns Hopkins, the organization has an integrated research and service center.

The departmental leader contacted an OS and identified a number of critical issues for the unit, including communication difficulties, severe interpersonal conflict, diversity issues and concerns, confusion about roles and job functions, ineffective leadership skills, unhealthy competition, and unprofessional and inappropriate behaviors in the workplace. These issues highlight the regressive forces internal to the organization that Kilburg, Stokes, and Kuruvilla (1997) refer to as IRFs that promote the organizational-regression process.

The leader although highly respected in his field, receives a great deal of pressure, as do most researchers, to establish and maintain fiscal independence by securing major grant funding. He recognizes that many of the staff are overworked, especially in terms of meeting increased work demands with fewer resources. In response to these circumstances, he has requested more financial resources to create more staff positions, which the university has not approved. Therefore, this unit has experienced the impact of what Kilburg, Stokes, and Kuruvilla (1997) call external regressive forces (ERFs), which are illustrated for this unit by way of resource limitations, competitive pressures, and demographic and environmental changes in service-delivery populations.

The OS conducted a formal needs assessment that involved individual and group meetings with all staff members. The findings of the assessment indicated that the leadership needed assistance and coordination with management issues. The two key leaders would often undermine one another's authority, creating confusion and triangulation issues with various staff members. In addition, the unit head's approach to managing others was to express firm orders and directives in a verbally aggressive manner and to voice overt criticisms of staff performance in front of other co-workers. The staff challenged these leadership approaches by engaging in regressed, inappropriate behaviors among themselves. Interpersonal interactions were often toxic, conflict-ridden, and disruptive to the functioning of the organization.

After assessing the problem, the OS requested a collaborative organizational counseling partnership with the EAP to assist with intervention design and implementation. The OS and the EA professional discussed the assessment findings and recommendations for the collaborative partnership with the two key leaders to foster commitment and participation in the intervention process. The OS provided feedback about the findings from the needs assessment and the intervention design to the entire unit during a staff meeting and introduced the EA professional, a psychologist, to the staff as a consultant who would be assisting in implementing the intervention.

The EA professional conducted a series of individual meetings with each staff member to further evaluate individual and system-level dynamics, which provided valuable insights about overall staff functioning and pertinent information that impacted the design of the OC intervention project.

The OS and the EA professional identified the core issues for the unit as ineffective communication, unhealthy competition issues, fiscal constraints, lack of clarity about the organizational mission, severe stress, interpersonal conflict, low tolerance of cultural differences, and limited management skills. According to the previously mentioned six-phase model of organizational functioning provided by Kilburg, Stokes, and Kuruvilla (1997), these behavioral patterns are indicative of Phase V of the organizational regression model, The Chaotic Organization. There was general consensus among the staff that conflicting coping methods, low morale, and chronic crisis management had become the normal level of functioning.

Implementing the Intervention

A collaborative intervention design that involved the leadership in the coordination process was developed. This intervention design incorporated three critical components that occurred concurrently: (1) The EA professional facilitated an OC intervention to assist staff in addressing intergroup and intragroup dynamics and in developing strategies for managing interpersonal conflict. This intervention included a series of group meetings and individual and paired sessions. (2) An executive-coaching intervention by the OS for the two key leaders of the unit addressed leadership issues, including diversity, enhanced supervisory effectiveness, and improvement in their partnership. This process involved the recruitment of another OS to facilitate individual and team coaching sessions for the leadership. (3) The OS and the EA professional facilitated an intervention with the organizational leaders to assist them in confronting key challenges interfering with work productivity.

The OC intervention was the most time-intensive process involving the entire unit. After an atmosphere of trust and safety were established in the group meeting, participants actively worked to develop more effective communication and conflict-management skills. The group process format worked well for this unit, for the staff seemed to value the opportunity for open, healthy communication and discussion.

Over time it became necessary to incorporate additional components to the intervention project. Additional human services staff were approached to join the collaborative team. Two trainers from the Training and Education Center facilitated educational workshops on stress management, team building, and organizational performance-enhancement tools. An EA professional provided brief counseling to one of the staff, who was dealing with transition issues as a new member of the unit.

The human services project took place over the course of 1 year, and, to date, the general feedback from the staff regarding the organizational intervention has been positive, highlighting improvements in communication and role clarity, increased tolerance of differences, and enhanced managerial skills. The staff reportedly have made significant improvements regarding communication, conflict management, and professionalism within the work environment. The leadership is pleased by the overall improvements in staff interactions and relationships in the research and service center. The team executive-coaching intervention continues to be a valuable component to the project and is scheduled as necessary. The entire organization remained committed to the goals and objectives of the intervention project throughout the process, which allowed this client system to move from a place of paralysis and regression to a position of empowerment.

Both of these examples represent actual case studies of the delivery of integrated human services in the workplace. EA professionals in each case actively collaborated with other members of the integrated human services team to provide both traditional EAP services and OC interventions. Such collaborative project teams provide a wide array of services that the EA professional could not provide alone. However, even if the EA professional were the only person available to provide services to these client systems, the OC approach described in this chapter would be more successful than a more traditional EA service-delivery model. An integrated human services model and the application of OC interventions are appropriate evolutionary steps for the ongoing development of the EA field. However, change is not easy, and the EA field will not shift in these suggested directions quickly. In order to expand the role of EA professionals, training and educational opportunities must be pursued for proper application of these and other similar interventions.

DEVELOPING NEW MODELS FOR PRACTICE, AND OVERCOMING BARRIERS FOR CHANGE

A shift from traditional EA practice to an integrated human services delivery structure and the application of an OC framework for EA practice will require overcoming a number of barriers to change. The context is akin to evolving organizations that are fighting the forces of resistance within the organization that inhibit change. The EA field is well established. It has a historically identified core technology, and many EA professional have been trained to practice within a prescribed model with limited degrees of freedom to deviate from the standards. The traditional model of assessment, triage, and referral, with its emphasis on chemical dependency and substance abuse, was useful and facilitated the early development of the EA field. This approach also provided important and necessary services to countless individuals and family members. But this model is antiquated with respect to scope. Although services traditionally provided by EA professionals are valuable, and a traditionally structured EA service is useful, during this era of rapid change within most organizations and most healthcare and mental healthcare systems, it is necessary that the EA field not remain stagnant and make changes in the range of services provided to its host organizations.

Ironically, most of the resistance to change will come from within the EA field itself. Most organizations would be receptive to EA professionals expanding their role after completing appropriate training and assuming the functions represented by an OC framework. Some may argue that this proposed role expansion will force them to "do more without an increase in resources." Others argue that EA professionals will do their work differently and perhaps shift their emphasis. Certainly, in the EA field, there is plenty of work to be done. Yet, in an era when strategic choices need to be made about the allocation and deployment of limited corporate resources, the provision of integrated human services, collaboration among a multidisciplinary team, and the application of the principles of an OC framework positions the EA professional differently within the organization and adds value for the EA field.

Assuming that many EA professionals choose to make the transition from a traditional EA service-delivery model to integrate within their practice principles of the OC model, there will be a critical need for training and ongoing case supervision. The integration of the OC approach will require EA professionals to study organizational behavior and development, as well as the field of organizational consultation. It also will be necessary to develop mentoring programs and opportunities for supervision. The availability of such training opportunities could be through university-based training programs that offer continuing professional development, as well as through professional associations such as EAPA.

It would be useful, whenever possible, to create multidisciplinary teams or ad hoc project teams that include EA professionals and others trained in related disciplines, including organizational development. Alternatively, in a manner similar to the evolution at Johns Hopkins, it would be appropriate to align existing organizational development-oriented units more closely with EA services. The creation of an integrated human services system within Johns Hopkins has prevented what easily could have developed into turf battles between services and has facilitated collaboration where there could have been competition. The development of an integrated human services system requires considerable resources and may be out of reach for many organizations. However, our model may serve as a useful platform on which to build a structure for the delivery of workplace human services programs.

SUMMARY AND CONCLUSION

This chapter has provided a theoretical perspective and several examples for an improved approach to EA practice, the integrated delivery of human services in the workplace, and an innovative framework for a new program emphasis—organizational counseling. The thrust of the interventions in the case examples presented, consistent with a human services systems approach, has been to understand the systemic functioning of these units with a particular focus on issues with respect to the interface between human development and organizational development. These case examples, in our view, represent exemplars for integrative and collaborative practice among human services professionals in the workplace. They also illustrate the conceptual framework for organizational counseling.

These constructs provide a useful direction for the ongoing development of the EA field. As organizations continue to change, as new generations of corporate benefits programs unfold, and as the health and mental health systems evolve, the EA field will also need to reflect on its own future. As the process of self-study for the EA field takes place, it would be prudent to carefully and critically focus on both the model for integrated human services in the workplace and the OC framework as a perspective for contemporary EA practice.

REFERENCES

Danish, S.J., D'Augelli, A.R., & Ginsberg, M.R. (1984). Life development intervention: Promotion of mental health through personal competence. In S.D. Brown & R.W. Lent (Eds.), *Handbook of counseling psychology.* New York: Wiley.

Espejo, R., Schuhmann, W., Schwaninger, & Bilello, U. (1996). *Organizational transformation and learning: A cybernetic approach to management.* New York: Wiley.

Ginsberg, M.R., Kilburg, R.R., & Gomes, P.G. (1994, August 8–10). Integrated human services and EAP's: The Johns Hopkins experience. *Employee Assistance Professionals Association (EAPA) Exchange.*

Kilburg, R.R., Ginsberg, M.R., & Gomes, P.G. (1997). *The characteristics and amelioration of organizational regression.* Paper presented at the annual conference of the International Association of Employee Assistance Programs in Education, Baltimore.

Kilburg, R.R., Stokes, E.J., & Kuruvilla, C. (1997). *Toward a conceptual model for organizational regression.* Paper presented at the annual convention of the American Psychological Association, Chicago.

Maloof, B.A. Governale, N., & Berman, D. (1997). The salvation of the EAP: How does direct corporate services sound? *Behavioral Health Management, 17*(4), 34–38.

Schulberg, H.C., & Baker, F. (1975). *Developments in human services* (Vol. 2). New York: Behavioral.

Smither, R.D., Houston, J.M., & McIntire, S.A. (1996). *Organizational development: Strategies for changing environments.* Reading, MA: Addison-Wesley.

Von Bertalanffy, L. (1950). An outline of general systems theory. *British Journal of the Philosophy of Science, 1,* 134–165.

CHAPTER 24

From Management Consultation to Management Development

JAMES K. ZIMMERMAN and JAMES M. OHER

> Catch a fish for a man and he will eat tonight. Teach a man to fish and he will feast for a lifetime.
>
> —Zen proverb

Employee assistance program (EAP) professionals, whether working as part of an organization or as outside consultants, are frequently approached by managers requesting advice or assistance in dealing with a problem employee. Typically, the manager wants to know what to do with this individual to solve the problem and wants to take quick ameliorative action. Often, this amounts to asking the EAP professional to figure out a way to fix the problem within a reasonable period of time. Termination is likewise an alternative; however, managers often consider this only as a last resort, particularly with previously high-functioning staff or those with a long employment relationship with the company.

Many EAP professionals feel compelled within this context to comply with the essence of the manager's request. If the EAP is internal, there are concerns about the position of the EAP in the organization, including how the EAP professional's behavior will affect his or her standing with upper management, where the manager making the request ranks in relation to the EAP professional, and what the functions and roles that the EAP plays in the organization include (i.e., whether status of the EAP is high or low, whether its value is respected). If the EAP professional is an external consultant or vendor, the aforementioned issues of status, role, and value will impinge upon his or her behavior, with the additional concern of how a response will affect the future relationship and contract with the organization. Further, in either case, a sophisticated EAP professional needs to assess how the problem employee is seen structurally and politically within the organization. (Is this a valued employee or a chronic thorn in management's side? Is there a diversity, Americans with Disabilities Act (ADA), or age-discrimination issue involved?) All of these factors will provide the background and the underpinnings of an EAP professional's reaction to a request for intervention of any kind.

Given this context, it is sometimes difficult or awkward for many EAP professionals to resist an immediate response. However, for the long-term sake of the employee, the manager, the organization, and the EAP professional as well, a more measured and broader response is more likely to be beneficial. This chapter will outline how to move from a request regarding an individual case (management consultation) to an intervention that considers the larger issues in the organization, the manager's abilities to bring out the best in employees, and the relationship between the manager and the specific employee involved. By contrast to consultation regarding only a specific current situation, this process, which takes into account the larger scale issues of the manager's skills and abilities, is what we consider management development. Management consultation is catching a fish for a manager; management development is teaching that manager to feast for a lifetime.

To provide the reader with a process-oriented sense of how a request for management consultation can be shifted to a management development intervention, a case study will be presented. This case will serve throughout this chapter as the basis for illustrating the phases of such a developmental intervention.

The Case of Sharon: Good Cop/Bad Cop

Sharon approached her human resources (HR) manager because of difficulty she was having with an employee. The HR manager suggested that she take up the problem with a workplace consultant who served an EAP function on a consultative basis.

Sharon discussed the problem employee's unsatisfactory performance with the EAP consultant: Specifically, for the past several months, the employee, Linda, had often come in late to work, had treated customers on the telephone without enthusiasm or respect, and had not completed projects that were expected of her. What made the situation more complex for Sharon and the organization was the fact that Linda, who had been employed with the company for approximately one year, was the victim of domestic abuse and the mother of three small children. During the period of the problematic behavior, she was living with her parents while trying to obtain a court order of protection to keep her husband away from her and her family.

Sharon was a manager of a technical support unit of employees and had worked for the firm for 3 years. She was recruited by her current employer because of her expertise in technical support and customer service, although her previous technical background was in a different specialty area than that for which she was now responsible.

In his effort to assess the present conflict at work between Sharon and Linda, the consultant gathered information about the historical relationship between the two that revealed a complex and entangled past. Initially, Sharon had gone out of her way to accommodate Linda because of her personal problems. She would ask others on her staff to cover Linda's shift, would help her on special projects, and would not fully report her tardiness and absences to human resources (HR). However, when Linda's behavior did not improve, Sharon began to feel unappreciated and taken for granted. Consequently, she became less tolerant with Linda. She shifted from acting as a flexible and empathic supervisor—behaving in ways that bordered on being an enabling influence that allowed Linda to avoid constructively addressing her own behavior—to being a strict, unsympathetic disciplinarian. Sharon's initial attitude of concern and subsequent feelings of anger, guilt, and resentment, along with behavior that shifted from enabling to harsh, had complicated and aggravated the situation, making problem resolution all the more difficult and intractable. Sharon's HR officer stated that other employees in the department were also concerned about Sharon's recent harsh treatment of Linda. In discussing the development of the current difficulty, Sharon readily admitted to the consultant: "I am all black or white; there is no gray with me." She was also aware that she tended to react quickly, sometimes without thinking through her responses before taking action.

To help Sharon address the present circumstances, the consultant helped Sharon to document Linda's pattern of unsatisfactory performance and to motivate her to seek professional assistance in solving her problems outside the workplace. The consultant was able to develop a specific action plan for Linda that included evaluation and treatment for depression, a safety plan for her and her family, and resignation from her job to devote more time to her children's welfare and development while relying on her parents for financial support. The consultant also arranged for the firm to offer Linda the opportunity to reapply for her job once her family conflicts were resolved to the point where she had adequate child support, a safe environment for her children, and full preparedness to focus on work.

During this process, it became clear to both Sharon and the consultant that she could benefit by assistance in developing a more consistent and balanced approach toward managing her staff, rather than functioning in the black-and-white world of "good cop/bad cop." Sharon's HR manager contributed information indicating that her managerial style could be too aggressive at times, with others perceiving her as stubborn and difficult to interact with. The HR manager noted further that Sharon did not have the full confidence of senior management, adding, "When she talks to you, you feel like she is backing you into a corner." With Sharon's permission, the EAP consultant sought senior management's approval for her to participate in a management development service at the company. The HR manager readily agreed, stating that if Sharon could improve her managerial style and hone her interpersonal skills, she would be more readily appreciated for what she was able to contribute to the firm.

CATCHING FISH

What is the essence of what has been described to this juncture about the intervention with Sharon and her employee Linda, and what allowed for or created the movement from consultation toward management development? There are several points that are worth emphasizing.

First, Sharon came to the consultant with a specific problem and in a state of need. It is well known and intuitively obvious that an intervention that has some relevance to the immediate needs of a manager is more likely to get a response and to be understood and incorporated by the manager into his or her "tool kit" of management skills (Daniels, 1994; Kinlaw, 1989). Because Sharon had reached a state of frustration, anger, and resentment, she was ready to accept the intervention that was provided. She also recognized that she was in over her head with Linda and did not know how to proceed on her own to ameliorate the situation.

Second, although Sharon was aware of problems she was having that were specific to the situation with Linda, she also knew that she had some difficulty with certain management skills in general. She knew that she was "all black-and-white" and that "gray" might sometimes be a useful place to be as a supervisor. She also recognized her inclination toward impulsive reactions that sometimes appeared not well thought out, leading her to seem less competent and knowledgeable than was the case. Her self-awareness in this regard and her willingness to work on the issue paved the way for the consultant to be able to intervene not only regarding the specifics of the situation with Linda, but also in more general ways regarding Sharon's management style. Without some sense on the client's part of a need for change, the shift to management development is tenuous at best. In Sharon's case, this had already occurred; in other cases, this desire for change needs to be created by the EAP consultant or is imposed by the organization in the form of a referral to the consultant by an HR professional or the client's supervisor.

Third, Sharon was a valued but problematic manager within the organization. Her HR manager and senior management were aware of her abilities in technical and customer support areas, but also of her tendency to be harsh, aggressive, and impulsive at times. They agreed readily with the consultant that Sharon's deficient interpersonal skills interfered with her ability to be a superior manager, inhibiting her effectiveness in the workplace. By implication, Sharon's advancement, and even her retention in her current managerial position, depended on enhancing these skills. In short, the organization was receptive to the idea of management development for Sharon, as was Sharon herself; in other cases, a client's supervisors or senior management must be sold on the idea so that a commitment to the process is made.

Finally, the consultant was able to act in such a way as to demonstrate concretely to Sharon the value of behaving in a certain way as a manager. The consultant "caught fish" for Sharon by helping her design and implement an intervention with Linda that resolved the problem in a way that was satisfactory to all parties involved. Sharon was also taught to fish by being encouraged to enroll in management development.

To summarize, the consultant's intervention was relevant to the issue at hand, immediately responsive to the needs of the clients (including, in this case, the organization, HR, Sharon, and Linda), and concrete and specific in form. These features allowed Sharon to find the intervention inherently useful; it reduced the level of urgency, guilt, and anxiety that she was experiencing regarding Linda. The consultant's response was also instructive for Sharon. It opened the door to addressing larger, more all-encompassing issues in her functioning in the workplace, including her resistance to confronting Linda initially, the complexity of her emotional responses to the situation, and the ways in which her managerial style interfered with her ability to be effective in coping with Linda's behavior. Of course, the support of higher levels of management was also crucial in allowing the consultant to intervene in the first place; clearly, this support is likewise central in moving from consultation to management development.

THE PROCESS OF MANAGEMENT DEVELOPMENT: LEARNING TO FISH

The initial stage of movement from consultation to management development is convincing the manager to commit to the idea of developing skills and tools to improve management style. By analogy, it is not possible to teach people to fish unless they experience the relevance of fishing to their lifestyle. Someone who is not hungry or who does not like the taste of the fish once it is prepared will be less likely to undertake the effort of learning how to be autonomous in providing that lifelong food source. By analogy, in their development and coaching guide, *For Your Improvement,* Lombardo and Eichinger (1996) maintained that their book would be of value only for individuals with a need for problem resolution, whether at work or in their personal lives. When the manager has accepted the concept of management development, the process can continue. Without this critically important commitment, little of real value will be learned or put into practice.

Once an agreement to engage in management development has been made, the phases of the process are as follows: assessment; creating developmental goals; designing measurements to evaluate goal attainment; and coaching to achieve goals.

Phase 1: Assessment

Assessment actually begins with the first consultative contact with a client, frequently before the idea of development has arisen. In Sharon's case, the consultant was assessing her management style and abilities from the outset by collecting information about the history of her relationship with Linda; by ascertaining the perception of Sharon by subordinates, the HR manager, and senior management; and by observing her behavior and responses in relation to himself and his interventions. Generally, the clinical acumen of the consultant will cause assessment to become an integral part of the ongoing process of any consultation.

Nevertheless, a more formalized assessment is essential in negotiating the transition from consultation to development. Effective assessment for management development includes several components: interviews with the client, interviews and surveys with others in the organization about the client, and standardized psychological assessment of the client.

Interview with the Client

This interview can be a loosely structured intervention akin to the initial session a psychotherapist undertakes with a new client or patient, or it can be more formally structured with a list of questions (for example, see Figure 24.1). In some cases, a paper-and-pencil questionnaire may be employed.

---

1. What is your management style? Describe how you tell employees what you need from them. How do you get them to perform up to standards? How do you develop excellence?

2. What problems have you run into with employees? How do you address problem areas? How have you tried to resolve them? Has it been successful?

3. What are your responsibilities as a manager? How many people do you manage? How are these people organized—as a team? As individuals working separately? How are your management responsibilities going at the present time? What challenges do you encounter as a manager?

4. What experiences with supervisors have you had as an employee that you felt were positive? Negative? Describe the best manager you ever had, and tell why that manager was so good. How has your management style been affected by your experience with supervisors? With supervisees?

5. What are some attributes of a good manager? Motivational style? The best interpersonal approach? The best ways of supporting the effort and output of employees?

6. What are your strengths as a manager? What areas need improvement?

Figure 24.1 Guidelines for assessment interview.

Overall, the following areas should be included in this interview, which is likely to take at least two hours to implement:

- Work history at current company.
- Previous employment and reasons for leaving past firms.
- Accomplishments in career, in both past and current positions.
- Other defining past experiences, within and outside the workplace.
- Frustrations in career.
- Relationships with manager, peers, subordinates, and other key employees.
- Goals/aspirations for the current job and the future.
- Expectations for the coaching/development process, including what the client would like to improve on and has been unable to accomplish to date.

A more clinically oriented approach may also be taken in concert with the preceding, as demonstrated in Figure 24.2.

Whatever the specific approach, structured or free-flowing, job-related or behavioral/psychological, when implementing an interview of this sort, it is essential for the consultant to follow the lead of the client where possible. This is salient for three reasons: First of all, as in more directly clinical circumstances, it is unlikely that the client will respond positively and openly to someone who does not seem to be listening attentively or responsively; second, the process is most effective when it is designed as a mutual exploration of the client's experience, allowing the client to come upon connections and insights with the support and guidance of the consultant (as opposed to being led or railroaded toward certain points of view); and finally, by attuning the interview to the client's thought processes, the consultant is modeling behavior that will help the client become a better manager. In other words, because hallmarks of good management style include the ability to listen attentively and responsively, to "resonate with" the experience of the employee, and to come to a mutual understanding of what needs to be done to resolve problems (Kinlaw, 1989; Tobias, 1990), the consultant is behaviorally demonstrating what he or she wants the client to absorb and to manifest later on.

Other Interviews and Surveys

Without having access to information from the point of view of others within the organization, the consultant is at a serious disadvantage in working with a specific client.

---

1. Cognitive style.
2. Approach to problem solving.
3. Personal/emotional style.
4. Life goals.
5. Workplace/management style.
6. Interpersonal style.
7. Fit of client to job.

Figure 24.2   In-depth behavioral interview (IBI)—areas covered.

This is because the client's point of view is likely to be skewed by his or her experience of interactions in the workplace, sometimes to the extent of being out of touch with the effect of his or her behavior on others. Hard data from others in the organization is, therefore, useful not only as information for the consultant, but also as a "wake-up call" for the client regarding sequelae of his or her actions. In the present case example, some of this information was gleaned informally from the HR manager, who notified the consultant about the opinions of Sharon voiced by supervisees and senior management. In turn, awareness of these opinions was part of what motivated Sharon to participate in management development.

It is frequently useful, if not essential, to implement brief interviews or structured surveys with direct reports not only of the client, but also of peers and supervisors. The clearest picture of a given client is likely to be provided through contact with a number of individuals in the organization who have different kinds of relationships with the client; this approach is known as a "360" because feedback is received from "360 degrees" around the client—from below through direct reports, from above through supervisors, and laterally through peers. Supervisees of the client can offer information about their manager's abilities and skills in delegation, exercise of authority, support, reinforcement of work well done, methods of addressing substandard performance, and so on. Peers will provide data regarding the client's ability to work on a team or within a unit or department and to collaborate and cooperate with others within the organization. Supervisors can report regarding the manager's ability to take direction, to respond to deadlines, to access and benefit from mentoring, and to produce measurable bottom-line results and outcomes in products or services. All can also offer information regarding the client's interpersonal style in general, including range and intensity of emotional reactions, functioning under stress, and degree of clarity and effectiveness in communication.

In brief, salient areas to be covered in interviews or surveys with others in the organization include the manager's abilities to communicate clearly and effectively; to delegate responsibility; to motivate supervisees to perform at optimal levels; to inspire trust and confidence; to get tasks completed in a timely, efficient manner, and at a high standard of quality; to respond to others in a respectful and mature way; to deal with requests to and from other units within the organization effectively; to work as an integral part of a team, unit, or division; to take direction and mentoring willingly; to approach others in a manner that is not offensive and that does not create defensiveness; to focus on the development of his or her own career as well as those of others; and to work within the organization with a general sense of purpose, focus, vision, and commitment.

Standardized Psychological Assessment

In principle, assessment with standardized psychological measures allows the consultant to gain a broader and deeper perspective on the client. In practice, such measures frequently affirm what a clinically astute consultant has already discovered through the interview process, and they are useful to confirm evidence as well as to extend the self-exploratory process of the client. They are also informative regarding discrepancies between what a client presents verbally to the consultant and what he or she reports in a more structured testing situation.

There are many standardized measures available, and there are more being created all the time. To engage in a discussion of the relative merits of various tests is beyond the scope of this chapter. However, one point should be made: It is important to consider one's goals in the use of a measure before the measure is chosen. For example, among widely used measures, the Myers-Briggs (Myers, 1975) compiles scores on four dimensions of personality, producing a quick and fairly simple picture, by character type, of how an individual tends to function. By contrast, the California Psychological Inventory (CPI; Gough, 1991; McAllister, 1988) offers scores on 20 scales and 3 vectors, which allow for a richer and more complex matrix of personality components. The simplicity of the Myers-Briggs is attractive in some circumstances, but the test can lead to something akin to an astrological "what's-your-sign" sense of personality and self-definition. On the other hand, the CPI is sometimes too complex for its results to be fully absorbed and integrated by a nonpsychologically sophisticated manager. Furthermore, some measures are restricted regarding who is permitted to administer them, in many cases requiring individuals with advanced training in psychology, which makes them inaccessible to some EAP professionals.

Although psychological assessment can be highly informative, there is a risk in placing too much importance on the results of standardized testing. At times, clients, HR officers, senior managers, and consultants see these results as having greater explanatory power than is actually the case, and these people use test scores and profiles in a way that constrains or "pigeon-holes" the consultation (such as in the "astrological" approach to the results of the Myers-Briggs). It is wise to remember at all times that standardized assessment data are provided by the client him- or herself and that results are therefore useful as summary descriptors of the *self-perception* of clients and how this *self-perception* compares with results from reference populations. In point of fact, results are *not* definitive, fully objective constructs that exist beyond the client's way of perceiving her- or himself.

Summary

Assessment of a candidate for management development is a tripartite, integrated process, which includes an extensive interview with the manager, interviews with others within the organization, and standardized psychological assessment of the manager. Interviews can be structured or free flowing, but in all cases the intent is to obtain a broad-based sense of who the manager is and how the manager interfaces with the work environment.

The interview with the client should also begin with the engagement of the client in the process of self-examination, which is vital to any successful management development; should promote the working alliance and trust between manager and consultant; and should provide a basis for the next steps in the process of development. Interviews and surveys with others within the organization are employed to obtain a view of the client from all angles (a "360"). Standardized psychological assessment is useful as one component of an integrated assessment of a candidate for management development and should be seen as one perspective among several. It should not be represented as a stand-alone method of understanding a manager because there is a risk that results can be misinterpreted or misused, either by the manager or by senior management to whom reports may be required to be submitted.

Phase 2: Creation of Developmental Goals

The assessment phase serves as the foundation of the second phase of management development, one in which goals for the intervention are created and delineated. In order to describe this phase of the process more fully, a return to the case example is necessary.

Feedback

Along with interviews with Sharon herself, information was obtained from her supervisor and colleagues and from direct reports. The following became clear:

Sharon intimidated colleagues and direct reports; her supervisor, Eliot, felt "she came on too strong." Eliot also noted that she seemed overwhelmed by her work at times and often did not seem to think through responses to immediate requests from him. He felt that she would frequently "shoot from the hip": Although she would often respond with correct information to requests, she would just as often be wrong. Sharon agreed that "shooting from the hip" caused credibility problems for her. She felt that this tendency grew out of the fact that she managed a large unit within the company, which had a fair share of crises on a daily or weekly basis. In response, she frequently experienced a need to act quickly, without necessarily stopping to think through what would be the best, most productive, or most incisive way to proceed. As a result, she was aware that she was not always a good model for her subordinates, sometimes "throwing things together" in a desultory way and subsequently feeling stupid or incompetent.

Sharon also recognized that she had difficulty delegating because she feared that the work would not be completed. She realized that in order to gain confidence in (and the confidence of) her staff, she needed to learn to respond in a more measured way and to trust her direct reports more. Sharon was decent at catching fish, but not as good at teaching fishing.

Sharon began the coaching process enthusiastically, but she recognized that she harbored some resentment toward Eliot and the company. She sought assistance in how to interact with Eliot, whom she felt undermined her by not being supportive and by encouraging her direct reports to criticize her. She also felt that her career was blocked because she was a "strong woman," and people like that did not do well in the organization.

Although not taking issue with Sharon's perceptions, the consultant tried to focus Sharon's attention on factors more likely to be within her control, such as what she did (and did not do) to interfere with her career and advancement in the company. He also helped her to experience some empathy for Eliot, with whom Sharon identified regarding pressures faced by managers in the organization. She began to recognize that she had options in responding to him beyond just getting angry and feeling thwarted.

In this phase of integration of feedback with the intent to set goals for management development, Sharon also became aware of the value of her relationship with a senior manager who had taken a liking to her. He proved to be an important role model for her, and she was able to avail herself of his function as a mentor. He set a good example, managing by delegating responsibilities and motivating others in a positive, encouraging manner. He was willing to come to Sharon and other subordinates in an open search for answers to problems. He had advised Sharon to "learn to trust people more" and to take her time in responding to crises.

Goal-Setting

Once the feedback from others was discussed and Sharon had examined her reactions to that feedback as well as to her own feelings about the areas in which she needed improvement, the consultant worked with her to construct goals for the intervention. In order for management development goals to be effective, they need to meet several criteria: They must be attainable, clearly delineated, specific and concrete, and capable of motivating the client to action.

If the consultant allows unattainable, pie-in-the-sky goals to be set, the manager will invariably end up feeling frustrated and losing self-confidence and self-esteem, and the consultation will fail. Although this appears patently obvious, it is not as easy in actual practice to design goals that are genuinely achievable or to avoid ones that are not. At times, a goal may appear attainable when actually it is not; for example, a manager may set a goal of becoming a vice-president in a family-owned company in which there are only two such positions, both occupied by young relatives of the owners. In other circumstances, the consultant may unwittingly compel the client toward a greater degree of personality change than is likely to occur; for example, allowing an anxious "bean-counter" to construct a goal that requires a free-spirited, entrepreneurial style. Clearly, designing attainable goals is a process that requires a realistic perception of oneself and of the current circumstances of the work environment. In Sharon's case, for example, it would have been unwise for the consultant, whatever his view of the situation, to encourage Sharon to set a goal of confronting the possibility of inherent gender bias in her place of work, at least not until other more accessible goals had been addressed and Sharon's management style had improved.

To the extent that goals are clearly delineated, specific, and concrete, they can be measured by objective methods. This is vitally important in the process of management development because measurement of achievements is what allows for a sense of accomplishment. Conversely, a lack of achievement of goals becomes the basis for a reexamination of the process, an analytic endeavor that itself creates a learning experience in which goals can be modified or reconstructed. Without specificity and objective measures, goals become vague and motivation can easily flag. Moreover, from the point of view of modeling the consultation process after an image of good management practices, clarity and specificity of goals help the client understand how to implement similar approaches in the workplace.

Goals that are attainable, clearly delineated, specific, and concrete are more likely to motivate managers to action as well. To return to the fishing metaphor, the consultant and the manager might agree that the manager will go to a specified, stocked pond and try to catch one fish per day at first, building up to a goal of three per day. By contrast, if the manager were told, "There are lots of fish in the world—go catch some," the motivation to persevere would be reduced by vagueness and lack of concrete criteria for success.

If Sharon's goals were "Be a better manager" or "Don't cause problems with your supervisor," consultation would be less likely to be effective because the generality of these goals could lead to miscommunication and confusion ("What does 'better' mean?" "What problems?" etc.). Sharon and the consultant chose to focus the work of development most directly on her tendencies to respond without first thinking incisively about a given situation, a behavior they felt was caused by anxiety regarding the quantity of work needed to be done and the quality of output required. They presumed that her aggressiveness was a consequence of feeling this anxiety and pressure. The consultant also felt that Sharon needed to learn to regard mistakes and failures as opportunities to learn and improve, which he felt would reduce her tendency to feel like she was running too fast all the time. Therefore, the goals set by Sharon and the consultant were as follows:

- Lessen strong aggressive stances and reactions to work events.
- Increase credibility in the workplace by making well-thought-out, considered responses to requests for information.
- Develop a methodical approach toward work tasks, and incorporate crises as opportunities in a continuous quality-improvement process.

Summary

Assessment in management development should include feedback from others within the organization in which the client works. This feedback then leads naturally into the phase of setting the goals for the developmental intervention. These goals should be constructed so as to take into account several features, including that they must be attainable, clearly delineated, specific and concrete, and capable of motivating the client to action. The establishment of goals for the intervention should flow seamlessly into the third phase of the management development process, in which ways of measuring progress are created and implemented.

Phase 3: Designing Measures to Evaluate Goal Attainment

Measures to evaluate progress toward and attainment of goals is crucial in effective management development. If such measures are not carefully designed to capture the essence of the goals that have been established, the energy of the consultation is likely to dissipate; if they are not also potent motivators for the client, momentum can easily be lost. Here again, specificity is paramount: Measures should be objective, behaviorally anchored, and quantifiable where possible.

By *objective,* we mean that the client and consultant (and others in the client's organization) can see, evaluate, and agree upon the content of a measure. For example, "Sharon is less aggressive" is not as objective as "Sharon has made fewer than three aggressive comments in the past week"; "Sharon is more credible" is less useful than "Sharon responded to at least 50% of my requests in a credible manner."

These examples also demonstrate the requirement of behaviorally anchored specificity as well; that is, either Sharon makes fewer than three aggressive comments per week or she does not; either she responds in a credible way more than half the time or she does not. Further, these examples are quantifiable: It would even be possible to maintain a chart of Sharon's levels of aggressiveness and credibility by tracking the behaviors that she manifested.

In Sharon's case, as she and the consultant reviewed the areas in which she needed improvement and development, it became clear that the underlying factors of impulsive responses (i.e., "shooting from the hip") and lack of organization and prioritization were most salient and in need of attention. As a result, the measures designed by Sharon and the consultant focused on these issues, as can be seen in Figure 24.3.

Likert Scales

A fairly simple method of creating quantifiability that is frequently employed in measuring behavioral change is the Likert scale (Likert, 1961). In essence, Likert scales delineate a list of responses along a conceptual continuum from one pole to its opposite (such as like–dislike or agree–disagree). They are best designed for statistical purposes to have a neutral midpoint so that there are an odd number of choices on the

1. Sharon does not try to immediately "fix" individuals or issues.
   Strongly Agree   Agree   Neutral   Disagree   Strongly Disagree

2. Sharon gives proper time, thought, and research to inquiries from senior management.
   Strongly Agree   Agree   Neutral   Disagree   Strongly Disagree

3. Sharon prioritizes and follows through on tasks based on their urgency and importance.
   Strongly Agree   Agree   Neutral   Disagree   Strongly Disagree

4. Sharon provides a comprehensive analysis and review of her service operations, including all relevant details and data components.
   Strongly Agree   Agree   Neutral   Disagree   Strongly Disagree

5. Sharon makes effective contributions to senior management that aim to optimize operational procedures throughout the company.
   Strongly Agree   Agree   Neutral   Disagree   Strongly Disagree

Figure 24.3   Evaluation of progress toward goals.

continuum. Each choice is then given a score; for example, a 5-point Likert scale may be scored 1 through 5 or −2 to +2 (see Figure 24.3).

By developing Likert scales to measure progress, a consultant provides the client with an opportunity to track movement toward goal attainment. Progress can be graphically demonstrated by noting changes in scores from week to week; further, differential progression toward goals can be noted as well. For example, Sharon may find that after 3 weeks, her mean score (on a −2 to +2 basis) on Item 1 in Figure 24.3 is +1.35, while her score on Item 2 is −0.44. This would suggest to her that she is doing a better job of responding in a more thoughtful way regarding her tendency to fix things immediately, but she has not improved substantively in the degree of careful consideration she gives to requests from senior management. In turn, this would allow her to focus on trying to develop her skills in interacting with senior management in a more effective manner.

"360" Revisited

It is generally useful to measure progress toward goal attainment in management development by obtaining information on a regular basis from the client's managers, peers, and direct reports, as is done in the assessment phase. For this purpose, Likert scales are well-suited for two reasons: (1) Each individual reports on the same issues, maintaining a high level of consistency in the information received by the client and consultant; and (2) the report is completed quickly and easily, increasing the likelihood of compliance among those from whom information is sought. Likert-based reports may be administered anonymously, by category (i.e., manager, peer, staff, etc.), or with each individual identified on the report. The advantage of anonymity is that individuals may feel more comfortable being honest in their responses because they will not feel constrained by reactions the client may have to their opinions; however, this approach does not allow for a more fine-grained analysis of the resulting data. Requiring individuals to identify themselves leads to a clear picture of the effects of management development on relationships with others in the organization; on the other hand, specificity may be gained at the expense of complete truthfulness, and the response rate (that is, the percentage of people who return the reports) may suffer because of the discomfort some individuals may feel as a consequence of the direct exposure of their opinions.

This dilemma may be avoided in two ways: First of all, those who complete the reports may be identified only to the consultant and not to the client, although this may lead to an erosion of trust within the client-consultant relationship. A second and perhaps preferable approach is to have reporters identified only by category and not individually. This method allows for a compromise between the advantages of anonymity and those of specificity, increasing the likelihood of honesty and of a higher response rate, while also permitting a finer analysis of the resulting data.

Summary

Measurement of progress toward goal attainment serves as a powerful feedback mechanism because information is gathered from individuals who interact with the client on a frequent basis. Weekly reports based upon quotidian contacts indicate graphically for the client and the consultant what progress is being made and what still needs to be accomplished. It is for this reason that progress measures must be designed to cleave closely to developmental goals and to be simple, quick, and objective. Hallmarks of good progress measures are that they are objective, behaviorally anchored, and quantifiable; Likert scales are widely used and recommended for this purpose. Again, as in the assessment phase of management development, gathering information from supervisors, peers, and staff is the most effective way of obtaining a clear, in-depth, and realistic picture of movement toward goal attainment.

Phase 4: Coaching to Achieve Goals

The process of coaching is not an entity separate within itself in management development. It is a method of interaction between consultant and client that mirrors the management style that the consultant (or coach) would like to instill in the client. Consequently, the coaching process begins with the onset of the relationship between consultant and client and inheres in that relationship through all phases of management development. It is not simply one phase of the relationship that occurs in a linear fashion after goals are set and measurement methods are designed, although it tends to take center stage once the first three phases of the process are in place. Presenting the coaching process as a phase of management development is therefore somewhat artificial, and it is done with the assumption that it will be kept in mind that this is the core of the client-consultant relationship.

A Coaching Model

Our approach to coaching is based upon that put forth by Dennis Kinlaw in his book, *Coaching for Commitment* (Kinlaw, 1989). As he defines it, Kinlaw regards *coaching* as the essence of superior management. The process of coaching develops management practices that include a focus on clear objectives and concrete actions, high productivity and quality standards, continuous quality improvement, close contact with direct reports, positive relationships within the organization and with outside contacts, ongoing career and competencies development, cooperation and commitment to common goals in the workplace, and high personal ethical and work standards. Kinlaw believes that these outcomes occur through the process of coaching, which centers on developing focus and commitment to one's career, position, and organization. Coaching is comprised of four processes: (1) counseling, (2) mentoring, (3) tutoring, and (4) confronting. The first three processes are directed at problem solving; the fourth is intended to improve performance. *Counseling,* with a focus on personal sensitivity to others, leads to increased self-sufficiency. *Mentoring,* focused on career development, increases a manager's commitment to the organization's goals and values. *Tutoring,* directed at skills development, deepens the appreciation of the value of continual learning. *Confronting,* intended to overcome performance deficiencies, increases the likelihood of a sustained, high level of quality in job-related activities (see Kinlaw, 1989, p. 25).

Coaching is implemented in a positive, respectful, mutually influential, future-oriented manner, with a confluence of attention paid to the process of interaction between coach and coachee. In other words, the attitude of the coach (or consultant) must include a nonjudgmental, positive regard for the coachee (or client); a respectful stance must be conveyed by encouraging the expression of the needs and concerns of the coachee with the intent to understand and develop information more thoroughly; the process must allow for the coachee to influence the coach, as well as vice versa; and the agenda must be to correct behavior in the future, not to affix blame for what was wrong with it in the past. Coaching also targets concrete behaviors—what the manager does, not what he or she intends—and is logical, objective, and descriptive. A revisiting of our case study should help clarify how this process operates in actual practice.

Coaching Sharon

To reiterate, the coaching process with a client should serve as a mirror image of the kind of management style that the consultant wants the client to develop. To this end, management development with Sharon explicitly focused on the four coaching processes: counseling, mentoring, tutoring, and confronting. In order to help identify Sharon's strengths and shortcomings in these processes, her direct reports were asked to complete the Coaching Skills Inventory (CSI; Kinlaw, 1989), an instrument that requested that they rate her use of a skill or behavior on a 5-point Likert scale. The scale ranges from "5"—indicating that a behavior was "very characteristic" of Sharon—to "1"—indicating that it was "very uncharacteristic" of her. Sharon was asked to complete the CSI about herself as well.

Overall, scores were in the range indicating that her direct reports thought Sharon was a good manager. However, her own self-report scores were higher than those of her supervisees. There were two coaching components—counseling and tutoring—in which her self-perception was statistically not congruent with the perception of her among her direct reports. This indicated that it was particularly in these areas that Sharon needed increased awareness and skill improvement.

When confronted with this information, Sharon was largely receptive. However, she began by placing some of the responsibility for the situation on the breakneck pace of work in her department, maintaining that this had compromised her ability to focus on and to understand the needs and concerns of her staff. Because this suggested some level of resistance to the consultant's confrontation, he shifted gears to a counseling stance, using Sharon's concerns as the subject of coaching, "dropping the agenda" of his own goals (Kinlaw, 1989, p. 96). This allowed Sharon to admit that intellectually she wanted to be more responsive to staff concerns and needs, but that she had difficulty doing so.

It became clear that Sharon brought an intensity of feeling to the current situation from past events and relationships in her life. For example, in one session, she vigorously complained about how insensitive, intrusive, and disruptive Eliot was. The consultant then asked her who else in her life had evoked such an intense reaction in her, which led Sharon into an emotionally laden description of her disappointing, unsatisfying, aggressive relationship with her parents. Sharon was able to recognize that she experienced Eliot as like her neglectful and hostile father and the majority of her staff as like her younger siblings. In childhood, she lived in a rural community with few other families nearby; both parents worked outside the home, and Sharon was left responsible for her younger siblings after school by the time she was 9 years old. The realization of the feeling of a repetition of family dynamics with her staff and supervisor was a profound experience for Sharon, and it took time and the consultant's assistance to work through this newfound awareness. She needed to remind herself frequently that she was no longer an abused, helpless child; she discovered that she could show restraint, a behavior not accessible to her as an angry latency-age girl.

The counseling process thus focused on increasing Sharon's awareness of the impact of the dynamics of her family of origin on her current behavior. Once this awareness began to flourish, the consultant was able to shift toward a mentoring and tutoring function, supporting Sharon's ability to react to circumstances and events in a more measured way. She learned how not to "shoot from the hip" and, subsequently, began to acknowledge that Eliot and other senior managers were actually more helpful than she had realized in the past.

The consultation process then moved toward assisting Sharon in integrating the results of her new understanding and experience into her own management style. She began working on taking a more balanced, less frenetic approach to the coaching process with her direct reports. She focused on developing a fuller understanding of the problem before reacting, on supporting staff in finding their own solutions, on structuring her conversations so that her logic was more easily understood, on increasing her staff's commitment to their own self-sufficiency, and on designing more effective methods for training them in technical competence. She also paid closer attention to her ability to serve as a resource for staff, peers, and senior management.

By employing a process of intervention that moves easily between counseling, mentoring, tutoring, and confronting, management development consultants can be flexible in taking advantage of whatever issue is most compelling and current in a client's experience. If the consultant in Sharon's case had not been able to shift gears, his confrontation of skills needing amelioration may have led to an impasse; because he was able to counsel Sharon on more deep-seated psychological issues that made her resistant to the consulting process, she was freed to examine ways in which she herself could improve as a manager. Practical tutoring and mentoring then allowed her to enhance her methods of leading and motivating her staff.

Summary

Coaching as an approach to management development can be highly effective because of its flexibility, immediacy to the issues at hand, and mirroring of the process of excellent management style. It serves to increase the client manager's self-awareness and psychological-mindedness, heightening understanding of management as a process founded on interpersonal relationships. As the manager becomes more effective, the effectiveness of individuals within the manager's unit is likely to improve because of the manager's more developed skills in counseling, mentoring, tutoring, and confronting. Because this process is respectful and interpersonally responsive, it also should allow for improved performance without removing or suppressing the qualities that make various individuals successful in the first place.

Finally, a more in-depth method such as this—a method that teaches managers to fish—is more likely to enhance the value of the consultant to the manager, to the unit, and to the organization. By contrast to one-shot, quick-fix approaches to isolated problems, management development by coaching can lead to genuine, systemic "sea changes" throughout the organization.

But I Don't Want to Fish: Managing Resistance

The consultation with Sharon proceeded relatively smoothly, with little resistance on her part and with receptivity to the process by senior management and others in the organization. This is not always the case, and the ability to manage and disarm various forms of resistance to the process is a vitally important function of a management development consultant. The following case is illustrative of the difficulties in addressing resistance to management development.

The Case of Nathan: "Just Fix It"

Nathan, the chief executive officer (CEO) of a semi-autonomous division of a financial services firm, contacted the consultant. Nathan and his chief operations officer (COO) partner had built the division from a mom-and-pop entrepreneurial boutique to a loosely structured corporate environment, increasing by 2,500% the amount of money they managed. Nathan recognized that he was having difficulty with some employees because they were too independent, "lone wolves," as he called them. At first, he appeared receptive to the idea that the shift in the corporate culture needed to be understood from a systems perspective, that he might need to make some changes himself, and that consultation should not be a quick fix. He acknowledged that although he needed to let go of the reins to some extent, he was a "control freak" who had a hard time delegating to others. At the same time, he did not want to be responsible for keeping people in line.

A younger employee who was a main concern for Nathan was Mike, who had a background as an options trader. Mike was accustomed to the "wild west" atmosphere of the trading pit and was not a very good team player. He tended to make investment-portfolio decisions on his own, without consulting others in the division who may have had valuable expertise to offer. Despite Nathan's attempts to rectify this situation, Mike seemed unreceptive.

The consultant implemented Individual Behavioral Interviews (IBIs; in Figure 24.2) with Nathan, the COO, Mike, and other key players in the division. He also administered the California Psychological Inventory (CPI) to the same people and, following assessment, scheduled feedback sessions with each. Finally, he interviewed individuals who reported to Nathan about their experience of the CEO as a manager. Nathan was somewhat uncomfortable during his feedback session, wanting to get to immediate, concrete solutions from the beginning. Further, he wanted to know "What's wrong with Mike," trying to understand right away what he should do to get Mike to become more responsive.

The consultant made an effort to help Nathan to become more aware of the systems issues involved and to see Mike's behavior in the context of an organization shifting from a successful entrepreneurial shop to a corporate behemoth. Nathan had difficulty grasping the concept that Mike's behavior was a symptom of an organizational problem and that Mike was in danger of being scapegoated. He was also unwilling to examine his own part in the problem, in that he had initially encouraged Mike's aggressive individualism, which reminded him of his own youthful exuberance. Now that that approach was no longer viable, Nathan felt uncomfortable in his role but was able to see it as problematic only in Mike's behavior. Ultimately, Nathan contacted the consultant and said: "Just tell me, should I fire Mike or not?" The consultant again tried to get Nathan to understand that the question was not that simple nor was the solution that clear-cut. The result was that the consultant was the next to go.

Resistances

Resistances can appear in a number of forms, some more subtle than others. Furthermore, some resistances reside more within the manager, whereas others more embedded in the culture of the organization itself. It is beyond the scope of this chapter to investigate the issue of resistance in detail and organizational resistances in particular; however, some fundamental forms of resistance and ways to address them will be outlined. These include: (1) client's unwillingness, (2) problem employee's intractability, (3) power imbalances, and (4) misconceptions and preconceptions.

Unwillingness

At times, the manager who would become the subject of development is not interested in moving beyond the specific issues that brought in the consultant in the first place. Often, as with Nathan, this amounts to a wish on the manager's part to have the consultant simply fix the identified problem employee. This is tantamount to wanting a fish dinner to be served without having to participate in the preparation of it. Such a potential client is likely to be unwilling to examine his or her own behavior and contributions to the problem situation. Frequently, guilt, anger, a sense of responsibility, and/or fear feed this unwillingness. Sharon, for example, initially had some difficulty directly facing her harsh treatment of Linda, in part because she felt responsible and guilty; this in turn made her angry when Linda was not responsive. Sharon's difficulty was also fed by her childhood experience with being responsible for others and feeling resentful and angry as a result. Likewise, although Nathan paid lip service to the idea that his division needed a consultant's help in making an organizational leap forward—he contacted and hired the consultant himself—he resisted any exploration of his own part in the problem. Certainly, his identification with Mike was ambivalent. On one hand, he saw in Mike the entrepreneurial spirit that made him (Nathan) successful; on the other hand, he felt threatened by Mike's youth and expansive future while he felt he was beginning his own decline. Uncomfortable with this vulnerability,

Nathan was unable to move forward with management development, preferring to retrench in the idea that a decision had to be made promptly about Mike's continued tenure in the organization.

Intractability

Sometimes the issue is not the inflexibility of the manager/client, but the resistance of the identified problem employee (IPE) to change. This may be caused by a response to a perceived threat in being confronted or challenged to improve. Certainly, in Nathan's case, Mike was not an easy employee to manage. He was resistant, suspicious, and guarded. In fact, he refused to sign off on the IBI report until his wife, an attorney, had looked it over. He returned to the consultant with requests for numerous rewordings of phrases that he thought might cast a negative light on him. He was unwilling, for the most part, to engage in an examination of the feelings he had about being portrayed as he was in the report, despite the fact that the information in the report all came from him. Mike was apparently overly conscious of the risk in the process of consultation, and his fear of negative repercussions detracted from the possibility that he could gain something from the experience.

Power Imbalances

Frequently, a consultant is brought into an organization from above; that is, the contracting is done with senior levels of management. A manager who approaches the consultant for assistance with a problematic employee may feel the need to be self-protective, in that there may be an implication that the manager is at fault for not being effective in the first place. This is even more likely to be the case when the consultant is told by senior management to contact the manager because of problems with a direct report. It is a common fact of life in organizations that power is an undercurrent to many interactions, and those implied threats to one's position are sometimes the context of communications from supervisors. Such is likely to have been part of what impelled Mike to be so self-protective, even hypervigilant, when approached by a consultant hired by Nathan. It is also likely to have been a substrate to Sharon's tendency to cast responsibility for her problems in Eliot's direction.

Misconceptions and Preconceptions

Some resistance occurs more because the client is unclear as to why the consultation is occurring or because he or she has inflexible ideas about what management consultation should be. Although there is some obvious overlap between this category of resistance and previous ones—because some lack of clarity and inflexibility is caused by cognitive "blinders," which themselves arise out of fear, guilt, anger, or resentment in the first place—there are some instances in which the requisite approach for the consultant needs to be more educational and informative than addressing resistances per se. Some managers, particularly those fairly new to management positions, can be quite naive regarding the interpersonal and psychological skills necessary for their work. In such cases, psychoeducational tactics (tutoring) are more appropriate than confrontational ones.

Working through Resistance

The essence of the first three forms of resistance described earlier is that they are founded upon fear, guilt, anger, and self-protection. In order to work through such resistances, it is first necessary to develop an alliance with the client founded upon trust, respect, and understanding. In fact, the word *resistance* is probably counterproductive in itself because it implies that the client is actively doing something that undermines the consultative relationship. Frequently it is more the case that the client is behaving in a way that is consistent with how he or she perceives the environment in which the consultation occurs, the circumstances that made it arise, and the relationships that need amelioration so that performance can improve. Without empathy for the client's position and point of view, the consultation will fail.

From this perspective, then, it is evident that addressing resistances first requires understanding them from the inside out, grasping what is the adaptive function of the behavior that appears to be an impediment to the consultation. Two objectives are accomplished by taking this stance: First of all, an empathic understanding of the client's experience requires the consultant to respond to the client in a nonjudgmental, essentially therapeutic, manner. This conveys a sense of respect for the client's view of his or her surroundings, which in turn promotes the client's ability to trust the consultant as an objective and compassionate individual. Second, by understanding the client's take on the situation, the consultant learns immensely valuable information about what is occurring not only within the client, but also in the workplace environment itself. This is because, in our view, a manager's experience invariably will be reflective of the interpersonal and cultural dynamics of the workplace in which he or she manages.

Therefore, the quality and nature of the manager's resistances—responses evolving from his or her interpretation of events and relationships within the organization—will inform the consultant regarding the workplace itself as well. For example, Mike's hypervigilance, although certainly partly a characterological trait, was also evidence for the likelihood that he was being scapegoated by Nathan because of Nathan's own ambivalence. Nathan's difficulty in easing up on the reins of management and his envy of younger employees and their "Dodge City" approach to their work were part and parcel of Mike's concerns about how he was represented by the consultant's reports. Without this level of understanding of the dynamics of the situation, the consultant would be less able to function in an effective systemic way; without empathy for Mike's position, the consultant would have been more likely to participate in the scapegoating, supporting the idea that Mike should be removed from his position in the company.

Clearly, then, when resistance arises, it behooves the consultant to regard it as an opportunity to understand what is occurring on a deeper level and to convey this understanding to the client in a respectful and empathic manner. An effective way of accomplishing this is to "drop the agenda" (Kinlaw, 1989, p. 96), reorienting the consultation away from the tasks at hand and toward an understanding of the client's present concerns and emotional state. By doing so, the consultant conveys respect for the client, underscores the value and importance of his or her feelings and concerns, and opens the consultation up to gaining vital information about the functioning of the client in the organization as well as the organization in the client.

Summary

Resistances arise in many forms and are generally best viewed as comprehensible responses by the client, given the client's experience of the workplace. From this perspective, resistances are taken as opportunities to propel the consultation forward by conveying a sense of respect for the client's point of view, deepening the consultant's understanding of the client and the organization, and enhancing the client's sense of trust in the consultant. Consequently, the consultant should act to address the resistance directly in an objective, nonjudgmental way, bringing that aspect of the client's experience to bear on the consultation itself.

CONCLUSION: BAITING THE HOOK

In the final analysis, the ability to shift one's stance as a consultant from case-by-case interventions with specific employees to a long-term developmental relationship with their manager is a practiced art. One frequently needs first to catch fish for the manager—to intervene in a given instance in such a way as to quickly ameliorate its most problematic aspects. If Sharon's consultant had not been effective in assisting her in managing Linda, it would have been far less likely that the relationship could have proceeded to one in which the focus was on developing Sharon's managerial abilities. Further, if the consultant had not been cognizant of the fact that his behavior would model for Sharon the methods and the techniques that he was trying to develop in her, there would have been less incentive for Sharon to acquire these methods and techniques for herself. By alleviating her management problem and modeling superior management approaches, the consultant convinced Sharon that his interventions had value for her.

Once a fish has been caught—once the pressing issue has been resolved—then the consultant can bait the hook—propose the idea of management development to the manager (or human resources officer or senior manager when appropriate). Having demonstrated the efficacy and utility of his or her approach, a consultant is in a far stronger position than if a course of action had been suggested and not implemented. Effective intervention in a specific case allows the manager to feel comfortable with the consultant's way of working and facilitates the necessary support of others in the organization (senior management, human resources, and so on) as well. Subsequently, the manager's comfort level is more likely to lead to the requisite degree of commitment to the process of management development, which can be difficult and arduous at times, particularly when issues of resistance are being confronted.

Finally, management development interventions, because of the depth and breadth of the process, can be very gratifying professionally and personally for the consultant—perhaps more so than case-by-case problem resolution, the traditional EAP role. To what extent EAP professionals will embrace this new role is open to question and beyond the scope of this chapter. However, the ability to observe and participate in the growth and development of a manager as manager and as human being makes management development a highly worthwhile pursuit. In the final analysis, the consultant can learn immensely valuable lessons from the manager: Teaching fishing sometimes leads to the reciprocal experience of being served a truly delicious seafood feast.

REFERENCES

Daniels, A.C. (1994). *Bringing out the best in people: How to apply the astonishing power of positive reinforcement.* New York: McGraw-Hill.

Gough, H.G. (1991). *California Psychological Inventory: Administrator's guide.* Palo Alto, CA: Consulting Psychologists Press.

Kinlaw, D.C. (1989). *Coaching for commitment: Managerial strategies for obtaining superior performance.* San Diego, CA: Pfeiffer.

Likert, R. (1961). *New patterns of management.* New York: McGraw-Hill.

Lombardo, M., & Eichinger, R. (1996). *For your improvement.* Lominger.

McAllister, L.W. (1988). *A practical guide to CPI interpretation* (2nd ed.). Palo Alto, CA: Consulting Psychologists Press.

Myers, I.B. (1975). *Manual: The Myers-Briggs type indicator.* Palo Alto, CA: Consulting Psychologists Press. (Original work published 1962)

Tobias, L.L. (1990). *Psychological consulting to management: A clinician's perspective.* New York: Brunner/Mazel.

APPENDIX

Responding Effectively to Traumatic Events at the Workplace

BARBARA FEUER

PROLOGUE

Throughout history, traumatic events have always happened in the workplace, and their consequences have affected countless workers and their loved ones. Despite this, the sequelae of work-related trauma have only been seriously addressed by employee assistance programs (EAP) in the past 10 or so years. And within this context, workplace violence has only recently emerged as a major workplace safety and health crisis that demands our attention.

But workplace trauma encompasses more than the very real threat of violence. In 1981, the author made a presentation at a safety and health training session at her work organization and had the opportunity to meet several flight attendants who had been in serious critical incidents—including crashes—where people had been injured and killed. Although these events had occurred many years earlier, when those involved began to discuss their experiences, it was painfully clear that many still had emotional wounds that had not healed; they were indeed walking wounded.

Because these individuals had not received any mental health assistance in the aftermath of their traumatic encounters, many issues still remained unresolved for them. Tragically, they were still victimized by the memories of their experiences.

The encounter with these survivors left an indelible impression on the author who began to research the literature on trauma psychology. At the time, she strongly believed these maladaptive outcomes were avoidable. Further review of the literature confirmed that if these individuals had received the appropriate emotional support they needed, their symptoms could have been minimized—or prevented altogether (Farberow & Gordon, 1979; Feuer, 1994; Hartsough & Myers, 1985; Mitchell, 1988).

In the mid-1980s, the author, then director of a well-respected EAP, designed one of the first workplace-trauma intervention models in the EAP field—an emergency response plan that provided an effective response to violence as well as to other traumatic events that occur all too often at the workplace.

Further impetus for incorporating this value-added service into the EAP was the desire to find the answers to a number of critical unanswered questions. What are the effects—immediate and long-term—of extraordinarily stressful events on victims/survivors and those who help them? What kinds of interventions are most effective in empowering those who have been traumatized so that they can recover and emerge as healthy survivors?

The importance of early recognition and treatment of post-traumatic stress responses is extensively documented in work with rape and violent-crime victims/survivors, survivors of natural disasters, and incest survivors (Kivens, 1980). In reviewing the literature, research confirmed that early intervention after the initial traumatic event appears to prevent—or significantly lessen—the post-traumatic effect on those involved. The literature also supports the author's hypothesis that crisis-intervention services offered as soon as possible after the traumatic event can minimize human suffering and later disabilities, as well as medical treatment, and legal costs (Mitchell, 1983; Barnett-Queen & Bergmann, 1988; Dunning, 1990; Lawson, 1987). These alone are certainly compelling reasons for including a workplace trauma-response component into an EAP's scope of services.

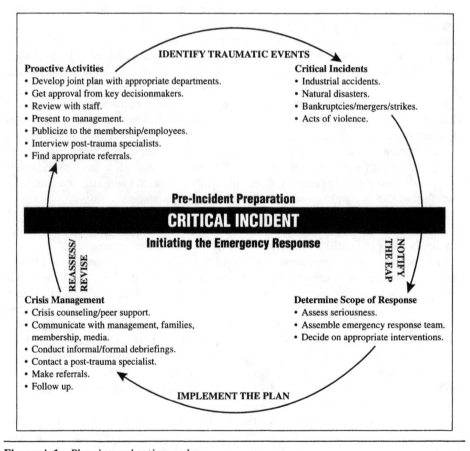

Figure A.1   Planning and action cycle.

The intervention paradigm presented in this chapter includes strategies for assisting coworkers and family members, as well as victim survivors. The model is operationalized via trauma-intervention training for coworkers trained as peer counselors, and builds on their already existing crisis-intervention skills. The model also offers EAPs the resources to:

- Proactively prepare for the eventuality of a critical incident.
- Assess the level of intervention necessary when a traumatic event occurs.
- Respond appropriately through proven intervention strategies, including formal and informal debriefings, one-on-one crisis counseling, education and information dissemination, and advocacy.
- Follow up with victims/survivors after the situation has stabilized. (Refer to Figure A.1.)

The author's model also addresses two important, but often overlooked issues—helping the helpers and secondary victimization (McCann, L. & Pearlman, L.A., 1990).

PART 1: A NONTRADITIONAL APPROACH

Though we usually respond adequately to life's demands and adapt accordingly, certain events are so significant in their human impact that even the most psychologically healthy worker will experience acute traumatic-stress reactions when exposed to them. These psychologically traumatic events are literally outside the range of normal human experience and can cause those involved in a critical incident to experience unusually intense emotional reactions that have the potential to interfere with their ability to function—either at the time of the event and later on. As an EAP professional, you may have observed this phenomenon with employees who are victims of sexual assault, domestic violence, and other crimes.

At the same time, you may have also noticed similar reactions among those who have been involved in a traumatic event on the job. Workplace trauma—from a minor mishap on the plant floor to a serious incident with loss of life—may precipitate traumatic stress reactions among those involved. You need to be aware of and to understand how a critical incident can impact those involved.*

Trauma is defined by a person's **subjective experience,** that is, if an individual experiences an event as life threatening (either actually life endangering or **perceived** as such), then she or he will experience traumatic stress reactions. It is important to understand that these are normal reactions to abnormal events—and no one is immune.

An underlying principle of this emergency response approach is the belief that crisis intervention and supportive treatment are the most effective post-trauma interventions. This approach differs from more traditional mental health models because

---

* A *critical incident* is defined as an unexpected event that causes suffering and loss and whose impact goes beyond the bounds of normal stress, for example, aircraft emergency, natural disaster, bankruptcy, strike, merger, and primary/secondary violence/threat.

it includes outreach and support **by peers** as well as by mental health professionals. It also assumes that the majority of people involved in critical incidents are normal, functioning human beings who are experiencing serious—but temporary—stress and trauma.

Thus, for most people, there will be no serious negative long-term repercussions in the aftermath. However, for those whose equilibrium is already upset by other stressors (e.g., health problems, illness, family problems or relationship issues), involvment in a critical incident could be the last straw. If a person continues to relive the memories of the event over and over again without meaningful resolution, one remains a victim, instead of becoming a survivor.

Peer Support: Coworkers Helping Their Peers

A common thread in the literature on trauma psychology is the importance of social support in the aftermath of a traumatic incident. What becomes clear is that the **disruption of social support** following an incident is one of the most damaging aspects for those directly impacted. Because the foundation of this model is based on peer support, the role of trained peer counselors is especially important.

Researchers have also found that when working with trauma victims, informal social networks have several advantages over professionals, including:

- A greater likelihood that informal social network members will intervene either prior to or soon after a problem develops (i.e., earlier identification and intervention—two basic EAP principles).
- The consistent availability of informal social networks (i.e., when a victim/survivor contacts a peer, she or he can be available as long as necessary).
- The help peer counselors offer is less costly, certainly less stigmatizing, and more comfortable for the survivors to accept (coworkers are part of the same subculture).

Thus, this approach optimizes chances for successful psychological outcome. And responding to critical incidents should be a natural by-product of any EAP's mandate.

BEING READY: PROACTIVE PLANNING AND PREPARATION

If a well-thought out emergency response plan is in place before a traumatic event happens, you're one step ahead of the game. Thus, the emphasis in this section is on what to do **before** an incident occurs. Being prepared is always the best defense.

What then are the essential elements of an effective trauma intervention plan? They include 7 important ingredients:

1. Crisis (one-on-one) counseling.
2. Debriefings: formal/informal.
3. Education and information dissemination.
4. Referrals to appropriate treatment providers.
5. Follow-up with all impacted groups.

6. A "helping the helper" component.

7. Evaluating—and revising—of the plan and of the process, as necessary.

Each of these elements is addressed in the pages that follow.

Who Should Be Involved?

An emergency-response plan works best if those whose areas of responsibility are affected are involved in the plan design. The EAP should take the following steps *before* a critical incident occurs:

1. Schedule a meeting(s) for EAP, safety and health, medical, human resources departments, and any other appropriate departments to:
   - Look at what emergency response plans and procedures already exist, if any.
   - Assess how they are working—or not (i.e., what needs to be changed, what can stay as is).
2. Collaborate on developing a plan of action for responding after critical incidents.
   - Spell out roles and responsibilities. For example, the safety and health department is the technical investigation experts after a critical incident. The EAP is the crisis (trauma) intervention expert.
   - Define common and functional specific goals and objectives. Be sure they're reasonable and do-able!
   - Commit to working together to provide the most helpful response to all those affected, e.g., survivors, coworkers, general employee population, families).
3. Meet with appropriate decision makers to define specific labor/management emergency response roles and clarify jurisdictional issues.
   - Get their commitment to notify the EAP whenever a critical incident happens—no matter how minor they think it is.
   - Be sure they have the contact phone numbers of those designated as the primary contacts.
   - Ask about degree of company/union involvement. Will they pay for—or help defray—the following costs?
     (1) Family members' transportation to the site, if necessary.
     (2) Trauma consultant's fees and expenses.
     (3) Meeting room rental/refreshments for debriefings (if incident is off-site).
     (4) Reproduction of resource materials/handouts.
     (5) Replacement of lost or ruined clothing and immediate-need toiletries.
     (6) Time off, if recommended by EAP.
     (7) Cost for any necessary treatment, if recommended by EAP.
   - Get their commitment to fully cooperate in providing a timely trauma-intervention response that is timely by:
     (1) Designating certain management staff, if appropriate as key contacts.
     (2) Making sure these individuals are aware of the chain of command and who the key EAP players are.

4. Finalize action plan by making sure all employees know:
   - Who to call and what to do when they hear about—or are involved in—a critical incident.
   - What critical incidents are, and are familiar with your work organization's emergency response plan.
5. Communicate critical information through written and face-to-face communication.
   - Company and/or union newsletter articles.
   - Bulletin board pieces in visible places.
   - Presentations at meetings, new-hire orientations, and in-house staff trainings and workshops.

Checklist

_____ 1. **Meet** with departmental counterparts.

_____ 2. **Develop** an action plan.

_____ 3. **Meet** with your boss(es).

_____ 4. **Meet** with top decision makers.

_____ 5. **Develop** outreach plan to reach all employees/members.

_____ 6. **Communicate** emergency response plan to same.

ROLES AND RESPONSIBILITIES

The Emergency Response Team

The first order of business is for team members to be prepared and ready to go to the scene when an incident occurs—no matter what time of the day or night.

- Clarify roles/responsibilities/chain of command/accountability issues **before** the incident so that everyone is as prepared as possible.
- The team must decide **who** will respond to **what** kinds of critical incidents.
  1. Some will be more comfortable responding to a **less** serious critical incident. (See Table A.1.)
  2. Others might want to be involved in any type of critical incident response.
- Because the response is more complex after a **serious** or **less serious** critical incident, decide who will have primary responsibility for coordinating emergency response activities.
  - At the site (if away from the workplace).
  - At the worksite.
  - Systemwide (if there are multiple worksites).

Table A.1 Assessing the Appropriate Response

	Serious (Loss of Life/Serious Injury)	Less Serious (Injury)	Least Serious
Critical Incident	• Crash • Industrial accidents • Bomb explosion • Natural disaster • Primary/secondary violence/threats*	• Industrial accidents • Natural disaster • Bankruptcies/mergers/ strikes • Primary/secondary violence/threats*	• Industrial accidents • Bankruptcies/mergers/ strikes • Primary/secondary violence/threats
	Crisis Counseling/Formal Debriefings for	Crisis Counseling and/or Formal/Informal Debriefings for	Within 24 Hours Contact
Intervention	• Those involved • Family members (optional) • General employee	• Involved employees • General employee group (optional)	• Involved employees
	Systemwide	Systemwide	Systemwide
	• EAP in employee cafeterias/lounges • Debriefings (optional) • Emergency response resource materials available	• EAP in cafeterias/ lounges (optional) • Informal debriefings (optional) • Emergency response resource materials available	• Optional
	At the Site (Off-Site)	Systemwide	At the Site (On-Site)
Emergency Response Team	• EAP • Post-trauma specialist	• EAP • Post-trauma specialists (optional)	• EAP
	EAP	EAP	EAP
Follow-Up	• For 1 year	• As needed	• As needed

*Robbery, homicide/suicide, sexual/physical assault.

Set up "mission control" operations for **at least** two days following the critical incident:

- Be available for crisis counseling/peer support to anyone who needs it;
- Distribute emergency response resource materials to employees coming and leaving work; and
- Assess the appropriate level of response in regards to any debriefing needs.

Team Leader (Primary EAP Staffperson)

After a **serious** critical incident he or she is the designated team leader(s) unless this responsibility is delegated to another staff member. The team leader is responsible for:

- Working with the trauma specialist during the critical-incident debriefing.
- Acting as the liaison between the involved employees and the company.
- Working with your company's communications department (or whoever coordinates media coverage).

Team Coordinator (responsibilities should be shared among team members)

- Primary logistical and administrative support person.
    - Locates meeting rooms for the scheduled debriefings.
- Provides backup support for the team leader.
- Keeps those who need to know apprised of the situation as it develops.
- Takes care of the needs of the trauma specialist.
    - Provides resource information about the work subculture.
    - Secures temporary I.D. badges to allow them on the site (if that is where debriefings are to be held).
- Makes sure that resource materials are copied and ready for distribution.
- Gets supplies ready for the general debriefing(s).
- Identifies local physicians with occupational injury expertise (for individuals who might file injury claims).

Team Members (Peer Counselors)

These individuals are the eyes and ears of the effort. They have primary contact with the involved employees up until, and after, the initial emergency response. In general, their role is to:

- Offer support and comfort in the immediate aftermath.
- Provide crisis counseling and peer support before and after any law enforcement and other necessary interviews and meetings.
- Encourage those involved and their family members to participate in scheduled debriefings.
- Ensure that referrals and follow-up will be done for those who need it.

The team also protects the victim/survivor from being retraumatized (a second injury) by acting as a buffer in response to the demands of the media, family, and others.

The EAP/Trauma Specialist Relationship

Before a Critical Incident

- Find your resources **before** a critical incident happens!
  1. The following can help you assess the suitability of potential trauma consultants:
     — Are they licensed mental health professionals?
     — Do they have post-trauma intervention experience?
     — Do they have debriefing experience?
     — What feedback have you gotten from professionals?
  2. When you find providers:
     — Describe the key elements of the emergency response plan.
     — Clarify their role:

     After **serious critical incidents**—he or she will colead the debriefing with the EAP.

     After **less serious critical incidents**—if a debriefing is necessary, the specialist will cofacilitate with an EAP staff member.
- Screen carefully and be selective! If potential consultants are not responsive to your needs, you don't need them!
- Discuss their fees as soon as possible.
  1. To segue into this discussion, be sure they understand what your expectations are about their involvement.
  2. Examples of usual and customary charges:
     — Facilitating the debriefing(s) (usually includes preparation time).
     — Expenses.
     — Travel.
     — Meals and hotels.
  3. If you would like them to be involved but their fees are too high for your budget, try negotiating a reduced rate based on the following arguments:
     — There is good potential for future business.
       • Referrals.
       • Workshops/trainings for the general employee population.
     — Your organization has a great population to work with!
  4. **Before** you hire a trauma specialist, always ask for references—and then check them.

REMEMBER

The best time to identify resources is
before you actually need them.

PART 2: WHEN THE EAP IS NOTIFIED

INITIATING THE EMERGENCY RESPONSE

1. Determine the seriousness of the critical incident (Refer to Table A.1)
   - According to the action plan the EAP must be notified as soon as possible after the incident occurs.
     - From 9–5, the office should be called directly.
     - After working hours, the designated EAP contact should be contacted by beeper or hotline number.
2. Organize the response team

   After a **Serious** Critical Incident
   - The team leader delegates responsibilities in person or by phone to the team.
     - She or he decides who will go to the site if the incident is off-site, and who will coordinate the efforts in-house.
   - When the critical incident is serious, part of the team is usually dispatched to the site.
   - The rest of the team coordinates activities at home.
   - The EAP staff also handles all logistical requirements.
     - Hotel reservations, car rentals.
     - Getting approval for trauma consultant, etc.
   - The peer counselors act as advocates for those affected.
     - Getting involved away from the scene as soon as possible.
     - Making sure they have access to medical care if warranted.
     - Offering emotional support and letting them know professional help is available, if necessary.
3. Implement the plan

   After **Serious/Less Serious** Critical Incidents

   Off-site
   - Setup a "mission control" center.
   - Dispatch designated team members to the site:
     - EAP from headquarters.
     - Local EAP staff, if incident takes place at another company location.
   - Begin dealing with affected employee groups immediately.
   - Decide if a debriefing specialist needs to be involved.
     - Have team members ready to meet with:
       - Victim/survivors
       - witnesses
       - coworkers
       - families members
   - Don't forget the injured victim/survivors!

—Try to organize makeshift debriefings for them (and their family members) in the hospital or at home.

—If not possible, try to schedule debriefings a week after incident (or as close to this time frame as possible).

In-house

• Set-up "mission control" center in the EAP offices.

• Dispatch EAP staff to support the victims/survivors during any interviews.

• Schedule debriefings within a week of the incident (24–72 hours is the optimal time frame).

Dispersed Workforce

• Committees should expect to be available on site in employee cafeterias or lounges for at least 2 days to:

—Talk with incoming and outgoing employees.

—Provide crisis counseling to those who ask for it.

—Answer any questions, quell rumors and hearsay.

• After the second day, teams can assess the need for additional coverage.

• Be ready to have debriefings if necessary.

• Reproduce *Resource Material* packets and have them available.

—Be sure the front page of the packets have EAP contact names and phone numbers.

—Include the names and phone numbers of EAP and other relevant contacts.

4. Contact trauma specialist (when necessary)

• Have the following information ready:

—Date, time, location of incident.

—Number of employees involved.

—Probable time(s) and location(s) of planned debriefings.

—Any other important information (e.g., deaths, injuries).

—A phone number where he or she can reach the designated emergency response team member.

• Clarify logistics and compensation:

—Consultation fees.

—Hotel/travel arrangements.

5. Clarify your relationship with the media

• If you don't have a Communications or PR Department, assign a team member to act as your media contact.

• Get agreement from all team members that they will not talk to the media.

• The media contact should coordinate all media activities with the team leader.

PART 3: THE EAP CONTINUUM OF CARE: SHORT-TERM CONCERNS

PUTTING THE TRAUMA EXPERIENCE INTO PERSPECTIVE

Mitigating Factors

When a critical incident occurs, it is usually sudden, apparently random, and often seems senseless. The event affects not only victims/survivors, but family members, coworkers, and the work organization as a whole. People's sense of safety and invulnerability are shattered, upsetting the apparent normalcy of everyday life, and often unleashing strong feelings of anger and grief.

The human response to a traumatic experience can be severe and disruptive. Those involved may find themselves coming back to work extremely stressed. They may blame themselves or the company. They may have trouble eating and sleeping and get annoyed with everyone in sight. The important thing to remember is that all these reactions are perfectly **normal** responses to an **abnormal** experience.

Some incidents are of such magnitude that they are experienced as traumatic by almost everyone exposed to them. Others may precipitate trauma reactions in some people because of specific life experiences and other mitigating factors (see Figure A.2), but will not cause significant reactions in others.

How is this possible? Because trauma is defined by our **subjective** experience of the event, rather than the event itself. In other words, if one experiences or perceives a situation as life-threatening, then he or she will probably have some traumatic stress reaction symptoms. The trauma response is simply the body and mind's way of reacting to a terrible shock.

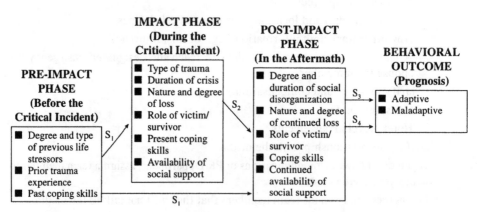

Stress$_1$ What happened in the past will affect what happens during and after the critical incident

Stress$_2$ Caused by the traumatic event

Stress$_3$ Caused by the traumatic event and subsequent community (workplace) and/or social systems (family, friends) disorganization

Stress$_4$ The result of community (workplace) and/or social system (family/friends) disorganization

Figure A.2   The effect of pre-impact, impact, and post-impact variables on outcome.

Although individuals react with different degrees of intensity and recover at varying rates, almost everyone close to a critical incident—and some not so close—will experience some traumatic stress reactions. Generally, the effects are not long lasting. But for some, they can continue in some form for months or years and if not detected and treated can cause severe psychological and behavioral problems.

The Phases of the Trauma Response

The trauma experience, from initial impact through recovery, is not a static one. Those who are traumatized progress through various stages, often moving back and forth among them until they have managed to resolve the effects of their experience. Different people progress at different speeds.

Researchers agree that there are 3 primary phases people move through as they progress from being victim to becoming a survivor.

1. **Pre-impact**—the period when a person realizes that something is about to happen. For the victim/survivor, it might be a matter of seconds, with no time to prepare, or hours, with time enough to prepare, coupled with the agony of waiting for the incident to finally happen.

2. **Impact**—the actual event. During this phase, survival efforts are initiated. People report being on automatic pilot and not remembering what they did during or right after the critical incident.

3. **Post-impact**—begins shortly after the incident and may last up to 2 years. Some researchers have divided this important period of time into 3 additional phases:

   a. **Honeymoon**—a brief period (hours to weeks) during which victim/survivors feel a sense of relief at having survived.

   b. **Disillusionment**—the time when those involved begin to realize that there has been a permanent disruption in their lives as a result of the incident. They sense that things will never be the same again, and this new reality is very hard to come to grips with for some. Feelings of anger, resentment, and frustration may surface. Some victim/survivors react by making dramatic changes—not always in their best interests (divorces, geographic changes, job changes). They may also become depressed and have difficulty coping. The connection with the critical incident is often overlooked by the victim/survivor and those close to him or her. The EAP can help make the critical connection.

   c. **Reconstruction**—During this stage, victims/survivors begin to take responsibility for rebuilding their lives, physically, emotionally, and spiritually. This can be a slow and difficult process, and support and understanding—along with large doses of patience—are essential.

The chart that follows (Figure A.2) presents an overview of factors to be addressed in the aftermath of a critical incident. These should be considered for each victim/survivor with whom you work. Other questions to consider are:

- How has he or she coped in the past—in a healthy, adaptive way or not?
- What kinds of trauma/crises has s/he had to deal with before?
- What about her/his support systems? Are they a help or a hindrance?

- What kind of personality type is he or she—calm, cool and collected, easily agitated, or a hot head?
- How long have they been working for the company?
- Has he or she been involved in any other critical incidents in the past? How serious were they?

Being aware that the whole person is greater than the sum of his or her parts will enhance what you do for those with whom you work.

PRIMARY INTERVENTION STRATEGIES (refer to Figure A.3)

"Yet truth, like love and sleep, resents
approaches that are too intense."
—Auden

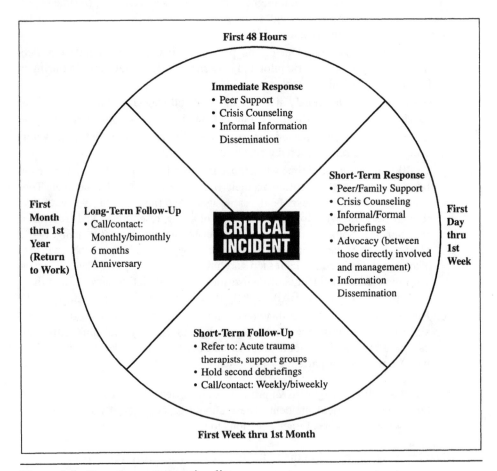

Figure A.3 Emergency response time line.

Peer Support

As soon as the team is in place and begins meeting face-to-face with those involved, peer counselors have their EAP hats on. At the site, in hotel rooms, at the hospital, before and after any interviews, and possibly during long days and evenings together—whenever they have an opportunity to meet with affected employee groups—there is an opportunity to do some important emotional band-aiding with victims/survivors. Peers are an important **buffer** between victim/survivors and the outside world.

As front line team members, peer counselors will have to function effectively in a pretty chaotic environment. Their primary role is one that encourages:

- **Normalization** of victim/survivor feelings, thoughts, and reactions as reasonable responses to an unreasonable, abnormal situation.

- **Validation** of the experience for each victim/survivor in his or her own terms and from his or her perspective.

- **Clarification** of facts versus rumors. Respond to their confusion and answer questions those involved may have about what happened, what will happen next, and what to expect in the very near future.

- **Ventilation** of their feelings of anger, frustration, "survivor guilt," self-doubt, and encouraging/giving them permission to communicate what they are feeling. Peer counselors are a "safe haven" for them to confidentially get these feelings out—perhaps the only one they have.

- **Advocacy:** Peer counselors function as mediators/negotiators/liaisons between those who have been hurt and those who are "supposed" to help.

Peer (one-on-one) Counseling Guidelines

1. *Establish Rapport*
   - Let survivors know that you know what you're doing. Though you might be unsure, don't let on!
   - Be respectful.
   - Be nonjudgmental.
   - Use active listening skills to move him or her from surface "content" issues to underlying "process" issues.
   - Build trust by promising only what you **can** do—not what you would like to do, or what he or she would like you to do.

2. *Be Empathic*
   - Put yourself in the victim/survivor's shoes. Convey to him or her that you understand and appreciate the experience—"I hear you."
     —Imagine what it would be like if it had happened to you.
     —If something similar has happened, remember how you felt and how you acted.

3. *Define and Focus on One Problem at a Time*
   - Identify specific problems.
     —Prioritize problems in order of importance.
     —Try to make whatever issues you chose to deal with as simple to resolve as possible—this gives the survivor a sense of control over an environment that seems out of control in the wake of the critical incident.

4. *Assess the Problem*
   - Carefully consider the seriousness of the situation for each member with whom you work. Try to find out if he or she:
     —Has been involved in a previous critical incident.
       When?
       What kind?
       How did he or she respond?
       Did he or she receive professional help?
     —What about other past traumatic experiences? (Was the EAP/other resources involved?)
   - Keep the focus on inner resources, personality, and present coping skills:
     —Is he or she usually calm, cool, and collected?
     —Or is he or she a hothead who deals with problems impulsively?
   - Answering these questions helps you to:
     —Establish priorities.
     —Assess the problem-solving capacity of the client.
     —Choose appropriate referral resources.

5. *Evaluate Available Resources*
   - When you're notified about a critical incident, contact several therapists with acute trauma experience with whom you've worked before.
   - Discuss a plan of action regarding expedited referral procedures and the EAP's role in follow-up.
   - Ask if other resources/support systems are available.

6. *Develop a Plan of Action*
   - In the wake of a critical incident, victims/survivors need to feel:
     —Useful.
     —Helpful.
     —That they can do something positive:
       a. Those who do, recover more quickly.
       b. Those who feel useless and helpless have more problems.
   - Having a sense of what's going to happen next gives survivors a sense of safety and security. Remember, their sense of vulnerability has been significantly increased, and that's scary.
   - A concrete plan, no matter how simple, is reassuring. The objective is for victim/survivor to think, "If I can come up with a plan, I'll be OK." This goes a

long way in helping them begin to deal with the myriad of feelings they are experiencing—guilt, sadness, being overwhelmed, confusion, fear, uncertainty.

7. *Move toward Closure*
  • Review what you've discussed and the next steps that will be taken by both you and the survivor.
  • Suggest to him or her that involvement in a critical incident can be an opportunity for growth and positive change.
    —When saying this, don't minimize the fact that his or her experience was a painful one.
    —Let the client know you'll follow-up during the next few weeks/months (depending on the seriousness of the critical incident).

The following will help the team distinguish between those who need a referral and those who don't. As with other cases, making a good referral requires that you act tactfully and sensitively.

Although a victim/survivor may have symptoms of physical and psychological stress, he or she may not be receptive to outside help for a host of reasons. If this is the case, she or he may respond more positively to a suggestion to contact a family physician or a trusted member of her/his support system. Follow-up is important to ensure the survivor is getting appropriate help.

Alertness and Awareness

You can probably handle the case if he or she:
  • Is aware of who he or she is, where he or she is, and what happened.
  • Is only slightly confused or dazed, or
  • Shows only slight difficulty in thinking clearly or concentrating on a subject.

Make a referral (psychiatric because of possible medical/neurological complications) if he or she:
  • Is unable to give his or her own name or names of people with whom he or she lives.
  • Cannot tell you the date, where he or she is, or what he or she does.
  • Cannot recall the events of the past 24 hours.
  • Complains about memory gaps.

Behavior

You can probably handle if he or she:
  • Wrings his or her hands, clenches fists, or is still and rigid.
  • Is restless, mildly agitated, and/or excited.
  • Has rapid or halting speech.
  • Has trouble sleeping.

Refer if he or she:
- Seems severely depressed.
- Is totally apathetic, immobile, or unable to rouse self to any movement.
- Describes or exhibits any self-mutilation.
- Talks about using alcohol or drugs excessively.
- Looks as if he or she is unable to care for self; isn't eating, drinking, bathing, or changing clothes (when there are clothes to change into!).

Emotions

You can probably handle if he or she:
- Cries and weeps, with continuous retelling of the incident.
- Has blunted emotions/affect, appears dazed, and doesn't react much to what is going on around her or him.
- Exhibits very high spirits, laughs excessively.
- Is easily irritated and angered about minor things.

Refer if he or she:
- Is unable to be aroused, despite your efforts, or is totally withdrawn.
- Is excessively emotional and exhibits extremely inappropriate emotional reactions.

Conversation

You can probably handle if he or she:
- Is able to express feelings of depression.
- Has doubts about her/his ability to recover.
- Is overly concerned with inconsequential things.
- Denies problems or wants to take care of everything alone.
- Blames problems on others, or articulates anger and resentment about what happened.

Refer if he or she:
- Hallucinates—hears voices, sees visions, or has imagined bodily sensations.
- States that his or her body feels unreal and that he or she fears losing his or her mind.
- Is excessively or obsessively preoccupied with one idea or thought.
- Is unable to make simple decisions or carry out everyday functions.
- Expresses paranoid thoughts; has the delusion that someone or something is out to get her or him and her or his family.
- Is incoherent and talks without making any sense.
- Is afraid of killing herself or himself or someone else (imminent risk).

SECONDARY INTERVENTION STRATEGIES

Debriefings: Formal and Informal

The debriefing process is rooted within a crisis-intervention framework—the cornerstone of this trauma response model. It is the author's experience that debriefings are useful intervention strategies, when "done right." At the same time, they are not magic bullets.

By definition, a debriefing is a psychoeducational group meeting that, although not group therapy is by its very nature naturally therapeutic. Its purpose is twofold:

1. To help reduce the possibility that those involved in a critical incident will experience long-term maladaptive effects, and
2. To assist their functioning to return to pre-impact level.

Participation gives survivors the chance to share what is on their minds without being judged or critiqued. Beginning the task of "working through" what happened in a safe, secure setting with other survivors can be a positive and healing experience.

What a Debriefing Is . . . and What It Isn't

In this model the post-trauma debriefing is a peer-driven process. This means that peer counselors are the backbone of this intervention strategy.

The goals are:

1. To meet the needs of those involved in the incident, as well as other affected employee groups.
2. To prepare participants for possible emotional after-effects.
3. To begin the process of moving those involved from victim to survivor status.

The objectives are:

1. To encourage ventilation of feelings.
2. To reinforce group cohesiveness.
3. To normalize feelings, thereby reducing the sense of abnormality/"craziness" that many often experience in the aftermath of a critical incident.
4. To identify those in need of a referral.
5. To underscore the fact that the EAP is there.
   a. As part of their support system.
   b. As advocates with families, the work organization, and others.
   c. As a knowledgeable resource which can refer them **confidentially** to appropriate mental health professionals.
   d. To follow-up.

Potential Client Populations

Involved Employees

1. Try to organize debriefing as quickly as possible.
   a. This includes those who are ambulatory and those who are hospitalized, if possible.
   b. Enlist coworkers, family members and friends to encourage them to attend.
   c. Be aware that those involved may decide they want nothing further to do with the EAP/the company after the incident.
      (1) Researchers have found that fear of affect (feeling) overload may make the survivors wary of any kind of mental health intervention.
      (2) Also, because victims may go through denial in response to the critical incident, it may be difficult to get through.
      (3) Nonetheless, still try to contact them, but be aware that some might refuse your help. Don't take it personally!

Family Members (after serious critical incidents only)

1. Shouldn't be included in the debriefing because their issues are often different. (Refer to the resource materials packet.)
2. Prepare resource materials and have them available at the time of the debriefing.

General Employee Group (usually only after a serious critical incident)

1. EAP should get the word out about the debriefings as soon as possible.
   a. Put notices on bulletin boards, in restrooms, in the cafeteria, and in employee lounges.
   b. Put an informational message on where and when these debriefings will be held on the EAP answering machine.
2. Have resource packets reproduced and available.
   a. Distribute in debriefings.
   b. Leave packets in a visible place in employee lounges for those who are unable to attend.

The Debriefing Process

Before

1. Debriefings are for all directly involved employees. After a serious and less serious critical incident, the EAP team will determine the need for general employee debriefings.
2. Be prepared. Put together some 5 × 7 index card "cheat sheets." Tell the group what the index cards are for (i.e., to help you remember the things you need to remember!).
3. They usually last from 2 to 4 hours, but may go longer.
4. Law enforcement, government agency, and company interviews usually take place before the debriefing.

5. All EAP team members should plan to have meals together. Use this important time to:

   a. Informally debrief.

   b. Discuss any problems or issues that have come up and need to be clarified.

   c. Plan and synchronize your schedules for the next few hours.

   d. Be supportive of one another's needs.

6. The team leader should meet with the debriefing specialist **before** the debriefings:

   a. To plan your strategy.

   b. To be sure that both of you understand your roles, and

   c. To discuss the possibility of a second debriefing.*

During

1. As difficult as it might be, the team leader (and any other members of the emergency response team who will be assisting) must control their emotions as much as possible until after the debriefing.

2. Be aware of unresolved grief issues—they can get in the way. When in doubt, have another team member take your place.

3. If possible, don't take part in a debriefing with employees you know personally—it's difficult to detach yourself.

4. Practice your listening skills and be a good listener/observer. You have an excellent opportunity to identify group members who might need professional help.

5. It's okay if there are some long pauses. Don't feel the need to jump in too quickly just for the sake of filling in the quiet spaces.

6. Maintain your composure and stay in control during a debriefing. Whether they express it or not, the employees may feel lost, and you're there to "help them find their way again." They'll look to you for the strength and assurance that they won't be feeling.

. . . *And After*

1. This isn't the time to be a martyr! Team members—including the debriefing specialist—should make sure to debrief themselves and discuss how they felt the session went:

   a. What parts went well?

   b. What didn't go as well as you would have liked?

   c. What was most difficult?

   d. What would you do differently next time?

   e. Who in the group do you need to pay special attention to?

2. Pay attention to the emotional impact that a critical incident has on supervisors and other management team members and offer them any assistance you feel is warranted.

---

* Some involved may be unable to attend the first debriefing because of injuries.

OUTLINE

Logistics

- Chairs should be in a circle or horseshoe.
  — Don't overwhelm participants with too many EAP staff.
  —A good ratio is one team member to four involved employees.
  —Team members can sit among participants.
- Be sure you have all necessary supplies, such as:
  —Flip chart or chalkboard.
  —Felt-tipped markers or chalk.
  —Tissues.
  —Noncaffeinated soft drinks and/or tea and coffee (if possible).
  —Handouts for all participants.
- Have a cup of coffee/tea/soda with you. Taking a sip during difficult moments can help you keep your composure.

Phase 1: Breaking the Ice

1. Begin with brief introductions. This should take no more than 10 to 15 minutes.
   a. EAP team.
   b. Trauma specialist.
2. If there are hospitalized employees, give a brief status report.
3. Establish ground rules.
   a. Clarify what a debriefing is—and what it isn't.
      (1) It is not a critique of the incident.
      (2) It is:
         (a) A safe place to discuss whatever they want to about what happened, and
         (b) An opportunity to ventilate.
   b. Explain the rationale for participating.
   c. Clarify confidentiality.
      (1) Group should share whatever they want.
      (2) No one can discuss other people's issues with anyone outside of the room.
   d. Get verbal commitments that all participants will honor confidentiality.
   e. Emphasize that no one is obligated to talk unless they want to.
      (1) Reassure them that people learn by listening as well.
      (2) But also let them know that people who participate have benefited from sharing their experience with the group.
   f. Formal breaks aren't scheduled, so if people need to go to the restroom, they should do so quietly.

g. There are no tape recorders or note taking by team leaders—and no media participation.

h. Ask them to do their best not to leave before the meeting is over.

Trainer Notes: *Structurally, this piece works best when done in a "round robin" format where facilitators ask each participant to respond. Though there is an expectation that everyone will contribute, if someone chooses not to, that's okay.*

At this point, team leaders should also be able to assess the level/intensity of emotions (as a result of the critical incident) of the participants.

Phase 2: Painting a Picture

During this part of the meeting, participants establish common ground by factually describing what they did during the incident. This is important for two reasons: (1) it helps group members establish a collective picture of what happened, and (2) participants learn about things they didn't know happened.

1. Ask them to discuss their experience in the context of the **technical** aspects of what happened. Some helpful questions are:
   a. Where were you when incident occurred?
   b. Do you remember what you were doing?
   c. What specifically happened to you?
2. Watch for any changes in body language.
   a. Squirming.
   b. Eyes down.
   c. Tears welling up.
   d. Crying.
   e. Clenched or wringing of hands.
   f. Increased agitation.
3. Again, though it's beneficial for everyone to participate, don't pressure participants into talking if they don't want to:
   a. Some will be helped just by being with their peers and listening and learning from their contributions.
   b. There will be those who may want to contribute, but feel inhibited by more articulate group members. Help them to feel comfortable sharing.
4. When—and if—it feels comfortable, one of the co-leaders can begin asking more probing questions:
   a. Can you recall your first thoughts after you stopped functioning on automatic pilot and did what you had to do?
   b. What sticks in your mind about the incident/that day?
   c. What were your first thoughts when you knew something was wrong?

5. When everyone who wants to has had a chance to share, and the group has finished reporting the facts, you're ready to move on.

Phase 3: Reactions (Feelings)

Begin the transition from the cognitive experience of the debriefing to the emotional phase. This is usually very powerful for participants, and not surprisingly, it often takes the most time. The group is establishing trust, and participants are beginning to feel it's safe to share feelings.

Why is this important? Because the ability to talk about what they felt before, during, and after the incident—and what they're feeling now—helps victims/survivors to begin putting the experience in perspective. And, that is an important element in the recovery process.

1. Keep the group focused:
   a. There may be a tendency to critique one's performance during the critical incident—or the immediate aftermath.
   b. Don't let them get sidetracked by blaming or pointing fingers at others.
2. One of the coleaders can ask:
   a. What was the worst part for you?
   b. If you could, what would you erase, if anything?
   c. What do you want to remember (if anything)?
3. Ask group members to describe their reactions at the scene, in the aftermath and right now, refer to all aspects:
   a. Physical.
   b. Emotional.
   c. Cognitive.
   d. Behavioral.
4. As participants talk about their feelings/reactions, use your communication skills to acknowledge and validate what is being said. For example:

Participant:	I'm really angry.
Team Leader:	I'm not surprised. It's a really normal feeling after going through what you have.
Participant:	I keep thinking I could've done better during the evacuation.
Team Leader:	I think we all understand that you think you could've done better. But you did the best you could—and that's all anyone could ask.

Trainer Notes: Move on when there's no more discussion and both leaders feel that everyone has had ample opportunity to say what they have to say about their fears, anger, guilt, or sadness as a result of their experience.

Phase 4: New Learning

This stage signals a transition from feelings/emotions back to the cognitive in the context of new learning based on their shared experience.

1. Go over post-traumatic stress reactions handout (see Resource Materials). Put the information that's beng shared within the context of how they felt during, and immediately after, the critical incident—as well as to how they're feeling now. This awareness relieves some of the apprehension and anxiety they might be feeling presently. Or might possibly experience in the future.
2. Reassure them that what they're feeling is absolutely normal—and to be expected.
3. Begin to discuss some survival techniques, such as:
    a. What's worked for them in the past;
    b. How to tell family members/significant others what they've been through;
    c. What reactions to expect from their families/significant others/coworkers, friends. (Refer to the emergency response resource materials.)
    d. The importance of taking care of themselves.
        (1) Asking for what they need.
        (2) Saying "no" to what they don't.
4. Hand out resource materials (wait until the very end of the meeting to do this so that participants won't be distracted).

The Final Phase: Reintegration, Action Planning, and Closure

1. Suggest to participants that they begin thinking about a plan—nothing too complicated, but some simple tasks that will help them to feel a sense of control and purpose. If they aren't forthcoming, offer a few:
    a. Encouraging family members to attend the family debriefing, if one is planned.
    b. Attending memorial services (if there have been line-of-duty deaths).
    c. Follow-up meetings for the group (offer the EAP as a resource).
    d. A group visit to where the incident occurred:
        (1) For some, it's healing and cathartic to revisit the site together several days/weeks removed from the traumatic experience.
        (2) A visit also offers an opportunity to challenge their initial impressions and to put the experience into perspective.
        (3) For others, a visit might trigger strong emotional reactions. If anyone isn't ready, their needs must be respected.
2. Once again, assure participants that whatever they're feeling is normal and reasonable.
3. Encourage them to reach out for help and support from:
    a. Family.
    b. Friends.

    c. Coworkers.

    d. The EAP.

    e. A therapist (if they're already in counseling or thinking about getting some professional help).

4. Make any other administrative announcements.

5. Ask survivors to think a moment about any positives that have happened since the incident. If they can't come up with specifics, the co-leaders can point out the following:

    a. Even if they aren't aware of it yet, the debriefing has the effect of "normalizing" their feelings by allowing participants to talk and share with one another. They now know they're not alone.

    b. The debriefing has also given them a sense of group cohesiveness (i.e., being connected to one another) by virtue of what they've gone through together. They can be support systems for one another because they've all "walked the same walk." And a support system is an important element in the healing process.

    c. It can also foster a commitment to make positive changes in their working conditions.

    d. They now have resource information about potential problem areas and know what to do—and where to go—if they need help in the future.

6. Let participants know that treatment resources are available. Be sure they have:

    a. Names of EAP team members,

    b. All EAP phone numbers.

    c. A participant list. (Optional, but in the author's experience, participants consistently request this.)

7. Before formally closing, reemphasize the need for confidentiality—they cannot discuss what others have shared outside the room.

8. Let the participants know that team members are always available if any of them wants to speak with someone individually.

SUGGESTED DEBRIEFING SUPPLIES

- Blackboard or newsprint pad and easel.
- Chalk and/or felt-tipped markers.
- Handouts.
- Tissues.
- Refreshments (decaffeinated coffee/tea, soft drinks, ice).

Red Flags

Be alert to the following and follow-up immediately if participants:

- Were unable to look anyone in the room in the eye, specifically if someone addressed her or him.
- Cried during the entire meeting.
- Were clearly agitated during the debriefing.
- Left the room before the debriefing was over (and didn't come back).
- Had monotone and flat effect—reacted to no one and nothing.
- Threatened violence to themselves or others.
- Appeared to be under the influence of a mind altering substance.

INFORMAL DEBRIEFING OUTLINE

Key Elements

- An informal debriefing is a scaled-down version of a formal debriefing. It is often the intervention response of choice after **less** serious critical incidents.
- Although it is usually facilitated by someone from the EAP, there are times that a trauma specialist should lead the meeting. It's the EAP's call.
- Like a formal debriefing, the EAP's role is to provide a time and place for the meeting to take place in a safe and confidential environment.
- Ideally, the debriefing should be held no more than 12 to 24 hours after the incident.
- Informal debriefings shouldn't be much longer than an hour or so. The goal is to get people in, then get them out, and home.

Introductions

1. Begin with a brief explanation of what an informal debriefing is, and its purpose:
   a. A confidential meeting with the EAP.
   b. A chance for people to ventilate and share what they just went through and how they feel about it.
2. Let the group know that the meeting will last for as long as is necessary for them to feel as if they've gotten what happened off their chest.
3. Emphasize confidentiality (repeat at the beginning and the end of the session).
4. Let the group know they don't have to talk if they don't want to.

Gathering Information

1. Ask some trigger questions, such as:
   a. What happened?
   b. What were the worst parts for you?

    c. How did/do you feel?

    d. What would you like to forget?

    e. What would help you the most right now?

2. As you do during a more formal debriefing, encourage the group to share, but underscore that no one is forced to talk unless they want to.

    a. Give them permission to discuss what is on their minds.

    b. Don't minimize—or interrupt—when they express their hurt or pain.

3. Next, ask a few leading questions, such as:

    a. What will you do when you get home?

    b. Who will be there?

    c. How will you let them know what happened to you?

4. Give them the time they need to ventilate. This will lessen their anxiety.

Closure

1. When they're done, let them know that the EAP is available to them whenever they need someone to talk to.

2. Be sure the participants have a list with appropriate names and phone numbers.

3. Let them know that the EAP will be in touch in the next week or two just to "check-in."

4. Also explain that you have referral resources if they feel a need to meet with a therapist.

5. Emphasize:

    a. Not to be hard on themselves.

    b. Even if they don't feel like it, try to eat well and take care of themselves—physically, emotionally, and spiritually.

        (1) Ask for some examples of what they plan to do.

        (2) Give them some concrete examples of self-nurturing. (Distribute the emergency response handouts.)

6. Solicit any additional thoughts, questions, or comments.

7. Don't leave without reviewing confidentiality one more time.

PART 4: THE EAP CONTINUUM OF CARE: LONGER TERM ISSUES (refer to Figure A.3)

FOLLOW-UP!—SOME PRACTICAL CONSIDERATIONS

1. After a formal or informal debriefing, case management responsibilities are the EAPs.

2. The status of those involved should be monitored at the following intervals:

    a. After a debriefing

        (1) Weekly, during the first month.

        (2) At least one a month for the next 11 months.

        (3) After announcement of any investigation findings.

        (4) On the one-year anniversary of the incident.

    b. After an informal debriefing

        (1) At least once during the first month.

        (2) After the first month, assess if further contact is necessary.

        (3) A phone call on the one-year anniversary date of the incident.

3. For those members involved in serious critical incidents, the committee should assist them in locating appropriate treatment providers as soon as possible.

4. Although treatment providers should be knowledgeable in working with victims of trauma, be aware that a critical incident can also trigger underlying—or situational—problems that need to be addressed (refer to the next section, "The Art of Making a Good Referral"):

    a. Loss and grief.

    b. Relationship problems—family/spouse/partner.

    c. Substance abuse, etc.

Other Factors

1. Some research seems to indicate that the longer a person is off the line, the less likely they are to return. If there are mitigating factors (physical injuries, litigation) their return to work may also be delayed.

2. People who enter therapy after a critical incident will often take longer to return to work.

3. When you make a referral, be sure to get a release of information form to speak with the treatment provider (in addition to the involved member) about a return-to-work timeline.

4. *A word to the wise:* As in all EAP work, watch out for the development of an unhealthy relationship between any of the survivors and yourself.

The "Art" of Making a Good Referral

Important Points

Recovery takes longer than most of us expect. Just as the body requires time and expert care to recover from trauma, the mind's healing process may also require both time and expert care. Therapy can be an important source of support for victims/survivors and their families. Involved members may want a referral soon after the critical incident if symptoms are especially painful, or when relationships become troubled.

    People respond differently to their involvement in a critical incident. There are a host of factors that mitigate their reactions, and each of these should be considered when making a good referral:

- **Choose referrals carefully!**
  During the first few visits, the victim/survivor is often still in shock. Nevertheless, no matter what the reason, therapy for those who have been involved in a

critical incident should always have a net positive effect. While painful sessions are inevitable, the goal of treatment is always to help the client feel better.

Victims/survivors need to feel and believe that their therapist is really "with them" emotionally. Her or his office should be a safe place where all feelings can be expressed and tolerated. It is really important that the therapist be sensitive to the emotional trauma that has been experienced. If he or she is critical, judgmental, or cold, he or she adds to the victim's/survivor's distress and can contribute to what is known as a "second injury."

- **The aftermath of a critical incident isn't the time for exploratory work that can weaken a person's defenses.**

  Because victim\s/survivors are trying to integrate a nightmare that seems both real and unreal, therapy should focus on the present reality and validate the survivor's perceptions. It's not until after the immediate trauma has lessened that it may be useful to address past events that have been triggered by the present trauma.

  In addition, because his or her sense of invulnerability and self-esteem is weakened, the therapist needs to affirm the victim's/survivor's wholeness and strength in a supportive and nurturing manner. The client should also feel comfortable that the therapist respects her or his pace in integrating what has happened.

- **Not all therapists can do acute trauma therapy effectively.**

  If therapy is not helpful (i.e., if the employee feels that the therapist does not understand), then a referral to another therapist should be considered. At its best, therapy can hasten the recovery process and help the victim find a healthy, meaningful way to use the experience to learn and grow.

Who—and What—to Look For

- Therapists who specialize in acute crisis/trauma counseling.
- Those who have experience working with traumatized/victimized clients.
- Those whose therapeutic orientation is:
  —Short-term, crisis-oriented;
  —Problem-solving oriented; and
  —Focused on the here and now.
- Those who have expertise in grief work if there were deaths.
- It's a good idea to try to find male therapists for male victims/survivors, and female therapists for female victims/survivors.

THE RECOVERY PROCESS

A Conceptual Framework

Think of the recovery process as one where involved people move from being victims to survivors.

- Victims are immobilized by a traumatic event.
- Survivors begin to make peace with the memories of the incident and move on.

Remember that survivors of human-induced and technological critical incidents can suffer long-term effects. That's why an EAP intervention is so important. When the critical incident also involves injury, loss of life and/or destruction, the long-term effects can be very serious. The reactions of those directly involved are also influenced by the following:

- The way victims died.
- The number and condition of bodies they saw.
- The duration of contact with these details.

Recovery rarely follows a predictable and orderly path. Rather, it's a process of working through—and coming to terms with—what happened. Like the stages of grief experienced by those who have lost a loved one, victim survivors also move through stages on their healing journey. Knowing what to expect can be helpful for them, and for their helpers as well:

- **Relief and Confusion**

  This is just what it says—a time of reflection immediately following the critical incident where one feels relief that it's over, but confusion about:

  —What really happened;

  —Why; and

  —What the consequences are.

- **Avoidance**

  Yes—it is okay not to deal with what happened immediately. Avoidance takes the pressure off, thus reducing anxiety and stress symptoms—though only temporarily.

- **Leaving Denial Behind**

  This is time when victims/survivors feel ready to confront the trauma and do the work necessary to become a survivor. For some, this may begin as early as the debriefing. For others, it will be a lifelong struggle. Some may never reach the final stage. There is no guarantee. What we do know is that an EAP intervention enhances the chances that the outcome will be positive.

- **Acceptance and Adaptation**

  Early intervention and adequate resources (e.g., personal, social, spiritual, and financial) are essential. During this time, victims/survivors begin to address some important questions. You can help by continued support and understanding, by helping them think/talk about:

  —What happened?

  —Why did it happen?

  —Why did I act as I did?

  —Why have I acted as I have since the critical incident?

  —What if I'm involved in another critical incident in the future?

Thinking about and beginning to answer these questions helps those involved re-define and reframe the event so that they can find some meaning in what they went through. Though they won't ever feel as "invulnerable" as they did before the critical incident, they'll be able to integrate the experience and not be victimized by it.

ADDITIONAL HINTS ON HOW TO HELP

Emotionally, we're all held together in part by our environment. If that environment is dangerous and unpredictable, it doesn't serve this supportive function. And if our external world falls apart, we fall apart inside. Usual ways of coping may no longer work. In the aftermath of a critical incident, there are many important questions to consider, including:

- What is the victim's usual way of coping with stress?
- What is the extent of her or his physical injuries?
- What are the present circumstances in the lives of those involved?
- How will their daily routines be altered?
- How supportive are family, friends, coworkers, and the company?
- What kind of coverage has the incident gotten from the media?

Always remember that a victim's/survivor's need to feel safe must be taken seriously. Whether rational or not, the fear of involvement in another traumatic event is real and terrifying to them. Any steps that you can take to make him or her feel safe—even symbolically—should be taken. These can include:

- Driving survivors home (if family or friends aren't available).
- Getting those involved time off from work.

Even if a request or behavior seems somewhat odd, refrain from sounding (even if you're feeling) judgmental. An empathic comment, such as "You must be feeling really scared," is much more helpful than an appeal to logic, such as "It doesn't make sense to think that this will happen to you again."

Victims/survivors are also sensitive about others presuming to know just how they're feeling. When those who are trying to be helpful make comments like "I know exactly how you feel," that's a surefire turnoff. Unless you've been in a critical incident, you really don't understand. Worse than saying the wrong thing, though, is failing to acknowledge what has happened.

SOME FINAL THOUGHTS ON THE HELPING PROCESS

"That which does not destroy me makes me strong."
Nietzche

Coping with Being Powerless

- Helping survivors regain a sense of personal power is essential. This may come about in a number of ways, including learning about post-traumatic stress symptoms, as well as developing a plan of action in one-on-one crisis counseling or in a debriefing.
- Acknowledging and accepting what has happened is also very important. This is one of those times when the *"Serenity Prayer"* can be helpful.

Seeking Meaning: Reframing the Experience

- When survivors consider the traumatic event as an opportunity for growth, they often become stronger.
- Remember, crisis means danger and opportunity. You can help victims/survivors to reframe their experience in a way that is growth-enhancing rather than negative.

Building and Sustaining Trusted Relationships

- Accepting of nurturance and support from those who care is critical.
- Encourage victims/survivors not to be afraid to say that something is bothering them and that they are hurting.
- Also persuade them to reach out to those who are able to give them "unconditional positive regard"—be nonjudgmental, supportive, and accepting of where they are in their recovery process.

Maintaining a Sense of Humor

- Laughing is healing, and it always helps not take oneself too seriously. Try to help get victims/survivors to a place where they can begin to not take themselves so seriously, but be careful not to minimize their experience.

PART 5: HELPING THE HELPERS

BE PREPARED

EAP work is difficult and challenging, and responding to critical incidents adds another layer of pressure and stress. When a critical incident happens, it's your job to put all other job responsibilities on the back burner so as to function effectively as part of the emergency response team. But what happens when you go home and have some time to think and decompress?

It's important to be aware of what's going on with *you* as well as with those with whom you work. Although trauma psychology research primarily focuses on reactions and symptoms as they relate to those directly involved, there is no question that EAP staff, both professional and peers, who respond after a critical incident are also affected. It's impossible to be a caring, compassionate person and not be touched in some way by the experience.

Emergency response team members can themselves go through a series of emotional phases quite similar to those of victim/survivors after a critical incident. While it's impossible to know exactly what a given individual will experience, an awareness of some of the possible reactions is helpful. (See Figure A.4.)

Alarm

The time it takes to comprehend and adjust to the news of the critical incident—collecting and making sense of whatever facts and information are available. EAP professionals, like victims, may initially feel shocked and stunned.

Mobilization

After recovering from your initial shock, you'll find yourself developing and coordinating a plan of action with the rest of the emergency response team members. Supplies, resources, and who's available are quickly reviewed and inventoried. The team moves into action.

Action

You're actively working at necessary tasks and functions. Although the team attempts to exert a sense of control in a chaotic situation, a high level of activity and stress often occurs simultaneously.

Feelings of frustration may also develop as a result of adverse conditions (e.g., your relationship with the company, other bureaucratic snafus). Being aware and prepared ahead of time can minimize the potential negative effects later on.

Letdown

The transition from an emergency-response mode back to the "real world" is often the most intense emotional period for emergency response team members. Feelings that were denied or pushed aside now begin to surface.

In addition, you may experience feelings of loss, resentment, and inadequacy as you transition from an emergency-response mindset back to a business-as-usual one. For some, the return to normalcy and the realization that life goes on is somewhat difficult.

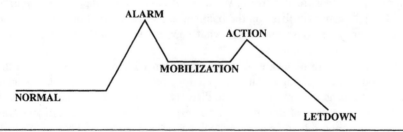

Figure A.4 Emotional phases possible following a critical incident.

How You're Affected

As has already been mentioned, all who are involved in the emergency-response effort are touched by the experience. The nature and magnitude of the critical incident play a part in determining your reactions. But no matter how serious the critical incident, it is not unusual for helpers to identify with what survivors are going through, and to imagine themselves in their place. "There but for the grace of God go I."

Trauma is always accompanied by a multitude of reactions. And you will probably experience some of them. As caring and concerned helpers, it's impossible not to work with involved members without being affected by them; this is the nature of human relationships.

At the same time, it can be painful to listen to and reexperience the event with victims/survivors. You may find that you experience feelings of helplessness, fear, and anger. Team members are normal people who usually function quite well under the responsibilities of doing EAP work. But like victims, if you're exposed to prolonged stress in the aftermath of a critical incident, it can begin to take its toll.

There is some evidence that persons close to the victim may suffer signs and symptoms of traumatization similar to those of the victim. This phenomenon has been described as secondary victimization. Some of the signs and symptoms include:

Psychological/Emotional

- Intensified feelings of fear, vulnerability, powerlessness, and lack of control of one's environment. A sense that the world isn't such a safe place after all.
- Guilt—"I should've/could've done better."
- Mood swings, which run the gamut from high highs to low lows—and everything in between.
- Psychic (emotional) numbing—disbelief, denial, and bewilderment. "I can't believe this really happened!" Feeling as if you were having a bad dream from which you might soon awake.*
- "Working through" simply means:
  - Confronting your feelings.
  - Experiencing the impact.
  - Expressing your feelings.
  - Allowing the intensity to diffuse and lessen.
  - Irritability and anger, which often manifest themselves as frustration, impatience, and intolerance.
  - Anxiety—an internal state of nervousness, often expressed as a feeling of "butterflies in my stomach." A free-floating sense of agitation or worry, often without knowing about what—or why.
  - Grief and sorrow—which come from experiencing a sense of loss.
  - Sadness comes and goes, and need not interfere with daily functioning.

---

*This protective defense mechanism provides relief from what might otherwise be emotionally overwhelming and debilitating. As the emotional impact of the incident lessens, painful feelings and thoughts associated with the experience can be dealt with and "worked through."

Cognitive

Coping with trauma demands a great deal of psychic energy. In addition to feeling anxious, distracted, and emotionally numb, this reallocation of energy can also affect your thinking, making it less accurate and dependable. You may experience:

- Temporarily impaired thought processes.
- Confusion.
- Difficulty setting priorities.
- Reduced trust in your own judgment and decision-making abilities.
- Lessened attention span.
- Intrusive, repetitious thoughts.

Physiological

Since the mind/body system is one, some physical reactions to psychoemotional trauma are inevitable. Except for those with preexisting conditions, don't be unduly concerned with temporary symptoms, such as:

- Reoccurring colds and flus.
- Sleep disturbances (too little or too much).
- Gastrointestinal problems.
- Tension headaches.

Behavioral

Being part of the response can also cause some of the following:

- Increased use of potentially abusing substances—alcohol/other drugs, food, nicotine, caffeine.
- Excessive "busyness" in an effort to avoid uncomfortable thoughts and feelings.
- Displacing anger onto others inappropriately. Jeopardizing relationships by provoking negative confrontations.
- Neglecting your health.
- Prematurely returning to anxiety-producing responsibilities before you're ready.
- Withdrawing and isolating yourself from your support systems (i.e., family, friends).

Attempts to relieve pain are normal. However, if after a critical incident you experience any of the preceding symptoms, take a long, hard look at what's going on—and then make the necessary changes. Helper, help thyself—and don't hesitate to get some professional assistance if necessary!

EVALUATING THE PLAN AND THE PROCESS

- Be aware of the rescuer mentality that lurks in all of us. Before you go into a debriefing, visualize/imagine yourself building internal resilience to protect yourself so that when you do a debriefing, you come out okay.
- After taking part in a debriefing, schedule a debriefing for the team. Do not leave this step out! It's as important as the debriefings for victims, their families, and the other employees.
- When you get home, take some time to put your thoughts and feelings down on paper to help you decompress. Spend some quiet time thinking about:
  —What went right.
  —What went wrong.
  —Lessons learned.
  —What you'll do differently next time.
- Make it a point to share your thoughts and feelings (including important insights, ideas, and new learning) with members of your team.

PART 6: RESOURCE MATERIALS/HANDOUTS

"The experience of life is broken."
Robert Jay Lifton

WHAT IS POST-TRAUMATIC STRESS DISORDER?

To most competently help those involved in critical incidents, it's helpful to have a working understanding of the concept of post-traumatic stress. The following information was adapted from the *Diagnostic and Statistical Manual*—the official diagnostic reference book used by psychologists, psychiatrists, clinical social workers, and other mental health professionals.

As you review the definition, you'll recognize that the reactions described are similar to many of the problems that troubled people experience. The following will give you a framework for understanding the nature of the problems that you are called upon to help others with:

A. The individual has experienced an event that is outside the range of usual human experience that would be markedly distressing to almost anyone (e.g., serious threat to one's life or physical integrity; serious threat or harm to one's children, spouse, or other close relatives and friends; sudden destruction of one's home or community; or seeing someone who is being (or has recently been) seriously injured or killed as the result of an accident or physical violence).

B. The distressing event is persistently reexperienced in at least one of the following ways:

1. Recurrent and intrusive distressing recollections of the event (which may be associated with guilty thoughts about behavior before or during the event).

2. Recurrent distressing dreams related to the event.

3. Sudden acting or feeling as if the event were recurring (includes a sense of re-living the experience, illusions, hallucinations, and dissociative (flashback) episodes, even those that occur upon awakening or when intoxicated).

4. Intense psychological distress at exposure to events that symbolize or resemble an aspect of the event, including anniversaries of the event.

C. Persistent avoidance of stimuli associated with the distressing event or numbing of general responsiveness (not present before the event), as indicated by at least three of the following:

1. Deliberate efforts to avoid thoughts or feelings associated with the event.

2. Deliberate efforts to avoid activities or situations that arouse recollections of the event.

3. Inability to recall an important aspect of the event (psychogenic amnesia).

4. Markedly diminished interest in significant activities.

5. Feelings of detachment or estrangement from others.

6. Restricted range of effect (feelings/emotions) (e.g., unable to have loving feelings).

7. Sense of a diminished future (e.g., child does not expect to have a career, marriage, children, or a long life).

D. Persistent symptoms of increased arousal (that were not present before the event) as indicated by at least two of the following:

1. Difficulty falling or staying asleep.

2. Irritability or outbursts of anger.

3. Difficulty concentrating.

4. Hypervigilance.

5. Physiological reactions at exposure to events that symbolize or resemble any aspects of the event (e.g., a woman who was raped in an elevator breaks out in a cold sweat when entering any elevator).

E. Duration of the disturbance of at least one month.

CHECKLIST OF POTENTIAL POST-TRAUMATIC REACTIONS

After a critical incident, you can refer to this checklist to help you decide if those involved need professional assistance. Make a prompt referral to a therapist with post-trauma stress experience for anyone displaying several of the following symptoms:

Cognitive

_____ Incoherence.

_____ Obsessive focus on fear of reoccurrence.

_____ Overintrusive and excessive efforts to assist others.

_____ Disbelief.

Physical

_____ Complaints or aggravation of prior physical symptoms.*

_____ Shortness of breath.

_____ Tightness of chest.

_____ Painful gastrointestinal problems.

_____ Blurred vision.

_____ Dizziness.

_____ Incapacitating or serious headaches.

Psychological

_____ Uncontrollable crying or trembling.

_____ Disorientation with reference to time, place, self-identity, or identity of others.

_____ Inability to respond to questions.

_____ Extreme anger (possibly acting out of same).

_____ Absence of any sign of fear/anxiety in market contrast to objective facts of involvement/exposure.

_____ Survivor guilt about own behavior during incident or about impact of incident on others.

_____ Emotional numbing/total withdrawal.

---

*Prompt medical attention is recommended if an involved member has a preexisting medical condition and any of these physical symptoms are present.

POST-TRAUMATIC STRESS REACTIONS

When people are involved in a traumatic event, it's not unusual to experience post-traumatic stress reactions. Some of you may experience none, some, or many of these. Keep in mind that they are **normal** reactions to an **abnormal** event. Over time, symptoms usually subside in frequency and intensity as you begin to try to make sense of what's happened. It's important to openly deal with what's going on. Rely on your support system to help you through this difficult time. If you need additional help, call the EAP. (See Table A.2.)

SOME DO'S AND DON'TS

- Within the first 24 to 72 hours—alternating periods of physical exercise with relaxation will alleviate some of the physical reactions.
- Structure your time—keep busy.
- You're normal and are having normal reactions—don't label yourself crazy.
- Talk to people—talk is the most healing medicine.
- Be aware of numbing the pain with overuse of drugs and alcohol—don't complicate the problem by abusing alcohol or other drugs.
- Reach out—people do care.
- Maintain as normal a schedule as possible.
- Spend time with others.
- Help the other involved coworkers as much as possible by sharing your feelings and checking out how they're doing.

Table A.2   Post-Traumatic Stress Reactions

Physical	
• Shock	• Sleep disturbances
• Agitation	• Startle reactions
• Diminished appetite	• Fatigue

Cognitive (Thought)	
• Disbelief	• Trouble remembering
• Flashbacks	• Poor concentration
• Nightmares	• Impaired decision making
• Self-blame	• Intrusive images

Emotional	
• Anxiety and fear	• Survivor guilt/remorse
• Depression	• Sorrow and grief
• Interpersonal problems	• Irritability and anger
• Feelings of helplessness	• Low stress tolerance
• Anxiety about recurrence	• Sense of vulnerability
• Crying spells	in another incident

- Give yourself permission to feel rotten and share your feelings with others.
- Keep a journal. Write your way through those sleepless hours.
- Do healthy things that feel good to you, not what others tell you is good for you.
- Realize that those around you are under stress.
- Don't make any big life changes.
- Do make as many daily decisions as possible which will give you a feeling of control over your life (e.g., if someone asks you what you want to eat, answer them even if you're not sure).
- Reoccurring thoughts, dreams, or flashbacks are normal—don't try to fight them—they'll decrease over time and become less painful.
- Eat well-balanced and regular meals (even if you don't feel like it).
- Get plenty of rest.

For Significant Others

Your loved one has been involved in a traumatic event (critical incident) and he or she may be experiencing post-traumatic stress responses. No one is immune—regardless of past experiences. Remember these important things about post-trauamatic stress:

- A post-traumatic stress response can occur at the scene, within hours, days, or even months after the incident.
- Your loved one may experience a variety of signs/symptoms (refer to the "Check-list of Potential Post-Traumatic Responses") or he or she may not experience any of them at this time.
- The symptoms normally subside and disappear in time if you and your loved one do not dwell upon them.
- All phases of life overlap and influence each other: personal, professional, fam-ily, etc. The impact of critical-incident stress can be intensified, influenced, or mitigated by personal, family, and current developmental issues.
- Talk is the best medicine. Encourage, but do **not** pressure, her or him to talk about the incident and her or his reaction to it. Your primary "job" is to listen and reas-sure. Remember that if an event is upsetting to you and your loved one, your chil-dren may be affected, also. They may need to talk, too. Encourage them to do so with you.
- You may not understand what the survivor is going through right now, but offer your love and support. Don't be afraid to ask what you can do that he or she would consider helpful.
- Accept the fact that life will go on. Maintain or return to a normal routine as soon as possible.
- If the stress symptoms your loved one is experiencing do not begin to subside within a few weeks, or if they intensify, consider seeking further assistance. The EAP is a confidential service that can help you find a professional who understands critical-incident stress and its impact on those involved.

Some Additional Tips on How to Help:

- Listen carefully.
- Spend time with the traumatized person.
- Offer your assistance and a listening ear—even if he or she has not asked for help.
- Reassure the survivor that he or she is safe.
- Help with the everyday tasks of cleaning, cooking, caring for the family, minding children.
- Give the survivor some private time.
- Don't take anger or other strong feelings personally.
- Don't tell the survivor that he or she is "lucky it wasn't worse." A traumatized person is not consoled by those statements. Instead, tell your loved one that you are sorry the event happened and you want to understand and help him or her any way you can.

REFERENCES

Barnett-Queen, T., & Bergmann, L.H. (1988). Critical incident training: I. *ISFSI Instructo-Gram: Training Keys for the Fire Officer, 9,* 4.

Braverman, M., & Gelberd, S.F. (1990). *Leadership skills for the critical incident.* Beaverton, OR: Great Performance.

Cohen, R.E., & Ahearn, F.L. (1980). General concepts in understanding disaster behavior. In *Handbook for Mental Health Care of Disaster Victims* (pp. 9–17). Baltimore: Johns Hopkins University Press.

Cohen, S. & Willis, T.A. (1985). Stress, social support and the buffering hypothesis. *Psychological Bulletin, 98,* 310–357.

Dunning, C. (1990). Mitigating the impact of work trauma: Administrative issues concerning intervention. In J.T. Reese, J.M. Horn, & C. Dunning (Eds.), *Critical incidents in policing* (pp. 73–82). Washington, DC: U.S. Government Printing Office.

Farberow, N.L., & Frederick, C. (1978). *Training manual for human service workers in natural disasters.* Rockville, MD: National Institute of Mental Health.

Feuer, B.A. (1994). The association of flight attendants employee assistance program responds to workplace trauma: A dynamic model. In B. Williams & J.F. Sommer, Jr. (Eds.), *Handbook of post-traumatic therapy* (pp. 310–324). Westport, CT: Greenwood Press.

Figley, C.R. (1983). Catastrophes: An overview of family reaction. In C.R. Figley and H. McCubbin (Eds.), *Stress and the family: Coping with catastrophe.* (Vol. 2). (p. 3–20). New York: Brunner/Mazel.

Figley, C.R. (1985). From victim to survivor: Social responsibility in the wake of catastrophe. In C.R. Figley (Ed.), *Trauma and its wake: The study and treatment of post-traumatic stress disorder* (pp. 398–415). New York: Brunner/Mazel.

Griffin, C.A. (1987). Community disasters and post-traumatic stress disorder: A debriefing model for response. In T. Williams (Ed.), *Post-traumatic stress disorders: A handbook for clinicians* (pp. 293–298). Cincinnati, OH: Disabled American Veterans.

Hartsough, D., & Myers, D.A. (1985). *Disaster work and mental health: Prevention and control of stress among workers.* Rockville, MD: National Institute of Mental Health.

Horowitz, M.J. (1985). Disasters and psychological responses to stress. *Psychiatric Annals,* 161–167.

Kivins, L. (1980). *Evaluation and change: Services for survivors.* Minneapolis, MN: Minneapolis Medical Research Foundation.

Lawson, B.Z. (1987). Work-related post-traumatic stress reactions: The hidden dimension. *Health and Social Work,* 250–258.

Lindy, J.D., & Grace, M.G. (1985). The recovery environment: Continuing stressor versus a healing psychosocial space. In B.J. Sowder (Ed.), *Disasters and mental health: Selected contemporary perspectives* (pp. 137–149). Rockville, MD: National Institute of Mental Health.

McCann, L. & Pearlman, L.A. (1990). Vicarious traumatization: A framework for understanding the psychological effects of working with victims. *Journal of Traumatic Stress Studies, 3,* 1.

Mitchell, J.T. (1983). When disaster strikes: The critical incident stress debriefing process. *Journal of Emergency Medical Services, 8*(1), 36–39.

Mitchell, J.T. (1988). The history, status and future of critical incident stress debriefings. *Journal of Emergency Medical Services, 8*(1), 36–39.

White, S.G., & Hatcher, C. (1988). Violence and the trauma response. *Occupational Medicine: State of the Art Reviews, 3*(4), 766–694.

Author Index

Aaron, W.S., 323
Aasland, O.G., 236
Abel, T., 77
Abramowitz, S.I., 80
Abrams, D.B., 259
Ahearn, F.L., 521
Alderfer, C.P., 72
Alexander, C.M., 73
Allen, M.M., 323
Allgier, P., 255
Amaral, T., 169, 171, 172, 422
Anderson, D.S., 241
Anderson, P., 224
Annis, H.M., 259
Anstadt, G., 319, 334
Armstrong, T.J., 343, 359
Aronoff, G.M., 346
Aschbacher, P., 409
Ashley, S., 286
Ator, N.E., 20
Austin, A.E., 36
Austin, B., 234

Babor, T.F., 233
Baker, F., 74, 456
Baldwin, D., 371
Barber, J., 251
Barnett-Queen, T., 480
Barney, C., 282
Barry, K., 234
Baruch, Y., 272
Basche-Kahre, E., 77
Bass, J., 319

Battie, M.C., 344
Baxter, A.K., 35, 37
Bazron, B., 73
Beehr, T.A., 361
Beidel, B.E., 93, 94, 95, 101, 106
Bell, Jr., C., 117
Bennett, N., 119
Bergmann, L.H., 480
Berkowitz, M., 342
Berman, D., 441
Berndt, E.R., 319
Berry, S., 325
Berwick, D.M., 118
Betzold, J., 20
Beyer, J., 38, 92, 105
Bezold, C., 268, 284
Bhagat, R.S., 361
Bien, T.H., 236
Bigos, S.J., 344
Bilello, U., 443
Binkoff, J.A., 259
Blazer, D.G., 320, 324
Blum, T., 119, 128, 339
Blum, T.C., 168, 169, 171, 173, 177, 249
Blum, T.T., 37
Blumenthal, R., 71
Bohn, M.J., 233
Bond, T., 410
Boodman, S.G., 19
Bowen, T., 36
Bowman, E.D., 317
Boyd, J.H., 320, 324
Brache, A.P., 346

523

Subject Index